"Situated critically in our age of identity politics and inclusion, this incisive and discerning study undermines a dichotomy between 'ethnic' Judaism and 'universal' Christianity perpetuated in various forms in modern New Testament scholarship to the present. Not itself pretending to have a view from nowhere, it invites further interrogation of its own conclusions. Both modest and profound, it marks a hermeneutical watershed in biblical studies, issuing a pressing summons to biblical scholars and Christian theologians alike to a reparative, self-critical approach to today's fraught issues of identity."

— SUSANNAH TICCIATI
King's College London

"In this hugely important and timely volume, David Horrell offers a fresh and persuasive account of early Christian identity creation. Deploying insights from whiteness studies, he convincingly demonstrates the unacknowledged and unreflective, yet influential, role that race has contributed to Christian exceptionalism endemic in scholarly accounts of the early church as uniquely open, inclusive, universal, and non-ethnic over and against the 'ethnic particularity' of Judaism. Through careful and wide-ranging readings of Jewish and New Testament texts, he shows there were in fact forms of non-ethnic inclusivism in Judaism, as well as ethnicization tendencies in early Christianity. In what is sure to become a classic text on early Christian identity, David Horrell issues a welcome challenge to all scholars (himself included) to be more attentive to our own racial locatedness and particularity."

— PAUL MIDDLETON
University of Chester

"Racism is perpetuated by claims about history, identity, and religion, especially within the Christian tradition. Resistance to racism must, then, include the reassessment of those claims, pressing back through the problematic history of interpretation to consider the biblical texts themselves in all their complexity and nuance. In this stunning work of engaged scholarship, David Horrell shows how ill-founded claims about early Christianity reveal our complicity in hermeneutical and theological discourses marked by racist assumptions and consequent practices. Horrell's careful survey of ancient identity construction makes this an important book for scholars and students of Jewish and Christian identity. But the final chapter on the endemic presence of whiteness in New Testament scholarship makes *Ethnicity and Inclusion* essential."

— SEAN WINTER
Pilgrim Theological College, University of Melbourne

Ethnicity and Inclusion

*Religion, Race, and Whiteness
in Constructions of Jewish and Christian Identities*

David G. Horrell

WILLIAM B. EERDMANS PUBLISHING COMPANY
GRAND RAPIDS, MICHIGAN

Wm. B. Eerdmans Publishing Co.
4035 Park East Court SE, Grand Rapids, Michigan 49546
www.eerdmans.com

26 25 24 23 22 21 20   1 2 3 4 5 6 7

ISBN 978-0-8028-7608-9

Library of Congress Cataloging-in-Publication Data

Names: Horrell, David G., author.
Title: Ethnicity and inclusion : religion, race, and whiteness in constructions of Jewish
    and Christian identities / David G. Horrell.
Description: Grand Rapids, Michigan : William B. Eerdmans Publishing Company, 2020.
    | Includes bibliographical references and index. | Summary: "A study of ethnic identity
    construction in Christianity and Judaism focused on New Testament texts"—Provided
    by publisher.
Identifiers: LCCN 2020017617 | ISBN 9780802876089 (hardcover)
Subjects: LCSH: Identification (Religion)—Biblical teaching. | Identity (Psychology)—
    Religious aspects. | Christians. | Jews in the New Testament. | Ethnicity in the Bible. |
    Racism—Religious aspects.
Classification: LCC BS2545.I33 H67 2020 | DDC 230.089—dc23
LC record available at https://lccn.loc.gov/2020017617

Arts and
Humanities
Research Council

Research for this book was funded by the UK Arts and Humanities Research Council.

For Stephen Plant
1 Peter 1:22–2:3

Contents

Foreword by Judith M. Lieu   xi

Acknowledgments   xv

Abbreviations   xix

Introduction   1

CONTEXTS OF RESEARCH

1. **A Persistent Structural Dichotomy:**
   Jewish Ethnic Particularism and Christian Inclusivism   21

   1.1   Ferdinand Christian Baur and the Making
   of Modern New Testament Scholarship   22

   1.2   E. P. Sanders and a New Perspective on Judaism   28

   1.3   Social-Scientific Perspectives on Ethnicity and Identity   37

   1.4   Conclusions   45

2. **Ethnicity, Race, and Ancient Jewish and Christian Identities:**
   Themes in Recent Research   47

   2.1   Ethnicity and Race in Antiquity: Jews/Judeans and Greeks   47

   2.2   Ethnicity and Race in Early Christian Discourse and Identity   56

   2.3   Conclusions   65

3. **Ethnicity, Race, and Religion in Social-Scientific Perspective**   67

   3.1   Ethnicity and Race in History and Theory   67

3.2 The Language of Race 75

3.3 Religion and Ethnicity 83

3.4 Conclusions 89

**COMPARISONS OF JEWISH
AND EARLY CHRISTIAN PERSPECTIVES**

4. **Shared Descent: Ancestry, Kinship,
Marriage, and Family** 95

4.1 Stories of Ancestors: Appeals to Genealogy and Descent 96

4.2 Kinship Relations: A Community of Brothers and Sisters 106

4.3 Marriage Rules: Endogamy as Norm 112

4.4 The Holiness of Children and the Passing on
of Christian Identity 123

4.5 Conclusions 133

5. **A Common Way of Life: Culture, Practice,
and the Socialization of Children** 136

5.1 Adhering to a Way of Life as Definitive for Jewish
and Christian Identity 137

5.1.1 *Way of Life and Jewish Identity* 137

5.1.2 *Way of Life and Christian Identity* 142

5.2 The Socialization of Children into a Way of Life 149

5.2.1 *Training Children in the Jewish Way of Life* 149

5.2.2 *Children and the Christian Way of Life* 152

5.3 Displaying a Way of Life through Practice 155

5.3.1 *Jewish Practices as Markers of Identity:
Circumcision, Food, and Sabbath* 157

5.3.2 *Christian Practices and Group Identity: Baptism,
Eucharist, and Sunday Meeting* 161

5.3.3 *Practices, Discourse, and Identity by Association* 173

5.4 Conclusions 175

6. Homeland: Territory and Symbolic Constructions of Space   178

6.1 Ideologies of Land and Constructions of Space
in Early Jewish Texts   183

6.2 Ideologies of Land and Constructions of Space
in New Testament Texts   194

   6.2.1 *Luke-Acts*   195

   6.2.2 *Paul*   196

   6.2.3 *1 Peter*   202

   6.2.4 *Hebrews*   206

   6.2.5 *Revelation*   211

6.3 Conclusions   214

**7. Becoming a People: Self-Consciousness
and Ethnicization**   217

7.1 People-Groups in Antiquity: ἔθνος, γένος, λαός   220

7.2 Jewish Peoplehood: The λαὸς θεοῦ   224

7.3 Becoming a People: Early Christian Self-Consciousness
and Ethnicization   228

7.4 Conclusions   246

8. Mission and Conversion: Joining the People   249

8.1 Proselytes, Sympathizers, and the Attractions of Judaism   251

   8.1.1 *From Missionary Zeal to Passive Attraction:
Shifting Perspectives*   251

   8.1.2 *Evidence for Judaism's Popularity*   255

   8.1.3 *Sympathizers, Godfearers, and Patrons*   257

   8.1.4 *Proselytes: Incomers and Joiners*   262

   8.1.5 *Leaving the People: Defectors and Apostates*   273

8.2 Early Christian Models of Mission   277

   8.2.1 *Matthew 28:18–20 and the Apostolic Commission*   280

   8.2.2 *Paul and the Earliest Communities*   283

   8.2.3 *Witness and Mission in 1 Peter*   287

8.3 Conclusions   293

REFLECTIONS ON LOCATION AND EPISTEMOLOGY

9. Implicit Whiteness and Christian Superiority:
   The Epistemological Challenge   299

   9.1   Retrospect, Summary, and Key Arguments Thus Far   300

   9.2   Insights and Questions from Whiteness Studies   310

   9.3   Particularizing (White, Western, Christian)
   New Testament Studies   318

     9.3.1   *Making Christianness Strange?*   319

     9.3.2   *Whiteness and Constructions of the Early
   Christian Vision*   325

     9.3.3   *Critique from the "Margins"—and the Center?*   335

   9.4   Moving Forward?   341

Bibliography   347

Cover Illustrations Credits   397

Index of Modern Authors   399

Index of Subjects   408

Index of Ancient Sources   410

Foreword

It is not surprising that the study of "what-would-become" New Testament texts and other early Christian writings has been inundated by the language of "identity" since the beginning of the twenty-first century. No doubt future generations will relate that to the various conflicts over group and personal identity that have dominated social and political life in this period, conflicts that in the public sphere have become focused in so-called, and now often-maligned, "identity politics" and in disputes over the nature and limits of sovereignty or autonomy. This location serves as a reminder that such concerns are not just "another intellectual approach" but intersect with, mask, expose, or challenge structures of power. Both as a mode of academic analysis and in this broader context, "identity" proves to be full of contradictions: the move away from essentialist toward constructivist definitions coexists with experienced and often militantly defended essentializing constructions; recognition of the artificiality of borders, whether physical or ideologically built, and of their actual porosity sits alongside the aggressive defense or "regaining control" of borders. Both in policymaking and in the social imagination, defense of the space for cultural multi-variety struggles with discomfort with or rejection of perceived nonconformity. It is often difficult to separate the act of differentiation demanded by the encounter with "the other" from the internal struggle for ownership or unity. In all this there is undoubtedly a two-way traffic between the wider mood generated around "identity" and the specific style of discourse or template for examining the discursive strategies of other groups and texts, which has become a major exercise in study of the past—not just, as sometimes is complained, a means of ventriloquizing them through our own dialects or accents, but a provocation for also rereading our present.

As so often, TRS (Theology and Religious Studies), and especially the study of the texts and history broadly associated with the Jewish and Christian Scriptures, has to some extent been merely following the example of her sister disciplines, even if a half-step behind. Classicists were already asking what it was that made "the Greeks" able so to speak of themselves and to recognize themselves, particularly subsuming, and extending beyond, city-state loyalties. The rhetorical strategies that constructed and essentialized Greekness or Romanness, often in contradistinction to unitary "barbarians," offered a primer for reading our texts. But as again has been the case in other reading styles, such as gender-based ones, TRS can also claim a distinct heritage. Mapping of the so-called parting of the ways predated the discovery of "identity" and owed much to the unavoidable challenges addressed by the Shoah to an unreflective Christian tradition of denigration and of a rarely questioned sense of superiority or, in more favored and scripturally legitimated terms, of "fulfillment." By focusing his attention on what he labels the "persistent structural dichotomy" of Jewish ethnic particularism and Christian inclusivism in a volume thoroughly invested in the language and scholarly analysis of identity, David Horrell ensures that this nonnegotiable heritage, with its challenging theological as well as historical legacy, is not relegated to the archives.

As Horrell's discussion of that "structural dichotomy" demonstrates, among the many questions posed by the "parting-of-the-ways" model is whether the two ways belong to the same dimension or stratum. The apparent complementarity of "particular–inclusive" is misleading, for the history of Christian thought shows that the question of how a universal/spiritual identity relates to any social formation continually reemerges in new forms and has never been conclusively answered: Is it antithetically positioned in relation to any terrestrial polity or (secular) state, or is it embodied in a particular local or trans-local entity? Yet, if the two ways effectively belong to different planes or dimensions, then the metaphorical pretensions of their "parting" are fatally undermined. Such a protest might seem naïve, for, perhaps contrary to the expectation of some early and subsequent believers, those who understood themselves in some way in relation to the story of (Jesus) Christ were born, lived, suffered, and died to all appearances in the same way as the rest of humankind, inhabiting the same four- (or ten-)dimensional world. Nonetheless, it is a reminder that, as metaphor, "parting" is a linguistic formulation and not a physical description, and indeed that the phenomenon it seeks to make sense of is as much linguistic practice as it is social articulation—or, rather, expresses the necessarily interpenetrating interplay between the two. Mistakes arise where what has been assumed to be Jewish social practice is immediately compared (or contrasted) with Christian linguistic articulation (or vice versa).

For the moment I would like to draw attention to just three of the possible aspects of the question about which Horrell provokes further thought: first, the "peoplehoodness" of those styled (by themselves or by others) "Jews," perceived as a social formation determined by "blood heritage" (even if one necessarily in various ways fictitious), especially when set alongside that of those similarly self- or hetero-styled "Christians," albeit as they adopted patterns of social formation that were already part of their broader socio-political context; second, whether the exclusivity of the shared cultural practices of the Jews, which had been articulated through a myth of blood heritage, came to achieve the status of an end in itself, which some would call "religion" (even if religion is not to be identified with the modern Western notion); third, the significance of the fact that (or perhaps why) Christians understood themselves not as individual, insular initiates but as corporately and reciprocally interdependent, both when adopting specific social formations or when transcending them, and in so doing, perhaps not surprisingly, adopted the corporate familial and spatial metaphors that were the stock-in-trade.

This foreword began with the conversation between contemporary and ancient discourses of identity. Such conversations can also lead to a mishearing. Whereas the language of "identity" has incurred the objection that it is a modern, or at most a premodern, term (and hence, it is argued, idea), it has to some extent ceded favored status to that of ethnicity, no less a modern category but one with the apparent virtue of being derived from a Greek noun, *ethnos*. This may be deceptive, liable to create a confusion of registers, using philology or etymology to join in contemporary anthropological and sociopolitical conversation. If "ethnicity" is a contemporary construction, both as concept and as claimed experiential mode, with a specific Western genealogy, then the presence (or absence) of the Greek term in our texts is irrelevant. This is even more true of whether and when *ethnos* is used in parallel to or in contrast to the Greek *genos*, from which, via the Latin, English gets "genus" but which is also regularly translated "race"; the etymological origins of the latter term are unclear, its function in modern ideologies is notorious, and its proper application in contemporary social analysis remains hotly disputed. The debate over whether in antiquity people had understandings of themselves or of others that are analogous to, or anticipatory of, Western concepts of biologically determined or articulated "race" is independent of the application of the Greek term *genos*, not least as "third," to Christians.

There can be little doubt of the fruitfulness for both sides of bringing contemporary discourses about ourselves as individuals and societies into conversation with the textual and material survivals from the past—themselves silent except as given voice by us; however, that last qualification already points to the self-critical alertness the exercise demands, the need, as it were, to listen as acutely to our own voice, to recognize its situatedness, taken for granted and therefore perhaps not heard by ourselves, even if grindingly obvious to others. Horrell addresses this in his inevitably tentative and exploratory closing reflections on "whiteness," a *genus* of criticism still more at home in North America than in Europe, although closely related to the emphasis on locatedness long familiar to feminist, queer, and postcolonial readings. Here "whiteness" is the taken-for-granted norm over against supposedly "minority" or "committed" perspectives and is reinforced as such by a particular political and social history in which those norms are effective. Horrell is concerned not just with the way scholarship on early Christianity has often functioned from an unexamined standpoint of the normativity of a Christian self-description, but also with the very practices of scholarship itself as it has developed within a Western political and intellectual environment. As was noted at the start of this foreword, that is very much the case with the questions and methods of identity analysis.

To take the terminology further, one might note that "white" is by definition achromatic, reflecting all the light that strikes it, and not absorbing it; "white noise," much celebrated for ensuring sleep for babies, and also, or perhaps thereby, for adults, blocks intrusive or discordant sounds, relaxing the brain and inducing a soporific state with its lack of differentiation or particularity. Horrell's study is far from being soporific, although this foreword deliberately avoids the conventions of a review or of a eulogy; his book takes the discussion of the intersecting issues tracked here, and others besides, a significant stage further, while also opening up a very necessary debate as to whom and what we serve in the pervasive politics of the various identities we all contest.

JUDITH M. LIEU

Acknowledgments

I first began to think seriously about the themes and issues addressed in this book in 2010 while working on the language of 1 Pet 2:9–10. This particularly rich and compact collection of "people" terms—not least the first application of the label γένος to the members of the earliest Christian communities—seemed highly significant in terms of the development of early Christian identity. A particular stimulus to my thinking about the "ethnoracial" significance of the phrases used in these verses was Denise Kimber Buell's seminal book *Why This New Race*, which remains a crucially generative work for the present project. Another stimulus was my earlier work on Pauline ethics in *Solidarity and Difference*; looking back on that project, I began to think more about the parallels between the structure of modern Western political liberalism and what scholars, including myself, see within the early Pauline assemblies, as well as about what those parallels might indicate. In a sense, this book seeks to develop and combine these insights by exploring how New Testament and early Christian texts, like (other) Jewish texts, construct identity in ethnic-like ways, and, in light of these explorations, reflecting on how far scholarly construals of the early Christian achievement are the product of a particular racial and religious location.

The opportunity to spend a concentrated time focused on this project came with the award of a leadership fellowship from the UK's Arts and Humanities Research Council (AHRC) from 2015 to 2017 (grant reference AH-M009149/1), which provided me with a year free from the usual demands of teaching and administration as well as resources to host two workshops, a conference, and various academic visitors. I am very grateful to the AHRC for their support and to the University of Exeter, and my colleagues in the Department of Theology and Religion in particular, for covering for my absence and allowing me a period of study leave in which to complete this volume during the first half of 2019. I am also indebted to many individuals whose support, input, advice, and help have been crucial in enabling this work to come to fruition. I am especially grateful to Katherine Hockey, who, with AHRC funding, was appointed as an associate research fellow to assist with the project. Katy was enormously efficient, capable, and wise in helping with a range of tasks from bibliographic research to workshop and conference organization, alongside developing her own research in a different area. She served as coeditor for the volume of essays that emerged from the events held under the auspices of the project, *Ethnicity, Race, Religion: Identities and Ideologies in Early Jewish and Christian Texts and in Modern Biblical Interpretation.* Bradley Arnold also provided some research support for which I would like to express my thanks, and Cherryl Hunt compiled the indexes, a laborious task for which payment, thanks, and cups of coffee are inadequate (but necessary) recompense. I would also like to express my sincere thanks to the two anonymous readers of the manuscript for their many very helpful comments and astute suggestions.

I am grateful, too, to those who agreed to present papers to the workshops and conference: John Barclay, Denise Buell, James Crossley, Gregory Cuéllar, Musa Dube, Kathy Ehrensperger, Ma. Marilou Ibita, Judith Lieu, Halvor Moxnes, Love Sechrest, and Tim Whitmarsh. I am especially grateful to Denise Buell, Musa Dube, and Love Sechrest, each of whom agreed to make a more extended visit to the University of Exeter's Centre for Biblical Studies. I am particularly indebted to Denise for taking the time to offer detailed feedback on an early outline of this book. I am conscious that I have not been able to do justice to all of her probing and insightful suggestions and that responsibility for the weaknesses that remain rests particularly on my shoulders. I am also grateful to all those who attended the various events and contributed to discussions from which I learned a great deal. They are too numerous to name, but I would like to mention Philip Esler and Steve Mason: we have debated our different views in print, but I have learned much from their work and also appreciate their willingness to engage in dialogue beyond the forum of published essays and to sustain collegial relationships despite our sometimes different perspectives. It is perhaps a cliché to say that rigorous and reasoned criticism is the lifeblood of any scholarly discipline, but it is good when robust interaction can be sustained alongside genuine and open collegiality.

I would also like to express my gratitude to those who have kindly taken the time to read and discuss various drafts of essays and chapters and to offer suggestions and share bibliography: Mark Brett, David Carr, William

Gallois, Helen John, my wonderful colleague Louise Lawrence (who read several draft chapters), Amy-Jill Levine, Andrew Mbuvi, Jon Morgan, Teresa Morgan (who also contributed an essay to our edited volume), Joan Taylor, Susannah Ticciati, David Tollerton, Wei Hsien Wan, and Daniel Weiss. Also among those who have offered valuable feedback are colleagues who have kindly hosted me during various occasions on which I have been able to present papers related to this project: Edward Adams, Reimund Bieringer, Simon Butticaz, Matthias Konradt, Steve Kraftchick, Bruce Longenecker, Emmanuel Nathan, Todd Still, Geoff Thompson, and Ekaterini Tsalampouni. Time spent in the wonderful libraries at Cambridge University, Heidelberg University, the Catholic University of Leuven, the Johannes Gutenberg University of Mainz, and Melbourne's University of Divinity was also enormously valuable, and I thank Reimund Bieringer, Matthias Konradt, Sean Winter, and Ruben Zimmermann for their kindness in facilitating some of those visits. I would also like to express my thanks for invitations to present plenary papers at the Studorium Novi Testamenti Societas annual meeting in Amsterdam in 2015 and the British New Testament Conference in Maynooth in 2017, where I took the opportunity to try out ideas related to this project. Some of these papers have been published, and I have drawn on them in this book, though none is substantially reproduced here (and the details of each are included in the bibliography). Finally, I would like to thank Michael Thomson for his long-standing interest in my work and enthusiasm to secure it for Eerdmans, Trevor Thompson, Jenny Hoffman, and all the other staff at Eerdmans who have so carefully and professionally guided this book to publication.

I cannot publish a book without expressing my profound and constant gratitude to Carrie, Em, and Cate, whose love and companionship mean so much to me. I would like to dedicate this book, however, to my friend Stephen Plant. We met just over thirty years ago, wrote our doctorates in neighboring flats, saw one another through hard times, and tolerate one another sufficiently (despite his snoring) to room together when we attend SBL/AAR meetings. A few years back, Stephen did me the honor of dedicating a book to me, and I am glad to return the compliment, especially as it gives me the opportunity to offer a dedication only he will understand (though either of us will be glad to let curious readers into the mystery).

Abbreviations

Abbreviations for primary texts and scholarly resources follow those given in *The SBL Handbook of Style*, 2nd ed. (Atlanta: Society of Biblical Literature, 2014) and are listed below for convenience. I prefer to define BCE and CE such that the "C" stands for "Christian," not "Common," for reasons given below on pp. 16–18.

AB	Anchor Bible
AJBI	*Annual of the Japanese Biblical Institute*
AnBib	Analecta Biblica
ANF	*The Ante-Nicene Fathers*. Edited by Alexander Roberts and James Donaldson. 1885–1887. 10 vols. Repr., Peabody, MA: Hendrickson, 1994
ASNU	Acta Seminarii Neotestamentici Upsaliensis
BBR	*Bulletin for Biblical Research*
BDAG	Danker, Frederick W., Walter Bauer, William F. Arndt, and F. Wilbur Gingrich. *Greek-English Lexicon of the New Testament and Other Early Christian Literature*. 3rd ed. Chicago: University of Chicago Press, 2000
BDF	Blass, Friedrich, Albert Debrunner, and Robert W. Funk. *A Greek Grammar of the New Testament and Other Early Christian Literature*. Chicago: University of Chicago Press, 1961
BECNT	Baker Exegetical Commentary on the New Testament
BETL	Bibliotheca Ephemeridum Theologicarum Lovaniensium
Bib	*Biblica*
BibInt	*Biblical Interpretation*
BibInt	Biblical Interpretation Series

BJRL	*Bulletin of the John Rylands University Library of Manchester*
BNTC	Black's New Testament Commentaries
BSac	*Bibliotheca Sacra*
BTB	*Biblical Theology Bulletin*
BZNW	Beihefte zur Zeitschrift für die neutestamentliche Wissenschaft
CBQ	*Catholic Biblical Quarterly*
CCSL	Corpus Christianorum: Series Latina. Turnhout: Brepols, 1953–
CRINT	Compendia Rerum Iudaicarum ad Novum Testamentum
CTR	*Criswell Theological Review*
CurBR	*Currents in Biblical Research*
EC	*Early Christianity*
ECC	Eerdmans Critical Commentary
EKKNT	Evangelisch-katholischer Kommentar zum Neuen Testament
EstBib	*Estudios bíblicos*
GCS	Die griechischen christlichen Schriftsteller der ersten [drei] Jahrhunderte
GLAJJ	*Greek and Latin Authors on Jews and Judaism.* Edited with introductions, translations, and commentary by Menahem Stern. 3 vols. Jerusalem: Israel Academy of Sciences and Humanities, 1974–84
HNT	Handbuch zum Neuen Testament
HTR	*Harvard Theological Review*
HUCA	*Hebrew Union College Annual*
IAph2007	*Inscriptions of Aphrodisias.* Edited by Joyce Reynolds, Charlotte Roueché, and Gabriel Bodard. 2007. http://insaph .kcl.ac.uk/iaph2007
ICC	International Critical Commentary
IG	*Inscriptiones Graecae. Editio Minor.* Berlin: de Gruyter, 1924–
JAAR	*Journal of the American Academy of Religion*
JBL	*Journal of Biblical Literature*
JECS	*Journal of Early Christian Studies*
JHebS	*Journal of Hebrew Scriptures*
JJS	*Journal of Jewish Studies*
JMJS	*Journal for the Study of the Jesus Movement in Its Jewish Setting*

JQR	*Jewish Quarterly Review*
JRE	*Journal of Religious Ethics*
JRS	*Journal of Roman Studies*
JSHRZ	Jüdische Schriften aus hellenistisch-römischer Zeit
JSJ	*Journal for the Study of Judaism in the Persian, Hellenistic, and Roman Periods*
JSJSup	Supplements to the Journal for the Study of Judaism
JSNT	*Journal for the Study of the New Testament*
JSNTSup	Journal for the Study of the New Testament Supplement Series
JSP	*Journal for the Study of the Pseudepigrapha*
JSPSup	Journal for the Study of the Pseudepigrapha Supplement Series
JSQ	Jewish Studies Quarterly
JTS	*Journal of Theological Studies*
LCL	Loeb Classical Library
LHBOTS	The Library of Hebrew Bible/Old Testament Series
LNTS	The Library of New Testament Studies
LSJ	Liddell, Henry George, Robert Scott, and Henry Stuart Jones. *A Greek-English Lexicon.* 9th ed. with revised supplement. Oxford: Clarendon, 1996
LSTS	The Library of Second Temple Studies
MAMA	*Monumenta Asiae Minoris Antiqua.* Manchester and London, 1928–1993
MM	Moulton, James H., and George Milligan. *The Vocabulary of the Greek Testament.* London, 1930. Repr., Peabody, MA: Hendrickson, 1997
Neot	*Neotestamentica*
NETS	*A New English Translation of the Septuagint.* Edited by Albert Pietersma and Benjamin G. Wright. Oxford: Oxford University Press, 2007
NICNT	New International Commentary on the New Testament
NIGTC	New International Greek Testament Commentary
NovT	*Novum Testamentum*
NovTSup	Supplements to Novum Testamentum
NTD	Das Neue Testament Deutsch
NTOA	Novum Testamentum et Orbis Antiquus
NTS	*New Testament Studies*
OBT	Overtures to Biblical Theology

OECS	Oxford Early Christian Studies
OTP	*Old Testament Pseudepigrapha.* Edited by James H. Charlesworth. 2 vols. New York: Doubleday, 1983, 1985
PG	Patrologia Graeca [= *Patrologiae Cursus Completus*: Series Graeca]. Edited by Jacques-Paul Migne. 162 vols. Paris, 1857–1886
PGL	*Patristic Greek Lexicon.* Edited by Geoffrey W. H. Lampe. Oxford: Clarendon, 1961
RAC	*Reallexikon für Antike und Christentum.* Edited by Theodor Klauser et al. Stuttgart: Hiersemann, 1950–
RB	*Revue biblique*
RBS	Resources for Biblical Study
RelSRev	*Religious Studies Review*
SBLDS	Society of Biblical Literature Dissertation Series
SC	Sources chrétiennes. Paris: Cerf, 1943–
ScrB	*Scripture Bulletin*
SD	Studies and Documents
SEÅ	*Svensk exegetisk årsbok*
SemeiaSt	Semeia Studies
SJT	*Scottish Journal of Theology*
SNTSMS	Society for New Testament Studies Monograph Series
SNTW	Studies of the New Testament and Its World
SP	Sacra Pagina
SR	*Studies in Religion*
ST	*Studia Theologica*
STAC	Studien und Texte zu Antike und Christentum
StBibLit	Studies in Biblical Literature (Lang)
SUNT	Studien zur Umwelt des Neuen Testaments
TAPA	*Transactions of the American Philological Association*
TBN	Themes in Biblical Narrative
TDNT	*Theological Dictionary of the New Testament.* Edited by Gerhard Kittel and Gerhard Friedrich. Translated by Geoffrey W. Bromiley. 10 vols. Grand Rapids: Eerdmans, 1964–1976
TDOT	*Theological Dictionary of the Old Testament.* Edited by G. Johannes Botterweck and Helmer Ringgren. Translated by John T. Willis et al. 8 vols. Grand Rapids: Eerdmans, 1974–2006
THNTC	Two Horizons New Testament Commentary

TLG	*Thesaurus Linguae Graecae: A Digital Library of Greek Literature* (University of California, Irvine; online at: http://stephanus.tlg.uci.edu)
TLNT	*Theological Lexicon of the New Testament.* Ceslas Spicq. Translated and edited by James D. Ernest. 3 vols. Peabody, MA: Hendrickson, 1994
TLZ	*Theologische Literaturzeitung*
TS	Texts and Studies
TSAJ	Texte und Studien zum antiken Judentum
TynBul	*Tyndale Bulletin*
TZ	*Theologische Zeitschrift*
VC	*Vigiliae Christianae*
VCSup	Vigiliae Christianae Supplements
WBC	Word Biblical Commentary
WUNT	Wissenschaftliche Untersuchungen zum Neuen Testament
WW	*Word and World*
ZKG	*Zeitschrift für Kirchengeschichte*
ZNT	*Zeitschrift für Neues Testament*
ZNW	*Zeitschrift für die neutestamentliche Wissenschaft und die Kunde der älteren Kirche*

Introduction

On Saturday, April 27, 2019, a man walked into a synagogue in Poway, California, and opened fire, killing one person and wounding others.[1] The attack came exactly six months after a mass shooting in a synagogue in Pittsburgh, Pennsylvania, in which eleven people were killed and others wounded—the deadliest antisemitic attack in US history and symptomatic of a recent rise in such incidents.[2] In May 2019, the German government's antisemitism commissioner, Felix Klein, warned that it could be unsafe for Jews to wear the *kippah* in public[3]—a warning that led to a moving call for solidarity with Jews on the part of the wider German public as Klein later urged "all citizens in Berlin and everywhere in Germany to wear the kippah on Saturday [May 31, Al-Quds (Jerusalem) day]."[4] The newspaper *Das Bild* provided a cut-out *kippah*, urging that "if just one person in our country cannot wear the kippa without putting themselves in danger, then the answer can only be that we all wear the kippa. The kippa is part of Germany."[5] In the UK, the parliamentary

---

1. See "San Diego Synagogue Shooting: One Person Dead in Poway, California," *BBC News*, April 28, 2019, https://www.bbc.co.uk/news/world-us-canada-48081535.

2. See Hugo Bachega, "The Threat of Rising Anti-Semitism," *BBC News*, November 2, 2018, https://www.bbc.co.uk/news/world-us-canada-46038438.

3. See "German Jews Warned Not to Wear Kippas after Rise in Anti-Semitism," *BBC News*, May 26, 2019, https://www.bbc.co.uk/news/world-europe-48411735.

4. Quoted in Emily Jones, "Germans Urged to Wear Kippah in Solidarity with Jewish Community," *CBN News*, May 29, 2019, https://www1.cbn.com/cbnnews/israel/2019/may/germans-urged-to-wear-kippah-in-solidarity-with-jewish-community. See also "Germans Urged to Wear Jewish Yarmulke in Solidarity," *Deutsche Welle*, accessed June 18, 2019, https://www.dw.com/en/germans-urged-to-wear-jewish-yarmulke-in-solidarity/a-48919776.

5. "Wenn auch nur einer in unserem Land nicht Kippa tragen kann, ohne sich in Gefahr zu bringen, kann die Antwort nur lauten, dass wir alle Kippa tragen. Die Kippa gehört zu Deutschland" (Julian Reichelt, "Die Kippa gehört zu Deutschland," *Das Bild*,

Labour Party is caught up in a long-running argument about the extent of antisemitism in its ranks.[6]

Clearly the risk of antisemitic violence and the existence of the underlying ideology has by no means disappeared from Western Europe and North America. But such attacks can also be part of a wider picture in which hostility and violence are targeted at those not part of what is perceived to be a threatened white Christian population, whose sense of threat heightened especially in the wake of terrorist attacks such as 9/11 in the USA and 7/7 in the UK. There are of course also tensions between Jews and Muslims, or Israelis and Arabs, that can exhibit such hostility (as the al-Quds day warnings indicate), but the white Christian Poway murderer compared his own synagogue attack with the deadly attack on mosques in Christchurch, New Zealand, just one month before, in which fifty-one people were killed.[7] Like the killer who attacked the Pittsburgh synagogue, these terrorists embody a form of extreme white nationalism, according to which Jews and Muslims represent a threat. Nor is this a form of hostility that can be categorized in purely religious terms: whiteness and Christianness here coalesce in the identity and ideology of the attackers. In some parts of the world, Christians, too, are a persecuted minority,[8] but on the principle of Matt 7:3–5// Luke 6:41–42 (of focusing on the log in my own eye rather than the specks

---

May 26, 2019, https://www.bild.de/politik/kolumnen/kolumne/kommentar-die-kippa -gehoert-zu-deutschland-62202206.bild.html). See also Julian Röpcke, "Kippa-Warnung für Juden im Land sollte 'aufrütteln,'" *Das Bild*, May 26, 2019, https://www.bild.de /politik/inland/kolumne/antisemitismus-beauftragter-kippa-warnung-fuer-juden-sollte -aufruetteln-62201624.bild.html.

6. The accusations, however contested, have been sufficient to initiate a formal investigation by the Equality and Human Rights Commission of the UK; see Lizzy Buchan, "Labour Antisemitism: Equality Watchdog Launches Formal Investigation into Party," *The Independent*, May 28, 2019, https://www.independent.co.uk/news/uk/politics/labour -antisemitism-jewish-members-mps-racism-equality-human-rights-commission-a8932876 .html. The Conservative Party, at the same time, faces calls for a comparable investigation into Islamophobia among its membership; see Lizzie Dearden, "Conservative Party Islamophobia Must Be Investigated by Equality Watchdog, Britain's Largest Muslim Group Demands," *The Independent*, May 28, 2019, https://www.independent.co.uk/news/uk/pol itics/conservative-party-islamophobia-racism-muslim-uk-investigate-tory-a8932851.html.

7. See "San Diego Synagogue Shooting." In these opening paragraphs, I have followed the lead of the New Zealand Prime Minister, Jacinda Ardern, in not naming any of the attackers whose actions I report. See Calla Wahlquist, "Ardern Says She Will Never Speak Name of Christchurch Suspect," *The Guardian*, March 19, 2019, https://www.theguardian.com/world/2019 /mar/19/new-zealand-shooting-ardern-says-she-will-never-speak-suspects-name.

8. See, e.g., Patrick Wintour, "Persecution of Christians 'Coming Close to Genocide'

in others' eyes), as well as on the basis of my own location and areas of competence, my focus in this work is on those contexts where both "white" and "Christian"—notwithstanding the problems and complexities of those labels—form the dominant majority. Indeed, despite aspirations that our research and writing be "international" in its relevance, I am conscious that this work is primarily shaped by the context of the UK, Western Europe, and the USA.

The connections between Christianness and whiteness are one indication of the ways in which religion and ethnicity or race—these are contested terms, as we shall see—are overlapping and intersecting facets of identity, implicated in enduring social conflicts around the globe. Whiteness itself is, of course, an ideological construct and not any kind of innate or objective category. We might also want to argue about whether Christianity, Judaism, and Islam are properly to be understood as religions, having nothing intrinsically to do with ethnic or racial identity. But these religious identities are often bound up—in complex and historically variable ways—with perceptions and constructions of ethnicity, race, and national identity (see §3.3 below). Indicative of this realization, a special issue of *Ethnic and Racial Studies* (36, no. 3 [2013]), edited by Nasar Meer, examines the connections between religion and racialization. Contributors argue for the need to integrate much more closely the study of race and racism on the one hand and antisemitism and Islamophobia on the other.[9]

The study of Christian origins, and of Christian theology more broadly, is much more relevant to this subject than it might initially appear. For a start, however distorted or objectionable, the justifications offered by some of the terrorists mentioned above draw on ideas from the field of Christian theology. The Poway synagogue killer left a seven-page letter detailing the reasons for his actions—a letter that included Reformed/Calvinist theol-

---

in Middle East—Report," *The Guardian*, May 2, 2019, https://www.theguardian.com/world/2019/may/02/persecution-driving-christians-out-of-middle-east-report.

9. See esp. the introductory essay, Nasar Meer, "Racialization and Religion: Race, Culture and Difference in the Study of Antisemitism and Islamophobia," *Ethnic and Racial Studies* 36 (2013): 385–98; also Nasar Meer, "Semantics, Scales and Solidarities in the Study of Antisemitism and Islamophobia," *Ethnic and Racial Studies* 36 (2013): 500–515. See also the section of readings on "Racism and anti-semitism" in Les Back and John Solomos, eds., *Theories of Race and Racism: A Reader*, Routledge Student Readers (London: Routledge, 2000), 191–252, which opens with the editors' remark that "one of the regrettable features of much contemporary theorising about race and racism has been the tendency to leave the question of anti-semitism to one side"; see also the comments in their introduction, pp. 10–11.

ogy as well as radical white nationalist ideology, thus causing shock and soul-searching among Christian pastors from the killer's denomination and beyond.[10] More broadly, a recent study of attitudes in Western European countries has shown that "both non-practicing and churchgoing Christians are more likely than the [religiously] unaffiliated to hold negative views of immigrants, Muslims and Jews." High percentages of Christians—the median figure across all countries surveyed is 49 percent of church-attending Christians, compared with 32 percent among the religiously unaffiliated—also consider Islam to be "fundamentally incompatible" with their national values and culture.[11] There remain, then, serious challenges in terms of addressing attitudes and prejudices among Christians, attitudes sometimes reinforced by preaching and biblical interpretation, despite what is by now quite a long history of efforts by church bodies and academics to confront and repudiate antisemitism, racism, and hostility to those of other religions, immigrants, refugees, and so on.[12]

But the issue runs even deeper than this. A notable common feature of a number of recent treatments of modern ideologies of race, and of the problematic constructions of whiteness in particular, is the claim that these ideologies find their roots in efforts to forge Christian identity over against Judaism, even if there is disagreement as to where and when the problematic moves took place.

In a major volume offering "a theological account of race," for example, J. Kameron Carter offers as a "fundamental contention . . . that modernity's racial imagination has its genesis in the theological problem of Christianity's quest to sever itself from its Jewish roots."[13] The *Rassenfrage*, Carter argues, is inextricably linked to the *Judenfrage*.[14] Carter thus speaks of "theology's complicity in forging a modern racial imagination" such that "the problem of whiteness itself"

10. See Julie Zauzmer, "The Alleged Synagogue Shooter Was a Churchgoer Who Talked Christian Theology, Raising Tough Questions for Evangelical Pastors," *The Washington Post*, May 1, 2019, https://www.washingtonpost.com/religion/2019/05/01/alleged-synagogue-shooter-was-churchgoer-who-articulated-christian-theology-prompting-tough-questions-evangelical-pastors/.

11. "Being Christian in Western Europe" (Pew Research Center, 2018), 20; PDF available at https://www.pewforum.org/2018/05/29/being-christian-in-western-europe.

12. For just one early example, see Vatican II's "Declaration on the Relation of the Church to Non-Christian Religions" (*Nostra Aetate*), available at http://www.vatican.va/archive/hist_councils/ii_vatican_council/documents/vat-ii_decl_19651028_nostra-aetate_en.html.

13. J. Kameron Carter, *Race: A Theological Account* (Oxford: Oxford University Press, 2008), 4; cf. 229, 285, 315, 372.

14. See Carter, *Race*, 40, 80–81, 104, 121.

is theological—"the core theological problem of our times."[15] Likewise, Willie James Jennings argues that "theology" became "the trigger for the classificatory subjugation of all non-white, non-Western peoples," with "whiteness" as "a way of organizing bodies by proximity to and approximation of white bodies."[16] For Jennings, too, "the most decisive and central theological distortion that exists in the church" is "the replacement of Israel, or, in its proper theological term, supercessionism."[17] This distortion plays out not only in relation to Jews but also in relation to non-white, non-Christian others: the "supercessionist problematic . . . expressed itself in the New World of colonialism."[18] According to Jennings, this supercessionist move leads to a kind of Christian "universalism" that "undermines all forms of identity except that of the colonialist."[19]

While Carter traces the problems particularly to Immanuel Kant (1724– 1804), seeing there the modern racializing of Christian supercessionism, Jennings examines narratives from the time of Portugese colonialism in the fifteenth century onward. James Thomas argues that the origins of modern Western racial ideology should be traced still further back, before the time of European colonialism and the European Enlightenment, to the "racial formation" of Jews in medieval Christian Europe.[20] In this way, Thomas suggests, "it was Christianity which provided the vocabularies of difference for the Western world," leading Meer to observe that "the category of race was co-constituted with religion."[21] How far back the problems begin is a moot point: Rosemary Radford Ruether long ago raised the provocative question of whether "anti-Judaism is too deeply rooted in the foundations of Christianity to be rooted out entirely without destroying the whole structure," noting in particular the enduring tendency to contrast the "particularism" of Judaism with the "universalism" of Christianity.[22] Denise Kimber Buell

---

15. Carter, *Race*, 8 and 6 respectively.

16. Willie James Jennings, *The Christian Imagination: Theology and the Origins of Race* (New Haven: Yale University Press, 2010), 87 and 59 respectively.

17. Jennings, *Christian Imagination*, 32.

18. Jennings, *Christian Imagination*, 251.

19. Jennings, *Christian Imagination*, 145. See further Jennings's reading of Colenso's thought, especially as expressed in his commentary on Romans and his "racialization of the soteriological vision" (138; see 132–50).

20. James M. Thomas, "The Racial Formation of Medieval Jews: A Challenge to the Field," *Ethnic and Racial Studies* 33 (2010): 1737–55.

21. Thomas, "Racial Formation of Medieval Jews," 1739; Meer, "Racialization and Religion," 389.

22. Rosemary Radford Ruether, *Faith and Fratricide: The Theological Roots of Anti-Semitism* (New York: Seabury; London: Search Press, 1975), 228, 233.

(whose work I shall describe more fully in chapter 2), focusing on texts from the second and third centuries, demonstrates how "ethnoracial" reasoning is deployed in the construction of early Christian identity such that there is an ethnoracial particularity to Christian identity from that time, even when it is depicted as an identity all people might potentially share.[23] It is not only in "heretical" or "gnostic" theologies that the potential problems might originate.[24] Further back still, the New Testament texts not only include polemic against (other) Jews—polemic that has a long and unfortunate history of effects (e.g., Matt 27:25; John 8:44)—but may also, as this book will seek to show, construct Christian identity by drawing on characteristics long associated with ethnic or racial groups. Moreover, as we shall see further in the course of this study, an enduring tendency, albeit in changing terminology, is to *depict* the Christian achievement as something that universalizes—offers to all humanity—that which was otherwise restricted or bound within Jewish ethnic particularity. While this might sound a note that can be used to challenge racism and break down barriers between people, it is also problematic, as Buell has stressed, since this vision of Christianity's transcendence of ethnic or racial distinctions is forged in contrast to a sense of Judaism's particularity, even its ethnocentrism. Christian inclusivism, we might suggest, is expressed in contrast to Judaism's exclusiveness.[25]

This focus on the interface between Judaism and Christianity—and specifically on the construction of Christian identity and theology in relation to Judaism—as at the heart of modern Western ideologies of race also begins to indicate specifically why the discipline of New Testament studies might be more crucially bound up with such issues than is often thought. For a start, the New Testament preserves the earliest documents that record the emergence of the movement centered around Jesus of Nazareth and the thought of some of its earliest proponents. That movement articulated its sense of identity within Judaism but also in tension and dispute with other Jews and in ways that eventually—much later—led to its distinct identity

---

23. Denise Kimber Buell, *Why This New Race: Ethnic Reasoning in Early Christianity* (New York: Columbia University Press, 2005).

24. As seems to be implied in Carter, *Race*, 11–36, which describes Irenaeus's engagement with the Gnosticism of his time. On the relation between modern racist ideas and aspects of early Christian discourse, see Denise Kimber Buell, "Early Christian Universalism and Modern Forms of Racism," in *The Origins of Racism in the West*, ed. Miriam Eliav-Feldon, Benjamin Isaac, and Joseph Ziegler (Cambridge: Cambridge University Press, 2009), 109–31.

25. See Buell, *Why This New Race*, 11–12, 28.

and existence. Moreover, the New Testament has long been a primary site for scholarly investigation of Christian origins, such that it is through readings of the New Testament and other contemporary evidence that scholars articulate their sense of the early Christian achievement—almost inevitably in comparison to the Judaism within which the Christian movement first formed. Two further factors add to the influence of the interpretation of this particular set of texts. First, the New Testament is, of course, part of the canon of Christian scripture such that it carries authority for Christians and is a prominent foundation for contemporary reflection, whether in preaching, Bible study, or church documents addressing issues of ethical or doctrinal concern, all of which are often informed, directly or indirectly, by scholarship on New Testament texts.[26] Second, the discipline of New Testament scholarship reflects a predominantly Christian perspective, whether that derives from the personal commitments of many of its practitioners or the institutional contexts in which they work. Given such a perspective, it is not difficult to see why it is likely that the Christian difference, as it were, will be constructed positively vis-à-vis Judaism. New Testament studies, in short, may be an important site—not the only one, to be sure—where we may explore the possible connections between the scholarly construals of early Christian identity in its relationship to Jewish identity and the epistemological foundations of Western European Christian self-identity, with all its wider implications for ideologies of religious and racial difference.

Outline of the Study

There are a number of ways in which one might begin to address these issues. My initial focus is to explore some of the major paradigms through which work in the field of New Testament studies has construed the potential achievement of earliest Christianity and the kinds of contrasts drawn between "Christianity" and "Judaism," contested terms for the early period, as I discuss in the next section. Developing in detail a point made by others, the opening chapter surveys work from the time of Ferdinand Christian Baur to the present day, seeking to show that, despite the shifts of paradigm

---

26. On the importance of the NT as canon "in shaping and implementing modern notions of race and ethnicity," see Denise Kimber Buell, "Challenges and Strategies for Speaking about Ethnicity in the New Testament and New Testament Studies," *SEÅ* 79 (2014): 34–37, quotation from 36.

and perspective and the changes in sociopolitical context, there remains in various forms a prominent tendency to reproduce a kind of structural dichotomy between an ethnically particular "exclusive" Judaism and an open, all-embracing "inclusive" Christianity. One of the main foundations underlying this dichotomy is a sense of Judaism as an ethnic or racial identity, such that its particularity is of an "ethnic" kind. Critically exploring the validity and value of this contrast invites consideration of what such a label might mean, how it might relate to the category of "religion," and in what ways, if at all, it might also characterize the particularity of early Christian identity.

Following in the footsteps of recent research (particularly the seminal work of Buell,[27] outlined in more detail in ch. 2), and informed by recent social-scientific work on ethnicity, race, and religion (ch. 3), the central chapters of the book offer a series of comparative studies of Jewish and early Christian perspectives on topics that are commonly seen as characteristics of ethnic groups (see §3.1): ancestry, kinship, and marriage (ch. 4); way of life, common culture, and the socialization of children (ch. 5); and homeland and territory (ch. 6). The sequence then continues with an examination of what is, explicitly or implicitly, at the heart of any sense of identity as an ethnic group, namely "self-consciousness" as a people (see §3.1): In what ways, where, and when do the early Christians begin to describe themselves as a "people," and what are the implications of such self-descriptions (ch. 6)? In all of these chapters, it becomes clear that these features of Jewish or early Christian identity cannot easily be categorized as either "ethnic" or "religious" in character; religious commitments and practices are, as elsewhere (see §3.3), inextricably bound up with a sense of "ethnic" identity as a people. The final comparative chapter (ch. 8) considers a topic—mission and conversion—that might more conventionally be assigned to the field of "religion," though even here there is no neat separation from ethnic or national identities.

These studies are inevitably selective in their engagement with early Christian and (especially) Jewish sources. In the former case, many of my detailed exegetical examples come from the letters of Paul and from 1 Peter, though the engagement also includes other New Testament texts and extends into early Christian literature of the first two centuries. In the latter case, aside from biblical texts, many of my examples are drawn from Josephus and Philo, each of whom is, of course, a distinctive figure representing a particular perspective on Judaism, albeit perspectives that are influential in

27. Buell, *Why This New Race.*

8

retrospect due to the scale of their literary output.[28] In relation to the Jewish sources, I make no claim to break new ground or to offer innovative analyses; indeed, I have tried to be guided by the contours of recent scholarship. With regard to the New Testament texts, I hope that the analysis of a range of texts in light of the comparisons with Jewish writings offers new insights into the ways in which ethnic—or ethnoreligious—discourse and practice might have featured in the construction of early Christian identities. As far as I can see, my argument does not depend on any assumption that the texts selected as case studies are "standard" or "representative," only that they illustrate the kinds of perspectives that can be found in both Jewish and Christian texts and thus offer examples from which comparisons may be drawn.

The findings of these central chapters, summarized in more detail in §9.1, suggest that both Jewish and early Christian traditions—differences and internal diversity notwithstanding—exhibit the kinds of discourse and social practice often associated with ethnic groups, such that both might be regarded, in certain ways, as "exclusive" or "ethnocentric." Aspects of the discourse and practice of early Christian identity-formation—such as self-description as a people or rules about marrying insiders—suggest impulses toward "ethnicization," though it is, I shall argue, not necessary or helpful to categorize Christian identity as "ethnic." Indeed, these modern categories can be a barrier to explanation as much as a route toward it, as both Max Weber and Rogers Brubaker, in their different ways, suggest.[29] In both Jewish and Christian traditions, "religious" convictions and practices are constitutive in defining identity and belonging, such that a distinction between "ethnic" or "religious" identity is hard to draw. This is particularly so given the evidence, explored in chapter 8, for various patterns of inclusion and possibilities for "joining" such that, contrary to frequent depictions and assumptions, Jewish communities at the time might be seen as more tolerant, inclusive, and welcoming than the early Christian assemblies. At least, that provocative comparison might pose questions about the pattern of contrast embedded in the traditions of New Testament scholarship. What does seem to characterize the early Christian movement is a more zealous sense

28. With regard to Philo, for example, Jennifer Otto illustrates the ambivalence of Philo's identity for early Christian writers (specifically Clement of Alexandria, Origen, and Eusebius) for whom Philo was both "like us" and "like them"—difficult to fit into the binary of "one of us" and "one of them" partly due to the overlapping and fluid identities of Jews and Christians. See Jennifer Otto, *Philo of Alexandria and the Construction of Jewishness in Early Christian Writings*, OECS (Oxford: Oxford University Press, 2018), quoted phrases from 197.

29. See §3.1, pp. 72–74 with nn. 24–30.

of missionary commitment, leading to more proactive forms of proselytization, though even here the picture needs to be carefully qualified (see ch. 8).

Reaching these conclusions returns us to the issues with which the book began and the question about the ways in which the modern discipline of New Testament studies—as an academic tradition developed and sustained in the West—might be enmeshed and implicated in constructions of both religious and racial identity that continue to reverberate in the world of today. Since the discipline developed in Europe during the time of Europe's major colonial expansion, the question requires us to consider how far it may have been shaped by the ideologies of that period and whether the contemporary discipline has sufficiently shifted from the patterns of thinking established during that formative era. In framing the question in this way, I hope it is clear that my concern is not with the intentions, commitments, or prejudices of any specific individuals, past or present, but rather with the ways in which our patterns of thought and structuring paradigms may be the product of their contexts of origin—more profoundly than many of us generally appreciate (see further in §9.1, pp. 309–10). Moreover, my use of the first person plural above is deliberate and indicates that I include myself within this established disciplinary tradition, such that this work is, in part, also an exercise in critical self-interrogation.

As I attempt this critical interrogation of the established mainstream of New Testament studies, with its European origins and its Euro-American dominance, I turn in the final chapter to whiteness studies, drawing on that discussion to pose questions for reflection (§9.2). Recalling the opening paragraphs above, I seek to explore these questions in a way that brings religious and ethnoracial concerns together, asking about both the Christianness and the whiteness of the dominant interpretative tradition and how these may be visible in our exegesis. One way to try to exhibit this enmeshedness of contemporary exegesis in a geopolitical and ethnoreligious context is to show some of the correspondences between contemporary Western liberal ideology and recent reconstructions (including my own) of early Christian visions and strategies. If this kind of enmeshedness can be shown, then it has implications for how we think about issues of epistemology. Feminist scholars have been prominent among those who have argued that "knowledge" is not, and cannot be, an innocent, neutral, disembodied production but is intrinsically bound up with the location of the knower, not only in individual terms but also in terms of broader disciplinary, sociopolitical, religious or racial contexts (see §9.2, pp. 316–17). What that means in this context is that fuller and richer insight into the New Testament, its history, legacies, and contemporary significance requires the contributions of a diverse body of interpreters—in both religious and ethnoracial terms. Moreover, the "alternative" perspectives brought by such scholars must not be policed at the margins, labeled by their specificity or their "minority" status in contrast to the unlabeled "core" of traditional white Christian exegesis; rather, they need to be seen as equally crucial sources of insight and knowledge.

As these remarks already indicate, the final chapter ranges widely, offering reflections that ripple out beyond the specific concern with the ethnicizing features of early Christian discourse and social practice. I confess—perhaps unwisely—that I remain somewhat unsure how successfully I have framed these final proposals or related them to the central chapters of the book. But I am at least convinced that conversation about such issues is important and that it is incumbent on "white" interpreters, as Greg Carey suggests, to "invest themselves in the conversation" that others have been urging for some time.[30]

I have also become conscious, partly through the conversations that have surrounded the work on this project, that the book's structure exhibits a particular style of argument in which (at least in my mind) each step leads to the next, such that the final chapter is the point at which, at last, the major claims and their wider implications are made clear. I am aware that this style is not everyone's preference and that some might wish the major claims to be put more squarely up front. This introduction serves at least to outline the contours of the landscape that lies ahead, but it remains my instinct not to present conclusions at the outset but to try to work toward them in the hope that readers may follow the evidence and arguments along the way to a point where they find themselves persuaded (or not) rather than judging the position *ab initio*. That said, I am conscious that the various parts of the book, though connected, can to some extent stand (or fall) separately and that some readers may be more (or less) convinced by one part than by another. Depending on their interests, readers might choose to approach the book in various ways. Of course, reading sequentially comes closest to following my intentions for the argument, but someone most interested in the broader issues of religious and racial identities shaping the field of New Testament interpretation might skip from chapter 1 to chapter 9. Readers

---

30. Greg Carey, "Introduction and a Proposal: Culture, Power, and Identity in White New Testament Studies," in *Soundings in Cultural Criticism: Perspectives and Methods in Culture, Power, and Identity in the New Testament*, ed. Francisco Lozada Jr. and Greg Carey (Minneapolis: Fortress, 2013), 6.

most interested in the historical and exegetical studies might focus their attention on chapters 4–8. Someone interested in the current landscapes of research might find chapters 2–3 valuable as a point of reference. Before we turn to the first stage in the argument, however, it is necessary to explain some decisions regarding terminology and method.

"Jews" and "Christians," AD or CE? Issues of Terminology

Already in outlining the chapters that lie ahead, I have referred to "Jewish" and "Christian" texts and traditions in ways that may have caused some readers to raise a suspicious eyebrow. The key labels "Jew" and "Christian" (and their related nouns and adjectives, Judaism, Jewish, Christianity, etc.) have been the subject of considerable critical discussion in recent years, and for some scholars, one or both terms (and their associated vocabulary) may be judged inappropriate and anachronistic for the first century CE (on the potentially problematic term "CE," see further below).

With regard to the term Ἰουδαῖος, there have been strong arguments mounted that the traditional translation "Jew" implies a modern category of "religious" identity, whereas ancient Ἰουδαῖοι should instead be seen as a "people," an ethnic group (or ἔθνος) like other ancient people-groups, with ancestral laws and customs (including religious practices), a homeland, and so on (see §2.1).[31] Assessing this case depends partly on considerations concerning the nature of Jewish/Judean identity at the time, on how "religious" and "ethnic" identities should be understood, and on whether there had already been, from, say, the Hasmonean period, a shift away from an ethnic kind of identity toward one that is more religiously or culturally defined (see chs. 2–3). But another objection raised by those who oppose the shift from "Jew" to "Judean" concerns the risk that any connection between contemporary Jews and their earlier forebears is thereby erased and that Jews thus effectively disappear from the historical records of the period, including the New Testament, leaving what Amy-Jill Levine calls a *Judenrein* New Testament. Contrary to the intentions of those who argue for the translation "Judean," there is, Levine argues, the potential for the shift to foster contemporary anti-Jewish or antisemitic ideologies.[32] This

31. Particularly influential in making this case is Steve Mason, "Jews, Judaeans, Judaizing, Judaism: Problems of Categorization in Ancient History," *JSJ* 38 (2007): 457–512.
32. Amy-Jill Levine, *The Misunderstood Jew: The Church and the Scandal of the Jew-*

in turn raises broader questions about the task and responsibility of the historian.[33]

One of the difficulties in deciding on any single translational equivalent is that the Greek word Ἰουδαῖος can indicate various groups in the ancient texts: the inhabitants of Judea; those from neighboring areas, such as the Idumeans, joined in political alliance with the Judeans; those scattered in the diaspora who identify as Ἰουδαῖοι and share a commitment to the Jewish (Judean?) way of life.[34] Acts 2:5–14 illustrates the multivalence of the term:[35] in v. 5 it seems to be an inclusive term denoting all those who identify themselves as Jewish (or, one might say, with the Judean way of life), whatever their geographical (or ethnic) origin (they come "from every nation" [ἀπὸ παντὸς ἔθνους]). Within this group of Ἰουδαῖοι, a distinction can be drawn

---

ish Jesus (New York: HarperOne, 2006), 159–66. Wolfgang Stegemann, for example, while accepting the arguments for taking Ἰουδαῖος to denote an ethnic rather than a religious identity, suggests that these concerns warrant retaining both "Jew" and "Judean" as translations of Ἰουδαῖος. See Wolfgang Stegemann, "Religion als Teil von ethnischer Identität: Zur aktuellen Debatte um die Kategorisierung des antiken Judentums," *Kirche und Israel* 25 (2010): 57–58; *Jesus und seine Zeit*, Biblische Enzyklopädie 10 (Stuttgart: Kohlhammer, 2010), 180–236, esp. 193, 204–7, 222, 234.

33. For an indication of the scope of the debate and the range of perspectives, see Timothy Michael Law and Charles Halton, eds., *Jew and Judean: A Forum on Politics and Historiography in the Translation of Ancient Texts* (Los Angeles: Marginalia Review of Books, 2014). A recent and mediating assessment is offered by John M. G. Barclay, "Ἰουδαῖος: Ethnicity and Translation," in *Ethnicity, Race, Religion: Identities and Ideologies in Early Jewish and Christian Texts and in Modern Biblical Interpretation*, ed. Katherine M. Hockey and David G. Horrell (London: Bloomsbury T&T Clark, 2018), 46–58. Note, too, the conciliatory comments of Steve Mason, *Orientation to the History of Roman Judaea* (Eugene, OR: Cascade, 2016), 278.

34. On the various meanings, see, e.g., Morton Smith, "The Gentiles in Judaism 125 BCE–CE 66," in *The Early Roman Period*, vol. 3 of *The Cambridge History of Judaism*, ed. William Horbury, W. D. Davies, and John Sturdy (Cambridge: Cambridge University Press, 1999), 210.

35. See the discussion in Daniel R. Schwartz, *Studies in the Jewish Background of Christianity*, WUNT 60 (Tübingen: Mohr Siebeck, 1992), 122–26, though his suggestion that v. 5a originally referred "to Judaeans (from various parts of Judaea) living in Jerusalem" and that the reference to those "from every nation" was added at a later stage of the story's development (see 125–26) seems unnecessarily complicated if one accepts both the multivalence of the term Ἰουδαῖος and the phenomenon of multiple Jewish ethnicities, on which see Cynthia M. Baker, "'From Every Nation under Heaven': Jewish Ethnicities in the Greco-Roman World," in *Prejudice and Christian Beginnings: Investigating Race, Gender, and Ethnicity in Early Christian Studies*, ed. Laura Nasrallah and Elisabeth Schüssler Fiorenza (Minneapolis: Fortress, 2009), 79–99; also pp. 189–91 below.

between those who are (in a more specific sense) Ἰουδαῖοι—meaning either from Judea or born "Jewish"—and those who are incomers or proselytes (προσήλυτοι, v. 11).[36] In v. 14, Ἰουδαῖοι are distinguished from "all who live in Jerusalem."

To use "Jew" for *all* such instances risks imposing a common (and predominantly religious) identity-label that conceals the diversity of use and meaning of the term Ἰουδαῖος. On the other hand, to avoid the term "Jew" entirely may elevate an ethnic-geographical designation (Judean) over a religio-cultural one in ways that are at least open to question (see §3.3) and may have problematic implications. These latter considerations have led me to retain the terms Jew, Judaism, and so on at various points in the chapters that follow, though I have also frequently chosen simply to transliterate the term *Ioudaios*.[37] This avoidance of a translation may be seen as merely evading the issue, but it is in keeping with the broader arguments of this book insofar as it leaves open and unspecified what kind of identity we are observing and the ways in which religious and ethnic facets of identity might intersect.

With regard to the term "Christian," also long standard in scholarship on New Testament texts, there are different reasons why some have argued that it is inappropriate as a designation for the followers of Christ who constitute the membership of the earliest assemblies.[38] It has become common to use alternative terms such as "Christ follower" or "Jesus groups." The two main reasons for the shift are related. The first is that the term "Christian" is anachronistic, since a distinctly identifiable entity (or "religion") called Christianity did not emerge until some time after the New Testament period, perhaps not until the fourth century. The second is that the term can be taken to imply that identity as a "Christian" was something distinct and separate from being a "Jew," whereas the early Christian movement is to be located firmly "within Judaism." The shift in terminology is in part, then,

---

36. For further discussion of the term προσήλυτος, see §8.1.4 below.

37. Following, for example, Caroline Johnson Hodge, *If Sons, Then Heirs: A Study of Kinship and Ethnicity in the Letters of Paul* (Oxford: Oxford University Press, 2007), 11–15, who offers a thoughtful consideration of the issues involved.

38. See, for example, Philip F. Esler, *Conflict and Identity in Romans: The Social Setting of Paul's Letter* (Minneapolis: Fortress, 2003), 12–13; John H. Elliott, "Jesus the Israelite Was Neither a 'Jew' Nor a 'Christian': On Correcting Misleading Nomenclature," *Journal for the Study of the Historical Jesus* 5 (2007): 147–48; Anders Runesson, "The Question of Terminology: The Architecture of Contemporary Discussions on Paul," in *Paul within Judaism: Restoring the First-Century Context to the Apostle*, ed. Mark D. Nanos and Magnus Zetterholm (Minneapolis: Fortress, 2015), 53–77.

intended to make clear both the historical misunderstanding and the potentially pernicious consequences of popular notions—such as the idea that Paul moved from being a Jew to being a Christian.[39]

I fully agree that we need to challenge anachronistic perspectives on the earliest followers of Christ and emphasize that the early Christian movement emerged within Judaism and is to be understood within that context. However, I am not entirely convinced that it is necessary or even preferable to drop the term "Christian" from our discussion of the New Testament and early Christian sources.

First, using the term "Christian" need not imply a separation of "Christianity" from "Judaism" or other such anachronistic notions. As the most concise designation of those who follow or believe in Christ, it could denote a group within Judaism, like "Essenes" or "Pharisees"; it at least leaves open the degree to which any distinction is presumed. We clearly need to challenge anachronistic assumptions, but changing the terminology is not necessarily the only way to do this. Terms mean different things in different historical and social contexts, and they change their meaning—sometimes drastically—over time. One way to avoid anachronism is to ensure that we attend to the particularities of what a term might mean in the context we are investigating.

The term "Christian" also has the advantage of being a term used within the New Testament, albeit only rarely and in relatively late documents (Acts 11:26; 26:28; 1 Pet 4:16). It is, unlike modern neologisms, the earliest specific term we have to identify those who profess allegiance to Jesus Christ; less specific labels, such as Luke's "the way" (ἡ ὁδός; e.g., Acts 9:2; 22:4; 24:14), only make sense within a wider literary context where it is clear which "way" is in view. Paul does not appear to know the term "Christian," but he does place a heavy focus on Christ as the defining mark of his and his converts' identity: he is an ἄνθρωπος ἐν Χριστῷ, an "in-Christ" (2 Cor 12:2; cf. 1 Cor 1:2; Gal 2:16–21; Phil 3:3–9).[40] We might use the label "in-Christ" to denote the members of Paul's assemblies—the "in-Christs" in Corinth, Rome, or wherever—but might also conclude that "Christian" is less clumsy and

---

39. Opposition to such views of Paul is signaled, for example, in the title of Pamela Eisenbaum's *Paul Was Not a Christian: The Original Message of a Misunderstood Apostle* (New York: HarperCollins, 2009) and in the scholarly coalition represented in Mark D. Nanos and Magnus Zetterholm, *Paul within Judaism.*

40. On this point, see David G. Horrell, "Grace, Race, and the People of God," in *One God, One People, One Future: Essays in Honour of N. T. Wright*, ed. John Anthony Dunne and Eric Lewellen (London: SPCK; Minneapolis: Fortress, 2018), 200–201.

functionally more or less equivalent. Moreover, just as Jews (rightly) want the translation of Ἰουδαῖος to signal some continuity between ancient and modern members of the people, Christians might legitimately want to signal a connection between the first believers in the resurrected Christ and those who identify with that same belief today.

I fully realize that not everyone will find these arguments persuasive. And I do not see anything crucial resting on this particular choice of terminology. So my final appeal on this point would be to ask those who find the use of the term "Christian" inappropriate in the context of discussing New Testament texts to mentally substitute their own preferred term in its place and to see if the observation or argument still stands.

More important in the context of the present study, however, is the categorization of these texts as "Christian" in such a way that comparisons are set out between "Jewish" and "Christian" documents. Whatever our terminology, some might ask whether this does not presume too great a distinction between what only later came to be two distinguishable traditions. There are various reasons why I think the categorization valid and pertinent here. First, notwithstanding their considerable diversity and their embeddedness within Judaism, New Testament (and other early Christian) texts are connected by their conviction, variously expressed, that Jesus is the Christ, God's anointed one, raised by God from the dead and exalted as Lord. Second, we read these texts from a retrospective standpoint in which the New Testament texts have been collected together and stand as a canon. It is in this form that they exercise their influence on modern ideologies of religion and race.[41] Third, it is the New Testament and other early Christian texts that form the particular focus for New Testament scholars seeking to discern and elucidate the particular character and achievement of earliest Christianity. In other words, in this context, whatever their diversity, it is the "Christian" texts that represent the early Christian perspective and will be compared with (other) Jewish texts on that basis. Testing the validity of the contrasts often drawn requires accepting the categorization on which it is based, if only heuristically.

There is one final terminological issue to be noted, even though it may pass unnoticed by the reader who skips this particular section of the introduction, and that is the categorization of dates with the labels BCE and CE. These terms, taken to refer to time before and into the "Common Era" have increasingly replaced BC and AD in biblical scholarship (and the related conventions or requirements of its publishers). The reasoning is clear and

---

41. Cf. the remarks of Buell, "Challenges and Strategies," 34–37.

explicit: the new labels neither presume nor express any Christian commitment but instead represent, as Robert Cargill suggests, "a standard that peoples of all nations and faiths can accept." By contrast, "the use of BC and AD perpetuates the stereotype that Christians are arrogant tyrants who insist on couching all of human history (including Jewish, Islamic, Indian, Chinese, etc.) as relative to the birth of Christ."[42]

The problem, as Wei Hsien Wan points out, is that this "change" retains precisely the Gregorian Christian system of dating—AD 70 simply becomes 70 CE—while concealing and universalizing the specifically Christian organization of history that is represented by the bifurcation of time at (around) the time of Jesus's birth.[43] Wan poses the question:

> Who, or what, then, makes it [*sic*] this Christian calendar "common," and for whom? That it is shared by almost all known societies, that it is ubiquitous and enjoys a dogmatic hold on societies all over the world, is a fact—but it is a fact that needs to be examined and explained, not simply repackaged so as to be more palatable.

"The answer," Wan suggests,

> is an uncomfortable one, for its dissemination is in turn tied to the emergence and spread of European modes and categories of knowledge under the conditions of modern colonialism. . . . The very notion of a "Common Era" carries with it a Christian—and, more importantly—Eurocentric pretense. Its status as the dominant way of measuring time was not acquired without material and ideological violence in many of the non-Western communities that have adopted it. The prerequisites of "common-ness" cannot simply be passed over.[44]

Equally important, not least in terms of issues to be addressed in the following chapters, is the concealment of particularity that occurs when a specifically Christian organization of time is (re)described as "common": this

---

42. Robert R. Cargill, "Why Christians Should Adopt the BCE/CE Dating System," *Bible and Interpretation*, September 2009, http://www.bibleinterp.com/opeds/why_3530.shtml.

43. Wei Hsien Wan, "Whose Time? Which Rationality? Reflections on Empire, 1 Peter, and the 'Common Era,'" *Postscripts: The Journal of Sacred Texts and Contemporary Worlds* 7 (2011): 288–93.

44. Wan, "Whose Time?," 291.

is a universalizing move that at the same time masks the specificity of the viewpoint that is being universalized. It does not signal its own particularity, and at the same time it brings other particularities under the organizing gaze of its "common" view from nowhere.[45]

My solution to this issue here is a somewhat minimal one. Accepting the acronyms BCE and CE rather than the faith-commitment implicit at least in AD (*anno domini*), I propose (as noted at the beginning of the list of abbreviations) to regard the "C" as denoting "Christian" rather than "Common," indicating that this organization of historical time is specifically Christian, even if, through a complex and often violent history, it has become widely adopted.

---

45. See Wan, "Whose Time?," 291–93.

PART I

Contexts of Research

A Persistent Structural Dichotomy: Jewish Ethnic Particularism and Christian Inclusivism

New Testament scholarship has developed and changed through the various phases of its modern history, and the shifts in the basic paradigms for the discipline have been considerable. Nevertheless, as this opening chapter will seek to show, despite these major changes and developments, influenced by changing sociopolitical contexts, there remains in various forms a frequent tendency to reproduce a kind of structural dichotomy between an ethnically particular or "exclusive" Judaism and an open, all-embracing "inclusive" Christianity. The specific terms and construals of this distinction vary, changing with different historical periods and approaches in scholarship, as we shall see; no single pair of terms captures the way in which the contrast is drawn. I refer to this distinction as "structural," echoing the use of this term in structuralist analysis of language, since despite the various terms used to depict the differences, there seems to me a broadly consistent structure underlying the contrast. Whether it is between particular and universal, exclusive and inclusive, or ethnic and trans-ethnic, a certain kind of dichotomy seems to remain, despite some critical voices along the way.[1]

---

1. For early questioning of the dichotomy between particular and universal, see Nils Alstrup Dahl, "The One God of Jews and Gentiles (Romans 3.29–30)," in *Studies in Paul* (Minneapolis: Augsburg, 1977), 178–91, esp. 191; Jon D. Levenson, "The Universal Horizon of Biblical Particularism," in *Ethnicity and the Bible*, ed. Mark G. Brett, BibInt (Leiden: Brill, 1996), 143–69; John M. G. Barclay, "Universalism and Particularism: Twin Components of Both Judaism and Early Christianity," in *A Vision for the Church: Studies in Early Christian Ecclesiology in Honour of J. P. M. Sweet*, ed. Markus Bockmuehl and Michael B. Thompson (Edinburgh: T&T Clark, 1997), 207–24; Anders Runesson, "Particularistic Judaism and Universalistic Christianity? Some Critical Remarks on Terminology and Theology," *ST* 54 (2000): 55–75; and more recently Gudrun Holtz, *Damit Gott sei alles in allem: Studien zum paulinischen und frühjüdischen Universalismus*, BZNW 149 (Berlin: De Gruyter, 2007). On the specific contrast between (Jewish) *ethnic* particularism and (Christian) universality,

The survey begins with Ferdinand Christian Baur, a founding figure of modern New Testament studies—at least in its historical-critical mode—whose influence continues to be felt within the discipline. We move next to consider the shift in perspective brought about particularly through the work of E. P. Sanders in the 1970s and '80s and the reinterpretation of New Testament texts—Paul in particular—in the work of "new perspective" scholars such as James D. G. Dunn and N. T. Wright. After this, our attention shifts to one of the perspectives generated by New Testament scholarship's engagement with the social sciences that began in the 1970s and gathered momentum through the following decades, namely the use of studies of ethnicity and social identity exemplified in the work of Philip Esler, among others. Similar recent perspectives on the "trans-ethnic" or inclusive character of the earliest Christian groups are also noted. Although there are certain figures whose important and influential work is highlighted in the survey that follows, my concern is not with individual biographies or the influence of personal identities but with the broader contexts in which the discipline of New Testament studies finds its shape.

1.1 Ferdinand Christian Baur and the Making of Modern New Testament Scholarship

It is hard to overestimate the influence of Ferdinand Christian Baur (1792–1860) and the Tübingen School of historical criticism on the making of modern New Testament scholarship. As Horton Harris remarks, "Within the two decades of its [the School's] existence the whole course of Biblical and especially New Testament criticism was fundamentally changed."[2] Despite much criticism and rejection of Baur's particular arguments (not least his arguments for the late dating and pseudonymity of many New Testament writings),[3] the agenda he pursued continues to shape the contours of the

---

see Stanley K. Stowers, *A Rereading of Romans: Justice, Jews and Gentiles* (New Haven: Yale University Press, 1994), 27–29, who casts this in terms of "an anachronistic distinction between religion and ethnicity" (27); Buell, *Why This New Race*, 10–13, 25–29; Johnson Hodge, *If Sons, Then Heirs*, 3–7; Cavan W. Concannon, *"When You Were Gentiles": Specters of Ethnicity in Roman Corinth and Paul's Corinthian Correspondence*, Synkrisis: Comparative Approaches to Early Christianity in Greco-Roman Culture (New Haven: Yale University Press, 2014), 1–7.

2. Horton Harris, *The Tübingen School* (Oxford: Clarendon, 1975), v.

3. For example, Baur accepted only four of Paul's letters as authentic—Romans, Gala-

discipline's landscape.[4] In his seminal article from 1831, on "the Christ-party in the Corinthian community, the opposition of Petrine and Pauline Christianity in the early church, the apostle Peter in Rome" (reproduced in part in his later book on Paul),[5] Baur developed the argument, earlier proposed by J. E. C. Schmidt, that the groups at Corinth to which Paul refers in 1 Cor 1:12 were essentially divided along a single fault line between Peter and Paul, with the Apollos group on Paul's side and the Christ group on Peter's.[6] This twofold division Baur saw as the basic fault line running through earliest Christian history: an opposition between Pauline (gentile) Christianity and Petrine (Jewish) Christianity that was eventually synthesized in catholic Christianity at the end of the second century. Baur saw later New Testament texts such as James, 1 Peter, Acts, and the Pastoral Epistles as indicative of the reconciling tendency that sought to establish this synthesis.[7]

That brief summary of Baur's central thesis might already indicate the profound influence on him of the philosopher Georg Wilhelm Friedrich Hegel (1770–1831), for whom the notion of dialectical opposition between thesis and antithesis resolving into synthesis is fundamental to understanding progress in history. There is some question as to whether Baur was already

---

tians, and 1–2 Corinthians—and dated the Pastoral Epistles late in the second century (as responding to the gnostic heresy). See the comprehensive treatment of Paul in Ferdinand Christian Baur, *Paul the Apostle of Jesus Christ: His Life and Works, His Epistles and Teachings*, 2nd ed., 2 vols. (London: Williams & Norgate, 1873–1875), and the integration of all the Pauline letters into Baur's view of church history in *The Church History of the First Three Centuries*, trans. Allan Menzies, 3rd ed., 2 vols. (London: Williams & Norgate, 1878–1879).

4. See, e.g., the recent essays in Martin Bauspiess, Christof Landmesser, and David Lincicum, eds., *Ferdinand Christian Baur und die Geschichte des Urchristentums*, WUNT 333 (Tübingen: Mohr Siebeck, 2014).

5. Ferdinand Christian Baur, "Die Christuspartei in der korinthische Gemeinde, der Gegensatz des paulinischen und petrinischen Christentums in der ältesten Kirche, der Apostel Petrus in Rom," *Tübinger Zeitschrift für Theology* 4 (1831): 61–206; reprinted in Baur, *Ausgewählte Werke in Einzelausgaben*, ed. Klaus Scholder, 2nd ed., 5 vols. (Stuttgart-Bad Cannstatt: Friedrich Frommann Verlag, 1963–1975), 1:1–146. For a partial ET, see Baur, *Paul the Apostle of Jesus Christ*, 1:267–320; and the extract with a brief introduction and further reading in Edward Adams and David G. Horrell, eds., *Christianity at Corinth: The Quest for the Pauline Church* (Louisville: Westminster John Knox, 2004), 51–59.

6. See Harris, *Tübingen School*, 181–85, who comments that "1831 marked the beginning of Baur's investigations into the historicity of the New Testament" and that "the cornerstone of this new approach was found in the opposition between Pauline and Jewish Christianity" (181).

7. See, e.g., Baur, *Das Christenthum und die christliche Kirche der drei ersten Jahrhunderte*, in *Ausgewahlte Werke*, 3:109–29; ET in Baur, *Church History*, 1:114–36.

influenced by Hegel at the time of his seminal article, but there is no doubt about the later impact of Hegel's philosophy on the framing of his work, particularly between 1833 and 1847.[8]

Hegel's philosophy is based on the idea that the history of the world is a history of progress toward freedom. "World history," he writes, "is the progress of the consciousness of freedom," a process of history oriented toward and directed by *Geist*, or spirit.[9] Hegel sets out a history in which this movement toward freedom has three basic phases. The first is found in "the Oriental World," in which the spirit, "still immersed in nature," is not truly free, except in the one person of the despotic ruler. The second is found in the Greek and Roman worlds, where an awareness of the spirit's own freedom begins to emerge: some (those participating in democracy) are free. The third phase comes with Christianity and "the Germanic age," in which the spirit can truly ascend to freedom.[10] It is important to stress, as Shawn Kelley has done, how thoroughly Hegel's is thus a racialized philosophy of history and of historical progress, articulating a narrative of Western European (and specifically Germanic) cultural, religious, and racial superiority.[11] The specific connections between racial and religious superiority in the story of progress toward freedom are clear. In Hegel's own words: "The Germanic nations, with the rise of Christianity, were the first to realise that man is by nature free, and that freedom of the spirit is his very essence."[12]

Judaism plays a particular role in this history, and a strictly limited one. As part of the Oriental world, and with its specific subservience to the Law, it "remains external, legalistic, ritualistic and ceremonial. . . . Jewish mono-

8. See Harris, *Tübingen School*, 25–27, 39–40, 155–58.

9. Georg Wilhelm Friedrich Hegel, *Lectures on the Philosophy of World History: Introduction; Reason in History*, trans. H. S. Nisbet (Cambridge: Cambridge University Press, 1975), 54.

10. Hegel, *Philosophy*, 130–31; cf. 54.

11. Shawn Kelley, *Racializing Jesus: Race, Ideology and the Formation of Modern Biblical Scholarship* (London: Routledge, 2002), 49: "Hegel explicitly racializes this process, outlining world history in three distinct, racial, progressively advancing phases: the non-Western Orient, where natural consciousness leads to despotism and cultural atrophy . . . the Greco-Roman infancy of the West, where spirit produces imperfect freedom . . . and the Germanic/European, where nature and spirit are reconciled in religion, absolute knowledge, and true freedom."

12. Hegel, *Philosophy*, 54. Kelley, *Racializing Jesus*, 49, offers his own rendering of the German original: "Only the Germanic nations (*die germanischen Nationen*) have in and through Christianity achieved the consciousness that man *qua* man is free, and that freedom of the spirit (*die Freiheit des Geistes*) constitutes his very nature."

theism and morality must be purged of its Jewish particularism and its Oriental despotism before it can become the foundation for Western culture and freedom."[13]

This is precisely the narrative of history that Baur sees played out in earliest Christianity: both Jesus and Paul in their different ways, with their spiritual insight and freedom, represent a stark contrast to their fellow Jews, with their outward rites and ordinances, legalism, and lack of true spiritual freedom. Judaism plays a unique and important role in the story of religious progress by which Christianity comes to triumph, but it is nonetheless a particular and limited one: "Judaism is nothing more than the religion of the law in contradistinction to Christianity, which is the religion of the spirit."[14] The profoundly Hegelian character of Baur's historical narrative is clear in his reflections on "Christianity as a new principle in the world's historical development": "Christianity is reached by the progress of the spirit to the freedom of its own self-consciousness, and humanity cannot arrive at this period till it has traversed that of unfreedom and servitude."[15] Paul claims a place of especial importance in Baur's view of this historical and theological development because of the way in which he takes up key elements of his Jewish heritage yet purges them of the particularism that characterized them in their Jewish form and context, which lacked true spirituality and

13. Kelley, *Racializing Jesus*, 58–59. Cf. Anders Gerdmar, "Baur and the Creation of the Judaism-Hellenism Dichotomy," in Bauspiess, Landmesser, and Lincicum, *Ferdinand Christian Baur*, 125–26. Gerdmar's particular focus is the creation and significance of the Judaism-Hellenism dichotomy, on which see also Dale B. Martin, "Paul and the Judaism/Hellenism Dichotomy: Toward a Social History of the Question," in *Paul Beyond the Judaism/Hellenism Divide*, ed. Troels Engberg-Pedersen (Louisville: Westminster John Knox, 2001), 29–61.

14. Baur, *Church History*, 1:58; see 1–43 (and on the superiority of Judaism to the "heathen" religions, but also its particularism, see 17–18). The overall shape of Baur's narrative is clear: "As against those special forms of religion it [Christianity] is therefore the absolute religion. . . . Christianity is elevated above the defects and limitations, the one-sidedness and finiteness, which constitute the particularism of other forms of religion. It is not polytheistic like Paganism: it does not, like Judaism, attach itself to outward rites and ordinances, nor identify itself with the positive authority of a purely traditional religion. . . . It is a more spiritual form of the religious consciousness than these are, and stands above them" (6). "But what is Christianity itself? What common unity . . . its spirituality. We find Christianity to be far more free than any other religion from everything merely external, sensuous, or material. It lays its foundations more deeply in the inmost essence of man's nature and in the principles of the moral consciousness" (9).

15. Baur, *Paul the Apostle of Jesus Christ*, 2:214. The preceding phrase is the title of chapter 6 in *Paul the Apostle of Jesus Christ*, vol. 2, from which this quotation is taken.

freedom.[16] Ernest Renan, in a broadly comparable view of the progress of the world's religious history culminating in Christianity, saw the historic development of "the pure spirit of religion" in Jesus;[17] in Baur's view, by contrast, Paul was pivotal:[18]

> The history of Christianity's development, after the departure of Jesus from the world, has in Paul a new point of commencement. . . . It was he who not only was the first to express explicitly and in definitive form the fundamental distinction between Christian universalism and Jewish particularism, but also from the beginning made this the task and guiding norm of his apostolic activity. . . . He broke through the bounds of Judaism and lifted Jewish particularism up into the universal idea of Christianity.[19]

16. Harris, *Tübingen School*, 195, notes that Baur's "book on Paul [published in 1845] was the work that he most prized. . . . With this book Baur's representation of the Apostolic Church received its final form, and was never altered in any essential points."

17. Ernest Renan, *The Life of Jesus* (London: Trübner, 1864), 304. There are nonetheless parallels with both Hegel and Baur in terms of Renan's sense of Jesus's (and Christianity's) place in world history. Though Jesus remained within the "restricted" world of Judaism (301), his was a crucial role (greater than that of Paul [306]) in the progress of humanity from superstitious paganism through Judaism to the universal and eternal pure religion of Christianity (see 35–45 for Jesus's place in world history cast in these terms). On the Orientalist racism woven into Renan's studies of Jesus, see Halvor Moxnes, *Jesus and the Rise of Nationalism: A New Quest for the Nineteenth-Century Historical Jesus* (London: I. B. Tauris, 2012), 121–47; Moxnes, "From Ernest Renan to Anders Behring Breivik: Continuities in Racial Stereotypes of Muslims and Jews," in Hockey and Horrell, *Ethnicity, Race, Religion*, 113–29.

18. Cf. Suzanne Marchand's comment: "Though understanding Christianity as an 'overcoming' of Judaism, which was characterized in his work as narrow, nationalist, and legalistic, compared with Pauline universalism, Baur did not doubt Jesus's Jewishness; indeed, one of the difficulties he bequeathed to later scholars was that of the transition from Jesus's ideas to those of the founders of the church, most critically Saint Paul." Suzanne L. Marchand, *German Orientalism in the Age of Empire: Religion, Race, and Scholarship* (Cambridge: Cambridge University Press; Washington, DC: German Historical Institute, 2009), 109.

19. Baur, *Ausgewählte Werke*, 3:44–45: "In Paulus hat die nach dem Hingang Jesu beginnende Entwicklungsgeschichte des Christenthums einen neuen Anfangspunkt. . . . Er war es somit auch, welcher den christlichen Universalismus in seinem principiellen Unterschied vom jüdischen Particularismus nicht nur zuerst ausdrücklich in seiner bestimmten Form aussprach, sondern auch von Anfang an sosehr zur Aufgabe und leitenden Norm seines apostolischen Wirkens machte . . . da er . . . auch die Schranken des Judenthums durchbrach und den jüdischen Particularismus in der universellen Idee des Christenthums aufhob." My translation differs somewhat from that in Baur, *Church History*, 1:46–47.

Thus the Galatian conflict, for Baur, was essentially a contest between Jewish particularism and Christian universalism; Paul's letter to the Romans fights a similar battle.[20] From Paul, moreover, develops the true and Christian form of spiritual freedom:

> The relation of Christianity to heathenism and Judaism is, as we have seen, defined as that between the absolute religion and the preparatory and subordinate forms of religion. We have here the progress from servitude to freedom, from nonage to majority, from the age of childhood to the age of maturity, from the flesh to the spirit. . . . It is only in Christianity that man can feel himself lifted up into the region of the spirit and of the spiritual life: it is only here that his relation to God is that of spirit to spirit. Christianity is essentially the religion of the spirit, and where the spirit is there is liberty and light, the clear and unshadowed identity of the spirit with itself.[21]

This, as we have already seen, is not only a narrative of *religious* superiority; what Kelley in particular demonstrates is the thoroughly *racialized* character of this pattern of thought. As he remarks:

> Lurking behind Baur's historical reconstruction is one of the central claims of Orientalism: freedom can only be found in the West because Orientals are spiritually and racially incapable of being free. Paul's theology is ultimately a rejection of, and purging of, the servile spirit of the East from the Western religion of Christianity.[22]

It is no coincidence that this kind of perspective on the relationship between Christianity and Judaism—and, more broadly, between Occident and Orient—develops in the particular sociopolitical context of nineteenth-century Europe. The Enlightenment had fostered a sense of the liberation and humanistic progress that (Western) reason could bring, though this "reason" was very much a European product and inextricably tied up with European colonialism.[23] An optimistic sense of the potential achievements

---

20. On the Galatian conflict, see Baur, *Church History*, 1:56–60. On the Christian universalism of Romans over against Jewish exclusivism, see Baur, *Paul the Apostle of Jesus Christ*, 1:322–54.

21. Baur, *Paul the Apostle of Jesus Christ*, 2:212. Cf. Kelley, *Racializing Jesus*, 77–78.

22. Kelley, *Racializing Jesus*, 77.

23. See Robert Young, *White Mythologies: Writing History and the West* (London: Routledge, 1990); see further in ch. 9 below. Even the (nineteenth-century) development of the

of Western European, and specifically Germanic, civilization provides the context in which a narrative about Christianity's superiority to Judaism, its universalizing fufillment of that which Judaism could only hint at in its limited and particular way, finds both legitimacy and influence.

1.2 E. P. Sanders and a New Perspective on Judaism

Much has happened in the years since Baur celebrated Paul's *Aufhebung* of Jewish particularism in the universal idea of Christianity. It is well known, at least in broad outline, how far German New Testament scholarship, and certain figures in particular, came to serve and support the antisemitic ideology of the National Socialist regime in the period leading up to and during the Second World War. Important archival research continues, however, to document and illuminate the activity and influence of scholars in that period. A notable example is Susannah Heschel's study of Walter Grundmann and the Institute for the Study and Eradication of Jewish Influence on German Church Life (*Institut zur Erforschung und Beseitigung des jüdischen Einflüsses auf das deutsche kirchliche Leben*), which he directed.[24] Other examples include Lukas Bormann's fascinating and disturbing research concerning the establishment of the international *Studiorum Novi Testamenti Societas* (SNTS), which shows not only how far the selection of proposed German members prior to the outbreak of the war was politically controlled, particularly through the activity of Gerhard Kittel in liaison with the German regime, but also how, even after the war, members of the committee in the

---

concept of "world religions," far from being a merely factual description of the phenomena, may be seen as bound up with what Tomoko Masuzawa calls "Europe's ever-expanding epistemic domain" (20), such that "the discourse on religion(s) [should] be viewed as an essential component, that is, as a vital operating system within the colonial disourse of Orientalism" (21). Masuzawa notes how, in the categorization of "world religions" versus indigenous or national religions, Christianity was seen as "uniquely universal" (23). See Tomoko Masuzawa, *The Invention of World Religions: Or, How European Universalism Was Preserved in the Language of Pluralism* (Chicago: University of Chicago Press, 2005).

24. Susannah Heschel, *The Aryan Jesus: Christian Theologians and the Bible in Nazi Germany* (Princeton: Princeton University Press, 2008). See also Susannah Heschel, "Historiography of Antisemitism versus Anti-Judaism: A Response to Robert Morgan," *JSNT* 33 (2011): 257–79. On Grundmann and his work, see also Roland Deines, Volker Leppin, and Karl-Wilhelm Niebuhr, eds., *Walter Grundmann: Ein Neutestamentler im Dritten Reich*, Arbeiten zur Kirchen- und Theologiegeschichte 21 (Leipzig: Evangelischer Verlagsanstalt, 2007).

UK and elsewhere expressed their sympathy for figures such as Kittel, who had lost his academic position and been interned due to his Nazi connections. Grundmann, Kittel, and Karl Georg Kuhn (one of Kittel's former students) remained members of the SNTS.[25] The processes of "de-Nazification" and of removing such views from academic life were by no means clear or uncomplicated.[26]

In the aftermath of National Socialism in Germany and the Holocaust in particular there is now—and has been for some decades—widespread commitment, not least in New Testament studies, to rejecting the antisemitic racial ideology that found such violent expression in the Nazi regime. Baur's "Orientalist" dichotomy between Jewish particularism and Christian universalism is often seen as part of that earlier, unfortunate, history, from which more recent studies have decisively departed. As we shall see, however, the story is not so straightforward.

Problems in the depiction of Judaism by New Testament scholars had long been pointed out—particularly by Jewish scholars—even in the time of Baur,[27] but it was not until they were subjected to thorough critique in the work of an American scholar from the (Protestant) Christian tradition, E. P. Sanders, that they received anything like their due attention in New Testament studies.[28] Those biographical facts alone are of significance: they

---

25. Lukas Bormann, "'Auch unter politischen Gesichtspunkten sehr sorgfältig ausgewählt': Die ersten deutschen Mitglieder der Studiorum Novi Testamenti Societas (SNTS) 1937–1946," *NTS* 58 (2012): 416–52. For the committee's letter to Kittel in 1947 and his name on the letterhead, see 448–49.

26. See, e.g., the discussion of the post-war fate of Günther Bornkamm (a member of the Confessing Church) and Karl Georg Kuhn (a member of the Nazi party, the NSDAP [National-Sozialistische-Deutsche-Arbeiter-Partei]) in Gerd Theissen, *Neutestamentliche Wissenschaft vor und nach 1945: Karl Georg Kuhn und Günther Bornkamm*, Schriften der Philosophisch-historischen Klasse der Heidelberger Akademie der Wissenschaften 47 (Heidelberg: Universitätsverlag, 2009).

27. Notably Abraham Geiger (1810–1874), on whom see Susannah Heschel, *Abraham Geiger and the Jewish Jesus* (Chicago: University of Chicago Press, 1998). See also, e.g., George Foot Moore, "Christian Writers on Judaism," *HTR* 14 (1921): 197–254; and the discussion of the work of Moore and others in E. P. Sanders, *Paul and Palestinian Judaism: A Comparison of Patterns of Religion* (London: SCM, 1977), 33–36. For a detailed review of Jewish engagement with Paul, see Daniel R. Langton, "Modern Jewish Identity and the Apostle Paul: Pauline Studies as an Intra-Jewish Ideological Battleground," *JSNT* 28 (2005): 217–58; Langton, "The Myth of the 'Traditional View of Paul' and the Role of the Apostle in Modern Jewish-Christian Polemics," *JSNT* 28 (2005): 69–104; Langton, *The Apostle Paul in the Jewish Imagination* (Cambridge: Cambridge University Press, 2010).

28. Near the end of *Jesus and Judaism* (London: SCM, 1985), Sanders indicates his debt

hint at both the shifting of the power center of New Testament studies from Germany to North America and also the tendency within an academic field dominated by (Protestant) Christian scholars to listen most attentively to those who share that religious location.

In two works from the 1970s and '80s, *Paul and Palestinian Judaism* and *Jesus and Judaism*, Sanders sought to expose the extent of Christian caricature and prejudice that underlay depictions of Jewish hypocrisy and legalism contrasted with Christian grace, mercy, and love. For example, in his pithy summary of findings at the end of *Jesus and Judaism*, Sanders—with a touch of wry humor directed at the caricatures often found in Christian scholarship—lists among the "incredible" points about Jesus, that "he was one of the rare Jews of his day who believed in love, mercy, grace, repentance and the forgiveness of sin" and that "Jews in general, and Pharisees in particular, would kill people who believed in such things."[29] In other words, it is inconceivable that there is any historical validity in such portraits. In *Paul and Palestinian Judaism*, Sanders sets out to establish, through a wide-ranging study of Jewish texts of the period, what the pattern of religion was in the Judaism of Paul's day. His conclusion is that the depiction of that religion as one of "legalistic-works-righteousness" is little more than Christian caricature. Instead, he proposes that Judaism's pattern of religion was one of "covenantal nomism." At its heart is the idea of covenant, a binding relationship between God and God's people, initiated by God in an act of undeserved grace. The appropriate *response* for those who are members of this covenant people is to live in obedience to God's law. In other words, obedience to the Law was not regarded as a means of earning one's salvation or of becoming a member of God's people but as a response to the gracious act of God in making a covenant with the people of Israel.

Moreover, Sanders refuses to see Paul's gospel as emerging from any intrinsic "problem" within Judaism—such as the traditional favorite, Paul's sense of guilt brought about by his inability to fulfill the law and thus secure righteousness by his own efforts.[30] Instead Sanders proposes that Paul

---

to a liberal, "social gospel" Protestantism: "I am a liberal, modern, secularized Protestant, brought up in a church dominated by low christology and the social gospel" (334).

29. Sanders, *Jesus and Judaism*, 326–27.

30. Seminal in challenging this particular view is Krister Stendahl, "The Apostle Paul and the Introspective Conscience of the West," *HTR* 56 (1963): 199–215; repr. in *Paul among Jews and Gentiles* (London: SCM, 1977), 78–96. In terms of understanding the extent of his influence, it may again be relevant to note that Stendahl was a member (later bishop) of the Lutheran Church of Sweden.

reasoned "from solution to plight." In other words, through his conversion experience, Paul became convinced that God had acted in Christ to save the world. Reasoning "backwards" from this new conviction, Paul concluded that all people must have needed saving (or otherwise Christ came for no good reason) and that the law was not the means by which they could be saved. In an oft-quoted summary, Sanders expresses in a nutshell what he sees as Paul's "criticism" of Judaism: "*This is what Paul finds wrong in Judaism: it is not Christianity*."[31] Once convinced that Christ is the answer, Paul then concludes (and attempts to demonstrate) that Judaism, and specifically the Jewish law, is not the way to attain salvation. In other words, there is no intrinsic reason, absent a prior commitment to Christ, why any Jew, Paul included, should have found their religion unfulfilling, impossible to live by, or theologically unsatisfactory.

There has been considerable debate concerning Sanders's proposals about the shape of Jewish religion in the period of Christian origins,[32] but what is of particular relevance here is the observation that Sanders's depiction of Judaism remains, for all its intended sympathy and refusal of any implicit Christian superiority, one cast in strongly Protestant terms. In a highly revealing phrase, for example, Sanders declares that "the Judaism of before 70 kept grace and works in the right perspective,"[33] where the evaluative use of "right" must imply something like "the way it is in Protestantism" on the presumption that therein lies the "correct" way to perceive such matters. Grace must come first, with clear priority, and works must be seen as the appropriate response to the saving initiative of God. As Philip Alexander has pointed out in a review of *Jesus and Judaism*:

> His [Sanders's] answer to the charge of "legalism" seems, in effect, to be that Rabbinic Judaism, despite appearances, is really a religion of "grace." But does this not involve a tacit acceptance of a major element in his opponents' position—the assumption that "grace" is superior to "law"? The correct response to the charge must surely be: And what is wrong with "legalism," once we have got rid of abusive language about "hypocrisy" and "mere externalism"? It is neither religiously nor philosophically self-evident that a

31. Sanders, *Paul and Palestinian Judaism*, 552, italics original.

32. For overviews of the scholarly discussion, see Stephen Westerholm, *Perspectives Old and New on Paul: The "Lutheran" Paul and His Critics* (Grand Rapids: Eerdmans, 2004); Magnus Zetterholm, *Approaches to Paul: A Student's Guide to Recent Scholarship* (Minneapolis: Fortress, 2009).

33. Sanders, *Paul and Palestinian Judaism*, 427.

"legalistic" view of the world is inferior to one based on "grace." If we fail to take a firm stand on this point we run the risk of seriously misdescribing Pharisaic and Rabbinic Judaism, and of trying to make it over into a pale reflection of Protestant Christianity.[34]

It is, then, highly significant that in work clearly intended to treat Judaism on its own terms, to free it from the caricatured judgments of Christian scholars, Sanders still ends up mired in the discursive presuppositions of Protestant theology.[35] Yet for all that, one thing remains particularly important and unusual in Sanders's approach: his refusal to see in Judaism any unresolved problem to which the Christian gospel articulates an answer, a move that removes much of the basis for implicit claims about Christianity's superiority.

It is precisely this stance, however, that is the main target for James Dunn's criticism of Sanders in his programmatic essay announcing the beginning of the "new perspective on Paul."[36] Although the iconic label "the

34. Philip S. Alexander, review of *Jesus and Judaism*, by E. P. Sanders, *JJS* 37 (1986): 105. A similar point is made much more sharply by Jacob Neusner, "Mr. Sanders' Pharisees and Mine: A Response to E. P. Sanders, *Jewish Law from Jesus to the Mishnah*," *SJT* 44 (1991): 92–95, who criticizes Sanders's "Protestant theological apologetic for a Judaism in the liberal Protestant model" (92). These authors are cited by Barry Matlock in a probing section on "a certain covert Protestantism" in the new perspective on Paul; R. Barry Matlock, "Almost Cultural Studies? Reflections on the 'New Perspective' on Paul," in *Biblical Studies/Cultural Studies: The Third Sheffield Colloquium*, ed. J. Cheryl Exum and Stephen D. Moore (Sheffield: Sheffield Academic Press, 1998), 444–47.

35. One of the significant gains from John Barclay's recent study of "grace" is to show that it is a concept that may be understood in a variety of ways and not only in the way it has been defined within Protestant Christianity. Thus, for Barclay, grace is everywhere present in Second Temple Judaism—including in the apostle Paul—but is defined and discussed in a variety of ways. This undercuts any simple contrast between Christian grace and Jewish legalism but also any assumption that grace, wherever it is to be found in Judaism (or indeed elsewhere), must always mean what it does in the Protestant tradition. See John M. G. Barclay, *Paul and the Gift* (Grand Rapids: Eerdmans, 2015).

36. James D. G. Dunn, "The New Perspective on Paul," *BJRL* 65 (1983): 95–122; repr. in James D. G. Dunn, *Jesus, Paul and the Law* (London: SPCK, 1990), 183–214. The phrase is also used in an earlier essay by N. T. Wright outlining a broadly comparable program in response to the earlier debate between Krister Stendahl and Ernst Käsemann, as well as to Sanders's work: "The Paul of History and the Apostle of Faith," *TynBul* 29 (1978): 61–88, esp. 64; repr. in N. T. Wright, *Pauline Perspectives: Essays on Paul, 1978–2013* (Minneapolis: Fortress, 2014), 3–20. This is acknowledged by James D. G. Dunn, *The New Perspective on Paul*, rev. ed. (Grand Rapids: Eerdmans, 2008), 7n24, who credits Wright as being "the first to recognise the significance of Sanders' work" and to offer a related "new perspective" on Paul.

new perspective" has thus come to be primarily associated with the study of Paul, what Sanders has essentially given—and what Dunn warmly welcomes—is what Dunn calls a *"new perspective on Second Temple Judaism."*[37] This new perspective rejects the anti-Jewish prejudices expressed in earlier ("Lutheran") readings, which depicted Jews as legalistic hypocrites striving to earn their salvation by doing good works. However, while accepting his depiction of Judaism itself, Dunn finds Sanders's Paul too arbitrary, simply abandoning one religious system for another with no good reason. Rejecting Sanders's "solution-to-plight" approach, Dunn seeks to rearticulate some sense of the "problem" with Judaism to which Paul provides an answer. This he does specifically through a reinterpretation of Paul's critique of "works of law." Dunn's key move is to interpret these works not as good deeds done in the hope of earning salvation but as markers of identity, badges of belonging that demarcated the (Jewish) people of God. Hence Dunn concludes that what Paul opposes is not legalism but ethnocentrism, nationalism, and xenophobia on the part of his fellow Jews. Paul's positive argument, thus construed, is to insist that

> the covenant should no longer be conceived in nationalistic or racial terms. . . . Rather it is broadened out as God had originally intended—with the grace of God which it expressed separated from its national restriction and freely bestowed without respect to race or work. . . . What he [Paul] is concerned to exclude is the *racial* not the *ritual* expression of faith; it is *nationalism* which he denies not *activism*. . . . It is works which betoken racial prerogative to which he objects.[38]

Thus, for Dunn, "Paul saw his own apostolic work not as a disowning of his heritage, but precisely as its fulfillment"; "his was the privilege of bringing Israel's promised destiny to its eschatological completion"; "Paul's criticism of Judaism was . . . a criticism of the xenophobic strand of Judaism, to which Paul himself had previously belonged. . . . Paul was in effect converting from a closed Judaism to an open Judaism."[39] And this new kind of "open" Judaism involved rejecting the importance of the "trappings of

---

37. James D. G. Dunn, *The New Perspective on Paul: Selected Essays*, WUNT 185 (Tübingen: Mohr Siebeck, 2005), 5, italics original.

38. Dunn, *Jesus, Paul and the Law*, 197–98, 200, italics original.

39. James D. G. Dunn, "Paul: Apostate or Apostle of Israel?," *ZNW* 89 (1998): 258, 264, and 261 respectively.

Jewish identity"—circumcision and food laws especially—in favor of an "essence" of Jewishness "determined from within."[40] In particular, this means that the positive achievements of Paul's "gospel" are seen precisely in terms of "breaking down barriers (not least of the law) between Jew and Gentile."[41]

A similar perspective is expressed in the work of N. T. Wright, also among the first to develop a form of the "new perspective" on Paul:[42] "Monotheism and election served, in the Judaism of Paul's day . . . as boundary markers round the community, as symbols of national and racial solidarity."[43] What Paul thus opposes is "a kind of meta-sin" on Israel's part, "the attempt to confine grace to one race."[44] And what Paul presents as God's offer of salvation in Christ is a fulfillment of the promise to Abraham that all nations would be blessed in him, a promise which it was Israel's (missed) vocation to bring to the world but which was achieved through her messiah, Jesus Christ.[45]

What is striking in such "new perspective" proposals—their variety and differences notwithstanding—is the extent to which they reproduce a di-

40. James D. G. Dunn, "Who Did Paul Think He Was? A Study of Jewish-Christian Identity," *NTS* 45 (1999): 192.

41. Dunn, *New Perspective*, rev. ed., 32, italicized in the original; cf. 16–17, 34.

42. See, e.g., Wright, "Paul of History" and other early essays collected in Wright, *Pauline Perspectives*.

43. N. T. Wright, *The Climax of the Covenant: Christ and the Law in Pauline Theology* (Edinburgh: T&T Clark, 1991), 13–14. See the same final phrase in an essay from 1980 in Wright, *Pauline Perspectives*, 31.

44. Wright, *Climax*, 240. For a critique of this language in Wright's work, though focused largely on the perceived problems of the notion of "race," see Calvin J. Roetzel, "No 'Race of Israel' in Paul," in *Putting Body and Soul Together: Essays in Honor of Robin Scroggs*, ed. Virginia Wiles, Alexandra Brown, and Graydon F. Snyder (Valley Forge: Trinity Press International, 1997), 230–44. On the Jewish "race" and its emphasis on "racial purity," see also N. T. Wright, *The New Testament and the People of God*, Christian Origins and the Question of God 1 (London: SPCK, 1992), 230–32. In his more recent work, Wright notes the potential difficulties with such language (though not Roetzel's critique specifically): see N. T. Wright, *Paul and the Faithfulness of God*, 2 vols., Christian Origins and the Question of God 4 (London: SPCK; Minneapolis: Fortress, 2013), 94n78. In this work, to a considerable extent, he follows Love L. Sechrest, *A Former Jew: Paul and the Dialectics of Race*, LNTS 410 (London: T&T Clark, 2009). Wright affirms the idea that Paul is in effect creating something like a "third race," whether or not one accepts that precise label (1443–49), a new form of "ethno-social particularity" (1449). Where Wright "parts company" with Sechrest is in regard to her claim that the church is a "*completely new* ethno-social particularity"; he emphasizes instead "that the new particularity *is the very thing God promised to Abraham in the first place*" (1448–49, italics original). For further reflections on this point, see Horrell, "Grace, Race."

45. See, e.g., Wright, *Climax*, 144–53, 67–74.

chotomy essentially similar to that which we observed in the work of Baur between Jewish particularism or ethnocentrism and Christian openness, universality, or inclusion.[46] The contrast between "old" and "new" perspectives has often been cast in terms of rejecting the older focus on Jewish "legalism." Even so, there remains a structural similarity. As Barry Matlock has astutely observed, "Substitute for 'legalism' in the traditional reading 'nationalism' in Dunn's, as the perverted attitude toward the law and its observance that is the real target of Paul's attack, and the old perspective fits Dunn right down to the ground."[47] Just as one might see a negative stereotype at work in Christian scholars' depiction of Jewish legalism, so too claims of ethnocentrism and xenophobia are equally negative, albeit in a different way. Thus, Jouette Bassler notes, "If a major objection to the old perspective was its depiction of Judaism as a soulless, legalistic religion, the new one provides no real improvement, for it caricatures Judaism as a racist, nationalistic religion."[48] Moreover, as we have seen in our brief survey of Baur's work, his fundamental yet broad contrast was between Jewish particularism and Christian universalism, within which legalism versus freedom formed just one specific contrast. Particularism versus universalism, ethnocentrism versus openness: the structure and nature of the dichotomy is strikingly similar. In the "new perspective" work too, it seems, Christianity has brought to the whole of humanity the positive promise that Judaism discovered but mistakenly kept constrained within the confines of its ethnic particularism.[49] While "new perspective" scholars may join with many in proclaiming that "the picture drawn by Baur has now been discredited" and suggesting that the model he promoted has largely been replaced in recent decades,[50] crucial elements of structural continuity remain. Thus,

46. For this point, see also Holtz, *Damit Gott*, who comments that this opposition "von universalistischem paulinischen Christentum und partikularistischem Judentum . . . zieht sich bis heute durch die neutestamentliche Forschung" (5; see further 538–65).

47. R. Barry Matlock, "Sins of the Flesh and Suspicious Minds: Dunn's New Theology of Paul," *JSNT* 72 (1998): 86.

48. Jouette M. Bassler, *Navigating Paul: An Introduction to Key Theological Concepts* (Louisville: Westminster John Knox, 2007), 16.

49. For a probing critique of the depiction of Jewish (Pharisaic) separatism as the backdrop to Paul's message in Wright's *Paul and the Faithfulness of God*, see Paula Fredriksen, review of *Paul and the Faithfulness of God*, by N. T. Wright, *CBQ* 77 (2015): 389–90.

50. N. T. Wright, *Paul and His Recent Interpreters: Some Contemporary Debates* (London: SPCK, 2015), 16. See also James D. G. Dunn, "Was Judaism Particularist or Universalist?," in *Judaism in Late Antiquity Part Three, Where We Stand: Issues and Debates in Ancient Judaism*, ed. Jacob Neusner and Alan J. Avery-Peck, vol. 2 (Leiden: Brill, 1999), 57–73. As

as Caroline Johnson Hodge has noted, despite the significant changes, this kind of new perspective continues to replicate what she concisely labels "the universal/ethnic dichotomy."[51]

The sociopolitical context for Sanders's new perspective on Judaism—and its resulting reinterpretations of Jesus and Paul—is of course rather different from that in which the Germanic tradition of Baur and others developed. Whether explicitly acknowledged or not, one key factor is the Holocaust and the resulting challenge to rid scholarship of the prejudicial caricatures of Judaism that fueled its pernicious ideology. Also pertinent is the founding of the state of Israel after the Second World War.[52] With the Allies' victory in that war and the concomitant shift of power to the victorious nations, it is perhaps no coincidence—even though it did not come about until the 1970s—that the new perspective emerged primarily in this new center of power, in the English-language scholarship of the USA and Great Britain. The fact that this turning point seems to occur in the 1970s may also be due, at least in part, to the influence on Anglo-American attitudes to Israel of the Six Day War in 1967, as James Crossley has argued.[53]

Yet, despite the change in both scholarly perspective and sociopolitical context, it is interesting that the structural dichotomy—an ethnically particular Judaism, an inclusively open Christianity—continues to dominate this new scholarly paradigm. The language and perspective have shifted, but the essential contrast remains.

Holtz, *Damit Gott*, 551, points out, despite Dunn's critical rejection of Baur's perspective at the opening of his essay, he ends up affirming a similar viewpoint: "Dunn wiederholt zwar nicht die traditionelle . . . christliche Perspektive . . . doch ist und bleibt der Apostel Jesu Christi auch für ihn derjenige, der die das Judentum kennzeichnende Spannung zwischen universalistichen und partikularistischen Tendenzen durch eine spezifisch christliche Form des Handelns löst." On the different narratives concerning Baur's influence, see James Carleton Paget, "The Reception of Baur in Britain," in Bauspiess, Landmesser, and Lincicum, *Ferdinand Christian Baur*, 335–86.

51. Johnson Hodge, *If Sons, Then Heirs*, 8.

52. These two key factors are mentioned as aspects of the context for doing NT studies and Christian theology by, e.g., Lloyd Gaston, *Paul and the Torah* (Vancouver: University of British Columbia Press, 1987), 2–3, 15; John G. Gager, *Reinventing Paul* (Oxford: Oxford University Press, 2000), 150–51.

53. See James G. Crossley, *Jesus in an Age of Terror: Scholarly Projects for a New American Century* (London: Equinox, 2008), 145–72; Crossley, "Jesus the Jew since 1967," in *Jesus beyond Nationalism: Constructing the Historical Jesus in a Period of Cultural Complexity*, ed. Halvor Moxnes, Ward Blanton, and James G. Crossley, BibleWorld (London: Equinox, 2009), 119–37, esp. 120–28.

1.3 Social-Scientific Perspectives on Ethnicity and Identity

It was not just the New Perspective on Judaism (and thence Paul) that was emerging in the 1970s and '80s. The 1970s was a period when a range of new perspectives was being developed in the field of New Testament studies, perspectives not obviously linked to one another but in part reflections of wider social changes and pressures: the civil rights movement, the women's movement, and other movements for greater liberation, social justice, and equality of opportunity.[54] Indeed, it so happens that three of these developments can be seen as reaching a significant point of development in 1983: the New Perspective with the publication of Dunn's essay of that title (cited above); feminist hermeneutics with the landmark publication of Elisabeth Schüssler Fiorenza's *In Memory of Her*; and social-scientific perspectives on early Christianity with another landmark book, Wayne Meeks's *The First Urban Christians*.[55]

Meeks's book exemplified the revival of interest in the social history of the earliest Christian communities and the creative deployment of social-scientific perspectives to illuminate the historical evidence.[56] Within this broad movement, one specific recent approach, pioneered by Philip Esler in particular but now much more widely adopted, involves the use of Social Identity Theory to illuminate the social processes at work among the early Christian groups and the strategic efforts of the authors of texts to construct a positive sense of in-group identity.[57] In the latest work, this social identity

---

54. For discussions of these social factors and influences, see Gerd Theissen, *Social Reality and the Early Christians: Theology, Ethics, and the World of the New Testament* (Edinburgh: T&T Clark, 1993), 15–29; Stephen C. Barton, "The Communal Dimension of Earliest Christianity: A Critical Survey of the Field," *JTS* 43 (1992): 399–427, esp. 399–406.

55. Elisabeth Schüssler Fiorenza, *In Memory of Her: A Feminist Theological Reconstruction of Christian Origins* (London: SCM, 1983); Wayne A. Meeks, *The First Urban Christians: The Social World of the Apostle Paul* (New Haven: Yale University Press, 1983).

56. On the history of these developments in NT scholarship, see David G. Horrell, "Social Sciences Studying Formative Christian Phenomena: A Creative Movement," in *Handbook of Early Christianity: Social Science Approaches*, ed. Anthony J. Blasi, Jean Duhaime, and Paul-André Turcotte (Walnut Creek, CA: Alta Mira, 2002), 3–28. For the reactions to Meeks's book and subsequent developments, see Todd D. Still and David G. Horrell, eds., *After the First Urban Christians: The Social-Scientific Study of Pauline Christianity Twenty-Five Years Later* (London: T&T Clark, 2009).

57. Among Esler's early deployments of Social Identity Theory, see Philip F. Esler, "Group Boundaries and Intergroup Conflict in Galatians: A New Reading of Galatians 5:13–6:10," in Brett, *Ethnicity and the Bible*, 215–40; Esler, *Galatians*, New Testament Readings

perspective has been combined with insights from the social-scientific study of ethnicity.

In a major work on Romans published in 2003, Esler's theoretical orientation for the reading of Romans is provided by Social Identity Theory (outlined in detail in chapter 2 of the book) and by a social-scientific understanding of ethnicity (outlined and applied to "the ancient Mediterranean world" in chapter 3).[58] Fundamental to the argument is the categorization of Jewish/Judean and Greek identities as ethnic. Esler therefore gives considerable space to arguing that "Greek" identity in the first century CE was, contrary to the arguments of Jonathan Hall, an ethnic form of identity and that the label *Ioudaioi* likewise denotes members of an ethnic group, like other territorially named groups in antiquity. As such, *Ioudaios* should be translated "Judean" and not "Jew," since the latter falsely and anachronistically implies that this was a religious identity when in fact it was ethnic.[59] Indeed, there seems more broadly to be a growing emphasis on Judaism in the Hellenistic and Roman period as an "ethnic" identity (see further §2.1).

What this means with regard to Romans, according to Esler, is that Paul is confronting a situation of inter-ethnic conflict—rivalry between Judeans and Greeks, with the tensions particularly visible, for example, in Rom 14:1–15:13.[60] Esler's overall thesis about Romans is that Paul is attempting to construct a new and positive form of group identity, a non- or trans-ethnic identity in Christ, that can encompass but not obliterate diverse ethnic identities: "In the language of modern social identity theory, Paul's strategy amounts to an exercise in recategorization, the creation (or perhaps invocation) of a common ingroup identity." The new identity in Christ "transcends the fundamental ethnic division among them between Judeans and Greeks."[61] Paul allows ethnic difference to remain but provides the foundations for a new "common identity."[62] The kind of trans-ethnic identity created by be-

---

(London: Routledge, 1998); Esler, "Jesus and the Reduction of Intergroup Conflict: The Parable of the Good Samaritan in the Light of Social Identity Theory," *BibInt* 8 (2000): 325–57. As evidence of the wider employment of such perspectives, see J. Brian Tucker and Coleman A. Baker, eds., *T&T Clark Handbook to Social Identity in the New Testament* (London: Bloomsbury T&T Clark, 2014).

58. Esler, *Conflict and Identity*, 19–39 and 40–76 respectively.

59. See Esler, *Conflict and Identity*, 54–61 (on Greek ethnicity) and 62–74 (on Judean ethnicity).

60. See Esler, *Conflict and Identity*, 74–76, 108, 339–56.

61. Esler, *Conflict and Identity*, 360.

62. Esler, *Conflict and Identity*, 355, 365.

lieving in Christ—being a "Christ follower"—thus belongs in a completely different category than that represented by the ancestrally constituted and territorially labeled "Judean" identity.

Esler has since mounted similar arguments regarding the strategy and achievements evident in the Gospels of Matthew and John. According to Esler, what John is doing in the famous prologue to the Gospel (specifically in John 1:9–13) "is contrasting a new identity that is non-ethnic, strongly marked by fictive kinship and intimate relations with God, with an original identity of an altogether different kind—one that was ethnic in character."[63] Likewise, "Matthew is writing for a group or groups of Christ-followers that embrace Judean and non-Judean members sharing a new, trans-ethnic, superordinate group identity in-Christ. This identity is quite distinct from that of the Judean ethnic group."[64] In all these cases, according to Esler, tension and rivalry between members of ethnic groups, *Ioudaioi* included, can (potentially, at least) be overcome by the adoption of an inclusive "superordinate" trans-ethnic identity such as is offered in Christ.

A broadly comparable proposal, also drawing on Social Identity Theory and concepts of ethnicity, has been made in relation to the goals of the author of Luke-Acts by Aaron Kuecker. In Luke-Acts, according to Kuecker, "the Holy Spirit emerges as *the central figure in the formation of a new social identity*."[65] In Acts 10–15 in particular, Kuecker sees Luke confronting "the most intractable intergroup barrier in his context: ethnic identity."[66] Luke does so

---

63. Philip F. Esler, "From *Ioudaioi* to Children of God: The Development of a Non-Ethnic Group Identity in the Gospel of John," in *In Other Words: Essays on Social Science Methods and the New Testament in Honor of Jerome H. Neyrey*, ed. Anselm C. Hagedorn, Zeba A. Crook, and Eric Stewart, Social World of Biblical Antiquity, Second Series 1 (Sheffield: Sheffield Phoenix, 2007), 127.

64. Philip F. Esler, "Judean Ethnic Identity and the Matthean Jesus," in *Jesus—Gestalt und Gestaltungen: Rezeptionen des Galiläers in Wissenschaft, Kirche und Gesellschaft; Festschrift für Gerd Theißen zum 70. Geburtstag*, ed. Petra von Gemünden, David G. Horrell, and Max Küchler, NTOA 100 (Göttingen: Vandenhoeck & Ruprecht, 2013), 208. See also Philip F. Esler, "Intergroup Conflict and Matthew 23: Towards Responsible Historical Interpretation of a Challenging Text," *BTB* 45 (2015): 38–59; Esler, "Giving the Kingdom to an *Ethnos* That Will Bear Its Fruit: Ethnic and Christ-Movement Identities in Matthew," in *In the Fullness of Time: Essays on Christology, Creation, and Eschatology in Honor of Richard Bauckham*, ed. Daniel M. Gurtner, Grant Macaskill, and Jonathan T. Pennington (Grand Rapids: Eerdmans, 2016), 177–96.

65. Aaron J. Kuecker, *The Spirit and the "Other": Social Identity, Ethnicity and Intergroup Reconciliation in Luke-Acts*, LNTS 444 (London: T&T Clark, 2011), 48, italics original.

66. Kuecker, *Spirit and the "Other,"* 181.

by offering "a new, allocentric, Spirit-formed superordinate group identity that affirms yet chastens and transcends ethnic identity."[67] It is important to note that Kuecker cautions against any "simple caricature of 'universalistic Christianity' over against 'particularistic Judaism,'" suggesting that

> the Jesus movement, as described by Luke, exhibits a "universal particularity," with its universal aspect defined by the cosmic lordship of the exalted Jesus. Jesus' lordship over all peoples is the prerequisite which allows all humans, regardless of class, ethnicity or gender, the opportunity to recognize, affirm and submit to Jesus' true identity.[68]

Thus "acknowledgement of the lordship of Jesus remains a very real boundary. . . . For Luke, one cannot be 'in' until one has submitted to Jesus' cosmic lordship."[69] This clear and candid acknowledgment of the firm requirement for group membership helps to make clear that this is not only a vision of tolerance and acceptance, however it is depicted. Yet the contrast between an ethnic Judean/Israelite identity and a trans-ethnic Christian one remains fundamental. Kuecker briefly contrasts Luke's vision with "the other trans-ethnic identity on offer in Luke's context—Roman citizenship," suggesting that Luke's view of Spirit-mediated encounter with Jesus as the basis for common identity is different from the kind of identity created through Rome's military dominion.[70]

Another comparable study that draws on social-scientific studies of ethnicity to illuminate the achievements of Jesus and his earliest followers is Joseph Hellerman's *Jesus and the People of God*.[71] Hellerman presents Jesus as a kind of "ethnic entrepreneur," deconstructing Jewish nationalism and challenging an ethnic understanding of the people of God, for example, through the alternative vision of a surrogate kinship group: "Jesus thus laid the conceptual foundation for his movement to transcend the boundaries of ethnic Judaism in the decades to follow."[72] Hellerman begins his conclu-

---

67. Kuecker, *Spirit and the "Other,"* 200; cf. 205 ("the construction of a group identity that transcends ethnic identities"), 215, 226 ("Luke's vision of Spirit-formed trans-ethnic social identity").

68. Kuecker, *Spirit and the "Other,"* 222.

69. Kuecker, *Spirit and the "Other,"* 222.

70. Kuecker, *Spirit and the "Other,"* 226.

71. Joseph H. Hellerman, *Jesus and the People of God: Reconfiguring Ethnic Identity*, New Testament Monographs 21 (Sheffield: Sheffield Phoenix, 2007).

72. Hellerman, *Jesus*, 308.

sion with a quotation from Graydon Snyder: "The Jesus tradition shattered Jewish exclusivism."[73]

The influence of this kind of perspective—and specifically of this kind of dichotomy between ethnic Judaism and trans-ethnic Christianity—can be seen in a wider range of recent works in the field. For example, Larry Hurtado's *Destroyer of the Gods*, published in 2016, aims to highlight the distinctive features of early Christanity in the Roman world.[74] In relation to most of these distinctives—the hostility early Christians faced, their exclusiveness, their beliefs about God, their ethics, and their "bookish" focus—Hurtado notes that these features are already found in Judaism (the exceptions would seem to be the veneration of Jesus and the preference for the codex form). But in each case there is a clear reason, for Hurtado, why the presence of this distinctive feature in Judaism does not "count" in the same way it counts as a distinctive achievement of early Christianity: Judaism was an ancient ethnic tradition whereas early Christianity was "translocal and transethnic."[75] Hurtado notes the phenomena of pagan sympathizers and proselytes to Judaism, and the widespread existence of Jews "all across the empire" but insists that "a genuinely Jewish religious identity required membership in the Jewish people, whether by birth or by full proselyte conversion." Diaspora Jews, likewise, "continued to think of themselves as part of the Jewish people."[76] By contrast, early Christianity "cut across ethnic lines": early Christian converts "retained their various ethnic identities" and took on "a new kind of religious identity that, uniquely, was both exclusive and not related to their ethnicity."[77] The distinction between an "ethnic" Jewish identity and a "trans-ethnic" Christian identity is thus crucial to Hurtado's claims that the key distinctives he identifies are to be attributed to Christianity and not to Judaism.[78] But the underlying importance of defining what we mean by

73. Hellerman, *Jesus,* 309. For a critical response to Hellerman's work, see Christoph Niemand, review of *Jesus and the People of God,* by Joseph H. Hellerman, *TLZ* 134 (2009): 1059–63. In view of the discussion to come in §2.2 below, it should also be noted that Hellerman briefly engages with, and in some measure accepts, the main insight of Denise Buell's work that "Christians saw themselves as ethnically inclusive, yet continued to utilize symbols and concepts related to ethnicity to define boundaries between themselves and other groups" (Hellerman, *Jesus,* 306–7n47).

74. Larry W. Hurtado, *Destroyer of the Gods: Early Christian Distinctiveness in the Roman World* (Waco: Baylor University Press, 2016).

75. Hurtado, *Destroyer,* 92; see further 52–56, 89–94.

76. Hurtado, *Destroyer,* 90.

77. Hurtado, *Destroyer,* 90, 92, 93.

78. See my review in *SJT* 71 (2018): 226–28.

"ethnic" identity, and clarifying what does and does not count as an "ethnic" identity, should also be apparent: In what sense, for example, might "membership of the people" also be required of converts to the Christian movement?

Other authors writing from quite different perspectives have also reinforced the case for seeing various New Testament texts as instances of efforts to create some kind of superordinate, inclusive group identity within which existing identities—and specifically identities as Jew and non-Jew/gentile—can legitimately remain, and indeed be valued. Paul's achievements in particular are widely seen as creating the basis for a diverse, inclusive community that values and preserves ethnic identities encompassed within a common unity in Christ. For example, according to William Campbell, "Paul's view of Jews and gentiles is that they remain two distinct entities, a distinction that abides, even though all is relativized in Christ."[79] "Thus there are differing identities in Christ."[80] Similarly, Kathy Ehrensperger argues that Paul's perspective is one in which "the distinction between circumcision and uncircumcision is to be maintained. Unity is not achieved by the eradication of cultural and ethnic distinctions, but by affirming their validity and value in Christ."[81] This positive vision of diverse ethnic and cultural identities incorporated in Christ is placed in stark contrast to the kind of "paradigm of sameness" promoted by the Roman Empire.[82] Comparable examples may be found in the work of some of those who have come to be seen as part of a "radical new perspective" on Paul— or, more informatively, the "Paul within Judaism" perspective—including work (notably by Caroline Johnson Hodge) that analyses Paul's efforts as a form of *ethnic* identity-construction (on which see ch. 2 below). Here too

79. William S. Campbell, *Paul and the Creation of Christian Identity*, LNTS 322 (London: T&T Clark, 2006), 100.

80. Campbell, *Creation of Christian Identity*, 120. A similar perspective is argued in J. Brian Tucker, *Remain in Your Calling: Paul and the Continuation of Social Identities in 1 Corinthians* (Eugene, OR: Pickwick, 2011).

81. Kathy Ehrensperger, *Paul at the Crossroads of Cultures: Theologizing in the Space-Between*, LNTS 456 (London: Bloomsbury T&T Clark, 2013), 158.

82. Ehrensperger, *Paul at the Crossroads*, 158: "The paradigm of sameness promoted by imperial power is exactly what these people from the nations were *not* to follow as followers of Christ." Later Ehrensperger is emphatic—repeating the phrase twice in two adjacent paragraphs—that the Roman discourse and that of Paul "could not be more different": in Paul's gospel "people from the nations" are called "in all their particularity and diversity" and "only what was incompatible with a way of life that should be guided by Christ (not copied) had to be given up" (172–73).

there is a tendency to depict Paul's achievements in terms of inclusion, albeit an inclusion that, as Campbell emphasizes, allows Jews to remain Jews (in Christ?).

Johnson Hodge rejects the common idea that Paul incorporates gentile converts alongside Jews into "a new group called Christians." Rather, "Christ-following gentiles are affiliated with Israel—sharing some characteristics but retaining a necessary separateness."[83] To develop this interpretation, Johnson Hodge outlines a model of multiple identities, one of which "can fit within—be nested inside—a more encompassing identity."[84] In Paul's scheme of "hierarchical identities," then, being "in-Christ" is "at the top." This "being in-Christ cuts across ethnic identities, including both *Ioudaioi* and non-*Ioudaioi*," such that "this 'in-Christness' [is] superimposed over other facets of identity."[85] Johnson Hodge sees Gal 3:28 from the perspective of a "model of multiple identities" as a means of seeking "unity while preserving difference."[86] Thus, "as Paul shapes the new identities of these gentiles, he places 'in-Christness' or 'keeping the commandments of God' at the top."[87] The focus here is on the reconfiguration of *gentile* identities, but Paul is nonetheless seen as envisaging the nesting of multiple identities while preserving difference. His message may thus be seen, as Pamela Eisenbaum suggests, as "a vision of inclusion that recognizes the legitimacy of difference."[88] Even in work where the abiding integrity and validity of Jewish identity is affirmed, then, it is in Paul or other early Christian writers that the possibility for inclusion is often found—and often found specifically on the basis of a trans-ethnic, superordinate, identity in Christ, within which Jews can remain Jews and gentiles gentiles.

The prominence of a focus on Paul's "inclusion" or trans-ethnic universalism can also be found in the very different secular philosophical engagements with Paul. Alain Badiou, for example, speaks of Paul's "passion"

---

83. Johnson Hodge, *If Sons, Then Heirs*, 117.
84. Johnson Hodge, *If Sons, Then Heirs*, 120.
85. Johnson Hodge, *If Sons, Then Heirs*, 125–26.
86. Johnson Hodge, *If Sons, Then Heirs*, 129.
87. Johnson Hodge, *If Sons, Then Heirs*, 134.
88. Pamela Eisenbaum, "Jewish Perspectives: A Jewish Apostle to the Gentiles," in *Studying Paul's Letters: Contemporary Perspectives and Methods*, ed. Joseph A. Marchal (Minneapolis: Fortress, 2012), 150.

for "universalism," which contrasts with Jewish "particularity."[89] Badiou declares:

> This is the driving force behind Paul's universalist conviction: that "ethnic" or cultural difference, of which the opposition between Greek and Jew is in his time, and in the empire as a whole, the prototype, is no longer significant with regard to the real, or to the new object that sets out a new discourse. . . . To declare the nondifference between Jew and Greek establishes Christianity's potential universality . . . by terminating the predicative particularity of cultural subjects.[90]

In the field of New Testament studies at least, arguments about the strategic achievements of Jesus, Paul, or other New Testament authors are generally presented as historical reconstructions—attempts to understand, using social-scientific resources and concepts, the discursive strategies and community-forming efforts of the authors of various New Testament texts.[91] But it is not hard to see that the achievements of these figures within earliest Christianity are seen as having positive value for the contemporary world too (hence, also, the appeal of Paul to contemporary political philosophers like Badiou). Indeed, this claim is often made explicitly. Esler announces near the beginning of his work on Romans that "the contemporary issue driving the current study of Romans is the nature of Christian identity . . . in a world rent by violent, often murderous conflict between groups, in particular those of an ethnic kind."[92] The argument comes full circle when the enduring value of Paul's strategy for overcoming inter-ethnic conflict is made clear in the closing sentence of the book: "In a world still torn by ethnic conflict, this is a message [about the overcoming of ethnic conflict through a new common identity in Christ] that will continue to resonate."[93] Similarly, Kuecker writes that "Luke's

---

89. Alain Badiou, *Saint Paul: The Foundation of Universalism*, trans. Ray Brassier, Cultural Memory in the Present (Stanford: Stanford University Press, 2003), 95: "universalism is Paul's passion." On Paul's stance toward "Jewish particularity," see 102.

90. Badiou, *Saint Paul*, 57. For critical discussion of these philosophical perspectives on Paul, not least concerning his supposed "universalism," see John D. Caputo and Linda Martin Alcoff, eds., *St. Paul among the Philosophers*, Indiana Studies in the Philosophy of Religion (Bloomington: Indiana University Press, 2009).

91. See, e.g., Esler, *Conflict and Identity*, 9; Campbell, *Creation of Christian Identity*, 174.

92. Esler, *Conflict and Identity*, 10.

93. Esler, *Conflict and Identity*, 365. Cf. Campbell, *Creation of Christian Identity*, 174–75.

Spirit-centered vision stands as a challenge for contemporary Christian faith and practice," a proclamation of "the possibility of a beautifully diverse community of peace that exists as an outpost of the eschatological new creation in the midst of a world marked by interethnic strife."[94] Paul's teaching may be seen as "a model for thinking about religious pluralism in the broader, more complex world in which we find ourselves."[95] My own earlier work makes a similar claim, finding in Paul's treatment of communal solidarity and tolerable difference resources of potential value in the context of contemporary plural societies.[96] This kind of observation, which celebrates the positive achievements of earliest Christianity—specifically its creation of diverse and inclusive community in Christ—and commends those achievements for the contemporary world, occurs with considerable regularity.

Again, these historical reconstructions emerging in the field of New Testament studies may be seen to reflect something of their sociopolitical context. The latter decades of the twentieth century have been an era of interfaith dialogue, supported by major religious bodies and international organizations such as the United Nations. They have also been a time when Western societies—often experiencing immigration from former colonies—have grappled with how to preserve and integrate diverse cultural, ethnic, and religious identities under such ideological banners as multiculturalism. Despite the Holocaust and the hope that such a uniquely grotesque program of annihilation might cement a determination to ensure that such genocide could never again occur, the late twentieth century also witnessed horrific inter-ethnic violence, notably in the 1990s in the former Yugoslavia and in Rwanda. It is clear that the reconstructions of the early Christian communities offered by scholars such as Esler both reflect and respond to such social challenges.

1.4 Conclusions

There are very considerable differences between the perspectives on Christian origins articulated by Baur, Dunn, and Esler, to take just three key representatives of the various phases and approaches surveyed above. It could

94. Kuecker, *Spirit and the "Other,"* 228, 230.
95. Eisenbaum, "Jewish Perspectives," 150.
96. David G. Horrell, *Solidarity and Difference: A Contemporary Reading of Paul's Ethics*, 2nd ed., Cornerstones (London: Bloomsbury T&T Clark, 2016 [1st ed. 2005]).

hardly be otherwise: the language of scholarship in the mid-nineteenth century, and the theoretical frameworks and sociopolitical contexts that shape such language, are inevitably far removed from the language of the late twentieth (and early twenty-first) century. Baur's Hegelian narrative about the progress of history is hugely different from James Dunn's rereading of Paul in the light of post-Holocaust reassessments of first-century Judaism; Esler's deployment of modern Social Identity Theory and social-scientific perspectives on ethnicity marks another kind of methodological innovation. The contrasting character of "Jewish" (or Judean) and "Christian" (or in-Christ) identities is depicted in different terms and with different vocabulary, just as the specific historical methods and exegetical approaches, as well as the sociopolitical contexts, have changed. Nonetheless, it seems that a certain structural dichotomy persists, one that contrasts an ethnically particular Judaism with an inclusive non-ethnic or trans-ethnic Christianity. For Baur, the particular achievement of the latter was to enable the flourishing of true spiritual freedom; later authors have, for reasons we shall return to, cast the achievement more in terms of the potential to transcend, encompass, and thus hold together without negating the particular (ethnic) identities of Jews and gentiles. But the potential to achieve this all-embracing inclusion, however it is cast, is found in the early Christian sources, and above all in the iconic figure of Paul.

How might we assess the validity of this enduring dichotomy? To what extent might it be challenged? To what extent is it a product of scholarship that reflects a particular context and tradition, however much that tradition has evolved and shifted over time? These are the issues to be explored in the studies that follow. First, however, we need to survey some further areas of recent research that are pertinent to either side of our dichotomy, particularly with regard to the category of "ethnicity" (and its relationship to "religion"). The next chapter will therefore summarize some of the main contours of recent research into ancient Jewish (or Judean) identity and also into the significance of ethnicity or ethnic terminology in New Testament and early Christian texts.

CHAPTER 2

Ethnicity, Race, and Ancient Jewish and Christian Identities: Themes in Recent Research

In the previous chapter we saw how a structural dichotomy between an ethnically particular Judaism and an open, inclusive, or trans-ethnic Christianity runs as a persistent theme through various phases of New Testament scholarship, from its early modern history in the nineteenth century to its latest formulations. The specific terms and expressions vary, unsurprisingly, with changing times and contexts, yet basic to the dichotomy—not least in its recent forms—is this contrast between an ethnic Judaism and a non-ethnic or trans-ethnic Christianity.

A critical assessment of this contrast evidently requires an informed sense of what it might mean to identify Judaism as "ethnic" (or, indeed, "racial") in character. Since a particular emphasis on ancient Judaism as an ethnic identity has emerged in recent research, it is important to outline the key points of that research and to locate it within the broader context of discussions of ethnicity and race in antiquity. This is the task of the first section of this chapter. We then move to a consideration of the other side of the dichotomy, and the categorization of early Christian identity. Here it is particularly pertinent to outline the range of recent research that has, in various ways, challenged the "non-ethnic" characterization of early Christian discourse.

2.1 Ethnicity and Race in Antiquity: Jews/Judeans and Greeks

Judaism has long been regarded—not least in the research outlined in chapter 1—as some kind of particular, ethnic, "national" or "racial" identity, though also as a kind of religion. However, recent years have seen a particular emphasis on the categorization of ancient Jewish identity as "ethnic." An influential landmark in this research is the seminal article from 2007 by

Steve Mason, in which Mason argues, *inter alia*, that in antiquity, Ἰουδαῖος connoted an ethnic identity (comparable to that of other ancient ἔθνη) in which cultural and religious practices were part of an ancestral way of life, regulated by laws and customs.[1] Mason's focus, it should be stressed, is not on modern social-scientific definitions of ethnicity but rather, from a rigorously historical and philological perspective, on the ancient terminology. In other words, *Ioudaioi* were recognized and labeled, like other people-groups at the time, as an ἔθνος. This (along with the πόλις) was a fundamental concept for the ordering of ancient society:[2]

> Each *ethnos* had its distinctive nature or character (φύσις, ἦθος), expressed in unique ancestral traditions (τὰ πάτρια), which typically reflected a shared (if fictive) ancestry (συγγενεία); each had its charter stories (μῦθοι), customs, norms, conventions, mores, laws (νόμοι, ἔθη, νόμιμα), and political arrangements or constitution (πολιτεία).[3]

It is anachronistic, Mason insists, to import the modern category of "religion" into the ancient world, and specifically into our study of ancient Judaism, since there is no ancient concept to which it properly corresponds.[4] From this perspective, then, it makes more sense to translate Ἰουδαῖος as "Judean," indicating an ethnic identity related to a particular land of origin as with other such groups in antiquity, rather than as "Jew," which connotes an essentially religious identification.[5]

Following Mason's proposals, Wolfgang Stegemann has forcefully argued for what he calls a "change of perspective" (*Perspektivenwechsel*) in

1. Mason, "Jews, Judaeans, Judaizing, Judaism."

2. For an extended presentation of the "classical paradigm" for "mapping peoples" in terms of *ethnos* and *polis*, see Mason, *History of Roman Judaea*, 97–146.

3. Mason, "Jews, Judaeans, Judaizing, Judaism," 484. For a similar definition, see Lukas Bormann, "Griechen und Juden—Skythen und Barbaren: Ethnizität, kulturelle Dominanz und Marginalität im Neuen Testament," in *Alternative Voices: A Plurality Approach for Religious Studies: Essays in Honor of Ulrich Berner*, ed. Afe Adogame, Magnus Echtler, and Oliver Freiberger, Critical Studies in Religion/Religionswissenschaft 4 (Göttingen: Vandenhoeck & Ruprecht, 2013), 121. Bormann also quotes Mason's definition on 119.

4. Mason, "Jews, Judaeans, Judaizing, Judaism," 460–80. Mason is followed, e.g., by Daniel Boyarin, "Rethinking Jewish Christianity: An Argument for Dismantling a Dubious Category (to Which Is Appended a Correction of My *Border Lines*)," *JQR* 99 (2009): 7–36; Douglas Boin, "Hellenistic 'Judaism' and the Social Origins of the 'Pagan-Christian' Debate," *JECS* 22 (2014): 167–96. For further examples of the influence of Mason's article, see below.

5. On the ongoing debate, see above, p. 13 n. 33.

studies of Judaism at the time of Christian origins, a shift of paradigm away from a "religion-model" in favor of an "ethnicity-model" (*Ethnizitätsmodell*).[6] While the significance of this shift—and of the recent debates about the translation of 'Ιουδαῖος—should not be underestimated, it is also the case, as we have seen in chapter 1, that a stress on Judaism as an essentially "ethnic" (or racial, or national) kind of ("particular") identity is by no means a recent development, even if the precise terminology has shifted with different phases of New Testament scholarship.[7]

A similar perspective on Judaism, but derived from an explicit application of social-scientific definitions of ethnicity, is found in the work of Philip Esler, as noted in chapter 1.[8] Using the six characteristics presented by Anthony Smith to identify (modern) ethnic groups (see §3.1), Esler argues that the presentation of Judean identity in Josephus's *Contra Apionem* includes all these aspects, indicating that ancient Judeans can best be seen as constituting an ethnic group—and were seen as such by Josephus and his contemporaries.[9] Like Mason, Esler argues on this basis that "Judean" is a more appropriate translation of 'Ιουδαῖος than "Jew."[10] One of Esler's arguments for using the term Judean is that, as with other territorially named groups in antiquity, the label reflects the people's attachment to a particular territory, Judea—attachment to a specific land or territory being one of the features of ethnic identity listed by Smith. This positive argument is also reinforced by a corresponding rejection of the possibility of the name denoting "a purely religious affiliation," since "in the ancient world," this notion would be "an anachronistic illusion."[11] This perspective on Judean ethnic identity, as noted in chapter 1, has since informed several other works in which Esler contrasts Judean ethnic identity with the "trans-ethnic" superordinate identity of "Christ followers."

6. Stegemann, *Jesus*, 180–236, esp. 210, 216, 234. For a concise overview of the key arguments, see also Stegemann, "Religion," 47–59.

7. See further, e.g., Halvor Moxnes's discussion of depictions of Jews in racial terms in the work of David Straus and Ernest Renan in Moxnes, *Jesus and the Rise of Nationalism*, 115–18, 137–41.

8. Their two approaches are combined in Steve Mason and Philip. F. Esler, "Judaean and Christ-Follower Identities: Grounds for a Distinction," *NTS* 63 (2017): 493–515.

9. Philip F. Esler, "Judean Ethnic Identity in Josephus' *Against Apion*," in *A Wandering Galilean: Essays in Honour of Seán Freyne*, ed. Zuleika Rodgers, Margaret Daly-Denton, and Anne Fitzpatrick McKinley (Leiden: Brill, 2009), 73–91.

10. See Esler, *Conflict and Identity*, 62–74.

11. Esler, *Conflict and Identity*, 73. Cf. also See Elliott, "Jesus the Israelite," 119–54. On the modern concept of religion and its inappropriateness in the ancient world, see §3.3 below, pp. 86–89.

In his commentary on Josephus's *Contra Apionem*, John Barclay expresses some skepticism about the use of a standard list such as Smith's to determine whether Josephus does or does not depict Judeans as an ethnic group,[12] but elsewhere he agrees that Judaism in the period was "primarily an ethnic tradition," though one which proselytes could join so as "to acquire in effect a new 'ethnicity' in kinship and custom."[13] Such comments indicate further agreement concerning ancient Judaism as a kind of ethnic identity but at the same time begin to indicate some of the complexities and questions involved in classifying it in this way: In what sense, for example, was it an ethnic identity that one could acquire by choosing to "join," and how unusual would this make Jewish identity in the landscape of antiquity? Equally important, how far are "ethnic" and "religious" aspects of this identity distinguishable?[14] This "ethnic" categorization is, nonetheless, a dominant one in contemporary scholarship.[15]

One significant challenge to this view of Jewishness as an essentially ethnic identity at the time of Christian origins is found in the work of Shaye Cohen. Cohen argues that a shift in the basis and character of Jewish identity took place in the Hasmonean period and is evident particularly in 2 Maccabees. He argues that "in the second century B.C.E., the metaphoric boundary separating Judaeans from non-Judaeans became more and more permeable. Outsiders could become insiders."[16] For Cohen, this represents

12. John M. G. Barclay, *Against Apion*, vol. 10 of *Flavius Josephus: Translation and Commentary* (Leiden: Brill, 2007), lv with n. 137. Expressing caution about Esler's use of Anthony Smith's criteria as "a template of ethnicity," Barclay insists that "we need to attend carefully to the precise ingredients of the image of 'Judeans' . . . without prior assumptions about what must, or must not, be embraced by this term." Esler, "Judean Ethnic Identity," 76n9, responds that "Barclay misunderstands the use of a social-scientific perspective in biblical interpretation." The criteria used "merely raise questions to put to the text, to which it must supply responsive data; they do not prescribe any particular conclusion." On these methodological issues, see §3.1 below.

13. John M. G. Barclay, *Jews in the Mediterranean Diaspora from Alexander to Trajan (323 BCE–117 CE)* (Edinburgh: T&T Clark, 1996), 408; see 402–13.

14. This issue is explored in Barclay, "Ἰουδαῖος," 46–58, and discussed further below (see §3.3).

15. For further examples, see Stewart Moore, *Jewish Ethnic Identity and Relations in Hellenistic Egypt: With Walls of Iron?*, JSJSup 171 (Leiden: Brill, 2015); Markus Cromhout, *Walking in Their Sandals: A Guide to First-Century Israelite Ethnic Identity* (Eugene, OR: Cascade, 2010); Hellerman, *Jesus*. For examples in German scholarship, see §2.2 below.

16. Shaye J. D. Cohen, *The Beginnings of Jewishness: Boundaries, Varieties, Uncertainties* (Berkeley: University of California Press, 1999), 110. For a broadly similar perspective on shifts in Jewish identity, see Schwartz, *Jewish Background*, 5–19.

a shift away from an ethnic "Judean" identity to a cultural-religious "Jewish" one.[17] Once again, issues of definition rapidly become crucial: since Cohen regards ethnicity as "closed, immutable, an ascribed characteristic based on birth," the shift of focus to cultural-religious commitments and practices as definitive of Jewish identity is seen as a move away from an ethnic notion of identity.[18] However, as critics have pointed out, Cohen's debatable definition of ethnicity underpins the categories of his argument.[19]

As we shall see in more detail in the next chapter, ethnicity may be—and indeed is most cogently—understood differently, as a constructed identity in which various factors may be invoked or made salient, notwithstanding the important developments to which Cohen draws attention.[20] It may therefore be more convincing to follow Love Sechrest in suggesting that Jewish notions of ethnicity/race in the first centuries BCE and CE make "religion" a central "criterion of identity" (though kinship and other factors remain significant) such that Jewish ethnicity is a group identity in which religio-cultural aspects play a dominant role.[21] Moreover, as Stewart Moore has re-

17. See also the more recent critical response to Mason (and also to Stegemann, among others) by Dieter Sänger, "'Ιουδαϊσμός—ἰουδαΐζειν—ἰουδαϊκῶς: Sprachliche und semantische Überlegungen im Blick auf Gal 1,13f. und 2,14," *ZNW* 108 (2017): 150–85. Sänger argues, based on a careful analysis of the relevant texts (and inscriptions) that 'Ιουδαϊσμός refers to adherence to the Jewish way of life and that identity as 'Ιουδαῖος, while it includes an ethnic dimension, cannot be limited purely to this but is more multifaceted and includes the notion of religion. This also partly affirms the arguments of Cohen. See also the discussion in Manfred Vogel, "Modelle jüdischer Identitätsbildung in hellenistisch-römischer Zeit," in *Religionsgemeinschaft und Identität: Prozesse jüdischer und christlicher Identitätsbildung im Rahmen der antike*, ed. Markus Öhler, Biblisch-Theologische Studien 142 (Neukirchen-Vluyn: Neukirchener, 2013), 43–68.

18. Cohen, *Beginnings*, 136. Cf. the straightforward statement at the opening of his chapter: "Ethnic (or ethnic-geographic) identity is immutable; non-Judaeans cannot become Judaeans any more than non-Egyptians can become Egyptians, or non-Syrians can become Syrians" (109).

19. For criticisms, see Denise Kimber Buell, "Ethnicity and Religion in Mediterranean Antiquity and Beyond," *RelSRev* 26 (2000): 243–49, 245–46; Buell, "Rethinking the Relevance of Race for Early Christian Self-Definition," *HTR* 94 (2001): 468–69; Buell, *Why This New Race*, 44–45, 162–63; Esler, *Conflict and Identity*, 68–74; Mason, "Jews, Judaeans, Judaizing, Judaism," 494–96.

20. On the importance of the developments that emerged in the context of the Maccabean crisis, as narrated especially in 1–2 Maccabees, see also Mason, "Jews, Judaeans, Judaizing, Judaism"; Boin, "Hellenistic 'Judaism.'"

21. Sechrest, *A Former Jew*, 97–105, esp. 104–5, 209. Also, though he pushes back somewhat harder against Mason's arguments against using the category "religion" to denote ancient Judaism, see Lee I. Levine, "Jewish Identities in Antiquity: An Introductory

cently stressed, the insights developed by Fredrik Barth (on which see §3.1) should help us to recognize that ethnic identities in general, and Judean ethnicity in particular, depend for their maintenance not on full adherence to all the practices and values that might be deemed to constitute the "cultural stuff"[22] enclosed within an ethnic boundary but rather on the specific values and practices deemed crucial to signaling this identity and maintaining the group boundary. Thus, Moore remarks, "Judean ethnic identity used specific religious behaviors as ethnic boundary markers."[23]

These debates and proposals begin to indicate something of the complexity of identifying ancient Jewish identity as "ethnic." It may clearly be "ethnic" in the sense that ancient authors, both Jews and non-Jews, recognized this group as a "people" (ἔθνος) with ancestral laws and customs and a homeland, but this leaves open to further consideration which factors (including "religion") played the largest part in determining Jewish identity, how joining and leaving might be understood, and how Jewish identity might relate to other (ethnic or non-ethnic) identities.

Indeed, similar issues and complexities surround the identities of other people-groups in antiquity.[24] Jonathan Hall, as well as exploring the construction of ethnic identity in Greek literature from the Archaic and Classical periods,[25] has argued in a later work—in a way not dissimilar to Cohen—that "the definitional basis of Hellenic identity shifted from ethnic to broader cultural criteria in the course of the fifth century [BCE]."[26] For example, Hall sees Herodotus's oft-quoted "definition" of Greekness (or "Hellenicity") as already an indication of this promotion of "cultural criteria (including

---

Essay," in *Jewish Identities in Antiquity: Studies in Memory of Menahem Stern*, ed. Lee I. Levine and Daniel R. Schwartz, TSAJ 130 (Tübingen: Mohr Siebeck, 2009), 30–32.

22. Fredrik Barth, "Introduction," in *Ethnic Groups and Boundaries: The Social Organization of Culture Difference*, ed. Fredrik Barth (Boston: Little, Brown, 1969), 15.

23. Moore, *Jewish Ethnic Identity*, 43.

24. For a recent overview of the energetic discussion of ethnicity in the Greek and Roman worlds, see Teresa Morgan, "Society, Identity, and Ethnicity in the Hellenic World," in Hockey and Horrell, *Ethnicity, Race, Religion*, 23–45.

25. Jonathan M. Hall, *Ethnic Identity in Greek Antiquity* (Cambridge: Cambridge University Press, 1997).

26. Jonathan M. Hall, *Hellenicity: Between Ethnicity and Culture* (Chicago: University of Chicago Press, 2002), 7; see 172–228. Cf. Cohen, *Beginnings*, 132, where he suggests that, from the fourth century BCE, the Greeks "deemphasized the immutable and emphasized the mutable elements" of their identity, such that "'Hellene' changed from an ethnic or ethnic-geographic term to a cultural term."

language and religion) to the same level as kinship"[27]—the latter ("fictive kinship") being, for Hall, "the *sine qua non* for ethnic consciousness."[28] Herodotus records the response of the Athenians to Spartan envoys, explaining why they reject the notion of an alliance with "foreigners" that would lead to the enslavement of other Greeks:

> For there are many great reasons why we should not do this . . . ; the kinship of all Greeks [τὸ Ἑλληνικόν] in blood and speech [ὅμαιμόν τε καὶ ὁμόγλωσσον], and the shrines of gods and the sacrifices that we have in common [θεῶν ἱδρύματά τε κοινὰ καὶ θυσίαι], and the likeness of our way of life [ἤθεά τε ὁμότροπα], to all which it would ill beseem Athenians to be false. (Herodotus, *Hist.* 8.144 [Godley, LCL])

While this characterization of Greekness mentions kinship (blood), language, religion, and way of life, it significantly omits, as Suzanne Saïd notes, "shared territory and shared history," commonly seen as crucial facets of "ethnic" identity.[29] Isocrates's statement from around 380 BCE, also discussed by Hall,[30] famously takes this cultural emphasis further, redefining Greekness in terms of shared culture rather than shared origin:

> The name "Greek" [τὸ τῶν Ἑλλήνων ὄνομα] seems no longer to connote the race [μηκέτι τοῦ γένους] but the mental attitude [ἀλλὰ τῆς διανοίας], and people are called "Greeks" who share our culture [τῆς παιδεύσεως τῆς ἡμετέρας] rather than our common origin [τῆς κοινῆς φύσεως]. (Isocrates, *Paneg.* 50 [Norlin, LCL])

However, as with Cohen's thesis about the transformation of Jewish identity, it seems that this transformation—significant though it is—may be understood in terms of the various potentially salient characteristics of ethnicity rather than as a move away from ethnicity per se. Esler, for example, insists, against Hall, that "a transition from ancestry to culture and language does not solemnize the disintegration of Greek ethnicity, but simply represents an alteration in the cultural indicia by which the

27. Hall, *Hellenicity*, 193.
28. Hall, *Hellenicity*, 26.
29. Suzanne Saïd, "The Discourse of Identity in Greek Rhetoric from Isocrates to Aristedes," in *Ancient Perceptions of Greek Identity*, ed. Irad Malkin, Center for Hellenic Studies Colloquia 5 (Cambridge, MA: Harvard University Press, 2001), 275.
30. See Hall, *Hellenicity*, 208–10.

boundaries of that ethnic group are negotiated."[31] (However, Esler's claim that Hall's case "rests on a single passage in Isocrates" is unfair.[32]) Denise Eileen McCoskey similarly—though using the language of race rather than ethnicity—sees Isocrates's statement as one indication that "cultural practice gained increasing authority in defining racial categories," though she also notes the "tensions and uncertainties that continued to accompany this shift, producing enduring concern over the relative roles of essence and practice."[33] A similar case is made by Edward Anson, who argues that language in particular played a key role in determining who was reckoned as Greek.[34]

A common theme in these discussions is the sense that ethnicity or race, whatever we mean by these terms, may be based on a range of indicators that vary in salience and prominence, including indicators that relate primarily to what we might call cultural practice rather than to biology or physiognomy. Further complicating this picture of ethnic identity are the indications that, as Teresa Morgan observes, "ethnic" designations in antiquity may be used of groups of various sizes, from cities or groups of cities to larger regions and kingdoms.[35] Morgan also documents multiple instances of individuals who either change their ethnic identity or acquire new identities alongside their existing ones in a process she labels "accretive."[36] This might be in relation to tax status, rising social status, or decisions to display their identity differently in different contexts or to different audiences—something Morgan, invoking a term from the field of linguistics, calls "code switching."[37] Likewise, Michael Peppard draws attention to evidence for "ethnic hybridity" in ancient Galilee.[38]

---

31. Esler, *Conflict and Identity*, 57.

32. Esler, *Conflict and Identity*, 56.

33. Denise Eileen McCoskey, *Race: Antiquity and Its Legacy*, Ancients and Moderns (London: I. B. Tauris, 2012), 63. Cf. Saïd, "Discourse of Identity"; David Konstan, "*To Hellēnikon ethnos*: Ethnicity and the Construction of Ancient Greek Identity," in Malkin, *Ancient Perceptions*, 29–50.

34. Edward M. Anson, "Greek Ethnicity and the Greek Language," *Glotta* 85 (2009): 5–30.

35. Morgan, "Society, Identity, and Ethnicity," 24–26.

36. Morgan, "Society, Identity, and Ethnicity," 35.

37. Morgan, "Society, Identity, and Ethnicity," 34–38.

38. Michael Peppard, "Personal Names and Ethnic Hybridity in Late Ancient Galilee: The Data from Beth She'arim," in *Religion, Ethnicity, and Identity in Ancient Galilee: A Region in Transition*, ed. Jürgen Zangenberg, Harold W. Attridge, and Dale B. Martin, WUNT 210 (Tübingen: Mohr Siebeck, 2007), 99–113.

As with Cohen's and Hall's stress on cultural or religious factors, even if we insist that such factors can still be a part of "ethnic" identity, this evidence suggests that "ethnic" identity could be a flexible, changeable, even multiple category. Furthermore, even if we accept that Jewishness at the time might be seen fundamentally as an ethnic identity—belonging to a recognized ancestral ἔθνος—we need to acknowledge that Jewish (and early Christian) groups are also described in other terms and categories: as associations, philosophical schools, ethnic groups, and so on.[39] To Galen, for example, Judaism and Christianity are examples of (defective) philosophies, deriving from the "schools" of Moses and Christ respectively (Galen, *De pulsuum differentiis* 2.4, 3.3).[40] Alternatively, the "religious" aspects may be more to the fore—if not separable from "ethnic" identity—as for example in Suetonius's report of when Tiberius "abolished foreign cults [*externas caerimonias*], especially the Egyptian and Jewish rites [*ritus*], compelling all who were addicted to such superstitions [*superstitione*] to burn their religious vestments [*religiosas vestes*] and all their paraphernalia" (Suetonius, *Tib.* 36 [Rolfe, LCL]).[41]

One of the issues clearly at stake in these various arguments is that of defining ethnicity and understanding its relationship to religion; both of these concepts are, after all, modern constructs. Whether Cohen's or Hall's theses are found convincing or not depends in part on whether their working definitions of ethnicity are appropriate. And what it means to define Judaism as an "ethnic" identity depends on how this categorization is understood. Another issue is the choice of the term "ethnicity" or "race" and the relationship between these modern concepts and ancient terms and near equivalents. All this indicates the need for a carefully considered theoretical framework, something that will occupy us in the following chapter. First, however, I turn to the other side of our dichotomy—namely, the construal of early Christian identity.

---

39. See further David G. Horrell, "Judaean Ethnicity and Christ-Following Voluntarism? A Reply to Steve Mason and Philip Esler," *NTS* 65 (2019): 4–7.

40. Text from Richard Walzer, *Galen on Jews and Christians*, Oxford Classical and Philosophical Monographs (Oxford: Oxford University Press, 1949), 14; see 37–56 for Galen's view of Judaism and Christianity as "defective" philosophies.

41. Cf. Tacitus, *Ann.* 2.85, who refers to "the proscription of Egyptian and Jewish rites [*sacris Aegyptiis Iudaieisque*]." For a longer account of the scandals that led to such actions, see Josephus, *A.J.* 18.65–84. The Egyptian cult specifically in view is that of Isis, which was popular in this period. See also Mary Beard, John North, and Simon Price, *A History*, vol. 1 of *Religions of Rome* (Cambridge: Cambridge University Press, 1998), 230–31.

2.2 Ethnicity and Race in Early Christian Discourse and Identity

Contrary to the enduring tendency to characterize early Christian identity as open, universal, or non-ethnic, some recent research has begun to explore how far, and in what ways, emerging Christian identity might itself be constructed and defined in ethnic or racial terms. Particularly important and influential in stimulating this focus in research is Denise Kimber Buell's ground-breaking study, *Why This New Race*, published in 2005. In this work, Buell explores the use of what she calls "ethnic reasoning" in early Christian texts from the second and third centuries. Rejecting the common dichotomy between Christian non-ethnic universalism and Jewish ethnic particularity, Buell insists that early Christians also exploited "ethnoracial" language to construct their identity, to describe the process of conversion and transformation, and to make universal claims about the potential for all humanity to enter this one, new people.[42] Buell uses "ethnicity" and "race" interchangeably and combines them in the term "ethnoracial," arguing that "race" in particular should be retained, not least in order to foreground (rather than evade) issues of racism.[43] She is "suspicious of the ways that certain modern concepts seem to be viewed as unproblematic for analysis of antiquity—religion, ethnicity, and gender, for example—whereas others have become 'off-limits' ('race' and increasingly also 'sexuality')."[44] Indeed, "replacing race with ethnicity," she insists, "has obscured the racist aspects of using ethnicity to distinguish Jews from Christians"; retaining the term helps us "to confront the elusive elasticity of race, since racism persists even when race has been exposed as a construct."[45]

Dismissing the notion that ethnicity and race are stable or concrete facets of identity, Buell insists that they are flexible, fluid categories that can be deployed in discourse in various ways. Indeed, for Buell it is precisely "the dynamic interplay between fixity and fluidity" that makes ethnicity/race

42. Buell, *Why This New Race*. For earlier presentations of aspects of the argument, see Buell, "Relevance of Race"; Buell, "Race and Universalism in Early Christianity," *JECS* 10 (2002): 429–68. Among her subsequent reflections, see Buell, "God's Own People: Specters of Race, Ethnicity, and Gender in Early Christian Studies," in Nasrallah and Schüssler Fiorenza, *Prejudice and Christian Beginnings*, 159–90; Buell, "Early Christian Universalism," 109–31; Buell, "Challenges and Strategies," 33–51.

43. Buell, *Why This New Race*, 13–21.

44. Buell, *Why This New Race*, 18. However, more recent work has increasingly also problematized the term "religion"; see §3.3 below.

45. Buell, *Why This New Race*, 14, 20.

a category of identity that can be deployed in these ways: while ethnic or racial identities are often *depicted*—and perceived—as fixed and given, they are also malleable and can be changed.[46] Thus, as she puts it in an earlier article, "instead of seeing conversion in contrast to ethnoracial identity, early Christians perceived ethnicity/race as concepts flexible enough to encompass both the radical transformation of identity attributed to the conversion process and the stability of identity hoped for in its wake."[47]

Drawing on the earlier work of Jonathan Hall, mentioned briefly above, Buell identifies both oppositional and aggregative strategies in early Christian texts—that is, strategies that, on the one hand, distinguish Christians from others (specifically from Jews and Greeks) and, on the other, depict Christianness as an identity that incorporates and includes others (potentially the whole of humanity).[48] Buell's focus, then, is not on whether early Christians did or did not, *qua* Christians, constitute an ethnic group—a formulation that implies too great a sense of essentialism—but rather on how ethnoracial terminology is deployed in early Christian discourse through "ethnic reasoning."[49]

Buell's study makes a number of important contributions. First and foremost, it has helped to bring the issues of ethnicity, race and their rhetorical and strategic deployment in texts to attention in the study of early Christianity.[50] Many subsequent works have taken up the agenda—and indeed the approach—highlighted by Buell. Second, Buell's work illustrates the diverse ways in which ethnoracial terms are employed in early Christian discourse, persuasively showing that the language of ethnicity or race forms a flexible resource for the construction of identity. Despite the sense of fixity and immutability that is often conveyed by appeals to notions of ethnic or racial identity, Buell demonstrates in multiple ways how the paradoxical fluidity of these notions enables their use for various strategic purposes. In particular, Buell shows how both exclusionary and universalizing strategies can

---

46. Buell, *Why This New Race*, 9.

47. Buell, "Race and Universalism," 436.

48. See Buell, "Race and Universalism," 441–50; Buell, *Why This New Race*, 138–65; cf. Hall, *Ethnic Identity*, 47.

49. For appreciation and critical reaction, see two extended reviews of Buell, *Why This New Race*: that of Stanley Stowers, *JAAR* 75 (2007): 727–30; and that of Erich S. Gruen, *CBQ* 72 (2010): 365–67.

50. Among other significant early pointers to the importance of this theme, see also Judith M. Lieu, "The Race of the God-Fearers," in *Neither Jew nor Greek? Constructing Early Christianity*, SNTW (Edinburgh: T&T Clark, 2002), 49–68; orig. *JTS* 46 (1995): 483–501.

draw upon ethnic terminology such that it is by no means contradictory for a group to conceive itself as open to all people while defining itself in ethnic terms.[51] Third, Buell's insistence on retaining the category of race, even for discussion of the ancient sources, marks an important, if controversial, stance, intended both to convey the inextricable interconnections between notions of ethnicity and of race and also to highlight the need to confront racism in scholarship and the wider world.

Buell's studies are, however, focused primarily on second- and third-century Christian texts,[52] examining discourses of identity-formation in the post-New Testament period. Indeed, she elsewhere expresses significant "hesitations" about applying the same approach to the New Testament texts due to complexities that arise because of the New Testament's canonical status and influence and its ambiguous character—when viewed from a later perspective—as a collection of originally intra-Jewish writings that "*become* and function as Christian documents."[53] An approach to the New Testament from the perspective of ethnicity would need, she suggests, to deal with the significance of the Bible as a whole, to "navigate both the Jewish and Christian character of the New Testament writings," and to consider the contemporary "stakes" of New Testament interpretation.[54] Her proposal is to do this through the notion of "haunting," which invites attention specifically to that which haunts New Testament texts in terms of their ongoing implications and legacies, not least in the history of race and racism.[55]

---

51. See also Buell, "Challenges and Strategies," 42.

52. The same goes for Judith Lieu's important studies, which also identify—though to a less prominent degree—the significance of "race" language in the construction of early Christian identity (see n. 50 above). See Lieu, *Neither Jew nor Greek?*; *Christian Identity in the Jewish and Graeco-Roman World* (Oxford: Oxford University Press, 2004). For similar interests in relation to the fourth century, see Aaron P. Johnson, *Ethnicity and Argument in Eusebius' "Praeparatio Evangelica,"* OECS (Oxford: Oxford University Press, 2006).

53. Buell, "Challenges and Strategies," 34–44, with quotation from 39, referring specifically to Paul's letters.

54. Buell, "Challenges and Strategies," 44.

55. Buell, "Challenges and Strategies," 45–50. In his critical response to this paper, James A. Kelhoffer ("Response to Denise Kimber Buell: A Plea for Clarity in Regard to Examining Ethnicity in, Based on, or in Scholarship on the New Testament," *SEÅ* 79 [2014]: 53–59) argues that Buell insufficiently distinguishes interpretation of the NT texts, the study of their history of reception, and critical interrogation of contemporary NT scholarship, but I assume Buell's point to be, in part at least, that these are inseparable tasks due precisely to the status and influence of the NT *qua* NT.

Other recent studies have, however, focused on New Testament texts, particularly on Paul, while taking a broadly similar perspective in relation to the ethnic or racial facets of early Christian identity-construction. For example, Caroline Johnson Hodge, whose work also includes close collaboration with Buell,[56] argues that Paul draws on discourses of kinship and ethnicity to create a new form of ethnic identity for gentile converts, reconfiguring their family histories such that they become Abraham's kin.[57] Following what has come to be called the "Paul within Judaism" perspective associated with Lloyd Gaston, John Gager, Stanley Stowers, and others,[58] Johnson Hodge argues that Paul is concerned specifically with gentile converts and does not similarly reconfigure the identities of Jewish believers in Christ. Different "nested" identities can continue,[59] and Paul envisages "two separate ethnic identities under the God of Israel, *Ioudaioi* and *ethnē*."[60]

By contrast, Love Sechrest, in a study that explores the diverse meanings of ethnicity/race by considering the terms and ideas with which it is associated in the ancient sources, sees Paul as more radically leaving behind his Jewish identity but similarly insists that he creates a new racial or ethnic identity for his converts, Jewish as well as gentile: Christian identity "is that of an *emergent, newly formed, Jewish-like racial group*."[61] Unlike many writers, Sechrest deploys the language of race to denote this group. In another recent monograph, Bruce Hansen, drawing on social-scientific studies of ethnicity and ethnogenesis, sees Paul as "concerned to cultivate concrete communities that embraced cultural diversity within a new ethnic solidarity."[62]

---

56. See Denise Kimber Buell and Caroline Johnson Hodge, "The Politics of Interpretation: The Rhetoric of Race and Ethnicity in Paul," *JBL* 123 (2004): 235–51.

57. Johnson Hodge, *If Sons, Then Heirs*.

58. On the roots, development, and significance of this perspective, see Zetterholm, *Approaches to Paul*, esp. 127–63; Nanos and Zetterholm, *Paul within Judaism*.

59. Johnson Hodge, *If Sons, Then Heirs*, 134.

60. Johnson Hodge, *If Sons, Then Heirs*, 138.

61. Sechrest, *Former Jew*, 206, italics original. For her critique of Johnson Hodge, see 217–24.

62. Bruce Hansen, *"All of You Are One": The Social Vision of Galatians 3.28, 1 Corinthians 12.13 and Colossians 3.11*, LNTS 409 (London: T&T Clark, 2010), 202; on ethnogenesis and the amalgamation of existing groups into a new unity, see 58–60. For another significant but shorter recent study, which interprets Ephesians's notion of the "one new humanity" through the lens of "ethnic reasoning" set in the context of "ancient cultural affirmations of the essential fluidity and changeability of all ethnicity," see J. Albert Harrill, "Ethnic Fluidity in Ephesians," *NTS* 60 (2014): 380–81.

Still more recently—and, like Buell, Johnson Hodge, and others, taking as his starting point the problematic distinction between Christian universalism and Jewish particularism—Cavan Concannon also takes up Buell's agenda, and specifically her stress on the fluidity and constructedness of ethnic identities and the consequent importance of appeals to ethnicity in discourse.[63] Setting his reading of Paul's Corinthian correspondence firmly in the context of the literary and archaeological evidence from Roman-era Corinth, Concannon explores Paul's appeals to a kind of ethnic malleability (1 Cor 9:19–23) and the Corinthians' possible reactions to this, both positive and negative, as well as the "uses of ethnic history"—including Jewish history (1 Cor 10:1–13; 2 Cor 3:7–18)—to construct identity.[64]

Other authors have addressed similar questions to other New Testament texts. Eric Barreto offers a study focused on Acts 16 in which he uses the concepts of ethnic fluidity and hybridity to illuminate the ways in which Luke "explores the fluid boundaries between 'Jews,' 'Greeks,' and 'Romans' while portraying these distinctions as inherent characteristics of identity of Jesus' followers."[65] Timothy, for example, is seen to be both "Jew and Greek," since "ethnicities are not either/or propositions but pliable constructions" (Acts 16:1–5). Likewise, Paul is depicted as both Roman and Jewish (Acts 16:35–40).[66] Unlike in some studies of Paul (such as Sechrest's, noted above), Barreto does not see Luke as imagining "the creation of a new ethnicity of Christians, gathered from among the many peoples of the world." Rather, he suggests that Luke "projects an interstitial ethnic space between the competing and overlapping ethnic claims of Jews, Romans, and Greeks, and the other peoples that populate the pages of Acts."[67]

The first letter of Peter has also offered fruitful material for reflection on these topics. In an earlier study applying some of Buell's ideas, I sought to show how 1 Pet 2:9 represents a particularly significant and influential move in the deployment of ethnoracial terminology to construct Christian identity as a "people."[68] In a similar way, Katherine Girsch (now Katherine Marcar)

63. Concannon, *"When You Were Gentiles,"* 1–7.

64. Concannon, *"When You Were Gentiles,"* 144.

65. Eric D. Barreto, *Ethnic Negotiations: The Function of Race and Ethnicity in Acts 16*, WUNT 2.294 (Tübingen: Mohr Siebeck, 2010), 181.

66. Barreto, *Ethnic Negotiations*, 61–118, 164–80.

67. Barreto, *Ethnic Negotiations*, 25.

68. David G. Horrell, "'Race,' 'Nation,' 'People': Ethnic Identity-Construction in 1 Peter 2.9," *NTS* 58 (2012): 123–43; revised in David G. Horrell, *Becoming Christian: Essays on*

has recently shown how the motif of divine regeneration (1 Pet 1:3–5, 23) is fundamental to 1 Peter's construction of a kind of ethnic identity for the letter's readers and undergirds in significant ways the letter's theology and ethical instruction.[69] Comparing 1 Peter's material with earlier Jewish precedents and Jewish and early Christian parallels, Girsch shows how other images in 1 Pet 1:3–2:10—notably those of "seed" (1:23), breast milk (2:1–3), and stones (2:5)—also contribute to this ethnic identity-construction. Girsch sees this use of ethnic identity markers as an "extended metaphor," though it seems to me that in light of Buell's work (and other social science to which we will turn in chapter 3) the distinction between metaphorical and literal uses of ethnic terminology cannot be so clearly drawn. Janette Ok argues similarly that the author of 1 Peter "constructs an ethnicity for his predominantly Gentile audience," specifically through establishing their shared relationship with God through election and new birth, instructing them to live according to a "new culture," linking them with a "heavenly homeland," drawing on Israel's "identity-defining designations" to construct their "ethnoreligious identity," and "strengthening their sense of communal identity."[70] Ok sees this work of ethnic identity-construction as an attempt "to provide a strong, distinct, cohesive, and positive in-group identity" in the face of hostility and stigma.[71] This construction of "Christian identity in ethnic terms" is intended to provide the means for gentile converts "to *disidentify* from their past . . . and *reidentify* as an entirely new people."[72]

This focus on constructions of early Christian identity in ethnic terms, using ethnoracial discourse or "ethnic reasoning," has featured less in German-language scholarship,[73] though there is growing interest in the theme of ethnicity and its relevance to understanding early Christian dis-

---

1 Peter and the Making of Christian Identity, LNTS 394 (London: Bloomsbury T&T Clark, 2013), 133–63.

69. Katherine Anne Girsch, "Begotten Anew: Divine Regeneration and Identity Construction in 1 Peter" (PhD diss., Durham University, 2015). Available at Durham E-Theses Online: http://etheses.dur.ac.uk/11349/. A revised version is to be published by Cambridge University Press: Katherine Marcar, *Begotten Anew: Metaphor, Divine Regeneration and Ethnic Identity Construction in 1 Peter*, in the SNTSMS series.

70. Janette H. Ok, "Who You Are No Longer: Constructing Ethnic Identity in 1 Peter" (PhD diss., Princeton Theological Seminary, 2018), 59; see 148–49.

71. Ok, "Who You Are No Longer," 99; see 102.

72. Ok, "Who You Are No Longer," 117, italics original.

73. On the relative lack of interest in the topic of ethnicity, see also Kathy Ehrensperger, "What's in a Name? Ideologies of *Volk, Rasse*, and *Reich* in German New Testament Interpretation Past and Present," in Hockey and Horrell, *Ethnicity, Race, Religion*, 104–9.

course. One contrast with some of the Anglo-American research is the absence of any use of the language of "race" (*Rasse*): while this is a prominent and politically-important term in the US context, it is largely avoided in the contemporary German context—one illustration of the importance of context and tradition in shaping scholarly approaches and vocabulary.[74] We have already noted Wolfgang Stegemann's enthusiastic promotion of an *Ethnizitätsmodell* for Judaism at the time of Christian origins.[75] Such a perspective is evident, for example, in Markus Öhler's analyses of the incident at Antioch. Öhler stresses the "ethnic" character of the conflict and specifically (following Mason, among others) the ethnic (not "religious") identity of the Jewish participants.[76] According to Öhler, Paul insists that "within the Christian community—as in most associations—ethnic origins [*die ethnische Herkunft*] must not play any role: 'Here there is no longer Jew or Greek'" (Gal 3:28).[77] Paul's efforts are thus seen as "an expression of the confrontation of an ethnos with a 'religion,' which pointedly seeks to free itself from an ethnic orientation, but is at the same time itself related to the religious traditions of this very ethnos."[78] As Ehrensperger notes, Öhler does not in this context treat Paul's construction of early Christian group identity as itself "ethnic" in character; but he does go on to discuss the use of eth-

---

74. See the discussion in Ehrensperger, "What's in a Name?" Although it is a crude indication, a Google Ngram survey of the use of *Rasse* in German literature between 1700 and 2008 clearly illustrates this trend: the frequency of the word's appearance rises from around 1840 and most rapidly after 1929, reaching a peak in 1940, then declines very sharply between 1941 and 1951, remaining low in frequency thereafter. By contrast, *Ethnizität* only begins to appear in the late 1970s, rising steeply thereafter. For a recent news item on this point, see "Don't Use the Term 'Race,' German Scientists Urge," *Deutsche Welle*, September 11, 2019, https://www.dw.com/en/dont-use-the-term-race-german-scientists-urge/a-50390582.

75. Stegemann, *Jesus*, 180–236; Stegemann, "Religion."

76. Markus Öhler, "Essen, Ethnos, Identität—der antiochenische Zwischenfall (Gal 2,11–14)," in *Der eine Gott und das gemeinschaftliche Mahl: Inklusion und Exklusion biblischer Vorstellungen von Mahl und Gemeinschaft im Kontext antiker Festkultur*, ed. Wolfgang Weiß, Biblisch-Theologische Studien 113 (Neukirchen-Vluyn: Neukirchener, 2011), 167–83. See also Öhler, "Ethnos und Identität: Landsmannschaftliche Vereinigungen, Synagogen und christliche Vereinigungen," in *Kult und Macht: Religion und Herrschaft im syropalästinensischen Raum: Studien zu ihrer Wechselbeziehung in hellenistisch-römischer Zeit*, ed. Anne Lykke and Fredrich T. Schipper, WUNT 2.319 (Tübingen: Mohr Siebeck, 2011), 237–46.

77. Öhler, "Ethnos und Identität," 246; cf. Öhler, "Essen, Ethnos, Identität," 199: "Ethnos in Christus keine Rolle spielt."

78. Öhler, "Essen, Ethnos, Identität," 199: "Ausdruck der Konfrontation eines Ethnos mit einer 'Religion,' die sich pointiert von einer ethnischen Orientierung lösen will, sich aber zugleich auf die religiösen Traditionen ebendieses Ethnos bezieht."

nic and "people-group" categories in the further development of Christian group identity, culminating in the later formulation of Christians as a *tertium genus* ("dritte Geschlecht").[79]

Other recent essays also approach the question of the role of ethnicity and ethnic identity in New Testament texts. Gudrun Guttenberger, informed by contemporary concepts of ethnicity, examines the topic of ethnicity in Mark's Gospel, considering the role of such established ethnic designations as Jew ('Ιουδαῖος), Galilean, Greek, and gentile. She investigates these designations, however, in relation to a central concern with "the ethnic self-understanding of the 'we-group'" depicted in the Gospel, seeing some indications, for example, of a self-understanding as Galileans.[80]

Lukas Bormann approaches the topic by relating the modern concept of ethnicity to the picture of ethnic identity in antiquity. He then considers the significance of ethnicity in the Gospels and Acts, emphasizing that there is no unified New Testament perspective on ethnic identity and that, in the Gospels and Acts, the community of Jesus followers appears as an inner-Jewish sect.[81] Turning to the theme of "universalism," Bormann suggests that this could only be found, if at all, in the letters of Paul.[82] Yet here, too, Bormann notes that, while Paul envisages a certain "inclusion" within God's people of non-Jewish members of Jesus communities, this is hardly "universalism" but remains defined by the ethnic categories of Paul's world: Paul's focus is on "Jews" and "Greeks," but the latter are another specific cultural and ethnic group within the non-Jewish peoples of antiquity.[83] For Bormann, one notable point of significance in the vision of the author of Colossians, then, is the stress on going beyond the world of Jews and Greeks and specifying also "barbarian, Scythian" (Col 3:11). Understood in concrete ethnic terms, this concerns "an expansion of the gospel-proclamation beyond the previous ethnic boundaries, designated by Jews and Greeks, to the indigenous

79. Ehrensperger, "What's in a Name?," 106. Öhler, "Ethnos und Identität," 247–48, extends and broadens the discussion beyond that in Öhler, "Essen, Ethnos, Identität." In the former, Öhler mentions Ephesians, Philippians, and 1 Peter before moving onto the later "third race" terminology. For example, regarding the πολίτευμα terminology in Philippians, he comments: "Dabei ist ein ethnischer Gedanke im Begriff durchaus impliziert, wenn auch nicht dominant" (247).

80. Gudrun Guttenberger, "Ethnizität im Markusevangelium," in Gemünden, Horrell, and Küchler, *Jesus—Gestalt und Gestaltungen*, 148; cf. 144–45.

81. Bormann, "Griechen und Juden," 122, 125.

82. Bormann, "Griechen und Juden," 125.

83. Bormann, "Griechen und Juden," 126.

peoples of Asia Minor."[84] Rather than lamenting the fact that the author of Colossians did not fully transcend such distinctions, as some have done, Bormann insists that in antiquity "ethnicity was an unquestionable [*unhinterfragter*] part of social, religious and political reality. What is much more significant is how one handled this category."[85] Bormann does not directly consider the construction of Christian group identity in ethnic terms, but he does insist, in conclusion, that early Christianity cannot sweepingly be seen as a "universal" form of Judaism nor as a movement in which ethnic categories and identities become irrelevant.[86]

The question about the potentially "ethnic" character of early Christian identity is addressed more directly in a series of essays resulting from a 2016 symposium at Lausanne—another indication of increasing interest in this topic in continental European scholarship.[87] For example, Michael Wolter concludes from his investigation of ethnicity and identity in Paul that the contrast between an ethnically particular Judaism and a "trans-ethnic" or "non-ethnic" Pauline Christianity cannot stand. Wolter does find a form of "Ethnizitätsdiskurs" in Paul but suggests that it is of a particular kind, rooted in a relationship to Israel: it is an "Israelizitätsdiskurs." Moreover, Wolter insists, the kind of "Ethnizität" that Paul ascribes to Christians is "categorically" different from a Jewish understanding of ethnicity: Paul constructs a "metaphorical ethnicity, which no Jew who does not believe in Christ would accept as an ethnic trait [*als ethnische Eigenschaft*]."[88]

Similarly nuanced arguments are presented by Samuel Vollenrieder and Simon Butticaz. For Vollenrieder, Paul, like the later author of the Epistle to Diognetus, can use ethnic discourse to draw a threefold distinction between Jews, Greeks/gentiles, and Christians, as in 1 Cor 1:18–25 and 10:32. But "there are clear limits to the representation [by Paul] of Christianity as an ethnicity." For example, original ethnic differences continue, though they are "abandoned in Christ," and "the community of believers goes beyond what might

---

84. Bormann, "Griechen und Juden," 129: "Die Ausweitung der Evangeliumsverkündigung über die bisherigen ethnischen Grenzen, die durch Juden und Griechen bezeichnet sind, hinaus zu den indigenen Völkern Kleinasiens."

85. Bormann, "Griechen und Juden," 130.

86. Bormann, "Griechen und Juden," 130–31.

87. The published papers form a themed issue on "Paul and Ethnicity" in *EC* 8, no. 3 (2017). Papers from a second symposium in 2018 held on a related theme—"Universality, Ethnicity and Spaces: Identity-Construction in Early Christianity"—were recently published in *Annali di Storia dell'Esegesi* 36, no. 2 (2019).

88. Michael Wolter, "Ethnizität und Identität bei Paulus," *EC* 8 (2017): 351–53.

be conceived of as an ἔθνος"; other kinds of description are more dominant. Indeed, rather like Wolter, Vollenrieder sees in Paul a "theo-ethnic" definition of the people, representing them in the category of the elected people of Israel.[89] Butticaz sees a contrast between Paul's discourse in relation to the incident at Antioch (Gal 2:11–21) and in relation to meals at Corinth (1 Cor 10:1–22). In the first case there is "a universalizing discourse which unites Jews and gentiles under the banner of a [christological] 'meta-identity' granted in baptism," a form of reasoning that is "not primarily ethnical [*sic*] but theo-anthropological";[90] in Corinth, by contrast, Paul is seen to be engaged in "a process of ethnicization," perhaps "a first attempt at an ethnicization of the early Christian movement."[91] Thus, for Butticaz, "it is difficult to speak unilaterally of an ethnic or a non-ethnic identity in the Pauline churches. . . . Ethnic features of identity could be either downplayed or promoted."[92]

All these studies, despite their differences and disagreements, indicate a growing interest in the topic of ethnicity, and specifically in the deployment of ethnic or racial terminology in early Christian texts and the consequences of this for our characterization of the early Christian groups. There are clear differences in perspective and approach, not only between English-language and German-language scholarship but also in relation to issues such as the choice of "ethnicity" or "race" as terms, whether early Christian identity is appropriately described in either way, and how this early Christian identity relates—perhaps differently—to gentile and to Jewish Christ-believers. Some of these differences, furthermore, also help us to see how contemporary contexts shape the categories and concerns of scholarship, whether this is intended and acknowledged or not: the language of "race" carries certain connotations and evokes a specific history in the USA, while in Germany the term *Rasse* has its own particular history, loading its contemporary usage in quite different ways.

2.3 Conclusions

The various areas of current research summarized in this chapter are lively and significant. As we have seen, there has been considerable recent em-

89. Samuel Vollenrieder, "Are Christians a New 'People'? Detecting Ethnicity and Cultural Friction in Paul's Letters and Early Christianity," *EC* 8 (2017): 303–4.

90. Simon Butticaz, "Paul and Ethnicity between Discourse and Social Practices," *EC* 8 (2017): 324.

91. Butticaz, "Paul and Ethnicity," 333–35.

92. Butticaz, "Paul and Ethnicity," 335.

phasis on Jewish identity as an "ethnic" identity from the perspectives both of an ancient designation as ἔθνος and a modern social-scientific category. There have also been some challenges to this classification that point to important questions about how ethnicity is best defined and whether "cultural" practices or the possibilities of joining (akin to some kind of "conversion") challenge or cohere with such a notion of ethnic identity. These issues are also relevant to the recent turn to questions of ethnicity and race in New Testament and early Christian texts. Some of this research, particularly following the stimulus of Buell's influential book, has sought to consider how early Christian texts deploy the language of ethnicity or race in constructing group identity, perhaps specifically for gentile converts. This is, in my view, an important new direction in research that I aim to pursue and assess in this study. There remains significant work to be done here: Buell's studies (like those of Judith Lieu, also notable for their treatment of early Christian identity) focus primarily on second- and third-century Christian texts rather than on the New Testament. Other work picking up Buell's agenda has focused on selected New Testament texts, most often in Paul, but has not yet provided a more systematic, wide-ranging examination of the evidence from New Testament and earliest Christian texts. Moreover, while some of the work surveyed has taken its critical point of departure from the tendency to contrast an ethnically particular Judaism with an open, inclusive, or universal Christianity, close comparison of Jewish and early Christian traditions related to various themes often identified as characteristic of ethnic identities has not been undertaken, to my knowledge.

All this begins to indicate a major part of the agenda and intended contribution of this study. One more preliminary but crucial task remains: defining what "ethnicity" (and "race") should be taken to mean, what kind of group identity the term(s) might denote, how they relate to the category of "religion," and how, if at all, these categories might relate to the forging of early Christian identity and the ways in which this is understood in modern scholarship. Running throughout much of the discussion thus far has been frequent reference to the concepts of ethnicity, race, and religion. It has also become clear that much hangs on how these terms are defined and understood and how we understand their interrelationships. Consideration of such issues is crucial to establishing an appropriate theoretical framework for the exegetical, historical, and critical analysis to follow. The next chapter therefore turns to these theoretical issues, engaging with social-scientific discussions of these central terms.

CHAPTER 3

Ethnicity, Race, and Religion
in Social-Scientific Perspective

We ended the previous chapter with a sense of the importance of understanding the key terms "ethnicity," "race," and "religion." Different perspectives on the description and categorization of groups in antiquity derive, at least in part, from different notions of what these key terms mean and how they relate to one another. In this chapter, therefore, we turn to a brief consideration of ethnicity, race, and religion in recent social-scientific discussion. The purpose is to inform and orient the exegetical investigations and critical reflections that follow. The first section of the chapter gives an overview of the history of the discussion of ethnicity and race and of contemporary theoretical perspectives on them. The second section specifically considers the term "race" and its relevance to discussions of antiquity. The third section turns to the topic of religion and its relationship to the categories of ethnicity and race. The chapter concludes by setting out an agenda for the chapters that follow, building both on the overviews of research given in the first two chapters and on the theoretical perspectives outlined here.

3.1 Ethnicity and Race in History and Theory

The terms "ethnicity" and "race" have a long, complex, and intertwined history. English words such as ethnic, ethnicity, and so on derive from the Greek ἔθνος, while race—when used to denote "a human group . . . connected by common descent or origin"—came into the English language only in the sixteenth century from the Middle French word, probably derived in turn from the Old Italian *razza*.[1] (The nearest equivalent in ancient Greek, though

---

1. *Oxford English Dictionary*, 2nd ed. (Oxford: Oxford University Press, 2004), s.v.

clearly without etymological connections to "race," is the term γένος, sometimes translated "race" in contexts where a human group based on descent is in view; e.g., Acts 7:19; 1 Pet 2:9; see §7.3.) The term "race" is bound up with an unfortunate history of prejudice and violence: the (pseudo-biological) theories of race and racial difference that developed from the seventeenth century onward were important in legitimating European colonialism and Nazi antisemitism specifically.[2] Indeed, the term "ethnicity" appears to have first been used in 1941, though previous discussion, not least by Max Weber, had begun to talk of "ethnic groups," or "ethnische Gemeinschaften."[3] It became established in modern English-language usage during the 1940s and '50s, in part as a deliberate alternative to the language of race at a time when the latter was perceived to have become "deeply compromised by 'racism.'"[4] Against this backdrop, the UNESCO statement on race of 1950—referring to "the injustices and crimes which give such tragic overtones to the word 'race'"—proposes explicitly that "it would be better when speaking of human races to drop the term 'race' altogether and speak of *ethnic groups*."[5] It is unsurprising, then, that the term race (and, even more so, its German equivalent, *Rasse*[6]) has tended to be abandoned in favor of ethnicity in much

---

"race." On the etymology of the term and its comparative newness in northern European languages, see Ivan Hannaford, *Race: The History of an Idea in the West* (Washington, DC: Woodrow Wilson Center; Baltimore: Johns Hopkins University Press, 1996), 5.

2. On these historical developments, see, e.g., Hannaford, *Race*; Colin Kidd, *The Forging of Races: Race and Scripture in the Protestant Atlantic World, 1600–2000* (Cambridge: Cambridge University Press, 2006).

3. See, e.g., Max Weber, *Wirtschaft und Gesellschaft*, vol. 3 of *Grundriss der Sozialökonomik*, 2nd ed. (Tübingen: Mohr Siebeck, 1925), 216–26 (though the subheadings include "die 'Rasse,'" and "Entstehung der 'Rassen'-merkmale"); Weber, *Economy and Society: An Outline of Interpretive Sociology* (New York: Bedminster Press, 1968), 385–98. For broader discussion, see David M. Miller, "Ethnicity Comes of Age: An Overview of Twentieth-Century Terms for *Ioudaios*," *CBR* 10 (2012): 295–96.

4. Werner Sollors, "Foreword: Theories of American Ethnicity," in *Theories of Ethnicity: A Classical Reader*, ed. Werner Sollors (New York: New York University Press, 1996), xxix; see p. x on the origin of "ethnicity" in the USA in 1941–42. For a more detailed discussion of the development of "ethnic" terminology and the reasons for it, see Miller, "Ethnicity," 295–96. See also John Hutchinson and Anthony D. Smith, "Introduction," in *Ethnicity*, ed. John Hutchinson and Anthony D. Smith, Oxford Readers (Oxford: Oxford University Press, 1996), 4, who comment that ethnicity is often seen as a "new term" in English from the 1950s onward but note its earlier derivation from Greek and its uses (from ancient times) to refer especially to "others."

5. UNESCO, "The Race Question" (Paris: UNESCO, 1950), 1, 6, italics original, https://unesdoc.unesco.org/ark:/48223/pf0000128291. See also Hannaford, *Race*, 386.

6. See p. 68 with n. 74.

academic discussion. As we have already noted, however (see §2.2, p. 65), this remains a contested point, and there are arguments—to which we shall return—for keeping the term "race" in use.

Past debates about both ethnicity and race often revolved around the alternative paradigms of what are broadly called primordialist and instumentalist views.[7] The former is the view that "ethnic or racial identities are fixed, fundamental, and rooted in the unchangeable circumstances of birth" while the latter is the view that ethnicity and race "are instrumental identities, organized as means to particular ends," a view that places primary weight upon the circumstances in which groups find themselves and the contextual reasons for classifying or claiming certain identities.[8] According to this latter view, rather than being some kind of natural, innate "given," ethnic and racial identities are a flexible cultural, political, and social resource, constructed and deployed in various ways.

In recent discussion, as we shall note in more detail below, a constructionist perspective has become dominant, not least under the influence of the work of Fredrik Barth.[9] This constructionist approach "focuses on the ways ethnic and racial identities are built, rebuilt, and sometimes dismantled over time. It places interactions between circumstances and groups at the heart of these processes."[10] As Kevin Avruch comments:

> For scholars of the postmodernist persuasion the great insight into ethnicity—ethnic identity, nationalism, culture, history, or most anything else that is social, for that matter—is that ethnicity is socially constructed: It is not a

---

7. See, e.g., Hutchinson and Smith, "Introduction," 8–9; Stephen Cornell and Douglas Hartmann, *Ethnicity and Race: Making Identities in a Changing World*, Sociology for a New Century (Thousand Oaks, CA: Pine Forge, 2007), 41–74, who give a wider survey of other proposals and alternatives.

8. Cornell and Hartmann, *Ethnicity and Race*, 51, 61.

9. In particular, Barth, *Ethnic Groups and Boundaries*. See, e.g., Cornell and Hartmann, *Ethnicity and Race*, 75–106 (a constructionist perspective "provides the conceptual foundation" for much of the book [76]); John Stone, "Max Weber on Race, Ethnicity, and Nationalism," in *Race and Ethnicity: Comparative and Theoretical Approaches*, ed. John Stone and Rutledge Dennis, Blackwell Readers in Sociology (Oxford: Blackwell, 2003), 33; Peter Jackson and Jan Penrose, "Introduction: Placing 'Race' and 'Nation,'" in *Constructions of Race, Place and Nation*, ed. Peter Jackson and Jan Penrose (London: UCL Press, 1993; Minneapolis: University of Minnesota Press, 1994), 1–23; Martha Augoustinos and Stephanie De Garis, "'Too Black or Not Black Enough': Social Identity Complexity in the Political Rhetoric of Barack Obama," *European Journal of Social Psychology* 42 (2012): 564–77.

10. Cornell and Hartmann, *Ethnicity and Race*, 75.

given but rather a thing which is made and thus potentially unstable, inconstant, and negotiable. . . . But what makes this insight worth pursuing (and it is, at least in the long run, essentially correct), is that it so sharply flies in the face of what most ethnic "actors," the players themselves, believe.[11]

This is why Stephen Cornell and Douglas Hartmann speak of "constructed primordialities":[12] ethnic identities are constructed, flexible, negotiable, and variously deployed, but they are often perceived and presented as natural and immutable, like a "given" of human identity.[13] As Jonathan Hall concisely encapsulates it, "Ethnic identity is a cultural construct, perpetually renewed and renegotiated through discourse and social praxis."[14]

Influential on definitions of ethnicity is the classic statement of Max Weber, who defines ethnic groups as those "which cherish a *belief* in their common origins of such a kind that it provides a basis for the creation of a community."[15] Crucially, for Weber, it is the shared *belief* in common origins that matters rather than any objective evidence concerning shared ancestry or parentage or, as John Stone makes clear, "any objective features of group

11. Kevin Avruch, "Culture and Ethnic Conflict in the New World Disorder," in Stone and Dennis, *Race and Ethnicity*, 73. On this "primordial" conviction on the part of ethnic actors themselves, see Francisco J. Gil-White, "How Thick Is Blood? The Plot Thickens . . . : If Ethnic Actors Are Primordialists, What Remains of the Circumstantialist/Primordialist Controversy?," *Ethnic and Racial Studies* 22 (1999): 789–820; Gil-White, "Are Ethnic Groups Biological 'Species' to the Human Brain? Essentialism in Our Cognition of Some Social Categories," *Current Anthropology* 42 (2001): 515–53.

12. Cornell and Hartmann, *Ethnicity and Race*, 93.

13. Cf. Buell's stress on the interplay between fluidity and fixity in Buell, *Why This New Race*, 6–10.

14. Hall, *Ethnic Identity*, 19. Cf. Mark G. Brett, "Interpreting Ethnicity: Method, Hermeneutics, Ethics," in Brett, *Ethnicity and the Bible*, 10: "Although *ethnie* can be exceptionally durable once formed, they are also symbolic constructions which have to be maintained by reiterated practices and transactions."

15. Max Weber, "Race Relations," trans. Eric Matthews, in *Max Weber: Selections in Translation*, ed. W. G. Runciman (Cambridge: Cambridge University Press, 1978), 364; also quoted in Stone, "Max Weber," 32. Weber continues, explaining the distinction between an "ethnic group" and a "kinship group": "The question whether they are to be called an 'ethnic' group is independent of the question whether they are objectively of common stock. The 'ethnic' group differs from the 'kinship group' in that it is constituted simply by the belief in a common identity" (364). See also Weber, *Economy and Society*, 387–93; Weber, *Wirtschaft und Gesellschaft*, 219, where he writes of the "Stammverwandtschaftsglaube," stressing that this is a "subjektive Glaube" that arises in an "artificial" way: "Diese 'künstliche' Art der Entstehung eines ethnischen Gemeinsamkeitsglaubens. . . ."

membership." As Stone remarks, for Weber, "it is this *sense* of common ancestry that is vital, but the identification with shared origins is largely, if not wholly, fictitious."[16]

Also influential on the prominence of the constructionist view of ethnicity, as we noted briefly above, is the seminal work of Fredrik Barth. Based on a wide range of empirical studies, Barth concluded that ethnic identities do not persist on the basis of isolation or wholesale cultural difference but rather through certain, specific "cultural features [which] are used by the actors as signals and emblems of differences."[17] Sustaining a group boundary—a key focus in Barth's work—requires "not only criteria and signals for identification, but also a structuring of interaction which allows the persistence of cultural differences."[18] In other words, distinctive ethnic identities are constructed and maintained through particular symbols, signals, and practices—through processes of intergroup interaction—and do not inhere somehow in the essence of group members.

Various characteristics, which vary in their prominence and salience, can undergird and express ethnic identities. Richard Schermerhorn, for example, offers a concise and influential definition: an ethnic group is "a collectivity within a larger society having real or putative common ancestry, memories of a shared historical past, and a cultural focus on one or more symbolic elements defined as the epitome of their peoplehood."[19] Schermerhorn's definition is adapted and extended in Anthony Smith's equally influential taxonomy of the characteristics of ethnic identity. First laid out in his 1986 work on the ethnic origins of nations and later summarized in a collaborative work with John Hutchinson, the following items constitute Smith's list of characteristics of ethnic groups:

1. a common *proper name*, to identify and express the 'essence' of the community;

2. a myth of *common ancestry*, a myth rather than a fact, a myth that includes the idea of a common origin in time and place and that gives an *ethnie* a sense of fictive kinship, what Horowitz terms a 'super-family' . . . ;

16. Stone, "Max Weber," 32, my emphasis.
17. Barth, "Introduction," 14.
18. Barth, "Introduction," 16.
19. Richard A. Schermerhorn, *Comparative Ethnic Relations: A Framework for Theory and Research* (Chicago: University of Chicago Press, 1978), 12. Schermerhorn's definition is adopted, e.g., by Cornell and Hartmann, *Ethnicity and Race*, 19–20.

3. shared *historical memories,* or better, shared memories of a common past or pasts, including heroes, events and their commemoration;

4. one or more *elements of common culture,* which need not be specified but normally include religion, customs, or language;

5. *a link* with a *homeland,* not necessarily its physical occupation by the *ethnie,* only its symbolic attachment to the ancestral land, as with diaspora peoples;

6. a *sense of solidarity* on the part of at least some sections of the *ethnie*'s population.[20]

Smith proposes that these "six 'components' of *ethnie* . . . afford a working definition of ethnicity," and even if "some of the elements or components vary in degree of clarity, scope and intensity . . . enquiry into these six dimensions will generally reveal the extent to which we are dealing with an *ethnie* or an ethnic category."[21] Also significant, though, is another, broader criterion noted by Schermerhorn: that there must be "consciousness of kind among members of the group."[22] Cornell and Hartmann, who also draw on Schermerhorn's definition in their own work, call this the "criterion of self-consciousness." As they explain: "Ethnic groups are self-conscious populations; they see themselves as distinct."[23]

More recent work, notably by Rogers Brubaker, has pressed the case for a subjectivist and constructionist perspective still further: lists of characteristics such as Smith's should not be taken to imply that ethnic groups exist as a clearly defined and identifiable category of human groups.[24] For a start, Brubaker is critical of what he terms "groupism," that is, "the tendency

20. Hutchinson and Smith, "Introduction," 6–7 (italics original), summarizing the more extended discussion of the "foundations of ethnic community" in Anthony D. Smith, *The Ethnic Origins of Nations* (Oxford: Blackwell, 1986), 22–31, for whom the roots of modern nations are to be found in a model of ethnic community (p. x). Among works that have employed this definition in work on early Jewish and Christian identities, see Esler, *Conflict and Identity,* 43–44; Philip F. Esler, *God's Court and Courtiers in the Book of the Watchers: Re-interpreting Heaven in 1 Enoch 1–36* (Eugene, OR: Cascade, 2017), 14; Sechrest, *A Former Jew,* 48–50; Horrell, *Becoming Christian,* 159.

21. Smith, *Ethnic Origins,* 30.

22. Schermerhorn, *Ethnic Relations,* 12.

23. Cornell and Hartmann, *Ethnicity and Race,* 19.

24. See, e.g., Rogers Brubaker, *Grounds for Difference* (Cambridge, MA: Harvard University Press, 2015), 48–84, esp. 48–49, 81–84.

to take bounded groups as fundamental units of analysis."[25] Instead, he insists, the focus of study should be on how various kinds of potential basis for "groupness" are invoked and claimed in different circumstances. Thus, "group-making" may be seen "as a social, cultural, and political project, aimed at transforming categories into groups of increasing levels of groupness."[26] Rather than seeing the identification of a certain group as "ethnic" as having achieved any kind of explanation, Brubaker argues that "ethnic common sense—the tendency to partition the social world into putatively deeply constituted, quasi-natural intrinsic kinds . . .—is a key part of what we want to explain, not what we want to explain things with; it belongs to our empirical data, not to our analytical toolkit."[27] Arguing for what he calls a cognitive approach, Brubaker suggests that "instead of asking 'what is race?', 'what is an ethnic group?', 'what is a nation?', a cognitive approach encourages us to ask how, when, and why people interpret social experience in racial, ethnic, or national terms."[28]

A second point Brubaker stresses is that ethnic or racial groupings are enormously diverse, such that it is much more important to investigate the specific forms and practices through which group identity is constructed in different circumstances than to invoke a standard model to classify groups as "ethnic" or "not ethnic":

> It may be that "ethnicity" is simply a convenient—though in certain respects misleading—rubric under which to group phenomena that, on the one hand, are highly disparate, and, on the other, have a great deal in common with phenomena that are not ordinarily subsumed under the rubric of ethnicity.[29]

25. Rogers Brubaker, *Ethnicity without Groups* (Cambridge, MA: Harvard University Press, 2004), 2. See also the earlier statement in Rogers Brubaker, "Ethnicity without Groups," *European Journal of Sociology* 43 (2002): 163–89.

26. Brubaker, *Ethnicity without Groups*, 13. Cf. Siân Jones, "Identities in Practice: Towards an Archaeological Perspective on Jewish Identities in Antiquity," in *Jewish Local Patriotism and Self-Identification in the Graeco-Roman Period*, ed. Siân Jones and Sarah Pearce, Journal for the Study of the Pseudepigrapha Supplement Series 31 (Sheffield: Sheffield Academic Press, 1998), 45: "Ethnic categories are based on a conscious reification of transient cultural practices taking place in different spatial and temporal contexts, and the 'group' only exists in the context of interpretation where it justifies and explains past practices and modes of interaction and informs future ones."

27. Brubaker, *Ethnicity without Groups*, 9.

28. Brubaker, *Ethnicity without Groups*, 87.

29. Brubaker, *Ethnicity without Groups*, 27.

Quoting Weber, Brubaker goes so far as to question the value of the category as such: "As Weber put it nearly a century ago . . . a precise and differentiated analysis would 'surely throw out the umbrella term "ethnic" altogether', for it is 'entirely unusable' for any 'truly rigorous investigation.'"[30]

This cognitive and constructivist approach may also help us to see why the kinds of features Smith lists—including religion and other features of cultural practice and way of life—may be more or less salient in sustaining a sense of identity as a people. Religion, which is itself notoriously hard to define and particularly problematic for the ancient world (see §3.3), may thus be more or less centrally bound up with what we might call an ethnic sense of peoplehood. As Brubaker again remarks: "Language and religion are both similar to ethnicity and nationalism and similarly intertwined with them. . . . Indeed ethnicity was constituted as an object of study precisely by abstracting from the specificities of language, religion, and other ascriptive markers such as phenotype, region of origin, and customary mode of livelihood."[31] It therefore makes no sense to separate such features off from the study of ethnicity—for in that case it would be hard to see what residual substance might be left to constitute the notion of ethnic identity.[32]

The direction of recent research seems, therefore, to lead to a stress on the fluidity and constructedness of ethnic identities—not unlike the kind of emphasis we noted in recent studies of ancient ethnic identities in the previous chapter. While lists of characteristics, such as Smith's, can help us identify the kinds of discursive features and social practices that might undergird a sense of ethnic identity, it is equally important to attend to the specific features and strategic goals of any particular articulation of such group identities.

---

30. Brubaker, "Ethnicity without Groups," 186n29. Weber is discussing the need to investigate the manifold bases for a sense of collective identity and for collective action on the part of a people-group, including common language, customs, religion, and a belief in shared kinship (*Blutverwandtschaftsglauben*). He comments: "Dabei würde der Sammelbegriff 'ethnisch' sicherlich ganz über Bord geworfen werden. Denn er ist ein für jede wirklich exakte Untersuchung ganz unbrauchbarer Sammelname" (Weber, *Wirtschaft und Gesellschaft*, 224; cf. Weber, *Economy and Society*, 394–95).

31. Brubaker, *Grounds for Difference*, 88.

32. Cf. Brubaker, *Grounds for Difference*, 88.

3.2 The Language of Race

A similar emphasis on the constructedness of identity is also dominant in contemporary discussions of race. Given the history of the terms "race" and "ethnicity," briefly sketched above, it is unsurprising that definitions of race overlap with those of ethnicity. Moreover, while some regard the two terms as essentially synonymous[33] or use the two terms more or less interchangeably,[34] others offer distinct but overlapping definitions (see below). But the most widely shared conviction—and the clearest point of (deliberate) distinction from the racial theories that legitimated such pernicious sociopolitical and colonial ideologies in the modern period—is that racial identities are constructed and believed rather than biologically or objectively real. As Brubaker remarks, "Race, ethnicity, and nationality exist only in and through our perceptions, interpretations, representations, classifications, categorizations, and identifications. They are not things in the world, but perspectives on the world."[35] A statement published by the American Anthropological Association in 1998 clearly confronts any biological or essentialist understanding of race, recognizing that (in the US context) "both scholars and the general public have been conditioned to viewing human races as natural and separate divisions within the human species based on visible physical differences." Against such an established viewpoint, they insist that "human populations are not unambiguous, clearly demarcated, biologically distinct groups. . . . Physical variations in the human species have no meaning except the social ones that humans put on them." The statement stresses the frequent ideological use of ideas about race as "a strategy for dividing, ranking, and controlling colonized people" though "not limited to the colonial situation."[36]

This broadly constructionist view of race (and of ethnicity) is widely held across a range of disciplines. For example, in his important study of the origins of racism in classical antiquity, Benjamin Isaac insists that "race" itself

33. See, e.g., Thomas H. Eriksen, "Ethnicity, Race, Class and Nation," in Hutchinson and Smith, *Ethnicity*, 28–31.

34. E.g., Brubaker, *Grounds for Difference*; Rogers Brubaker, *Trans: Gender and Race in an Age of Unsettled Identities* (Princeton: Princeton University Press, 2016).

35. Brubaker, *Ethnicity without Groups*, 79; cf. 17.

36. American Anthropological Association, "AAA Statement on Race," May 17, 1998, https://www.americananthro.org/ConnectWithAAA/Content.aspx?ItemNumber=2583.

"does not exist."[37] What remains important, for Isaac, is *belief* in the shared characteristics of what is defined as "race": "This, however, is a sociological fact, not a biological one."[38] Or as Colin Kidd remarks in his historical study of ideas of race from 1600 to 2000, "Race is in the eye of the beholder; it does not enjoy a genuine claim to be regarded as a fact of nature."[39]

The recent and ongoing breakthroughs in the analysis of human DNA might appear to offer new grist to the mill of those who consider that race is a biologically meaningful category and that the world's human population can be cogently assigned to distinct racial or ethnic groups.[40] The rise of companies offering insights into ancestry through DNA analysis—informing someone their ancestral profile is, say, 8 percent Ireland, 21 percent Scandinavia, 36 percent Britain, and so on—might be taken to reflect just such newfound ability. Yet while DNA analysis can provide information about shared characteristics, familial connections, and geographically-based affinities, it does not support the notion that there are definable or distinct racial groups that can be classified on the basis of variations in DNA.[41] As geneticist Steve Jones bluntly insists, "The genes do show that there are no separate groups within humanity."[42]

> Man [*sic*], it transpires, is the most boring of mammals, varying scarcely at all from place to place. . . . DNA bears a simple message; that individuals are the repository of most variation. A race, as defined by skin colour, is no more an entity than is a nation, whose personality depends only on a brief shared history. The notion that humanity is divided up into a series of distinct groups is wrong.[43]

37. Benjamin Isaac, *The Invention of Racism in Classical Antiquity* (Princeton: Princeton University Press, 2004), 30; cf. 32–33, 515.

38. Isaac, *Invention of Racism*, 33.

39. Kidd, *Forging of Races*, 3.

40. For important reflections on the findings of recent biology and an insistence that they must not be ignored in sociology, see Brubaker, *Grounds for Difference*, 48–84. Brubaker nonetheless concludes by reiterating the case for an essentially constructionist view of race/ethnicity.

41. For a popular warning about the false promises of this new commercial venture—branded "genetic astrology"—see Nick Collins, "DNA Ancestry Tests Branded 'Meaningless,'" *The Telegraph*, March 7, 2013, http://www.telegraph.co.uk/news/science/science-news/9912822/DNA-ancestry-tests-branded-meaningless.html.

42. Steve Jones, *The Language of the Genes: Biology, History and the Evolutionary Future*, rev. ed. (London: Flamingo HarperCollins, 2000), 255.

43. Jones, *Language of the Genes*, 62–63. Cf. also Hall, *Hellenicity*, 14–15; Kidd, *Forg-*

"All that can be said," Ivan Hannaford remarks, "is that each individual is a complex organism of phenetic relationships, and the term 'race' now obscures more than it illuminates."[44] As Jones insists, from a geneticist's perspective "the idea of pure races is a myth."[45] Indeed, the kind of ancestral profiling offered through DNA analysis, as mentioned above, might be taken to demonstrate what Brubaker refers to as "universal mixedness"—that we are all, in a sense, "multiracial."[46]

More significantly, this should make clear that decisions about what kind of racial or ethnic categories to use—where to draw lines, what groups to define, and so on—is a matter of social construction and sociopolitical decision, not biological classification, as becomes clear when one considers the history of efforts to make such categorizations: whether the Nazi identification of Jews, the American "one drop of blood" principle, the classification of racial groups in Apartheid South Africa or in contemporary Malaysia, and so on.[47] Of course there are observable differences in skin tone and other physical characteristics shared by some population groups, such that people whose ancestral families come from Namibia look different to those who come from Norway. But as we have already noted, these variations in skin tone and physical appearance do not indicate the existence of genetically distinct racial groups: "Gene geography shows that people from different places do not differ much and that colour says little about what lies under the skin."[48] So as soon as we begin on this (fragile and illusory) basis to attempt to classify "races," we are immediately back

---

ing of Races, 3–13; Eloise Hiebert Meneses, "Science and the Myth of Biological Race," in *This Side of Heaven: Race, Ethnicity, and Christian Faith*, ed. Robert J. Priest and Alvaro L. Nieves (Oxford: Oxford University Press, 2007), 35–39. I am grateful to Cherryl Hunt for introducing me to the basics of the science of DNA.

44. Hannaford, *Race*, 7.

45. Steve Jones, *Language of the Genes*, 266.

46. See Brubaker, *Grounds for Difference*, 73: "Autosomal tests . . . reveal that virtually everyone derives genetic ancestry from a variety of ancestral populations. This emphasis on universal mixedness undermines typological forms of racial thinking" (the use of the term "multiracial" above is my own).

47. In the nineteenth century, measurement of skull size was a common basis for the identification of supposed racial types, but this is now recognized as an entirely spurious form of pseudoscience; see Jones, *Language of the Genes*, 256–58. On the American "one drop" principle, see Alan H. Goodman, Yolanda T. Moses, and Joseph L. Jones, *Race: Are We So Different?* (Chichester: Wiley-Blackwell, 2012), 52, 160; on contemporary Malaysia, see Sharmani P. Gabriel, "The Meaning of Race in Malaysia: Colonial, Post-Colonial and Possible New Conjunctures," *Ethnicities* 15 (2015): 782–809.

48. Jones, *Language of the Genes*, 262.

to the point about choosing categories, drawing boundaries, and the discursive and practical significance of these: any such categorizations are always the product of politically and ideologically loaded acts of social construction. Thus, one must always ask: Why is this particular categorization being made? For what purposes, and by whom? Why is a line drawn *here* and not elsewhere?

Consequently, contemporary definitions of race—like Weber's classic definition of ethnicity—also stress the importance of belief and perception. Isaac, for example, defines a "race" as "a group of people who are *believed* to share imagined common characteristics, physical and mental or moral, which cannot be changed by human will, because they are thought to be determined by unalterable, stable physical factors: hereditary, or external, such as climate or geography." For Isaac it is belief in the reality of race that is crucial, even if such beliefs are inevitably false.[49] While some writers, as we have noted, do not see any meaningful distinctions between the concepts of ethnicity and race, Cornell and Hartmann, for example, offer distinct, if overlapping, definitions of each.[50] They pick up Weber's classic definition of ethnicity but criticize the subsequent tendency in sociology "to equate ethnicity with shared culture" and follow Schermerhorn in their own elucidation of the term.[51] When it comes to race, they agree that it should be dismissed as a meaningful biological category but offer a definition focused primarily—and in my view, too singularly—on *perceived* physical characteristics: "a human group defined by itself or others as distinct by virtue of perceived common physical characteristics that are held to be inherent. A race is a group of human beings socially defined on the basis of physical characteristics."[52] Thus, put concisely: "Ethnicity refers to perceived common ancestry, the perception of a shared history of some sort, and shared symbols of peoplehood. Race refers to a group of human beings socially defined on the basis of physical characteristics. A human group might well meet both sets of criteria at once."[53]

A further distinction, in their view, is that the term "race" is typically used to assign status to others—to "them" (especially by a dominant group to

49. Isaac, *Invention of Racism*, 34, my italics.

50. See Cornell and Hartmann, *Ethnicity and Race*, 15–40. See their summary table of "definitional distinctions" between ethnicity and race on 36.

51. Cornell and Hartmann, *Ethnicity and Race*, 17; see 17–21.

52. Cornell and Hartmann, *Ethnicity and Race*, 25.

53. Cornell and Hartmann, *Ethnicity and Race*, 33.

a less powerful one).[54] Ethnicity is more commonly a reflection of an identity that a group claims for itself. Put concisely, race is often assigned, ethnicity asserted.[55] Thus, "When a racial group sets out to construct its own version of its identity, it makes itself both a race and an ethnic group at once."[56] Their definitions of two related processes epitomize this distinction between race as a label applied by some to others and ethnicity as what group members claim or perceive of their own group identity:

> *Racialization* is the process by which groups of persons *come to be classified* as races. Put more precisely, it is the process by which certain bodily features or assumed biological characteristics are used systematically to mark certain persons for differential status or treatment. . . .
>
> Ethnicization is the making of an ethnic group. It is the process by which a group of persons *comes to see itself* as a distinct group linked by bonds of kinship or their equivalents, by a shared history, and by cultural symbols that represent . . . the "epitome" of their peoplehood. It is a coming to consciousness of particular kinds of bonds: the making of a people.[57]

Cornell and Hartmann express a general preference for the terminology of ethnicity, since it is hard to overcome the implications in the colloquial use of "race"—that it refers to a natural, inherent, immutable identity—while ethnicity "more readily conveys something variable and changing" and rooted in people's self-consciousness.[58] But their treatment of both ethnicity *and* race is helpful not least in identifying how both terms might usefully be employed to distinguish between the "racializing" processes by which some are labeled by others and the "ethnicizing" processes by which groups forge and express their own identities. Richard Jenkins suggests that "'racial' differentiation and racism should perhaps best be viewed as historically-specific forms of the general—perhaps even universal—social phenomenon of ethnicity."[59]

Cornell and Hartmann's stress on physical or biological characteristics in a definition of race may, however, be somewhat restrictive. In part, this

54. Cornell and Hartmann, *Ethnicity and Race*, 30. Cf. Richard Jenkins, "Rethinking Ethnicity: Identity, Categorization, and Power," in Stone and Dennis, *Race and Ethnicity*, 67.

55. Cornell and Hartmann, *Ethnicity and Race*, 105.

56. Cornell and Hartmann, *Ethnicity and Race*, 31.

57. Cornell and Hartmann, *Ethnicity and Race*, 34–35 (except for the initial italicization of "racialization," the italics are mine).

58. Cornell and Hartmann, *Ethnicity and Race*, 39.

59. Jenkins, "Rethinking Ethnicity," 67.

is because attempts (often by those in power) to differentiate races on the basis of physical characteristics often prove impossible in practice since no such distinctions can, in the end, be meaningfully employed. But it is also because a key feature of racialization is the association of (perceived) physical or biological characteristics with "mental or moral" ones, as Isaac rightly stresses. It hardly needs to be said that the classification of races in practice has not been concerned merely with group-allocation according to physical characteristics but with the intellectual, moral and behavioral qualities *believed* to be associated with racial identity—whether a predisposition to laziness, criminality, moral laxity, or whatever—and, of course, the superior qualities generally claimed to belong to those doing such classifying.

The association of the term race with biological characteristics, and the particular development of racial theories in the modern period, has led some writers to insist that race is not a category that can properly be applied to the ancient world and should therefore be abandoned in scholarship on New Testament (and other ancient) texts.[60] To be sure, we must be aware that distinctively modern theories of race (and their relationship to skin color) cannot and must not be presumed for the ancient world.[61] Yet the kinds of racializing often associated with such theories—linking physical appearance to place of origin and to moral and behavioral characteristics— are certainly evident in ancient sources. Hence, in his major study of the origins of racism in classical antiquity, Isaac—with due caution (hence his term "proto-racism")—shows from a wide range of sources how far such ideas can be found in the ancient world.[62] To give just one prominent exam-

---

60. Among NT scholars, see, e.g., Roetzel, "No 'Race of Israel' in Paul," 230–44; Esler, *Conflict and Identity*, 40, 55; Esler, "Giving the Kingdom," 182–83; Kathy Ehrensperger, "Paulus, sein Volk und die Rasseterminologie: Kritische Anfragen an den 'Race'-Diskurs in neuerer englischsprachiger Paulus-Forschung," *Kirche und Israel* 27 (2012): 119–33; ET in Ehrensperger, "Paul, His People and Racial Terminology," *Journal of Early Christian History* 3 (2013): 17–32. Cf. Ehrensperger, "What's in a Name," 103.

61. On the distinctively modern developments of the idea, see Hannaford, *Race*. But for important arguments that the notion of race is also powerfully relevant to understanding medieval Europe, see Geraldine Heng, *The Invention of Race in the European Middle Ages* (Cambridge: Cambridge University Press, 2018). For the argument that the ancient world was not characterized by a specific prejudice against those with dark or black skin, see Frank M. Snowden Jr., *Before Color Prejudice: The Ancient View of Blacks* (Cambridge, MA: Harvard University Press, 1983). On the other hand, on the negative uses of "blackness" to symbolize sin and vice in early Christian literature, see Gay L. Byron, *Symbolic Blackness and Ethnic Difference in Early Christian Literature* (London: Routledge, 2002).

62. Isaac, *Invention of Racism*. An important counterbalance to the stress on ethno-

ple, the second-century CE astronomer, geographer, and astrologer Claudius Ptolemy—highly influential right up to the Renaissance[63]—describes and explains the different ethnic characteristics of the peoples of different regions as follows:

> The demarcation of ethnic characteristics (ἐθνικῶν ἰδιωμάτων) is established in part by entire parallels and angles, through their position relative to the ecliptic and the sun. . . . The people who live under the more southern parallels . . . since they have the sun over their heads and are burned by it, have black skins (μέλανες τὰ σώματα) and thick, woolly hair, are contracted in form and shrunken in stature, are sanguine of nature, and in habits are for the most part savage (ἄγριοι). . . .
>
> Those who live under the more northern parallels, since they are far removed from the zodiac and the heat of the sun, are therefore cooled; . . . they are white in complexion (λευκοί τε τὰ χρώματά), straight-haired, tall and well-nourished, and somewhat cold by nature; these too are savage (ἄγριοι) in their habits because their dwelling-places are continually cold. . . .
>
> The inhabitants of the region between the summer topic and the Bears, however, since the sun is neither directly over their heads nor far distant at its noon-day transits, share in the equable temperature of the air. . . . They are therefore medium in colouring, of moderate stature, in nature equable, live close together, and are civilized in their habits. (Ptolemy, *Tetrabiblos* 2.2 [Robbins, LCL; slightly amended])

Not for the last time, an attempt to classify and explain the diverse characteristics of the various peoples of the world finds the author's own location and people to be the most favorable.[64] Indeed, within this last group, those who come from Ptolemy's own particular area—"the southernmost

---

centrism and proto-racism among ancient writers is, however, provided by Erich S. Gruen, *Rethinking the Other in Antiquity*, Martin Classical Lectures (Princeton: Princeton University Press, 2011), who stresses the ways in which ancient peoples also found or invented links and commonalities between one another.

63. F. E. Robbins, introduction to Ptolemy, *Tetrabiblos* (LCL), v, comments: "From his own day well into the Renaissance Claudius Ptolemy's name was well-nigh pre-eminent in astronomy, geography, and astrology alike."

64. This quotation also illustrates, however, Frank Snowden's point (see n. 61 above) that negative prejudice was not (necessarily) directed specifically toward black skin color: here peoples both "white" (to the north) and "black" (to the south) are seen as "savage."

of them"—are said to be "in general more shrewd and inventive, and better versed in the knowledge of things divine" (*Tetrabiblos* 2.2 [Robbins, LCL]).

What terminology should we then use in our discussions of early Christian and Jewish texts, and what are the implications of our choice? Contrary to those who see the notion of race as only apposite to post-Enlightenment contexts, the term may be relevant, as the example above suggests, to the discussion of ancient texts as well as modern history, particularly if it is understood to refer to physical characteristics and their association with both geographical or ancestral origins on the one hand and intellectual and moral qualities on the other. It may also have a particular pertinence, as Cornell and Hartmann suggest, in situations where others are labeling—or "racializing"—a specific group on this basis, whether in ancient or modern contexts, such as when the author of John's Gospel insists that the *Ioudaioi* are descendants of the devil whose collective characteristics are to lie and to kill (John 8:39–44). Of course, the pseudoscientific theories that have undergirded pernicious modern ideologies of race are unknown to ancient writers, but that kind of difference applies to many concepts routinely used in discussion of ancient texts, including gender, ethnicity, and religion.[65]

Nonetheless, I have come to accept that there are good reasons to make "ethnicity" the default term we use for discussing the kind of constructed group identity that is built on beliefs about the range of issues Anthony Smith and others have presented: kinship, ancestry, homeland, culture, language, and so on.[66] "Ethnicity" is more readily—and, in both popular and academic discourse, actually—taken to refer to an identity that is socially and culturally defined. By contrast, as we have seen above, "race" is often *taken* to refer to physical or biological characteristics, even when it is stressed that such characteristics cannot form a cogent or objective basis on which to assign people to "races" except insofar as such groups are socially constructed on the basis of beliefs. Following Cornell and Hartmann, insofar as we are seeking to probe "insider" constructions of identity, we may perhaps better speak of "ethnic" identity and "ethnicization"; "race" and "racialization" might better be applied to "outsider" designations, especially if these attribute particular moral qualities to a group on the basis of physiognomy or ancestry.

Yet there remains one particularly important point made by some of

65. Cf. Buell, *Why This New Race*, 18.
66. To this extent, then, I accept the arguments made by Esler, "Giving the Kingdom," 182–83, and Ehrensperger, "Paul, His People."

those who advocate retaining the language of race in our discussions. This is the insistence that a mere change in terminology—as promoted in the 1950 UNESCO report cited above—does not solve the problems of racism, whether in our texts or in our traditions of interpretation. As noted in chapter 2, Buell insists that "replacing race with ethnicity has obscured the racist aspects of using ethnicity to distinguish Jews from Christians." As she remarks, "Racism persists even when race has been exposed as a construct."[67] Sara Ahmed makes a similar point: "We cannot do away with race, unless racism is 'done away.' . . . Thinking beyond race in a world that is deeply racist is a [*sic*] best a form of utopianism, at worse [*sic*] a form of neo-liberalism."[68] Just as with "antisemitism," so too with "race," the insistence that such modern ideologies have no direct counterparts in the ancient world, and should therefore be replaced with alternative terms, can too easily serve to remove them, by definition, from critical consideration.[69] To this extent, at least, we must remain ready to address constructions and ideologies of race and forms of racism in both our sources and our traditions of scholarship.

3.3 Religion and Ethnicity

A final consideration is how the category of religion relates to those of ethnicity and race. This is an important issue in the contemporary world, even though it is somewhat neglected in the standard handbooks on ethnicity and race[70]—perhaps due to the implicitly secular character of much social science and its consequent difficulty in adequately dealing with religion.[71] In the modern world, a notion of religion has developed such that, in theory at

67. Buell, *Why This New Race*, 14, 20.

68. Sara Ahmed, "Declarations of Whiteness: The Non-Performativity of Anti-Racism," *Borderlands* 3.2 (2004): §48.

69. Cf. Horrell, "Grace, Race," 195–97.

70. For example, Stone and Dennis, *Race and Ethnicity*, despite occasional mention of religious affiliations (e.g., Catholic/Protestant) in various chapters, contains no section or chapter in which religion is a prominent topic, nor does "religion" feature in the index. Hutchinson and Smith, *Ethnicity*, in a book of sixty-three excerpts, has a section on "Ethnicity, Religion, and Language" that contains seven excerpts, only three of which centrally address religion and ethnicity. Similarly, see Rodolfo D. Torres, Louis F. Mirón, and Jonathan Xavier Inda, eds., *Race, Identity, and Citizenship: A Reader* (Malden, MA: Blackwell, 1999).

71. On the marginalization of theology and religion in the construction of modern social science, see John Milbank, *Theology and Social Theory: Beyond Secular Reason* (Oxford: Blackwell, 1990). For reflections on the connections between secularism and modernity,

least, it is possible to conceive of religious affiliation as a category independent of nationality, race, or ethnicity—a notion that owes much to the later interpretation of the achievements of early Christianity.[72] Indeed, as Brent Nongbri has recently argued, this modern construction of the category of "religion" has a particular history and reflects its context of production in the sixteenth and seventeenth centuries: "The idea of religion is not as natural or universal as it is often assumed to be. Religion has a history. It was born out of a mix of Christian disputes about truth, European colonial exploits, and the formation of nation-states."[73] This particularly Christian influence on the modern definition of the concept of "religion" is also central to the earlier argument in Wilfred Cantwell Smith's classic study from 1962, *The Meaning and End of Religion*. Smith argues that "religion" as a concept (specifically, a modern, Western, Christian one) is confusing and inappropriate: "The word 'religion' has had many meanings; it . . . would be better dropped. This is partly because of its distracting ambiguity, partly because most of its traditional meanings are, on scrutiny, illegitimate."[74]

Despite the (modern) notion of religious affiliation as a matter of personal conviction or belief separable from other facets of identity, it is evident that religion is often profoundly and inextricably woven into contemporary perceptions of national, ethnic or racial identity. A recent Pew Research Center survey revealed that in some of the predominantly Christian countries surveyed, "being a Christian" was felt by a significant proportion of the population to be "very important" in order truly to share the national identity.[75] In a wide-ranging and comparative study across a large span of

---

see Talal Asad, *Formations of the Secular: Christianity, Islam, Modernity*, Cultural Memory in the Present (Stanford: Stanford University Press, 2003), esp. 1–17, 181–201.

72. Cf. Buell, *Why This New Race*, 66. On the history of the idea of religion and the relatively recent origins of the modern concept, see the recent study of Brent Nongbri, *Before Religion: A History of a Modern Concept* (New Haven: Yale University Press, 2013).

73. Nongbri, *Before Religion*, 154. See also the overview of the term's history and complexities in Jonathan Z. Smith, "Religion, Religions, Religious," in *Critical Terms for Religious Studies*, ed. Mark C. Taylor (Chicago: University of Chicago Press, 1998), 269–84.

74. Wilfred Cantwell Smith, *The Meaning and End of Religion* (Minneapolis: Fortress, 1991), 194. On the point that "religion" is not an ancient category but a modern, Christian one, see 15–50.

75. See Bruce Stokes, "What It Takes to Truly Be 'One of Us'" (Washington, DC: Pew Research Center, 2017), 21–22; PDF available at http://www.pewglobal.org/2017/02/01/what-it-takes-to-truly-be-one-of-us/: 54% of Greeks, 34% of Poles, and 32% of Americans interviewed (57% for white, evangelical Protestants in the USA) agreed on this point. Other countries—such as Spain (9%), the Netherlands (8%), and Sweden (7%)—exhibited much

historical periods, Anthony Smith shows how religion is bound up with the formation of a sense of national identity, whether this be through the integration of a religious tradition into the sense of nationhood (as with Protestantism—specifically Anglicanism—in England) or through a kind of secularized religious focus on the nation itself (as in the post-revolutionary focus on *la patrie* in France). Smith also shows how influential on the development of the modern, Western European model of the nation is the biblical picture of the election of Israel, seen as a kind of paradigmatic precedent.[76]

A specific example of the interconnections between religious and ethnic identities is found in Claire Mitchell's sociological work on "religion and social identification in Northern Ireland."[77] In this context, Mitchell discusses religion as "an ethnic marker"[78] and notes widespread agreement among sociologists that "religion *can* be a basis of ethnic identity."[79] Her key argument, against a widespread tendency to downplay religion's social significance, is that religion is not *merely* a marker of what is "really" an ethnic identity but is crucial in social identification and community construction such that "religion often constitutes the fabric of ethnic identity."[80]

The prominence of religion in a sense of ethnic and national identity is often clear. One does not need to look hard to see how religion, culture, politics, and nationhood are intertwined, influencing such things as who is deemed appointable for political office, the ceremonies they must participate in, perceptions of who "belongs," and so on, even in countries where such discrimination is officially illegal. In such contexts, religion is often closely connected with popular perceptions of ethnicity and race.[81] As noted

---

lower levels of conviction. For a micro-scale ethnographic analysis of these intersections in a northern English town, see Ingrid Storm, "'Christianity Is Not Just about Religion': Religious and National Identities in a Northern English town," *Secularism and Nonreligion* 2 (2013): 21–38.

76. Anthony D. Smith, *Chosen Peoples* (Oxford: Oxford University Press, 2003).

77. Claire Mitchell, "Behind the Ethnic Marker: Religion and Social Identification in Northern Ireland," *Sociology of Religion* 66 (2005): 3–21; Mitchell, "The Religious Content of Ethnic Identities," *Sociology* 40 (2006): 1135–52. See also the discussion of the racializing of the Irish and the significance of the Catholic/Protestant divide in this in Siobhán Garrigan, "Irish Theology as White Theology: A Case of Mistaken Identity?," *Modern Theology* 30 (2014): 193–218.

78. Mitchell, "Behind the Ethnic Marker," 8–10; Mitchell, "Religious Content," 1138–40.

79. Mitchell, "Religious Content," 1136, italics original.

80. Mitchell, "Religious Content," 1137; see further 1143–48.

81. Perceptions concerning such interconnections are evident, for example, in discussions about Barack Obama's religious identity, however insubstantial the claims. See

in the introduction, in a recent issue of *Ethnic and Racial Studies* focused on the theme of religion and racialization—and specifically on perceptions of Jews and Muslims—Nasar Meer argues not only for the importance of recognizing this interconnection but also for an integration of "the contemporary study of antisemitism and Islamophobia squarely within the fields of race and racism."[82] Religious affiliation and ethnic identity are not the same thing, but they are often connected in socially and politically significant ways. Moreover, religion—and Christianity in particular—has clearly been intimately bound up with the construction of racial and ethnic categories and perspectives.[83] The genealogical tables (derived from the Table of Nations in Genesis 10) commonly printed in the King James (Authorized) Version of the Bible from the seventeenth century onward, tracing humanity's ancestry to the three sons of Noah—Japeth, Shem and Ham (allocated, respectively, to Europe, Asia, and Africa)—provide one obvious indication of the correlations.[84]

When it comes to the ancient world, it is now widely accepted that the modern concept of religion—and specifically the idea of its separability from other facets of cultural, ethnic, political, or familial identity and practice—is anachronistic and inappropriate. As Edwin Judge comments, "We merely retroject onto the Greeks and Romans something that has become necessary to our understanding of life, thus turning history into a hall of mirrors in which we contemplate ourselves under the illusion that we are looking at the Greeks and Romans."[85] There is no word in Greek or Latin

---

Will Bredderman, "'No Doubt' President Obama Is a Muslim, Donald Trump's New York Campaign Chair Says," *Observer Online*, August 4, 2016, http://observer.com/2016/08/no-doubt-president-obama-is-a-muslim-donald-trumps-new-york-campaign-chair-says/.

82. Meer, "Racialization and Religion," 386. Another way of getting at these overlaps is through the concept of intersectionality, originally developed to highlight the reinforcing and inseparable implications of being multiply disadvantaged in terms of gender, race, and class. For an overview and discussion of the applications of this theory to biblical studies, see Ute E. Eisen, Christine Gerber, and Angela Standhartinger, "Doing Gender—Doing Religion: Zur Frage nach der Intersektionalität in den Bibelwissenschaften; Eine Einleitung," in *Doing Gender—Doing Religion: Fallstudien zur Intersektionalität im frühen Judentum, Christentum und Islam*, ed. Ute E. Eisen, Christine Gerber, and Angela Standhartinger, WUNT 302 (Tübingen: Mohr Siebeck, 2013), 1–33.

83. See pp. 3–7; also Buell, *Why This New Race*, 21–29.

84. On the complex interactions between the Bible, Christian theology, and developing ideas of race—some of which (such as polygenesis, the idea that different human races came from different originators) were challenges to what was seen as orthodox biblical (Adamic) theology—see Kidd, *Forging of Races*.

85. Edwin A. Judge, *Jerusalem and Athens: Cultural Transformation in Late Antiquity*,

that corresponds exactly to the modern notion of religion—though there are various words that overlap in some way with this broad domain: εὐσέβεια, δεισιδαιμονία, θρησκεία, *religio, pietas, supplicatio,* etc. Carlin Barton and Daniel Boyarin, in a study focused in particular on *religio* (in Tertullian) and θρησκεία (in Josephus), illustrate the different meanings, uses, and nuances of such particular words, making the argument that to translate simply with "religion" obscures the richness and particularity of the ancient discourse.[86] More broadly, what we might identify as religion, it has often been pointed out, frequently had more to do with cultic practice and dutiful obligation than allegiance to a set of beliefs and doctrines, as the modern notion might be taken to imply.[87] As we have already seen in our brief discussion of notions of Jewish and Greek identities (see §2.1), what we would call religious practices—offering sacrifices to the gods and so on—were seen as part of what constituted "ethnic" identity.[88] Hence Paula Fredriksen insists that, in antiquity, "gods run in the blood."[89] In other words, "gods also attached to particular *peoples*; 'religion' ran in the blood. . . . Ethnicity expressed 'religion' (acknowledging the anachronism of both terms for our period), and religion expressed 'ethnicity.'"[90] This bald assertion needs some nuance, not least in terms of the incorporation of "foreign" deities, such as the Egyptian Isis, into the sphere of popular Roman "religious" devotion.[91] But the broader point stands.[92] As Esler puts it: "'Religious' phenomena . . . certainly do occur [in the ancient world] but they are connected with, or rather embedded in, a wider identity that is best described as 'ethnic' in character."[93]

WUNT 265 (Tübingen: Mohr Siebeck, 2010), 264; see 264–75, esp. 264–66.

86. Carlin Barton and Daniel Boyarin, *Imagine No Religion: How Modern Abstractions Hide Ancient Realities* (New York: Fordham University Press, 2016).

87. See, e.g., Smith, *Meaning and End,* 20–21; Buell, *Why This New Race,* 59.

88. For Greek, Christian, and other forms of religious practice as sites for the performance of ethnoracial difference, see Buell, *Why This New Race,* 42–62.

89. Paula Fredriksen, "Mandatory Retirement: Ideas in the Study of Christian Origins Whose Time Has Come to Go," *SR* 35 (2006): 232.

90. Paula Fredriksen, "What 'Parting of the Ways'? Jews, Gentiles, and the Ancient Mediterranean City," in *The Ways That Never Parted: Jews and Christians in Late Antiquity and the Early Middle Ages,* ed. Adam H. Becker and Annette Yoshiko Reed, TSAJ 95 (Tübingen: Mohr Siebeck, 2003), 39; cf. also Paula Fredriksen, "Judaizing the Nations: The Ritual Demands of Paul's Gospel," *NTS* 56 (2010): 234–40.

91. On the incorporation of "foreign" cults into Roman religion, see Beard, North, and Price, *History,* 245–60.

92. Larry Hurtado, *Destroyer,* 82–87, refers to cults such as that of Isis under the label "voluntary religion" while accepting the broader point made by Fredriksen (see 78–79).

93. Esler, *God's Court,* 15.

This widely held conclusion about the place of "religion" in the ancient world is often presented as a contrast to the modern situation—and of course there are vast differences. Nonetheless, given the extent to which religion remains complexly entwined into modern perceptions of ethnic, cultural, and national identities, the distinction should not be overdrawn.[94] As we noted above, Wilfred Cantwell Smith's classic study argues that "religion" is a problematic category for both the ancient and the modern world.[95] In both contexts, religion is frequently—though not uniformly—woven into perceptions and constructions of ethnic identities. In the modern world, religion is thus also connected with perceptions of national identity and the racializing of the "other."

Does this then mean that the term "religion" should simply be abandoned in studies of ancient texts? This is probably too drastic a move, not least because we would need to invent some other (equally flexible and questionable) term to replace it in order to denote the particular aspects of human behavior we wish to specify. It is hard to come up with an alternative word to capture what we might want to talk about in relation to this kind of topic. As Jonathan Z. Smith notes, having surveyed the complex history and varied definitions, "'Religion' is not a native term; it is a term created by scholars for their intellectual purposes and therefore is theirs to define"—but as such is crucial, he insists, in "establishing a disciplinary horizon."[96] Yet it remains the case that, within this broad horizon, the category of religion is in danger of obscuring as much as it reveals.[97] In particular, we should be ready and willing to treat religion and ethnicity (and race) as potentially and frequently overlapping terms, with religion often being one more or less prominent component of what is taken to constitute the distinctive identity of an ethnic group. To argue for replacing the paradigm of "religion" with one of "ethnicity," then, is to risk reinscribing the notion that these are separable concepts rather than studying their interconnections. In Anthony Smith's list of characteristics, set out above, religion is one of the aspects of the "common culture" that an ethnic group shares, and this, *mutatis mutandis* (a qualification that should be heavily stressed),

94. Cf. Asad's (*Formations of the Secular*, 200) comment on contemporary modernity: "The categories of 'politics' and 'religion' turn out to implicate each other more profoundly than we thought."

95. Smith, *Meaning and End*.

96. Smith, "Religion, Religions, Religious," 281.

97. Cf. the remarks of Barton and Boyarin on Jonathan Z. Smith's comments (Barton and Boyarin, *Imagine No Religion*, 5–6).

characterizes such groups in both the ancient and the modern world. Religion is closely bound up with ethnic and racial identities, albeit in various and historically contingent ways.

3.4 Conclusions

It remains, finally, to stand back from the theoretical discussion and consider how it should shape the approach to be taken in the chapters that follow. Four points are particularly significant.

First, the definitions and characteristics of ethnic groups set out by authors such as Schermerhorn and Anthony Smith provide a valuable taxonomy of the kinds of factors that may play a part in making and maintaining a sense of ethnic identity. These characteristics provide some orientation to the themes we might look for in discerning whether, and in what ways, it might be meaningful to describe early Christian and Jewish identities as constructed using ethnic (or racial) categories. Rather than being neatly separable or distinct, religion will be one of those aspects of common culture that may play a (greater or lesser) part in sustaining a sense of shared ethnic identity. However, it is important not to regard such lists of characteristics as the basis for a kind of tick-box exercise through which we can determine whether such and such a group is or is not an ethnic group. It is vital to attend carefully to the *particular* ways in which appeal is made to any one of the characteristics in particular texts, whether in modern or ancient contexts. We should also be open to consider other facets of group identity that do not feature on such lists but may be crucial to a particular group's sense of its own identity. Fundamental, too, is the point made by Schermerhorn, though not included in Smith's list of characteristics, concerning the self-consciousness of ethnic groups: it is important to note evidence as to whether the members of the group understand themselves—and/or are understood by others—to constitute a "people."

Second, we have seen that there is widespread agreement in contemporary social science that ethnic and racial identities are socially constructed rather than natural or inherent, fluid and flexible rather than biologically or genetically determined. This points us to the importance of discourse and social practice as means by which such identities are constructed and maintained. As Cornell and Hartmann remark in the closing sentence of their book, "The critical issue for the 21st century is not so much whether ethnicity and race will continue to serve as categories of collective identity, but what kinds of ethnic and racial stories we choose to tell and how those stories are put to use."[98] For ancient groups in particular, this highlights the importance of texts. As Hall remarks, "Since ethnicity is discursively constructed through the employment of symbols such as fictive kinship, literary evidence will normally constitute the initial point of departure in any analysis of ancient ethnicity."[99] Furthermore, one of the implications of this "constructionist" view of ethnic and racial identities is that it becomes much more difficult to distinguish between "real" ethnic or racial groups and those that use ethnic discourse in a fictive or metaphorical way. All claims to kinship at the scale of ethnic or racial group are, in some sense, fictive. And if all such ethnic or racial identities are, at the end of the day, discursively and practically constructed, then it becomes more pertinent to ask how the language of ethnicity or race—and the associated facets of such identities—is *used* in discourses that construct the identities of insiders and outsiders, to ask how social practices function to maintain such identities, and to critically probe these discursive and practical foundations.[100]

Third, and following on from this, it is important to appreciate that ethnic and racial identities are always in process, by which I mean that they are produced, maintained, and transformed through the ongoing processes of social reproduction and are never static or immutably fixed—even if they remain relatively stable over significant periods of time or (more likely) are perceived to be so by in-group or out-group members. (Appeals to past history are almost inevitably particular constructions of past history in service of contemporary interests.) It is in the context of such a perspective that the processes of ethnicization and racialization are to be understood—as processes, following Cornell and Hartmann, by which a group comes to see itself in ethnic terms or comes to be identified by

---

98. Cornell and Hartmann, *Ethnicity and Race*, 266.

99. Hall, *Hellenicity*, 19, clarifying and defending the position set out in Hall, *Ethnic Identity*, 111–42, which argues against the view that artifacts (discovered and interpreted through archaeology) can be used to identify ethnic groups, since, in Hall's view, "artefacts never served as defining criteria of ethnic identity in the past" (142). He writes, "If one's ethnic identity cannot be determined in the first place by physiognomy, language or religion, then it is illusory to imagine that inanimate objects will prove to be a better candidate" (131). A similar insistence on the priority of the "literary evidence" that constitutes the "discursive channels" through which ethnicity is "actively proclaimed, reclaimed and disclaimed" is found in Hall, *Ethnic Identity*, 182.

100. Cf. Buell, *Why This New Race*, 69–70.

others in racial terms. Since the main focus of the exegetical studies to follow is on the "insider" perspectives of early Jewish and Christian texts, and since earliest Christianity in particular is a new movement forging a sense of group identity in the world, it will be particularly pertinent to consider evidence for processes of "ethnicization" in New Testament and early Christian texts.

Fourth, it needs to be stressed that the historical study of ancient ethnicity and identity-construction is likely to be—albeit in ways not easy to discern—bound up in contemporary ideologies and convictions concerning ethnic, racial, or religious identities. As much of the scholarship reviewed in this chapter makes clear, constructions of ethnic and racial groups—drawing classificatory lines, claiming or assigning identities—are often imbued with strategic purpose and ideological conviction. Study of ancient ethnicity, and especially study of early Christian identity in its relationship to Jewish identity, is inextricably connected to contemporary commitments and concerns. The socio-historical studies of early Jewish and Christian texts that follow are therefore undertaken within the context of a critical and reflective analysis of modern New Testament scholarship, which seeks to locate that scholarship within its specifically religious and racial contexts in modern Western democracies. This is a theme to which we shall return explicitly in the final chapter of this study.

These various points begin to indicate the agenda for the studies that follow. Following some of the key areas of ethnic identity-construction outlined above, we shall explore how these feature in early Christian texts and how the appeals to such characteristics compare with those found in Jewish texts from a similar period. We shall also consider a theme more often connected with "religion," namely that of "mission and conversion," or joining the people. I want to explore how such characteristics play a part in early Christian identity-construction and what the discourse of the texts and the social practices the texts presume or prescribe indicate about the character of emerging Christian and Jewish identities. At the same time, this inquiry entails a critical assessment of the ways in which modern scholarship has construed the nature of Christian identity and depicted its contrasts with Judaism, picking up the issues raised in the opening two chapters. How far and in what ways is early Christian identity constructed in ethnic terms, how far might we see processes of ethnicization going on, and how far does what we find indicate contrasts or similarities between earliest Christianity and Judaism in the same period? The insights gained will enable us to return, finally, to the structural dichotomy with which we began and to ask what its prevalence and particular constructions might tell us about the religious and ethnoracial location of that tradition of scholarship.

PART II

Comparisons of Jewish
and Early Christian Perspectives

Shared Descent: Ancestry, Kinship, Marriage, and Family

Notions of shared descent and kinship are central to most attempts to define ethnic identities. For Max Weber, as we have already noted, it is "a belief in . . . common origins" that is at the heart of the constitution of an ethnic or racial group.[1] Hence Jonathan Hall goes so far—rather too far—as to claim that "fictive kinship" is "the *sine qua non* for ethnic consciousness."[2] Yet no single factor should alone be seen as definitive or constitutive of ethnic or racial identities; various characteristics can acquire greater or lesser salience in different contexts and can be deployed for various rhetorical purposes. Nonetheless, appeals to shared ancestry and descent—and the sense of shared kinship that is built on such bases—are an obvious focus of attention for any study of ethnic identity-construction (and any study of the intersections between ethnic/racial and religious identities). Moreover, as both Weber's and Hall's comments indicate, the kinship bonds established through such appeals are essentially fictive, a matter of belief and perception more than objective lines of blood-connection, even if the latter is how the bonds are depicted and commonly understood. Indeed, ancestry is a particularly interesting locus for the interplay between fixity and fluidity to which Buell in particular has drawn attention,[3] since it is, in one sense, something that is unalterable—one cannot (as children often bemoan) change one's biological parents, nor they theirs, and so on—but in reality genealogies are constructed and presented in diverse ways for various purposes, as we shall see.[4] In addition to the rhetorical uses of genealogy, ancestry, descent, and so

1. Weber, "Race Relations," 364.
2. Hall, *Hellenicity*, 26.
3. Buell, *Why This New Race*, 6–10.
4. I owe this particular observation about the collocation of fixity and fluidity in depic-

on to construct notions of shared ethnic or racial identity, it is also important to consider the social norms and practices that reinforce and reproduce the sense of shared descent and kinship. Particularly important here are norms about marriage and the raising of children.

In this chapter, then, we shall examine how notions of shared ancestry and genealogies feature in both Jewish and early Christian texts and how a sense of shared kinship is deployed to express and develop group identity. We shall then turn to Jewish and Christian rules regarding marriage and assumptions regarding the identity of children.

4.1 Stories of Ancestors: Appeals to Genealogy and Descent

An interest in genealogies—recording who begat whom—is prominently displayed in the Jewish scriptures. Right from the early chapters of Genesis there is a clear concern to record lines of descent: from Adam via Cain and then Seth, from Seth to Noah (see Gen 4:17–5:32), on through Noah's three sons, Japheth, Shem, and Ham (Gen 10:1–32), then from Shem to Abram (Gen 11:10–29), and from Abram (now Abraham, see Gen 17:5) to Isaac and his two sons Esau and Jacob. Jacob later comes to be called Israel, father of the twelve sons from whom the twelve tribes take their names (see Gen 25:19–26; 32:28; 37:2–3; 49:1–28). The first eight chapters of 1 Chronicles consist of little else than versions of such genealogical records. Needless to say, such records do not exist merely for antiquarian interest but rather because they root the identity of the people for whom the text is intended in stories of their ancestors. Abraham, Isaac, and Jacob become the most prominent ancestors on whom the identity of the people of Israel is founded.[5] Abraham in particular is appealed to as the progenitor of Israel, "the rock from which [they] were cut" (Isa 51:1–2).

Echoing the promise from Gen 17:5, Abraham is sometimes celebrated as a "father of many nations" (e.g., Sir 44:19–21).[6] Josephus draws genea-

---

tions of ancestry, and specifically genealogies, to Katherine Marcar, in conversation. On the kinds of appeal made to ancestry, both for groups and individuals in the Roman empire, see Christopher Jones, "Ancestry and Identity in the Roman Empire," in *Local Knowledge and Microidentities in the Imperial Greek World*, ed. Tim Whitmarsh (Cambridge: Cambridge University Press, 2010), 111–24.

5. See, e.g., Gen 50:24; Exod 3:16; Deut 1:8; 6:10; 9:5; 2 Kgs 13:23; 2 Macc 1:2; 4 Macc 7:19; 13:17; 16:25; Matt 8:11; Acts 3:13.

6. Birgit van der Lans, "Belonging to Abraham's Kin: Genealogical Appeals to Abra-

logical connections between Abraham and various other peoples (e.g., *A.J.* 1.214, 221, 239, 241), and repeats the tradition that both Jews and Spartans are members of the γένος of Abraham (*A.J.* 12.225–27; see also 1 Macc 12:21: ἐκ γένους Αβρααμ).[7] This latter example in particular shows how such genealogical connections—even when implausible—can be (strategically) invoked in order to forge alliances (1 Macc 12:1–7). But a more prominent kind of genealogical appeal is to Abraham as the originator of the Jewish γένος, which is specifically seen as the seed of Abraham (σπέρμα Αβρααμ, Isa 41:8; Pss. Sol. 9:9; 18:3).[8] Josephus describes Abraham as "our father" (ὁ πατήρ ἡμῶν) (*A.J.* 1.158). As Birgit van der Lans notes, appeals to the people's Abrahamic descent are prominent in 4 Maccabees, which refers to them as "Abraham's children" (οἱ Αβρααμ παῖδες) (6:17, 22; cf. 17:6) and, in a more developed formulation, as "Israelite children, offspring of the seed of Abraham" (τῶν Αβραμιαίων σπερμάτων ἀπόγονοι παῖδες Ισραηλῖται) (18:1).[9]

One indication of the significance of such ancestral claims is found in cases where the conduct of the ancestors and their consequent rewards serves as a motivation for action deemed congruent with this inheritance (e.g., 1 Macc 2:51–61; 4 Macc 6:17–22; 14:20; 15:28; 18:1; this is a theme we shall examine in more depth in the following chapter). Ancestral traditions, and venerated burial places in particular, are also significant in territorial claims.[10] Another indication of the significance of claims about ancestors is exemplified in Josephus's *Contra Apionem*. The "extreme antiquity" of the Jewish γένος (*C. Ap.* 1.1), which Josephus is concerned to establish—and which, he says, he has fully documented in the *Antiquities*—is, he argues, demonstrable due to the great care and accuracy with which the Jews keep their ancestral records and cherish their scriptures, compared with Greek and other historians (*C. Ap.* 1.1–46). Especially in the case of priests, strict regulations about whom a priest may marry—in order to keep the lineage "unmixed and pure" (ἄμικτον καὶ καθαρόν)—have necessitated careful and

---

ham as a Possible Background for Paul's Abrahamic Argument," in *Abraham, the Nations, and the Hagarites: Jewish, Christian, and Islamic Perspectives on Kinship with Abraham*, ed. Martin Goodman, Guert Henrik van Kooten, and Jacques T. A. G. M. van Ruiten, TBN 13 (Leiden: Brill, 2010), 308–9.

7. More broadly on the ways in which Jewish writers found or made genealogical connections with Greeks and other peoples, see Gruen, *Rethinking the Other*, 302–7.

8. See Van der Lans, "Belonging," 309–12.

9. Van der Lans, "Belonging," 310.

10. See Francesca Stavrakopoulou, *Land of Our Fathers: The Roles of Ancestor Veneration in Biblical Land Claims*, LHBOTS 473 (London: T&T Clark, 2010).

accurate records, which cover "the last two thousand years" (*C. Ap.* 1.30–36). Here the Jewish claim to authentic and venerable peoplehood is made on the basis of claims about ancestral records, which purportedly demonstrate this identity as γένος.

Also significant are indications that ancestral identity can be changed or abandoned, for good or ill. Philo, with his focus on the importance of virtue, depicts ancestral identity as defined and, indeed, gained or lost through the practice of virtue. In *De Virtutibus* he remarks, on the one hand, on those among "the founders of the [Jewish] race" who did not profit from "the virtues of their ancestors" (αἱ τῶν προγόνων ἀρεταί) and, by failing to reproduce these virtues, were "denied any part in the grandeur of their noble birth [εὐγενεία]" (*Virt.* 206–7). On the other hand, he depicts Abraham, the founder of the Jewish people, as leaving behind the vices of his ancestors—indeed, leaving his race (γενεά) itself—to attain true virtue (*Virt.* 211–216).[11] Thus it seems that kinship and ancestry are defined—and changed—by conduct rather than blood (cf. *Virt.* 195; see further in ch. 5).

The New Testament, of course, begins in its canonical form with its own "book of Genesis" (Βίβλος γενέσεως) (Matt 1:1), which itself opens precisely with a lengthy genealogy (Matt 1:1–16) intended to recount the lineage of Jesus the Messiah, identified initially, and fundamentally, as both son of Abraham and son of David (Matt 1:1). Matthew's genealogy is clearly stylized, with its three blocks of fourteen generations (Matt 1:17). It contains certain striking features: the tracing of Jesus's lineage through Joseph, not Mary, despite the account of miraculous conception that follows (Matt 1:18–25); and the inclusion of four women—Tamar, Rahab, Ruth, and "the wife of Uriah"—who fit somewhat uneasily into such a deliberately constructed Israelite lineage.[12]

---

11. Cf. Philo, *Abr.* 67; and, more generally on the importance of virtue rather than birth, *Abr.* 31–39. Note also the description of Hagar in *Abr.* 251: "an Egyptian by birth [descent/race], but a Hebrew by deliberate resolution" (γένος μὲν Αἰγυπτίαν, τὴν δὲ προαίρεσιν Ἑβραίαν).

12. See the discussion of the reasons for the inclusion of these four women in W. D. Davies and Dale C. Allison, *A Critical and Exegetical Commentary on the Gospel According to Saint Matthew*, 3 vols., ICC (Edinburgh: T&T Clark, 1988–1997), 1:170–72. They cautiously suggest that the most compelling explanations may be "that the women in 1.2–16 reflect an interest in the salvation of the Gentiles" and that their "irregular, even scandalous" marital unions "prefigure the situation of Mary" (171). It may also be that Matthew sees the patrilineal line as most crucial in terms of determining identity-by-descent.

Luke's genealogy of Jesus is significantly different, naming different lines of paternity, which are traced backward through time rather than forward, ending up with Adam, rather than Abraham, born "of God" (Luke 3:23–38). Again, the line is traced through Joseph, even though Luke signals that this was only what people "supposed" was Jesus's paternal lineage (ὡς ἐνομίζετο, Luke 3:23). This is significant insofar as it indicates that the setting out of Jesus's ancestral lineage is deemed valuable, even if it does not—even for the writer—pretend to convey his actual "blood-line." Such a genealogy can, as it were, valuably insert him into a line of ancestors, giving him the identity of son of David, Jacob, Isaac, Abraham, Adam (among others), and ultimately God. Indeed, just as Jewish writers can connect Jewish ancestral claims to other peoples for strategic purposes, as we noted above, so a comparable (universalizing) move is made in Acts 17:28–29, which stresses the idea that all humanity is "God's offspring" (γένος) as the basis of an appeal to accept the Christian message.

In polemical contexts, New Testament authors can also seek to undermine Jewish ancestral claims: John the Baptist is recorded as challenging his hearers not to rely on their status as Abraham's descendants since "God is able from these stones to raise up children for Abraham" (Matt 3:9//Luke 3:8). The image of stones as descendants is an interesting one to which we shall return. In the notoriously polemical John 8, Jesus goes much further, denying the claims of the *Ioudaioi* to have Abraham, and indeed God, as their "father" and insisting instead that their opposition to him reveals them to be children of the "devil" (ὁ διάβολος) (John 8:39–44). In turn, the *Ioudaioi* dispute Jesus's identity as *Ioudaios*: "You are a Samaritan and have a demon" (John 8:48). From both sides, at least as presented in this dialogue, there is an attempt to deny and discredit the ancestry of the other.

In John, the identity of those who believe in Jesus is defined not in terms of being, or becoming, Abraham's descendants (cf. John 8:37) but rather in terms of being children of God. This is explicitly described as having come about by God's fatherly "siring" or begetting of these children (John 1:12–13, ἐκ θεοῦ ἐγεννήθησαν). Indeed, referring to God as "the Father" (with Jesus as "the Son") is especially frequent in John, and the motif of new birth and of being born of God is a prominent Johannine theme (John 3:3–8; 1 John 2:29; 3:9; 4:7; 5:4, 18).[13] Claiming God's paternity as a basis for the people's

---

13. On this theme in the Johannine literature, see Girsch, "Begotten Anew," 69–82. On this construction of what he calls "cosmological race" in John, and the ways in which this new layer of "racialized identity" impacts on "historical-geographical race," see Andrew

identity is not often found in Hebrew Bible and Second Temple Jewish texts, as Katherine Girsch (now Katherine Marcar) has shown, though it is occasionally evident (e.g., Deut 32:18; less directly, Num 11:12; Isa 66:7–9) and seems to become somewhat more prominent in Jewish thought by the first century CE.[14] Elsewhere in the New Testament, there is a brief allusion to the specific idea of rebirth, or regeneration, in Titus 3:5 (παλιγγενεσία) and more prominently in 1 Peter, to which we shall shortly return.

Two particular motifs of ancestral descent thus seem especially significant in terms of the construction of early Christian identity in the New Testament: being Abraham's descendants and being God's offspring. In both cases, the language of "seed" (σπέρμα) is used—a point of interest to which we shall return. The former motif is prominent in Paul's letters, while the second appears in 1 Peter. We shall consider each in turn, focusing on the particular examples of Gal 3 and 1 Pet 1–2.

In Gal 3, seeking to convince his recalcitrant Galatian gentile converts that membership of the righteous, Spirit-filled people comes not by works of law but through faith in Christ (Gal 2:16–3:5),[15] Paul turns—as he does in Rom 4—to the figure of Abraham. Quoting Gen 15:6 (as, again, in Rom 4:3), Paul depicts Abraham as someone whose righteousness came by faith (ἐπίστευσεν τῷ θεῷ) such that those who share this characteristic (οἱ ἐκ πίστεως) "are sons of Abraham" (υἱοί εἰσιν Ἀβραάμ) (Gal 3:7).[16] The foundational promise to Abraham, that "all the nations will be blessed in you" (Gen 12:3; 18:18; Gal 3:8),[17] is seen as an anticipation of the "good news"

Benko, *Race in John's Gospel: Toward an Ethnos-Conscious Approach* (Lanham: Lexington, 2019).

14. See Girsch, "Begotten Anew," 58–68.

15. By referring to "faith in Christ" here, I do not imply a decision to take all πίστις Χριστοῦ references in Galatians as objective genitives; rather, I mean to indicate that, however we take these references, there is indisputably a reference to the importance of converts placing their trust in Christ (e.g., ἡμεῖς εἰς Χριστὸν Ἰησοῦν ἐπιστεύσαμεν, Gal 2:16).

16. Johnson Hodge, *If Sons, Then Heirs*, 79–91, argues for the subjective genitive understanding of πίστις Χριστοῦ and renders οἱ ἐκ πίστεως literally as "those out of faithfulness"—that is, "those whose line of descent springs from faithfulness and promise" (79, 91). See also the discussion in Matthew Thiessen, *Paul and the Gentile Problem* (Oxford: Oxford University Press, 2016), 110–11. Insofar as the phrase likely characterizes the identity of those who are labeled this way (using a common Greek construction to do so), it does seem also to point to their "trust," which mirrors Abraham's own "trust"; see Peter Oakes, *Galatians*, Paideia Commentaries on the New Testament (Grand Rapids: Baker Academic, 2015), 105–6.

17. Paul's phrase πάντα τὰ ἔθνη is closest to Gen 18:18 (where, however, the phrase concludes with τῆς γῆς). Gen 12:3 has πᾶσαι αἱ φυλαὶ τῆς γῆς.

(προευηγγελίσατο) that God would "righteous" (δικαιοῖ) the gentiles by faith, through Christ (3:8). After explaining how Christ redeems people from what Paul sees as "the curse of the law" (3:13), Paul turns to develop the idea that this promise was made to Abraham καὶ τῷ σπέρματι αὐτοῦ (3:16), focusing in particular on the reference to "seed." Observing that the word is singular, not plural, enables Paul to make the claim, however implausible it might be as a reading of Genesis, that this refers to one person, and specifically to Christ (3:16).[18] Implicitly at least, this undercuts claims that anyone else, in the intervening years, has been Abraham's descendant, interrupting any ancestral narrative by drawing the line of descent directly from Abraham to Christ.[19] The final step in this particular elucidation of the idea of descent from Abraham is to claim that all who are in Christ are, on this basis, "Abraham's seed" (τοῦ Ἀβραὰμ σπέρμα) (3:29)—here the fact that a singular σπέρμα denotes a plural group (σπέρμα ἐστέ) does not, presumably, seem to Paul to undercut his previous exegesis of Genesis. Nor does their being declared σπέρμα Ἀβραὰμ prevent the group from also being identified as υἱοὶ θεοῦ (3:26).

As Caroline Johnson Hodge has argued, Paul is here engaged in "rewriting" the genealogies of his gentile converts: "They are adopted into a new lineage and granted a new heritage."[20] Paul constructs a form of ancestral identity for his converts by inserting them into a narrative of descent in which they become Abraham's offspring through Christ. This is one effective deployment of ideas of ancestry and descent. While this is clearly a line into which these converts have been inserted rather than one that stems from their physical birth, we should be wary of drawing any clear distinction between "real" and "fictive" descent. Even genealogies are constructed and manipulated to specific ends,[21] and as Weber's

18. On the logic of Paul's exegesis here, and its connecting Gen 13:15 and 17:8 with the Davidic promise in 2 Sam 7:12, see Thiessen, *Paul*, 122–27. Francis Watson, *Paul and the Hermeneutics of Faith* (London: T&T Clark, 2004), 191–92, also finds a logical connection between the Genesis texts and Paul's exegesis: Genesis probably suggests that, of Abraham's many "seeds," "only one is true heir to the promises: Isaac." Thus, for Paul, "Isaac is a type of Christ." For a broader discussion of Paul's use of scriptural quotations here and the level of audience competence they require to work, see Christopher Stanley, *Arguing with Scripture: The Rhetoric of Quotations in the Letters of Paul* (London: Continuum, 2004), 114–35.

19. Likewise, Paul's depiction of the law here relegates its role to an interim one (via an intermediary), which cannot nullify the original promise (Gal 3:17–20). See Barclay, *Paul and the Gift*, 400–418.

20. Johnson Hodge, *If Sons, Then Heirs*, 33.

21. See Johnson Hodge, *If Sons, Then Heirs*, 19–42, on the ways in which claims to patri-

classic definition makes clear, all appeals to shared kinship at the scale of the ethnic group are fictive.

Where I find Johnson Hodge's argument less convincing is in her claim that this is an identity constructed specifically and only for Paul's gentile converts—one that enables them to be inserted into a narrative of Abrahamic descent alongside, but distinct from, the *Ioudaioi*.[22] According to Johnson Hodge, while "being in-Christ" requires a reconfiguring of ethnic identity for gentile converts, it "does not involve shifting or mixing for Jews; it is already a Jewish identity."[23] However, in Galatians at least, identity as Abraham's "seed" is (re)configured by connection to Christ as Abraham's singular seed such that both gentiles and Jews (now) attain this identity, according to Paul, in Christ (cf., e.g., Gal 3:27–29; Rom 11:23).[24] As Love Sechrest remarks, "Paul thinks that God creates a kinship between Abraham, uncircumcised Gentile believers, and circumcised Jewish believers that is as real as any claims about kinship κατὰ σάρκα."[25]

In 1 Peter, the idea of being Abraham's descendants is only indirectly apparent—in the declaration that the wives who conduct themselves in an appropriate way have become Sarah's daughters (1 Pet 3:6). Nonetheless, this particular appeal to ancestry is significant. In his attempt to legitimate the pattern of conduct demanded of the wives—especially their submission to husbands—the author appeals to "the holy women of old," particularly to Sarah (3:5–6). These women also submitted to their husbands, the author claims, basing this assertion in Sarah's case on a highly selective and slanted reading of Genesis (cf. Gen 16:2!).[26] Insofar as they do good and fear no terror—that is, follow the central demands of ἡ ἀγαθὴ ἐν Χριστῷ ἀναστροφή (3:16, on which see pp. 145–46)—they show themselves to be Sarah's descen-

---

lineal descent are constructed and employed as part of what she calls "the ancient practice of reconfiguring family histories" (33).

22. See Johnson Hodge, *If Sons, Then Heirs*, 117–35.

23. Johnson Hodge, *If Sons, Then Heirs*, 150.

24. For a probing critique of Johnson Hodge and the "Paul within Judaism" perspective, related specifically to the theme of being Abraham's descendants, see Karin B. Neutel, "'Neither Jew nor Greek': Abraham as a Universal Ancestor," in Goodman, Van Kooten, and Van Ruiten, *Abraham, the Nations, and the Hagarites*, 291–306.

25. Sechrest, *A Former Jew*, 126.

26. Apart from Gen 18:12, where Sarah says, "My master is old" (ὁ δὲ κύριός μου πρεσβύτερος), she is nowhere depicted in these terms. Gen 16:2 gives a contrary impression: ὑπήκουσεν δὲ Αβραμ τῆς φωνῆς Σαρας. The addressing of Abraham as κύριος is much more prominent in the Testament of Abraham, as Troy Martin has shown. See Troy W. Martin, "The TestAbr and the Background of 1 Pet 3,6," *ZNW* 90 (1999): 139–46.

dants (3:6). The aorist verb ἐγενήθητε may point to the event of conversion and/or of baptism/initiation, but the participial phrase—ἀγαθοποιοῦσαι καὶ μὴ φοβούμεναι μηδεμίαν πτόησιν (3:6)—also carries a sense of exhortation and conditionality: identity as Sarah's children is displayed by exhibiting a pattern of behavior like hers and, by implication, depends upon continuing to do so.[27] Furthermore, while the specific focus here is clearly upon the wives within the Christian community, the generic designation τέκνα (not θυγατέρες, despite many translations),[28] allows the possibility that all the addressees, insofar as they follow the approved pattern of conduct, may be regarded as Sarah's descendants (cf. Gal 4:26–31). This is particularly so given that the pattern of conduct here demanded of wives is in large part demanded also of the whole community in 3:13–17; the wives, like the domestic slaves, are in a sense paradigmatic.[29]

Abraham himself is only mentioned once, as the husband whom Sarah, a model for Christian wives, (supposedly) "obeyed, calling him lord" (3:6). More prominent in 1 Peter is the motif of divine paternity, and specifically divine regeneration, which is introduced at the very beginning of the letter's

27. Commentators have debated how exactly to understand the participial phrase. J. Ramsey Michaels, *1 Peter*, WBC 49 (Waco: Word, 1988), 166, takes the participles as imperatival in force. A conditional sense is favored by Francis W. Beare, *The First Epistle of Peter*, 3rd ed. (Oxford: Blackwell, 1970), 157. Paul J. Achtemeier, *1 Peter*, Hermeneia (Philadelphia: Fortress, 1996), 216, interprets them as participles of "attendant circumstance," with effectively a temporal sense. John H. Elliott, *1 Peter: A New Translation with Introduction and Commentary*, AB 37B (New York: Doubleday, 2000), 573, suggests that the participles "describe the present conduct and confidence consequent upon becoming Sarah's spiritual children through conversion." Leonhard Goppelt, *A Commentary on I Peter* (Grand Rapids: Eerdmans, 1993), 224, insists that the participles "express not the *ground* but a *demonstration* of this relationship to Sarah"; but there is nonetheless some conditionality bound up with this demonstration—this lifestyle is, in a sense, constitutive of their identity as Sarah's children. See also Jacques Schlosser, *La première épître de Pierre*, Commentaire biblique: Nouveau Testament 21 (Paris: Cerf, 2011), 191.

28. Among older translations, see Geneva, Tyndale, KJV, LutherBibel (1912); among recent translations, see NIV, NRSV (a change from RSV), LutherBibel (1984).

29. There is a series of close parallels between 3:1–6 and 3:13–17: pattern of conduct (3:1–2//3:16); fear (3:2//3:16); the heart (3:4//3:15); gentleness (3:4//3:16); hope (3:5//3:15); doing good (3:6//3:17); not being afraid (3:6//3:14). See Elliott, *1 Peter*, 619 with n. 230, who elsewhere makes the point about the domestic slaves being paradigms (see 523); Michaels, *1 Peter*, 166: "Nothing in this statement applies exclusively to women." Achtemeier, *1 Peter*, 217, likewise suggests "that these Christian wives are paradigmatic for the way all Christians are to live within a hostile cultural situation," noting (in n. 158) that the admonition not to fear is addressed to all believers in 3:14. See David G. Horrell, "Fear, Hope, and Doing Good: Wives as a Paradigm of Mission in 1 Peter," *EstBib* 73 (2015): 409–29.

opening blessing (1:3–12). There, the God who is "father" of Jesus Christ is also declared to be the one who has fathered (ἀναγεννήσας) the Christian recipients of the letter, causing them "to be begotten again into a living hope" (1:3). The resurrection of Christ is explicitly the basis (δι᾽) for this rebirth into the hope of salvation (1:3–5). The motif occurs again in 1:23, where the readers' regeneration (ἀναγεγεννημένοι) is declared to be of imperishable (divine) seed (ἐκ σπορᾶς . . . ἀφθάρτου), brought about through the λόγος θεοῦ.

As Girsch has persuasively argued, this appeal to divine paternity and regeneration provides the foundation for 1 Peter's construction of Christian identity in ethnic terms.[30] Here the focus is on God the Father as the one from whom the members of the Christian communities trace their lineage. Other images and motifs in 1 Peter can also be seen to cohere around this focus. Girsch draws attention to the use of the image of newborn babies and their craving spiritual milk (1 Pet 2:1–3). In particular, following Cynthia Chapman, she shows how breastfeeding is widely connected with the transmission and formation of ethnic identity and the forging of kinship.[31] Chapman also notes ancient stories about divine breastfeeding.[32] She highlights the somewhat surprising references to nursing or weaning in three important Hebrew Bible narratives: the indication in Gen 21:7 that, despite her age and high status, Sarah herself breastfed Isaac; the ironic (and unlikely) appointment of Moses's biological (Hebrew) mother as his wet-nurse (Exod 2:7–9); and Naomi's feeding of Obed (Ruth 4:13–17), again despite her age (Ruth 1:8–12). Naomi is not Obed's mother, but she is, unlike Ruth (the Moabite, his biological mother), a Judahite.[33] As Chapman argues, "if one understands breast milk as a constitutive substance in the formation of the ethnic identity and ritual status of a child, the three seemingly preposterous breastfeeding narratives make perfect sense."[34] Breastfeeding is, in Chapman's words, "ethnicity-forming."[35] Moreover, as Girsch remarks, "The births of Isaac, Moses, and Obed are all endowed with national significance; their births and upbringing, therefore, are part of Israel's national foundation

30. Girsch, "Begotten Anew."

31. Girsch, "Begotten Anew," 145–51; Cynthia R. Chapman, "'Oh That You Were Like a Brother to Me, One Who Had Nursed at My Mother's Breasts': Breast Milk as a Kinship-Forging Substance," *JHebS* 12 (2012): 1–41.

32. Chapman, "Breast Milk," 8–11.

33. Chapman, "Breast Milk," 26–39.

34. Chapman, "Breast Milk," 26.

35. Chapman, "Breast Milk," 40.

story."[36] One can understand, then, why there was a particular concern to show that these male sons were nourished by "properly" ancestral women. Furthermore, breastfeeding was understood in the ancient world to impart not only physical nourishment but also moral character.[37] While the image of regeneration stresses the male role of "begetting," the image of feeding milk to infants highlights the female role, indicating how the author of 1 Peter can use both male and female images to depict God's parenting.[38] The breastfeeding imagery in particular finds even more striking expression in Odes Sol. 8:14 (cf. 19:1–4).[39]

The image of believers in Christ as "living stones" may also, as Girsch shows, have points of connection to the theme of ethnic identity-construction.[40] Deuteronomy 32:18 describes the people's origins from "the rock that bore you" and "the God who gave you birth," an image picked up in Isaiah's appeals to the Israelites to "look to the rock from which you were hewn, and to the quarry from which you were dug . . . to Abraham your father and to Sarah who bore you" (Isa 51:1–2, ESV). Just as the addressees of 1 Peter are newborn infants craving God's nourishing milk, so too they are stones hewn from a quarry—even if this latter implication is not explicitly drawn. The construction of the addressees' identity as a "people" reaches a climax at the culmination of the first main part of the letter (2:9–10), a text to which we shall return in chapter 7.

These two particular and limited examples indicate some of the ways in which discourses of ancestry and lineage were developed in early Christian literature and used to construct the identity of those who belonged to these

36. Girsch, "Begotten Anew," 150.

37. See Girsch, "Begotten Anew," 164; Philip L. Tite, "Nurslings, Milk and Moral Development in the Greco-Roman Context: A Reappraisal of the Paraenetic Utilization of Metaphor in 1 Peter 2.1–3," *JSNT* 31 (2009): 371–400. For example, Aulus Gellius, reporting a discourse of the philosopher Favorinus, sees breast milk as a form of blood that shapes not only the physical body of the infant but also their character in body and mind (*Noct. att.* 12.1.1–24; cf. also Macrobius, *Sat.* 5.15). Plutarch (*Mor.* 5E [*De lib. ed.*]) advises that a mother should rear her own children but that if a foster-mother or nurse must be employed, she should be Greek in character (τοῖς ἤθεσιν Ἑλληνίδας), in order properly to form and regulate the character of the children (τὰ τῶν τέκνων ἤθη). (I owe these ancient references to one of the anonymous readers of the manuscript.)

38. Girsch, "Begotten Anew," 151–61.

39. See David G. Horrell, *The Epistles of Peter and Jude*, Epworth Commentaries (London: Epworth, 1998), 37–8; Girsch, "Begotten Anew," 151–61. The pun on χρηστός/Χριστός in 2:3, drawing on Ps 34:8, also contributes to the image of feeding on Christ.

40. See Girsch, "Begotten Anew," 205–12.

Christian communities. It is clear, unsurprisingly, that these adaptations of what we might call "ancestral reasoning" are profoundly rooted in Jewish scripture and tradition, albeit adapted distinctively to center on Christ.

4.2 Kinship Relations: A Community of Brothers and Sisters

Sharing ancestral lineage is one basis for kinship relations: through a common ancestor, members of a group are in some sense believed to be linked by familial bonds. In the case of ethnic groups, as Weber makes clear, these bonds go far beyond those of immediate family and close relations and constitute a fictive bond—a bond that is *believed*—between a much wider group of people, who see themselves as sharing an identity as descendants of certain ancestors or founding figures. As we have seen in the use of the language of ancestry and lineage, these lines of descent can be constructed, reconfigured, and manipulated for specific purposes. Adoption and breastfeeding, among other things, can serve to integrate people into a particular ethnic identity.

Perhaps the most obvious indication of these bonds of kinship is the use of the language of siblinghood—brother/sister, ἀδελφός/ἀδελφή, /אח אחות—to denote fellow members of the people.[41] It is no surprise, then, that such terms are regularly used in the Hebrew Bible to denote fellow Israelites (e.g., Exod 2:11; 4:18; Lev 10:6; 25:46; Deut 15:3–7). As Lev 10:6 makes clear, "your brothers and sisters" can indicate "the whole house of Israel."[42] Such a conventional designation continues into later Jewish literature, being prominent in the Greek texts from the LXX written around the first two centuries BCE (e.g., Tob 4:13; 1 Macc 2:40–41; 2 Macc 1:1) and apparent also among a range of family terms used for community members in the DSS (e.g., 1 QS 6.10; 6.22; CD 6.20; 7.2). Josephus also reports that the Essenes related to one another like siblings (ἀδελφοί) (*B.J.* 2.122).

It is unsurprising, then, that such language is taken up into early Christian discourse. As H. F. von Soden insists: "There can be no doubt . . . that

41. For overviews of the material, see *TDOT* 1:188–93; *TDNT* 1:144–46; Reidar Aasgaard, *"My Beloved Brothers and Sisters!" Christian Siblingship in Paul*, JSNTSup 265 (London: T&T Clark, 2004), 112–15.

42. As is common in ancient literature, the male forms (οἱ ἀδελφοὶ ὑμῶν / אחיכם) are used here to indicate the whole community (though in some contexts, only the men might be in view). Given the patriarchal assumptions that such language reflects, it is debatable whether this is best conveyed by retaining the masculine form ("brothers"; so, e.g., ESV) or by using a more inclusive rendering ("your kindred"; so NRSV as I have done here).

ἀδελφός is one of the titles of the people of Israel taken over by the Christian community."[43] While we might demur at the designation of this label as a "title"—as if it carried some special status as such, rather than being one of a range of familial terms used in a rather everyday way for members of the people—this Jewish usage would seem likely to be the most direct influence on the New Testament authors. The designation of members of the Christian community as ἀδελφοί is indeed common.[44] In the Gospels, there are, for obvious reasons, few direct references to the Christian groups as ἀδελφοί, though there are some (esp. Matt 18:15–22; John 21:23; less directly, Matt 5:22–24; Luke 22:32). In Acts, οἱ ἀδελφοί is one of the quasi-technical designations for the members of the Christian movement (e.g., Acts 1:15; 9:30; 14:2; 15:1); in such cases one sees something approaching von Soden's "titular" use. In the Epistles, the label is again widely established (e.g., Heb 3:1; 13:22; Jas 1:2; 4:11; 1 John 2:9–11; 3:10–17; 3 John 10). It is particularly prominent in James (20 times, including one use of ἀδελφή in 2:15), 1 John (15 times), and the undisputed Pauline letters (93 times; also in 2 Thessalonians, with 9 occurrences).[45] Indeed, as Robert Banks rightly observes, the designation ἀδελφός "is far and away Paul's favorite way of referring to the members of the communities to whom he is writing."[46] His conventional address for members of the Christian communities, especially when making an appeal to them, is ἀδελφοί (e.g., Rom 1:13; 11:25; 15:30; 1 Cor 1:10; 16:15; Gal 1:11; Phil 1:12; 1 Thess 5:14).[47]

Paul does not simply employ the designation ἀδελφοί as a conventional address but uses the term with particular intensity when appealing for relationships among community members to be shaped by the kind of regard appropriate to that between siblings (see esp. Rom 14:10–21; 1 Cor 6:5–8; 8:11–13).[48] In his short letter to Philemon, Paul not only addresses Philemon

43. *TDNT* 1:145. Cf. Meeks, *The First Urban Christians*, 87.

44. See Paul R. Trebilco, *Self-Designations and Group Identity in the New Testament* (Cambridge: Cambridge University Press, 2014), 16–67.

45. For a careful tabulation of the occurrences, see Aasgaard, *"My Beloved Brothers and Sisters"*, 313–14. For the Pauline letters, see David G. Horrell, "From ἀδελφοί to οἶκος θεοῦ: Social Transformation in Pauline Christianity," *JBL* 120 (2001): 311; repr. in David G. Horrell, *The Making of Christian Morality: Reading Paul in Ancient and Modern Contexts* (Grand Rapids: Eerdmans, 2019), 75–96.

46. Robert Banks, *Paul's Idea of Community: The Early House Churches in Their Historical Setting*, rev. ed. (Peabody, MA: Hendrickson, 1994), 50–51.

47. It is a more common address in Paul's letters than either "holy ones" (ἅγιοι) or "believers" (οἱ πιστεύοντες, κτλ.); see Horrell, *Solidarity*, 121–26.

48. On Paul's deployment of ἀδελφός language in these particular contexts, see Hor-

(individually) as ἀδελφέ (Phlm 7, 20) but also urges that he welcome back his slave Onesimus as a "beloved brother" (ἀδελφὸν ἀγαπητόν) (Phlm 16), a request given added force and scope by Paul's insistence that this should be "both in the flesh and in the Lord" (καὶ ἐν σαρκὶ καὶ ἐν κυρίῳ, Phlm 16).[49] As Reidar Aasgaard has suggested, the term ἀδελφός thus functions for Paul not only as an identity-designation for members of the Christian group but also as a means to evoke a set of ethical expectations—behaviors appropriate to the "role" of ἀδελφός.[50]

In 1 Peter, ἀδελφός is not used except to denote Silvanus as ὁ πιστός ἀδελφός (5:12). This does not mean, however, that the notion of Christians as a kinship group has dropped out of sight. On the contrary, the author twice refers to the Christian movement as an ἀδελφότης—a word difficult to render into gender-inclusive English (2:17; 5:9).[51] Similarly, the exhortation to demonstrate love for community members (cf. 1:22; 3:8; 4:8; 5:14) is denoted as φιλαδελφία (1:22; cf. 3:8).[52]

As John Elliott notes, in using the term ἀδελφότης, the author of 1 Peter employs "a unique *collective* term for the entire *community of brothers and sisters*, consonant with his employment of collective terms elsewhere in the letter."[53] The use of -οτης to form abstract substantive nouns from "adjec-

---

rell, "From ἀδελφοί to οἶκος θεοῦ," 300–303; Horrell, *Solidarity*, 121–133; Aasgaard, *"My Beloved Brothers and Sisters,"* 151–260; K. Schäfer, *Gemeinde als "Bruderschaft": Ein Beitrag zum Kirchenverständnis des Paulus*, Europäische Hochschulschriften 333 (Frankfurt: Peter Lang, 1989), 330–52.

49. On the implications of this request, see Norman R. Petersen, *Rediscovering Paul: Philemon and the Sociology of Paul's Narrative World* (Philadelphia: Fortress, 1985), 266–70, 288–89; Aasgaard, *"My Beloved Brothers and Sisters,"* 237–60. On the ambiguities and complexities of the situation and the opacity of Paul's request to Philemon, see John M. G. Barclay, "Paul, Philemon and the Dilemma of Christian Slave-Ownership," *NTS* 37 (1991): 161–86.

50. Reidar Aasgaard, "'Role Ethics' in Paul: The Significance of the Sibling Role for Paul's Ethical Thinking," *NTS* 48 (2002): 513–30.

51. ESV has "brotherhood" in both cases while NRSV opts for "the family of believers" in 2:17 and "brothers and sisters" in 5:9.

52. On this community focus for the exhortation to love in 1 Peter, see Runar M. Thorsteinsson, *Roman Christianity and Roman Stoicism: A Comparative Study of Ancient Morality* (Oxford: Oxford University Press, 2010), 105–16. The material in the following two paragraphs draws on David G. Horrell, "'Honour Everyone. . .' (1 Pet. 2.17): The Social Strategy of 1 Peter and Its Significance for the Development of Christianity," in *To Set at Liberty: Essays on Early Christianity and Its Social World in Honor of John H. Elliott*, ed. Stephen K. Black (Sheffield: Phoenix, 2014), 198–200.

53. Elliott, *1 Peter*, 499.

tives and substantives of the second declension" is common in later Greek.[54] But ἀδελφότης is unusual, especially prior to 1 Peter, and its occurrence here may constitute the first time it is used in the concrete sense to denote a community of ἀδελφοί—"the brotherhood" or "the siblinghood"—as distinct from the abstract sense of "familial affection" or "brotherly bonds" (as in 1 Macc 12:10, 17; 4 Macc 9:23; 10:3, 15; 13:19, 27; Dio Chrysostom, *Nicom.* 15 [ἡ ἀδελφότης τί ἄλλο ἐστὶν ἢ ἀδελφῶν ὁμόνοια]; Vettius Valens, *Anth.* 1.1.45, 89; Hermas Mand. 8.10).[55] The word occurs only very rarely in inscriptions from Asia Minor, and when it does, in the period prior to 1 Peter's composition, it is used in the abstract sense: "the Peoples . . . who have taken oaths over newly-burnt offerings and made blood-offerings for their natural alliance, eternal concord, and brotherhood with each other" (ὑπὲρ τῆς πρὸς ἀλλήλους φ[ύσει] συμμαχίας καὶ ὁμονοίας [αἰ]ωνίου καὶ ἀδελφότητος).[56]

In subsequent Christian literature, however, the term becomes common as a designation for the Christian community, perhaps, at least in part, under the influence of 1 Peter. As F. J. A. Hort noted long ago, "The word does not earlier [than 1 Peter] occur in this [concrete] sense (indeed it is rare even in the abstract sense), but was speedily taken up into Christian literature, Latin as well as Greek."[57] For example, in Polycarp's letter to the Philippians (*Phil.* 10.1), which is almost certainly influenced by 1 Peter (cf. Eusebius, *Hist. eccl.* 4.14.9),[58] the addressees are urged to be "lovers of the brotherhood" (*fraternitatis amatores*—this section of his letter being

---

54. See BDF §110.1.

55. LSJ, 21, lists only 1 Pet 2:17 and 5:9 for the substantive "the brotherhood." Some of the instances in 4 Maccabees (10:3, 15) could be seen as acquiring a more substantive sense, but phrases such as οὐκ ἀρνήσομαι τὴν εὐγενῆ ἀδελφότητα (10:15) are best understood in the sense of "our noble family ties" (so NRSV). In any case, the date of 4 Maccabees may well be around, or slightly later than, the date of 1 Peter; for a date of 90–100 CE, see Barclay, *Jews*, 449; Hans-Josef Klauck, *4. Makkabäerbuch*, ed. Hermann Lichtenberger, JSHRZ 3/6 (Gütersloh: Gütersloher Verlagshaus, 1989), 668–69.

56. *IAph2007* 8.210. A search of the Packard Humanities inscriptions database for Asia Minor (at http://epigraphy.packhum.org/inscriptions) yielded only this example from the first century CE and earlier. Other (Christian) examples date from the third century (see below p. 110 with n. 61) and the sixth to seventh centuries (*MAMA* 4.37[1]).

57. F. J. A. Hort, *The First Epistle of St. Peter I.1–II.17: The Greek Text with Introductory Lecture, Commentary, and Additional Notes* (1898; repr. Eugene, OR: Wipf & Stock, 2005), 146.

58. For the connections between 1 Peter and Pol. *Phil.*, including some "virtually certain citations," see Elliott, *1 Peter*, 143.

extant only in Latin—roughly equivalent to the Greek οἱ τὴν ἀδελφότητα ἀγαπῶντες).[59] In 1 Clem 2.4, the addressees are praised for their efforts ὑπὲρ πάσης τῆς ἀδελφότητος. Other instances occur in patristic litera-ture, where the word is used to denote the Christian community in gen-eral, the local congregation (as in *Hist. eccl.* 6.45.1), or a religious or mo-nastic community, or, somewhat more specifically, as a form of address to members of councils, groups of bishops, or clergy.[60] Likewise, a late third-century Christian inscription from a cemetery in Phrygia, although somewhat incomplete, wishes "peace to all the brotherhood" (εἰρήνη πάση τῇ ἀδελ[φότητ]ι). A similar cemetery stone has the functionally equivalent phrase εἰρήνη πᾶσι τοῖς ἀδελφοῖς.[61] So, while the author of 1 Peter does not replicate the common custom of referring to Christians directly as ἀδελφοί, he reinforces the sense of kin-based group identity by initiating a substan-tive use of ἀδελφότης that would then become common Christian vocab-ulary. Indeed, while there are notable variations in terminology, and in the prominence of sibling terminology vis-à-vis other familial and household terms, the characterization of members in familial terms continues broadly within early Christianity in the first two centuries of its existence, as Joseph Hellerman has shown.[62]

The mere use of sibling or kinship terminology does not, of course, mean that early Christian groups—or any other groups, for that matter—are to be regarded straightforwardly as "ethnic." For a start, kinship terminol-ogy (ἀδελφός/ἀδελφή specifically) was used in a wide variety of contexts where some kind of sibling-like bond was felt or sought, such as among the

---

59. Cf. Theophylact, *Expositio in Epist. 1. Pet.* 363 (in PG 125, col. 1216): πάντας τιμήσατε, τὴν ἀδελφότητα μὲν ἀγαπῶντες, τὸν δὲ θεὸν φοβούμενοι, τὸν βασιλέα τιμῶντες. Also cited in Troy W. Martin, *Metaphor and Composition in 1 Peter*, SBLDS 131 (Atlanta: Scholars, 1992), 204n236.

60. See *PGL*, 31.

61. See William M. Ramsay, *The Cities and Bishoprics of Phrygia*, 2 vols. (Oxford: Clar-endon, 1897), 720, §655 and §654 respectively.

62. Joseph H. Hellerman, *The Ancient Church as Family* (Minneapolis: Fortress, 2001). Drawing on Hellerman's work, S. Scott Bartchy, "Undermining Ancient Patriarchy: The Apostle Paul's Vision of a Society of Siblings," *BTB* 29 (1999): 76–77, thus comments: "Both the brother-sister rhetoric and sibling values continued to characterize a wide va-riety of Christian groups throughout the Roman empire for more than 250 years." Given the shifts in emphasis, not least within the Pauline corpus (on which see Horrell, "From ἀδελφοί to οἶκος θεοῦ"), less compelling is Bartchy's view that it was Constantine who was essentially responsible for introducing "a virulent form of hierarchy and patriarchy" into Christianity.

members of the various associations that were so common in the Greek and Roman world.[63] It could be used between spouses[64] or when a cooperative relationship was sought, such as between a king and a hoped-for ally (see, e.g., Josephus, *A.J.* 13.45). Once again, we cannot draw a clear distinction between "real" kinship bonds and those that are "fictive" or metaphorical. Once we have moved beyond the scale of immediate blood brothers and sisters ("son of the same mother" as LSJ, 20, first defines ἀδελφός),[65] then, as Aasgaard makes clear, we are dealing with various kinds of fictive or metaphorical deployments of these terms.[66] Indeed, as the above examples show—not least those highlighted in Paul's letters—sibling language is deployed in particular contexts for particular and varied purposes. Rather than ask whether the use of sibling language does or does not denote an ethnic group, we do better to ask—following the kind of approach taken by Jonathan Hall and Denise Kimber Buell[67]—how such essentially ethnic, kin-group language is discursively deployed. And it is clear that just as the early Christians used discourses about ancestry and lineage to construct their group identity, so, too, they made extensive use of the language of kinship and family.

These notions help to construct and sustain a sense of peoplehood, of belonging to a group connected through shared descent and bound together with sibling-like bonds. Yet equally important to consider are the social practices by which such a discursively constructed sense of group identity is maintained. In this regard, there are two areas of particular interest: marriage and children.

63. On the use of ἀδελφός terminology in associations, see Philip A. Harland, *Dynamics of Identity in the World of the Early Christians: Associations, Judeans, and Cultural Minorities* (London: T&T Clark, 2009), 63–81; LSJ, 20 (s.v. ἀδελφός [3]); G. H. R. Horsley, ed., *A Review of the Greek Inscriptions and Papyri Published in 1977*, vol. 2 of *New Documents Illustrating Early Christianity* (North Ryde: Macquarie University, 1982), 49–50; Dennis C. Duling, "The Matthean Brotherhood and Marginal Scribal Leadership," in *Modelling Early Christianity*, ed. Philip. F. Esler (London: Routledge, 1995), 159–82. On the terminology in Greco-Roman religious contexts, see K. H. Schelke, "Bruder," *RAC* 2:632–34.

64. E.g., P.Lond. 42; and for the term ἀδελφή used by a husband of his wife, see P.Oxy. 120, 528, 744.

65. *TDOT* 1:188 offers a similar definition for the Hebrew term אָח: "a person's own blood brother."

66. Aasgaard, *"My Beloved Brothers and Sisters,"* esp. 107–16.

67. See Jonathan M. Hall, *Ethnic Identity*, 19, 182; Buell, *Why This New Race*, 69–70; §3.4 above.

4.3 Marriage Rules: Endogamy as Norm

There is plenty of evidence from both Jewish and non-Jewish texts to indicate a widespread ancient view that Jews did not marry non-Jews. As Tacitus observes, "They sleep apart, and . . . abstain from intercourse with foreign women [*alienarum concubitu abstinent*]" (*Hist.* 5.5 [Moore, LCL]). That Tacitus's remarks are, however, something less than unvarnished description should be clear from his hostile (and racializing?) remarks that this is despite the fact that "as a race [*gens*], they are prone to lust [*proiectissima ad libidinem*]" and that "toward every other people they feel only hate and enmity" (*Hist.* 5.5). His remarks on views of the Christians are similarly negative, referring to their "hatred of the human race" (*Ann.* 15.44).[68] Yet Jewish authors also refer to a Jewish custom of endogamy. Philo, for example, refers to Moses's prohibition of entering "into the partnership of marriage with a member of a foreign nation [ἀλλοεθνεῖ]" (*Spec.* 3.29). Josephus likewise refers a number of times to the legal prohibition against marrying foreign women, even though the context for these remarks is often stories about Jewish figures who had precisely not kept this injunction (e.g., *A.J.* 8.191–92; 11.140, 151–52; 12.187; 18.349). Indeed, a gap between norm and practice is evident in the case of Josephus himself: while he can declare that the careful scrutiny of ancestral records is necessary to keep the priestly line pure and unmixed (*C. Ap.* 1.30–36), he elsewhere records that he himself married, though at Vespasian's command, a captive from Caesarea, one of at least three wives he had (*Vita* 414–15, 426–27).[69]

Even in theory, however, matters are not quite so straightforward, and we must be careful to define what endogamy is taken to mean. The relevant legislation in the Torah prohibits intermarriage with the seven Canaanite peoples (ἔθνη/גוים) in the land that the people are promised, and the reason for the prohibition (as in many subsequent repetitions) is that it will lead people to turn away to other gods—that is, to idolatry (Deut 7:1–4; cf. Gen 24:3; Exod 34:11–16; Deut 23:2–3). More rigorous standards apply to a priest, who may marry only "a virgin [בתולה, παρθένος] from his own people" (Lev 21:14; Josephus, *C. Ap.* 1.30–36). As Shaye Cohen has pointed out, for the

---

68. See John Granger Cook, *Roman Attitudes toward the Christians: From Claudius to Hadrian*, WUNT 261 (Tübingen: Mohr Siebeck, 2010), 62–65, on this stereotypical accusation and its application to both Jews and Christians.

69. See Adele Reinhartz and Kim Shier, "Josephus on Children and Childhood," *SR* 41 (2012): 365.

people in general, "neither Exodus nor Deuteronomy prohibits intermarriage with all non-Israelites, and both of them prohibit intermarriage with Canaanites only because it might lead to something else that was prohibited (idolatry)."[70] This helps to explain the range of attitudes and practices that seem thereafter to have emerged.

As Christine Hayes has shown, in Second Temple Judaism there are two somewhat distinct perspectives on intermarriage.[71] One of these represents a strict prohibition of all intermarriage on the basis of a "holy seed" ideology. Fundamental here is Ezra's polemic against the Israelites' "mixed marriages," precisely on the grounds that these have led to "the holy seed" (σπέρμα τὸ ἅγιον/זרע הקדש) being mixed (ταρήχθη) with that of the peoples of the land (Ezra 9:2).[72] Using similar terms, the book of Tobit warns against marrying foreign women and exhorts marriage only with a woman who is ἀπὸ τοῦ σπέρματος τῶν πατέρων σου ("from the seed of your fathers"). The ancestors are also said to have followed precisely this custom and to have been rewarded for it (Tob 4:12–13). The author of the book of Jubilees is likewise keen to show that the patriarchs adhered to the norm of endogamy (4:15, 16, 20, 27, 28, 33; 8:6; 11:7, 14).[73] Hayes gives particular attention to the ban on intermarriage in Jubilees 30.[74] Drawing on Exod 19:5–6, Jubilees "establishes that the entire nation of Israel is categorically distinct from other peoples, that all Israel are holy priests" (cf. Jub. 16:17–18). And once this move is made, "the application to all Israel of priestly standards of ritual and marital purity is a next logical step."[75] In particular, Jubilees reinforces the "holy seed"

70. Cohen, *Beginnings*, 261.

71. Christine E. Hayes, *Gentile Impurities and Jewish Identities: Intermarriage and Conversion from the Bible to the Talmud* (Oxford: Oxford University Press, 2002). On the various perspectives, see also Christl M. Maier, "Der Diskurs um interkulturelle Ehen in Jehud als antikes Beispiel von Intersektionalität," in Eisen, Gerber, and Standhartinger, *Doing Gender*, 129–53.

72. For a recent study of Ezra's approach to intermarriage informed by theoretical perspectives on ethnicity, hybridity, and migration, see Katherine E. Southwood, *Ethnicity and the Mixed Marriage Crisis in Ezra 9–10: An Anthropological Approach* (Oxford: Oxford University Press, 2012).

73. Cf. S. Safrai, "Home and Family," in *The Jewish People in the First Century*, ed. S. Safrai and M. Stern, vol. 2, CRINT 2 (Assen: Van Gorcum, 1976), 754. Nonetheless, the author of Jubilees preserves the tradition that Joseph married an Egyptian (Jub. 40:10).

74. Hayes, *Gentile Impurities,* 73–81. See also Cana Werman, "Jubilees 30: Building a Paradigm for the Ban on Intermarriage," *HTR* 90 (1997): 1–22.

75. Hayes, *Gentile Impurities*, 74.

ideology, insisting that any mixing with gentile seed constitutes an act of sexual immorality that defiles and pollutes the children of Israel (Jub. 30:7–15). Conversion of the gentile partner cannot alleviate this problem.[76] Hayes finds a similar position in 4QMMT (B75–82), a text, she argues, that "adopts the holy seed thinking of Ezra and so objects to any and all unions between Israelites and Gentiles."[77]

But this "holy seed" ideology was by no means the only, nor even the majority, position among Jews of the period. Indeed, Hayes argues that Jubilees and 4QMMT are precisely opposing a widespread alternative view: that "Israelites (unlike priests) were permitted to marry foreigners as long as the latter had renounced idolatry and assimilated or converted to Judaism."[78] In other words, the concern in such a view is not so much with what Hayes calls "genealogical purity"; rather, it is a "moral-religious"concern, focused on the avoidance of idolatry and immorality.[79] If the gentile partner converts to the Jewish way of life, the latter concern can (at least in theory) be avoided, while the former concern can never be addressed in this way. We shall turn to the subject of "conversion"—a problematic term, as we shall see—in chapter 8.

In the Hebrew Bible, the paradigmatic story of a non-Israelite being joined to an Israelite in marriage is found in the book of Ruth, while in later Jewish literature it is expressed in the story of Joseph and Aseneth (written sometime between around 100 BCE and the early second century CE).[80] Ruth's turn from her own people to Naomi's people is explicitly described in what we might call ethnoreligious terms: from one people to another, and from old gods to a new one (Ruth 1:15–16).[81] As Ruth affirms to Naomi: "Your people shall be my people, and your God my God" (v. 16). Even in the positive story of Ruth's joining with Boaz, there is, as we noted above, a hint of concern with maintaining proper genealogical continuity in the otherwise surprising declaration that Ruth's child Obed was breastfed by the

76. See Werman, "Jubilees 30," 16–17.

77. Hayes, *Gentile Impurities*, 84. For the text and ET, see Florentino García Martínez and Eibert J. C. Tigchelaar, *The Dead Sea Scrolls Study Edition*, 2 vols. (Leiden: Brill; Grand Rapids: Eerdmans, 2000), 797–99.

78. Hayes, *Gentile Impurities*, 86; see 78, 81–83.

79. Hayes, *Gentile Impurities*, 8–9, 68.

80. On the date, see Christoph Burchard, "Joseph and Aseneth," in *OTP*, 2:187–88.

81. As David Daube, *Ancient Jewish Law: Three Inaugural Lectures* (Leiden: Brill, 1981), 5, notes in relation to this text, "The unity of nation and religion could not be expressed more clearly."

aged Naomi (Ruth 4:16).[82] But the story as a whole affirms the possibility that a non-Jew could join the people by marriage.

Joseph and Aseneth is a work of historical fiction, a kind of romantic novel built on the basis of the brief reference in Gen 41:45–50 to Joseph's marriage to Aseneth, "the daughter of Potiphera, priest of On" (MT; in the LXX, she is "the daughter of Petephres, priest of Heliopolis").[83] It was evidently a successful and popular piece of writing that circulated widely in various forms.[84] Central to the story is Aseneth's repentance, her turn from idolatry to the God of Israel, and her marriage to Joseph. Indeed, the theme of Aseneth's "conversion" dominates the narrative.[85] Despite the work's fictional, legendary character, and despite uncertainties about its purpose and intended readership, it seems clear enough that the narrative accepts and strongly legitimates both the idea of "coming in" to Judaism, or joining the Jewish people, and the consequent acceptability of a Jew marrying someone who has turned from idolatry and "converted" to join the people in this way.[86]

Josephus also indicates his awareness of the possibility of marriage when the non-Jewish partner agrees to convert (*A.J.* 16.225; 20.139). Thus, Martin Goodman observes that the "assumption by Jews that marriage partners should convert before union does indeed seem to have been general by the

---

82. As Chapman notes, qualifying Cohen's argument that the shift from patrilineal to matrilineal lineage as determinative for Jewishness occurs only Mishnaic period, such references indicate the crucial role of the mother—or, more precisely, the breastfeeder—in defining identity. See Chapman, "Breast Milk," 41; Cohen, *Beginnings*, 263–307.

83. On the genre of the work, see Burchard, "Joseph and Aseneth," 186–87; Randall D. Chesnutt, *From Death to Life: Conversion in Joseph and Aseneth*, JSPSup 16 (Sheffield: Sheffield Academic Press, 1995), 85–92. Marc Philonenko, *Joseph et Aséneth: Introduction, texte critique, traduction et notes*, Studia Post-Biblica (Leiden: Brill, 1968), 43–44, calls it a "roman d'amour."

84. On the various texts and recensions, see Burchard, "Joseph and Aseneth," 178–81; Philonenko, *Joseph et Aséneth*, 3–16.

85. As Barclay, *Jews*, 205, remarks, the narrative, despite its character as romance, "has been overwhelmed by the theme, and the elongated description, of Aseneth's conversion."

86. Cf. Barclay, *Jews*, 214–15; Randall D. Chesnutt, "The Social Setting and Purpose of Joseph and Aseneth," *JSP* 2 (1988): 21–48; Chesnutt, *Death to Life*, 256–65; Burchard, "Joseph and Aseneth," 194–95, all of whom doubt that the work was intended as a missionary document but see it as affirming the value and validity of conversion. For a recent treatment, see Jill Hicks-Keeton, *Arguing with Aseneth: Gentile Access to Israel's Living God in Jewish Antiquity* (Oxford: Oxford University Press, 2018), who sees *Joseph and Aseneth* as providing a myth of origins for gentile inclusion into Israel set in the context of Jewish debate and disagreement about the possibility and the means of gentile incorporation.

first century."[87] The reality that Jews not infrequently married non-Jews is evident throughout the period, even when the practice is a cause for criticism (see, e.g., Exod 2:16–21; 1 Kgs 11:1–4; Ezra 10:10–11; Neh 13:23–27). Indeed, as Hayes suggests, the polemical argument of Ezra, and later Jubilees, only makes sense against such a backdrop.[88]

Jewish custom, then, strongly favored endogamy, but this was inconsistently practiced and variously understood. While some prohibited all intermarriage so as not to "mix" the holy seed of Israel, others regarded intermarriage as acceptable if the non-Jewish partner assimilated or converted to the Jewish way of life. In this way, the risk of the Jew abandoning their way of life and turning away to what is seen as idolatry could be avoided.[89] This is a form of endogamy, but one that presumes that outsiders can enter the group prior to marriage and thus become acceptable partners. Such a definition of endogamy illustrates clearly one way in which what we might distinguish as religious or ethnic considerations overlap in the complex ideological and practical facets of making and sustaining group identity.

In the earliest Christian sources, the only topic concerning marriage that is regularly addressed is that of divorce (and remarriage after divorce). Given its multiple attestation in two essentially different forms—one long, one short—it is highly likely that Jesus himself spoke against divorce (Matt 19:3–9//Mark 10:2–12; Matt 5:31–32//Luke 16:18).[90] All these versions of the prohibition of divorce reflect a particular concern with remarriage after divorce, or divorce in order to remarry, declaring—with the one qualification of the Matthean clause μὴ ἐπὶ πορνείᾳ—that marrying after divorce is adultery.[91] In one of his rare references to Jesus's teaching, Paul reiterates

---

87. Martin Goodman, *Mission and Conversion: Proselytizing in the Religious History of the Roman Empire* (Oxford: Clarendon, 1994), 77. Cf. also Hayes, *Gentile Impurities*, 83.

88. Hayes, *Gentile Impurities*, 78.

89. Cf. Barclay, *Jews*, 107–8 (on Philo's concern in this regard) and 410–12 (on the broader issue). Yet in view of Hayes's work, we need to note the potential distinction between two positions Barclay describes together when he notes "the concern among Diaspora Jews to keep marriage bonds within the nation, or at least to accept only Gentiles committed to join it" (410).

90. See, e.g., E. P. Sanders and Margaret Davies, *Studying the Synoptic Gospels* (London: SCM, 1989), 324–28.

91. On the tradition-historical issues, see David Catchpole, "The Synoptic Divorce Material as a Traditio-Historical Problem," *BJRL* 57 (1974–75): 92–127; and on the emphasis on remarriage, see John Nolland, "The Gospel Prohibition of Divorce: Tradition History and Meaning," *JSNT* 58 (1995): 19–35.

this prohibition (1 Cor 7:10–11) and develops it in his own terms to address the particular situation of so-called mixed marriages within the Christian community (7:12–16). We will return to this latter passage in the next section to discuss its use of holiness language, particularly in relation to children. For now, our interest is in rules and principles regarding the initiation of marriage. And here it seems clear—despite some varying interpretations (discussed below)—that Paul's concern is with existing marriages (εἴ τις ἔχει . . .) rendered "mixed" by the conversion of one partner.[92] His striking declaration that the unbelieving partner in a marriage is "sanctified" (ἡγίασται) by the Christian spouse (1 Cor 7:14) refers to existing marriages and is intended to give one among several reasons why the marriage need not end—along with the possibility of the unbeliever's conversion (7:16),[93] and the holiness of any children (on which see below)—quite possibly in opposition to some of the Corinthians, perhaps especially women, who thought differently about their existing marriages.[94] As Tertullian observes,

---

92. Hayes, *Gentile Impurities*, 94: "It is clear [in 1 Cor 7:12–14] that the continuance of such a marriage is a concession and that Paul does not mean to say that marriage to an unbeliever is permitted at the outset." On this as the dominant understanding of vv. 12–16, see Wolfgang Schrage, *1 Kor 6,12–11,16*, vol. 2 of *Der erste Brief an die Korinther*, EKKNT 7.2 (Neukirchen-Vluyn: Neukirchener, 1995), 121. One can see why the text left room for Christians to disagree about whether or not it was permissible to marry a non-Christian— so Caroline Johnson Hodge, "'Mixed Marriage' in Early Christianity: Trajectories from Corinth," in *Corinth in Contrast: Studies in Inequality*, ed. Steven J. Friesen, Sarah A. James, and Daniel N. Schowalter, NovTSup 155 (Leiden: Brill, 2014), 227–44; Shaye J. D. Cohen, "From Permission to Prohibition: Paul and the Early Church on Mixed Marriage," in *Paul's Jewish Matrix*, ed. Thomas G. Casey and Justin Taylor, Bible in Dialogue 2 (Rome: Gregorian and Biblical Press, 2011), 259–91. But Tertullian's insistence (*Ux.* 2.2) that this section of Paul's instruction applied only to already existing marriages seems to have a much firmer exegetical basis. See further discussion below.

93. Commentators have long discussed whether Paul's comment in v. 16 is optimistic or pessimistic concerning the unbelieving partner's salvation. It seems best to accept that the questions leave the implied answer open but hopeful. As J. B. Lightfoot, *Notes on Epistles of St. Paul from Unpublished Commentaries* (New York: Macmillan, 1904), 227, wisely remarks: "These expressions [τί οἶδας . . . εἰ], so far from emphasizing a doubt, express a hope . . . implying that there is a reasonable chance." Cf. also Gordon D. Fee, *The First Epistle to the Corinthians*, rev. ed., NICNT (Grand Rapids: Eerdmans, 2014), 337–38; Schrage, *1 Kor 6,12–11,16*, 112.

94. Cf. Margaret Y. MacDonald, "Women Holy in Body and Spirit: The Social Setting of 1 Corinthians 7," *NTS* 36 (1990): 161–81; MacDonald, *Early Christian Women and Pagan Opinion: The Power of the Hysterical Woman* (Cambridge: Cambridge University Press, 1996), 189–95; Antoinette C. Wire, *The Corinthian Women Prophets: A Reconstruction through Paul's Rhetoric* (Minneapolis: Fortress, 1990), 85. For later examples of such

Paul refers in 1 Cor 7:12-13 to anyone who "has" (*habet*) an unbelieving spouse, not "takes" (*ducit*) one (*Ux.* 2.2.2).[95] Whether Paul regards the Christian as free to remarry if their unbelieving spouse chooses to separate is unclear (οὐ δεδούλεται ὁ ἀδελφὸς ἢ ἡ ἀδελφὴ ἐν τοῖς τοιούτοις, 1 Cor 7:15),[96] though his remarks have provided the basis in Catholic teaching for annulment and remarriage in such situations, under the so-called *privilegium Paulinum* or "Pauline privilege."[97]

There is only one New Testament text that gives explicit guidance on whom a Christian may legitimately marry, and even this text is specifically concerned only with widows. Toward the end of 1 Corinthians 7, a chapter devoted to instruction regarding marriage and divorce, Paul reinforces the point that marriage is a bond for life but then advises concerning the case of a widow, "If her husband dies, she is free to be married to whom she wishes," with the crucial proviso, μόνον ἐν κυρίῳ (v. 39). Exactly what this phrase implies is open to some debate. J. B. Lightfoot, for example, insists, against the view that it indicates that any future marriage partner must be a Christian, that "the expression cannot be so pressed" but "will only signify that she must remember that she is a member of Christ's body." Lightfoot does concede, however, that marrying a Christian might be "the consequence" of her remembering this.[98] This, however, seems to give insufficient weight to the fact that it is the marrying—the word adjacent to the crucial phrase (and using the passive infinitive, γαμηθῆναι)—that must be ἐν κυρίῳ, not merely the freedom to act that is defined and limited in this way. Given parallel uses of ἐν κυρίῳ elsewhere in Paul, it seems most plausible to take the phrase to mean something like "within the sphere of belonging to the

---

separations, see Justin Martyr, *2 Apol.* 2; Acts of Peter 34. For discussion, see MacDonald, *Early Christian Women*, 205-13; Johnson Hodge, "Mixed Marriage."

95. Chrysostom later makes the same point: Οὐ γὰρ εἶπεν, Εἴ τις βούλεται λαβεῖν ἄπιστον, ἀλλ', Εἴ τις ἔχει ἄπιστον (*Hom. 1 Cor* 19.4).

96. For discussion, see Fee, *1 Corinthians*, 338-39; Anthony C. Thiselton, *The First Epistle to the Corinthians*, NIGTC (Grand Rapids: Eerdmans, 2000), 540-43.

97. See Augustus Lehmkuhl, "Divorce I: In Moral Theology," in *The Catholic Encyclopedia*, ed. Charles G. Herbermann et al. (New York: Robert Appleton, 1909), 60.

98. Lightfoot, *Notes*, 235; followed by C. K. Barrett, *The First Epistle to the Corinthians*, 2nd ed., BNTC (London: A & C Black, 1971), 186. Schrage, *1 Kor 6,12-11,16*, 205-6, follows Lightfoot and Barrett to the extent of insisting that the key point of Paul's instruction concerns the woman's living in the Lord, which is more encompassing than an instruction about whom she may marry. Nonetheless, this "Grundorientierung des Lebensstils am Kyrios . . . soll auch bei Wieder 'heirat' beachtet werden," and in practice this means, Schrage concludes, that Paul would regard it as "sinnvoll und nützlich" to marry a Christian.

Lord."[99] In other words, as many scholars and commentators have agreed, both parties to the marriage should be believers in Christ, members of the Christian community.[100]

This interpretation would also fit well with what Paul elsewhere reveals about his perspective on marriage specifically and "the gentiles" in general. In 2 Cor 6:14–7:1, we find the instruction not to be "unequally yoked with unbelievers" (6:14, ESV) (μὴ γίνεσθε ἑτεροζυγοῦντες ἀπίστοις). This text is notoriously enigmatic and so distinctive in character and content that some have questioned whether it is Pauline at all.[101] It does not directly mention marriage. But it is unsurprising that it was taken to express a principle that applied to marriage, reinforcing the notion that entering a marriage with a non-Christian was forbidden (see below).[102] While noting that the text "is unspecific and therefore widely comprehensive" in its scope, Margaret Thrall cautiously concludes that Paul "doubtless . . . does have in view the contraction of a marriage between a believer and an unbeliever," but also other associations and relationships.[103] Aside from 2 Cor 6:14–7:1, in 1 Cor 6:16, Paul quotes the

99. The phrase is frequent and used with somewhat diverse senses, but see esp. 1 Cor 11:11; Phil 4:1–2; 1 Thess 3:8; 5:12; Col 3:18; 4:7; Eph 2:21; 5:8; 6:1. This is also one indication that the crucial social boundary is between those who are and are not "in Christ"; there is no corresponding evidence that such an identity-defining boundary exists between Jewish and gentile Christians, *pace* Johnson Hodge, *If Sons, Then Heirs,* 138, 146, et passim. On Paul's distinguishing of his own "in-group" from both Jews and gentiles, see E. P. Sanders, "Paul's Jewishness," in Casey and Taylor, *Paul's Jewish Matrix,* 64–73; N. T. Wright, *Paul and the Faithfulness of God,* 1443–49 (though Wright stresses that this group is a fulfilment of God's promises to Abraham and to Israel and so is in that sense continuous with the story and identity of Israel).

100. So, e.g., O. Larry Yarbrough, *Not Like the Gentiles: Marriage Rules in the Letters of Paul,* SBLDS 80 (Atlanta: Scholars Press, 1985), 109; Thiselton, *First Epistle,* 604; Fee, *1 Corinthians,* 392 with n. 379. This becomes the dominant interpretation from the earliest times, though not the only one; see further Cohen, "Permission to Prohibition," 260–63; Schrage, *1 Kor 6,12–11,16,* 210–11; and discussion below.

101. E.g., Jerome Murphy-O'Connor, *Keys to Second Corinthians: Revisiting the Major Issues* (Oxford: Oxford University Press, 2010), 116–39.

102. See further Hayes, *Gentile Impurities,* 97–100; Cohen, "Permission to Prohibition" (but for critique of Cohen's wider argument, see n. 115 below).

103. Margaret E. Thrall, *A Critical and Exegetical Commentary on the Second Epistle to the Corinthians,* vol. 1, ICC (Edinburgh: T&T Clark, 1994), 473; similarly Victor Paul Furnish, *II Corinthians,* AB 32A (New York: Doubleday, 1984), 372. Thomas Schmeller, *2 Kor 1,1–7,4,* vol. 1 of *Der zweite Brief an die Korinther,* EKKNT 8.1 (Neukirchen-Vluyn: Neukirchener; Ostfildern: Patmos, 2010), 373, sees v. 14 as encapsulating a warning against *Gemeinschaft* with "pagan" non-Christians. The present tense verb γίνεσθε is probably best

COMPARISONS OF JEWISH AND EARLY CHRISTIAN PERSPECTIVES

same phrase from Gen 2:24 that is quoted in the long version of the Synoptic teaching on divorce (Matt 19:5–6//Mark 10:7–8): "The two shall become one flesh." He thus illustrates his conviction that union with Christ is incompatible with union with a πόρνη. Here, too, he sees sexual immorality as uniquely defiling the body, describing the body as a temple (ναός) of the Holy Spirit.[104] It is clear how such a theology of sex could be taken to favor continence or, as a second best option, to allow marriage only to another Christian, ἐν κυρίῳ. A similar concern for holiness and sexual control is apparent in 1 Thess 4:3–8, with its exhortation not to live "like the gentiles" (v. 5).[105]

Understanding Paul to recommend marriage only to another Christian became the dominant interpretation of 1 Cor 7:39 in early Christian literature, and one that underpinned a widely shared expectation that Christians should marry only other Christians.[106] Ignatius, for example, indicates that the bishop should sanction marriage partnerships in order that marriage may be κατὰ κύριον and not κατ' ἐπιθυμίαν and that all things may be done "to the honor of God" (Ign. Pol. 5.2). As William Schoedel comments, "This development contributes to the exclusiveness of the Christian community and puts in the hands of the clergy one of the most potent instruments of social control—namely, 'group endogamy.'"[107]

Most emphatic in insisting that Christians should marry only other Christians, and drawing on Paul to make this case, is Tertullian:

---

taken to refer to the (potential) beginning of a new association; so Schmeller, *2 Kor 1,1–7,4*, 373; Furnish, *II Corinthians*, 361; Thrall, *Second Epistle*, 473n2001. On the complex and much discussed questions concerning the origins, affinities, and original location of this text, see Furnish, *II Corinthians*, 375–83; Schmeller, *2 Kor 1,1–7,4*, 378–82 (and the literature listed on 366–67).

104. Klaus Berger, *Das Buch der Jubiläen*, JSHRZ 2/3 (Gütersloh: Gerd Mohn, 1981), 473ng, suggests that an analogy with Jub. 30:15 is "unübersehbar." In Jubilees, Berger comments: "Die Mischehe ist daher als direkte Beflekung der Heiligkeit des Tempels verstanden."

105. On which, see Yarbrough, *Not Like the Gentiles*; Abraham J. Malherbe, *The Letters to the Thessalonians*, AB 32B (New York: Doubleday, 2000), 224–41.

106. See, e.g., Hayes, *Gentile Impurities*, 92–103; Peter Brown, *The Body and Society: Men, Women and Sexual Renunciation in Early Christianity*, 20th anniv. ed., Columbia Classics in Religion (New York: Columbia University Press, 2008), 147: "Marriage with pagans was severely discouraged."

107. William R. Schoedel, "Theological Norms and Social Perspectives in Ignatius of Antioch," in *The Shaping of Christianity in the Second and Third Centuries*, vol. 1 of *Jewish and Christian Self-Definition*, ed. E. P. Sanders (Philadelphia: Fortress, 1980), 50.

For fear we should make an ill use of what he says, "Let her marry whom she wishes," he has added, "only in the Lord," that is, in the name of the Lord, which is, undoubtedly, "to a Christian." . . . To this condition alone does he concede the foregoing of continence. "Only," he says, "in the Lord:" [*sic*] he has added to his law a weight—"*only*." Utter that word with what tone and manner you may, it is weighty: it both bids and advises; both enjoins and exhorts; both asks and threatens. It is a concise, brief sentence; and by its own very brevity, eloquent. . . . For who but could understand that the apostle foresaw many dangers and wounds to faith in marriages of this kind, which he prohibits? and that he took precaution, in the first place, against the defilement of holy flesh in Gentile flesh? (*Ux.* 2.2 [*ANF* 3:45]).[108]

Tertullian is stern in his condemnation of those who act otherwise: "Believers contracting marriages with Gentiles are guilty of fornication, and are to be excluded from all communication with the brotherhood, in accordance with the letter of the apostle" (*Ux.* 2.3 [*ANF* 3:45], citing 1 Cor 5:11).[109] Cyprian quotes 1 Cor 7:39, 1 Cor 6:15–17, and 2 Cor 6:14, along with Tob 4:12 and 2 Kgs 11:4, and appeals to the example of Abraham and the book of Ezra as the basis for the instruction "that marriage is not to be contracted with Gentiles" (*Test.* 3.62 [*ANF* 4:550]).[110]

There is some evidence that this is not an entirely unanimous view, not least the force with which Tertullian and others argue their case for prohibiting mixed marriage.[111] Origen, in an extended and somewhat opaque set of comments (extant only in fragments), appears to argue that Paul's instruction is open to various interpretations in terms of marriage decisions and does not in any case carry the same authority as the Lord's own commands: "It is better to obey laws from the Lord than to obey laws of Paul the apostle" (καὶ καλόν ἐστιν ἀκούειν νόμων ἀπὸ κυρίου ἢ ἀκούειν νόμων Παύλου τοῦ ἀποστόλου) (*Fr. 1 Cor.* 35.70–71).[112] On the one hand,

---

108. For Tertullian's perspective on marriage, see Hayes, *Gentile Impurities*, 98–99.

109. See further *Ux.* 2.2–5. Other places where Tertullian specifically appeals to 1 Cor 7:39 include *Cor.* 13 [*ANF* 3:101]; *Marc.* 5.7 [*ANF* 3:443]; *Mon.* 7, 11 [*ANF* 4:64, 68].

110. See also Cohen, "Permission to Prohibition," 260–61.

111. See esp. Johnson Hodge, "Mixed Marriage"; Cohen, "Permission to Prohibition."

112. The Greek text of the fragments was first published in four parts by Claude Jenkins, "Origen on I Corinthians," *JTS* 9–10 (1908): (I) 9:231–47, (II) 9:353–72, (III) 9:500–514, (IV) 10:29–51 (now available via the *TLG*). The line numbers above refer to the numbering in Jenkins's publication of the Greek. For the Greek text and English translation of the relevant fragments (35–36), quoted above, see Cohen, "Permission to Prohibition," 287–91. I

Origen seems to query Paul's assumption (1 Cor 7:14) that the holiness of the believing spouse sanctifies their unbelieving partner: the danger is that the opposite might take place (*Fr. 1 Cor.* 36). He appears to agree with Paul, therefore, that not marrying at all is the best course of action and that, if one does marry, then marrying a Christian is advised. But it seems possible, in Origen's view, that Paul has also left room for the possibility that a Christian has the freedom to marry whom they wish: "He [Paul] has permitted us to think otherwise" (ἀφῆκεν ἡμῖν τὸ ἄλλο νοεῖν) (36.20). Thus Shaye Cohen suggests that Origen sees Paul presenting three possibilities: "not to marry at all (most preferred option); to marry in the Lord (that is, to a fellow Christian); to marry a non-Christian, in the uncertain hope that the Christian" will win over the non-Christian partner.[113] The obscurity of Origen's comments, however, hardly justifies Cohen's positive conclusion "that Origen understands 1 Cor 7:12–14 as Pauline permission to enter into a mixed marriage";[114] the thrust of Origen's point seems mainly to be that Paul is too optimistic in his view that the believer sanctifies the unbeliever. Given the danger that marriage will operate the other way around and pollute the believer, it is better not to marry at all, and certainly better to avoid marrying an unbeliever. The instruction in 1 Cor 7:39, then, brief though it is, is best understood as recommending that a widow "remain as she is"— reiterating a theme of the whole of 1 Cor 7—but allowing remarriage only to a fellow Christian.[115]

---

am also grateful to Bradley Arnold for sharing his own English translation of relevant parts of the text.

113. Cohen, "Permission to Prohibition," 290n69. The footnote is incomplete in the published version of the chapter, breaking off where my quotation ends, but see 276 for Cohen's interpretation on this point.

114. Cohen, "Permission to Prohibition," 277.

115. Cohen, "Permission to Prohibition," exaggerates the ambiguities of Paul's instructions greatly when he argues that "not a single verse in the Pauline correspondence explicitly and unambiguously prohibits a believer from marrying a non-believer" (284). He goes on to conclude "that Paul did not prohibit mixed marriage, and that such a prohibition was the work of formative Christianity only in the second century C.E." (285), and he even turns the possible ambiguity of Paul's comments into a positive claim: "Paul is the only Jew of antiquity who argued on principle against a prohibition of mixed marriage" (285n60). However we interpret his remarks, Paul does not argue *against* such a prohibition, and Cohen makes an unlikely case for Pauline exceptionalism, making Paul uniquely different from both the Judaism that preceded him and the early Christians who followed him. The critique of the criterion of "double dissimilarity" used in the quest for the historical Jesus and the argument for an alternative criterion of plausibility is relevant here. See Gerd Theissen and Dagmar Winter, *The Quest for the Plausible Jesus: The Question of Criteria* (Louisville:

New Testament writers show little concern with formulating rules about whom one may marry. In part this is due to a sense of eschatological expectation: such concerns are irrelevant for a community that does not expect to last for more than a generation (cf. 1 Cor 7:29–31; 15:51–52; 1 Thess 4:13–18). It is also due in part to a not-unrelated tendency to favor asceticism and sexual continence.[116] There were of course other Jewish groups with similarly ascetic convictions.[117] Yet insofar as the New Testament gives any hints about such marriage rules, they point in the direction of favoring endogamy, partnerships between fellow Christians rather than between what is holy and what is deemed unholy. The only exception to this, given the strong opposition to divorce, is in the case of already existing marriages, which may—indeed should, if possible—continue. Although brief and concise, the clearest remark specifically about entering into a marriage specifies that this should be ἐν κυρίῳ, that is, a partnership within the bounds of those in Christ, members of the Christian community. Early Christian teaching broadly follows this lead, though with some diversity of practice and interpretation of Paul. The general rule was that, if a Christian married at all, they should marry another Christian.

4.4 The Holiness of Children and the Passing on of Christian Identity

The primary purpose of marriage, across many cultures and time-periods, has been seen as procreation—the bearing of children. Paul is rather unusual in depicting marriage as a guard against sexual immorality rather than a means to ensure reproduction (1 Cor 7:2–5).[118] Indeed, he strikingly shows no interest in the production and rearing of children, no doubt due to both his imminent eschatological expectations and his preference for celibacy. But in ancient Judaism, children are seen as a blessing, and childlessness, correspondingly, as a curse (often presented, with patriarchal prejudice, as due to the woman's barrenness). The Mishnah emphasizes the duty to procreate, placing particular responsibility upon the man in this regard (m.

Westminster John Knox, 2002), 212 (on the wider applicability of this criterion, note the comment on p. xviii).

116. See esp. Brown, *Body and Society*.

117. See Stephen C. Barton, *Discipleship and Family Ties in Mark and Matthew*, SNTSMS 80 (Cambridge: Cambridge University Press, 1994), 23–47.

118. See Brown, *Body and Society*, 55; Roy B. Ward, "Musonius and Paul on Marriage," *NTS* 36 (1990): 284–87; Yarbrough, *Not Like the Gentiles*.

Yebam. 6.6).[119] In the following chapter, we shall consider both Jewish and early Christian depictions of the socialization of children, the responsibilities of parents and other teachers, and how far the socializing of children into a particular way of life—and their subsequent adherence to that way of life—is or is not seen as constitutive of their identity. Our concern here is with the more specific question of whether Jewishness and Christianness, as identities, are in any sense seen as passed on through the family, from parents to children.

In the case of Judaism, it is at least clear that the children of marriages between Jews are themselves regarded as Jews (though to what extent the continuation of that status depends on following the Jewish way of life is a question we shall consider in the next chapter and in ch. 8).[120] Matters become somewhat less clear cut when one or the other parent is not Jewish. As Shaye Cohen has shown, in what he calls "the biblical period" a patrilineal principle is dominant, in keeping with the presuppositions of a patriarchal society: a woman who marries enters the household of her husband, becoming part of his property.[121] In such cases, Cohen remarks, "the act of marriage was functionally equivalent to the later idea of 'conversion'" and "it never occurred to anyone to argue that her children were not Israelites."[122] In the case of Israelite women marrying foreign men, Cohen suggests—appealing to texts such as Lev 24:10; 1 Kgs 7:13–14; 1 Chr 2:17; 2:34–36; 2 Chr 2:12–14, but noting the lack of attention given to this issue—that the children of such unions "were judged matrilineally," that is, as Israelite, "only if the foreign husband joined the wife's domicile or clan."[123] In other words, it seems that the location of the child's upbringing—the household or clan in which it is reared—was in practice decisive for judgments about its identity. Indications of the mother's influence on the child's (perceived) identity are also given, as Chapman notes, in references to the crucial role of breastfeeding in defining identity (see pp. 104–5).[124]

Developing views of the identity of children also depend, of course, on underlying views of marriage, which we have briefly explored above.

---

119. See Safrai, "Home and Family," 750.

120. See also Daniel H. Weiss, "Born into Covenantal Salvation? Baptism and Birth in Early Christianity and Classical Rabbinic Judaism," *JSQ* 24 (2017): 324–27.

121. On the prominence of such "property" principles, see also L. William Countryman, *Dirt, Greed, and Sex: Sexual Ethics in the New Testament and Their Implications for Today*, rev. ed. (Minneapolis: Fortress, 2007), 144–63.

122. Cohen, *Beginnings*, 265; cf. Daube, *Ancient Jewish Law*, 3–7.

123. Cohen, *Beginnings*, 266.

124. Chapman, "Breast Milk," 41.

From the perspective of the "holy seed" ideology evident in Ezra, it is understandable that children of mixed marriages may themselves be regarded as unholy—hence the declaration of the men of Israel in Ezra 10:3 that they will "send away all these [foreign] wives and their children."[125] Even here, however, it is notable that Ezra's exhortation in 10:11 does not require the expulsion of children, only of wives, whatever may have been the response.[126] Also, "the sons of the priests who had married foreign women"—that is, descendants from mixed marriages—were not expelled, but instead "pledged to put away their wives" and to make a guilt offering (Ezra 10:18–19). The ideology at work here seems as much patriarchal as it is concerned for ethnic or racial "purity." Nonetheless, this text was, as we have seen, influential upon a view that sought to maintain, however impossibly or inconsistently, what Hayes calls a "genealogical purity" by avoiding any "mixing" of the holy seed. From the perspective of a different ideology of purity and consequently of intermarriage, however, conversion on the part of the non-Jewish partner— often the woman, but not always—renders the marriage licit and the children legitimately Jewish.[127] The description "bastard" (νόθος/ממזר) is sometimes applied to children of unequal unions, specifically where the gentile partner has not converted, as in Philo, *Mos.* 2.193, discussing Lev 24:10–16.[128] Here,

---

125. As Cohen, *Beginnings*, 267–68, argues, the reason for this focus on the men is unlikely to be because the matrilineal principle was already established, such that the children of Israelite women, even with foreign husbands, were clearly regarded as Israelites. Much more likely is that the text represents the general (patriarchal) focus on the male-led household.

126. Ezra 10:44 concludes a list of those who had "married foreign women," some of whom had borne children. Some modern English translations draw on the Greek text of 1 Esd 9:36 here to clarify this obscure verse (e.g., NRSV: "They sent them away with their children"); others do not (e.g., ESV: "Some of the women had even borne children"). It is at least clear that 1 Esdras envisages the sending away of both wives and children as part of the response to Ezra's exhortation.

127. Cf. Cohen, *Beginnings*, 272. It is significant, for example, that what is notable for Josephus is not that Herod's son Alexander's offspring were born of a mixed marriage but that they "abandoned the observance of the ways of the Jewish land" (*A.J.* 18.139–41). See further Mireille Hadas-Lebel, "Les mariages mixtes dans la famille d'Hérode et la Halakha prétalmudique sur la patrilinéarité," *Revue des Etudes Juives* 152 (1993): 397–404, who confirms that the patrilineal principle continued into the first century CE (403). Note also Cohen's wider argument that the specifically matrilineal principle develops only in the Mishnaic period (*Beginnings*, 263–307). On the late and ambivalent emergence of the notion that the child of a Jewish woman was Jewish, see Hadas-Lebel, "Mariages mixtes," 403; Daube, *Ancient Jewish Law*, 24–32.

128. See further Daube, *Ancient Jewish Law*, 23; Cohen, *Beginnings*, 271–73.

though, it seems not only to be parentage that determines the label: Philo specifically comments that the νόθος—the child of an Egyptian father and a Jewish mother—had "set at naught the ancestral customs of his mother and turned aside . . . to the impiety of Egypt" (Colson, LCL; cf. *Mos.* 1.147).

If the New Testament shows little interest in rules about marriage, except in terms of the prohibition of divorce and remarriage, then it shows an equal lack of interest in instruction concerning the bearing and rearing of children. Again, eschatological expectation and ascetic inclinations may help to explain this neglect. As we shall see in the next chapter, there is some relevant material concerning the socialization of children within the (Christian) family and household, but for now our interest is in the question about the identity bequeathed to children by their parents.

With regard to this specific question, there is one New Testament text of particular interest—a text already mentioned in the discussion of marriage rules above. When Paul is giving reasons why a "mixed" marriage between believer and unbeliever may (indeed should, ideally) continue, he explains: "The unbelieving husband is made holy [ἡγίασται] by [or 'in,' ἐν] his wife, and the unbelieving wife is made holy [ἡγίασται] by [or 'in,' ἐν] her husband. Otherwise your children would be unclean, but as it is, they are holy" (1 Cor 7:14). Paul's main focus of concern, having turned so unusually and momentarily to children, quickly returns to the question of divorce and separation: despite this conveying of holiness to the spouse and children, the Christian spouse should allow the unbelieving spouse to leave, if they wish, and is "not bound" in such cases (7:15). But the possible salvation of the unbelieving spouse is another good reason to maintain the marriage, if possible (7:16).

Many aspects of this text are enigmatic and somewhat opaque, and commentators have struggled to make sense of Paul's declaration that the unbelieving spouse and the children are "holy." Gerhard Delling's comment is indicative: "So many minds, so many meanings" (*so viele Köpfe, so viele Sinne*).[129]

In an early attempt to break through the mass of "bewildering" and "unsatisfactory" interpretations of this verse, Jerome Murphy-O'Connor distinguishes between πίστις and ἁγιασμός in Paul, arguing that holiness is

---

129. Gerhard Delling, *Studien zum Neuen Testament und zum hellenistischen Judentum: Gesammelte Aufsätze 1950–1968* (Göttingen: Vandenhoeck & Ruprecht, 1970), 257. However, Delling's suggestion that the "children" in view are of adult age seems unlikely; see the comment of Andreas Lindemann, ". . . ἐκτρέφετε αὐτὰ ἐν παιδείᾳ καὶ νουθεσίᾳ κυρίου (Eph 6.4): Kinder in der Welt des frühen Christentums," *NTS* 56 (2010): 172.

an essentially ethical quality, which "is not given once and for all" but "demands a continuous effort of fidelity which involves both truth and behavior."[130] The unbelieving partner is thus ἅγιος and ἄπιστος at the same time; they can be described as holy because they exhibit "a pattern of behaviour that is analogous to the conduct expected of the *hagioi*," specifically by consenting to continue the marriage and thus avoid divorce.[131] When it comes to the children's holiness, this status is again, Murphy-O'Connor claims, based on their behavior: "Paul's basis here is the simple fact of experience that children assimilate the behaviour pattern of their parents."[132] This ethical and behavioral view of what constitutes holiness here has been followed by Anthony Thiselton, who comments: "If the spouse falls under the influence of the Christian partner's faith, lifestyle, prayer, and living out of the gospel, how much more shall not [*sic*] the children? . . . Even if only one parent is Christian the children will be marked by an element of shaping and 'difference' from the wholly pagan environment."[133]

In terms of how the term ἅγιος functions in Paul, this moralizing interpretation is unsatisfactory, as we shall see below. But a more immediate problem can be seen in Murphy-O'Connor's argumentation: if the (ethical) holiness of the unbelieving spouse is specifically predicated on their maintaining a marriage and avoiding divorce, then this is clearly not a pattern of behavior that can (yet) be copied by the children. More broadly, only children who have reached a certain age could plausibly be reckoned to "assimilate the behavior" of their parents in any ethically substantive way; yet Paul gives no indication that his conviction applies only to older children rather than to babies or infants. Many of the attempted explanations of this phrase are too much shaped by a desire to avoid finding in Paul a theology at odds with later church conviction, and specifically a status for children that, in John O'Neill's words, "seems to depend neither on belief nor on the sacrament of baptism."[134]

---

130. Jerome Murphy-O'Connor, "Works without Faith in I Cor., VII, 14," *RB* 84 (1977): 349, 355; repr. in Jerome Murphy-O'Connor, *Keys to First Corinthians: Revisiting the Major Issues* (Oxford: Oxford University Press, 2009), 43–53, with a postscript on 53–57.

131. Murphy-O'Connor, "Works," 356.

132. Murphy-O'Connor, "Works," 361.

133. Thiselton, *First Epistle*, 530.

134. John Cochrane O'Neill, "1 Corinthians 7,14 and Infant Baptism," in *L'Apôtre Paul: Personnalité, Style et Conception du Ministère*, ed. A. Vanhoye, BETL 73 (Leuven: Peeters, 1986), 357. E.g., Craig Keener, "Interethnic Marriages in the New Testament (Matt 1:3–6; Acts 7:29; 16:1–3; cf. 1 Cor 7:14)," *Criswell Theological Review* 6 (2009): 43, asserts that

A rather different perspective on the problem is presented by Yonder Moynihan Gillihan, who proposes a "halakhic interpretation" of this verse based on comparisons with Jewish *halakhot*, particularly insofar as these refer to the act of betrothal as one of "sanctification" that indicates that the marriage is licit.[135] By insisting that the believing partner "sanctifies" the unbelieving spouse, Paul is effectively ruling "that mixed marriages are, in fact, licit."[136] As such, the children of the union are also holy—"that is, eligible to participate in the religious life of the community."[137] This is an illuminating discussion, particularly in relating the issues of holiness to those of legitimate membership of, and participation in, the community. Gillihan does note a key difference, however: the Jewish parallels he cites deal with betrothal and thus with the issue of marriages that may legitimately be undertaken. Paul, by contrast, as Gillihan notes, is dealing with pre-existing marriages and how they (and their offspring) should be regarded.[138]

Margaret MacDonald and Leif Vaage criticize Gillihan for implying "a vision of the house church that too closely resembles the later religious congregations of both Jews and Christians, with firmly established social boundaries rather than the often messy life of the first-century Pauline com-

---

"Paul . . . is not claiming that the children are saved because they have Christian parents, nor that infant baptism saves"). O'Neill's own solution is equally implausible and infused with theological assumptions: the perfect ἡγίασται, he suggests, refers to a future possibility for the unbelieving spouse, which is more easy for God than sanctifying children, who are not yet capable of believing and must be reckoned to be "unclean" naturally but are sanctified precisely through infant baptism. It is interesting to see John Calvin grapple with the difficulties, particularly the tension between the conviction that all humans are born unregenerate and under the sentence of condemnation and that the children of believers seem to have a special privilege in this regard. See John Calvin, *The First Epistle of Paul the Apostle to the Corinthians*, Calvin's Commentaries (Edinburgh: Oliver & Boyd, 1960), 149–50.

135. Yonder Moynihan Gillihan, "Jewish Laws on Illicit Marriage, the Defilement of Offspring, and the Holiness of the Temple: A New Halakic Interpretation of 1 Corinthians 7:14," *JBL* 121 (2002): 717–18.

136. Gillihan, "Jewish Laws," 716; cf. 727–28, 738.

137. Gillihan, "Jewish Laws," 735.

138. Gillihan, "Jewish Laws," 729. Another difference is that the active sanctifying in the Mishnaic *halakhot* is done by the man, and the women is "sanctified" for "licit marital union" (717). Thus, Gillihan argues, "Paul's usage puts the believer, male or female, in the more powerful 'male' role of sanctifying/causing licit betrothal, while the unbeliever implicitly becomes 'feminized'" (718). This kind of allocation of (potential) power to both male and female parties would fit with Paul's style elsewhere in this passage, most notably in 7:4 (also 7:10–16).

munities."[139] Their sense of this messiness, and specifically of the ambiguous location of children within it, is based on a rather different construal of the grammar and translation of 7:14c. In an earlier article, on which the collaborative essay depends for this point, Vaage challenges the established interpretation of the first clause as a contrary-to-fact condition and argues instead, given the indicative mood of the verb ἐστιν (repeated in the second clause), that both clauses depict true conditions. He thus proposes as the "simplest translation": "Since therefore your children are unclean, but now they are holy."[140] Paul thus "flatly contradicts himself—or, better stated, he speaks paradoxically."[141] The status of the children, like that of members of the Pauline communities generally, is seen as a kind of "labile" or "tensive social identity":[142] their holiness is fragile. If the marriage were to dissolve, then the children would "logically" revert to the status of "unclean."[143]

This last point is an interesting one, though it is not one on which Paul gives any ground for coming to a clear judgment. The question of what would happen to the status of the children if the marriage were to end—Would it continue to be determined by the Christian parent or not?—is simply not considered. But the broader arguments about the translation of the phrase are problematic and unconvincing. One of the conditions is clearly hypothetical (and contrary-to-fact), as in Heb 9:26 and 1 Cor 7:10–11 (where ἐπεί . . . νῦν/νυνὶ δέ constructions also appear), despite Vaage's arguments to the contrary.[144] If the unbelieving partner were not sanctified by their

139. Margaret Y. MacDonald and Leif E. Vaage, "Unclean but Holy Children: Paul's Everyday Quandary in 1 Corinthians 7:14c," *CBQ* 73 (2011): 526–46.

140. Leif E. Vaage, "The Translation of 1 Cor 7:14C and the Labile Social Body of the Pauline Church," *RB* 116 (2009): 564; cf. 567. Vaage's argument is also accepted by Murphy-O'Connor, *Keys to First Corinthians*, 57: "Corinthian children . . . were both 'unclean' and 'holy' *at the same time*" (italics original).

141. Vaage, "Translation of 1 Cor 7:14C," 568.

142. Vaage, "Translation of 1 Cor 7:14C," 570–71.

143. Vaage, "Translation of 1 Cor 7:14C," 569.

144. See Vaage, "Translation of 1 Cor 7:14C," 564–65. Hebrews 9:26 describes two scenarios, each of which would be true if another condition were to be the case: if Christ were offering a sacrifice repeatedly, he would (truly) then have to suffer many times. But since the former is not true, neither is the latter. Christ offers himself once, so he suffers once. Vaage's suggestion that 1 Cor 5:10 "is a straightforward description of the early Christian project as he [Paul] understood it" (565)—that is, that Paul *does* mean that Christians should come out of the world—runs completely counter to the sense of the passage. The broader context is the threat to the community's purity posed not by immoral unbelievers but by a "so-called brother" who is guilty of sexual immorality (5:1–3, 11). Paul does not mean them to avoid all sexually immoral people but sexually immoral people within the

spouse, the children would be unclean. But since this is not the case, they are holy. It is fallacious to assume that verbs in the indicative mood must reflect factual conditions and cannot be used of hypothetical or contrary-to-fact statements; Daniel Wallace better summarizes the mood's use for what is "assumed true for the sake of argument."[145]

The various elements of the phrase in 7:14c—the (standard) meaning of ἐπεί as "otherwise,"[146] the strong contrast conveyed by ἐπεὶ ἄρα and νῦν δέ, and the two identical verbs (ἐστιν . . . ἐστιν)—are therefore best conveyed in the standard translation: "Otherwise your children would be unclean, but as it is, they are holy" (ESV, NRSV, NIV, etc.).[147]

What is clear and emphatic in Paul's phrasing, then, is that in their present state, the children are holy. Indeed, underlying his conviction regarding the sanctification of the unbelieving partner is a prior and more fundamental conviction about the holiness of the children of such a marriage. This serves, indeed, as supporting evidence for the holiness of the unbelieving partner.[148] It is, Larry Yarbrough comments, "the presupposition of Paul's argument."[149] Thus, interestingly, it seems also to be something Paul can take as a basis for his reasoning, implying that it would be assumed by his audience.[150]

Christian community. Here then, in Paul's only other ἐπεὶ ἄρα . . . νῦν δέ construction, the indicative verb, quite unproblematically, refers to a hypothetical conclusion that would follow (but does not) if some logically prior condition were true (which it is not).

145. See further Daniel B. Wallace, *Greek Grammar beyond the Basics: An Exegetical Syntax of the New Testament* (Grand Rapids: Zondervan, 1996), 442–61, 689–94; Stanley E. Porter, *Idioms of the Greek New Testament*, 2nd ed. (Sheffield: Sheffield Academic Press, 1994), 50–52. The use of the indicative for what is "assumed true for the sake of argument" (Wallace, *Greek Grammar*, 692), even when the assumption is, from the speaker's point of view, false, is well illustrated by Matt 12:27–28 (691, 693), or, in a construction with ἐπεί, Rom 11:6.

146. See BDF §456.3: "for otherwise." This is its most common sense in Paul: leaving aside 1 Cor 5:10 and 7:14, see Rom 3:6; 11:6; 11:22; 1 Cor 14:16; 15:29. The meaning "since" is required in a few instances: 1 Cor 14:12; 2 Cor 11:18; 13:3.

147. The hypothetical nature of the first clause could even be indicated with indicative verbs, as in Hayes's rendering: "For otherwise your children are unclean, but now they are holy" (Hayes, *Gentile Impurities*, 94).

148. Cf. also Gillihan, "Jewish Laws," 714–15: "As evidence that this principle [that the unbelieving spouse is sanctified by the believing spouse] is true Paul points to the fact that the children are holy, not impure." Indeed, Paul may be presuming a Jewish perspective on the way in which children are born into the covenantal community: see Weiss, "Born into Covenantal Salvation?"

149. Yarbrough, *Not Like the Gentiles*, 111.

150. So, similarly, Lindemann, "Kinder," 172.

What does it mean to designate these children as "holy"? As is well known, ἅγιος is one of the most common Pauline designations for members of the assemblies, frequently used in the opening epistolary greetings (e.g., Rom 1:7; 1 Cor 1:2; 2 Cor 1:1; Phil 1:1).[151] As 1 Cor 6:1–2 makes clear, it draws the boundary between "in" and "out," or between church and world.[152] Ἅγιος functions as a designation of identity, and specifically in relation to this boundary issue: when the circle is drawn to determine in and out, those who are ἅγιος are within the community; they share the identity of insider. There may be some significance in the difference between Paul's description of the unbelieving spouse and that of the children:[153] the former is "made holy" by (or even "in," ἐν) the believer, despite remaining ἄπιστος, such that the union is licit (not immoral), as are its offspring. Only the children are emphatically described as ἅγιος.

Despite his eschatologically motivated preference for singleness and his lack of interest in what was often seen as the key purpose of marriage—to bear children—by setting down the presumption that the children of Christians are holy, Paul is in effect establishing a principle of identity and heredity: children with at least one Christian parent already belong within the Christian community. Lightfoot puts this clearly and concisely: "Plainly the children of mixed marriages were regarded as in some sense Christian children. We cannot say more or less than this."[154] This passage has understandably been a crux for the discussion of infant baptism, despite the fact that it is silent on the issue. Lightfoot again notes wisely that the passage "enunciates the principle which leads to infant baptism, viz., that the child of Christian parents shall be treated as a Christian."[155] Christian identity can be conveyed by either parent, since, even in situations of mixed marriage, their holiness is the dominant characteristic. As Daniel Weiss has recently suggested, Paul

151. On this self-designation, which is much more frequent in Paul than elsewhere in the NT, see Trebilco, *Self-Designations*, 122–63.

152. See Horrell, *Solidarity*, 147–82; Trebilco, *Self-Designations*, 135: "Οἱ ἅγιοι functions to establish boundaries *around* the Christian community."

153. Pace Fee, *1 Corinthians*, 333, who seems more concerned than Paul to insist that the children's status can only be derived from and dependent on their ongoing link to the (adult) "believer": "Through their relationship with the believer, who maintains the marriage and thus keeps intact the relationship with the children, they too can be understood to be 'holy' *in the same way as the unbelieving spouse*" (my emphasis). It is not hard to see that theological convictions shape the exegesis at this point.

154. Lightfoot, *Notes*, 226. Cf. Barrett, *1 Corinthians*, 165: "The children are within the covenant; this could not be so if the marriage itself were unclean."

155. Lightfoot, *Notes*, 226.

(and other early Christians) may here be assuming and continuing a Jewish perspective: "Children born to those already inside are treated as inherently already inside."[156] This does not, of course, rule out the possibility that children may reject this affiliation and apostasize (something also possible for Jews: see ch. 8), but it does indicate that the default position, the starting point for their enculturation, is their sharing in the Christian identity of their parent(s).

As products of a movement growing primarily through conversion, it is understandable that earliest Christian texts do not give much attention to questions of family heritage and inherited identity. Moreover, decisions to convert not infrequently led to the disruption of established household and family structures (see, e.g., Mark 3:31–35; Luke 14:26; 1 Cor 7:12–16; 1 Pet 3:1–7).[157] Yet we find, as we shall see in the next chapter, considerable evidence that the early Christians placed weight on the importance of socializing children into the Christian tradition in the context of family and household. We also find indications, as the first generation gives way to the second and third, that Christianness might pass through the generations (cf. 2 Tim 1:5). Later, this conviction becomes expressed in the custom of infant baptism, the most obvious sacramental institution for passing Christian identity on from parents to children. First Corinthians 7:14 is only a brief and passing reference to the identity of children, but insofar as it reveals instincts from the first generation—Paul's instincts, but ones he apparently

---

156. Weiss, "Born into Covenantal Salvation?," 324. On 1 Cor 7:14, see 334–35, where Weiss's proposals cohere closely with those presented here. Weiss also comments on Tertullian's famous comment that "Christians are made, not born" (*Apol.* 18.4 [LCL]), interpreting this as indicating that "the task of becoming more and more Christ-oriented was a life-long effort, not something completed at birth" (335). The phrase would not therefore imply that Tertullian "viewed children born to Christian parents as standing in need of baptism or conversion" (336). However, the apologetic context is probably crucial to understanding this phrase: Tertullian is noting that Christians, too, once laughed at the ideas they now embrace, since they—as a collective group, as it were—emerged from among "you" (*de vestris sumus*), i.e., his "pagan" addressees. The comment thus relates to the relationship of Christianity to paganism rather than the identity of individual Christians born to Christian parents, since not every Christian individually—and especially not those born into Christian families—would previously have regarded Christian convictions as ridiculous.

157. See further John M. G. Barclay, "The Family as the Bearer of Religion in Judaism and Early Christianity," in *Constructing Early Christian Families: Family as Social Reality and Metaphor*, ed. Halvor Moxnes (London: Routledge, 1997), 73–75; Barton, *Discipleship*; Stephen C. Barton, "The Relativisation of Family Ties in the Jewish and Graeco-Roman Traditions," in Moxnes, *Constructing Early Christian Families*, 81–100.

could assume would be shared—it is a significant glimpse into ideas about the identity of children in relation to that of their parents. In terms of community membership, they were deemed to belong by virtue of being born to one or more parents who belonged.

4.5 Conclusions

In this chapter, we looked first at some of the ways in which both Jews and early Christians appealed to notions of ancestry and descent in developing and sustaining their group identity. It is clear that the earliest Christian writers made various kinds of use of such genealogical claims. Prominent among them is Paul's interpretation of the promise to Abraham's seed such that all who are in Christ—who is the (individual) "seed of Abraham"—themselves become Abraham's descendants. Another significant motif, developed by the author of 1 Peter, is the theme of divine parenting, in which Christians find their common identity in their begetting and nurturing by God, their father. These claims to shared ancestry and common descent form the basis for a sense of shared kinship, something which we also find as a widespread theme in early Christian literature. Just as the people of Israel regarded (and addressed) one another as brothers and sisters, so the early Christians frequently used this self-designation, such that the author of 1 Peter could initiate a description of the movement as simply "the community of brothers and sisters" or (more concisely, but in gender-exclusive language) "the brotherhood" (ἡ ἀδελφότης).

Naturally, Jewish claims to shared descent and common kinship can appeal to the antiquity of the people (as Josephus does) in ways that the early Christians cannot insofar as they come to be distinguished from Judaism as some kind of *novum*. But this does not mean that claims to kinship among Christians should be seen as fictive in a way that Jewish claims are not. Perhaps it would be better to see them as *differently* fictive. Both kinds of claim, their differences notwithstanding, are fictive insofar as they invoke a sense of close familial kinship for groups much wider than immediate blood-siblings, and which in reality contain a wide range of members, some of whom have joined from other people-groups, with or without the approval of the authors of our texts (e.g., Ezra 10:10–19).

It is also significant to consider how these discursive appeals to ancestry, descent, and shared kinship are concretized in the social practices that are crucial for sustaining such a sense of shared group identity—namely those concerning marriage and the bearing of children. The custom of endogamy—common, of course, to many ethnoreligious groups in the past and present—was prominent among Jews in antiquity, though understood in various ways. While some opposed any "mixing" of the holy seed of Israel, many apparently accepted the idea of marriage to a gentile if the gentile converted to Israel's way of life. The intersections between "ethnic" and "religious" identity here become apparent.

The earliest Christian literature, with its imminent eschatological expectation and tendency to favor asceticism, shows little interest in the choice of marriage partners, but what little evidence there is (Paul's advice to widows in 1 Cor 7:39 and his wider views on union between holy and unholy bodies) also indicates that endogamy—that is, in Paul's terms, marriage (only) ἐν κυρίῳ—was the norm. Indeed, early Christian teaching largely followed Paul's lead in this respect, often promoting celibacy and, for those who wished to marry, permitting only marriage to a fellow Christian.

Likewise, the earliest Christian texts give scant attention to the identity of children or to the priority to reproduce, generally the main rationale for marriage. Again, eschatological and ascetic convictions influence the focus of priorities. But the tantalizing indication we find in 1 Cor 7:14 suggests a conviction—shared by others as well as Paul—that children with at least one Christian parent belong within the Christian community, just as (*mutatis mutandis*) children of Jewish parents belong within the community of Israel. The default position, so to speak, is that they are inside the circle of the ἅγιοι even if they later reject this affiliation.

Those who are "in Christ," according to Paul, not only share Abraham as their distant ancestor and thus become fellow kin but also pass this identity on through family, and specifically to their children. In other words, the broader discourse of sharing ancestry and kinship is here concretized and instantiated in the smaller-scale context of family life. We will turn in the following chapter to further consideration of the evidence concerning the rearing and socialization of children. What is significant to note for now is that even in the first-generation situation, Paul outlines, albeit *in nuce*, two principles and correlative social practices that are crucial to the creation and maintenance of an ethnoreligious form of group identity: restricting marriage to within the group (endogamy) and establishing Christianness as a form of identity that is conveyed to the next generation through the children of Christian parents. These moves might well be seen as evidence of "ethnicization"—that is, both discursive and practical impulses toward "the making of a people" whose identity is understood and reproduced in ancestral and inter-generational terms and reinforced by the practice of endogamy.

There are, then, considerable overlaps and similarities in the various kinds of appeals Jews and early Christians make to ideas of ancestry and descent, in the ways in which they express a sense of shared kinship, in their strong preference for endogamy, and in their sense that children belong within the community. In part, of course, these are entirely unsurprising, since the earliest Christian groups formed within Judaism and, even as they became visible as something distinct, expressed their group identity in ways grounded in the interpretation of Jewish scripture and Jewish modes of self-identification. Yet it is also important to stress that—quite apart from their intricate connections and the internal diversity of both traditions—I do not intend to suggest on the basis of the material surveyed above that Jews and Christians made identical use of discourses of ancestry and kinship or followed exactly the same customs concerning the choice of marriage partners and the identity of children. Nor do I want to be taken to imply that the similarities indicate that Jewish and early Christian identities may equally be regarded as "ethnic" in character. Our earlier discussions (see ch. 3) should already have suggested that such a clear and categorical label might not be adequate or illuminating in either case. But I defer to a final chapter (ch. 9) what the significance of these overlapping discourses and practices might be in relation to such categories. Instead, we turn next to consider a further cluster of ideas and practices that are commonly associated with ethnic identity though also intrinsically connected with what we call religion: those related to a shared way of life, or common culture, and to the socialization of children into that way of life.

CHAPTER 5

A Common Way of Life: Culture, Practice, and the Socialization of Children

In his famous statement about the name "Greek" (see p. 53), Isocrates claims that culture, παίδευσις—a tradition of education in the sense of the German *Bildung*—has become central to determining who shares Greek identity (*Paneg.* 50). Greeks are those who share a common culture, a particular mental disposition (διάνοια). Whether or not this marks a shift in the notion of Greekness, and whatever other factors (family origins, place of birth) might continue to carry significance, it is unsurprising that adherence to a common culture—a particular "way of life"—is prominent in defining what constitutes Greek identity.[1] As we have already seen (p. 72), one of the characteristics of ethnic groups listed by Anthony Smith is "elements of common culture," which, Smith suggests, "normally include religion, customs, or language."[2] Here in particular, the intersections between what we have come to call religion (closely interwoven with "customs") and ethnicity/ race are explicit.

In this chapter, we shall therefore explore the extent to which, and the ways in which, identity as Jew or Christian—both disputed terms for this period, as we have already discussed (pp. 12–16)—was conceived in terms of adherence to a particular way of life.[3] We shall then consider evidence

1. See further Saïd, "Discourse of Identity," 275–99.

2. Hutchinson and Smith, "Introduction," 6–7.

3. An exploration of the idea of following a "way of life" could of course go well beyond the comparison of Jewish and Christian traditions and beyond the particular consideration of "ethnic" and "religious" categories, for example in terms of ancient philosophy as a "way of life," as influentially explored by Pierre Hadot, *Philosophy as a Way of Life: Spiritual Exercises from Socrates to Foucault* (Oxford: Blackwell, 1995). Broader comparison might help illuminate why, in certain contexts, both Judaism and early Christianity can be depicted as philosophies or philosophical schools and would further reinforce the point—explored

concerning the socialization of children into such a way of life and the importance attributed to this. (Questions about "converts," or incomers, and their [re]socialization will occupy our attention in ch. 8.) Finally, we shall discuss the particular practices that express these different ways of life and assess their importance in terms of both the marking and the sustaining of collective identity.

5.1 Adhering to a Way of Life as Definitive for Jewish and Christian Identity

5.1.1 *Way of Life and Jewish Identity*

Central to Judaism from its early biblical formulations onward was a sense of calling to follow a particular way of life, to "walk in the way that the Lord your God has commanded" (Deut 5:33). Indeed, this particular expression—"walking in the way," using הלך/πορεύεσθαι[4]—becomes idiomatic for the pattern of life and conduct to which the people are called or, indeed, for other possible ways of life they are warned against (see, e.g., Exod 18:20; Deut 13:5; Judg 2:22; Prov 2:20; Jer 6:16; 7:23). The opening of Ps 119 specifies this as walking "in the law of the Lord" and, as Exod 18 and Deut 5 show, the context for these exhortations is a call to both religious devotion (to the one God of Israel) and obedience to the law (the code of conduct set down for the people of Israel). Indeed, since the first command of the Decalogue is for exclusive devotion to the God of Israel, the two are inextricably bound together (Exod 20:2–6; Deut 5:7–10).

One of the iconic and enduringly influential periods in which this "way of life" came under particular pressure was during the era of Seleucid rule over Judea, when the Jewish revolt led by Judas Maccabeus and his brothers broke out (c.167 BCE). Although Hellenism had been influencing the region for some time already, the actions of Antiochus IV brought the conflict between Hellenism and the Jewish way of life to a head, at least from the perspective of those whose refusal and resistance are heroized in the books

---

below—that "way of life" cuts across (as well as going beyond) the categories of ethnicity and religion.

4. See the long list of uses of πορεύεσθαι in Edwin Hatch and Henry A. Redpath, *A Concordance to the Septuagint and the Other Greek Versions of the Old Testament (Including the Apocryphal Books)*, 2 vols (Graz, Austria: Akademische Druck, 1954), 1189–94, the large majority of which correspond to הלך in the MT.

of 1, 2 and 4 Maccabees. Under Antiochus's rule, Jews were pressurized to abandon their ancestral customs, particularly the practices of circumcision and avoidance of pork, and to adopt the values and customs of Hellenism (represented by gymnasium education and Greek dress).[5] Some Jews clearly accepted such demands and embraced the new culture (1 Macc 1:11–15) while others resisted, convinced that this entailed abandoning their ancestral covenant and Torah-based way of life (1 Macc 2:20–21). What is particularly significant for our purposes here is to see how this confrontation led to certain developments in the discursive articulation of what it meant to be Jewish.

One significant linguistic innovation that we owe to the author of 2 Maccabees—or, more specifically, to either the author of the original narrative, Jason of Cyrene, or his subsequent epitomist (see 2 Macc 2:23)[6]—is the word Ἰουδαϊσμός (2 Macc 2:21; 8:1; 14:38). It is also in this text that we first encounter the word Ἑλληνισμός (2 Macc 4:13), to which Ἰουδαϊσμός stands in contrast and opposition. The word Ἰουδαϊσμός should not, despite frequent comments to this effect, be taken simply as a newly coined designation for "the whole system of belief and practice of the Jews"[7] as if "Judaism," as just such a system, had now been conceptually articulated. It remains a rarely used word even after this time.[8] Rather, as Mason has shown, Ἰουδαϊσμός represents "a certain kind of *activity* over against a pull in another, foreign direction."[9] Mason continues, "The contest becomes clearer when the author invokes Ἑλληνισμός, which is also not a static system or culture, but an en-

---

5. See 1 Macc 1:13–15; 2 Macc 4:9–12; 6:7–9; 4 Macc 5:1–6:30.

6. On the composite nature of 2 Maccabees and the issue of the relationship of our extant text to the earlier work of Jason, see Robert Doran, *2 Maccabees: A Critical Commentary*, Hermeneia (Minneapolis: Fortress, 2012), 1–14; also, more briefly, Robert Doran, "2 Maccabees," in *The Oxford Bible Commentary*, ed. John Barton and John Muddiman (Oxford: Oxford University Press, 2001), 734–35.

7. William R. Schoedel, *Ignatius of Antioch: A Commentary on the Letters of Ignatius of Antioch*, Hermeneia (Philadelphia: Fortress, 1985), 118. On the frequency of such comments, see Mason, "Jews, Judaeans, Judaizing, Judaism," 465.

8. A point made by Mason, "Jews, Judaeans, Judaizing, Judaism," 465. The argument that the notion of "Judaism"—and, indeed, the category "religion"—is a much later Christian construction, is developed at length by Daniel Boyarin, *Judaism: The Genealogy of a Modern Notion*, Key Words in Jewish Studies 9 (New Brunswick, NJ: Rutgers University Press, 2019). For discussion of Boyarin's book, see Annette Yoshiko Reed and Shaul Magid, eds., "Daniel Boyarin's *Judaism*: A Forum," *Marginalia: Los Angeles Review of Books*, July 5, 2019, https://marginalia.lareviewofbooks.org/daniel-boyarins-judaism-forum/.

9. Mason, "Jews, Judaeans, Judaizing, Judaism," 466. See also Mason's discussion of the verb ἰουδαΐζω/ἰουδαΐζειν (461–64). On the range of possible meanings for this verb, see Cohen, *Beginnings*, 175–97.

ergetic movement away from one's own traditions to embrace foreign ones: a 'Hellen*izing*.'"[10] In 2 Macc 4:10–15, the scenario is one of people being "shifted over" (μεθίστημι) (4:10) to Greek ways—a move depicted as an ἀκμή τις Ἑλληνισμοῦ (4:13)—and consequently abandoning their ancestral ways. The first occurrence of the term Ἰουδαϊσμός, by contrast, is in reference to those who "fought bravely ὑπὲρ τοῦ Ιουδαϊσμοῦ" (2:21; cf. 8:1; 14:38). As Douglas Boin has argued, the terms are therefore deployed in 2 Maccabees to rhetorical effect in an attempt to establish and police boundaries against assimilation—to urge Jews, in effect, to imitate those virtuous and heroic Jews who resisted the pull of Hellenism and instead focused their commitment and practice toward Ἰουδαϊσμός.[11] As such language makes clear, there was evidently considerable diversity in Jewish responses to Hellenism, various levels of assimilation and cultural accommodation: what was acceptable to some was apostasy to others.[12] Even the Maccabean literature, after all, is written (in its extant forms) in Greek, and in some cases (especially 4 Maccabees) shows an especially strong influence of Greek philosophical and ethical ideas. In other words, a high level of acculturation may be evident, even in literature that expresses resistance to that very same cultural influence.[13] As Martin Hengel has famously demonstrated, the encounter with Hellenism shaped Judaism and its Jewish literature both in the diaspora and in Judea.[14] But the clear perception of the authors of this literature is that the Maccabean crisis represents a battle for the survival of the Jews' established and ancestral way of life—a battle to maintain Jewish identity.

Given this context, it is no surprise that the threat of Ἑλληνισμός is depicted in precisely these terms; it is equivalent to ἀλλοφυλισμός (2 Macc 4:13)—that is, adopting the customs and practices of another φυλή, or people-group (NRSV: "the adoption of foreign ways").[15] This is another

10. Mason, "Jews, Judaeans, Judaizing, Judaism," 466.

11. Boin, "Hellenistic 'Judaism,'" 176–80.

12. For a systematic study of the diverse levels of assimilation, acculturation, and accommodation expressed in Jewish literature from the period, see Barclay, *Jews.*

13. For discussion of these categories and issues, see Barclay, *Jews,* 92–98, 192–203, 369–80.

14. See Martin Hengel, *Judaism and Hellenism: Studies in Their Encounter in Palestine During the Early Hellenistic Period,* trans. John Bowden, 2 vols. (London: SCM Press, 1974); see also the briefer treatment in Hengel, *The "Hellenization" of Judaea in the First Century after Christ,* trans. John Bowden (London: SCM; Philadelphia: Trinity Press International, 1989).

15. In 4:13, the word's only other occurrence in the LXX, ἀλλοφυλισμός stands alongside Ἑλληνισμός. T. Muraoka, *A Greek-English Lexicon of the Septuagint* (Leuven: Peeters, 2009), 29, suggests "alien, foreign culture."

-ισμος word that finds its first and only LXX occurrences—indeed, virtually all of its occurrences in Greek literature[16]—in 2 Maccabees (4:13; 6:24), though its cognate, ἀλλόφυλος, appears frequently in the LXX (and elsewhere in Greek literature).

One of the ways in which 2 Maccabees denotes the Jewish way of life is with the word ἀναστροφή, which can refer to a pattern of life or conduct, the orientation of one's behavior.[17] In the LXX, this word appears only three times, two of which are in 2 Maccabees (5:8; 6:23).[18] In one of these instances, it indicates, by implication, the Jewish way of life:[19] in 2 Macc 6:23, Eleazar's refusal to be compelled to eat pork is said to reflect a resolve worthy of his excellent ἀναστροφή from childhood (τῆς ἐκ παιδὸς καλλίστης ἀναστροφῆς). In the following verse, he is said to insist on this, lest any of the young think he has gone over (μεταβεβηκέναι) εἰς ἀλλοφυλισμόν—which the NRSV here translates "to an alien religion,"[20] but which clearly conveys a broader ethno-cultural sense, as noted above.

Another innovative tendency in 2 Maccabees in relation to other Jewish literature in Greek is the move to describe that which is under threat as specifically an *ancestral* way of life, using the adjective πάτριος. In the LXX, this adjective occurs almost exclusively in 2–4 Maccabees, and mostly in 2 and 4 Maccabees.[21] Indeed, the aim of 2 Maccabees as a whole may be

16. According to the *TLG*, it appears elsewhere only in a derivative reference in Origen, *Mart.* 22.13.

17. On the range of meanings, see LSJ, 122. Mason, "Jews, Judaeans, Judaizing, Judaism," 469n21, helpfully observes that it generally indicates some sense of "inclination" or "turning toward" something.

18. It is also rare in Josephus and Philo, with only five occurrences in Josephus (*A.J.* 17.345; 18.173, 359; 19.28, 90), only one of which means "conduct" (19.28; see Karl Heinrich Rengstorf, *A Complete Concordance to Flavius Josephus*, 5 vols. [Leiden: Brill, 1973–83], 1:110), and one in Philo (*Deus* 72), where it means something like "the reverse order." As we shall see below, these authors use other terms to refer to the Jewish way of life.

19. In 2 Macc 5:8, it seems to mean something like "reversal of fortune"; so Muraoka, *Lexicon*, 46. The other reference is in a series of admonitions addressed to the παιδίον in Tob 4:14 (only in GI, the shorter text-form), where it refers to a pattern of conduct: ἴσθι πεπαιδευμένος ἐν πάσῃ ἀναστροφῇ σου ("be disciplined in all your conduct," RSV).

20. Joachim Schaper, NETS, 508, 511, evades the difficulty of translation by rendering it "allophylism," though a footnote glosses this as "alien ways."

21. Along with nineteen instances in 2, 3, and 4 Maccabees (though 4 Macc 16:16 is textually unlikely), Hatch and Redpath, *Concordance*, 1112, list only two other occurrences, one in the prologue to Sirach and the other—textually doubtful—in Isa 8:21 (this is more likely to have read παταχρα). Only two of these instances are in 3 Maccabees. See also Bernd Schröder, *Die "väterlichen Gesetze": Flavius Josephus als Vermittler von Halachah an Griechen*

summarized as an attempt "to move its audience to commit to faithfully following the ancestral traditions of Judaism."[22] In 2 Macc 7:24, Antiochus offers inducements to the youngest brother—the only one of the seven remaining alive—if he will turn from his ancestral ways (μεταθέμενον ἀπὸ τῶν πατρίων). Elsewhere in 2 Maccabees, the adjective is linked with various other terms that denote central facets of this ancestral way of life: οἱ πάτριοι νόμοι (6:1; 7:2, 37); ἡ πάτριος φωνή (7:8, 21, 27; 12:37; 15:29). A comparable expression is found in 11:25, where the *Ioudaioi* are given freedom to live "according to the customs of their ancestors" (κατὰ τὰ ἐπὶ τῶν προγόνων αὐτῶν ἔθη) (NETS). Fourth Maccabees also makes significant use of such terminology: for example, describing Antiochus's "failure" in terms of inability to persuade the Jews ἀλλοφυλῆσαι—which the NRSV here renders "to become pagans"[23]—or to turn away from τῶν πατρίων ἐθῶν (18:5; cf. 4:23; 5:33; 8:7; 9:1, 24, 29; also 3 Macc 1:3; 6:32).

Such terminology for referring to the Jewish way of life (and to the ancestral ways of other peoples, such as τὰ Ἕλλησι πάτρια [Josephus, *A.J.* 18.141]) is also widespread and standard in Josephus.[24] Πάτριος is generally linked with other words, such as νόμος, νόμιμος, and especially ἔθος (τὰ πάτρια ἔθη). This is what the Maccabean heroes sought to defend (*A.J.* 12.280, 303), what conquered peoples were forced to adopt (*A.J.* 13.397; cf. 13.258), what Julius Caesar permitted the Ἰουδαῖοι to follow (*A.J.* 14.194, 213–14), and so on. In *Contra Apionem*, Josephus opines concerning the wise person's duty to be faithful to their own customs and not slander those of others (*C. Ap.* 2.144),[25] underlines the Jews' commitment to their original laws and customs (2.182–83, 237), and also notes that many non-Jews are apparently eager to follow Jewish practices (2.282–83). Indeed, in relation to welcoming non-Jews into the Jewish way of life (on which see ch. 8), Josephus comments: "To all who desire to come and live under the same

---

und Römer, TSAJ 53 (Tübingen: Mohr Siebeck, 1996), 207–16, specifically on οἱ πάτριοι νόμοι. Πάτριος is used in this way (to mean "ancestral customs") in Greek literature more generally—most often in the plural but also in the singular (see LSJ, 1348; on this and related terms as "standard terminology . . . for the laws and customs of ethnic groups," see Mason, "Jews, Judaeans, Judaizing, Judaism," 480; Schröder, *Die "väterlichen Gesetze*," 159–206).

22. Doran, 2 *Maccabees*, 1.

23. Again (cf. n. 20), the NETS evades the difficulty of translation (here by Stephen Westerholm) by rendering this "to become allophyles."

24. See further Schröder, *Die "väterlichen Gesetze*."

25. Though as Barclay, *Against Apion*, 242n521, notes, Josephus himself does not exactly follow his own maxim in this regard.

laws with us, he [our legislator, Moses] gives a gracious welcome, holding that it is not descent alone [οὐ τῷ γένει μόνον] that constitutes relationship [οἰκειότης] but also the deliberate choice of a way of life [ἀλλὰ καὶ τῇ προαιρέσει τοῦ βίου]" (C. Ap. 2.210 [Thackeray, LCL; slightly amended]).[26]

Philo, in his Legatio ad Gaium, for example, talks similarly of the Jews' determination to abide by their ancestral customs (τὰ πάτρια; e.g., Legat. 117, 153, 155, 200, 208), their νόμοι καὶ ἔθη (Legat. 115, 134, 170, 210). Not least, then, when defending the Jewish way of life to outsiders and seeking tolerance for its ongoing practice, Jewish writers described it as a set of ancestral laws and customs comparable to those to which other peoples were rightly committed but which Jews were especially concerned to uphold (a perspective also reflected, e.g., in Acts 6:14; 21:21; 28:17; Gal 1:14). Like Josephus, Philo enunciates the principle that sharing a way of life is crucial to the ethnic bond: "Kinship is not measured only by blood, but by similarity of conduct and pursuit of the same objects" (τὸ συγγενὲς οὐχ αἵματι μετρεῖται μόνον . . . ἀλλὰ πράξεων ὁμοιότητι καὶ θήρᾳ τῶν αὐτῶν) (Virt. 195; cf. Spec. 1.317). Indeed, such a principle is also confirmed by comments on those who abandoned their ancestral way of life and thus forfeited their place among the people (see §8.1.5).

5.1.2 Way of Life and Christian Identity

It is unsurprising that the New Testament writers do not describe their own pattern of life following Christ as an ancestral tradition. The adjective πάτριος does not appear;[27] and ἔθος is used only to denote Jewish customs (Luke 1:9; 2:42; John 19:40; Acts 6:14; 15:1; 21:21; 26:3; 28:17), Roman customs (Acts 16:21; 25:16), or specific "habits" (Luke 22:39; Heb 10:25).[28] Early Christian writers do, however, often make the claim, in various ways, that the movement of those following Christ represents the true fulfillment of Jewish hopes and expectation such that what later comes to be known as Christianity stands in some kind of continuity with—and makes

26. Cf. Barclay, Against Apion, 291: "not only a matter of birth but also of choice in life style." The context for these remarks is that of the welcome offered to proselytes ("those who choose to share our ways," 2.209), on which see ch. 8.

27. Nor does it appear in the entries for the Apostolic Fathers in Henricus Kraft, Clavis Patrum Apostolicorum (Munich: Kösel, 1963).

28. See Schröder, Die "väterlichen Gesetze," 243–58, who examines the comparable phrases in the NT and notes their marginal place (262).

a claim regarding—the ancestral traditions of Judaism.[29] Indeed, as previously noted (§4.1), Paul inserts his gentile converts into a Jewish ancestral lineage not only in calling them Abraham's offspring (Gal 3:29) but also in claiming the Jewish ancestors more generally as theirs (1 Cor 10:1; cf. Rom 11:17–24). But insofar as the Christian movement also distinctively focused its identity on Christ, it is in certain ways also engaged in distinguishing itself—and being distinguished by others—from the Judaism within which it emerged (see below).

There are indeed some indications that following Christ comes to be seen as a way of life comparable with—and specifically juxtaposed as alternative to—other (former or competing) ways of life; "the way" (ἡ ὁδός) is, after all, one of its early designations (see, e.g., Acts 9:2; 22:4; 24:14). In what is probably the earliest New Testament writing, 1 Thessalonians, Paul offers a compact summary of the Thessalonians' response to his message in 1:9–10, which is perhaps best seen as Paul's own summary statement rather than a pre-Pauline missionary tradition:[30] "You turned [ἐπεστρέψατε] to God from idols" (1 Thess 1:9b). As Traugott Holtz notes, this short summary does not merely deal with a specific theme or topic but seeks to depict the "conversion" event as a whole.[31] Commentators frequently note that the verb ἐπιστρέφω is here a technical term for the process of "conversion," as it is elsewhere in the New Testament, especially in Acts (e.g., 9:35; 11:21; 14:15; 15:19): turning to God or to the Lord is an established expression in such contexts.[32] But as with the comparable discussion of turning to or from the Jewish way of life, we might ask to what extent we should understand this "turning" as a purely "religious" matter rather than a broader change in "way

29. Among the most obvious examples are Matthew's so-called fulfillment quotations (e.g., Matt 1:22; 2:15; 8:17), Luke's depiction of the Christian movement as a fulfillment of Israel's hopes (e.g., Luke 1:1; 24:25–27; Acts 2:14–36), and Paul's insistence that the promise made to Abraham's seed is fulfilled in Christ (Gal 3:6–29). On Luke's attempts to present the Christian movement's "ancestral" validity, see, e.g., Philip F. Esler, *Community and Gospel in Luke-Acts: The Social and Political Motivations of Lucan Theology*, SNTSMS 57 (Cambridge: Cambridge University Press, 1987), 215–17.

30. See Morna D. Hooker, "1 Thessalonians 1.9–10: A Nutshell—But What Kind of Nut?," in *Frühes Christentum*, vol. 3 of *Geschichte—Tradition—Reflexion: Festschrift für Martin Hengel zum 70. Geburtstag*, ed. Hermann Lichtenberger (Tübingen: Mohr Siebeck, 1996), 435–48.

31. Traugott Holtz, *Der erste Brief an die Thessalonicher*, EKKNT 13 (Zürich: Benziger; Neukirchen-Vluyn: Neukirchener, 1986), 54: "sie [1 Thess 1:9b–10] will . . . das ganze Bekehrungsgeschehen aussprechen."

32. E.g., Holtz, *Thessalonicher*, 59; Malherbe, *The Letters to the Thessalonians*, 119.

of life" and in affiliation to a people. The same term is also used in the classic tale of "conversion" in Jewish literature, the story of Joseph and Aseneth (11.11: καὶ ἐπιστρέψω πρὸς αὐτόν).[33] In this romantic novel, Aseneth's conversion is bound up with her desire to marry Joseph, and, more broadly, with joining his people: this turn, enacted through repentance and commitment to Joseph's God, makes their marriage legitimate.

Our earlier discussions about the intersections between "ethnicity" and "religion" and about the nature of "religion" in the ancient world may already suggest that "turning to God from idols" may be more than a matter of religious realignment—such commitments can hardly be neatly separated from other aspects of identity and practice. Rather, the "turn" involves a more socially consequential withdrawal from a set of practices that were part of everyday life and constitutive of a sense of identity—encompassing what we might define as religious, political, social, cultural, and ethnic aspects.[34] That this was the case is indicated in the letter by the report that the Thessalonians have suffered hostility from their people (τῶν ἰδίων συμφυλετῶν, 2:14). In other words, this transfer of allegiance has involved some kind of rupture with "their people" comparable to those we find in the accounts of Jewish proselytism presented by Philo and Josephus (see §8.1.4). One could describe them, echoing Philo's language, as having abandoned "their kinsfolk by blood [γενεὰν μὲν τὴν ἀφ᾽ αἵματος] . . . their customs [ἔθη] and the temples [ἱερὰ] and images of their gods [ἀφιδρύματα θεῶν]" (Virt. 102). Or one might well imagine them being accused of such things.

If ἐπιστρέφω, as the language of "turning," depicts a wide-ranging rupture with a previous way of life, then the language of περιπατέω encapsulates the positive way of life to which the Thessalonian converts are now

33. The parallel is noted by many commentators on 1 Thessalonians; e.g., Malherbe, *The Letters to the Thessalonians*, 119; Holtz, *Thessalonicher*, 57–58 ("Der wichtigste Vergleichstext"). Greek text from Christoph Burchard, *Joseph und Aseneth*, Pseudepigrapha Veteris Testamenti Graece 5 (Leiden: Brill, 2003). Cf. Tob 14:6: πάντα τὰ ἔθνη ἐπιστρέψουσιν.

34. Cf. Jeffrey A. D. Weima, *1–2 Thessalonians*, BECNT (Grand Rapids: Baker Academic, 2014), 108–9: "In a society where cultic and social activities were intimately connected, there was nothing simple about turning to God from idols. Such a total renunciation of all pagan deities also meant a complete rejection of a variety of social events closely associated with the worship of these gods. . . . The conversion of the Thessalonian Christians involved a truly radical break with their previous way of life—a break that naturally incurred the resentment and anger of their fellow citizens (2:14)." Of course, it is open to question how far any individual converts did or did not make the kind of break that Paul's rhetoric implies; though the indications that they encountered opposition and hostility (assuming these too reflect some degree of social reality) imply some degree of noticeable disruption.

committed. Echoing in particular the Jewish use of such "walking" language to refer to the conduct of one's life, the "way" one should live, Paul recalls his urging them "to walk worthily of God" (περιπατεῖν . . . ἀξίως τοῦ θεοῦ) (2:12). This same language recurs in the headline of the ethical appeal to a way of life that is pleasing to God (4:1), characterized by sexual purity and intense community-love, distinguished from that of τὰ ἔθνη (4:5) who are ignorant of God. Again, we might compare the way in which Philo urges that incomers to the Jewish community be "loved" (ἀγαπᾶν) such that they become fully part of "a single living being" characterized by "fellowship" (κοινωνία) (*Virt.* 103).

One specific point of interest in regard to following Christ as a way of life is the New Testament uses of ἀναστροφή. As we have already seen, this word occurs only rarely in the LXX but is used in 2 Maccabees to denote the Jewish way of life, particularly insofar as it represents a particular orientation of one's life in the face of perceived threats or alternatives. It appears somewhat more often in the New Testament (thirteen times, confined to the Epistles), where it refers consistently to behavior, conduct or way of life.[35] In the undisputed Pauline letters, it appears only once, significantly, where Paul describes his former "way of life" in Judaism: τὴν ἐμὴν ἀναστροφήν ποτε ἐν τῷ Ἰουδαϊσμῷ (Gal 1:13). As with the uses of Ἰουδαϊσμός in 2 Maccabees, here too (where we find the only uses of Ἰουδαϊσμός in the New Testament, twice in Gal 1:13–14) it is clear that this is not simply a neutral descriptor for "Judaism" but rather a term that captures the active orientation of Paul's former life, his ἀναστροφή. He specifically recalls his zealous persecution of the ἐκκλησία.[36] The noun is also used to denote a "former way of life" (τὴν προτέραν ἀναστροφήν) in Eph 4:22, where this is one way to depict a dramatic transformation, a "putting off of the old self" (τὸν παλαιὸν ἄνθρωπον) and a putting on of the new (τὸν καινὸν ἄνθρωπον) (Eph 4:22–24; cf. Col 3:9–10). Elsewhere it is used to describe the positive pattern of conduct expected of Christians (1 Tim 4:12; Heb 13:7; Jas 3:13; cf. 2 Pet 3:11).

The word ἀναστροφή is a particular favorite of the author of 1 Peter: six of its New Testament uses are in this letter. Here it denotes both a futile past way of life as ἔθνη received from one's ancestors (1:18: ἐκ τῆς ματαίας ὑμῶν ἀναστροφῆς πατροπαραδότου; cf. 4:2–3: τὸ βούλημα τῶν ἐθνῶν; Eph 4:22) and, by contrast, the holy and good way of life that is required for the people

---

35. On the variety of meanings, see LSJ, 122. The NT references are Gal 1:13; Eph 4:22; 1 Tim 4:12; Heb 13:7; Jas 3:13; 1 Pet 1:15, 18; 2:12; 3:1, 2, 16; 2 Pet 2:7; 3:11.

36. See Mason, "Jews, Judaeans, Judaizing, Judaism," 469.

of God (1:15; 2:12; 3:1–2). What Christians are to display in their patterns of conduct is ἡ ἀγαθή ἐν Χριστῷ ἀναστροφή (3:16).

This is a significant designation of the Christian way of life. Just as Paul and 2 Maccabees can speak of Judaism as an ἀναστροφή, from which one might conceivably turn to the customs and way of life of another people (εἰς ἀλλοφυλισμόν), so 1 Peter depicts life in Christ as requiring both an abandonment of an ancestral way of life (1:18) and a commitment to a new pattern of living, an ἀναστροφή ἐν Χριστῷ (3:16). Unsurprisingly, this way of life ἐν Χριστῷ is not—and could hardly be—described as "ancestral," unlike the appeals to τὰ πάτρια ἔθη we have seen in contemporary Jewish writers. But it is equally clear that it cannot be placed in an entirely different *category* than such ancestral ways of life, since it requires—at least for gentile converts—an abandonment of a former (ancestral) way of life in order to participate in a new one; and it is precisely this, according to the author, that is the cause of surprise, resentment, and hostility on the part of their contemporaries (cf. 1 Pet 4:2–4). It is understandable that there was antipathy to such abandoning of ancestral customs and way of life.[37] If "religious" practices are indeed bound up with, even constitutive of, a sense of "ethnic" identity or of belonging to a "people" (see ch. 7)—as many have argued for both the ancient and the modern world (see §3.3)—then the adoption of the way of life required in Christ would seem to affect, cut across, and redefine the "ethnic" identity of those who enter it. We might thus see 1 Peter's stress on the adoption of this ἀναστροφή ἐν Χριστῷ as another contribution to the ethnicizing of Christian identity: the construction of a sense of being a people who share a common set of customs and practices (see ch. 7).

Interestingly, the word ἀναστροφή does not appear in the Apostolic Fathers, so the author of 1 Peter can hardly be claimed to have initiated an influential or widespread specific designation of the Christian way of life. Nonetheless, there are—as there are elsewhere in the New Testament— plenty of indications that belonging to the Christian movement could be conceived as following a particular way of life associated with a particular body of people (cf., e.g., Phil 1:27; Eph 4:1; Col 1:10; 1 Thess 4:1–11; Did. 1–4; Diogn. 1.1 [ἐπιτήδευμα]; Pol. *Phil.* 5.1–2; on the language of peoplehood, see ch. 7).[38] Luke's standard label for believers in Christ is as followers of "the way" (ἡ ὁδός; e.g., Acts 9:2; 22:4; 24:14). Another significant example is

---

37. See Mason, "Jews, Judaeans, Judaizing, Judaism," 462, 497–501.
38. On the Epistle to Diognetus, and specifically its claim that Christians are *not* distinguishable by their lifestyle, see §5.3 below.

the use of the language of citizenship (πολιτεία, κτλ.): Ephesians proclaims that those who were once "aliens and strangers" have now become "fellow citizens [συμπολῖται] with the saints and members of the household of God [οἰκεῖοι τοῦ θεοῦ]" (Eph 2:19, ESV; cf. Phil 3:20).[39] Similarly, 1 Clement describes the Corinthian Christians as having followed "a highly virtuous and honorable way of life [πολιτεία]" (1 Clem. 2.8 [Ehrman LCL]). The verb πολιτεύομαι, used together with the adverb ἀξίως of the Christian way of life in Phil 1:27, becomes something of a standard way to refer to this manner of life, with ἀξίως or similar adverbs such as ὁσίως or καλῶς (1 Clem. 21.1; 44.6; Pol. *Phil.* 5.2; cf. 1 Clem. 3.4; 6.1; 51.2; 54.4).

To describe belonging to the Christian movement as something that entails the adoption of a particular "way of life" does not, however, mean that this pattern of life is wholly distinctive or even easily visible—still less separate from the patterns of life characteristic of other groups and peoples at the time. After all, to take just one example, the New Testament household codes (Col 3:18–4:1; Eph 5:22–6:9; 1 Pet 2:18–3:7) commend a largely conventional and widely established pattern of relationships within the household, affirming the subordination of wives, children and slaves to the male household heads, albeit with distinctively Christian motivations. It is in the *significance* attributed to certain orientations, practices, and values that the sense of a distinctive way is located—a point to which we shall return when we consider the particular practices that might most clearly serve to construct and consolidate a sense of Jewish or Christian group identity (see §5.3 below). The Epistle to Diognetus, for example, insists that Christians are *not* distinctive in terms of their country, language, or customs (Diogn. 5.1). Yet this apologetic claim is followed precisely by indications as to ways in which Christian practice does differ at certain points from that which was common in wider society (for example, in the censure of the practice of abandoning infants [Diogn. 5.6], something also rejected by Jews [e.g., Philo, *Spec.* 3.110–16; Josephus, *C. Ap.* 2.202]) and makes clear that Christians nonetheless face hostility from both Jews and Greeks (Diogn. 5.17). Moreover, the epistle opens with a designation of Christians as a "new race or way of life" (καινὸν γένος ἢ ἐπιτήδευμα) (1.1) in the world and spends its

---

39. Here, as Benjamin Dunning points out, identity as aliens and strangers in the world (cf. 1 Pet 1:1, 17; 2:11) is transposed into the language of citizenship as a way of constructing the language of group-belonging; Benjamin H. Dunning, "Strangers and Aliens No Longer: Negotiating Identity and Difference in Ephesians 2," *HTR* 99 (2006): 3–4. Cf. also Öhler, "Ethnos und Identität," 247.

opening chapters showing how Christians are distinguished in their own religious worship (θεοσέβεια, 4.6) from both the idolatry of the "Greeks" (3.3) and from the worthless practices of the Jews (Diogn. 2.1–4.6).[40]

Also relevant here is a linguistic innovation on the part of Ignatius, bishop of Antioch. Just as the author of 2 Maccabees coined the word Ἰουδαϊσμός to address a particular situation—a perceived threat from Ἑλληνισμός that called for a determined orientation toward the Jewish way of life and its ancestral traditions—so Ignatius makes a derivative move in coining the term Χριστιανισμός. Again, it is significant to note that all of Ignatius's uses of this word come in contexts where a commitment to Χριστιανισμός is undertaken in the face of some opposing alternative. "Let us learn to live according to Christianity" (μάθωμεν κατὰ Χριστιανισμὸν ζῆν), Ignatius urges the Magnesians (Ign. *Magn.* 10.1), evidently concerned to persuade them against any notion that practicing Judaism—or moving in a Judaizing direction—would be acceptable: "It is misplaced [ἄτοπον] to proclaim Jesus Christ and to judaize [ἰουδαΐζειν]. For Christianity [Χριστιανισμός] did not believe in Judaism [οὐκ εἰς Ἰουδαϊσμὸν ἐπίστευσεν], but Judaism in Christianity" (Ign. *Magn.* 10.3 [Ehrman, LCL; slightly amended]).[41] Elsewhere, urging the Philadelphians not to hear (μὴ ἀκούετε) anyone who interprets Judaism (Ἰουδαϊσμὸν ἑρμηνεύῃ) to them, Ignatius exclaims that "it is better to hear Christianity from a man who is circumcised [παρὰ ἀνδρὸς περιτομὴν] than Judaism from one who is uncircumcised" (Ign. *Phld.* 6.1).[42] Better, in other words, to be directed toward Christianity—to Christianize—than to move toward Judaism.[43] As Mason comments: "Whereas the author of 2 Macca-

40. On the subtle ways in which the Epistle of Diognetus invokes the terminology of ethnic belonging and religious practice, see Judith M. Lieu, "Identity Games in Early Christian Texts: The *Letter to Diognetus*," in Hockey and Horrell, *Ethnicity, Race, Religion*, 59–72. Cf. also Benjamin H. Dunning, *Aliens and Sojourners: Self as Other in Early Christianity*, Divinations: Rereading Late Ancient Religion (Philadelphia: University of Pennsylvania Press, 2009), 67–70.

41. On these somewhat enigmatic remarks, see Schoedel, *Ignatius*, 126: "The curious remark that Judaism 'believed in' Christianity makes sense only if Ignatius is recalling the first generation of Jewish Christians referred to in *Mag.* 9.1 who left their old (essentially godless) ways and turned to Christ."

42. The only other use of Χριστιανισμός in Ignatius's letters is in *Rom.* 3.3 (where some texts read Χριστιανός), and a comparable perspective emerges here: orientation to Christianity is laudable in the face of hatred from the world.

43. Cf. Schoedel, *Ignatius*, 202–3: "What Ignatius is saying is this: Any entanglement with Judaism is unfortunate, but how much better to have moved . . . from Judaism to Christianity than in the reverse direction."

bees had championed Ἰουδαϊσμός as response to the threat of Ἑλληνισμός, Ignatius coins Χριστιανισμός as remedy for a threatening Ἰουδαϊσμός."[44] The coining of the term Χριστιανισμός, like its precursor Ἰουδαϊσμός, does not then indicate that some (religious?) system called Christianity had now been invented or recognized to exist[45] but rather that the notion of an orientation of life toward Christ was being discursively invoked in the face of a perceived threat. As Éric Rebillard has stressed, following Rogers Brubaker in particular, group identities—and facets of group identity such as ethnicity or religion—do not exist or prevail in the abstract but rather are deployed and made salient in particular contexts by particular actors for particular reasons.[46] Just as Judaism's ancestral traditions and particular way of life are invoked and defended in the face of particular threats, disputes, and alternatives, so too are those of emerging Christianity.

5.2 The Socialization of Children into a Way of Life

5.2.1 *Training Children in the Jewish Way of Life*

For ancient Judaism, as for many other cultures and peoples, the main purpose of marriage was to bear children; thus children, especially sons, were seen as a blessing (e.g., Ps 127:3–5; Sir 25:7).[47] One clear indication of the importance placed on family life and relationships is the inclusion within the Decalogue of the commandment to "honor your father and mother" (Exod 20:12; cf. Deut 5:16; Lev 19:3). As the author of Ephesians points out, this is the first commandment with a promise attached, an explicit incentive to obey it (Eph 6:2; cf. Sir 3:1–18). Indeed, in terms of negative incentives, Deuteronomy specifies capital punishment as the consequence for children who are incorrigibly disobedient (Deut 21:18–21), and writers in the Wisdom tradition

---

44. Mason, "Jews, Judaeans, Judaizing, Judaism," 470. See also Boin, "Hellenistic 'Judaism,'" 181–83.

45. Cf. Schoedel, *Ignatius*, 126n1, who suggests that the coining of the term is unsurprising given the analogous Ἰουδαϊσμός, which "provided a ready model for the creation of a noun to describe the distinctive identity of the Christian movement."

46. Éric Rebillard, *Christians and Their Many Identities in Late Antiquity, North Africa 200–450 CE* (Ithaca: Cornell University Press, 2013). On Brubaker's work, see §3.1 above.

47. See O. Larry Yarbrough, "Parents and Children in the Jewish Family of Antiquity," in *The Jewish Family in Antiquity*, ed. Shaye J. D. Cohen, Brown Judaic Studies 289 (Atlanta: Scholars Press, 1993), 41–42; Safrai, "Home and Family," 750.

particularly stress that parents should discipline their children firmly (e.g., Prov 13:24; 19:18; 22:15; Sir 7:23; 22:3–6; 30:1–13). It is difficult to know how frequently, if ever, the killing of disobedient children was carried out, but both Josephus and Philo affirm the validity of such punishment, probably indicating their awareness in this regard of the Roman custom of *patria potestas* (Philo, *Spec.* 2.232–33; 2.247–48; Josephus, *A.J.* 4.260–65; *C. Ap.* 2.216–17).[48]

While the commandment of the Decalogue specifies a duty of children toward parents—most likely, as Larry Yarbrough points out, focused on the duties of adult "children" toward their parents[49]—the Jewish scriptures frequently indicate the responsibilities of parents toward their children. Most relevant for our concerns here is the emphasis upon a parent's (and especially a father's) responsibility to teach their children the right way to live (see Prov 22:6). A prominent term for this instruction, particularly in the Wisdom literature (esp. Proverbs and Sirach) is παιδεία, an emblematic term for Greek cultural education and one we shall find in significant places in early Christian instruction too (see below). For example, Prov 1:8 urges a son to heed his father's παιδεία (and his mother's rules [θεσμοί]; cf. Prov 4:1; Sir 6:18). Prov 4:13 stresses the value of παιδεία (similarly, Prov 8:10; 10:17), which is often closely linked with wisdom, σοφία (Wis 6:17; Sir 1:27; 4:24). At the heart of this teaching on parents' responsibility toward their children is education in the commandments, which stipulate moral and religious duties, including the central obligation to worship God (see, e.g., Deut 6:7; 11:19; Prov 4:1–4; Tob 4:3–19; 4 Macc 18:9–19). Thus, as Yarbrough comments on the basis of a wider and more extended survey, "in almost all of the sources treating the obligations parents owe their children the emphasis is clearly on moral and religious instruction."[50] Jewish schools, mostly evidenced from later rabbinic writings, place learning within a similarly religious framework. As S. Safrai notes: "All stages of education are centred around the study of the Torah. Even the initial learning of the letters of the alphabet was understood as a religious act, as was children's further study."[51]

An emphasis on the training of children in their way of life—and on the exceptional thoroughness with which Jews do this—is also clear in Josephus

---

48. See Yarbrough, "Parents and Children," 51; Adele Reinhartz and Kim Shier, "Josephus on Children," 369–70.

49. Yarbrough, "Parents and Children," 53.

50. Yarbrough, "Parents and Children," 48.

51. S. Safrai, "Education and the Study of the Torah," in Safrai and Stern, *The Jewish People*, 945. The Mishnah specifies five as the age to begin study of scripture, ten for the Mishnah, and so on (m. 'Abot 5.21).

and Philo.[52] "Above all," Josephus writes, "we take pride in raising children [παιδοτροφίαν],[53] and make keeping the laws and preserving the traditional piety [εὐσέβιαν] that accords with them the most essential task of our whole life" (*C. Ap.* 1.60 [Barclay]; cf. *C. Ap.* 2.204). As this remark makes clear, this kind of training or παιδεία is not only something for children but something that governs the whole Jewish way of life (cf. *C. Ap.* 2.171).[54] Philo similarly notes how the *Ioudaioi* are "trained in a certain way of life from the cradle [δεδιδαγμένους ἐξ αὐτῶν τρόπον τινὰ σπαργάνων], by parents and tutors and instructors and by the far higher authority of the sacred laws [τῶν ἱερῶν νόμων] and also the unwritten customs [τῶν ἀγράφων ἐθῶν], to acknowledge one God who is the Father and Maker of the world" (*Legat.* 115 [Colson, LCL; slightly amended]; cf. *Legat.* 210; *Spec.* 2.228–31).[55]

Thus John Barclay comments that despite the diversity of first-century Judaism, "all our evidence suggests that the Jewish religious tradition was deeply woven into the fabric of Jewish family life" not only through the passing on of moral and religious instruction but also through practices connected with meals, social interaction, and the pattern of work and rest. Barclay sees these practices—to which we shall turn in the following section—as contributing to "an ethos in which [children's] ethnic distinctiveness was continually reinforced."[56] As others have noted, such an emphasis on the familial context and its importance for the (culturally) proper nurturing and rearing of children is by no means unusual in antiquity.[57]

---

52. For an overview of Jewish material on the child-parent relationship around the era of Christian origins, see Peter Balla, *The Child-Parent Relationship in the New Testament and Its Environment*, WUNT 155 (Tübingen: Mohr Siebeck, 2003), 80–111.

53. As Barclay, *Against Apion*, 43n241, notes, this may refer to either a Jewish rejection of abortion and exposure of infants or to the education of children (as in Thackeray's ET in LCL) or both.

54. See the extended discourse on the superiority of the Jewish system of education and moral training (παιδεία) in Josephus, *C. Ap.* 2.171–89. As Georg Bertram (*TDNT* 5:617) comments, for Josephus "παιδεύειν and παιδεία have the sense of education and culture." Likewise, "For Philo παιδεία is primarily the education and culture of the individual and people. He has in mind the general culture which transcends and gathers up the specialised training and which consists in the moral establishment of character and the fulfilment of man's nature as *humanitas*" (612–13).

55. For Philo's perspective on parents and children, and specifically the obligations of parents to instruct their children, see Adele Reinhartz, "Parents and Children: A Philonic Perspective," in Cohen, *The Jewish Family*, 61–88, esp. 73–74.

56. Barclay, "The Family," 68, 71.

57. See, e.g., Yarbrough, "Parents and Children," 53–57; Reinhartz, "Parents and Children," 86–88.

5.2.2   *Children and the Christian Way of Life*

We have already noted that the New Testament displays little interest in instruction concerning the bearing and rearing of children (see §4.4). Given both the eschatological expectation and asceticism that were prominent in the early Christian movement, this is an understandable gap, especially in the first generation. Jesus was recorded to have declared that "this generation" would see the fulfillment of the final eschatological events (Mark 13:30; cf. Mark 9:1), and Paul clearly expects the return of Christ to occur during the lifetime of at least some of the first converts (1 Thess 4:13–5:11; 1 Cor 15:51–52; cf. Mark 9:1; 13:30). The present generation, for Paul, was the one on which the ends of the ages had fallen (1 Cor 10:11).

Some indications of a developing concern for the rearing of children are, however, evident in the so-called household codes, particularly in the most complete and formulaic examples: the parallel codes in Col 3:18–4:1 and Eph 5:21–6:9. These codes seem most likely to represent concerns for stability and continuity in the time around or in the decades immediately after the death of Paul.[58] Specifically, they are representative of those strands of early Christianity that focused, unlike some of the more ascetically oriented strands, on the well-ordered household as a key basis for both family life and the ἐκκλησία.[59]

In Colossians and Ephesians, the direct vocative address to each of the household members—wives, husbands, children, fathers, slaves, masters— presumes an allegiance to Christ on the part of all those addressed, not only by the very fact of the direct address but also by the explicitly Christian motivation given for each group's conduct.[60] Thus, children are to obey their parents because this is pleasing ἐν κυρίῳ (Col 3:20; expanded with a scriptural command and promise in Eph 6:1–3). In Ephesians, the admonition to fathers is to raise their children "in the training and instruction of the Lord"

---

58. See, e.g., Margaret Y. MacDonald, *The Pauline Churches: A Socio-Historical Study of Institutionalization in the Pauline and Deutero-Pauline Writings*, SNTSMS 60 (Cambridge: Cambridge University Press, 1988), 102–20.

59. See, e.g., 1 Tim 3:1–15; Titus 2:1–10. On this particular trajectory, see Horrell, "From ἀδελφοί to οἶκος θεοῦ," 293–311. On the renunciation of family, also preserved in the earliest Christian traditions, see, e.g., Barton, *Discipleship*; Theissen, *Social Reality*, 33–59.

60. On this unusually direct appeal, see the comments of Margaret Y. MacDonald, *The Power of Children: The Construction of Christian Families in the Greco-Roman World* (Waco: Baylor University Press, 2014), 7, 18. More broadly on the instruction here concerning the relations of children and parents, see Balla, *Child-Parent Relationship*, 165–78.

(ἐν παιδείᾳ καὶ νουθεσίᾳ κυρίου) (Eph 6:4, NIV). Here in particular, as Barclay has pointed out, we find a developing sense of the family as the place for "the Christian socialization of children" and "a key site for the practice of a distinctly Christian life-style."[61] This concern for the socialization of children into the Christian way of life is, as Margaret MacDonald notes, a "deliberate attempt to incorporate the next generation via education."[62]

The household is here depicted as a social unit that shares a common Christian identity and passes on that identity to the next generation through the training that is provided to children. In such a depiction, we see, in a sense, the instantiation in practice of the principle expressed *in nuce* by Paul: that the children of Christian parents (even one Christian parent) are reckoned to belong within the Christian community (1 Cor 7:14; see §4.4), a principle that infant baptism would also come to embody.[63] The children continue to belong, however, not by the mere fact of their birth into a Christian household but rather by their integration into the Christian community and their training in the customs, practices, and beliefs of the Christian movement. As in the case of Judaism, there is a strong sense that children need to be trained in the "right" ways.

Later versions of household code material, though less formally structured than in Colossians and Ephesians, repeat this emphasis on the training of children. In 1 Clement, the author's direct addressees are the senior male householders ("We should instruct the youth. . . . We should set our wives along the straight path," 1 Clem. 21.6 [Ehrman, LCL; slightly amended]; cf. 1 Clem. 1.3).[64] Notable in the exhortation concerning the youth is the language of παιδεία, emphasized by the combination of verbal and nominal forms: τοὺς νέους παιδεύσωμεν τὴν παιδείαν τοῦ φόβου τοῦ θεοῦ ("Let us train the youth in the discipline of the fear of God"). Wives and children are addressed indirectly (and at some length) with third-person imperatives

61. Barclay, "The Family," 76–77, though cast, one should note, under the rubric of the family as "bearer of religion" rather than of ethnicity (but see 69 for Judaism as "fundamentally an ethnic tradition"). Cf. also Lindemann, "Kinder," 181–83.

62. MacDonald, *Power of Children*, 75. On the concern for the socialization and education of children, see 67–107.

63. Cf. Lindemann, "Kinder," 178.

64. See David G. Horrell, *The Social Ethos of the Corinthian Correspondence: Interests and Ideology from 1 Corinthians to 1 Clement*, SNTW (Edinburgh: T&T Clark, 1996), 269; on the household code in 1 Clement, see 263–72. Children, however, are largely ignored in this analysis, exemplifying the wider lack lamented and addressed by MacDonald, *Power of Children*.

(21.7–8). The instruction concerning children is substantial and, again, is characterized as παιδεία:

> Let our children partake of the upbringing that is in Christ [τῆς ἐν Χριστῷ παιδείας]. Let them learn the strength of humility before God and the power of pure love before God. Let them learn how the reverential awe [φόβος] of him is beautiful and great, and how it saves all who conduct themselves [ἀναστρεφόμενους] in it in a holy way, with a clear understanding. (1 Clem. 21.8 [Ehrman, LCL; slightly amended])

Similarly, in Polycarp's *Epistle to the Philippians*, instruction concerning wives and children is addressed directly to the men ("We should teach our wives . . .") and encapsulates the duty toward children in words almost identical to 1 Clement's: "to train the children in the discipline of the fear of God" (τὰ τέκνα παιδεύειν τὴν παιδείαν τοῦ φόβου τοῦ θεοῦ) (Pol. *Phil.* 4.2).

A somewhat different household code tradition appears in the Didache and the Epistle of Barnabas, but it conveys substantially the same message concerning the instruction of children (almost identically worded in both texts[65]): "Do not remove your hand[66] [οὐκ ἀρεῖς τὴν χεῖρά σου] from your son or your daughter, but from their youth [ἀπὸ νεότητος] teach them [διδάξεις] the reverential fear of God" (Did. 4.9; cf. Barn. 19.5).

To use the language of παιδεία to characterize what it is that children should be trained in, as do Ephesians, 1 Clement, and Polycarp's *Philippians*, is to echo one of the central notions of the Greek cultural tradition (cf. the reference to παίδευσις in the quotation at the opening of this chapter),[67] though this is also a prominent notion in Jewish writings in Greek, as we have noted above. Like the German word *Bildung*, παιδεία is difficult to render adequately into English and impossible to capture in a single word.

---

65. The opening phrase in Barnabas differs slightly from the version quoted below from the Didache, using the emphatic double negative with aorist subjunctive instead of the future to convey the command: οὐ μὴ ἄρῃς. The only other difference is that the nouns in the final phrase are arthrous in Barnabas and anarthrous in the Didache (φόβον θεοῦ).

66. As Ehrman's glosses indicate, this phrase, and "hand" in particular, may be understood to refer either to discipline or to responsibility (LCL, 1.425; 2.77). The use of "hand" in Ps 39:10 [LXX 38:11] may suggest that discipline is most likely in view. By contrast, Kurt Niederwimmer, *The Didache*, Hermeneia (Minneapolis: Fortress, 1998), 110, stresses "the acceptance of responsibility for them and their παιδεία."

67. Thus Georg Bertram (*TDNT* 5:597) comments that "the word group [παιδεύω, παιδεία, κτλ.] characterises Greek culture."

Needless to say, the word can carry a range of meanings and connotations depending on its context of use, but when used to describe the formation of children (and adults), it conveys a sense of training, education, instruction and discipline (including correction),[68] not merely in the sense of learning facts or telling right from wrong but also in a more "cultural" sense (again, *Bildung* is comparable)—hence the gloss "cultural nurture."[69] To acquire παιδεία is to be socialized, enculturated, and trained in a particular tradition of cultural norms and practices. Thus Tim Whitmarsh, for example, discusses παιδεία as a key means to acquire Hellenic identity in the Roman Empire and comments that, in terms of this Hellenic identity, "at root, *paideia* is the primary means of creating adult identity."[70] Similarly, we might say that for children in Christian households, at least according to the ideal model set out in the household codes, παιδεία—specifically ἡ ἐν Χριστῷ παιδεία, as 1 Clem. 21.8 puts it—is the way to be formed in the Christian way of life, to be socialized, disciplined, and enculturated as a Christian. Once again, we might see this as a move with ethnicizing potential, developing a sense of identity as a people that passes through the generations.

5.3 Displaying a Way of Life through Practice

Having considered how Jewish and early Christian sources depict their respective identities in terms of a way of life and how they value the socialization of children in their respective ways of life, it is important next to consider how particular practices are taken to embody and express these ways of life and the distinctive group identities that they represent. What marks out, in visible or practical ways, those following a particular way of life? In turning to this subject, it is worth recalling one of the seminal insights of Fredrick Barth in his work on ethnic groups and boundaries: that the maintenance of group identity does not depend on distinctiveness or, still less, isolation in all aspects of social life but rather on certain "cultural features" that "are used by the actors as signals and emblems of differences."[71] As Barth stresses, it is not

---

68. Παιδεία quite frequently carries this sense of corrective discipline in Jewish and Christian texts; see, for example, Prov 22:15; 2 Macc 6:12; 7:33; Heb 12:11; Pss. Sol. 7.9; Herm. Vis. 2.3 (7.1).

69. BDAG, 748.

70. Tim Whitmarsh, *Greek Literature and the Roman Empire: The Politics of Imitation* (Oxford: Oxford University Press, 2001), 130; see 90–130.

71. Barth, "Introduction," 14. See §3.1 above.

that such group-defining cultures are isolated or entirely distinct from those around them but rather that there are certain signals or practices by which the boundary and thus integrity of the group's identity is maintained. It is, as we shall see, the significance attributed to certain features and aspects of practice that matters as much as the practice itself.

It is of course impossible to do justice to the internally diverse and manifold aspects of Jewish and early Christian practice and their functions in terms of group identity and boundaries—let alone the scholarly discussion and debate—in a short section devoted to the topic, but we can at least identify a few key features.[72] One obvious feature, central to both Jewish and Christian traditions, is the commitment to worship only one God—a commitment that carried both positive and negative practical implications. Despite the divergence from Jewish monotheism that takes place over time through the distinctively Christian devotion to Christ and the eventual formulation in Christianity of a trinitarian conception of the one God, this monolatry was a shared feature of both Judaism and early Christianity and meant that Jews and Christians could face similar issues in the wider world. Positively, it meant that those who counted themselves as either Jews or Christians would, at least in theory, be committed to the exclusive worship of their God and would meet with others for this purpose. Negatively, it meant a refusal to join in the worship of other gods in the Greek or Roman pantheon, a stance that drew accusations of "atheism" from external critics (see, e.g., Mart. Pol. 9.2; Dio Cassius, *Hist. Rom.* 67.14.2; Tacitus, *Hist.* 5.5, who records that Jews "despise the gods" [*contemnere deos*]).[73] One point where this stance came to a head for both Jews and Christians was in the worship of the emperor (and his family) in the imperial cults: Philo describes at length Gaius's claims to divinity (*Legat.* 74–113) and explains Gaius's hostility toward the Jews on the basis that they alone opposed his claims due to their commitment to acknowledge only the one God (*Legat.* 115). Early Christians soon found themselves negotiating similar difficulties and articulated a similarly limited acceptance of the emperor's position. They prayed for him but not to him (1 Tim 2:1–2) and were willing to offer him honor

72. Cf., e.g., the overview and comparison of Jewish and early Christian boundary markers in James D. G. Dunn, "Boundary Markers in Early Christianity," in *Gruppenreligionen im römischen Reich: Sozialformen, Grenzziehungen und Leistungen*, ed. Jörg Rüpke, STAC 43 (Tübingen: Mohr Siebeck, 2007), 49–68.

73. See further Geoffrey E. M. De Ste. Croix, "Why Were the Early Christians Persecuted?," *Past and Present* 26 (1963): 24–25; Stephen Benko, *Pagan Rome and the Early Christians* (Bloomington: Indiana University Press, 1985), 1–29.

but not worship (1 Pet 2:17). This latter stance in particular was often used to define the Christian position—and the limits of acquiescence to imperial demands—in the decades to follow.[74]

Our main concern in this section, however, is with the more practical dimensions of the ways of life to which Jews and Christians were committed. In terms of Judaism in the period with which we are concerned, both internal and external sources highlight three specific and particularly prominent practices or customs by which Jews displayed their distinct group identity: circumcision, food regulations, and observance of Sabbath.[75]

5.3.1 *Jewish Practices as Markers of Identity:*
Circumcision, Food, and Sabbath

The obligation to circumcise male children to signify their belonging to the Jewish people derives from Gen 17:9–14, where it is required of Abraham and his descendants. In the context of the Maccabean revolt, this is evidently one of the bodily sites where the cultural conflict is played out, heightening the significance of the practice as a marker of Jewishness.[76] Some (hellenizing) Jews apparently removed the signs of circumcision (1 Macc 1:15) while others were killed for circumcising their children (1 Macc 1:60–61; 2 Macc 6:10; 4 Macc 4:25). By contrast, opponents of the moves toward hellenization are said to have forcibly circumcised boys who had not previously been circumcised (1 Macc 2:46). Josephus responds to criticism of the Jewish practice, indicating that it was known as a particular custom of the Jews (*C. Ap.* 2.137), and Philo insists on both the spiritual significance and physical importance of the rite (*Migr.* 92). A prominent dispute in the

---

74. See further Horrell, "Honour Everyone."

75. These three features are identified as the key markers of Jewish identity by, e.g., Dunn, *Jesus, Paul and the Law*, 191–94; see also, more recently, Dunn, "Boundary Markers," 50–55. For all three together in ancient (non-Jewish) sources, see Petronius, *Frag.* 37 (*GLAJJ*, §195); Juvenal, *Sat.* 14.96–106 (*GLAJJ*, §301). See Diogn. 4.1 for early Christian polemic against precisely these practices.

76. Cf. Benedikt Eckhardt, "'An Idumean, That Is, a Half-Jew': Hasmoneans and Herodians between Ancestry and Merit," in *Jewish Identity and Politics between the Maccabees and Bar Kokhba: Groups, Normativity, and Rituals*, ed. Benedikt Eckhardt, JSJSup 155 (Leiden: Brill, 2012), 91–115; Eckhardt also notes that "circumcision is of special interest to 1 Maccabees" compared with 2 Maccabees (108). The removal of the marks of circumcision is mentioned among the indications of adopting Greek ways in the former (1 Macc 1:15) but not the latter (2 Macc 4:12).

earliest Christian movement concerned whether gentile converts needed to be circumcised (see, e.g., Acts 15:1–2; Gal 5:1–4). There may already have been some debate among Jews at the time as to whether circumcision was essential (or, indeed, effective) for proselytes (see ch. 8).[77] Circumcision was not in any case unique to the *Ioudaioi* but was also practiced by other peoples in the eastern parts of the Roman Empire and beyond, notably Egyptians, as both Philo (*QG* 3.47; *Spec.* 1.2) and Josephus (*C. Ap.* 1.169–71; 2.141–42) note.[78] Yet corresponding to the prominence given to circumcision as a mark of (male) belonging among Jewish authors, Greek and Roman writers also identify circumcision as a key marker of the *Ioudaioi* (e.g., Petronius, *Satyricon* 102 [*GLAJJ*, §194]). Suetonius records how this could be used to identify whether someone was Jewish in the context of ascertaining liability

77. There is debate about this among modern scholars. Among those who argue for such a diversity of opinion among ancient Jews are Francis Watson, *Paul, Judaism and the Gentiles: Beyond the New Perspective*, rev. and expanded ed. (Grand Rapids: Eerdmans, 2007), 75–79; J. Albert Harrill, *Paul the Apostle: His Life and Legacy in Their Roman Context* (Cambridge: Cambridge University Press, 2012), 55–57; Neil J. McEleney, "Conversion, Circumcision and the Law," *NTS* 20 (1974): 323–24. For the contrary view that circumcision was presumed as necessary for all converts, see John Nolland, "Uncircumcised Proselytes?," *JSJ* 12 (1981): 173–94; Paula Fredriksen, "Judaism, the Circumcision of Gentiles, and Apocalyptic Hope: Another Look at Galatians 1 and 2," *JTS* 42 (1991): 536n11. Especially crucial in terms of primary evidence is Philo, *QE* 2.2, which seems to indicate that the προσήλυτος undergoes a spiritual rather than a physical circumcision, and *Migr.* 89–93, which suggests that some at least may have argued that the spiritual significance of circumcision was what mattered, such that the physical act was unnecessary. Philo, however, firmly rejects this point of view. Cf. Josephus, *A.J.* 20.38–46 (on which see §8.1.4 below). Another dimension to this debate has been highlighted by Matthew Thiessen, who points to evidence that some Jews—albeit a minority—regarded only eighth-day circumcision as valid and therefore disputed the validity of proselyte circumcision; see Matthew Thiessen, *Contesting Conversion: Genealogy, Circumcision, and Identity in Ancient Judaism and Christianity* (Oxford: Oxford University Press, 2011). Thiessen argues that Paul's objections to gentile converts' circumcision may best be understood within this matrix of Jewish perspectives; see Thiessen, *Paul*.

78. See, e.g., Herodotus, *Hist.* 2.104.2 (*GLAJJ*, §1, with further references there); Diodorus Siculus, *Bib. Hist.* 1.28.3; 1.55.5 (*GLAJJ*, §§55, 57); Strabo, *Geogr.* 16.4.9; 17.2.5 (*GLAJJ*, §§118, 124). The same goes for the Idumaeans (cf. Jer 9:25–26); see Aryeh Kasher, *Jews, Idumaeans, and Ancient Arabs: Relations of the Jews in Eretz-Israel with the Nations of the Frontier and the Desert during the Hellenistic and Roman Era (332 BCE–70 CE)*, TSAJ 18 (Tübingen: Mohr Siebeck, 1988), 56–57; Peter Richardson, *Herod: King of the Jews and Friend of the Romans* (Edinburgh: T&T Clark, 1999), 55. Hence, while Barclay, *Jews*, 411–12, is right to highlight the importance of circumcision as a marker of Jewish identity when marriage was being contemplated, this physical sign cannot alone securely connote identity: the discursive and cultural context is significant too.

to pay the *fiscus Iudaicus* (*Dom.* 12.2 [*GLAJJ*, §320]).[79] For many both inside and outside the Jewish people, it was a significant marker of Jewish identity, albeit one that was generally unseen.

Jews' observance of particular customs with regard to food was another practical feature of life that was important to a sense of shared identity as well as something that was noted (and ridiculed) by outsiders. Prominent among these food rules was abstention from pork, the consumption of which is depicted as a paradigmatic instance of turning away from right ways (cf. Isa 65:4; 66:17). Again, this is evident in the Maccabean literature, where a resolve "not to eat unclean food" is a particular mark of resistance (1 Macc 1:62–63) and attempts to compel Jews to eat pork are repeatedly recorded (2 Macc 6:18; 7:1; 4 Macc 5:2, 6; 6:15). Similarly, Josephus lists among Apion's criticisms of the Jews their refusal to eat pork (*C. Ap.* 2.137). The prominence of such customs is also reflected in the New Testament, where, as with circumcision, questions about how far Jewish food laws must be followed by those converted to Christ quickly becomes an issue of debate (see, e.g., Mark 7:19; Acts 15:19-20, 28-29; Rom 14:1-7; 1 Cor 10:25-32; Rev 2:20). It is also worth pointing out that abstention from certain foods, notably meat, can be found among other groups at the time (such as some Pythagoreans and Stoics) such that, once again, the practice itself—avoiding meat, or pork specifically—is not in itself definitive of Jewish identity.[80] In replying to Apion's criticisms, Josephus notes that Egyptian priests generally abstain from pork (*C. Ap.* 2.141) and even reports, likely with a degree of exaggeration, a widespread adoption of Jewish food rules (*C. Ap.* 2.282).[81] When Philo reports Gaius's question, "Why do you refuse to eat pork?," he comments that this topic caused great laughter among those listening. But he also reports someone observing that "just as many don't eat lamb" (*Legat.* 361–62). Yet, as this dialogue reveals, external observers frequently noted and discussed as a specifically Jewish custom the commitment to abstain from pork.[82]

---

79. For further references among ancient authors, see Molly Whittaker, *Jews and Christians: Graeco-Roman Views*, Cambridge Commentaries on Writings of the Jewish and Christian World, 200 BC to AD 200, 6 (Cambridge: Cambridge University Press, 1984), 80–85.

80. See, e.g., Seneca, *Ep.* 108.17–22. On abstinence from meat in first-century Rome, see Mark Reasoner, *The Strong and the Weak: Romans 14.1–15.13 in Context*, SNTSMS 103 (Cambridge: Cambridge University Press, 1999), 75–84, who concludes that "vegetarianism was popular in Rome" (84).

81. Cf. Barclay, *Against Apion*, 240n500, 241n513.

82. For an extensive collection of non-Jewish sources on this point, see Whittaker, *Jews and Christians*, 73–80.

Plutarch, for example, records a lengthy discussion concerning "whether the Jews abstain from pork because of reverence or aversion for the pig" (*Quaest. Conv.* 4.4.4 [*GLAJJ*, §258]): the reasons are open to discussion, but the custom itself is well known.[83]

The third key practice is that of Sabbath observance, mandated in the Decalogue (Exod 20:8–11; Deut 5:12–15; cf. Exod 31:13–17; Lev 19:3; 23:3) and again a test case of Jewish loyalty (see, e.g., Neh 9:14; 10:31; 13:15–22; Isa 56:1–6; 58:13; Jer 17:19–27). Once again, the emblematic status of this custom is evident in the Maccabean literature. In 1 Maccabees, Jews who assimilate to a Hellenistic way of life are said, among other things, to have desecrated the Sabbath (1 Macc 1:43–45). Loyal Jews, on the other hand, refuse to fight on the Sabbath and are consequently slaughtered (1 Macc 2:34–38; cf. 2 Macc 5:25–26; 15:1–5). In 1 Maccabees it is reported that this policy was then overturned (1 Macc 2:41), though in 2 Maccabees there are reports of successful Jewish fighters keeping Sabbath (2 Macc 8:24–28; 12:38).[84] Keeping Sabbath is among the key practices Philo highlights, insisting that its symbolic meaning does not justify any abrogation of the laws for its observance (*Migr.* 91). Again, the issue is one that soon appears as a cause of some disagreement in the earliest Christian movement (Rom 14:5–6; Col 2:16).[85] Furthermore, it is clear from a range of non-Jewish authors that the observance of Sabbath was a well-known marker of Jewish identity (see, e.g., Plutarch, *Superst.* 8 [*GLAJJ*, §256]; Suetonius, *Aug.* 76.2 [*GLAJJ*, §303]). Josephus also records such external recognition of the Sabbath custom (*A.J.* 12.259; 16.163–4). Although the custom was often misunderstood (e.g., as a day of fasting) and derided as a symptom of sloth and inactivity,[86] it is also interesting to note some evidence for the popularity of Sabbath observance among gentiles. Josephus may well exaggerate somewhat when he claims that there is "no city [οὐ πόλις] . . . nor any nation [οὐδὲ ἓν ἔθνος],

---

83. For other ancient discussions of the reasons why Jews abstained from pork, see, e.g., Tacitus, *Hist.* 5.4.2 (*GLAJJ*, §281).

84. See also the reports on this matter in Josephus, *A.J.* 12.274–78; 13.12; 14.64; 18.354.

85. On Rom 14:5–6 as focused on the issue of Sabbath observance, see John M. G. Barclay, "'Do We Undermine the Law?': A Study of Romans 14.1–15.6," in *Paul and the Mosaic Law*, ed. James D. G. Dunn, WUNT 89 (Tübingen: Mohr Siebeck, 1996), 287–308; repr. in John M. G. Barclay, *Pauline Churches and Diaspora Jews*, WUNT 275 (Tübingen: Mohr Siebeck, 2011), 37–59, esp. 39.

86. See the extended compilation of references in Whittaker, *Jews and Christians*, 63–73.

to which the custom of the seventh day, when we abstain from work [τὸ τῆς ἑβδομάδος, ἥν ἀργοῦμεν ἡμεῖς, ἔθος], has not spread" (*C. Ap.* 2.282 [Thackeray, LCL; slightly amended];[87] cf. Philo, *Mos.* 2.21–22), but for the claim to be plausibly made at all—not least in an apologetic work—it must at least have some basis in a recognizable popularity of Jewish customs and practices (see §8.1.2).

These customs and practices structured—that is, both enabled and limited—social interaction. We should not stress only the latter part of that effect: Jewish separatism, polemically reported by ancient non-Jewish authors (e.g., Tacitus, *Hist.* 5.5), has often been exaggerated in contemporary New Testament scholarship, where emphasizing such separatism serves to highlight the contrasting inclusiveness of early Christianity.[88] As many authors have pointed out, there is plenty of evidence for Jews being integrated—albeit (unsurprisingly) to various degrees—into their wider civic societies.[89] Gentiles could join in the Jewish communities in various ways and to various extents (as we shall see in ch. 8). Indeed, in all these cases there is evidence to suggest that comparable customs could be found among other peoples or that Jewish practices were attractive to many, despite the ridicule to which they were subject. Nonetheless, these particular practices were perceived—not exclusively, but prominently—by both Jews and non-Jews to characterize the Jewish way of life, and they attained high significance precisely in that regard.

5.3.2 Christian Practices and Group Identity: Baptism, Eucharist, and Sunday Meeting

When it comes to the early Christian movement, it is equally impossible to consider the full range of practices—still less the variety of such practices in different times, places, and groups—that might be deemed to constitute and embody the Christian way of life and to mark group-belonging in visible

87. See Barclay, *Against Apion*, 327n1135, on the textual variants and possible readings with regard to the description of the cities and nations as Greek and barbarian—which do not, however, affect the key point of the quotation given above.

88. For one recent critique of the focus on Jewish separatism, see Fredriksen, review of *Paul and the Faithfulness of God* (by N. T. Wright), 389–90.

89. For example, see Philip A. Harland, *Associations, Synagogues, and Congregations* (Minneapolis: Fortress, 2003), 200–228; Erich S. Gruen, "Kinship Relations and Jewish Identity," in Levine and Schwartz, *Jewish Identities*, 101–16.

and practical ways.[90] Yet just as we considered three key Jewish practices as particularly emblematic for displaying the Jewish way of life, so we may consider three broadly corresponding Christian practices—also dealing with the sign of belonging, the consumption of food, and the structuring of time—on which to focus our attention: baptism, eucharist, and the weekly (Sunday) gathering.

There are plenty of complex and disputed issues concerning the origins and character of baptism in the name of Jesus Christ: To what extent, if at all, does it derive from Jewish customs of immersion, and specifically the requirement of baptism for proselytes?[91] To what extent was it seen as a development from, or a distinctly different thing compared with, the baptism offered by John the Baptist?[92] How early did the custom of infant baptism develop, and were infants included in the household baptisms that are recorded in the New Testament?[93]

These and other issues have been the subject of extensive discussion that cannot be considered here. What matters most in this context is the more basic observation that in the early Christian sources, baptism (into the name of Jesus/Christ) seems to be widely presumed as a rite of entry into the movement.[94] Even this has been recently disputed by Richard DeMaris, but it seems unduly skeptical to doubt it—though we may grant DeMaris's point that baptism was subject to disagreement and conflict and not simply

90. For a valuable discussion of this in the context of second-century Carthage, see Rebillard, *Christians and Their Many Identities*, 12–20.

91. For an overview of the evidence and the difficulty of dating the origins of the Jewish practice, see Everett Ferguson, *Baptism in the Early Church: History, Theology, and Liturgy in the First Five Centuries* (Grand Rapids: Eerdmans, 2009), 76–82.

92. Acts 19:1–6 records an intriguing instance of a Christian group of disciples that has apparently not received the Spirit, having only received John's baptism. After receiving baptism into Christ's name, this lack is rectified—"the only example in the New Testament of a 're-baptism'" (Ferguson, *Baptism*, 181). In Acts 10:44–48 the evidence of the Spirit's outpouring appears before baptism, but baptism is undertaken immediately.

93. For the baptism of households, see, e.g., Acts 16:15; 18:8; 1 Cor 1:16. Origen attributes to the apostles the custom of baptizing infants (*Comm. Rom.* 5.9.11), while Tertullian is against the practice (*Bapt.* 18). For an extended survey of the evidence from the NT through to the fifth century, see Ferguson, *Baptism* (see 362–79 on the origins of infant baptism specifically). See also Lindemann, "Kinder," 185–90, who argues that children were likely included in the early household baptisms.

94. On this, and specifically the baptismal formulae using the name of Jesus, see Lars Hartman, *"Into the Name of the Lord Jesus": Baptism in the Early Church* (Edinburgh: T&T Clark, 1997), esp. 37–50.

taken for granted as a ritual with self-evident meaning.[95] A presumption that converts have been baptized seems clear, for example, in Paul's comments about his own apostolic activity in 1 Cor 1:13–17 and his exhortations in Rom 6:1–11 (see also 1 Cor 12:13; Gal 3:27–28). Likewise, his appeal to the experiences of the Israelites in the wilderness to warn the Corinthians against complacency and the risks of idolatry is shaped by an assumption that baptism and eucharist are established and accepted practices of the group; hence Paul narrates the Israelites' experiences in precisely these terms—"baptized into Moses," consuming "spiritual food" and "spiritual drink" (1 Cor 10:1–11). The deutero-Pauline letters continue to reflect this presumption: Colossians assumes the baptism of believers (Col 2:12), relating it, like Romans 6, to dying and rising with Christ; Ephesians includes "one baptism" among the foundational elements of the church's unity (Eph 4:5). Similarly, the author of 1 Peter seems to presume that the addressees have been baptized when presenting his famously enigmatic comments on how baptism "saves" (1 Pet 3:21) analogously to the way in which Noah and his family "were saved through water" (διεσώθησαν δι᾽ ὕδατος) (1 Pet 3:20; cf. Herm. Vis. 3.3 [11.5]).[96]

A presumption that Christians have been baptized continues to be reflected in post-New Testament literature (e.g., Barn. 11.1; 2 Clem. 6.9; Ign. *Pol.* 6.2; Herm. Vis. 3.7 [15.3]). Ignatius's characteristic efforts to strengthen the authority of the bishop include comments on baptism: "It is not permitted to baptize without the bishop" (Ign. *Smyrn.* 8.2; cf. Tertullian, *Bapt.* 17). Concise summaries of the Christian missionary message also include baptism as one of the key elements (e.g., Matt 28:19; Mark 16:16 [part of the longer ending added to Mark's Gospel]; Acts 2:38; 8:36). Matthew's famous closing missionary exhortation also indicates how developing trinitarian formulations were expressed in baptismal lit-

95. Richard E. DeMaris, *The New Testament in Its Ritual World* (London: Routledge, 2008), 14–36.

96. Elliott, *1 Peter*, 668, notes the innovative move made by the author of 1 Peter in drawing a parallel between the flood and Christian baptism. The grammar of 3:21 is difficult, however, and the precise construal of the crucial phrase has been much discussed. See, e.g., Bo Reicke, *The Disobedient Spirits and Christian Baptism: A Study of 1 Pet. III.19 and Its Context*, ASNU 13 (Copenhagen: Ejnar Munksgaard, 1946), 143–201; William J. Dalton, *Christ's Proclamation to the Spirits: A Study of 1 Peter 3:18–4:6*, 2nd ed., AnBib 23 (Rome: Pontifical Biblical Institute, 1989), 189–214; Chad T. Pierce, *Spirits and the Proclamation of Christ: 1 Peter 3:18–22 in Light of Sin and Punishment Traditions in Early Jewish and Christian Literature*, WUNT 2.305 (Tübingen: Mohr Siebeck, 2011), 227–36.

urgy ("baptizing them in the name of the Father, and of the Son, and of the Holy Spirit," Matt 28:19).

The earliest instruction concerning the details of baptismal practice is found in the Didache (Did. 7.1–4).[97] Again, there is a presumption that baptism will be practiced, and the same trinitarian formula found in Matt 28:19 is prescribed (cf. Tertullian, *Bapt.* 6).[98] The baptizand is instructed to fast prior to their baptism, along with the baptizer and some others (Did. 7.4). But the major concern is to give instruction that will provide guidance about the kind of water that is needed. Running water is ideal, but if water is scarce, then pouring it on the head (three times) is sufficient (Did. 7.2–3). These instructions imply that immersion was the standard and preferred mode of baptism, as would also be suggested by both the records of John's practice (Mark 1:9–10) and the imagery of death, burial, and emergence to new life as well as of unclothing and reclothing (Rom 6:3–4; Gal 3:27; Col 3:9–10; Eph 4:22–24).[99] Tertullian's later discourse on baptism combines immersion and sprinkling as standard parts of the ritual (*Bapt.* 2). This discourse indicates some debate and diversity of opinion concerning the necessity and status of baptism, as Tertullian replies to several potential objections to the practice (*Bapt.* 11–14), but it also confirms the importance of baptism for Tertullian and its prominent place in his conception of church practice.

Unlike circumcision, baptism leaves no permanent mark on the body, cannot be "verified" outside the context of the rite and any records of it, and was undertaken by both males and females. There are clear and obvious differences between the two rites. Yet this does not mean they are entirely incomparable as marks of belonging—bodily practices that signify membership in the community. For a start, as we have noted above, the physical fact of circumcision could not alone identify someone as Jewish since other peoples practiced the custom as well. Rather, it is the practice combined

---

97. On baptism in the Didache, see Hartman, *Into the Name*, 172–77; Ferguson, *Baptism*, 201–6.

98. The agreement concerning this formula may (as Niederwimmer, *Didache*, 127, suggests) reflect "their common dependence on the liturgy" rather than the Didache's dependence on Matthew directly—though there are many points of contact between Matthew and the Didache, often assumed to reflect the Didache's knowledge of Matthew or of traditions contained in Matthew. The alternative case, namely Matthew's dependence on Didache, has been argued by Alan Garrow, *The Gospel of Matthew's Dependence on the Didache*, JSNTSup 254 (London: T&T Clark, 2004).

99. On this imagery, and its enactment in ritual, see Meeks, *The First Urban Christians*, 150–57.

with a discursive and cultural focus on its significance that together constituted its identity-defining function such that both insiders and outsiders saw it—that is, assigned it significance—as a particularly Jewish marker of identity. Second, as we have also noted above, circumcision was not generally or publicly visible, except in intimate or very particular circumstances (cf. 1 Macc 1:14–15; Suetonius, *Dom.* 12.2). Third, circumcision was prescribed only for males, yet this does not mean that Jewish women were not reckoned as Jews, even if the means by which this identity was marked is less easily defined—a point of relevance especially in the case of proselytes.[100] Indeed, as Judith Lieu remarks, the fact that the Christian movement adopted baptism as its rite of entry and administered it to both men and women does not necessarily mean that the position of women was different compared with Judaism.[101] After all, as Lieu notes, despite the famous declaration that there is "no longer male and female" in Christ (Gal 3:28), Paul continues to define the issue of belonging in relation to the issue of circumcision, constructing his implied readership as male and leaving unanswered the question about how women's belonging and status might be affected: "If you have yourselves circumcised, Christ is of no benefit to you" (Gal 5:2).[102] What seems clear from Gal 3:26–29, though, is that just as circumcision was taken to define belonging to the Jewish people, so too baptism, as a visible bodily practice, marked a person's belonging to Christ.

With regard to customs concerning food, these did not have an identity-defining significance within the Christian movement in the same way they did in Judaism. That bold statement conceals an enormous amount of diversity and uncertainty, however, not least because there was no clear boundary or distinction between what we now call "Judaism" and "Christianity" at the time, and some whom we label "Christian" were also Torah-observant Jews (such as the author of Matthew's Gospel). Paul, though, is surprisingly clear that "everything sold in the marketplace" can, indeed should—the πᾶν plus imperative is emphatic—be eaten (1 Cor 10:25).[103] He is convinced "in the Lord Jesus that nothing is unclean in itself" (Rom 14:14). Whether Paul

100. See the discussion in Judith M. Lieu, "Circumcision, Women and Salvation," *NTS* 40 (1994): 358–70; repr. in Lieu, *Neither Jew nor Greek?*, 101–15.

101. Lieu, "Circumcision," 368–70.

102. Lieu, "Circumcision," 369.

103. See David G. Horrell, "Idol-Food, Idolatry and Ethics in Paul," in *Idolatry: False Worship in the Bible, Early Judaism and Christianity*, ed. Stephen C. Barton (London: T&T Clark, 2007), 23–24; this essay also appears in somewhat expanded form in Horrell, *Making of Christian Morality*, 117–42.

knows or is influenced by Jesus's teaching on the source of uncleanness (Mark 7:1–23) is difficult to say, but the author of Mark—rightly or wrongly—understands Jesus to have "declared all foods clean" (Mark 7:19).[104] For Paul, there is a distinction between sex and food such that the former has identity-defining significance in a way the latter does not.[105] Even so, Paul is equally clear in his lengthy and somewhat contorted discussion of food offered to idols that idolatry itself is strenuously to be avoided (1 Cor 8:1–11:1), and early Christian teaching was generally swift to prohibit such idol-food explicitly, whether or not Paul himself intended to do so (cf. Rev 2:20; Did. 6.3).[106]

In terms of an identity-defining practice concerning food, there is, however, an obvious point of focus in the earliest Christian movement—namely, the community "thanksgiving" meal that came to be known as the eucharist (εὐχαριστία).[107] The fact that Christian groups met for a meal is by no means unusual or unexpected: as Dennis Smith and others have shown, in eating

104. Strong arguments have been raised against reading Mark 7:1–23 as indicating Jesus's rejection of aspects of Jewish law, whether on purity or on food. See, e.g., James G. Crossley, *The Date of Mark's Gospel: Insight from the Law in Earliest Christianity*, JSNTSup 266 (London: T&T Clark, 2004), 191–93; Yair Furstenberg, "Defilement Penetrating the Body: A New Understanding of Contamination in Mark 7.15," *NTS* 54 (2008): 176–200; John van Maaren, "Does Mark's Jesus Abrogate Torah? Jesus' Purity Logion and Its Illustration in Mark 7:15–23," *JMJS* 4 (2017): 21–41. Making sense of Mark's editorial comment in 7:19 is another matter. For example, Maaren, "Does Mark's Jesus," 38–39, argues that "7:19c must refer to *kosher* food" such that Jesus's point is that "permitted food does not convey impurity"; cf. Crossley, *Date of Mark's Gospel*, 192–93. But it is at least arguable whether this restriction to already *kosher* food fits the context of Mark's addressees. Moreover, the fact that Matthew, the earliest interpreter of Mark, concerned to present Jesus as affirming every detail of the Law (Matt 5:17–20), excluded Mark's comment (Matt 15:17–18), suggests that it was understood, problematically for Matthew, to imply "that the observance of the food laws for followers of Jesus is not obligatory" (Adela Yarbro Collins, *Mark: A Commentary*, Hermeneia [Minneapolis: Fortress, 2007], 356; cf. also Joel Marcus, *Mark 1–8: A New Translation with Introduction and Commentary*, AB 27 [New York: Doubleday, 1999], 457–58). Both Collins and Marcus stress that this is an editorial comment of Mark's and note the parallels in Paul.

105. See Horrell, "Idol-Food," 130–34; Alistair S. May, *"The Body for the Lord": Sex and Identity in 1 Corinthians 5–7*, JSNTSup 278 (London: T&T Clark, 2004), 106–10.

106. On the early Christian stance toward "idol food," see Alex T. Cheung, *Idol Food in Corinth: Jewish Background and Pauline Legacy*, JSNTSup 176 (Sheffield: Sheffield Academic Press, 1999), 165–295.

107. For a recent overview of the evidence and developments in the first three centuries, see Valeriy A. Alikin, *The Earliest History of the Christian Gathering: Origin, Development and Content of the Christian Gathering in the First to Third Centuries*, VCSup 102 (Leiden: Brill, 2010), 103–46.

a meal together at their gatherings, early Christians did what any group in the ancient Mediterranean would do when meeting for social or religious purposes.[108] Indeed, Smith's key claim is "that earliest Christian meals developed out of the model of the Greco-Roman banquet."[109] Moreover, there was, as in so many other areas of early Christian belief and practice, considerable diversity in eucharistic custom and the elements of food and drink, as Andrew McGowan has valuably shown.[110]

Yet the eucharistic gathering clearly has special significance as a practice that expresses and reinforces a sense of belonging to the Christian community. Like other practices we have mentioned, it is a practice imbued with significance by the discourse that surrounds and interprets it. For example, in the same context where Paul expresses his vehement opposition to participation in the worship of idols, noted above, he makes equally emphatic mention of the significance of sharing in the bread and wine that represent Christ's body and blood:

> Flee from idolatry. . . . The cup of blessing that we bless, is it not a participation [κοινωνία] in the blood of Christ? The bread that we break, is it not a participation in the body of Christ? Because there is one bread, we who are many are one body [ἒν σῶμα], for we all partake of the one bread. . . . You cannot drink the cup of the Lord and the cup of demons. You cannot partake of the table of the Lord and the table of demons. (1 Cor 10:14–21, ESV)

The participation in this Christian meal, then, and the corresponding non-participation in other "idolatrous" sacrifices, is a practical and located embodiment of the rejection of idolatry of which early Christian sources so frequently make mention (e.g., 1 Thess 1:9–10; 1 Cor 10:14; Diogn. 2).

Paul can evidently presume—as he does later in 1 Cor 11—that the Corinthians are meeting for a communal meal, which can be referred to as "the Lord's Supper" (1 Cor 11:20) and which is probably a central feature of the gathering for worship.[111] The only reason Paul comes to repeat the tradition

---

108. Dennis E. Smith, *From Symposium to Eucharist: The Banquet in the Early Christian World* (Minneapolis: Fortress, 2003), 1, 174, 176, et passim.

109. Smith, *Symposium to Eucharist*, 287.

110. Andrew B. McGowan, *Ascetic Eucharists: Food and Drink in Early Christian Ritual Meals*, OECS (Oxford: Clarendon, 1999).

111. The activities Paul describes and seeks to regulate in 1 Cor 12–14 probably correspond to the kind of "after-dinner" activities (the *symposion*) that might typically follow a meal. See, e.g., Peter Lampe, "Das korinthische Herrenmahl im Schnittpunkt hellenistisch-

of words from the Last Supper is because of his indignation at the factional divisions that have become evident during such meals. Yet this is precious evidence of the spread of this particular tradition, also recorded in somewhat different forms in each of the Synoptic Gospels (of which Luke's is closest to Paul's).[112] It was presumably recalled at such meals, though Paul does not explicitly indicate—still less instruct—that it is or should be so used. Paul also gives some indication of the special significance of this κυριακὸν δεῖπνον when he warns that the Corinthians' malpractice is the cause of sickness and even death: the eucharist represents an encounter with the divine that brings threat and risk as well as embodying participation in the community (1 Cor 11:27-30).

It is difficult to know whether Luke's references to "the breaking of bread" as the fellowship meal indicate a practice significantly different from that which Paul reports at Corinth (Luke 24:30, 35; Acts 2:42, 46; 20:7, 11; 27:35).[113] But it seems most plausible to take Luke's phrase (in most instances at least) to refer to eucharistic celebrations;[114] the Didache indicates that "breaking bread" had this association (κλάσατε ἄρτον καὶ εὐχαριστήσατε, Did. 14.1), as does Ignatius (*Eph.* 20.2).[115] The early references to "love-feasts" (ἀγαπαί, Jude 12) also seem most likely to refer to the same communal meal, at least at this early stage in Christian history.[116]

---

römischer Mahlpraxis und paulinischer Theologia Crucis (1 Kor 11, 17–34)," *ZNW* 82 (1991): 183–213, esp. 188–91, 200–201; Hal Taussig, *In the Beginning Was the Meal: Social Experimentation and Early Christian Identity* (Minneapolis: Fortress, 2009), 47.

112. See 1 Cor 11:23–26; Matt 26:26–29; Mark 14:22–25; Luke 22:15–20.

113. A distinction between the "Pauline" meal and the "Jerusalem" type (focused on bread alone) was famously argued by Hans Lietzmann, *Mass and Lord's Supper* (Leiden: Brill, 1979). For a critique, see McGowan, *Ascetic Eucharists*; Smith, *Symposium to Eucharist*, 4–5. On Luke's references, see, e.g., the brief remarks of C. K. Barrett, *A Critical and Exegetical Commentary on the Acts of the Apostles*, vol. 2, ICC (London: T&T Clark, 1998), xcii–iii.

114. See Alikin, *Christian Gathering*, 112–13. One exception, for example, may well be Acts 27:33–36, though there is at least eucharistic imagery and allusion in the description of Paul's action with the bread (v. 35).

115. On these two texts, see, respectively, Niederwimmer, *Didache*, 195–96, who suggests that the two expressions constitute "a hendiadys, together describing the meal celebration culminating in the Eucharist" (196), and Schoedel, *Ignatius*, 97–98.

116. See Alikin, *Christian Gathering*, 80–81. Ign. *Smyrn.* 8.1–2 would seem to imply that they are still—at least in Ignatius's eyes—terms to refer to one and the same meal, or that the two are still intrinsically combined. As Schoedel, *Ignatius*, 244, comments, "Nor can there be much doubt that the love-feast was thought of as including the eucharist, since baptism and love-feast are juxtaposed as the cardinal liturgical acts of the church." For a contrary argument, see Justin J. Meggitt, *Paul, Poverty and Survival*, SNTW (Edinburgh: T&T Clark,

Whatever the extent of diversity in practice and custom, the prominent place of a significant "ritual" meal as a focal point for Christian meeting is difficult to deny. Ignatius, for example, can broadly assume that the Christians to whom he writes do celebrate eucharist, though he is typically keen to ensure that this is done in a unity under the authority of the bishop (Ign. *Phld.* 4.1; *Smyrn.* 8.1-2; perhaps also *Eph.* 13.1).[117] It is uncertain whether those said to be abstaining from the eucharist (Ign. *Smyrn.* 7.1) are really abstaining from the ritual meal or whether Ignatius rather denies its validity since such people apparently "do not confess that the eucharist is the flesh [σάρξ] of our savior Jesus Christ" (Ign. *Smyrn.* 7.1 [Ehrman, LCL]).

As with baptism, the Didache provides the earliest record of an attempt to regulate the practice of the eucharist and to set down a liturgy to be used. Words of thanks are prescribed for both cup and bread, and only the baptized are to be allowed to participate (Did. 9.1-5). Also prescribed is a prayer of thanksgiving for the conclusion of the meal, which is presumed to be a real and satisfying meal (Did. 10.1-6). These instructions conclude with the perhaps surprisingly permissive remark that "the prophets"—itinerant figures who evidently carry some authority but are to be welcomed with caution (Did. 11-13)—should be permitted to give thanks (or "hold eucharist": εὐχαριστεῖν) "as much as they wish" (ὅσα θέλουσιν) (Did. 10.7).[118]

Indeed, the timing and frequency of eucharistic celebrations is closely connected with a third area of early Christian practice: the focus on Sunday as the day of meeting. The emergence of this Christian custom has been the subject of considerable scholarly discussion and continues to be a matter of some controversy. The New Testament evidence for the establishment of Sunday as the day of meeting is sparse and somewhat inconclusive. Three

---

1998), 189-93, but his attempt to argue for an early distinction, and that the Lord's Supper at Corinth was not a real meal, seems to presume the separation between eucharist and love-feast that needs to be demonstrated.

117. It is not entirely clear whether the exhortation to "be eager to come together more frequently εἰς εὐχαριστίαν θεοῦ καὶ εἰς δόξαν" (Ign. *Eph.* 13.1) should be taken to refer specifically to the eucharist or whether, in view of καὶ εἰς δόξαν, it should be understood as referring more generically to giving thanks and glory to God (probably in the context of the eucharist). Note Ehrman's translation and gloss (LCL, 1.233) and see the comments of Schoedel, *Ignatius*, 74.

118. On the complexities of this verse, see Niederwimmer, *Didache*, 164, who takes this phrase to indicate that the prophets are granted a degree of liturgical freedom in the prayers of thanksgiving. Whether ὅσα indicates temporal freedom ("as often as. . ."; so Lake and Ehrman, LCL) or liturgical freedom ("in whatever way," or "as much as. . ."; so Niederwimmer) is difficult to determine and not crucial to the point.

texts in particular are often discussed: 1 Cor 16:2; Acts 20:7 and Rev 1:10.[119] First Corinthians 16:2 seems likely to reflect the custom of meeting on "the first day of the week" (κατὰ μίαν σαββάτου)—that is, Sunday, the first day after the Jewish Sabbath—though it is not entirely beyond doubt that the setting aside of funds by each individual for Paul's collection project is intended to happen in the context of the community-gathering. Acts 20:7 (ἐν δὲ τῇ μιᾷ τῶν σαββάτων) also adds weight to the notion that Sunday had become the regular day of meeting for the Christian meal, though again there is some room for doubt as to whether Luke implies this or simply indicates that this particular meeting happened to take place on this day.[120] Revelation 1:10 represents the first use of the adjective κυριακός to denote "the Lord's day" (ἐν τῇ κυριακῇ ἡμέρᾳ), rather than using the phrase that relates this day to the Jewish Sabbath (as ἡ μία τῶν σαββάτων). This usage invites comparison with the only other New Testament use of the adjective: Paul's description of the Christian meal as κυριακὸν δεῖπνον (1 Cor 11:20). Again, this may point to the establishment of Sunday as a standard day of Christian meeting, but this is less than certain and hinges largely on later evidence for the use of κυριακή for Sunday, to which we shall turn below. John 20:19 and 26 offer further hints that Sunday, "the first day of the week," had already acquired special significance and become the established day of meeting.[121] None of

---

119. See, e.g., the exchange between S. R. Llewelyn, "The Use of Sunday for Meetings of Believers in the New Testament," *NovT* 43 (2001): 205–23, and Norman H. Young, "'The Use of Sunday for Meetings of Believers in the New Testament': A Response," *NovT* 65 (2003): 111–22. In an earlier major treatment, Samuele Bacchiocchi, *From Sabbath to Sunday: A Historical Investigation of the Rise of Sunday Observance in Early Christianity* (Rome: Pontifical Gregorian University Press, 1977), 90–131, also examines the same texts and concludes skeptically, as does Young, that "no probative value can be derived from them" concerning "Sunday observance in apostolic times" (131). For a contrary perspective, see the essays collected in D. A. Carson, ed., *From Sabbath to Lord's Day: A Biblical, Historical and Theological Investigation* (Grand Rapids: Zondervan, 1982).

120. The latter interpretation is claimed by Young, "Use of Sunday," 118. However, it is not entirely clear whether the comment he quotes in support of this interpretation from Barrett, *Acts*, 2:952, intends this meaning or rather implies that meetings on this day are already standard practice: "Luke's reference to the first day of the week is made in passing, as a natural explanation of the fact that the Christians were taking supper together. It does not appear that he is pressing the observance of the day as something that he wishes to commend to his readers; rather he assumes that they will fully understand what is going on."

121. Cf. C. K. Barrett, *The Gospel According to St. John* (London: SPCK, 1955), 476: "There may be a special intention in John's account of the Lord's special presence on the first day of the week, the day of the Church's regular assembly." Similarly, D. A. Carson,

these references alone is decisive, but overall, the New Testament evidence combines to suggest strongly that Sunday, as the day of Christ's resurrection, had already become significant as a regular day of (weekly) meeting.[122]

This impression is reinforced and confirmed in other early Christian literature. The designation "the Lord's day" (ἡ Κυριακή) becomes established as a way to refer to the day of Christ's resurrection (see Gos. Pet. 35, 50) and is specifically the day when the Christians meet (e.g., Acts John 106; Acts Pet. 30).[123] The Didache gives this as a clear instruction, using a "striking and obviously pleonastic" expression:[124] "On the Lord's day of the Lord [Κατὰ κυριακὴν δὲ κυρίου] when you come together [συναχθέντες], break bread [κλάσατε ἄρτον] and give thanks [or celebrate the eucharist: εὐχαριστήσατε]" (Did. 14.1 [Ehrman, LCL; slightly amended]). Also apparent are polemical contrasts between (Jewish) Sabbath and (Christian) Sunday:[125] after warning the Magnesians against living "according to Judaism" (κατὰ Ἰουδαϊσμόν) (Ign. *Magn.* 8.1), Ignatius speaks of those who are "no longer keeping Sabbath [μηκέτι σαββατίζοντες] but are living according to the Lord's day [ἀλλὰ κατὰ κυριακὴν ζῶντες]," the day of resurrection on which "our life rose up" (Ign. *Magn.* 9.1). Here it is clear that the distinction in the marking of time—Sabbath versus "Lord's Day"—serves to distinguish the two group identities, albeit for groups that are still closely intertwined.

The Gospel According to John (Grand Rapids: Eerdmans, 1991), 657: "a subtle allusion to the origins of Christian worship on this particular day."

122. So also Llewelyn, "Use of Sunday," 223; Alikin, *Christian Gathering*, 40–49.

123. See the detailed study of this term and its use in early Christian literature by Richard J. Bauckham, "The Lord's Day," in Carson, *From Sabbath to Lord's Day*, 221–50. As Bauckham notes (225), the reason the term κυριακός was used most often to refer to the Lord's *Day* (often with ἡμέρα) is that the alternative phrase ἡ ἡμέρα τοῦ κυρίου could not be used without confusion, given that it was established as a phrase to refer to the final eschatological day.

124. Niederwimmer, *Didache*, 195. Niederwimmer comments further that "Κυριακή here . . . is already a familiar term for the day of the week that is consecrated by the resurrection of the Lord. The community is accustomed to gather on that day."

125. On the issue of these juxtapositions, see Richard J. Bauckham, "Sabbath and Sunday in the Post-Apostolic Church," in Carson, *From Sabbath to Lord's Day*, 251–98. Note, however, Bauckham's arguments against Bacchiocchi's thesis that the origin of Sunday worship lies in the desire to distinguish Christian worship from Jewish Sabbath observance (270–73). As Bauckham remarks: "Christian Sunday worship did not originate as the Christian replacement for the Jewish Sabbath, but as the new, specifically Christian day of worship even before the Gentile mission and before the church's differentiation from Judaism. As such it was already normal Christian practice at the beginning of the second century" (273).

This kind of polemical juxtaposition of Sabbath and Sunday, giving explicit reasoning to support the Christian practice of meeting on Sunday, is also found in the Epistle of Barnabas. After a lengthy discussion of Sabbath, both in terms of the eschatological symbolism of the six "days" and the inability of people to keep Sabbath holy, the author argues that this is why Sabbath observance is no longer acceptable and why Christians gather on "the eighth day": this "eighth day" marks the beginning of a new world (Barn. 15.8). "Therefore," he writes, "we also celebrate with gladness the eighth day [τὴν ἡμέραν τὴν ὀγδόην] on which Jesus also rose from the dead [ὁ Ἰησοῦς ἀνέστη ἐκ νεκρῶν]" (Barn. 15.9). Such texts suggest that one effect of the adoption of Sunday as the Christian day of meeting was, at least eventually, to differentiate the Christian movement from Judaism, albeit in a context where such differentiation is neither established nor presumed.[126]

It is impossible to ascertain from non-Christian writers how far external observers might confirm that these practices were notable or prominent markers of Christian identity in the first decades of the Christian movement. Our earliest external comments on the Christians only begin to appear in the early second century (with the exception of the much disputed *Testimonium Flavianum* in Josephus, *A.J.* 18.63–64, which records that "the tribe of the Christians [τὸ φῦλον τῶν Χριστιανῶν] has still to this day not disappeared" [Feldman, LCL]) and then give only the barest of information. Pliny learns from the Christians he interrogates that they worship Christ *quasi deo* and share a meal together (Pliny, *Ep.* 10.96.7), while Tacitus and Suetonius merely tell us—polemically—of the Christians' antisocial behavior, their "hatred of the human race" (Tacitus, *Ann.* 15.44), and their belonging, as a particular *genus hominum*, to a "new and wicked superstition" (*superstitionis novae ac maleficae*, Suetonius, *Nero* 16.2). Comments on what the Christians do are heavily shaped by conventional polemic against suspicious groups, though the specific elements may reflect some knowledge of distinctive Christian customs and practices.[127] The accusations of incest, for example,

126. Cf. Bacchiocchi, *From Sabbath to Sunday*, 234–35, who labels this kind of deliberate distinguishing, beginning in Barnabas, an "anti-Judaism of differentiation" (305). He suggests that this kind of break with Judaism—and the focus on Sunday as the day of meeting—first occurred in second-century Rome, but he seems unduly sceptical about the NT evidence for Sunday-meeting (see n. 119 above), and it is unlikely that the original focus on Sunday reflects such a concern for differentiation (see n. 125 above).

127. For reports of such polemical criticism, see, e.g., Eusebius, *Hist. eccl.* 4.7.11; 5.1.14, 26; 9.5.2; Justin, *1 Apol.* 26; *2 Apol.* 12; Tertullian, *Apol.* 2.5; 6.11–7.5; De Ste. Croix, "The Early Christians," 20–21; Craig S. de Vos, "Popular Graeco-Roman Responses to Christian-

may have some basis in the prominence of kinship language among Christians (see §4.2) and their custom of the kiss;[128] the charge of cannibalism may be rooted in eucharistic practice, and specifically the idea of eating Christ's flesh and drinking his blood (cf. John 6:53–56). But such references can give only brief glimpses of the ways Christians were perceived, and it is on the internal sources that we have largely to depend.

5.3.3   *Practices, Discourse, and Identity by Association*

These various Jewish and Christian practices, covering key aspects of culture and custom—signs of belonging, food and meals, and marking time—seem to serve as broadly comparable ways in which the particular identity of the people-group was marked. Without in any way minimizing the significant differences, it is also interesting to draw attention to another respect in which such identity-defining practices are comparable: in none of these cases is there an unambiguous visual signifier sufficient, *eo ipso*, to confirm that a person is Jewish or Christian. As we noted above, the Epistle to Diognetus insists that Christians are *not* distinctive in terms of their country, language, or customs (Diogn. 5.1), though it does describe them as a "new race" (1.1) and spends its opening chapters distinguishing them and their practices from both Greek idolatry and from Judaism. Shaye Cohen gives a strikingly similar answer to his question about how, in antiquity, one could tell who was a Jew:

> The diaspora Jews of antiquity were not easily recognizable—if, indeed, they were recognizable at all. Jews looked like everyone else, dressed like everyone else, spoke like everyone else, had names and occupations like those of everyone else, and, in general, closely resembled their gentile neighbors. Even circumcision did not always make male Jews distinctive, and as long as they kept their pants on, it certainly did not make them recognizable. . . . How, then, did you know a Jew in antiquity when you saw one? The answer is that you did not.[129]

---

ity," in *The Early Christian World*, ed. Philip F. Esler (London: Routledge, 2000), 877–85; Marta Sordi, *The Christians and the Roman Empire* (London: Routledge, 1994), 32–33.

128. See Rom 16:16; 1 Cor 16:20; 2 Cor 13:12; 1 Thess 5:26; 1 Pet 5:14. On the kiss as a possible "sign of identification" (in the context of late second-century North Africa), see Rebillard, *Christians and Their Many Identities*, 17. On the "holy kiss" as a ritual action among the early Christians, see Alikin, *Christian Gathering*, 255–60.

129. Cohen, *Beginnings*, 67. See also, in agreement on this point, Joseph Geiger, "The

It seems, then, that neither Jews nor Christians would have been identifiable merely from visual clues—unlike modern ethnic or racial identifications made (however questionably) on the basis of visual signifiers such as
skin color, even though these visual signs are also too varied and flexible to
allow unambiguous identification. Given this conclusion, Cohen suggests
that there are two ways in which Jews could plausibly have been identified:
by association and by ritual practices. The quotation above continues:

> But you could make reasonably plausible inferences from what you saw.
> First, if you saw someone associating with Jews, living in a (or the) Jewish
> part of town, married to a Jew, and, in general, integrated socially with
> other Jews, you might reasonably conclude that that someone was a Jew.
> Second, if you saw someone performing Jewish rituals and practices, you
> might reasonably conclude that that someone was a Jew.[130]

Cohen continues, however, by noting that uncertainty would continue
and that cases of mistaken identity were likely.[131] In a similar way, Éric Rebillard, discussing the particular context of second-century Carthage, suggests
that Christians could only have been identified "by association"—that is, by
the fact that they associated with other Christians as a group and identified
themselves as such.[132] Their identity-defining practices—such as baptism,
eucharist, and Sunday meeting—would have constituted significant aspects
of this "identity by association."

One implication of this is that the lines of demarcation between Jew and
non-Jew, and also between Christian and non-Christian, are not necessarily
easy to draw and are dependent on the observer, the self-identification of
the individual, and the judgment of groups themselves as to whether or not
so-and-so is a genuine member.[133] Even circumcision, the most enduringly
physical, if generally hidden, of the identity-defining practices we have considered, did not, as we have already noted, *ipso facto* constitute a badge of
Jewishness, not only because it could serve to identify only the male mem-

---

Jew and the Other: Doubtful and Multiple Identities in the Roman Empire," in Levine and
Schwartz, *Jewish Identities*, 135–46.

130. Cohen, *Beginnings*, 67–68; cf. 53–62.

131. Cohen, *Beginnings*, 68.

132. Rebillard, *Christians and Their Many Identities*, 14. Similarly, Geiger, "The Jew and
the Other," 142–43.

133. Cf. Joshua D. Garroway, *Paul's Gentile-Jews: Neither Jew nor Gentile, but Both* (New
York: Palgrave Macmillan, 2012), 15–43.

bers of the community but also because it was practiced by other peoples at the time. What this means is that, in all these cases, the discursive and social contexts that surround and interpret any such practice are crucial for its significance.

5.4 Conclusions

In this chapter, we have explored three distinct but closely related facets of early Christian and Jewish discourse and practice: the depiction of belonging to the group as constituted by the adoption or practice of a particular way of life, the importance of socializing children into that way of life, and the most significant practices that were taken to be indicative of that way of life. Quite apart from all the internal variety among both Jewish and Christian writers and groups and the complex and inextricable connections between the two identities, it is clear that there are considerable differences between Jewish sources on the one hand and Christian sources on the other in terms of the ways these aspects of group identity are construed and depicted. Though I have set out comparisons in this chapter, as in others, it is not my intention to suggest any neat equivalence. To take one clear example, the idea of following ancestral ways (τὰ πάτρια) is prominent as a way to encapsulate what it means to live a Jewish life in a number of Jewish sources, but the same terminology is not used of the Christian way of life in the earliest Christian writings (for some obvious reasons). Following Christ is not—and is not presented as—a "way of life" in exactly the same way that Judaism is, just as Judaism is not depicted as a way of life in precisely the same way that Hellenism or Greekness is.

But there are also sufficient indications that the various depictions of Jewish and Christian identity as constituted by following a particular way of life are at least comparable in significant ways. First, the stress placed on the need to follow a certain "way of life" indicates that this is seen, in both Jewish and Christian contexts, as crucial to maintaining and displaying one's identity—indeed as constitutive of that identity. Second, in both traditions, we find a stress on the importance of socializing children into this way of life, indicating the intention that identity as Jew or Christian will be passed on down the generations as children are enculturated into the appropriate patterns of conduct and practice. Third, there are various distinctive practices that are seen to function as important signs of belonging, though in each case these practices are given significance by discursive and social context. Visual clues and social practices are not sufficient in themselves to define identity but may be confirmed as such either by the discourse that surrounds and gives meaning to these practices or by the power of "association." As Cohen and Rebillard suggest, Jews and Christians were most likely to be identified "by association."

The stress placed upon following a "way of life," displayed in particular through certain salient practices, and passed on to the next generation especially through the family, also suggests once again that the modern categories of "religion" and "ethnicity" are inextricably woven together in what the ancient sources depict as a way of life. In both Jewish and Christian sources, whatever the precise terms used to depict ancestral customs and patterns of conduct, what we would call "religious" convictions and practices are central; in neither case can "ethnic" and "religious" be neatly separated.

Indeed, however much there might be differences in their depictions of this way of life, it would not seem appropriate to assign "Jewish" and "Christian" ways of life to entirely different categories, such as "ethnic" on the one hand and "non-ethnic" or "socio-religious" on the other. Even if Jewishness is an "ethnic" identity, it is clearly not an identity simply and sufficiently given by birth but one that depends on maintaining and adhering to a Jewish way of life; there is a certain self-consciousness about the possibility of acquiring or losing such identity through appropriate or inappropriate conduct (see ch. 8). Early Christian depictions of allegiance to Christ as a way of life suggest, notwithstanding the significant differences, that this way of life belongs in a similar category, since turning to a new way of life in Christ is explicitly depicted as requiring the abandonment of "ancestral" ways, a move that disrupts ethnic identity insofar as this is constituted not by birth alone but also by the adherence to a particular way of life with its customs, culture, and religious practices. This, indeed, was one reason why the Christian movement faced hostility.

The focus of this chapter on "way of life" and its maintenance through practice and across the generations is not, however, intended to imply an answer to the question whether either Jewish or early Christian identity might best be categorized as "ethnic" (or, indeed, as "religious"). Rather, the question itself is to some degree thereby problematized, since both modes of belonging seem to focus on what are generally seen as key features of ethnic groups—a common culture, customs, and way of life passed on through the generations—though in different and distinctive ways and with "religious" convictions and practices at their core.

What the comparisons do suggest, though—their significant differences notwithstanding—is that both Jewish and Christian texts depict belonging in terms of adherence to a way of life that demarcates and bounds the group in particular ways, distinguishing it from others. Given the structural similarities in discourse and practice, it would seem questionable to draw any contrast between the two traditions in terms of particular versus universal, exclusive versus inclusive, closed versus open, or even ethnic versus trans-ethnic or non-ethnic. There is one respect, however, in which the contrast might seem more likely to hold, and that is in relation to homeland or territory, to which we turn in the next chapter.

CHAPTER 6

Homeland: Territory and Symbolic Constructions of Space

Among the characteristics commonly seen in ethnic groups, according to Anthony Smith, is some kind of "*link* with a *homeland*, not necessarily its physical occupation by the *ethnie*, only its symbolic attachment to the ancestral land, as with diaspora peoples."[1] Many—though not all—of the names assigned to "peoples," or ἔθνη, in antiquity as well as the present day reflect a (perceived) connection with a land of origin or homeland: Egyptians from Egypt, Syrians from Syria, Idumaeans from Idumea, and so on.[2] As Josephus remarks, "Those who think highly of their own homelands are proud to be named after them"—though what he goes on immediately to say indicates that people did not always stick to this principle (*C. Ap.* 2.30 [Barclay]).[3] This, then, is an initially important and obvious difference between the group-names Ἰουδαῖοι and Χριστιανοί: the former encodes a link with a land—the Ἰουδαῖοι are connected with Ἰουδαία—while the latter expresses adherence to a person, as do other names of the (Latin-derived) -ιανος formation.[4] Does this basic distinction indicate, as has often been suggested, that Judaism—and Jewish identity—is inextricably bound to a particular

---

1. Hutchinson and Smith, "Introduction," 7, italics original. See p. 72 above.

2. For these examples, see Steve Mason, "Das antike Judentum als Hintergrund des frühen Christentums," *ZNT* 19 (2016): 20; see also Esler, *Conflict and Identity*, 63. Not all ethnic group names derive from territory; on the varieties of ethnic names, see R. R. R. Smith, "Simulacra Gentium: The Ethne from the Sebasteion at Aphrodisias," *JRS* 78 (1988): 50–77, esp. 57–58; for one literary example, see Strabo, *Geogr.* 2.5.33.

3. On this text and the wider issue, see Barclay, "'Ἰουδαῖος," 46–47; Barclay, *Against Apion*, 183–84n101.

4. On the etymology of the name Χριστιανός, see David G. Horrell, "The Label Χριστιανός: 1 Pet 4:16 and the Formation of Christian Identity," *JBL* 126 (2007): 362–67; revised and expanded in Horrell, *Becoming Christian*, 164–210.

land, while early Christian identity is essentially detached from territorial claims and allegiance, "deterritorialized" since "Jesus becomes 'the place' which replaces all holy places"?[5] In attempting to probe this distinction, the task of this chapter is to explore the kinds of orientation to place and territory we find in Jewish and early Christian texts. The broader concern is to consider how far these various orientations support or query the contrast between an ethnically particular Judaism—linked to a specific homeland—and a trans-ethnic, universal Christianity, freed from such territorial constraints.

Before we turn to specific evidence and textual examples, we may note some initial reasons why any simple contrast may at least be open to question. First, as we have noted previously, no single factor, including attachment to a specific land, should be taken as a *sine qua non* for ethnic identity. It is striking, for example, that Herodotus's famous "definition" of Greekness (8.144) makes no mention of shared territory (see §2.1 above). Various factors can be invoked—can become or be made salient for group identity—at different times and in different places. As Love Sechrest has demonstrated, different characteristics and factors are associated in ancient literature with particular ethnic or racial groups; in the case of the Jewish texts Sechrest surveys, it is religious factors that loom largest in conjunction with the topic of ethnic group identity.[6] Second, the linking of territory and people is sometimes further complicated by a connection with myths of eponymous ancestors from whom the people and thus the place derive their names: Romulus and Hellen are perhaps among the most famous examples; Plutarch records a less famous legend that a certain Ἰουδαῖος was the ancestor of the Ἰουδαῖοι.[7] Third, it is important to stress Anthony Smith's emphasis on "symbolic at-

---

5. These phrases are taken from W. D. Davies, *The Gospel and the Land: Early Christianity and Jewish Territorial Doctrine* (Berkeley: University of California Press, 1974), 173n19 (on Paul), 318 (on John's Gospel). They are also cited by Georg Strecker, "Das Land Israel in frühchristlicher Zeit," in *Das Land Israel in biblischer Zeit*, ed. Georg Strecker, Göttinger Theologische Arbeiten 25 (Göttingen: Vandenhoeck & Ruprecht, 1983), 189–90. See further Davies, *Gospel and the Land*, 179, 219–20, 366–75; and the overview of Davies's work in Strecker, "Das Land Israel," 188–92. For a recent revisiting of the issues raised, see Amy-Jill Levine, "*The Gospel and the Land* Revisited: Exegesis, Hermeneutics, and Politics," in *Peace and Faith: Christian Churches and the Israeli-Palestinian Conflict*, ed. Cary Nelson and Michael C. Gizzi (forthcoming).

6. Sechrest, *A Former Jew*, 54–109, esp. 104–5, also 209.

7. Plutarch records the belief that the Egyptian god Typhon gave birth to two sons, named Ἱεροσόλυμος and Ἰουδαῖος, but dismisses this as an attempt "to drag Jewish traditions into the legend" (τὰ Ἰουδαϊκὰ παρέλκοντες εἰς τὸν μῦθον) (*Mor.* 363D [Babbitt, LCL]).

tachment" to land rather than physical occupation necessarily. Indeed, one key difference he suggests between "*ethnie*" and "nation" as concepts is that the latter occupies a homeland while the former may have only a symbolic attachment to it.[8]

All this gives us initial reasons to suspect that a sharp dichotomy between Jewish territoriality and a "deterritorialized" early Christianity may not be adequate to understanding the evidence—and in particular the various kinds of significance attributed to space and place. This is especially so in light of recent theoretical approaches to space and place that may also help to frame and inform our discussion.[9]

Fundamental to contemporary critical spatial theory is the complex and difficult work of the French philosopher Henri Lefebvre in *The Production of Space*, which has been developed by the human geographers David Harvey and Edward Soja.[10] This work has been taken up in recent biblical studies.[11] Emblematic of such interest is the five-volume project on constructions of space emerging from the work of an SBL seminar devoted to the theme.[12]

8. See, e.g., Anthony D. Smith, *National Identity* (London: Penguin; Reno: University of Nevada Press, 1991), 40; *Nationalism: Theory, Ideology, History*, Key Concepts (Cambridge: Polity, 2010), 12–15.

9. The following paragraphs are adapted from David G. Horrell, "Re-Placing 1 Peter: From Place of Origin to Constructions of Space," in *The Urban World and the First Christians*, ed. Steve Paul Walton, Paul R. Trebilco, and David Gill (Grand Rapids: Eerdmans, 2017), 278–80. An earlier version of some of the material in this chapter appears in David G. Horrell, "Physical and Symbolic Geography: Constructions of Space and Early Christian Identities," *Annali di Storia dell'Esegesi* 36 (2019): 375–92.

10. Henri Lefebvre, *The Production of Space*, trans. Donald Nicholson-Smith (Oxford: Blackwell, 1991 [French original 1974]); David Harvey, *The Condition of Postmodernity: An Inquiry into the Origins of Cultural Change* (Oxford: Blackwell, 1989); Edward W. Soja, *Thirdspace: Journeys to Los Angeles and Other Real-and-Imagined Places* (Oxford: Blackwell, 1996).

11. For a recent overview, see Eric C. Stewart, "New Testament Space/Spatiality," *BTB* 42 (2012): 139–50, esp. 145–47 on works in NT studies. On the theoretical developments since the early appropriations of Lefebvre by Harvey and Soja, see Matthew Sleeman, "Critical Spacial Theory 2.0," in *Constructions of Space*, vol. 5: *Place, Space and Identity in the Ancient Mediterranean World*, ed. Gert T. M. Prinsloo and Christl M. Maier, LHBOTS 576 (London: Bloomsbury T&T Clark, 2013), 49–66. On the wider theoretical developments in geography and the challenge to biblical studies, see Matthew Sleeman, *Geography and the Ascension Narrative in Acts*, SNTSMS 146 (Cambridge: Cambridge University Press, 2009), esp. 22–56.

12. Jon L. Berquist and Claudia V. Camp, eds., *Constructions of Space*, vol. 1: *Theory, Geography, and Narrative*, LHBOTS 481 (London: T&T Clark, 2007); Berquist and Camp, eds., *Constructions of Space*, vol. 2: *The Biblical City and Other Imagined Spaces*, LHBOTS 490 (London: T&T Clark, 2008); Jorunn Økland, J. Cornelis de Vos, and Karen J. Wenell,

The starting point for such theoretical refection is a concern to challenge the common-sense perception, based in Newtonian science and Cartesian philosophy, that space, like time, is simply there, a given, an empty physical container with fixed parameters within which human action takes place. Lefebvre's *Production of Space*, for example, begins, "Not so many years ago, the word 'space' had a strictly geometrical meaning: the idea it evoked was simply that of an empty area."[13] By contrast, these theorists insist, space is produced and reproduced: constructed, shaped, represented. This insistence on the constructedness of space underpins what has been labeled a spatial turn, in which much greater attention is paid to what Soja calls "the *spatiality of human life*."[14]

A second key point, which follows from the first, is that the study of space needs to engage with various ways in which space is produced, experienced and conceived. Lefebvre, Harvey, and Soja all present somewhat different threefold categorizations of spatial perspectives and practices.[15] Lefebvre's schema is adapted by Harvey in the following three categories: "material spatial practices" (the realm of "experience"), "representations of space" (the realm of "perception"), and "spaces of representation" (the realm of "imagination").[16] Soja's scheme, though also inspired by Lefebvre, is somewhat different: he speaks of "firstspace" as "focused on the 'real' material world" and "secondspace" as a "perspective that interprets this reality through 'imagined' representations of reality."[17] "Thirdspace" is deliberately and explicitly a loosely defined category but is intended to break down the

---

eds., *Constructions of Space*, vol. 3: *Biblical Spatiality and the Sacred*, LHBOTS 540 (London: Bloomsbury T&T Clark, 2016); Mark K. George, ed., *Constructions of Space*, vol. 4: *Further Developments in Examining Ancient Israel's Social Space*, LHBOTS 569 (London: Bloomsbury T&T Clark, 2013); Prinsloo and Maier, *Constructions of Space*, vol. 5: *Place, Space and Identity in the Ancient Mediterranean World*, LHBOTS 576 (New York: Bloomsbury T&T Clark, 2013).

13. Lefebvre, *Production of Space*, 1. See Harvey, *Condition of Postmodernity*, 201–203; David Harvey, *Spaces of Hope* (Edinburgh: Edinburgh University Press, 2000), 182; Liam Kennedy, *Race and Urban Space in Contemporary American Culture*, Tendencies: Identities, Texts, Cultures (Edinburgh: Edinburgh University Press, 2000), 8–9; Sleeman, *Geography*, 24.

14. Soja, *Thirdspace*, 2, italics original. For an overview of this turn and both the early and more recent developments in spatial theory, see Sleeman, "Critical Spacial Theory 2.0."

15. A concise tabular overview is provided by Sleeman, *Geography*, 43.

16. See Lefebvre, *Production of Space*, 38–39; Harvey, *Condition of Postmodernity*, 218–23, esp. table 3.1 on 220–21.

17. Soja, *Thirdspace*, 6; cf. 10–11, 66–68, 74–82.

binary dichotomy between the two first categories, between material space and imagined space, and to create new space and new possibilities for resistance—hence Soja's emblematic designation of "real-and-imagined places" (in the subtitle of his book entitled *Thirdspace*).[18] Drawing on Lefebvre, Soja speaks of "spaces of representation"—Lefebvre's third category—as "the terrain for the generation of 'counterspaces,' spaces of resistance to the dominant order arising precisely from their subordinate, peripheral or marginalized positioning."[19] Indeed, drawing on radical thinkers such as Jacques Derrida, bell hooks, and Homi Bhabha, as well as Lefebvre, Soja stresses the ways in which thirdspace can, from the margins, challenge "all conventional modes of spatial thinking," disorient and disrupt, and fundamentally offer "an alternative envisioning of spatiality."[20]

One of the key contributions of such critical spatial theory is to challenge and disrupt any binary distinction between physical space on the one hand and symbolic, imagined or represented space on the other. The two are always intertwined in complex and significant ways. This is not to downplay the importance of physical space—given the basic human need for space to inhabit, a place for the body to live in—but it is to insist that the (often contested) claims to physical space are intrinsically bound up with perceptions about the significance of space, about its meaning and symbolic power. This theoretical orientation might already begin to indicate one reason to be cautious concerning any overly simple contrast between Jewish attachment to the land and Christian detachment from, or spiritualization of, such connections.

My aim in this chapter, then, is to explore some of the ways in which land, territory, or place are construed and constructed in Jewish and early Christian texts and to consider the significance of these for notions of identity. These explorations will be selective and illustrative only, not least in relation to the Jewish sources, which are the subject of the first main section below. On this subject in particular, one can hardly fail to be aware of the contemporary resonances of the issue in the conflicts over land in Israel/Palestine, which are evident (and explicitly discussed) even in works whose

18. Cf. Soja, *Thirdspace*, 81: "*Thirdspace epistemologies* can now be briefly described as arising from the sympathetic deconstruction and heuristic reconstitution of the Firstspace-Secondspace duality, another example of what I have called thirding-as-Othering. Such thirding is designed not just to critique Firstspace and Secondspace modes of thought, but also to reinvigorate their approaches to spatial knowledge with new possibilities heretofore unthought of inside the traditional spatial disciplines."

19. Soja, *Thirdspace*, 68.

20. Soja, *Thirdspace*, 163.

primary focus is the ancient biblical period.[21] My particular concern here leaves such issues largely at the margins, though the problematizing of any neat contrast between Jewish territoriality and Christian a-territorial universalism might at least raise questions about both the nature of the link between Jewishness and territory[22] and any implication that Christianity rises innocently above territorial claims.

6.1 Ideologies of Land and Constructions of Space in Early Jewish Texts

According to the biblical accounts, just as Abraham was promised that he would become a "great nation" (גּוֹי גָּדוֹל; ἔθνος μέγα) (Gen 12:2) and have many descendants (Gen 15:5; 17:4–7), so too he was promised a land—the land of Canaan—to be given to him and his descendants forever (e.g., Gen 12:1; 15:7; 17:8; cf. 2 Chr 20:7; Neh 9:7–8). While the specific label "land of promise," or "promised land" (γῆ τῆς ἐπαγγελίας) was apparently coined by the author of Hebrews (Heb 11:9),[23] the motif forms a prominent thread in the narrative(s) of the Jewish scriptures, albeit presented and understood in various ways.[24] Richard Vair, for example, draws attention to two major and contrasting traditions in the Jewish scriptures, one of which stresses the unconditional promise of the land to Abraham and his descendants, the other of which stresses the conditionality of the occupation of the land, contingent upon obedience to the Mosaic covenant. Norman Habel has detailed six distinct "biblical land ideologies."[25]

---

21. For some highly contrasting examples, see Keith W. Whitelam, *The Invention of Ancient Israel: The Silencing of Palestinian History* (London: Routledge, 1996); David Frankel, *The Land of Canaan and the Destiny of Israel: Theologies of Territory in the Hebrew Bible*, Siphrut: Literature and Theology of the Hebrew Scriptures 4 (Winona Lake, IN: Eisenbrauns, 2011); Stavrakopoulou, *Land of Our Fathers*; Marie-Theres Wacker and Ralf Koerrenz, eds., *Heiliges Land*, Jahrbuch für Biblische Theologie 23 (Neukirchen-Vluyn: Neukirchener, 2009); Walter Brueggemann, *The Land: Place as Gift, Promise, and Challenge in Biblical Faith*, 2nd ed., OBT (Minneapolis: Fortress, 2002).

22. For one example of reflections on this link, see Daniel Boyarin, *A Radical Jew: Paul and the Politics of Identity* (Berkeley: University of California Press, 1994), 251–60.

23. An observation noted by Robert L. Wilken, *The Land Called Holy: Palestine in Christian History and Thought* (New Haven: Yale University Press, 1992), 52; cf. Harold W. Attridge, *The Epistle to the Hebrews*, Hermeneia (Philadelphia: Fortress, 1989), 323.

24. See W. D. Davies, *The Territorial Dimension of Judaism* (Berkeley: University of California Press, 1982), 6–14.

25. See Richard James Vair, "The Old Testament Promise of the Land as Reinterpreted

Among the prominent concerns in the Hebrew Bible, the land is the final goal of the escape from Egypt narrated in Exodus and the basis for the covenant set out in Deuteronomy (see, e.g., Deut 1:8).[26] A strong sense of interconnection between God, the people, and the land is frequently evident, not least in Leviticus, with its promises and threats about the need to live obediently and properly so that both people and land may flourish (e.g., Lev 25:18; 26:3–13, 27–33).[27] It is a land taken by conquest, which is extensively narrated in the book of Joshua. In various contexts of threat, defeat, exile, and perceived infidelity, prophets express hope for a restoration of the people to flourishing in the land (e.g., Amos 9:14–15); in reaction to the Babylonian exile, visions of the people restored to the land are declared, even if the prophet Jeremiah sees no particular urgency to anticipate the end of exile (Jer 29:4–14).[28] Some of the visions of so-called Second and Third Isaiah give expression to what Robert Wilken calls "a new cartography of hope" with "sublime language and soaring images" of the people flourishing in the land, and in particular of a renewed and glorious Jerusalem.[29] The prophet Zechariah, also expressing visions of hope for restoration, is the first to use the expression "holy land" (אדמת הקדש; τὴν γῆν τὴν ἁγίαν) (Zech 2:12; cf. 2 Macc 1:7), though this motif is found in other references to the "holy mountain" within the land.[30] The idea of a land promised to the people that they shall inhabit and flourish in, so long as they are faithful and obedient, is both a partly fulfilled reality and an aspect of eschatological hope.

Already in such a brief sketch, we can discern that there is symbolic representation and imaginary construction of space woven into the depictions of—and claims over—the land. Just as literary and cartographic descriptions in other contexts, ancient and modern, have placed their own focal point at the center of the world—Rome, London, or wherever—so it is no surprise to find depictions of Israel, or more specifically Jerusalem and its temple,

---

in First and Second Century Christian Literature" (PhD diss., Graduate Theological Union, 1979), 1–17; Norman C. Habel, *The Land Is Mine: Six Biblical Land Ideologies*, OBT (Minneapolis: Fortress, 1995).

26. Cf. Wilken, *Land Called Holy*, 4.

27. See, e.g., Jonathan Morgan, "Transgressing, Puking, Covenanting: The Character of Land in Leviticus," *Theology* 112 (2009): 172–80; Morgan, "Land, Rest and Sacrifice: Ecological Reflections on the Book of Leviticus" (PhD diss., Univesity of Exeter, 2010).

28. See Davies, *Territorial Dimension*, 21–28.

29. Wilken, *Land Called Holy*, 17; see, e.g., Isa 52:1–9; 60:11–22; 66:10–20; cf. Isa 2:1–4; Mic 4:1–3.

30. E.g., Ps 78:54; Isa 27:13; 57:13; Jer 31:23; Ezek 20:40; Joel 2:1.

as the center of the earth, its navel (ὀμφαλός, Ezek 38:12; cf. 5:5; Jub. 8:12, 19).[31] This orientation to Jerusalem and the temple is a kind of symbolic construction of space.

There are various aspects of these traditions and their developments in subsequent Jewish texts that further nuance and complicate the sense of physical-and-symbolic connections between the people, their identity, and the land.

First, we might note the insistence that the land belongs to YHWH such that the people themselves do not ever own it (Lev 25:23).[32] One corollary of this is that the people can be described as "strangers and aliens" (גרים ותושבים; προσήλυτοι καὶ πάροικοι) even in this "promised" land (Lev 25:23). The phrasing is reminiscent of Abraham's self-description as "a stranger and an alien" (גר ותושב; πάροικος καὶ παρεπίδημος) (Gen 23:4) among the Hittites (in the land described as Canaan; cf. Gen 15:18–20).[33] Further texts, echoing this self-description, indicate a kind of broadening or spiritualizing of this description such that it conveys a sense of dislocation or "not-at-home-ness" in the world. Perhaps the clearest example is in 1 Chr 29:15: "For we are strangers before you and sojourners, as all our fathers were. Our days on the earth [על־הארץ/ἐπὶ γῆς] are like a shadow, and there is no abiding" (ESV; cf. Ps 39:12 [39:13 MT; 38.13 LXX]).[34] This kind of depiction of human

31. See Davies, *Territorial Dimension*, 1–3. See further Philip S. Alexander, "Jerusalem as the *Omphalos* of the World: On the History of a Geographical Concept," in *Jerusalem: Its Sanctity and Centrality to Judaism, Christianity, and Islam*, ed. Lee I. Levine (New York: Continuum, 1999), 104–19, who argues that this image of Jerusalem as the navel of the world originates in the Hasmonean period with Jubilees, whose implied map of the world reflects and supports "the political propaganda of the Hasmonean state" (110). On the influence of the geographical construction of Jub. 8–9, which he sees as stemming from the "table of nations" in Genesis 10, see James M. Scott, *Geography in Early Judaism and Christianity: The Book of Jubilees*, SNTSMS 113 (Cambridge: Cambridge University Press, 2002). On the ideological dimensions of modern Bible maps, see Burke O. Long, "Bible Maps and America's Nationalist Narratives," in Berquist and Camp, *Constructions of Space*, 1:109–25.

32. On this theme, see Davies, *Territorial Dimension*, 15–21.

33. Cited also by Philo, *Conf.* 79. On the Hebrew coupling, see Joyce Reynolds and Robert Tannenbaum, *Jews and God-Fearers at Aphrodisias: Greek Inscriptions with Commentary*, Cambridge Philological Society Supplementary Series 12 (Cambridge: Cambridge Philological Society, 1987), 48, 58–59.

34. While ארץ and γῆ can refer to the earth in general or to the land of Israel (or some other particular land), the surrounding imagery here suggests that it is existence on the earth that is in view rather than life in the land of Israel specifically. On this issue, see Martin Vahrenhorst, "Land und Landverheißung im Neuen Testament," in Wacker and Koerrenz, *Heiliges Land*, 125–26, who notes, e.g., the ambiguity of the term in Matt 5:5, 13. On Matt

life—as a brief and temporary residence on the earth—is not infrequently echoed in other ancient Greek literature, as Reinhard Feldmeier has shown.[35] Philo reiterates the self-description of Abraham in Gen 23:4, contrasting the human's heavenly πατρίς with their residence on earth as ξένος; the wise person dwells in the body as a stranger and finds their true home in the virtues (*Conf.* 78–82; see further below).

A second point to note, closely connected to this first one, is that in the Hebrew Bible's own stories, whatever their historical veracity, the land Israel claims is not depicted as the people's land of origin. As W. D. Davies notes, "In the Hexateuch, the Land is invariably referred to as 'the land of Canaan.' Not until 1 Sam. 13:19 does the phrase 'the land of Israel' appear."[36] Some later writings indicate a concern to explain or justify the occupation of the land:[37] the Wisdom of Solomon suggests that God hated the idolatry and child-murder of the previous inhabitants in God's "holy land" (τῆς ἁγίας σου γῆς), so they were, by God's will (ἐβουλήθης), destroyed "through the hands of our ancestors" (διὰ χειρῶν πατέρων ἡμῶν) (Wis 12:3–7). Philo records that the people left Egypt because the land there was insufficient to contain their vast population and because they yearned for "their ancient fatherland" (τῆς πατρίου καὶ ἀρχαίας γῆς) (*Hypoth.* 6.1).[38] His readers are asked to choose which they prefer from two explanations as to the reasons for the Jews' success in occupying the land (6.6): either their superior force or, rather, that they were weak and few after their migration but "won the respect of their opponents, who voluntarily surrendered their land to them" (αἰδέσεως δὲ τυχεῖν παρὰ τούτοις καὶ τὴν γῆν λαβεῖν ἑκόντων). Philo seems clear that he finds this latter alternative more reasonable despite the historical narratives (6.5).[39]

In this regard, it is interesting to observe a shift in perspective and description over time: only in later biblical writings, such as the books of

---

5:5, see Wilken, *Land Called Holy*, 47–48, who suggests the translation "possess the land" given the parallels in the LXX (e.g., Isa 60:21; 61:7).

35. Reinhard Feldmeier, *Die Christen als Fremde: Die Metapher der Fremde in der antiken Welt, im Urchristentum und im 1. Petrusbrief*, WUNT 64 (Tübingen: Mohr Siebeck, 1992), 23–38.

36. Davies, *Territorial Dimension*, 15. See, e.g., Gen 12:5; 17:8; 37:1.

37. See further Wilken, *Land Called Holy*, 30–33.

38. The text is extant only in quotations in Eusebius, *Praep. ev.* 8.6.1–9; 7.1–20; quoted above from Colson, LCL, which uses the chapter and verse numbers from Eusebius.

39. Cf. also Berndt Schaller, "Philon von Alexandria und das 'Heilige Land,'" in *Das Land Israel in biblischer Zeit*, ed. Georg Strecker, Göttinger Theologische Arbeiten 25 (Göttingen: Vandenhoeck & Ruprecht, 1983), 176.

the Maccabees, does the land begin to be described as πατρίς, an ancestral homeland (see esp. 2 Macc 8:21, 33; 13:10, 14; 14:18; 4 Macc 1:11; 4:20; 17:21; 18:4).[40] Sixteen of the twenty-six occurrences of the word in the LXX come in 2 and 4 Maccabees (cf. Josephus, *C. Ap.* 1.210, 212; 2.277).[41] In 1 Macc 15:33, Simon insists: "We have neither taken foreign land nor seized foreign property, but only the inheritance of our ancestors" (NRSV) (τῆς κληρονομίας τῶν πατέρων ἡμῶν). Although there are of course claims to the land on the basis of the ancestors made in the Hebrew Bible,[42] it is notable that these are expressed in terms of a land given or promised to the ancestors, especially Abraham, not simply as homeland or ancestral land. Indeed, Nehemiah, for example, is candid that this land, given to Abraham's offspring, was "the land of the Canaanite, the Hittite, the Amorite, the Perizzite, the Jebusite, and the Girgashite" (Neh 9:8; cf. Gen 15:18–21; Exod 3:8, 17; Deut 7:1). Thus, noting these developments in the Maccabean literature, Wilken comments: "As the Land of Israel came to be viewed as a native land, Jews learned to legitimate their residency in the land *without* reference to the land promises in the Scriptures. The right to possess the land rested on tenancy, on having lived on the land for as long as anyone could remember."[43] Furthermore, it is worth noting, following W. D. Davies, that in post-biblical Jewish writings, references to the land are comparatively infrequent, though Davies immediately qualifies this with the observation that references to Jerusalem and the Temple are very frequent and that these are, in a sense, the "quintessence" of the land.[44] A number of writers also note the relative lack of interest in the land in Hellenistic Jewish writings from the diaspora, a point to which we shall return below.[45]

A third point of interest is to consider the ways in which diaspora writers such as Josephus and Philo depict the lands in which Jews live—and where

40. Wilken, *Land Called Holy*, 27–29.

41. For the list, see Hatch and Redpath, *Concordance*, 1112; two of those listed outside 2 and 4 Macc are textually uncertain. Occurrences in Jer 22:10; 26:16 LXX (MT 46:16); and Ezek 23:15 refer to the notion of "native land" but do not denote Israel's land in this way.

42. On this subject, see Stavrakopoulou, *Land of Our Fathers*.

43. Wilken, *Land Called Holy*, 29.

44. Davies, *Territorial Dimension*, 33.

45. Schaller, "Philon," 173; J. Cornelis de Vos, "Die Bedeutung des Landes Israel in den jüdischen Schriften der hellenistisch-römischen Zeit," in Wacker and Koerrenz, *Heiliges Land*, 97; Vahrenhorst, "Land und Landverheißung," 143; and Doron Mendels, *The Rise and Fall of Jewish Nationalism*, 2nd ed. (Grand Rapids: Eerdmans, 1997), 255, who makes this observation also about literature from Palestine and associates the change especially with the Roman occupation from 63 BCE.

they were often born and raised—in relation to Judea, Jerusalem, and the Temple. Philo, for example, draws a distinction between the "motherland" (μητρόπολις) to which the *Ioudaioi* look—with its center in Jerusalem— and their homeland or πατρίς, which is the place of their own origin. This usage may reflect the Greek tradition of referring to the capital city—"mother-city" in relation to colonies (ἀποικίαι)—as μητρόπολις.[46] Sarah Pearce argues that a particular influence on Philo's usage is Jewish scripture, with its image of Jerusalem as mother and (a single) reference to Jerusalem (Zion) as μητρόπολις (Isa 1:26 LXX).[47] In his treatise on Flaccus, criticizing Flaccus's part in provoking hostility against the Jews of Alexandria, Philo comments concerning "the Jews" (ʼΙουδαῖοι) that

> while they hold the Holy City where stands the sacred Temple of the most high God to be their mother city [μητρόπολιν], yet those [χῶραι, lands/ countries] which are theirs by inheritance from their fathers, grandfathers, and ancestors even farther back, are in each case accounted by them to be their fatherland [πατρίδας] in which they were born and reared, while to some of them [that is, these lands] they have come at the time of their foundation as immigrants to the satisfaction of their founders. (*Flacc.* 46 [Colson, LCL]; cf. *Conf.* 78; *Contempl.* 18; *Legat.* 281)[48]

Pearce argues that in this text, Philo "does not portray Jerusalem as having greater or less significance than the fatherlands or colonies" that Philo and his fellow Jews inhabit. "There is," she suggests, "no tension between the notion of Jerusalem as mother-city and Alexandria as home."[49] The sig-

46. See Sarah Pearce, "Jerusalem as 'Mother-City' in the Writings of Philo of Alexandria," in *Negotiating Diaspora: Jewish Strategies in the Roman Empire*, ed. John M. G. Barclay, LSTS 45 (London: T&T Clark, 2004), 21.

47. Pearce, "Jerusalem as 'Mother-City,'" 33. For other uses in the LXX related to other cities, see Josh 10:2; 14:15; 15:13; 21:11; 2 Sam 20:19; Esth 9:19. For references in Josephus, see n. 60 below.

48. On this point in Philo, see Schaller, "Philon," 174–75: "Jerusalem, die Heilige Stadt, gilt ihnen [Juden] nach wie vor als Mutterstadt (μητρόπολις), weil sie die Stätte des Tempels, den allen Juden gemeinsamen Kultort, beherbergt. Das Vaterland, die πατρίς, aber liegt nicht mehr im Land, das die Vorväter einst verließen; Vaterland (πατρίς) ist der Ort, in dem man aufgewachsen ist und die Familie seit Generationen lebt." See also Wilken, *Land Called Holy*, 34–37. On both Josephus and Philo, see de Vos, "Bedeutung," 91–93; Vahrenhorst, "Land und Landverheißung," 143. By contrast, reiterating this distinction, Philo does have Agrippa describe Jerusalem as his πατρίς (*Legat.* 278).

49. Pearce, "Jerusalem as 'Mother-City,'" 32, 36.

nificance of the two places, we might suggest, is different, given Jerusalem's ancestral and cultic importance, but clearly Alexandria, like other diaspora places, can become πατρίς. Moreover, Pearce stresses, Philo displays "fierce loyalty to Alexandria as home, fatherland, for himself and for other Alexandrian Jews."[50] Indeed, part of the offence of Flaccus's action against the Jews, according to Philo, was precisely to attempt to deny their true Alexandrian citizenship, to cut away their "ancestral customs" (πατρίων) and political rights, and to denounce them as "foreigners and aliens" (ξένους καὶ ἐπήλυδας) (*Flacc.* 53–54).[51] One of the results of this was that Jews were driven out from the neighborhoods they inhabited. This racializing of the Jewish population of Alexandria—an attempt to insist that they were not genuinely compatriots of their Alexandrian neighbors and to deny their ancestral roots there—bears ominous comparison with much later efforts to identify, isolate and eliminate Jews from within a population. Scholarly insistence that Jews (including diaspora Jews) constitute a *distinct* ethnic group can potentially—albeit contrary to what is intended—reinforce such a perspective insofar as it might imply that they are not truly also members of their local populace.

By contrast, drawing on the criteria of ethnicity employed by Jonathan Hall (similar to those of Richard Schermerhorn, Anthony Smith, and others; see §3.1), Cynthia Baker has used these and other passages to argue—convincingly in my view—that writers such as Philo "depict Jews as a multi-ethnic or multiracial people."[52] Commenting on Philo's depiction in particular, Baker remarks that

> Jews, in their many disparate fatherlands, subscribe to narratives of "descent and kinship" associated with each ancestral fatherland or "specific territory" and that territory's "sense of shared history," often back to its very foundation. At the same time, this diverse array of Jews of diverse fatherlands

50. Pearce, "Jerusalem as 'Mother-City,'" 23. See further Sarah Pearce, "Belonging and Not Belonging: Local Perspectives in Philo of Alexandria," in Jones and Pearce, *Jewish Local Patriotism*, 97–105. Similarly, Erich S. Gruen, *Diaspora: Jews amidst Greeks and Romans* (Cambridge, MA: Harvard University Press, 2002), 243: "Diaspora Jews, in Philo's formulation at least, held an intense attachment to the adopted lands of their ancestors."

51. On Philo's outrage at this attempt, see Pearce, "Belonging and Not Belonging," 98.

52. Baker, "From Every Nation," 81; see 81–82 on Hall's "definitional criteria," with reference to Hall, *Hellenicity*, and Hall, *Ethnic Identity*. On the multiplicity and complexity of ethnic affiliation for Jews in Egypt, see Sylvie Honigman, "*Politeumata* and Ethnicity in Ptolemaic and Roman Egypt," *Ancient Society* 33 (2003): 89–102.

nevertheless shares with other Jews a sense of cultic piety toward a Holy City, broad patterns of worship, and other ancient customs.[53]

As Baker goes on to show, this perspective of Philo's is similar to that found in the depiction of events in Jerusalem in Acts 2. Here, the crowd, drawn from those "living in Jerusalem" (εἰς Ἰερουσαλὴμ κατοικοῦντες) is made up of "devout Jews [Ἰουδαῖοι . . . εὐλαβεῖς] from every nation [ἀπὸ παντὸς ἔθνους]" (Acts 2:5).[54] Those present are later specified as including:

Πάρθοι καὶ Μῆδοι καὶ Ἐλαμῖται, καὶ οἱ κατοικοῦντες τὴν Μεσοποταμίαν, Ἰουδαίαν τε καὶ Καππαδοκίαν, Πόντον καὶ τὴν Ἀσίαν, Φρυγίαν τε καὶ Παμφυλίαν, Αἴγυπτον καὶ τὰ μέρη τῆς Λιβύης τῆς κατὰ Κυρήνην, καὶ οἱ ἐπιδημοῦντες Ῥωμαῖοι, Ἰουδαῖοί τε καὶ προσήλυτοι, Κρῆτες καὶ Ἄραβες.

Parthians and Medes and Elamites and residents of Mesopotamia, Judea and Cappadocia, Pontus and Asia, Phrygia and Pamphylia, Egypt and the parts of Libya belonging to Cyrene, and visitors from Rome, both Jews and proselytes, Cretans and Arabians. (Acts 2:9–11, ESV)

As Baker suggests, noting the tendency of modern scholarship to resist such a conclusion, this is a depiction of "broad Jewish ethnic diversity."[55] The self-description Luke puts into the mouth of Paul is also comparable: εἰμι Ἰουδαῖος, Ταρσεύς; "I am a *Ioudaois*, a Tarsian" (Acts 21:39).[56] And Luke describes other *Ioudaioi* in the narrative of Acts as having specific (other) ethnic or racial identities: Aquila is both Ἰουδαῖος and Ποντικὸς τῷ γένει ("Pontican by descent/race," Acts 18:2); Apollos, exemplifying the kind of dual identity Philo insists on, is both Ἰουδαῖος and Ἀλεξανδρεὺς τῷ γένει ("Alexandrian by descent/race," Acts 18:24). Similarly, Josephus refers to a certain Atomos, who is both a Ἰουδαῖος and also "Cyprian by descent/race" (*A.J.* 20.142: Ἄτομον . . . Ἰουδαῖον, Κύπριον δὲ τὸ γένος). As Esler has noted, dual or nested ethnicity is not uncommon.[57] Indeed, elsewhere Josephus is

53. Baker, "From Every Nation," 88–89.
54. Baker, "From Every Nation," 91–95.
55. Baker, "From Every Nation," 93. For a detailed discussion of Acts 2:9–11, arguing that it is "based on the Table of Nations tradition" and "anticipates the later mission to the nations," see Scott, *Geography*, 68–84 (quotations from 84).
56. Luke does not write "from Tarsus" despite most English translations. He does have Paul immediately go on to specify his identity as "citizen" (πολίτης) of this "city" (πόλις).
57. Esler, *Conflict and Identity*, 72–74, disputing the claim of Shaye Cohen that this

explicit about the fact that Jews living in various places are rightly referred to by the names of those places—as Alexandrians, Antiochenes, Ephesians, Romans, and so on (*C. Ap.* 2.38–42).[58]

With regard to Josephus's broader perspectives on the Jewish homeland, Betsy Halpern Amaru suggests that, in his presentation of the biblical sources in the *Antiquities*, Josephus reshapes and relatively neglects the topic of land, "down-playing acquisition of the land from gift to providential assistance, and replacing the land stress with a law stress."[59] Amaru concludes that Josephus's vision is one of "a glorious people whose eternal existence is assured by divine blessing and promise; a people who have a motherland, but whose population is so great that they overflow into every island and continent."[60]

As this last observation makes clear, these kinds of dual identifications reflect the existence and experience of a Jewish diaspora, a context that shapes attitudes toward homeland, as we have seen. While Josephus and Philo retain a sense of the focal importance of "the holy land"[61]—and of Jerusalem in particular—they both depict life in diaspora in positive ways that hardly suggest that this existence is to be characterized by a yearning to return to this land "from exile."[62] Jeremiah, as we have noted, urges the Babylonian exiles to pursue a mode of positive engagement in their exilic land since time there may be quite extensive (Jer 29:4–14); for Josephus and Philo, the diaspora may be characterized as an enduring indication of the flourishing of the Jewish peo-

---

example from Josephus indicates that by this period Ἰουδαῖος has become a "religious term" rather than an ethnic one; see Cohen, *Beginnings*, 79.

58. See also *C. Ap.* 1.179–80, where Josephus quotes from Clearchus, who reports an anecdote apparently told by his master Aristotle (1.176), concerning a Ἰουδαῖος (by γένος) who is said to be descended from philosophers in India (where they are known by a different name) and who is thoroughly Greek. On the complexity of identity evident here and the territorial connection attributed to the Ἰουδαῖοι, see Barclay, "Ἰουδαῖος," 46–47.

59. Betsy Halpern Amaru, "Land Theology in Josephus' 'Jewish Antiquities,'" *JQR* 71 (1981): 216, commenting on the depiction in *A.J.* 3.86–87 in comparison with Deut 9:6; cf. also *C. Ap.* 2.160.

60. Amaru, "Land Theology," 228. Josephus regularly refers to Jerusalem as the μητρόπολις (e.g., *B.J.* 2.400, 421; 4.239, 267–68; 7.375; *A.J.* 7.289; 11.160), though this is a standard term he uses of other capital cities too (e.g., *B.J.* 3.29; *A.J.* 10.269; 11.340).

61. For the phrase ἡ ἱερὰ χώρα, see Philo, *Legat.* 202, 205. For further references and comparable phrases in Philo, see de Vos, "Bedeutung," 90n76. Vos also notes that the phrase is absent from Josephus ("Bedeutung," 92 with n. 84). For Josephus's focus on the land of Israel, referred to as "our land" (using χώρα) see, e.g., *C. Ap.* 1.60, 103, 174; see also Barclay, "Ἰουδαῖος," 46–48.

62. See Gruen, *Diaspora*, 232–52.

ple and the appeal of their customs (Philo, *Flacc.* 45; *Legat.* 281–84; Josephus, *C. Ap.* 2.282; *A.J.* 4.115–16). Such references suggest that an orientation to the land of Judea, and specifically to Jerusalem and its temple, remained significant for *Ioudaioi* living in the diaspora but that this could coexist indefinitely with a sense that life—and, indeed, homeland (πατρίς)—were (permanently and genuinely) elsewhere.[63] Since these two important figures were writing from both sides of the Jewish War and the destruction of the temple—Philo before, Josephus after—these attitudes cannot be attributed specifically to the changed circumstances after 70 CE.

A final point of some significance is to consider the ways in which the land (or its temple) is spiritualized or similarly reinterpreted in some Jewish writings of the time.[64] Again, this is not simply a post–70 CE development, so it cannot be taken to indicate reaction to the momentous events of the first Jewish war, important though those were. Given the common focus on Jerusalem and its temple as the central place of significance, it is notable, for example, that the writings from Qumran give expression to the idea of the community itself as temple, an alternative to the corrupted one in Jerusalem (e.g., 1QS 8.4–11),[65] though the community also looked for an eschatological return to worship in Jerusalem and a new, divinely built temple.[66] Perhaps the most extended and often-noted example of a kind of spiritualizing or metaphorical application of the notion of the land comes in the work of Philo. With his focus on the philosophically defined notion of the virtuous life, Philo depicts "entrance to the land" as "entrance into philosophy." This is "a good land and fertile in the pro-

---

63. Cf. Schaller, "Philon," 175, who comments (in relation to texts such as *Flacc.* 45): "Das Leben in der Diaspora . . . erscheint hier als eine zumindest ebensogute Lebensmöglichkeit wie das Leben im angestammten Land, wie im 'Heiligen Land.'" See also Baker, "From Every Nation," 86–89; Gruen, *Diaspora*, 252.

64. On this general theme, see Davies, *Territorial Dimension*, 78–91; Mendels, *Rise and Fall*, 255–56.

65. See Girsch, "Begotten Anew," 177–92; Schwartz, *Jewish Background*, 37–38; Lawrence H. Schiffman, "Community without Temple: The Qumran Community's Withdrawal from the Jerusalem Temple," in *Gemeinde ohne Tempel/Community without Temple: Zur Substituierung und Transformation des Jerusalemer Tempels und seines Kults im Alten Testament, antiken Judentum und frühen Christentum*, ed. Beate Ego, Armin Lange, and Peter Pilhofer, WUNT 118 (Tübingen: Mohr Siebeck, 1999), 272–74; Davies, *Gospel and the Land*, 188.

66. See Schiffman, "Community without Temple," 276–80; Davies, *Gospel and the Land*, 188. See also George J. Brooke, "Miqdash Adam, Eden, and the Qumran Community," in Ego, Lange, and Pilhofer, *Gemeinde ohne Tempel*, 285–301, esp. 297: the Qumran community "viewed its worship as an anticipation of what would take place in Jerusalem at the end of days and beyond, at the time of the recreation of all things."

duction of fruits, which the divine plants, the virtues, bear" (*QE* 2.13 [Marcus, LCL]). Elsewhere, as Wilken remarks, "Abraham's migration" from his kinfolk and homeland is interpreted as "an allegory of a soul that loves virtue in search of the true God" (*Abr.* 60–68).[67] As Berndt Schaller comments, "The promised Land appears as a symbol of wisdom, virtue, or philosophy."[68]

Such metaphorical and spiritualizing interpretations of the significance of the land of Israel have led Samuel Sandmel to remark, "It cannot be over-emphasized that Philo has little or no concern for Palestine."[69] However, as both Schaller and Wilken are concerned to show, this is an overly one-sided remark.[70] Schaller points in particular to works from the later period of Philo's life, especially such apologetic works as *De Legatione ad Gaium* and *In Flaccum*, in which a concrete historical or eschatological interest in the land comes to the fore, while the texts in which the land is essentially symbolic come predominantly from the early and middle periods of his activity.[71] For example, in *Legat.* 200–202, Philo describes the actions of the non-Jewish inhabitants of Jamnia to provoke the Jews by erecting an altar to the emperor Gaius, knowing that, as Philo puts it, the Jews "felt it intolerable that the sanctity [ἱεροπρεπής] which truly belongs to the Holy Land [τῆς ἱερᾶς χώρας] should be destroyed," so they pulled the altar down (*Legat.* 202 [Colson, LCL]). Schaller's explanation for this is that it is during this time that Philo's political concern came to the fore, given the threats to Jews in Alexandria. He concludes, overall, that Philo's various statements indicate

> that for Jews in the hellenistic diaspora, the biblical promises and expectations concerning the Land, under the pressure and the necessity to assimilate, could easily pale into symbols of individual piety. They show equally impressively, however, that the biblical promises and expectations concerning the Land could and did again come alive, when historical conditions placed into question the realities and possibilities of Jewish life in the diaspora.[72]

67. Wilken, *Land Called Holy*, 35.

68. Schaller, "Philon," 173. Cf. Pearce, "Belonging and Not Belonging," 89.

69. Samuel Sandmel, "Philo's Place in Judaism: A Study of Conceptions of Abraham in Jewish Literature: Part II," *HUCA* 26 (1955): 237. The phrase is also quoted by Schaller, "Philon," 173, and Wilken, *Land Called Holy*, 35, both of whom go on to qualify the claim.

70. See Schaller, "Philon"; Wilken, *Land Called Holy*, 34–37; also de Vos, "Bedeutung," 90–91.

71. Schaller, "Philon," 181.

72. Schaller, "Philon," 182.

In other words, particularly for those living in the diaspora, the signifi-cance—symbolic and/or physical—attached to the "holy land" could and did vary according to sociopolitical circumstance.

As we stand back from this brief and selective sketch of a wide range of diverse material, our first response must be precisely to stress the diver-sity of constructions of the land and its significance. A certain orientation toward the land of Canaan/Israel, and to Jerusalem and its temple in par-ticular, seems to be a broadly consistent feature: there is a clear "link with a homeland," variously physical or symbolic in form. At different times and places, for a range of reasons, the land and the people's relationship to it are construed and depicted in a wide variety of ways. It is also clear that physical and symbolic space—broadly equivalent to Soja's first and second kinds of space—are inextricably woven together in the various ways in which the land is constructed, imagined, and represented. The prominent focus on Jerusalem and its temple as the holy city or the holy mountain, for ex-ample, represents a mode of spatial imagination, a construction of space that configures the world around a central core, a physical "navel," a sacred site of divine habitation and encounter. Seeing this as a "real-and-imagined" space—to use Soja's phrase—helps us to understand how this "holy land" can become the subject of eschatological vision, in which depictions range beyond the realms of human experience and imagine a future of glorious flourishing and bliss. It also helps us understand how Jews living in diaspora, for whom this land was not treated or regarded as homeland or ancestral land (πατρίς), could nonetheless retain and reiterate—especially at times when it became politically relevant—an orientation toward Jerusalem and the land as motherland, a significant point of reference in their construction of the world, even if they held no hope or even desire to relocate there. Equally important to stress is the insistence that other places—places where diaspora Jews reside and trace their origins—can also be "homeland" and that what we might call "ethnic" allegiance can be assigned to these places among members of what Baker calls a "multi-ethnic" Jewish people.

6.2 Ideologies of Land and Constructions of Space in New Testament Texts

In considering perspectives on the land, and on Jerusalem and its temple, in the earliest Christian writings, it is important to reiterate that no clear distinction can be drawn between Jewish and early Christian perspectives in this regard for reasons noted in the introduction (see pp. 14–15). Moreover, just as with the Jewish sources surveyed above, so too this brief survey of early Christian perspectives on land will necessarily be selective and illustrative. Because of this, and because my concerns are with "Christian" perspectives—that is, with the perspectives on the land expressed by those who hold Jesus to be the Christ/Messiah (see p. 16)—I shall not attempt to consider the historical Jesus's attitude to the land of Israel, to Jerusalem, or to its temple, and I will not pay much attention to the Gospels' depictions of these attitudes.[73] After a brief consideration of Luke-Acts, my main case studies will come from Paul, 1 Peter, Hebrews, and Revelation.

6.2.1 *Luke-Acts*

The geographical interest that shapes Lukan redaction has long been recognized. As Hans Conzelmann classically showed, Luke's reordering and editing of his sources is strongly influenced by both eschatological concerns (specifically, according to Conzelmann, the delay of the parousia) and a geographical theology (or a theological geography).[74] Conzelmann's work is, of course, dated and open to significant critique, but his identification of this geographical interest in Luke (and Acts) remains important.[75] One of the characteristics of Luke 9:51–19:28, the central section of the Gospel, is the depiction of Jesus's travels as part of a deliberate and determined journey to Jerusalem (see, e.g., Luke 9:51; 13:22; 17:11; 18:31; 19:28). This particular organization is not evident in either Mark or Matthew. Indeed, Luke's distinctive focus on Jerusalem is reinforced in the contrasting messages given to the women who encounter angelic messengers at the empty tomb: in Mark and Matthew the disciples are to be told to return to Galilee to meet the risen Jesus there (Matt 28:7; Mark 16:7); in Luke the reference to Galilee is edited into an earlier recollection of Jesus's words "while he was still in

73. On this subject, see the classic work of Davies, *Gospel and the Land*. Among more recent contributions, see Karen Wenell, *Jesus and Land: Sacred and Social Space in Second Temple Judaism*, LNTS 334 (London: T&T Clark, 2007).

74. Hans Conzelmann, *The Theology of St Luke*, trans. Geoffrey Buswell (London: Faber and Faber, 1960). The title of the German original, *Die Mitte der Zeit*, conveys the central thesis with regard to eschatological revision much more clearly, if not the geographical emphasis.

75. For critique of Conzelmann's (dated) approach to geography, see Sleeman, *Geography*, 30–33.

Galilee" (Luke 24:6). In Luke's scheme they must remain in Jerusalem, from where the good news will go to the nations (Luke 24:47–49, 52; Acts 1:4).

This theological geography continues to be expressed in Acts, where the narrative of the early church's development is presented as an expansion from the focal center of Jerusalem "to the end of the earth" (Acts 1:8; 13:47).[76] The journey of the message about Christ from Jerusalem to Rome, in the person of Paul, is particularly significant, indicating the journey to the heart of the Roman Empire, another focal and symbolically important geographical location (cf. Acts 19:21; 23:11; 28:14, 16). This is a symbolic geography in which Jerusalem continues to function as a focal center, the place of resurrection and ascension, in which the gathered crowds first hear the proclamation (Acts 2:14).[77] Moreover, as Norbert Brox has shown, Luke's depiction of the earliest Christian community in Acts 2:42–47 and 4:32–37 makes the Jerusalem community a model and ideal for Christian communities thereafter.[78] We find a comparable geographical focus in the letters of Paul.

6.2.2 Paul

According to W. D. Davies, Paul's "Christological logic" means that "the land, like the Law, particular and provisional, had become irrelevant. . . . Theologically he [Paul] had no longer any need of it."[79] Davies does note

---

76. On the meaning of this phrase, see Scott, *Geography*, 58–61. For further reflections on the "universality" of the Lukan vision, but also the "theological ethnicity" and specific territorial orientation of the church's identity, see Simon Butticaz, "The Church in Acts: Universality of Salvation, Ethnicity, and Philanthropy," *Annali di Storia dell'Esegesi* 36 (2019): 433–52.

77. As Scott, *Geography*, 57, remarks, in Acts—and specifically in the ascension narrative—"Jerusalem is the omphalos connecting heaven and earth, a veritable axis mundi of intersecting horizontal and vertical planes." This focus is to some extent challenged in Sleeman, *Geography*, which argues that the ascended Christ provides a kind of "heavenly thirdspace," an "ascension geography," which orients a (re)configuration of space in the narrative of Acts, though I think this can combine with a physical-and-symbolic focus on Jerusalem as an important aspect of Luke's structuring of space. On the various "mental maps" that shape Luke's presentation in Acts, see Loveday Alexander, "Mapping Early Christianity: Acts and the Shape of Early Church History," *Int* 57 (2003): 163–73.

78. Norbert Brox, "Das 'irdische Jerusalem' in der altchristlichen Theologie," *Kairos* 28 (1986): 163–68: "Die Christen, die Ortsgemeinden überall, mußten sich an der Kirche von Jerusalem messen (lassen): Jerusalem war Kriterium und Norm" (163).

79. Davies, *Gospel and the Land*, 179, 220.

Paul's continued focus on Jerusalem but sees this as something of a relic of his "geography of eschatology," now "otiose" in the light of the pan-ethnic and universal reality of life "in Christ."[80] For Mark Strom, Paul's lack of interest in the land is due to his transposition of the story of God's saving deeds to a "worldstory" freed from its geographical context: "The hope of a renewed land had been absorbed and eclipsed in the reconciliation of the cosmos." Paul's legacy is thus "the transposition of land to cosmos."[81] Yet we may wonder whether Jerusalem, the focal point of much Jewish land ideology, continues to hold a rather more important physical-and-symbolic significance in Paul's construction of the world and his ordering of space. We might also wonder whether these positively framed (Christian) claims about Paul's cosmic vision are more troubling than their proponents intend.

In Romans, one of his later letters, Paul gives a concise geographical overview of his missionary career as one in which he has accomplished (πεπληρωκέναι) the good news of Christ from Jerusalem around to Illyricum (ἀπὸ Ἰερουσαλὴμ καὶ κύκλῳ μέχρι τοῦ Ἰλλυρικοῦ, Rom 15:19).[82] Despite Paul's earlier reticence to associate himself too strongly with Jerusalem—in a context where he needs to stress his independent authority (Gal 1:16–24)—here he construes the spatial pattern of his apostolic activity as something that finds its point of orientation in Jerusalem. Furthermore, he is now planning to return to Jerusalem with the offering "for the poor among the saints" he has raised from his largely gentile churches (Rom 15:25–27). As many authors have pointed out, this offering is more than a sharing of material aid between congregations, meeting a need for those most impoverished at the time—though it is certainly that.[83] It also symbolizes the cen-

---

80. Davies, *Gospel and the Land*, 220; on Jerusalem in Paul's thought and writing, see 195–208; on salvation in Paul as "pan-ethnic," see 176–77.

81. Mark Strom, "From Promised Land to Reconciled Cosmos: Paul's Translation of 'Worldview,' 'Worldstory,' and 'Worldperson,'" in *The Gospel and the Land of Promise: Christian Approaches to the Land of the Bible*, ed. Philip Church et al. (Eugene, OR: Pickwick, 2011), 14–27; quotations from 23 and 27.

82. See James M. Scott, *Paul and the Nations: The Old Testament and Jewish Background of Paul's Mission to the Nations with Special Reference to the Destination of Galatians*, WUNT 84 (Tübingen: Mohr Siebeck, 1995), 136–62.

83. For the argument that the collection forms part of a broader Pauline commitment to meeting the material needs of the poor and that Gal 2:10 may refer to this broader concern and not—contrary to established opinion—to the collection specifically, see Fern K. T. Clarke, "God's Concern for the Poor in the New Testament: A Discussion of the Role of the Poor in the Foundation of Christian Belief (Early to Mid First Century CE)" (PhD diss., University of Exeter, 2000), 188–93; Clarke, "'Remembering the Poor': Does Galatians 2.10a

tral significance of Jerusalem as the origin of the "spiritual blessings" that have emanated from there to the gentiles (Rom 15:27). Whether this planned journey is envisaged by Paul as initiating a final, eschatological pilgrimage of the nations to Zion, as has sometimes been suggested, is at least open to doubt, not least since he is preparing to travel from Jerusalem to Rome and thence on to Spain (Rom 15:23–24).[84] Yet a comparable eschatological focus is evident elsewhere: citing scripture, Paul brings his complex discussion of Israel's place in God's mysterious saving plans to a climax with the affirmation that the "deliverer will come from Zion [ἐκ Σιών]" (Rom 11:26). Paul's choice of preposition here is striking, given that the original of Isaiah 59:20, which is quoted here, has ἕνεκεν Σιων/לְצִיּוֹן ("for/to/on account of Zion").[85] Sze-kar Wan sees this as Paul's "declaration that Jerusalem shall be the Messiah-king's new seat of power. Jerusalem is not the redeemer's final destination, but his starting point, the center of his authority, indeed his capital."[86] Without denying Paul's heavy "Christ-focus"—perhaps inviting a study of Paul's construction of space along the lines of Sleeman's "ascension geography" in Acts[87]—such references indicate how far Paul's geographical construction of the world places Jerusalem at its center, just as do those of the earlier Jewish writers who described it in similar terms, even as the navel of the earth.[88] A potentially worldwide mission to the nations finds its orientation from this point outward, and the return of gratitude embodied

---

Allude to the Collection?," *ScrB* 31 (2001): 20–28; Bruce W. Longenecker, *Remember the Poor: Paul, Poverty, and the Greco-Roman World* (Grand Rapids: Eerdmans, 2010). For an overview of the collection project and scholarship on it, see Horrell, *Solidarity*, 254–65.

84. See, e.g., Johannes Munck, *Paul and the Salvation of Mankind* (London: SCM, 1959), 303–4; and the criticisms of Davies, *Gospel and the Land*, 201–8. More recently, on Paul's focus on the eschatological incoming of gentiles, see Paula Fredriksen, *Paul: The Pagans' Apostle* (New Haven: Yale University Press, 2017), 73–77, 159–66.

85. The specific phrasing may echo Ps 14:7 (LXX 13:7), or perhaps Ps 53:6 (MT 53:7; LXX 52:7) or Isa 2:3, but the main source of Paul's quotation is clearly Isaiah 59:20–21, so the reformulation remains significant as an indication of Paul's perspective. See further James D. G. Dunn, *Romans 9–16*, WBC 38B (Waco: Word, 1988), 682; Robert Jewett, *Romans*, Hermeneia (Minneapolis: Fortress, 2007), 703–4.

86. Sze-kar Wan, "'To the Jew First and Also to the Greek': Reading Romans as Ethnic Construction," in Nasrallah and Schüssler Fiorenza, *Prejudice and Christian Beginnings*, 141.

87. Sleeman, *Geography*.

88. See Scott, *Paul and the Nations*, who sees the Table of Nations in Gen 10 and the appropriation of this in early Judaism as a key influence on Paul's Jerusalem-centered construction of space.

in the collection comes back to this center. This seems clearly to reflect a topocentric worldview.

A rather different perspective on Jerusalem is expressed in Paul's infamous allegory in Gal 4:21–31. Here Paul contrasts "two covenants" (δύο διαθῆκαι) represented by the two women, the slave-girl (παιδίσκη)[89] Hagar and the free woman Sarah, and the two children to whom they gave birth, Ishmael and Isaac (4:22–24; cf. Gen 16:1–4; 21:1–18). Both are children of Abraham, but one is a child "born according to the flesh" (κατὰ σάρκα γεγέννηται), the other "through a promise" (δι᾽ ἐπαγγελίας). Strikingly and scandalously, Paul identifies the line of Hagar and her children as corresponding (συστοιχεῖ) to "the present Jerusalem" (τῇ νῦν Ἰερουσαλήμ), "for she is in slavery with her children" (δουλεύει γὰρ μετὰ τῶν τέκνων αὐτῆς) (Gal 4:25). By contrast, Paul insists, "the Jerusalem above is free, and she is our mother" (ἡ δὲ ἄνω Ἰερουσαλὴμ ἐλευθέρα ἐστίν, ἥτις ἐστὶν μήτηρ ἡμῶν) (4:26). After quoting from Isaiah's vision of a restored Jerusalem, to which we shall return, Paul explicitly identifies the recipients of his letter—the gentile converts in Galatia whom he is warning against adopting the Jewish law, particularly the demand for circumcision—as "children of promise" (ἐπαγγελίας τέκνα) like Isaac (4:28), an identification he reiterates in contrast to the "children of the slave-girl" (4:31). Thus the (superior) "freedom" that is the possession of these converts to Christ is what Paul urges them to hold on to, refusing circumcision in particular (5:1–4).

This passage has traditionally been seen as a stark condemnation of Judaism on Paul's part, a daring contrast rooted in creative exegesis of Genesis: in J. B. Lightfoot's now chilling and oft-cited words, it sounds "the death-knell of Judaism."[90] According to Hans Dieter Betz, "Paul's intention is clear; he wants to create a dualistic polarity between 'Judaism' and 'Christianity,' in order to discredit his Jewish-Christian opposition."[91] This final phrase is cru-

---

89. Most modern English translations render παιδίσκη "slave woman" (e.g., ESV, NIV, NRSV), yet this rendering, while slightly less objectionable to modern ears, does not do justice to the likelihood that the diminutive term indicates a young female, one who would in modern categorizations be a girl rather than a woman.

90. J. B. Lightfoot, *St. Paul's Epistle to the Galatians: A Revised Text with Introduction, Notes, and Dissertations* (London: Macmillan, 1869), 181; quoted, e.g., by Susan Eastman, "'Cast Out the Slave Woman and Her Son': The Dynamics of Exclusion and Inclusion in Galatians 4.30," *JSNT* 28 (2006): 310; Brendan Byrne, "Jerusalems Above and Below: A Critique of J. L. Martyn's Interpretation of the Hagar-Sarah Allegory in Gal 4.21–5.1," *NTS* 60 (2014): 215n1.

91. Hans Dieter Betz, *Galatians: A Commentary on Paul's Letter to the Churches in Ga-

cial here and indicates a focus, developed in more recent exegesis, on Paul's specific (Jewish-)Christian opponents. Such exegesis has frequently sought to rescue Paul's text from anti-Jewish implications, notably in J. Louis Martyn's insistence that the target of Paul's critique is not Judaism as such but rather Paul's Jewish-Christian opponents, the teachers, who are vying for the loyalty of his Galatian gentile converts.[92] Martyn's reinterpretation, as Susan Eastman notes, has virtually become the basis of a new consensus.[93] Yet shifting the focus to an inner-Christian conflict between Jewish-Christian teachers and Paul does not entirely remove the problematically negative implications about Judaism, as Mark Nanos has shown.[94] Moreover, there are aspects of Martyn's exegesis that seem unconvincing, however attractive the reinterpretation. As Brendan Byrne has recently argued, the language of covenant (διαθήκη) in v. 24, for example, is most likely, as in Paul's other provocative and problematic contrast between the fading glory of "the old covenant" and the surpassing glory of the new one (2 Cor 3:4–18), meant to express a contrast between the covenant at Sinai and the new covenant Paul sees inaugurated in Christ (cf. 1 Cor 11:25).[95]

Space does not permit an attempt to resolve the many difficult exegetical and interpretative issues concerning this passage.[96] In any case, my particular interest is in Paul's striking references to Jerusalem and what these indicate about his geographical ideology and constructions of space. It is clear that, in invoking a contrast between two covenants, one of flesh and slavery, the other of promise and freedom, Paul relates these to two Jerusalems, one "the present" (νῦν) Jerusalem, enslaved with her children, the other "above" (ἄνω) and free. In drawing this contrast, he invokes the Isaianic vision of a renewed Jerusalem liberated from barrenness and freed to flourish and rejoice, thus picking up the prophetic tradition of escha-

---

latia, Heremeneia (Philadelphia: Fortress, 1979), 246; quoted by Byrne, "Jerusalems Above and Below," 216.

92. See J. Louis Martyn, *Theological Issues in the Letters of Paul*, SNTW (Edinburgh: T&T Clark, 1997), 191–208; J. Louis Martyn, *Galatians: A New Translation with Introduction and Commentary*, AB 33A (New York: Doubleday, 1997), 117–26.

93. Eastman, "Cast Out the Slave Woman," 311.

94. See Mark D. Nanos, "How Inter-Christian Approaches to Paul's Rhetoric can Perpetuate Negative Valuations of Jewishness—Although Proposing to Avoid that Outcome," *BibInt* 13 (2005): 255–69.

95. Byrne, "Jerusalems Above and Below," 221–24.

96. For a recent argument that Paul's particular target here is the notion that gentiles can benefit from circumcision, see Thiessen, *Paul*, 73–101. Like Martyn, Thiessen sees the argument in terms of two competing approaches to the gentile mission.

tological visions of the city and the land that move above and beyond the earthly realities, as we noted above. Paul thus offers another example of the kind of spiritualizing and eschatologizing tendencies we noted above in some Jewish perspectives on the land. Moreover, just as Josephus and Philo can refer to Jerusalem as the mother-city, so too for Paul, the city is "our mother," a depiction that gives Jerusalem a fundamental role in birthing the people whose identity takes its orientation from her—another evocation of Isaiah's imagery of the city.

Thus, Paul's (gentile) converts in Christ are a people whose identity is spatially (re)configured, as it were, around Jerusalem. Paul's polemical contrast between the two covenants—one of slavery represented by being ὑπὸ νόμον (4:21) and accepting circumcision (5:2), the other of freedom brought by Christ (5:1–4)—leads him to the stark contrast between the two Jerusalems, the present earthly one and the eschatological one above. But this contrast does not indicate that Paul's eschatological geography is simply "otiose" in light of the Christ-event. The theoretical perspectives on the construction of space outlined briefly above provide a better way of approaching this issue: Paul's spatial imagination is centered on Jerusalem, and his evocation of a "Jerusalem above" as mother of the free represents a particular kind of construction of space, a sort of thirdspace, in Soja's terms, which constitutes both a positive (maternal) source of shared identity and a space of polemical resistance to the "present Jerusalem," which in this text at least represents the covenant of slavery Paul is desperate to dissuade his gentile converts from adopting.

As Davies notes, it is clear that Paul does not make any significant use of the promise of the land to the people of Israel, except perhaps indirectly in his references to the promises to Abraham and the patriarchs (e.g., Rom 4:13; 9:4).[97] But this does not mean, as Martin Vahrenhorst rightly insists, that the land of Israel had lost its particular significance for Paul.[98] In the conceptualizing of his apostolic activity—his travel plans, his collection project, his depiction of his converts as birthed by mother Jerusalem—he reveals a physical-and-symbolic construction of the world in which Jerusalem remains a place of central significance, a place that is represented and imagined

---

97. Davies, *Gospel and the Land*, 166–79. See also the discussion in Vair, "Promise of the Land," 45–51. As Vahrenhorst, "Land und Landverheißung," 139, points out, Paul's use of the word κόσμος in Rom 4:13 indicates a certain "universalising of the promise of the land."

98. Vahrenhorst, "Land und Landverheißung," 140. See also the remarks of Brueggemann, *Land*, 166–67, who gives various reasons to question Davies's assertion.

in eschatological terms; as such, it has an identity-defining role not only for Paul himself but also, importantly, for his predominantly gentile converts.

6.2.3   1 Peter

A somewhat different kind of theological geography is apparent in 1 Peter. In the letter's opening greeting, the addressees are identified as παρεπίδημοι (1 Pet 1:1). Later in the letter, at the opening of a major section within the letter body, this identification is reiterated, this time using (in the plural) the same pairing used in Gen 23:4 of Abraham (see above): πάροικοι καὶ παρεπίδημοι ("strangers and aliens," 1 Pet 2:11). Along with the reference to the Christians' present lives as a time of παροικία (1:17), these phrases invoke a theme we have already noted in the Jewish scriptures (see also Acts 7:6, 29), where they convey both the sense that the Israelites (like Abraham, their forefather) are only temporary residents in the land, not its owners as such, and also the broader notion that they are not fully at home in the world. As well as in 1 Peter, where it is particularly emblematic, comparable designations of the early Christians are found in Ephesians—a letter with significant points of similarity with 1 Peter[99]—and Hebrews, to which we shall turn below (see Eph 2:19: ξένοι καὶ πάροικοι; Heb 11:13: ξένοι καὶ παρεπίδημοι).

In his classic social-scientific exegesis of 1 Peter, John Elliott argues that this designation of the recipients of the letter indicates their sociopolitical status as "resident aliens and transient strangers" who "shared the same vulnerable condition of the many thousands of Jewish and other ethnic πάροικοι of Asia Minor and throughout the Roman empire."[100] Thus, Elliott continues, "they may have been included among the numerous immigrant artisans, craftsmen, traders, merchants residing permanently in or temporarily traveling through the villages, towns and cities of the eastern provinces."[101]

---

99. For discussion of these similarities and the contrasting arguments about whether or not this indicates literary dependence, see, e.g., C. Leslie Mitton, "The Relationship between 1 Peter and Ephesians," *JTS* 1 (1950): 67–73, who argues for the use of Ephesians by 1 Peter; and Kazuhito Shimada, "Is I Peter Dependent on Ephesians? A Critique of C. L. Mitton," *AJBI* 17 (1991): 77–106; repr. in Kazuhito Shimada, *Studies on First Peter* (Tokyo: Kyo Bun Kwan, 1998).

100. John H. Elliott, *A Home for the Homeless: A Social-Scientific Criticism of 1 Peter, Its Situation and Strategy*, 2nd ed. (Minneapolis: Fortress, 1990), 37; cf. 129.

101. Elliott, *Home*, 48.

Elliott's proposal, however, has not convinced many on this point,[102] and Elliott himself acknowledges that such a precarious socioeconomic and political status may not have characterized all within the Christian communities addressed; the labels πάροικοι and παρεπίδημοι could be both literal and figurative, indicating "religious as well as social circumstances."[103] Nonetheless, what these designations do together express, as Elliott has rightly stressed, is a sense of alienation and estrangement from society; indeed, the author's depiction of the addressees in these terms constructs and reinforces this sense of dislocation.[104] It is, as Wei Hsien Wan has explored in some detail, a significant aspect of the author's construction of space, albeit one that functions in negative terms to distance the readers from their contemporary society.[105]

Also part of this geographical designation of the recipients of 1 Peter in the opening greeting is the assertion that they are located in the diaspora (διασπορά, 1:1), and specifically in areas of the Roman provinces of Asia Minor.[106] This term represents a distinctively Jewish description of location, found elsewhere in the New Testament only in a comparable opening address in James 1:1 and (less relevantly) in John 7:35. It conveys a sense of dislocation from a homeland, and in 1 Peter, read alongside the letter's closing reference to Babylon (5:13), likely evokes the narrative of Israel's Babylonian defeat and exile, casting Rome in the role of Babylon.[107] As we

102. For discussion of the criticisms, see David G. Horrell, "Aliens and Strangers? The Socioeconomic Location of the Addressees of 1 Peter," in *Engaging Economics: New Testament Scenarios and Early Christian Reception*, ed. Bruce W. Longenecker and Kelly Liebengood (Grand Rapids: Eerdmans, 2009), 176–202; revised in Horrell, *Becoming Christian*, 100–32.

103. Elliott, *Home*, 42; cf. his later remarks: "The experience of many as actual strangers and resident aliens provided an existential basis for the depiction of all believers as strangers and resident aliens in a metaphorical sense" (Elliott, *1 Peter*, 482).

104. On the construction of identity in these terms in 1 Peter, see also Dunning, *Aliens and Sojourners*, 9–12; David G. Horrell, "Between Conformity and Resistance: Beyond the Balch-Elliott Debate Towards a Postcolonial Reading of 1 Peter," in *Reading 1 Peter with New Eyes: Methodological Reassessments of the Letter of First Peter*, ed. Robert L. Webb and Betsy Bauman-Martin, LNTS 364 (London: T&T Clark, 2007), 111–43; revised in Horrell, *Becoming Christian*, 211–38.

105. See Wei Hsien Wan, "Reconfiguring the Universe: The Contest for Time and Space in the Roman Imperial Cults and 1 Peter" (PhD diss., University of Exeter, 2016), now published in revised form as *The Contest for Time and Space in the Roman Imperial Cults and 1 Peter: Reconfiguring the Universe*, LNTS 611 (London: Bloomsbury T&T Clark, 2019); Horrell, "Re-Placing 1 Peter."

106. See Horrell, "Re-Placing 1 Peter," 272.

107. See Horrell, *Becoming Christian*, 223–27; "Re-Placing 1 Peter," 280–84.

have seen in the writings of Josephus and Philo, however, references to life in diaspora do not necessarily view this location negatively.

If the references in 1 Peter to the recipients as strangers and aliens scattered in the diaspora convey a kind of negative geographical construction of the world—in the sense that this is a place where the readers are not at home—what, if anything, does the author offer by way of a positive counterpart? As with Paul, it is notable that the author does not make positive reference to inheriting the land, except perhaps indirectly with the mention of an inheritance (1:4). And just as Paul's mother Jerusalem is the (eschatological) Jerusalem "above" (Gal 4:26), so this inheritance, according to the author of 1 Peter, is "kept in heaven for you," part of a hope for salvation, which will be revealed "at the last time" (ἐν καιρῷ ἐσχάτῳ, 1:5), even though there is no explicit or implicit reference to Jerusalem in the letter.[108] Once again, this "heavenly" construction of the place where the readers will finally reach their goal (cf. 1:9), after completing the time of their παροικία (1:17), does not imply an absence of spatial construction or geographical ideology. On the contrary, it may be seen to function as a kind of thirdspace which both configures life in the spaces of here and now in a particular way and also orientates the readers' identity toward a shared future place. Indeed, this kind of spatial imagination, as Wan has shown, constitutes a particular form of political resistance, an "alternative spatiality" in contrast to the rather more concrete manifestations of Roman domination in urban environments throughout the οἰκουμένη, not least in Asia Minor.[109]

There is also, as Elliott insightfully observes, a positive counterpart to the addressees' alienation and dislocation from society in the author's indications that they find a new "home" in the household of God (οἶκος τοῦ θεοῦ, 4:17; cf. 2:5).[110] The juxtaposition of this positive image alongside that of the readers as aliens and strangers is also found in Eph 2:19.[111] As critics have

108. Thus Vair, "Promise of the Land," 61, comments: "The concept of inheritance . . . in 1 Peter 1:4, is emptied altogether of its earthly connotation and filled with the meaning of salvation in the eternity beyond history." As I attempt to show, however, such comments despatialize the significance of these ideas too much.

109. See Wan, "Reconfiguring the Universe."

110. Thus, Elliott's thesis is encapsulated *in nuce* in the title of his book: *A Home for the Homeless.*

111. On this latter text and its spatial dimensions, see Carmen Bernabé Ubieta, "'Neither *xenoi* nor *paroikoi, sympolitai* and *oikeioi tou theou*' (Eph 2:19): Pauline Christian Communities: Defining a New Territoriality," in *Social Scientific Models for Interpreting the Bible: Essays by the Context Group in Honor of Bruce J. Malina*, ed. John J. Pilch (Leiden: Brill, 2001), 260–80. The essay depicts this new household in terms of a "'spiritual' territoriality"

noted, two aspects of Elliott's proposal seem doubtful, however. One is the stress placed upon the οἶκος image given that the exact terminology occurs in the letter only at the two places cited above, though we might also include the uses of οἰκοδομέω (2:5, 7), the stone and building imagery (2:4–8), and the particular designation of the slaves addressed in the household code as οἰκέται (2:18). Nonetheless there remains a suspicion that Elliott may overly stress the positive significance of the "house/home" motif.[112] The second aspect open to criticism is Elliott's insistence that this οἶκος—specifically, in 2:5, an οἶκος πνευματικός—is a "house" or "household" and not a (cultic) "temple."[113] Since this building—despite the author's somewhat awkward mixing of metaphors and images—is not only "spiritual" but also one where sacrifices are offered and a priesthood operates (2:5, 9), this seems an unlikely case to sustain. As Ramsey Michaels sagely remarks, "It is difficult to imagine a house intended for priesthood as being anything other than a temple of some sort."[114] The author of 1 Peter, then, depicts the recipients of the letter as the stones of a building, specifically a temple of which Christ is cornerstone (2:4–7). As has often been observed, 1 Peter's notion of the community as a kind of living temple also invites comparison with the expression of a similar theme in the Qumran literature, as noted briefly above.[115] While this image in 1 Peter has often been understood and interpreted as a metaphor,[116] it is important also to draw attention to its material and spatial aspects. It is, as Wan notes, "a way of envisioning Christian solidarity: a temple made up of material bodies, both those of believers and of the vindicated Jesus." He continues:

> To read οἶκος πνευματικός in this way is not to take the expression in a wooden, literalistic sense, but rather to think of it as robustly material, spa-

---

(279) that embodies the inclusivity and trans-ethnic welcome of the Pauline communities in contrast to the treatment of "foreigners" in Greco-Roman cities. For reasons that this book as a whole seeks to make clear, the contrast between a trans-ethnic Pauline model of inclusion and more "exclusive" ancient groups and institutions may be open to serious question.

112. For a critique, see Feldmeier, *Christen als Fremde*, 203–10, esp. 205–6.

113. John H. Elliott, *The Elect and the Holy: An Exegetical Examination of 1 Peter 2:4–10 and the Phrase* basileion hierateuma, NovTSup 12 (Leiden: Brill, 1966), 156–59.

114. Michaels, *1 Peter*, 100. See also the more detailed arguments on this point in Wei Hsien Wan, "Repairing Social Vertigo: Spatial Production and Belonging in 1 Peter," in Walton, Trebilco, and Gill, *Urban World*, 295–99.

115. For a recent exploration of the considerable points of similarity, see Girsch, "Begotten Anew," 171–212.

116. E.g., Girsch, "Begotten Anew," 173, 210, et passim.

tial, imaginative. It tells us that Christian bodies, spread throughout the Anatolian terrain in their respective communities, are simultaneously asked to conceive of themselves as a single, trans-spatial temple joined in Christ and animated by God's spirit.[117]

As Wan stresses, this alternative spatial construction is politically significant, structuring and orientating the readers' lives in a particular way, connecting them across what we might call trans-national space as a community of siblings (ἀδελφότης, 1 Pet 5:9).[118]

In 1 Peter, then, we find a number of specific points of contact with some of the facets of Jewish land ideology and constructions of space that we explored briefly above. The dislocation of the community members from society, or more broadly from the world, is expressed, using scriptural language, in their identification as πάροικοι καὶ παρεπίδημοι. They are described as living in diaspora. Positively, they are seen as living stones which together comprise the "spiritual house" in which praise and sacrifice are offered to God. These are not merely spiritual or metaphorical ideas but may better be seen, following recent spatial theory, as representations and constructions of space that configure the readers' identity and location in particular ways. As Soja has stressed, such "imagined" constructions of space are politically and socially significant; they structure and orient life and practice in the world. To imagine the community as a living temple, for example, may in one sense be metaphorical and imaginary; but in another sense this construction both interprets and structures the physical existence of the embodied Christians who comprise this temple—in what Sleeman calls "believer-space"[119]—and reshapes their sense of relationship to the social spaces they inhabit, to other kinds of temples and shrines—not least those that represent the imperial rule of Rome.

6.2.4 Hebrews

Among the writings of the New Testament, the letter to the Hebrews is, as Wilken remarks, the only one to give a prominent place to the promise of the land.[120] Indeed, Wilken suggests that it "is the first systematic effort by

---

117. Wan, "Repairing Social Vertigo," 300.
118. See Wan, "Repairing Social Vertigo"; Wan, "Reconfiguring the Universe."
119. E.g., Sleeman, *Geography*, 259.
120. Wilken, *Land Called Holy*, 52; cf. also Vahrenhorst, "Land und Landverheißung,"

a Christian to interpret the land tradition in light of the new circumstances that came into being after the death and resurrection of Christ."[121] In seeking to make sense of these "new circumstances," scholars again draw a contrast between Jewish ethnocentric particularism and Christian universalism, as in Knut Backhaus's remarks on the *Heilsuniversalismus* of Hebrews:

> The soteriologically grounded universal perspective in Hebrews excludes "once and for all" (ἐφάπαξ) any topocentric and also ethnocentric restriction [*Engführung*] of salvation. The promised land, understood in the sense of the author of Hebrews, thus leads all earthly land-promises [*Landverheißungen*] to be understood as a salvation-historical anachronism.[122]

Thus, Philip Church suggests, Hebrews may be seen to mention the "promised land" only "to negate it in favour of the eschatological goal of the whole people of God."[123] To what extent are these characterizations valid? As we have already noted, it is in Hebrews that we first encounter the phrase "promised land" (Heb 11:9), and there are two passages within Hebrews where the biblical traditions about the promise and possession of the land are explicitly discussed: 3:7–4:11 and 11:8–16.

In the first of these, the author comments in particular on the depiction of the Israelites' rebellion in the wilderness in Ps 95:7–11 (LXX 94:7–11), which itself encapsulates traditions from the narratives in Exodus, Numbers, and Deuteronomy. Of especial significance for Hebrews is the depiction of entering the land as an entry into "rest" (κατάπαυσις) (cf. Deut 12:9–10;

136–39. Whether Hebrews is properly or originally a letter is open to question since it lacks any epistolary opening; and it has often been seen as more homiletic in character, perhaps originally a sermon. But the closing greetings (13:22–25) give the current text an epistolary character. I retain the traditional description of it as a "letter" for convenience. Barnabas Lindars, *The Theology of the Letter to the Hebrews* (Cambridge: Cambridge University Press, 1991), 6–7, insists that it is genuinely a letter, while Attridge, *Epistle to the Hebrews*, 14, finds "homily" a more specific and useful identification of its genre, since the epistolary genre can encompass so much. Erich Grässer, *An die Hebräer (Hebr 1–6)*, EKKNT 17.1 (Zürich: Benziger; Neukirchen-Vluyn: Neukirchener, 1990), 16, prefers to consider Hebrews in quite general terms as a "theologische Meditation" in which the dominant style is more that of speech (*Redestil*) than of writing (*Schreibstil*).

121. Wilken, *Land Called Holy*, 52.

122. Knut Backhaus, "Das Land der Verheißung: Die Heimat der Glaubenden im Hebräerbrief," *NTS* 47 (2001): 187.

123. Philip Church, "'Here We Have No Lasting City' (Heb 13:14): The Promised Land in the Letter to the Hebrews," in Church et al., *Gospel and the Land*, 57.

Ps 95:11).[124] After a lengthy quotation of this passage from the LXX Psalm (Heb 3:7–11), the author proceeds to apply the lessons of this paradigmatic story to his contemporary addressees, urging them in particular not to lose their initial confidence in and commitment to Christ (3:12–15), a concern also evident elsewhere in the letter (6:4–8). The Israelites' failure to enter into the land of God's promise—"into his rest" (εἰς τὴν κατάπαυσιν αὐτοῦ, 3:18)—is seen as an instance of sinful disobedience (3:17–18; 4:11), attributed specifically to infidelity, or a lack of faith(fulness) (ἀπιστία, 3:19).[125]

The promise of entering this rest is depicted as something still unfulfilled—a promise that remains open (4:1).[126] The disobedient Israelites were prevented by God from entering (4:2–5); indeed, the idea of a promised and attainable rest is seen as deferred to the future, even on the Jewish scriptures' own terms. Quoting the appeal of Ps 95:7–8 not to harden hearts against God's voice—seen as spoken through David much later than the time of the wilderness wanderings (4:7)—the author argues that the people cannot therefore yet have attained their promised rest: "For if Joshua had given them rest [κατέπαυσεν], he [that is, God, speaking through David] would not speak about another day afterwards [μετὰ ταῦτα]" (4:8). Having linked the

---

124. The noun occurs eight times in this passage (Heb 3:11, 18; 4:1, 3 [2x], 5, 10, 11) and only once elsewhere in the NT (Acts 7:49).

125. It is probably better to think of this in terms of a lack of faithfulness rather than "unbelief," as most modern translations render ἀπιστία. The lexicon of πίστις in the NT as well as in other Greek and Roman texts is, as Teresa Morgan has shown, centrally to do with trust and faithfulness rather than with propositional belief. See Teresa Morgan, *Roman Faith and Christian Faith:* Pistis *and* Fides *in the Early Roman Empire and Early Churches* (Oxford: Oxford University Press, 2015).

126. On the depictions of "heavenly access" in Hebrews, and the (near) future (rather than present) realisation of this hope, see Nicholas J. Moore, "'In' or 'Near'? Heavenly Access and Christian Identity in Hebrews," in *Muted Voices of the New Testament: Readings in the Catholic Epistles and Hebrews,* ed. Katherine M. Hockey, Madison N. Pierce, and Francis Watson, LNTS 565 (London: Bloomsbury T&T Clark, 2017), 185–98. Matthew J. Marohl, *Faithfulness and the Purpose of Hebrews: A Social Identity Approach,* Princeton Theological Monograph Series (Eugene, OR: Pickwick, 2008), 149–80, examines the theme of promised rest in Hebrews from the perspective of a "present temporal orientation" that is argued to characterize the ancient Mediterranean, though whether this brings new insight is open to question. The distinction drawn on this basis between the promised future as a "consequence" of faithfulness, not a motivation for continued faithfulness, does not seem to be consistently sustained: cf., e.g., "the author never attempts to motivate the addressees to remain faithful by emphasizing a future goal" (168) and "this understanding [that the consequence of faithfulness was the promised rest] was meant to motivate the addressees to continue in their faithfulness" (170).

idea of "rest" with God's rest on the seventh day of creation (Gen 2:2; Heb 4:4), the author therefore concludes that a "sabbath rest" (σαββατισμός)[127] still remains "for the people [τῷ λαῷ] of God" (4:9), a rest that brings an end to one's labors (4:10). The exhortation to the recipients of Hebrews is to "make every effort [σπουδάσωμεν] to enter that rest [εἰσελθεῖν εἰς ἐκείνην τὴν κατάπαυσιν]" (4:11).[128]

The second passage to deal with the promised land comes in the lengthy catalogue of paradigms of faith presented in Heb 11.[129] Following the sequence from Abel through Enoch and Noah, we reach Abraham, "who obeyed when he was called to depart for a place [ἐξελθεῖν εἰς τόπον] he was about to receive as an inheritance [εἰς κληρονομίαν]" (11:8). Echoing the description of Abraham from Gen 23:4, noted above (see §6.1), the author describes him as having "lived as a stranger [παρῴκησεν . . . ὡς ἀλλοτρίαν] in the land of promise [εἰς γῆν τῆς ἐπαγγελίας]" (11:9). Echoing again the spiritualizing of this notion of temporary residence in the Jewish scriptures, also noted above, the author explains (γάρ . . .) the character of Abraham's sojourn in the land on the basis that he was "anticipating [ἐξεδέχετο] a city with foundations [τὴν τοὺς θεμελίους ἔχουσαν πόλιν]," built by God (11:10). The eschatological, heavenly focus of this deferred hope is made clear in 11:13–16, where all the paragons of faith are seen as having died without seeing God's promises fulfilled. Abraham's identity as a stranger and an alien is generalized to all these characters: "They declared that they were strangers and temporary residents on the earth" (ὁμολογήσαντες ὅτι ξένοι καὶ παρεπίδημοί εἰσιν ἐπὶ τῆς γῆς) (11:13). What this self-identification indicates, the author continues, is that they were seeking a "homeland" (πα-τρίς) (11:14). As noted above (see n. 34), γῆ can refer to the earth in general or to the land (of Israel) in particular, but here (as in 1 Chr 29:15, quoted above) it clearly refers generically to the character of life on earth, since the author goes on to make clear that their identity as "strangers" indicates that this πατρίς they are seeking is not any other land to which they can return but rather a "better," "heavenly" (ἐπουράνιος) homeland, a "city" (πόλις) prepared by God (11:15–16).

---

127. This word occurs only here in the LXX and NT; and this is its first occurrence in Greek literature (so Attridge, *Epistle to the Hebrews*, 131 with n. 103).

128. Attridge, *Epistle to the Hebrews*, 126–28, offers an overview of the "rest" image in Hebrews, seeing it as "a complex symbol for the whole soteriological process that Hebrews never fully articulates, but which involves both personal and corporate dimensions" (128).

129. For an overview of this text on the subject of the "promised land," see Backhaus, "Das Land der Verheißung," 172–76.

Just as these ancestors in faith looked forward, on the author's interpretation, to a homeland, a place of rest (to recall the language of Heb 3–4) that is an object of eschatological hope, so too the recipients of this letter—or the hearers of the original homily[130]—have no abiding residence here and now but are "looking for the city [πόλιν] that is to come [τὴν μέλλουσαν]" (13:14). Such language in 11:16 may already have called to mind the city of Jerusalem, but this identification is made explicit in 12:22, where the author, building on the catalogue of the exemplars of faith (12:1), encourages the addressees with the assurance that they "have come [προσεληλύθατε] to Mount Zion, the city of the living God, the heavenly Jerusalem ['Ιερουσαλὴμ ἐπουρανίῳ]." The formulation here might almost suggest that the recipients of this affirmation have already arrived at this heavenly home, but the closing exhortations include the unambiguous statement that they, with the author, are "looking forward" (ἐπιζητοῦμεν) to it (13:14, quoted above). Not unusually for the New Testament, the eschatological hope is presented as already close or in the process of realization (cf. 1 Pet 1:6–9).

Long ago, Ernst Käsemann drew attention to the importance of the theme of "the wandering people of God" in Hebrews. Certainly in the passages that feature the themes of rest, promised land, and abiding city there is a clear sense that the followers of Christ are called to be faithful and obedient during their time as exiles and strangers on earth so as to arrive in the end at their heavenly homeland, the city of Jerusalem.[131] Once again, themes from the Jewish scriptures are fundamental to the author's presentation: the notion of a land of promise, a place of (final) rest, the sense of an alien, estranged existence on the earth, and the eschatological hope for a new Jerusalem that is flourishing and glorious beyond anything yet seen. Given the extent to which such themes are already spiritualized and eschatologized in the Jewish scriptures and in the works of other Jewish writers, as we have seen, we should query any sharp distinction, at least in Hebrews' presentation, between a territorial Judaism and a deterritorialized Christianity.

It is clear enough that the letter to the Hebrews orientates its recipients not toward renewed possession of or dominion over an ancestral or divinely promised portion of the earth but rather toward an eschatological homeland that is explicitly described as heavenly.[132] Yet, as in Gal 4:21–31,

---

130. See n. 120 above on the genre of Hebrews.

131. Ernst Käsemann, *The Wandering People of God: An Investigation of the Letter to the Hebrews* (Minneapolis: Fortress, 1984); cf. also Backhaus, "Das Land der Verheißung," 182.

132. Nonetheless, Wilken, *Land Called Holy*, 52–55, pushes back against an over-

the orientation of the readers' identity toward a Jerusalem above represents a symbolic construction of space, an ideological geography that continues to place Jerusalem at its heart (and, as such, imbues the earthly Jerusalem with ongoing significance). This remains a topocentric perspective, albeit one in which the symbolic and spiritual construction of place is more prominent than the physical. The orientation toward Jerusalem may be toward an eschatological, heavenly Jerusalem, but that does not mean that this "symbolic attachment" to a homeland—to use Smith's phrase (see p. 72 above)—is without consequence for the construction and perception of existence in the physical spaces of the here and now. As in 1 Peter, the spatial ideology of Hebrews configures the Christians' current existence in society as one of παροικία, of estrangement, thus inculcating a stance of distance from their wider civic spaces, with social and practical implications.[133] Those who yearn for a homeland are not, as the author of Hebrews stresses (11:13–14), at home where they are.

6.2.5 Revelation

The New Testament writing that most extensively, explicitly, and influentially depicts this eschatological, heavenly Jerusalem is the book of Revelation, which concludes with a striking description of this glorious city coming down to earth from heaven (Rev 21:1–22:5).[134] Already in the collection of letters to the churches with which the book opens, there is included, within the letter to the angel of the Christian assembly in Philadelphia (3:7–13), the assurance that the one who holds fast and endures until Christ comes, "the one who conquers" (ὁ νικῶν), will be made "a pillar in the temple of my God" and will have written upon them "the name of my God, and the name of the city of my God [τὸ ὄνομα τῆς πόλεως τοῦ θεοῦ μου], the new Jerusalem which comes down from heaven [τῆς καινῆς Ἰερουσαλήμ, ἡ καταβαίνουσα ἐκ τοῦ οὐρανοῦ]" (3:12). As with the extended vision at the close

---

spiritualizing of Hebrews and its land theology in particular, suggesting that the author may, for example, envisage a city (Heb 11:16) that "would majestically come down from the heavens to its resting place in the promised land" (55).

133. On this construction of identity as alien other in Hebrews, see Dunning, *Aliens and Sojourners*, 46–63.

134. For an overview of the description of the new Jerusalem here, see Richard Bauckham, *The Theology of the Book of Revelation*, New Testament Theology (Cambridge: Cambridge University Press, 1993), 132–36.

of the book, here too there is an allusion to Ezekiel's vision of the city and its name (Ezek 48:35).

The culmination of the prophetic visions of the book in chapters 21–22 commences with the Isaianic eschatological anticipation of a new heaven and a new earth (Rev 21:1; Isa 65:17; 66:22). However earthly the vision of the new Jerusalem, it is nonetheless clearly located within some kind of new (or at least radically renewed; cf. Rev 5:5) cosmos, since "the first heaven and the first earth [ἡ πρώτη γῆ]" have passed away (ἀπῆλθαν) and the sea no longer exists (οὐκ ἔστιν ἔτι) (21:1).[135] Picking up the prophetic words of Ezekiel and Isaiah, the city is declared to be a place where God dwells with his people and where death, suffering, and pain are no more (21:3–4; cf. Ezek 37:27; Isa 25:8; 65:19). Much of the description, echoing comparable material in Ezekiel 40–48, focuses on the splendor and size of the city. While Ezekiel's material has a heavy focus on the temple itself, set within the city (Ezek 48:30–35) and the land (Ezek 47:13–48:29), Revelation's new Jerusalem strikingly has no temple as such, since God's very presence removes the need for one (Rev 21:22).[136] John's new Jerusalem is bizarrely massive in its dimensions, extending to 12,000 stadia (about 1,400 modern international miles) in all directions, even upward, forming a cube (21:16).[137] With its thick, bejewelled walls—again extending to implausible dimensions (21:17)—it is evidently the city to dwarf all others in size and splendor, an embodiment of the incomparable power and victory of John's God and his son, Jesus Christ.[138]

John's vision is explicitly one of a "new" Jerusalem that comes down from heaven. In a sense, therefore, as Richard Bauckham remarks, this Jerusalem "is not the actual city which the Romans had captured and sacked some time before Revelation was written."[139] But this should not be taken to imply that there is no real connection between earthly Jerusalem and

135. On the cosmic destruction and replacement or renewal assumed here, see Edward Adams, *The Stars Will Fall from Heaven: Cosmic Catastrophe in the New Testament and Its World*, LNTS 347 (London: T&T Clark, 2007), 237–39.

136. See Bauckham, *Book of Revelation*, 136; Wilfrid J. Harrington, *Revelation*, SP 16 (Collegeville: Liturgical Press, 1993), 217–18.

137. See Wes Howard-Brook and Anthony Gwyther, *Unveiling Empire: Reading Revelation Then and Now* (Maryknoll, NY: Orbis, 1999), 187–88, who stress the symbolic nature of this description and its allusions to perfection.

138. On this gigantic urban vision (and the consequent problems with appeal to it as an ecological resource) see Stephen D. Moore, *Untold Tales from the Book of Revelation: Sex and Gender, Empire and Ecology*, RBS 79 (Atlanta: Society of Biblical Literature, 2014), 235–38.

139. Bauckham, *Book of Revelation*, 126.

heavenly vision, nor that earthly Jerusalem loses its significance as place. It is, of course, precisely *Jerusalem* that is depicted in a renewed, paradisal form pervaded by the presence of God; and this identification continues to imbue the earthly Jerusalem with special significance and symbolic centrality within John's vision. Though differently from Paul and Hebrews, Revelation also configures space around Jerusalem, since it is precisely here—in concretely geographical space, it would seem—that the final and glorious arrival of God's new and enduring city will take place. It is no surprise, then, that Revelation's vision was of ongoing influence in the development of Christian chiliasm and other forms of eschatological belief that looked for the arrival on earth of God's new messianic kingdom.[140] Indeed, as Lorenzo Perrone, following Stefan Heid, remarks, "The widespread presence of chiliastic ideas from the second to the fourth centuries shows that early Christianity had, in fact, much more interest in Jerusalem and the Holy Land than the *communis opinio* would allow us to think."[141] Justin Martyr, for example, later declares his conviction that "I and every other completely orthodox Christian feel certain that there will be a resurrection of the flesh, followed by a thousand years in the rebuilt, embellished, and enlarged city of Jerusalem, as was announced by the Prophets Ezekiel, Isaiah, and the others" (*Dial.* 80.5; see further 80.1–5; 81.4; 113.3–5).[142] Indeed, after Constantine's adoption of Christianity as the religion of the Roman Empire, when Christians came to hold imperial power in Judea, the "earthly" Jerusalem continued to have

140. See Stefan Heid, *Chiliasmus und Antichrist-Mythos: Eine frühchristliche Kontroverse um das Heilige Land*, Hereditas: Studien zur Alten Kirchengeschichte 6 (Bonn: Borengässer, 1993).

141. Lorenzo Perrone, "'The Mystery of Judaea' (Jerome, *Ep.* 46): The Holy City of Jerusalem between History and Symbol in Early Christian Thought," in Levine, *Jerusalem*, 226; see also 223–28. Perrone is building on the work of Brox, "Das 'irdische Jerusalem,'" and Heid, *Chiliasmus und Antichrist-Mythos*.

142. Ἐγὼ δέ, καὶ εἴ τινές εἰσιν ὀρθογνώμονες κατὰ πάντα Χριστιανοί, καὶ σαρκὸς ἀνάστασιν γενήσεσθαι ἐπιστάμεθα καὶ χίλια ἔτη ἐν Ἰερουσαλὴμ οἰκοδομηθείσῃ καὶ κοσμηθείσῃ καὶ πλατυνθείσῃ, ὡς οἱ προφῆται Ἰεζεκιὴλ καὶ Ἠσαΐας καὶ οἱ ἄλλοι ὁμολογοῦσιν. Greek text from Philippe Bobichon, ed., *Justin Martyr, Dialogue avec Tryphon: Édition critique, traduction, commentaire*, 2 vols., Paradosis 47/1–2 (Fribourg, Switzerland: Academic Press Fribourg, 2003), 406; ET (slightly altered) from Thomas B. Falls, *Writings of Saint Justin Martyr*, The Fathers of the Church 6 (Washington, DC: Catholic University of America, 1948). On Justin's beliefs in this regard, see Brox, "Das 'irdische Jerusalem,'" 156–57; Heid, *Chiliasmus und Antichrist-Mythos*, 31–51; Wilken, *Land Called Holy*, 56–59. More broadly, on the diverse perspectives in early Christian literature, see Vair, "Promise of the Land"; Heid, *Chiliasmus und Antichrist-Mythos*; Perrone, "Mystery of Judaea."

special significance, "venerated," Andrew Jacobs remarks, "as the earthly manifestation of 'Jerusalem above.'"[143]

6.3 Conclusions

There are some points of contrast—notwithstanding their variety and diversity—between the kinds of reference to the land found in Jewish and early Christian sources. Jewish sources frequently refer, albeit in various ways, to the ancestral homeland that has Jerusalem at its center. Even for writers such as Philo, who can either spiritualize the notion of promised land or insist that diaspora Jews are firmly rooted in ancestral lands elsewhere where they (and their forebears) live, the "holy land," with Jerusalem at its center, remains a concrete, material point of reference. Nowhere in the New Testament is the land of Israel described in such concrete terms as "ancestral homeland" (πατρίς) for those who follow Christ—unsurprisingly, we might add, since, like Philo's Alexandrian Jews, they mostly originate from other places.

Yet there are also, as we have seen, considerable similarities and points of contact in the various ways Jewish and early Christian sources depict the land of Israel and Jerusalem in particular, often due to the use of scriptural phrasing and imagery in these early Christian texts. Jewish views of the land include eschatological and spiritualizing perspectives, a sense of detachment or alienation from the "world," and clear indications that diaspora Jews could identify their ancestral homeland elsewhere while retaining an orientation toward Judea and Jerusalem. All these features find parallels and echoes in New Testament and early Christian texts. Like Philo, for example, some New Testament texts take up the scriptural image of living on the earth as "strangers and aliens" to depict the Christians as "not at home" while yearning for an eschatological heavenly "homeland." First Peter adopts and adapts the scriptural motif of living as aliens and strangers in the world, specifically in the diaspora, and constructs the trans-national community of Christians as a new (temple) space. We also find examples of a clear spatial orientation toward Jerusalem that can encompass both physical and spiritual/escha-

---

143. Andrew S. Jacobs, *Remains of the Jews: The Holy Land and Christian Empire in Late Antiquity*, Divinations: Rereading Late Ancient Religion (Stanford: Stanford University Press, 2004), 105. See also Andrew S. Jacobs, "The Remains of the Jew: Imperial Christian Identity in the Late Ancient Holy Land," *Journal of Medieval and Early Modern Studies* 33 (2003): 23–45; Wilken, *Land Called Holy*, 82–100.

tological dimensions, as in the letters of Paul. Visions of an eschatological new Jerusalem, rooted in the visions of the prophets Isaiah and Ezekiel and briefly articulated in Hebrews, culminate in Revelation's final depiction of the city coming down from heaven to earth. These early Christian constructions of space are clearly (and unsurprisingly) imbued with Jewish theological geography, reflective of ongoing modes of symbolic attachment and orientation to Judea and Jerusalem.

Discussions of homeland and territory are another area in which a contrast is often drawn between Jewish ethnic particularism—ethnic, earthy, tied to territory—and Christian trans-ethnic universalism, which has moved beyond such limitations to a vision of heavenly salvation that transcends all specific territorial and ethnic boundaries. Yet the material we have surveyed, albeit briefly and selectively, illustrates that such a clear distinction is difficult to sustain, at least in these terms.

First, as we have already noted, no single criterion can reliably function as a *sine qua non* for ethnic identity, which is multi-faceted and flexible. A concrete connection to homeland is not necessarily present or prominent in all cases. Second, even on Anthony Smith's criterion, the attachment to a homeland can be "symbolic." This point becomes even more significant in the light of contemporary theories of space, which emphasize the intrinsic connections between physical and symbolic, or "real-and-imagined," space. Indeed, in both Jewish and early Christian texts, we have seen how inextricably connected are the physical and symbolic dimensions of the construction of space, most often expressed in a configuration of the world around the center of Jerusalem, a kind of theological geography. Even such motifs as the "heavenly homeland," which might appear to express a detachment from the material earth, both reflect and shape particular construals and constructions of place, as critical theories of space help us to see. These symbolic and ideological constructions of the world have consequences for the perception and practice of existence in the physical spaces of the here and now.

A further contrast is sometimes built on the distinction between Jewish attachment to a physical land and the transcending of this particularity in early Christianity, with its universal, cosmic, or heavenly hope. In such scholarship, Jewish attachment to land is sometimes described in crudely material terms, referring to the promised land as a piece of "real estate," for example—an expression Wilken criticizes as "vulgar."[144] More troubling still is when such a perspective is linked with an interpretation of the early

144. Wilken, *Land Called Holy*, 272n50.

Christian vision as aiming for the whole world. In Philip Church's view, for example, "Paul has evidently interpreted the land promise to Abraham not as a promise that his descendants would inherit a slice of real estate at the eastern end of the Mediterranean, but rather a promise that Abraham's descendants (both Jew and Gentile) would inherit the entire world."[145]

While such comments may be intended to present the Christian perspective as a critique of Israel's land policies and of Christian Zionism in particular,[146] they suggest an uncomfortable correlation between such biblical interpretation and Christian imperialism, which has indeed laid claim to the whole world.[147] Rather than aiming for a mere "slice" of "real estate," the Christian gospel apparently legitimates a claim to it all. Brueggemann comments critically, for example, on the connections between "land entitlement" and "earth occupation," suggesting that such a biblical ideology played a clear part in European/Western colonialism.[148] At the very least, the studies presented in this chapter should indicate that early Christian perspectives and their interpretive legacy, despite their tendency to spiritualize or eschatologize orientation to the promised land, and to Jerusalem in particular, are implicated in shaping concrete attitudes to land and territory just as Jewish ones are. The intersections between ethnicity and religion, and their connections with land, here become especially significant. Comments on Christianity's aim to encompass the whole earth also invite a consideration of perspectives on mission and conversion and of the ways in which ethnoracial and religious contexts shape scholarly constructions. We shall turn to such issues in later chapters. Before that, however, we address a fundamental topic that has been implicit through much of what has been said thus far: the evidence for a sense of being a "people."

145. Church, "No Lasting City," 50.

146. See the wider context of the essays collected in Church et al., *Gospel and the Land*, and in particular the comments of Tim Meadowcroft, "The Gospel and the Land of Promise: A Response," 162–63.

147. Cf. Philip Church, "'God Has By No Means Rejected His People': A Response to the Accusation of 'Replacement Theology,'" in Church et al., *Gospel and the Land*, 157: "It is the worldwide expansion of Christianity rather than the rise of Zionist nationalism that continues to fulfill the purposes of God."

148. Brueggemann, *Land*, xv.

CHAPTER 7

Becoming a People: Self-Consciousness and Ethnicization

A sense of being a "people" is probably as close as one might get to an essential criterion for ethnic identity, albeit a somewhat tautologous one. As noted in chapter 3, Richard Schermerhorn makes "self-consciousness" key to the identification of ethnic groups. Equally important though, as Rogers Brubaker's critique of "groupism" makes clear, is that such self-consciousness need not by any means be a constant, influential, or settled feature of life for any given individuals. Indeed, a sense of ethnic identity or peoplehood can be invoked—or provoked—by particular circumstances or actors, not least when external pressure or hostility induces the activation or construction of an identity that may not otherwise have been salient or even, on a constructionist model, existent. As Brubaker insists, "Participants' accounts . . . often have what Pierre Bourdieu has called a performative character. By invoking groups, they seek to evoke them, summon them, call them into being. Their categories are for doing—designed to stir, summon, justify, mobilize, kindle and energize."[1]

In the modern world, the Western European model of the nation-state has become a primary locus for the identification of peoplehood and the key mode of engagement in global politics, even if the collocation of peoplehood with existing nation-states is artificial and ill-fitting in many places and for various historically specific reasons. So it is, for example, that Tommy Givens adopts as the title of his book on the election of Israel and Christian peoplehood the opening words of the US Constitution: "We the people."[2] Indeed, just as J. Kameron

1. Rogers Brubaker, "Ethnicity without Groups," 166.
2. Tommy Givens, *We the People: Israel and the Catholicity of Jesus* (Minneapolis: Fortress, 2014). For the US Constitution (of 1787), see https://www.archives.gov/founding-docs/constitution.

Carter identifies supercessionist constructions of Christianity's relationship to Judaism as the root of the modern ideology of race,[3] so Givens, influenced by Carter, sees the modern (Western) construction of the nation and peoplehood as a secularized Protestant creation based on a particular appropriation of the notion of divine election and a negative view of Judaism: "Jewishness functioned as the negative foundation on which Christian powers found themselves constructing race and nation as the basic, mutually informing sociopolitical structures of the modern world."[4] Givens's concern, building on the work of John Howard Yoder and Karl Barth, is both to challenge the identification of nations as "the most determinative form of human community"—"the primary basis for killing"[5]—and to develop an account of God's elect people that sees Jews, Christians, and others as part of this people and prohibits premature and exclusionary attempts to determine who counts as "in" or "out."[6]

It is clear that the model of the nation-state that dominates the contemporary political scene is a particular one, a development of a distinctively Western European tradition. While Anthony Smith stresses the origins of nations in ethnic groups and communities,[7] it is also important to emphasize the other side of the coin: that the formation and maintenance of a nation requires a certain kind of ethnicization, the *construction* of a sense of peoplehood. Étienne Balibar, for example, sees the nation-state as a community based on a "fictive ethnicity":

No nation possesses an ethnic base naturally, but as social formations are nationalized, the populations included within them, divided up among them or dominated by them are ethnicized—that is, represented in the past or in the future *as if* they formed a natural community, possessing of itself an identity of origins, culture and interests which transcends individuals and social conditions.[8]

3. Carter, *Race*; see the introduction (p. 4 above).

4. Givens, *We the People*, 137. For a study of the role of religion in the formation of nations and national identities that foregrounds the paradigmatic influence of Israel's election as a people/nation, see Smith, *Chosen Peoples*.

5. Givens, *We the People*, 1.

6. See, e.g., Givens, *We the People*, 413–19; note also the comment on Muslims on 361n28.

7. Smith, *Ethnic Origins*.

8. Étienne Balibar, "The Nation Form: History and Ideology," in *Race, Nation, Class: Ambiguous Identities*, ed. Immanuel Wallerstein and Étienne Balibar (London: Verso, 1991), 96, italics original.

There has been considerable discussion as to whether there were nations in antiquity or, better put, whether terms like nation, nationalism, and so on are apposite to the study of ancient people-groups.[9] This is in part a question of definition (not unlike similar questions with regard to "race" or even "ethnicity"): if one defines "nation" in terms of the modern (Western) nation-state, then it is clear that nations and nationalisms belong to the world's modern history and cannot be retrojected into antiquity. On the other hand, if one adopts a broader model of nationhood, then a case can at least be made that some of the various ancient peoples who lived in an ancestral homeland, under some set of laws and customs and a ruler of some kind, constituted a type of nation.[10]

Nevertheless, there is a risk that such a designation obscures or distorts as much as it illuminates. It should be clear that none of the ancient people-group terms—in particular ἔθνος, γένος, and λαός—directly corresponds to our term "nation," even if translation sometimes requires the use of this and other less-than-adequate equivalents.[11] Nor does any of these terms—including ἔθνος, despite the etymological link—directly equate to the modern sociological category of the ethnic group or *ethnie*. What is also clear, though, is that such terms were frequently used to identify people-groups in the ancient world. The task of the current chapter, then, is, first, to outline briefly the range of meanings and uses for these crucial "people" words; second, to consider their uses to display a sense of Jewish peoplehood; and finally, to explore the gradual appearance of such terms to indicate a developing self-consciousness concerning Christian peoplehood.[12] In previous chapters, we explored some of the main features of what was taken to characterize being a

9. See, e.g., the overview and discussion in Anthony D. Smith, *The Antiquity of Nations* (Cambridge: Polity, 2004).

10. So Smith, *Antiquity of Nations*, 127–53. Cf. Mendels, *Rise and Fall*, who argues for the appropriateness of the term "nationalism" for the study of ancient Judaism.

11. On the sense that γένος, ἔθνος, and λαός together represent the three crucial terms in regard to this topic, see Buell, *Why This New Race*, 62, 69, 87, et passim.

12. It is important, though, to acknowledge Teresa Morgan's point that study of these words will not necessarily take us specifically to "ethnic" identity since the "terminology is so multivalent" and may refer to "almost any kind of group." See Morgan, "Society, Identity, and Ethnicity," 25. These terms nonetheless constitute one way in which we may search for a *conscious* sense of identity as some kind of "people" (notwithstanding the diverse meanings that each of the key words can carry, on which see below), but we also need to attend to the substantive ways in which such "people-group" identities can be constructed and maintained, as the previous chapters have sought to do.

member of the Jewish people or a member of the early Christian groups. The focus here is on the evidence for self-consciousness about being "a people."

7.1 People-Groups in Antiquity: ἔθνος, γένος, λαός

Each of the words commonly used to denote some kind of people-group in ancient Greek has a considerable range of meaning and application; none can be unproblematically or univocally identified with a modern equivalent, whether nation, race, or *ethnie*. As Jonathan Hall remarks, "The ancient Greeks possessed no single term that might equate to our word 'ethnicity.'"[13] Nonetheless, the term ἔθνος, from which the modern vocabulary of ethnicity derives, is a good place to start, since it is widely used as a standard way to denote people-groups. The word broadly denotes "a class of beings who share a common identification," human or animal, and in Homer it is used of groups of birds and bees, for example, as well as of humans.[14] Even when it comes to human groups, the types that can be designated as an ἔθνος are quite diverse, ranging from larger populations or inhabitants of a particular πόλις[15] to members of smaller groups such as clubs, guilds, and associations.[16] As Jeremy McInerney notes, "'ethnos' served as a conveniently loose label equivalent to the vague English term 'people.'"[17] More generally, as Teresa Morgan observes, "ethnic" designations may be used of groups of various sizes, from cities or groups of cities to larger regions and kingdoms.[18]

That ἔθνος served as a standard, if loosely defined, term to denote various "peoples" can be illustrated briefly from both inscriptional and literary evidence.[19] For example, in the Sebasteion at Aphrodisias, a series of stat-

13. Hall, *Hellenicity*, 17.

14. Hall, *Ethnic Identity*, 35. See also Jeremy McInerney, "Ethnos and Ethnicity in Early Greece," in Malkin, *Ancient Perceptions*, 55–56; Homer, *Il.* 2.459 (birds); 2.87 (bees); 2.469 (flies); 2.91; 3.32 (warriors).

15. Hall, *Ethnic Identity*, 34–35; Herodotus, *Hist.* 1.57; 5.77; 7.161; 8.73.

16. LSJ, 480; Anthony J. Saldarini, *Matthew's Christian-Jewish Community* (Chicago: University of Chicago Press, 1994), 59–60; Matthias Konradt, *Israel, Church, and the Gentiles in the Gospel of Matthew*, Baylor-Mohr Siebeck Studies in Early Christianity (Tübingen: Mohr Siebeck; Waco: Baylor University Press, 2014), 181.

17. McInerney, "Ethnos and Ethnicity," 56.

18. Morgan, "Society, Identity, and Ethnicity," 24–26.

19. For an extended survey of the prominence of *ethnos* (and *polis*) as key categories in the organization of ancient societies, see Mason, *History of Roman Judaea*, 97–146.

uary reliefs stand on inscribed bases that identify the figures as, in many cases, personified ἔθνη, including, for example, the ἔθνους Ἀιγυπτιων, the ἔθνους Πιρουστων, the ἔθνους Δαρδανων, and the ἔθνους Ἰουδαιων. The series is part of a wider complex dedicated to the Julio-Claudian emperors and exhibiting the dominion of Rome over a range of peoples and lands.[20] Steve Mason notes the widespread use of ἔθνος in ancient Greek literature and draws attention to examples, such as in Pseudo-Skylax's fourth-century BCE geographical description of the world of the Greeks.[21] In this account, as Graham Shipley notes, Pseudo-Skylax "composes his world out of building blocks that he defines as *ethnē*"; these are, in effect, geographical areas—"ethnically defined political units"—within which are various πόλεις, noted along with harbors, rivers, mountains, and distances in travel times.[22] Shipley describes the account as having a somewhat "formulaic quality": "After *ethnos* X is *ethnos* Y, in it are the following *poleis*."[23] For example, in the section describing the land from Mysia to Cilicia, the following extracts give a flavor of the pattern:

> And past Karia is Lykia, a community [ἔθνος]: and the Lykioi have the following cities [πόλεις]: Telmissos with a harbour and the river Xanthos. . . .
> And after Lykia is Pamphylia, a community [ἔθνος], and in it the following cities [πόλεις]. . . .
> And after Pamphylia is Kilikia [Cilicia], a community [ἔθνος], and in it the following cities [πόλεις]: Selinous; Charadrous, a city [πόλις] with a harbour; Anemourion, a cape with a city; Nagidos, a city: and it has an island. . . .
> And out of Sinope in the Pontos, through the mainland and Kilikia to Soloi, the road from sea to sea is of days, 5. (Pseudo-Skylax, *Periplous* 100.1–102.2 [ET Shipley])

Strabo, in his own geographical survey, offers one illustration of the flexibility of the term ἔθνος, using it to denote both smaller tribal peo-

---

20. See Smith, "Simulacra Gentium." For one engagement with such visual imagery in NT interpretation, see Davina C. Lopez, *Apostle to the Conquered: Reimagining Paul's Mission*, Paul in Critical Contexts (Minneapolis: Fortress, 2008).
21. Mason, *History of Roman Judaea*, 103–4. For the date (of c. 338–37 BCE), see Graham Shipley, *Pseudo-Skylax's* Periplous: *The Circumnavigation of the Inhabited World: Text, Translation and Commentary* (Exeter: Bristol Phoenix, 2011), 6–8.
22. Shipley, *Pseudo-Skylax's* Periplous, 14.
23. Shipley, *Pseudo-Skylax's* Periplous, 18.

ples like the Cataonians and Pisidians and larger "nations," such as India (Strabo, *Geogr.* 2.5.32). McInerney shows how this traditional use of the term ἔθνος—as a broad, flexible, and imprecise term for various kinds of "people" groups—continued in Greek literature into the Byzantine era.[24] It is also worth noting, not least because of its prominence in Biblical Greek, the occasional use of ἔθνος to denote "people groups foreign to a specific people group."[25]

In a fruitful analysis of the term ἔθνος (and also of γένος, on which see below), Love Sechrest explores "the features associated with ethnic and racial identity in the early Christian period" by examining the words or topics that are associated with these key terms in the contexts where they appear.[26] She concludes that conflict (or war) and territory are most frequently associated with the term ἔθνος in her selected non-Jewish writers from the period (Diodorus Siculus, Dionysius of Halicarnassus, Strabo, and Plutarch).[27] This association of ἔθνη with both territory and conflict or conquest is likewise evident in the depictions at Aphrodisias.[28] More broadly, as Mason notes, ἔθνη are often associated with such things as particular laws, customs, ancestral claims, and religious or cultic practices, which together constitute ancestral ways of life (see ch. 5).[29] As such, the characteristics associated with ἔθνη, at least in these contexts, correlate closely with those linked with ethnic groups in modern social science.[30] Mason also notes how new ἔθνη

24. McInerney, "Ethnos and Ethnicity," 54–57.

25. BDAG, 276 §2; also MM, 181, who note uses of ἔθνη to denote the rural barbarians living outside the *polis*. For non-biblical "pagan" uses, see e.g. Aristotle, *Pol.* 7.2.5 (1324b): τοῖς ἔθνεσιν ("the non-Hellenic nations" [LCL]); Dio Cassius, *Rom. hist.* 36.41.1; for its use of foreign groups in Rome, see Appian, *Bell. civ.* 2.2.13, 26.107; 3.35.140. See also *IG* 2.1283 (240–39 BCE), in which ἔθνος is used of immigrant groups and specifically of an association of Thracians in Athens; I am grateful to John Kloppenborg for alerting me to this inscription, now available in Richard S. Ascough, Philip A. Harland, and John S. Kloppenborg, *Associations in the Greco-Roman World: A Sourcebook* (Berlin: De Gruyter, 2012), 26–28.

26. Sechrest, *A Former Jew*, 90–91. For the analysis, see 54–109 and summary charts on 232–33.

27. See Sechrest, *Former Jew*, 66–70, 94–96.

28. See Smith, "Simulacra Gentium," 55–59.

29. Mason, "Jews, Judaeans, Judaizing, Judaism," 484; Mason, *History of Roman Judaea*, 107.

30. Cf. Mason and Esler, "Judaean and Christ-Follower Identities," 499. For a specific mapping of the modern criteria onto an ancient depiction of the Jewish/Judean people, see Esler, "Josephus' *Against Apion*."

could be formed out of existing ones or through migration.[31] Likewise, contemporary social science has analyzed various forms of ethnogenesis.[32]

Like ἔθνος, γένος can be applied to both human and non-human groups, to sorts and kinds of things as well as to what we might call ethnic or racial groups.[33] As Hall notes, however, it has a somewhat "more specialised meaning" than ἔθνος, "with its focus on the notion (however fictive) of shared descent."[34] Sechrest, while not utilizing the category of descent as such, finds that "kinship" ideas are most frequently associated with uses of γένος in the non-Jewish authors she studies.[35] While γένος (or the closely related γενεά/γενεή) can be used as "a subdivision of ἔθνος,"[36] it need not be so, and the two terms can be used as synonyms.[37] A common term to denote the "tribes" that might together constitute a broader ἔθνος is φυλή, which often refers to a group connected by descent.[38]

Unlike ἔθνος and γένος, λαός seems always to refer to groups of human beings such as soldiers, sailors, country-folk, or a gathered crowd, the assembled inhabitants.[39] Sometimes the specific sense is of the people in distinction from the leaders[40]—hence the established meaning of the "common folk" or peasants.[41] But λαός came also to be used to refer to the whole

---

31. Mason, *History of Roman Judaea*, 105, 108.

32. See the discussion and application to the field of NT studies in Hansen, *"All of You Are One,"* 55–60.

33. See Homer, *Il.* 12.23: ἡμιθέων γένος ἀνδρῶν ("the race of men half-divine" [Murray, LCL]); *Il.* 2.852: "the race [γένος] of wild she-mules" (LCL); Ael. Arist., *Or.* 45.1: "the race of poets" (τὸ τῶν ποιητῶν γένος). See MM, 124, for the common use in the papyri for "a species or class of things" as well as uses corresponding "to *gens*, a tribe or clan."

34. Hall, *Ethnic Identity*, 36. Cf. Homer, *Il.* 13.354: "Both were of one stock [γένος] and of one parentage [πάτρη]"; *Od.* 15.267: ἐξ Ἰθάκης γένος εἰμί ("Of Ithaca I am by birth" [Murray, LCL]), which seems to mean, in effect, "I am an Ithacan"; Sophocles, *Oed. Tyr.* 1383: γένους τοῦ Λαΐου ("of the race of Laius" [Lloyd-Jones, LCL]).

35. See Sechrest, *Former Jew*, 84–87, 94–96.

36. LSJ, 480; cf. 344 (γένος), 342 (γενεά/γενεή); as in, e.g., Herodotus, *Hist.* 1.101: "Deioces, then, united the Median nation [τὸ Μηδικὸν ἔθνος]. . . . The Median tribes [Μήδων γένεα] are these . . ." (Godley, LCL).

37. Hall, *Ethnic Identity*, 36; Sechrest, *Former Jew*, 90; see, e.g., Herodotus, *Hist.* 1.56–57; Ael. Arist., *Or.* 1.50 (173D).

38. See LSJ, 1961.

39. See LSJ, 1029.

40. E.g., Homer, *Il.* 2.365; 13.108; *Od.* 3.305. See *TDNT* 4:30.

41. See Polybius, *Hist.* 4.52.7; *TLNT* 2:373; MM, 370. Note, however, *TLNT*'s discussion of the Egyptian papyri, in which Spicq suggests that λαός may refer to a "superior stratum of the . . . population . . . farmers, for example, as distinct from the mass of farm laborers" (*TLNT* 2:373).

population, which might equally be described as an ἔθνος or γένος—"the people" as a collective whole.[42]

None of these terms corresponds consistently or precisely to the modern vocabulary of ethnicity, not least due to their variety of use. But it is equally clear that these are the key terms with which ancient Greek authors referred to people-groups, and (particularly in the cases of ἔθνος and γένος) specifically those that from a modern perspective would be labeled as ethnic (or racial) groups.

7.2 Jewish Peoplehood: The λαὸς θεοῦ

In the LXX, ἔθνος is frequently used (in the plural) to denote outsiders—"the nations" as distinct from "the people"—often (but by no means always) rendering גוים (e.g., Exod 34:24; Lev 18:24).[43] This pattern is also common in the New Testament.[44] In Exod 1:9, Pharoah speaks τῷ ἔθνει αὐτοῦ (אֶל־עַמּוֹ) concerning τὸ γένος τῶν υἱῶν Ισραηλ (עַם בני ישראל).[45] Deuteronomy 7:6-7 describes Israel as a people (λαός, עַם) holy, chosen, and special to God, set among the nations (ἔθνη, גוים; cf. Deut 32:8-9). The book of Judith also provides a clear example: "Woe to the nations [ἔθνεσιν] that rise up against my people [τῷ γένει μου]" (16:17). Second Maccabees 8:9 describes Nicanor as in charge of "twenty thousand Gentiles of all nations [παμφύλων ἔθνη]"; his task is "to wipe out the entire Judean race" (τὸ σύμπαν τῆς Ιουδαίας γένος; cf. Wis 10:15). As these examples indicate, and as is briefly detailed below, λαός and γένος are standard terms for the people of Israel, often in juxtaposition to the (other) ἔθνη.[46]

---

42. *TDNT* 4:31. Cf. Plutarch, *Rom.* 26.3; *TLNT* 2:373.

43. On ἔθνος in the LXX and later Jewish sources, see the extensive and detailed survey in Scott, *Paul and the Nations*, 58–121. Also see *TDNT* 2:364–69; Hatch and Redpath, *Concordance*, 368–73, who list fifteen Hebrew words for which ἔθνος can stand as an equivalent.

44. For clear examples where the contrast is drawn, see Luke 2:32; Acts 4:27; 14:5; 26:23; Rom 15:10; 2 Cor 11:26; Gal 2:14–15.

45. Cf. Isa 42:6 and 49:6 (in some MSS) for the contrast between the διαθήκη γένους (ברית עם) and the ἔθνη (גוים); Georg Bertram (*TDNT* 2:367) insists that ברית עם "refers to the chosen people."

46. Φυλή (rendering various Heb. words; see Hatch and Redpath, *Concordance*, 1444–46) is most frequently used in the LXX of the twelve tribes or clans of Israel (e.g., Exod 24:4; 28:21; Num 1:4–49) or of such groupings among other peoples (e.g., Gen 10:18) or among people in general (e.g., Gen 10:5; 12:3). This pattern continues in the NT (see n. 73 below).

Yet ἔθνος can also be used of the people of Israel, not least in later writings.[47] As James Scott notes, the Table of Nations (ἔθνη) in Gen 10 is a comprehensive description of "the 'nations' of the world, including Israel."[48] The foundational promise to Abram is to make of him "a great nation" (ἔθνος μέγα/גוי גדול, Gen 12:2) and to bless all the nations (ἔθνη/גוים) of the earth in him (Gen 18:18; 22:18; 26:4).[49] A number of times in the book of Exodus, for example, Israel is described as an ἔθνος (23:11; 33:13 [גוי] 32:10; [עם]). In Exod 19:6 (quoted in 1 Pet 2:9), God declares that the people will be a holy nation, the Greek here—with ἔθνος rather than the more usual λαός—being a rendering of the Hebrew with what Georg Bertram calls "philological accuracy" (ἔθνος ἅγιον/גוי קדוש; contrast Deut 7:6).[50]

This use of ἔθνος to denote the people of Israel is prominent in later Jewish texts.[51] Indeed, to take just Philo and Josephus as examples, this is the dominant referent of the word—not because of any particular distinction in their use of such terms but simply because they speak of the Jewish people more frequently than of any other. Scott reports that of the roughly 280 uses of ἔθνος in Philo's works, the majority refer to the Jewish people: τὸ Ἰουδαίων ἔθνος, or simply τὸ ἔθνος, etc.[52] Likewise, according to Scott, of the 413 uses of ἔθνος in Josephus, the great majority refer to the Jewish people, using a similar range of phrases.[53] In the New Testament, in both Luke-Acts and John, there are a number of uses of ἔθνος to refer to the Jewish "people."[54] Indeed,

---

47. See 1 Esd 1:4 (τὸ ἔθνος αὐτοῦ Ἰσραήλ); 8:66 (τὸ ἔθνος τοῦ Ἰσραήλ); cf. 1:32, 34, 49; 2:5; 5:9; 8:10, 13, 64.

48. Scott, *Paul and the Nations*, 58. For NT examples of general, inclusive uses of ἔθνη, see, e.g., Matt 28:19; Mark 11:17; Luke 12:30; Acts 14:5; 26:23; Rev 2:26.

49. In Gen 12:3 and 28:14 the same promise is made using φυλαί rather than ἔθνη.

50. *TDNT* 2:366. Cf. F. J. A. Hort, *First Epistle of St. Peter*, 126. However, ἔθνος ἅγιον (as opposed to λαὸς ἅγιος) is not quite "unique" here; see Exod 19:6; 23:22; Wis 17:2.

51. See Scott, *Paul and the Nations*, 74–121.

52. Scott, *Paul and the Nations*, 84. See also the detailed discussion in Sarah Pearce, "Notes on Philo's Use of the Terms ἔθνος and λαός," *The Studia Philonica Annual: Studies in Hellenistic Judaism* 28 (2016): 209–26. In addition to the examples given by Scott, see further, e.g., Philo, *Legat.* 117, 119, 137, 161, 279, and the full list of 287 occurrences in Peder Borgen, Kåre Fuglseth, and Roald Skarsten, *The Philo Index: A Complete Greek Word Index to the Writings of Philo of Alexandria* (Grand Rapids: Eerdmans, 2000), 104.

53. Scott, *Paul and the Nations*, 99. In addition to the examples given by Scott, see further, e.g., Josephus, *C. Ap.* 2.220; *B.J.* 1.232, 581; 2.282; *A.J.* 14.290; 18.6, and the full list in Rengstorf, *Complete Concordance*, 2:15–18.

54. τὸ ἔθνος ἡμῶν, τὸ ἔθνος τῶν Ἰουδαίων, κτλ.; e.g., Luke 7:5; 23:2; Acts 10:22; 24:2, 10, 17; 26:4; 28:19.

all of the five uses of ἔθνος in the Gospel of John have this referent (John 11:48, 50–52; 18:35).[55]

In contrast to non-biblical Greek literature, where the term λαός is relatively infrequent, it is a very common term in the LXX, with over two thousand occurrences, generally rendering the Hebrew עַם.[56] Hermann Strathmann notes the strong tendency in the LXX to use λαός for עַם when referring to Israel and "a corresponding inclination to use ἔθνος instead when עַם does not refer to Israel."[57] These tendencies are not always followed; nonetheless, as Strathmann puts it, "the truly distinctive feature of the LXX usage is the careful restriction of the use of the term to Israel. All else is subsidiary."[58] In the New Testament too, the predominant use of λαός, particularly in Luke-Acts[59] and almost always in the singular form, is in reference to the people of Israel, following the Septuagintal custom.[60] Both Josephus and Philo also use the term in this way, often when echoing scriptural texts.[61]

Septuagintal usage of γένος reflects the term's established range of meanings, noted briefly in the previous section; hence it is used to denote different kinds of things—plants, animals, and so on (Gen 1:11–12, 21, 24–25; Wis 19:11); specific kin-groups, tribal groups, or lines of descent (Lev 20:17–18; 21:13–14, 17; 1 Macc 5:2; 12:21; 2 Macc 5:22); or people in general as one

55. Cf. Hort, *First Epistle of St. Peter*, 126, who notes that ἔθνος is never used of Israel in the NT Epistles and the Apocalypse and that in most cases in the Gospels and Acts (John 11:50–52 is the exception) "it is so used only in sentences spoken by, or of persons of another nation."

56. See *TDNT* 4:29–32; Pearce, "Notes," 206; Hatch and Redpath, *Concordance*, 853–62; of the seventeen Hebrew words listed as possible equivalents, עַם is the term in the vast majority of cases.

57. *TDNT* 4:33.

58. *TDNT* 4:34.

59. Over half (83 of 142) of the NT uses of the word appear in Luke-Acts.

60. For especially clear examples, see Acts 26:17, 23; Rom 11:1–2; 15:10; 2 Pet 2:1. For the plural λαοὶ Ἰσραήλ, see Acts 4:27. By contrast, in Rom 15:11, it is used in the plural of the nations in general.

61. On Philo's usage, see Pearce, "Notes," 206–9, who notes that it is most often used in connection with "citations from the Greek Torah" (207) and "never . . . in accounts of the Jewish people as a whole in the context of contemporary events" (209). The word appears only 90 times in Philo's writings (Borgen, Fuglseth, and Skarsten, *Philo Index*, 204). Josephus also uses the word (ca. 291 times in total; see Rengstorf, *Complete Concordance*, 3:13–15) with its established range of meanings: the surrounding crowd (*B.J.* 1.122), the populace (*B.J.* 1.550), and other people(s), such as the λαός of Egypt (*A.J.* 2.301; cf. Philo, *Migr.* 62).

(human) "race" (Gen 11:6; 2 Macc 7:28).[62] But by far the most frequent use, and one that becomes especially prominent in writings of the first two centuries BCE, is to denote the people of Israel.[63] As Judith Lieu puts it, "The sense of being a race or people is one proudly held in Jewish literature from the Maccabaean period, often in a context of suffering and persecution. . . . Γένος joins the more widespread and older λαός in proclaiming a sense of identity in the midst of hostility and attempted annihilation."[64] Sometimes this is with the full and explicit label τὸ γένος Ισραηλ, sometimes with simply τὸ γένος or τὸ γένος ἡμῶν. In the book of Judith, for example, γένος is used around twelve times to refer to the people of Israel; 2 and 3 Maccabees also have a significant number of such occurrences.[65] As with λαός, while context is necessary for interpretation—the word cannot by itself signify "the people of Israel"—γένος has clearly become a standard term with which to designate that people. As we have just seen, both Josephus and Philo use ἔθνος standardly to denote the Jewish people, often with Ἰουδαῖος as a specific identity-designation. But they also commonly use γένος in this way (as well as to denote other people-groups) in such phrases as τὸ γένος ἡμῶν, τὸ Ἰουδαϊκὸν γένος, κτλ. (see, e.g., Josephus, *C. Ap.* 1.1–2, 59, 106, 130, 160; 2.8, 288; Philo, *Legat.* 3–4, 201; cf. Philo, *Legat.* 265, for Jews among all the human "races").[66]

There are, then, some distinctive features of the Jewish use of "people" language, especially in the LXX's focus on λαός in contrast with ἔθνη, echoing the Hebrew Bible's use of עַם and גּוֹים. But in later scriptural and post-scriptural writing, ἔθνος and γένος become prominent as labels for

62. It is most frequently used to render the Heb. מִין ("kind" or "species") and עַם ("people"); Hatch and Redpath, *Concordance*, 239, list seventeen instances for מִין and sixteen for עַם.

63. E.g., Exod 1:9; 5:14; Josh 4:14; 11:21; Isa 22:4; 42:5; 43:20; Jer 38:1, 35, 37; 1 Esd 1:32; Esth 3:13; 6:13; Add Esth 8:21; Pss Sol 7:8; 17:7; cf. Lieu, *Neither Jew nor Greek*, 58–60.

64. Lieu, *Neither Jew nor Greek*, 58.

65. Jdt 5:10; 6:2, 5, 19; 8:20, 32; 9:14; 11:10; 12:3; 13:20; 15:9; 16:17; 2 Macc 5:22; 6:12; 7:16; 7:38; 8:9; 12:31; 14:8–9; 3 Macc 3:2; 6:4, 9, 13; 7:10. Interestingly, the NRSV variously uses "people," "nation," "race," and "descendants" to render γένος in Judith. There is a further reference in Jdt 16:24, though this seems most likely to refer more specifically to Judith's kin (NRSV: "kindred"; cf., possibly, 12:3).

66. Tessa Rajak, *The Jewish Dialogue with Greece and Rome: Studies in Cultural and Social Interaction* (Leiden: Brill, 2002), 138, offers this summary comment concerning Josephus: "For him, the Jews are an ἔθνος or γένος, to which affiliation in differing degrees is possible by conversion." Josephus uses γένος around 360 times (see Rengstorf, *Complete Concordance*, 1:352–55), Philo some 535 (Borgen, Fuglseth, and Skarsten, *Philo Index*, 74).

the Jewish people, just as they are standard terms to refer to other people-groups, whether large "nations" or smaller "tribes." In part, the abundant use of such language simply seems to reflect the assumption that this group forms a "people," and non-Jewish sources also affirm this—a modest and uncontroversial conclusion. However, we may also recognize the function of such language in reinforcing and sustaining such a "group" identity—in Brubaker's terms, evoking "groupness" and mobilizing such a consciousness. The frequency of such language represents, in part, a concern to emphasize the salience of this particular identity.

7.3 Becoming a People: Early Christian Self-Consciousness and Ethnicization

The earliest writings known to us from the Christian movement—the letters of Paul—use a variety of labels to denote the in-group. The most common is "siblings" (ἀδελφοί). Also prominent are "holy ones" (ἅγιοι) and "those who trust/have faith" (οἱ πιστεύοντες).[67] Echoing language frequently found in the Jewish scriptures (e.g., Deut 7:6-7; 32:8-9, cited above, p. 224), Paul refers to his addressees as "called" or "elected" to be "holy" (e.g., Rom 1:7; 1 Cor 1:2; cf. 1 Pet 1:1, 15; 2:9). When it comes to the use of "people" terms applied to the Christian communities, it is only λαός that appears in this way in Paul's letters, and then only in the context of scriptural quotations (cf. Rom 9:25-26; 1 Cor 14:21; 2 Cor 6:16).[68] In Rom 9:25-26, discussing God's calling of "us" (ἡμᾶς) not only from the Jews (ἐξ Ἰουδαίων) but also from the gentiles (ἐξ ἐθνῶν) (v. 24), Paul quotes from Hosea: "Those who were 'not my people' I will call 'my people'" (καλέσω τὸν οὐ λαόν μου λαόν μου) (v. 25). Scriptural quotation is also the source in another instance in which Paul implicitly identifies his readers, in the context of exhortation, as the λαὸς θεοῦ (2 Cor 6:16, quoting Lev 26:12; Ezek 37:27; cf. Jer 31:33). In this oddly

---

67. On these and other identity labels in earliest Christianity, see Trebilco, *Self-Designations*.

68. Γένος occurs six times in Paul's letters, three times denoting "kinds" of tongues or languages (1 Cor 12:10, 28; 14:10), three times referring to the Jewish people (as the people to which Paul belongs: 2 Cor 11:26; Gal 1:14; Phil 3:5; cf. Acts 7:19; 13:26). Ἔθνος is more common, generally in the plural form to denote either "the nations" in a broad and potentially inclusive sense (e.g., Rom 1:5; 4:17-18; Gal 3:8) or, more frequently, gentiles as distinct from Jews (for especially clear examples where the distinction is evident, see Rom 2:14; 3:29; 11:11-13; 15:10; 1 Cor 1:23; 2 Cor 11:26; Gal 2:14-15).

disjunctive passage calling for distinction and separation from unbelievers (2 Cor 6:14–7:1), Paul describes himself and his readers as the temple of God (cf. 1 Cor 3:16), relating the scriptural declaration "I will be their God and they shall be my people" to his Corinthian addressees (described in 1 Cor 12:2 as formerly gentiles). The same language is taken up in the climactic vision of the new Jerusalem in the closing chapters of Revelation (21:3). Scriptural phrasing also provides the language for the appeal of Rev 18:4: "Come out of her, my people" (ὁ λαός μου) (cf. Jer 51:45).

There are two examples in the book of Acts where the word λαός seems to be applied to those who have come to believe in Christ. In Acts 15:14, when James begins to speak about Peter's experience of the conversion of gentiles, he describes this conversion in terms of God's taking "from among the gentiles [ἐξ ἐθνῶν] a people [λαός] for his name." Slightly more cryptic is Acts 18:10, in which Paul is encouraged in a vision not to be afraid, "for there are many in this city who are my people [λαός ἐστί μοι πολύς]." Given the opposition Paul is depicted as facing from the *Ioudaioi* in Acts, including in this very context (see 18:5–6 and, e.g., 13:44–46; 14:19; 17:5–9), it is unlikely that this reference is intended to refer to them, but on the other hand, this is hardly a clear indication that Luke regards the followers of Christ as a distinct λαός.[69]

A number of uses of λαός in Hebrews are interesting in that they illustrate how a term rooted in scriptural language about the people of Israel comes to be applied to the Christian communities precisely through the application of this whole discursive tradition to the latter, seen by the author as part of the one people of God, past and present.[70] This process is common in the New Testament and intrinsic to the formation of Christian discourse (cf., e.g., Rom 15:4; 1 Cor 10:1 [οἱ πατέρες ἡμῶν]; 10:11). The term λαός is comparatively frequent in Hebrews (13x), often in the context of describing Jewish practice (5:3; 7:5, 11; 9:7, 19 [2x], 25) or quoting scripture (8:10; 10:30). But precisely because of the way the writer sees these Jewish practices and scriptures as foreshadowing and describing the achievements of Christ, there are also uses of λαός that evidently apply to the community presently addressed, the people for whom Jesus the great high priest has

69. For example, Barrett, *Acts of the Apostles*, 2:870, sees this as a reference to "the Lord's people" but elaborates that "λαός is here the people of God; and it includes both Jews and Gentiles."

70. On the question of the identity of God's people in Hebrews, see Ole Jakob Filtvedt, *The Identity of God's People and the Paradox of Hebrews*, WUNT 2.400 (Tübingen: Mohr Siebeck, 2015).

finally made effective sacrifice (2:17; 4:9; 7:27; 13:12).[71] Indeed, the extent to which there is an identification of the one people of God, past and present, is illustrated in 11:25–26: as a hero of faith, Moses is described as having chosen to endure mistreatment with "the people of God" (τῷ λαῷ τοῦ θεοῦ); yet his suffering is also strikingly described as "the reproach of Christ" (τὸν ὀνειδισμὸν τοῦ Χριστοῦ), which Moses chose rather than the wealth of Egypt (cf. 1 Cor 10:4; 1 Pet 1:11).[72]

There are, then, a number of places in the New Testament where λαός is used, albeit loosely, and largely through the use of scriptural phrasing, to denote the communities of believers in Christ. The same cannot be said of ἔθνος and γένος (nor of φυλή).[73] It is no surprise that λαός is the first such "people" word to come into the discourse of Christian identity in this way: it is the loosest of the "people" terms insofar as it can be used to describe various kinds of assembled groups, such as an assembled crowd, whereas γένος most clearly implies a specifically "ethnic" type of identity with its focus on the idea of shared descent, and ἔθνος itself standardly denotes what we would call ethnic groups or (albeit anachronistically) "nations." More significantly, λαός is a standard Septuagintal word to denote the people of God, especially in distinction from τὰ ἔθνη, and thus most naturally enters into early Christian discourse through scriptural quotations.[74]

There are, however, two—but only two—New Testament texts to consider in terms of their use of other "people" words: Matt 21:43 and 1 Pet 2:9-10. (James 1:1 is in a somewhat different category since the address "to the twelve tribes [φυλαῖς] in the Diaspora" evidently recalls the description of Israel's tribes, whatever its referent in the letter.)[75] At the conclusion

---

71. Cf. 1 Clem. 59.4; 2 Clem. 2.3; Barn. 13.1–6.

72. See the discussion of this text in Filtvedt, *Identity of God's People*, 201–3.

73. Apart from Jas 1:1 (on which see below with n. 75), addressed to "the twelve tribes in the Diaspora"—conceivably an application of this Jewish designation to "Christian" addressees—all other uses of φυλή in the NT refer either to tribes of Israel (e.g., Luke 22:30; Rom 11:1; Phil 3:5; Heb 7:14; Rev 5:5; 7:4-8) or to human tribes in general—the latter mostly in Revelation (e.g., Matt 19:28; Rev 1:9; 5:9; 7:9; 14:6).

74. As Hort, *First Epistle of St. Peter*, 128, notes, commenting on 1 Pet 2:9, λαός "in the Gospels, Acts, and Hebrews frequently denotes the Jewish people," and "with the exception of two or three transitional instances in Hebrews [citing 4:9; 11:25; 13:12], its transference to the new Israel [a term that begs questions, needless to say] is likewise throughout the N. T. confined to quotations and . . . borrowed phrases [citing Titus 1:14 and Rev 18:4 as instances of the latter]."

75. Many commentators take this as an application to the Christian community of Israel's identity. Christoph Burchard, *Der Jakobusbrief*, HNT 15/1 (Tübingen: Mohr Sie-

of Matthew's version of the parable of the tenants of the vineyard (Matt 21:33–46; cf. Mark 12:1–12; Luke 20:9–19), Matthew places into the mouth of Jesus what is most likely his own redactional comment (unique to Matthew's version of the parable):[76] "The kingdom of God will be taken away from you and given to a people [ἔθνει] producing its fruits" (Matt 21:43). This has long been understood to signal the view that Israel has been replaced as the people of God by the church.[77] Graham Stanton, for example, comments that "the evangelist considered his readers to be a 'new people'—in effect a 'third race' (*tertium genus*) over against both Jews and Gentiles."[78] Some recent scholarship, however, has pushed back against such an interpretation. Matthias Konradt, for example, argues strongly that the parable is directed against Israel's Jerusalem-based leadership, not against Israel as a whole, and that it is these leaders who will be replaced (by the followers of Jesus).[79] More broadly, there is extensive and long-running scholarly debate about whether Matthew conceives the "church" (his is the only gospel to use the term ἐκκλησία [16:18; 18:17]) as within or outside Judaism and about how his focus on universal (post-Easter) mission (Matt 28:19: πάντα τὰ ἔθνη)

---

beck, 2000), 6, for example, states: "Jak meint damit aber nicht das jüdische Volk oder die Jesus-anhänger in ihm . . . sondern die Christenheit." Others, however, insist that James's address is focused on the people of Israel and expresses hopes for Israel's messianic and eschatological renewal. See, e.g., Patrick J. Hartin, *James*, SP 14 (Collegeville: Liturgical Press, 2009), 51–55; similarly, see Richard J. Bauckham, *James: Wisdom of James, Disciple of Jesus the Sage*, New Testament Readings (London: Routledge, 1999), 14–15, who comments that "reference to the tribal constitution of Israel, which had no equivalent in the new Israel, seems inherently unsuitable for transference to the church. . . . The phrase is a natural way of referring to Israel outside the land" (14).

76. On this comment as Matthean, see, e.g., Davies and Allison, *Gospel According to Saint Matthew*, 3:186; Ulrich Luz, *Matthew 21–28: A Commentary*, Hermeneia (Minneapolis: Fortress, 2005), 36; Konradt, *Israel*, 168.

77. See, e.g., Donald A. Hagner, *Matthew 14–28*, WBC 33B (Grand Rapids: Zondervan, 1995), 623, who speaks of the "setting aside of the privilege of Israel as the unique people of God in favour of another people, namely the church," which he calls "the new people of God." For an extensive list of representatives of this position, see Konradt, *Israel*, 168n2.

78. Graham N. Stanton, *A Gospel for a New People: Studies in Matthew* (Edinburgh: T&T Clark, 1992), 11–12, noting the use of ἔθνος in 21:43; see 85–107 for the basis for this conclusion in Stanton's sociological perspective on Matthew's notion of the Christian community. Otherwise see Saldarini, *Matthew's Christian-Jewish Community*, 58–63, who reads ἔθνος here as a reference to a group within Judaism, contrasted with the Jerusalem leadership, who are the rejected ἔθνος.

79. Konradt, *Israel*, 172–92, 373. For earlier interpretations along these lines, see, e.g., Saldarini, *Matthew's Christian-Jewish Community*, 58–63; David C. Sim, *The Gospel of Matthew and Christian Judaism*, SNTW (Edinburgh: T&T Clark, 1998), 148–49.

relates to the ongoing status of the people of Israel.[80] Without needing to adjudicate these complex issues and competing perspectives, it is at the very least striking that Matthew uses the word ἔθνος to denote the group to which "the kingdom of God" will be given.[81] As we have seen, the word can denote various kinds of groups and so need not necessarily connote a whole "people" in a sense equivalent to the "people" of Israel.[82] But whether the "group" to which Matthew attaches this label is to be seen as within or outside Israel,[83] its designation as an ἔθνος marks a significant move, not least given the predominant use of the word to refer to peoples or nations in general and the *Ioudaioi* in particular.[84]

If Matthew's use of ἔθνος is somewhat allusive and enigmatic, 1 Peter's use of combined "people" terms is forceful and emphatic. The wider passage, 1 Pet 2:4–10, forms a climax to the opening main section of the letter, drawing together the affirmations and the exhortations found in 1:3–2:10 and laying the foundation for the instruction which is to follow in the second major section of the letter (2:11–4:11). As John Elliott puts it, the writer of 1 Peter here brings "to a resounding climax the line of thought begun in 1:3."[85] The passage is also characterized by a rich and extensive use of Jewish scripture.[86] After a concise summary of the themes of the passage in vv. 4–5,

80. Contrast, for example, the perspectives of Stanton, *Gospel for a New People*, and Saldarini, *Matthew's Christian-Jewish Community*. For extensive discussion engaging recent (and older) scholarship on this topic, see Konradt, *Israel*. For broader reflections on the "election of Israel" according to Matthew, see Givens, *We the People*, 295–343.

81. Konradt, *Israel*, 178, refers to it as "a *crux interpretum*" and cites a comment of Ulrich Luz (*Matthew 21–28*, 42) to this effect: "Most important and most difficult is the interpretation of 'nation' (ἔθνος)."

82. So Konradt, *Israel*, 178–83.

83. Luz, *Matthew 21–28*, 43, wisely stresses that "Matthew leaves open the question of who the 'nation' is."

84. Konradt's comment (*Israel*, 178) that "ἔθνος in the sense of 'a people' signifies a national, not a religious, entity and is thus, in this sense, poorly suited to the concept of the Church" rather begs the question about the character of early Christian identity. His remark that λαός would have been the natural choice had Matthew "wanted to bring in the theme of the people of God" (*Israel*, 178; similarly, Luz, *Matthew 21–28*, 43), while rightly reflecting the dominant Septuagintal usage, perhaps insufficiently acknowledges the common use of ἔθνος (and γένος) to denote the people of Israel, as indicated briefly above (§6.2).

85. Elliott, *1 Peter*, 407.

86. Elliott, *Elect and Holy*, 16–49; Richard J. Bauckham, "James, 1 and 2 Peter, Jude," in *It Is Written: Scripture Citing Scripture*, ed. D. A. Carson and Hugh G. M. Williamson (Cambridge: Cambridge University Press, 1988), 303–17. More generally on 1 Peter's use of scripture, see William L. Schutter, *Hermeneutic and Composition in 1 Peter*, WUNT 2.30

vv. 6–8 present three scriptural quotations and interpretative comments focused on the theme of Christ as λίθος. In vv. 9–10, the author's attention turns to the identity of the addressees (ὑμεῖς δέ . . .). Weaving together a series of phrases drawn from Isa 43:20–21, Exod 19:5–6, and Hos 1–2 (specifically 1:6, 1:9, 2:3 [LXX], and 2:25 [LXX]) he declares:

> ὑμεῖς δὲ γένος ἐκλεκτόν, βασίλειον ἱεράτευμα, ἔθνος ἅγιον, λαὸς εἰς περιποίησιν, ὅπως τὰς ἀρετὰς ἐξαγγείλητε τοῦ ἐκ σκότους ὑμᾶς καλέσαντος εἰς τὸ θαυμαστὸν αὐτοῦ φῶς· οἵ ποτε οὐ λαός, νῦν δὲ λαὸς θεοῦ, οἱ οὐκ ἠλεημένοι, νῦν δὲ ἐλεηθέντες.

> But you are a chosen race, a royal priesthood, a holy nation, a people for his own possession, that you may proclaim the excellencies of him who called you out of darkness into his marvelous light. Once you were not a people, but now you are God's people; once you had not received mercy, but now you have received mercy. (1 Pet 2:9–10 ESV)

As with Paul's much more limited moves to denote the Christian communities as a λαός, here, too, the author's language and phrasing are dependent on his scriptural sources.[87] Yet the move he makes here is much more deliberate and emphatic than was the case in Paul's uses of λαός. For a start, the passage is artfully constructed using a series of scriptural phrases drawn from various sources. Furthermore, the focus on "people" terms is striking: no other New Testament text even approaches this concentration of terms, and the occurrence of all three key words (γένος, ἔθνος, λαός) here suggests a deliberate attempt to pack the verse with "people-group" labels.[88] Indeed, the author of 1 Peter also adds the resonant designation λαὸς θεοῦ to the phrases taken from Hosea. Being called a priesthood—a designation of the

---

(Tubingen: Mohr Siebeck, 1989); Benjamin Sargent, *Written to Serve: The Use of Scripture in 1 Peter*, LNTS 547 (London: Bloomsbury T&T Clark, 2015).

87. The number of scriptural allusions shared with Rom 9 (cf. also 1 Pet 2:6–8 and Rom 9:33) is striking, though many commentators do not see the similarities as indicating direct literary dependence. For example, Elliott, *1 Peter*, 442, concludes that the "differences between Paul and 1 Peter" in their uses of Hosea "argue against any literary dependency of one upon the other." Cf. Elliott, *Elect and Holy*, 45–46, where he suggests that the explanation for the similarities is "the use of common Christian tradition" (45).

88. A deliberate attempt to bring together the main "people" words might explain why the author selects the phrase ἔθνος ἅγιον from Exod 19:5 rather than the more common λαὸς ἅγιος (Deut 7:6; 14:2, 21; Hos 12:1 [LXX]; Isa 30:19).

community that is also unique to 1 Peter in the New Testament (cf. also 1 Pet 2:5)—also implies an identity based on ancestry and descent (cf. Justin, *Dial.* 116.3, cited more fully below). Of particular significance, as we shall see, is the fact that this is the only New Testament text in which the term γένος is used to denote the identity of the Christian people.[89]

As with Matt 21:43, older commentators were often inclined to see in these verses in 1 Peter an indication that the church had replaced Israel as the people of God.[90] More recent commentators have tended to avoid such a "replacement" interpretation but nonetheless see the author as appropriating scriptural language to denote the identity of these Christian communities.[91] Betsy Bauman-Martin has criticized the author's appropriation of Jewish identity markers as a kind of colonizing move on the part of the author.[92] Certainly it is striking how closely the author picks up not merely the "people" words γένος, ἔθνος, and λαός but also scriptural phrases that are foundational to a sense of Jewish identity: "holy," "elect," "a people who belong to God, God's 'special possession'" (cf. Deut 7:6; Exod 19:5-6; also Titus 2:14).[93] Yet without denying the extent to which the author applies these identity-designations to his Christian (and probably largely gentile) address-

89. A point noted, e.g., by F. Büchsel (*TDNT* 1:685); Peter Richardson, *Israel in the Apostolic Church*, SNTSMS 10 (Cambridge: Cambridge University Press, 1969), 172n8.

90. See, e.g., Hans Windisch, *Die Katholischen Briefe*, 2nd ed., HNT 15 (Tübingen: Mohr Siebeck, 1930), 61; Johannes Schneider, *Die Briefe des Jakobus, Petrus, Judas und Johannes: Die Katholischen Briefe*, NTD 10 (Göttingen: Vandenhoeck & Ruprecht, 1961), 61-62. On the shifting perspectives in German commentaries, see David G. Horrell, "'Das im Unglauben verharrende Judenvolk': 1 Pet 2:4-10 and Its History of Interpretation in Germany (1855-1978), and the Important Contribution of Leonhard Goppelt," in *Bedrängnis und Identität: Studien zu Situation, Kommunikation und Theologie des 1. Petrusbriefes*, BZNW 200, ed. David S. Du Toit (Berlin: De Gruyter, 2013), 327-51.

91. See, e.g., Michaels, *1 Peter*, 107. Also see Achtemeier, *1 Peter*: "For our author the Christian community has now become God's elect and chosen people" (167); "Israel has become the controlling metaphor for the new people of God, and as such its rhetoric has passed without remainder into that of the Christian community" (72). Achtemeier equally insists that this "is evidently not an instance of anti-Semitism" (72) since it lacks negative invective and gives no indication that the Jews have been rejected as God's people nor any clear indication as to the current "relationship between Jewish and Christian communities" (167).

92. Betsy J. Bauman-Martin, "Speaking Jewish: Postcolonial Aliens and Strangers in First Peter," in Webb and Bauman-Martin, *Reading 1 Peter*, 144-77.

93. For these three fundamental "identitätsgründende Aussagen," see Eberhard Schwarz, *Identität durch Abgrenzung: Abgrenzungsprozesse in Israel im 2. vorchristlichen Jahrhundert und ihre traditionsgeschichtlichen Voraussetzungen: Zugleich ein Beitrag zur Erforschung des Jubiläenbuches*, Europäische Hochschulschriften 162 (Frankfurt: Peter Lang, 1982), 53-57.

ees, we should also note that the author does not specify that this identity has been taken away from the Jewish people, unlike plenty of other early Christian writings that explicitly draw the contrast between "old" and "new" and suggest that the former is obsolete (e.g., Heb 7:18–19; 8:6–13; 9:11–15; Barn. 16.5–8; Melito, *Peri Pascha*, 43).[94] It may be, as Elliott suggests, that he sees the believers in Christ as "incorporated into God's ancient covenantal people."[95] The author of 1 Peter is simply (if strikingly) silent about the ongoing identity of what Paul calls "Israel according to the flesh"—ὁ Ἰσραὴλ κατὰ σάρκα (1 Cor 10:18).[96] What kind of relationship the author sees between Jewish and Christian communities—and how distinct or interwoven those communities might be in practice—remains unspoken. But the key point, for our purposes here, is that the author emphatically and unambiguously describes the communities of Christians to which he writes in terms of their identity as a people. Indeed, the artful force with which these phrases are constructed suggests a deliberate concern to evoke a sense of "being a people"; we might see the author, in Brubaker's terms, as a kind of "ethnopolitical entrepreneur," evoking, summoning, and kindling a sense of peoplehood among the Christian assemblies in Asia Minor.[97] Again, this seems a kind of "ethnicizing" move, contributing to the "making" of a people, a construction of this of shared identity among the recipients of the letter.

It would be overly bold to propose that 1 Pet 2:9 is somehow the lynchpin for later talk of Christians as a γένος, ἔθνος, or λαός.[98] Nonetheless,

---

94. Even in an old commentary that interprets this whole passage as reflecting a contrast between the "hardened," unbelieving Jews and the gentiles who have come to faith, G. Wohlenberg, *Der erste und zweite Petrusbrief und der Judasbrief*, Kommentar zum Neuen Testament 15 (Leipzig: Deichert'sche Verlagsbuchhandlung, 1915), 64, notes, for example, the lack of a definite article before γένος ἐκλεκτόν (v. 9) despite the articular forms in Isa 43:20 LXX. Thus, he suggests, one cannot simply conclude "daß er [the author of 1 Peter] die Heidenchristen ohne weiteres an die Stelle des atl Gottesvolkes setzte."

95. Elliott, *1 Peter*, 443.

96. See, e.g., the comments on this point of Wolfgang Schrage, "Der erste Petrusbrief," in *Die "Katholischen" Briefe: Die Briefe des Jakobus, Petrus, Johannes und Judas*, by Horst Balz and Wolfgang Schrage, NTD 10 (Göttingen: Vandenhoeck & Ruprecht, 1993), 85; Michaels, *1 Peter*, 107; Richardson, *Israel*, 173 ("there is no hint of interest in Israel in 1 Peter"); Achtemeier, *1 Peter*, 72, 167; Lieu, *Christian Identity*, 40, who comments on 1 Pet 2:9–10: "There is no hint that there were others, also of 'the Dispersion' (1.1), who claimed the same epithets and appealed to the same Scriptures." For further reflections on the broader question of 1 Peter's stance toward Israel, see David G. Horrell, *1 Peter*, New Testament Guides (London: T&T Clark, 2008), 102–5.

97. Brubaker, "Ethnicity without Groups," 166.

98. Charles Bigg, *A Critical and Exegetical Commentary on the Epistles of St. Peter and St.*

whatever the precise routes of influence, talk of Christians as a people—particularly as a γένος—seems to have become firmly established during the second century.[99] The Martyrdom of Polycarp describes Christians as a "godly and pious race" (τοῦ θεοφιλοῦς καὶ θεοσεβοῦς γένους τῶν Χριστιανῶν) (Mart. Pol. 3.2). Elsewhere in the same text, and also in Hermas, they are "the race of the righteous" (τὸ γένος τῶν δικαίων) (Mart. Pol. 14.1; 17.1; Herm. Sim. 9.17.5). Justin Martyr describes them as "the true high-priestly race of God" (ἀρχιερατικὸν τὸ ἀληθινὸν γένος . . . τοῦ θεοῦ) (Dial. 116.3) and as a "holy people" (λαὸς ἅγιός ἐσμεν) (Dial. 119.3).[100]

A number of texts use γένος language in the context of a threefold classification: Greeks,[101] Jews, and Christians—a classification already found embryonically in Paul, though without the language of peoplehood or "race" or the specific designation "Christians" (1 Cor 10.32).[102] Examining some of these examples will give us valuable indications as to how this language and conceptuality became established in Christian discourse.

The earliest—but also somewhat difficult—example of the phrase τρίτον γένος is found in what is almost certainly a quotation from the Kerygma

---

Jude, ICC (Edinburgh: T&T Clark, 1901), 134, however, suggests regarding γένος that "from its use here [in 1 Pet 2:9] possibly comes the expression τρίτον γένος, applied to Christians."

99. On this topic, see esp. Buell, "Rethinking"; Buell, "Race and Universalism"; Buell, Why This New Race; Lieu, "Race"; Lieu, Christian Identity, 239–68. For a brief overview of some of this material, see David F. Wright, "A Race Apart? Jews, Gentiles, Christians," BSac 160 (2003): 134–37.

100. Text from Bobichon, Justin Martyr.

101. Insofar as this designation is used, it shows that the ethnic worldview remains one focused on the Greek world rather than on the various "barbarian" peoples beyond, as Lukas Bormann has stressed in the NT context. See Bormann, "Griechen und Juden."

102. This text is probably the one where a threefold classification is most apparent in Paul (see also 1 Cor 1:22–24). Elsewhere, Michael Wolter points out, Paul is concerned to depict the new, Christian identity as a new reality (a "new creation") beyond the existing distinction between Jew and Greek (or Gentile) (e.g., Gal 3:28; 5:6; 6:15). Michael Wolter, "Ein neues 'Geschlecht'? Das frühe Christentum auf der Suche nach seiner Identität," in Ein neues Geschlecht? Entwicklung des frühchristlichen Selbstbewusstseins, NTOA/SUNT 105, ed. Markus Lang (Göttingen: Vandenhoeck & Ruprecht, 2014), 295–97. Wolter's "rein hypothetisch" suggestion that Paul could have known the later threefold distinction but chose not to use it since it did not fit his theological perspective (295) seems to me highly unlikely given the lack of any evidence that Paul knew the term "Christian," at least when he wrote his letters. He may have become aware of it during his trial, where Helga Botermann suggests the term originated. See Helga Botermann, Das Judenedikt des Kaisers Claudius: Römischer Staat und Christiani im 1 Jahrhundert, Hermes Einzelschriften 71 (Stuttgart: Franz Steiner, 1996), 171–77. On the date of origin of the term, see Horrell, Becoming Christian, 171–76.

Petrou (frag. 5) in Clement of Alexandria's *Stromateis*. The context is one in which Clement uses quotations from this earlier source to show that Greeks and others also knew God but did not know or worship him in the right way. In other words, Clement claims that the Christians are not announcing a new God but a new way (rightly) to worship him (echoing Jer 31:31–32 and Heb 8:8–10 on the new covenant).[103] In this differentiation of old and new ways of worship, distinctions are drawn between three groups of people and three modes of worship:

> He made a new covenant with us; for what belonged to the Greeks and Jews is old. But we, who worship him in a new way, τρίτῳ γένει, are Christians.

> νέαν ἡμῖν διέθετο· τὰ γὰρ Ἑλλήνων καὶ Ἰουδαίων παλαιά, ἡμεῖς δὲ οἱ καινῶς αὐτὸν τρίτῳ γένει σεβόμενοι Χριστιανοί.

Clement continues with his own comment:

> For clearly, as I think, he showed that the one and only God was known by the Greeks in a gentile way [ἐθνικῶς], by the Jews in a Jewish way [Ἰουδαϊκῶς], and in a new and spiritual way by us. (*Strom.* 6.5.41.6–7)[104]

Two main issues complicate this text. One is the question of whether the crucial phrases are taken from the Kerygma Petrou or are Clement's own words. This is not entirely clear, but the Kerygma Petrou is usually taken to include the reference to worshiping τρίτῳ γένει.[105] This seems most plausible, given the signaling of the return to Clement's voice with "as I think"

---

103. Thus, as Wolter, "Ein neues 'Geschlecht'?," 285, comments: "Die 'Christianer' befinden sich nicht in einer Äquidistanz zu 'Griechen' und 'Juden,' sondern sie gehören in die Abfolge der Generationen Israels hinein."

104. Text from GCS 52 (Clem II), 452. That given by Michel Cambe, *Kergyma Petri: Textus et Commentarius*, Corpus Christianorum: Series Apocryphorum 15 (Turnhout: Brepols, 2003), 63, has ὑμῖν and ὑμεῖς in place of the first-person plurals in the GCS edition.

105. See Wilhelm Schneemelcher, "The Kerygma Petrou," in *New Testament Apocrypha*, ed. E. Hennecke and Wilhelm Schneemelcher, vol. 2 (London: Lutterworth, 1965), 100; Patrick Descourtieux, ed., *Clément d'Alexandrie, Les Stromates: Stromate VI*, SC 446 (Paris: Cerf, 1999), 144–45; Cambe, *Kergyma Petri*, 63; Lieu, *Christian Identity*, 261–62 with nn. 87–88. For a wide-ranging study of the Kergyma Petri, see Henning Paulsen, "Das Kerygma Petri und die urchristliche Apologetik," *ZKG* 88 (1977): 1–37; repr. in Henning Paulsen, *Zur Literatur und Geschichte des frühen Christentums*, WUNT 99 (Tübingen: Mohr Siebeck, 1997), 173–209.

(οἶμαι). The second, more crucially, is the question about the sense of γένος here, which I left untranslated above: Does it denote a distinct Christian "kind" or "form" of worship[106] or a distinct Christian identity "as a third race"?[107] Most recent interpreters seem to agree that it should be taken here to refer to the Christian manner of worship as representing a third kind. As Adolf von Harnack observed long ago: "Still, it is to be noted that here the Christians do not yet call themselves 'the third race' [das dritte Geschlecht], but rather their form of worship [Gottesverehrung] counts as the third. Our author does not divide humanity into three peoples [Völker] but into three classes of god-worshippers [in drei Klassen von Gottesverehrern]."[108] This seems indeed the most plausible construal of the Greek, taking the phrase τρίτῳ γένει to modify the immediately following participle, σεβόμενοι.[109] Nonetheless, while the threefold distinction is thus focused on the patterns of what we might call religious devotion and practice, it remains significant that it distinguishes the three groups in this way. As Harnack also remarks: "The striking thing [das Bemerkenswerte] is, however, that he [the author] quite specifically asserts three kinds, not more and not less, and explicitly designates Christianity [das Christentum] as the new, third kind [genus] of worship [Gottesverehrung]."[110]

A similar threefold classification of peoples is found in the Greek version of Aristides's *Apology*, where it is said "that there are three races [γένη] of people in the world, which are those known among us as worshippers of gods, and Jews, and Christians [θεῶν προσκυνηταὶ, καὶ Ἰουδαῖοι, καὶ

---

106. Adolf von Harnack, *Die Mission und Ausbreitung des Christentums in den ersten drei Jahrhunderten*, 4th ed., 2 vols. (Leipzig: Hinrich, 1924), 1:264 ("auf die dritte Weise"); Cambe, *Kerygma Petri*, 63 ("selon un troisième type").

107. Schneemelcher, "Kerygma Petrou," 100 ("But we are Christians, who as a third race worship him in a new way"); Descourtieux, *Clément, Stromate VI*, 145 ("comme une troisième race").

108. Harnack, *Mission und Ausbreitung*, 1:265. Similarly, Wolter, "Ein neues 'Geschlecht'?," 283–85; Paulsen, "Kerygma Petri," 20.

109. See Wolter, "Ein neues 'Geschlecht'?" 283n4. Sechrest, *Former Jew*, 16, comments in favor of the "third race" interpretation that "the only thing standing in the way of such an understanding [of this passage as a reference to "the third race"] is Harnack's assumption . . . that *the word 'race' cannot refer to people-groups classified by religion*" (italics original). This does not sufficiently engage the difficulties here, nor does it do justice to Harnack's comments and choice of vocabulary (*Geschlecht*, not *Rasse*). See further below and the discussion of Harnack in Ehrensperger, "What's in a Name?," 100–103.

110. Harnack, *Mission und Ausbreitung*, 1:265, italics original. Cf. Paulsen, "Kerygma Petri," 20–21.

Χριστιανοί]" (2.2).[111] The writer proceeds to classify the "worshippers of gods" into three races (τρία γένη): Chaldeans, Greeks, and Egyptians. Here, as Michael Wolter remarks, "it is not merely the form of Christian worship that is described as 'new,' or counts as a 'third kind,' but the Christians themselves are described as a γένος." As Wolter notes, it is the form of religious devotion that is the key factor in this differentiation, but a focus on their identity as people is apparent, a people "descended [γενεαλογοῦνται] from the Lord Jesus Christ" (*Apol.* 15.1).[112] A similar threefold distinction between Greeks, Jews, and Christians is also the context for an explicit description of Christians as "this new race" (καινὸν τοῦτο γένος) in Diogn. 1.1.[113] Here again, the focus of the author's interest is the distinctiveness of the Christians' religious devotion (θεοσέβεια, 1.1): the opening chapters proceed to distinguish their worship from Greek idolatry (ch. 2) and from Jewish practice (chs. 3–4).[114] This emphasis on kinds of religious practice does not mean, however, that this classification of people-groups can be separated from the category of ethnic identity. On the contrary, as we have previously noted, "religion"—gods, cult, ritual, devotion, and so on—formed a central aspect of a people's identity as an ἔθνος or γένος.[115]

The specific labeling of Christians as a third race or kind of humans, a τρίτον γένος or *tertium genus*, is nowhere explicit in these sources (despite the phrase τρίτῳ γένει in the Kerygma Petrou, as we have seen), but the

---

111. For the text, see J. Rendel Harris and J. Armitage Robinson, *The Apology of Aristides on Behalf of the Christians*, TS 1.1 (Cambridge: Cambridge University Press, 1891); Bernard Pouderon et al., *Aristide, Apologie: Introduction, Textes Critiques, Traductions et Commentaire*, SC 470 (Paris: Cerf, 2003). For a recent overview, see Michael Lattke, "Die Wahrheit der Christen in der Apologie des Aristides: Vorstudie zu einem Kommentar," in Lang, *Ein neues Geschlecht?*, 215–35. For discussion of this particular text and its implications, see Lieu, "Race," 55–56; Lieu, *Christian Identity*, 260–61. Cf. also Joseph Clifford Fenton, "New Testament Designations of the Catholic Church and of its Members," *CBQ* 9 (1947): 142, who cites Aristides's *Apology* as an indication "that the term γένος, used by St. Peter as a designation of the Church, was an important factor in the teaching of the early Christian society." The Syriac version lists four races: "Barbarians and Greeks, Jews and Christians"; see Harris and Robinson, *Apology of Aristides*, 36; Lieu, *Christian Identity*, 260.

112. Wolter, "Ein neues 'Geschlecht?,'" 286.

113. Cf. Barn. 5.7: τὸν λαὸν τὸν καινόν.

114. See Lieu, "Identity Games," 59–72; Clayton N. Jefford, *The Epistle to Diognetus (with the Fragment of Quadratus): Introduction, Text, and Commentary*, Oxford Apostolic Fathers (Oxford: Oxford University Press, 2013), 203–17; Horacio E. Lona, "An Diognet," in *Die Apostolischen Väter: Eine Einleitung*, ed. Wilhelm Pratscher (Göttingen: Vandenhoeck & Ruprecht, 2009), 214–15.

115. Cf. Mason, "Jews, Judaeans, Judaizing, Judaism," 484.

threefold division of humanity into Greeks, Jews, and Christians expresses this idea, albeit focused on their differing patterns of religious devotion and practice. The explicit label is found, as a positive and self-defining Christian claim, in the somewhat later Pseudo-Cyprianic work *De Pascha computus*, dated to 243 CE,[116] in which Christians ("we") are positively identified as "the third race of humankind" (*tertium genus hominum*) (*De Pascha comp.* 17). The phrase is also found a number of times in the writings of Tertullian, though mostly as a rather negative designation used by outsiders and one he treats with some scorn. "Clearly, we are called the third race" (*Plane, tertium genus dicimur*) (*Nat.* 1.8.1), he reports, while ridiculing the idea that Christians are somehow a different species: "Have Christians teeth of a different sort from others? Have they more ample jaws? I don't think so [*non opinor*]!" (*Nat.* 1.7.34). He poses the rhetorical challenge: "If you attach any meaning to these names, pray tell us what are the first and second race, that so we may know something of this 'third'" (*Nat.* 1.8.1). These comments are interesting not only because they indicate that Christians had come to be seen (critically) as a distinct *genus* of people (cf. Suetonius, *Nero* 16.2; Josephus, *A.J.* 18.64 [τῶν Χριστιανῶν . . . τὸ φῦλον][117]) but also because Tertullian's ridiculing of the notion reveals that the term *genus* might indeed be taken to refer to the kinds of physical characteristics that much later theories of "race" would highlight—though, as Tertullian makes clear, such a physiognomic definition of Christian peoplehood would make no sense.

Elsewhere, rather less polemically, though clearly still in the context of discussing persecution, Tertullian describes Christians as a third race (*genus tertium*), in contrast to synagogues of the Jews (*synagogas Iudaeorum*) and peoples of the nations (*populos nationum*), from whom comes the cry to be rid of "the third race" (*genus tertium*) (*Scorp.* 10.10). He also finds a parallel to the logic of Christians existing as a third race in the existence of what he calls "a third race in sex"—that is, eunuchs—alongside male and female

---

116. See J. Quasten, *The Ante-Nicene Literature after Irenaeus*, vol. 2 of *Patrology* (Utrecht: Spectrum, 1958), 369. Adolf von Harnack, *The Expansion of Christianity in the First Three Centuries*, vol. 1 (London: Williams and Norgate; New York: Putnam, 1904), 313, gives 242–43 CE.

117. The authenticity of this text in Josephus has long been doubted, or interpolations at least suspected. Since the text is cited by Eusebius (e.g., in *Hist. eccl.* 1.11.7–9), it would remain relevant here in terms of its depiction of the early Christians, even if the phrase is not Josephus's own. See the extended and learned discussion in James Carleton Paget, "Some Observations on Josephus and Christianity," *JTS* 52 (2001): 554–606, who leans cautiously toward authenticity (including this phrase), though in an amended form.

(*Nat.* 1.20.4).[118] These latter examples suggest that the description of Christians as the third race was not necessarily something Tertullian rejected[119]—though his use of the example of eunuchs, a destabilizing "third" category that threatens a clear distinction between the two sexes, suggests that the notion retains an unsettling edge. Indeed, there is perhaps a tacit indication in Tertullian of the tension implicit in describing Christians as members of a *genus*: in one sense this is ridiculous and in another sense not—something that hints at a deeper and more general tension between the apparent fixity yet real fluidity of "ethnic" or "racial" categorizations.[120]

As Harnack observed in his classic treatment of this subject, the description of Christians as a third race or kind of people thus seems to exist both as an internal self-description and as a label apparently used by opponents. Harnack thought it unlikely that the opponents borrowed the phrase from Christian literature and concluded that "the term rose as spontaneously to the lips of Christians as of their opponents," noting the "chronological succession of its occurrences" in the Kerygma Petrou (early second century),[121] Tertullian (197 CE), and later Pseudo-Cyprian (243 CE).[122] "Christians," Harnack comments, "held themselves to be the new People and the third race of mankind."[123]

---

118. "You too have your 'third race' [*tertium genus*] not as a third religious rite [*tertio ritu*], but a third sex [*tertio sexu*]." Latin texts here and in the citations above from CCSL 1–2; ET in *ANF* 3.

119. Wolter, "Ein neues Geschlecht?," 288, thus goes a little too far in suggesting that the designation is, for Tertullian, "nicht christliche Selbstbezeichnung, sondern Fremdbezeichnung." Wolter also overstresses the (nonetheless significant) difference between Tertullian's treatment of the "third race" in terms of an abusive outsiders' label and the other texts (surveyed above) in which an inner-Christian claim about religious distinctiveness is made (see 288–91, esp. 290).

120. This interplay between fluidity and fixity is central to the approach developed by Buell, *Why This New Race*.

121. For the date of 100–120 CE, see Paulsen, "Kerygma Petri," 13.

122. Harnack, *Expansion*, 1:347–48n2. See also Lieu, "Race," 57–59, who sees "two trajectories . . . [that] lead to the designation of Christians being a 'race'" (57): one arising from the slurs of opponents, the other from Christian appropriation of Jewish identity-designations. She tentatively suggests, "It is possible that the Jews already spoke of themselves as the *third* race, only to have the epithet taken over by the Christians" (59); see, similarly, Lieu, *Christian Identity*, 262–66. Origen's use of the phrase τρίτον γένος in *Cels.* 5.61 is interesting, though somewhat opaque. Harnack, *Expansion*, 1:350n1, regards it as irrelevant, as it refers to a third kind of sect-grouping among the Christians, which Origen identifies as the Valentinians. Since the phrase seems to come from Celsus, it may perhaps be a further indication of the currency of the label among the non-Christian critics of Christianity.

123. Harnack, *Expansion*, 1:335.

We should pause at this point, however, and briefly consider the issue of translating γένος, often rendered "race" as in the translations above, not least in discussion of Christians as the "third race." Harnack, as Kathy Ehrensperger notes, did not use the German *Rasse* ("race") but rather *Geschlecht*—generally used to denote sex, gender, lineage, or race.[124] In the Kerygma Petrou, as discussed above, γένος most likely describes a "kind" or mode of religious devotion. Similarly, in many of the instances discussed here, we might take the word to indicate a particular "kind" or "type" of humans, classified primarily on the basis of their religious allegiance. This might caution against retaining the translation "race"—though there are other reasons why we might want to retain this word in our discourse (see §3.2). But however we translate γένος, it is at least important to emphasize that its use in texts to label the Christian people is comparable to its use to denote other peoples, not least the *Ioudaioi*—frequently described as a γένος, as we saw above. In both contexts, it is used to distinguish and label a people-group (and often, in general, with a focus on the notion of common descent).

We should also acknowledge the relative rarity of the specific designation of the Christians as a "third race," as well as the extent to which—at least in Tertullian's perspective—it is a questionable and often hostile label.[125] Yet beyond the specific uses of the "third race" motif, there is widespread use of "people" terminology as a self-identification in second-century Christian sources, as Buell in particular has shown.[126] Clement of Alexandria not infrequently uses γένος language to talk specifically of the way in which those from among both Greeks and Jews have been brought together into what he calls "the one race of the saved" (τὸ ἓν γένος τοῦ σῳζομένου) (*Strom.* 6.5.42.2; cf. 3.10.70.1–2; 6.13.106.4). Significantly, this particular phrase comes immediately after the quotation from the Kerygma Petrou, discussed above, suggesting that there is, at least for Clement, no sharp distinction between the γένος that denotes the specific "kind" of Christian worship and the people themselves as a γένος.

Sometimes this divine calling into the one new people is expressed as encompassing both Greeks and Barbarians: there is, Clement asserts, since the coming (παρουσία) of Christ, "the catholic/universal calling [ἡ κλῆσις ἡ καθολική] to be a special people of righteousness [εἰς περιούσιον δικαιοσύνης λαόν] . . . brought together by one Lord, the only God of both

124. Ehrensperger, "What's in a Name?," 100–103.
125. So Wolter, "Ein neues 'Geschlecht'?," 291.
126. Buell, *Why This New Race*.

Greeks and Barbarians, or rather of the whole human race [παντὸς τοῦ τῶν ἀνθρώπων γένους]" (*Strom.* 6.17.159.9).[127] Here, as Buell has shown, using Jonathan Hall's terminology, Clement uses one particular kind of ethnic reasoning: an "aggregative" or universalizing strategy, suggesting that all can be incorporated into this new people of God.[128]

A second, and contrasting, strategy is what Buell labels an "oppositional" one, which uses similar "people" language to distinguish Christians from others—whether from outsiders or from those would-be Christians who are deemed to be heretical—as in the threefold division of humanity that we have seen in various forms in the Kerygma Petrou, Aristides, and Diognetus.[129] For example, in *Strom.* 5.14.98.4, Clement refers to "three polities [τρεῖς πολιτείας] . . . that of the Jews . . . that of the Greeks . . . and that of the Christians." Clement's echoes of 1 Pet 2:9–10 provide one particular illustration of the significance of such language for him.[130]

For example, in the *Protrepticus* (4.59.3), Clement quotes much of 1 Pet 2:9–10 in the context of an address rejecting the sexual immorality and idolatry of the Greco-Roman world (Homer is cited in the immediately preceding verses) and depicting the new Christian identity to which he calls the addressees: "We are the chosen race, the royal priesthood, a holy nation, a special people, who once were no people, but are now the people of God" (ἡμεῖς τὸ γένος τὸ ἐκλεκτόν, τὸ βασίλειον ἱεράτευμα, ἔθνος ἅγιον, λαὸς περιούσιος, οἱ ποτὲ οὐ λαός, νῦν δὲ λαὸς τοῦ θεοῦ).[131] A less extensive allusion is found in the *Paedagogus* (1.6.32.4), where Clement draws a contrast between the Christian's old and new identity, describing the putting off of the old person and the putting on of the immortality of Christ "in order that we may become new, a holy people, born again" (ἵνα καινοὶ γενόμενοι, λαὸς ἅγιος, ἀναγεννηθέντες).[132] Commenting on 1 Pet 2:9 in his *Adumbrationes*

127. Cf. Clement, *Protr.* 12.120.2, where Christ summons "countless tribes [μυρία φῦλα], all people of reason, both Barbarians and Greeks, I call on the whole human race [τὸ πᾶν ἀνθρώπων γένος καλῶ]" (GCS 12 [Clem I], 84).

128. Buell, "Race and Universalism," 441–50; Buell, *Why This New Race*, 138–65; cf. Hall, *Ethnic Identity*, 47.

129. See Buell, "Race and Universalism," 442.

130. These citations and allusions are discussed in more detail in Horrell, *Becoming Christian*, 145–52.

131. Greek text from GCS 12 (Clem I), 46.

132. Greek text from GCS 12 (Clem I), 109. One might perhaps question how secure this is as an allusion to 1 Pet 2:9 given the phrase λαὸς ἅγιος rather than ἔθνος ἅγιον. However, it is notable that the surrounding words contain a number of points of contact with the language of 1 Peter, making an allusion to the letter likely, though hardly beyond

(extant only in Latin), Clement affirms: "That we are a chosen race by the election of God is abundantly clear" (*Quoniam electum genus sumus dei electione, abunde clarum est*).[133]

Also significant are a number of allusions to 1 Pet 2:9 in the *Stromateis*, in which Clement refers to Christians as a γένος. Those who revere and honor God continually in every way, thus displaying true *gnōsis*,[134] are "the elect race" (τὸ γένος τὸ ἐκλεκτόν) (*Strom.* 7.7.35.2).[135] Similarly, those who seek God are described as τὸ γένος τὸ ἐκλεκτόν (*Strom.* 7.10.58.6). Later, echoing the words βασίλειος and γένος from 1 Pet 2:9,[136] Clement describes the decision to be righteous as taking "the royal road [ἡ ὁδὸς λέγεται βασιλική], which the royal race travels [ἣν τὸ βασιλικὸν ὁδεύει γένος]" (*Strom.* 7.12.73.5). Further, in his own contributions to the *Excerpts from Theodotus*, Clement describes "the Church" as "the chosen race" (τὸ γένος τὸ ἐκλεκτόν) (*Exc.* 4.1).[137] Here, γένος ἐκλεκτόν—with the definite

---

question. Apart from ἀναγεννηθέντες in the phrase quoted above (see 1 Pet 1:3, 23, only here in NT), the quoted sentence continues immediately as follows: ἀμίαντον φυλάξωμεν τὸν ἄνθρωπον καὶ νήπιοι ὦμεν ὡς βρέφος τοῦ θεοῦ κεκαθαρμένον πορνείας καὶ πονηρίας. This is strongly reminiscent of 1 Pet 2:1–2.

133. Latin text from GCS 17 (Clem III), 204, lines 21–22.

134. On Clement's view of *gnōsis* as the goal of the mature Christian life, see John Behr, *Asceticism and Anthropology in Irenaeus and Clement*, OECS (Oxford: Oxford University Press, 1999), 185–207; Henny Fiskå Hägg, *Clement of Alexandria and the Beginnings of Christian Apophaticism*, OECS (Oxford: Oxford University Press, 2006), 32, 150–52.

135. Greek texts in this paragraph from GCS 17 (Clem III). In this and the following reference, where only the phrase γένος ἐκλεκτόν is echoed from 1 Pet 2:9, it is conceivable that the allusion might be to Isa 43:20. However, given Clement's clear use of 1 Pet 2:9–10 elsewhere, including in his *Adumbrationes*, where he highlights just this phrase (see below), this is unlikely (insofar as the influence of the two biblical texts can neatly be separated). Although the phrase in 1 Pet 2:9 is anarthrous (contrast Isa 43:20 LXX), it is unsurprising that Clement used the definite article, and the possessive pronoun of the phrase in Isaiah (τὸ γένος μου τὸ ἐκλεκτόν) is not included. Among the early citations of Isa 43:20, Clement, *Strom.* 6.6.50.4, and Tertullian, *Marc.* 3.5.3, do not include the γένος ἐκλεκτόν phrase, and two references in Cyprian that do include it are focused on the water imagery and its baptismal relevance (Cyprian, *Ep.* 63.8; *Test.* 1.12). The reference to Job's children as "a chosen and honored race from the seed of Jacob" (γένος ἐκλεκτόν ἔντιμον ἐκ σπέρματος Ιακωβ, Testament of Job 1:5) may reflect the influence of the Jewish scriptures generally and Isa 43:20 in particular and need not be a sign of Christian editing, nor of the influence of 1 Pet 2:9, though the Testament as a whole is thought to show at least some signs of Christian redaction; see *OTP* 1.833–34.

136. This combination of words means that 1 Pet 2:9, rather than Isa 43:20, has to be the scriptural influence here.

137. On the reasons to take *Exc.* 4–5 as Clement's own work, see François Sagnard,

articles—seems to have become a concise way to describe and define the church (and in a context where distinctiveness from the surrounding society is not the topic). Clement's reference to the one, singular church is both emphatic and polemical. As Annewies van den Hoek notes, "Clement's concept of church has a strongly polemical orientation. When he speaks about the gatherings of heretics, he is eager to use the plural ἐκκλησίας in order to deny their claim to be ἐκκλησία in the singular, the one and true church, in which the just assemble."[138]

These are only selected examples, needless to say, but they give some indication of the ways in which "people" language came to prominence in early Christian discourse—and in the often hostile discourse of their opponents.[139] It is entirely understandable that such language is barely evident in the New Testament itself, and then only through the appropriation of scriptural phrases, since what came to be a movement with a distinct sense of its own self-identity over against both Jews and gentiles began as a messianic Jewish movement that understood itself not as a new or distinct "people" but rather, in diverse ways, as playing a role in the fulfillment of Israel's eschatological hopes, including the salvation of the gentiles. Though composed of scriptural phrases, 1 Pet 2:9–10 represents a strikingly emphatic and artful expression of the "peoplehood" of the Christians, and one that seems to mark a point at which the discourse of Christians as a γένος begins and a self-consciousness of being a "people" is evoked. Whatever the specific influence of 1 Pet 2:9–10, Christian literature of the second century gives ample evidence of the influence of such "people" language on early Christian self-identification and also some evidence of this categorization being used, from the outside, in a hostile manner. Indeed, it may not be a coincidence

---

Clément d'Alexandrie, Extraits de Théodote: texte grec, introduction, traduction et notes, SC 23 (Paris: Cerf, 1970), 59n2 (and for the agreement on this, see 8–9); Werner Foerster, *Patristic Evidence,* vol. 1 of *Gnosis: A Selection of Gnostic Texts,* trans. R. McL. Wilson (Oxford: Clarendon, 1972), 223, who omits *Exc.* 4–5. For the Greek text with English translation, see Robert Pierce Casey, *The Excerpta ex Theodoto of Clement of Alexandria,* SD 1 (London: Christophers, 1934).

138. Annewies van den Hoek, "The 'Catechetical' School of Early Christian Alexandria and Its Philonic Heritage," *HTR* 90 (1997): 72.

139. For the trajectory into later examples, see, e.g., on the ethnic construction of Christian identity in Eusebius's *Praeparatio Evangelica,* Johnson, *Ethnicity and Argument,* esp. 198–233. Elsewhere, Eusebius describes the Christians as "a new nation" (νέον . . . ἔθνος, *Hist. eccl.* 1.4.2) and cites an imperial edict in which they are variously labeled an ἔθνος, a δεισιδαιμονία ("superstition"), and a θρησκεία ("cult") (*Hist. eccl.* 9.9a.1–6); see Goodman, *Mission and Conversion,* 101.

that such language is used both to define the group's identity in a context of hostility and opposition and in the battle for internal self-definition and the drawing of boundaries, as is evident in Clement of Alexandria, for example.[140]

7.4 Conclusions

The fact that words like ἔθνος and γένος can be used to denote ancient people-groups, including the *Ioudaioi*, and that such words also came to be used of the Christians does not, it hardly need be said, mean that all these groups are to be seen as precisely equivalent—members of a standard category—whether we label the category "nation," "race," "people," or even *ethnie*. The Greek words themselves are much too diverse in their usage to permit such a crude conclusion. But we may draw more constructive conclusions from the preceding survey.

It is clear that the various "people" words are standardly and frequently used to denote the Jewish people, with some distinctive emphases, such as the LXX's strong preference for λαός. Such language both presumes and reinforces a sense of peoplehood, which was evidently recognized from both internal and external perspectives. It is also clear that a sense of self-consciousness as a "people" emerges in the early Christian sources—embryonically in the New Testament itself and much more prominently in later Christian literature. This is significant not only as an indication of this emerging self-consciousness but also because—whatever the diversity of nuance and meaning—Christian identity is described using the terms also standardly used of other people-groups. Indeed, the threefold distinction not infrequently encountered, from its embryonic form in Paul through to more explicit articulation in Clement of Alexandria and beyond, between Jews, Greeks (or, more generally, gentiles or "pagans"), and Christians, indicates how this people-language played a part in the boundary-making crucial to self-definition.[141] Indeed, equally importantly, it shows that this was done precisely by describing "Christian" identity in the same terms as those other competing people-groupings, the terms standardly used to organize

---

140. Cf. Judith Lieu's comment (*Neither Jew nor Greek*, 58) on the use of such language in Jewish literature, quoted above (p. 227).

141. On the ways in which the language of Jewishness and Greekness (and the evolving language of "paganism") was used in attempts to define boundaries around the developing Christian community, see Boin, "Hellenistic 'Judaism.'"

the social world. Turning to the Christian way of life was explicitly seen to cut across those previous identifications such that—as the threefold categorization broadly confirms—being Christian is deemed to stand in distinction from being Jewish or being Greek. Whatever Christian self-consciousness as a "people" implies, then, it seems in at least some ways to correspond to whatever it might mean to be a part of some other people-group, since it stands—or is presented as standing—in contrast to and competition with those other identities.

We have also seen how far the Christian sources, in making this distinction among different kinds, or races, of people, focus on Christian religious devotion as different from (and, needless to say, superior to) that of Jews and Greeks. As we have previously noted, this does not mean that we can plausibly separate off such concerns as belonging to the realm of "religion" rather than that of "ethnicity" or even "nationality." For a start, such a distinction founders on the general point that religious traditions are frequently bound closely into forms of ethnic and national identity, as Anthony Smith shows through a wide range of diverse examples.[142] Even in the modern period, as we have already seen (§3.3), religion, ethnicity, and national identity are much more closely intertwined than the modern Western model of religion would imply. All the more in the ancient world, the focus on "religious" devotion and practice—specifically central to Jewish identity, as previous chapters have shown—operates in a context where such cultic and religious practices (part of a "way of life"; see ch. 5), were constitutive of identity as a people. Unlike other people-groups, the early Christians could not easily claim ancestral roots for their Christian way of life (except insofar as they identified themselves with Judaism or appropriated Jewish identity), this sense of novelty being a significant reason for hostility toward them. Indeed, the kind of insistent emphasis on being a "people" found in 1 Pet 2:9–10 represents an attempt to evoke this kind of identity in the face of what the author depicts as an estranged and vulnerable existence in a hostile world. This particular example, and the wider discourse that follows, represents a certain kind of ethnicization, a sort of ethnogenesis: the construction and creation of a self-consciousness of identity as a people. The making of new peoples is, after all, not an uncommon phenomenon.

The generation of such self-consciousness about shared identity as a people does not necessarily mean that we should place them into the same kind of "ethnic" group category as other ancient peoples—not least because,

142. See Smith, *Chosen Peoples*.

as we have seen, there is a wide variety in the kinds of groups that could thus be labeled. What we can say is that early Christian texts deployed "people" terminology in the discursive construction of their group identity and that they placed this group identity alongside, as competing with, other "people" identities, specifically those of Jews and Greeks (or gentiles). Moreover, as we have seen, following Buell's work in particular, this people-language could be deployed in various ways, both (in "oppositional" mode) to stress the distinctiveness and boundedness of the Christian people and (in "aggregative" mode) to make a more missionary appeal: that all may (potentially) join this one new race, "the one race of the saved." That evocative self-description leads us to consider one final aspect of early Christian discourse and practice, one that most obviously seems to indicate its universal, trans-ethnic, inclusive character: a mission to all the peoples of the earth.

CHAPTER 8

Mission and Conversion: Joining the People

The idea that one might join a group through what we call conversion seems inherently to belong to the sphere of religion and not ethnicity or race. Religions, it seems, might in some cases have a sense of mission, a desire to reach out to non-members and encourage or persuade them to join. But missionary outreach is less likely to be associated with an ethnic or racial group. Is it not clearly the case that the early Christian movement must be categorically different from "ethnic" groups, including the ancient *Ioudaioi*, if it is growing through the entry of converts and driven by a sense of universal mission that transcends ethnic (and other) distinctions, as classically expressed in Gal 3:28?

As with the other topics we have covered thus far, the distinction between religion and ethnicity (or race, or nationhood) that such a presumption implies may skate over the complex intersections between these facets of group identity. In his analysis of the ways in which religious ideas and traditions contribute to the formation of national identities, for example, Anthony Smith characterizes certain peoples as "missionary" (in contrast to "covenanted peoples"): "Missionary peoples," he suggests, "are equally dedicated to what they see as the true faith and the word of God, but they seek to expand into and transform the world, by example, persuasion, or force, or a combination of these."[1] Commenting later on English identity and the sense of being a chosen people—what he calls "ethnic chosenness"[2]—he remarks on "the rise of a 'British' national identity in the eighteenth century":

> Despite the unevenness of religious affiliation and conviction across Britain, and much resistance to the idea of British political and religious unity, the

1. Smith, *Chosen Peoples*, 95.
2. Smith, *Chosen Peoples*, 117.

dominant current remained "Protestant" (or, more accurately, Anglican) and it greatly reinforced the sense of national exclusiveness that expressed itself, not only in anti-Popery riots at home, but also in colonial attitudes of cultural (and, much later, racial) superiority and paternalism overseas. One strand of the growth of an expansionist and imperial British nationalism, with its mission of conquest, civilization, and Christianization, can be traced back to the effects of this Protestant belief in English missionary election.[3]

It is perhaps no coincidence, then, that Brooke Foss Westcott, in 1885, declared, "The English nation cannot but be a nation of Missionaries," or that Henry H. Montgomery spoke in 1901 of the aim to "make the ancient Church of England more completely an Imperial Church—the unit being the world and not the United Kingdom."[4] Indeed, as Adrian Hastings shows, Christian mission in the nineteenth and twentieth centuries more generally was often characterized by a certain kind of "missionary nationalism," expressed, for example, in "the anxiety to retain a given 'field' for one's own country and one's own religious order."[5] This changed significantly, of course, with the processes of decolonization and the rise of new African nationalisms in the 1950s and '60s. Nonetheless, Hastings comments critically that

> What none of us anticipated at the time was that the gravest nationalist threat to Christianity by the late twentieth century might come from the United States, essentially a rehash of the traditional Christian imperialism of western European countries. It is just the latest example of a self-appointed "chosen people" carrying forth a gospel message reshaped by its own values and bonded to its own political expansion. . . . The dual temptation of late-twentieth-century America, basking in a prosperity and imperial power beyond anything hitherto known, has been to see itself in terms of God's preferred people and to see the American brand of universalism "as simply universalism itself."[6]

3. Smith, *Chosen Peoples*, 122.

4. Quoted in Stephen S. Maughan, *Mighty England Do Good: Culture, Faith, Empire, and World in the Foreign Missions of the Church of England, 1850–1915* (Grand Rapids: Eerdmans, 2014), 1, 378; see 378–410 on this short-lived period of particular ambition, in which there was also awareness of the competition from Islam (398).

5. Adrian Hastings, "The Clash of Nationalism and Universalism within Twentieth-Century Missionary Christianity," in *Missions, Nationalism, and the End of Empire*, ed. Brian Stanley, Studies in the History of Christian Missions (Grand Rapids: Eerdmans, 2003), 18.

6. Hastings, "Clash of Nationalism," 32–33. The phrase "as simply universalism itself"

Thus, claims Hastings, "the story of white imperialist nationalism and its relationship to missionary Christianity is one that did not end around 1960, the 'Year of Africa.' It merely shifted its shape."[7] Such observations indicate something of the connections between religion, nationalism, and race and suggest that investigations of constructions of Christian "peoplehood"—often cast in relation to Jewish peoplehood—are by no means irrelevant to understanding the functioning of modern Western states and their appeal to a sense of identity as "people."[8]

In one sense, then, this chapter's focus on mission and conversion marks a shift from the previous chapters, with their treatments of various topics typically linked to ethnic identity. Yet in another sense, considering such things as a commitment to outward mission, the opportunities or encouragement offered to outsiders to join, the idea of a "people" that might expand as others become members of it, and so on is highly relevant to our broader comparison of Jewish and early Christian identities and scholarly approaches to them in relation to issues of ethnicity, religion, and race.

There has been considerable discussion and debate about the nature and extent of missionary activity and the means of gaining adherents and converts, particularly insofar as Judaism is seen in comparison with early Christianity. In the following investigation, we turn first to questions about Jewish missionary activity and proselytism before moving on to a consideration of selected examples from the early Christian evidence.

8.1 Proselytes, Sympathizers, and the Attractions of Judaism

8.1.1 *From Missionary Zeal to Passive Attraction: Shifting Perspectives*

Early in the twentieth century, there appears to have been a strongly established view, not least in Protestant scholarship on Christian origins, that Judaism at the time of Christian origins was characterized by energetic missionary zeal.[9] Adolf von Harnack is an early and influential representative of

---

is reused here, having appeared in earlier lines in a quotation regarding the tendency of a typical French missionary "to impose around him an extremely French brand of universalism which he regards as simply universalism itself" (Jean de Menasce, quoted on 32).

7. Hastings, "Clash of Nationalism," 33.

8. See Givens, *We the People*.

9. For a detailed and nuanced review of early scholarship and its roots back to the time of Calvin, see Rainer Riesner, "A Pre-Christian Jewish Mission?," in *The Mission of the Early*

this perspective.[10] He sees evidence for a strong missionary impulse among Jews of the time: "Proudly [*stolz* (*sic!*)] the Jew felt that he had something to say and bring to the world, which concerned all men. . . . It was owing to the consciousness of this . . . that he felt missions to be a duty."[11] For Harnack, the evidence for the presence of Jews spread throughout the Roman Empire indicated that "Judaism, as a religion, was already [*bereits*] blossoming out by some inward transformation."[12] As Harnack's revealing use of the word "already" indicates, his perspective on Jewish missionary activity was, as is often the case, driven primarily by a concern to explain the missionary commitment and religious success of early Christianity.[13] Thus, as Harnack comments, at least part of Christianity's "missionary zeal was inherited by Christianity from Judaism."[14] And Christianity, of course, represents the successful culmination of the "blossoming out" that Judaism began but failed to fulfill—due, in Harnack's view, to the fact that it failed to allow a gentile, "in the first generation at least," to "become a real son of Abraham." (This revealing comment helps to explain how such a view could coexist with the structural dichotomy between particularistic Judaism and inclusive Christianity we surveyed in chapter 1.) "The religion which will repair this omission," he ominously remarks, "will drive Judaism from the field."[15]

Subsequent scholars, such as Joachim Jeremias and Dieter Georgi, reiterate a similar view of Judaism's energetic missionary activity.[16] Jeremias, for example, speaks of "the time of Jesus's appearance" as "an unparalleled

---

Church to Jews and Gentiles, ed. Jostein Ådna and Hans Kvalbein, WUNT 127 (Tübingen: Mohr Siebeck, 2000), 211–17.

10. Harnack, *Expansion*, 1:1–18. German original: Adolf von Harnack, *Die Mission und Ausbreitung des Christentums in den ersten drei Jahrhunderten* (Leipzig: J. C. Hinrichs, 1902).

11. Harnack, *Expansion*, 1:12; *Mission und Ausbreitung*, 7.

12. Harnack, *Expansion*, 1:12; *Mission und Ausbreitung*, 7, italicized in the original.

13. Edouard Will and Claude Orrieux, *"Proselytisme Juif"? Histoire d'une erreur* (Paris: Les Belles Lettres, 1992), 13, 291n4, comment that this theory of a Jewish converting mission is Christian in origin, though it is also found in some Jewish scholarship. They turn to the question of the origins of this theory on 211–89. But for earlier origins in Calvin, see Riesner, "Jewish Mission?," 213. For examples of both Christian and Jewish scholars who have supported the theory, see the works (some of which are cited below) listed by James Carleton Paget, "Jewish Proselytism at the Time of Christian Origins: Chimera or Reality?," *JSNT* 62 (1996): 66 with nn. 4–9.

14. Harnack, *Expansion*, 1:11.

15. Harnack, *Expansion*, 1:15.

16. Dieter Georgi, *The Opponents of Paul in Second Corinthians: A Study of Religious Propaganda in Late Antiquity* (Edinburgh: T&T Clark, 1987), 83–151.

period of missionary activity . . . in Israel. . . . Judaism was the first great missionary religion to make its appearance in the Mediterranean world."[17] This is, moreover, a missionary zeal against which Jesus (in Matt 23:15) pronounces "a stern judgement," though Jeremias notes "the riddle . . . why this harsh saying about converts should be the only utterance of Jesus which we possess concerning the Jewish mission," despite its "unparalleled" level of activity.[18]

Criticism of such a view of Judaism's missionary attitude may be found, so Rainer Riesner notes, as early as the 1930s and '40s, particularly in Scandinavian scholarship; and what Riesner labels a "full attack" is found in the 1951 monograph by Sverre Aalen, though mission and proselytism is only one theme in Aalen's study of "light" and "darkness" and associated motifs in ancient Judaism.[19] Since then, a considerable number of studies have challenged the view of an active Jewish "mission," notably the monographs of Scot McKnight, Martin Goodman, and Edouard Will and Claude Orrieux.[20] The dominant perspective in contemporary scholarship—though far from unanimous—has shifted significantly toward the view that Judaism at the

17. Joachim Jeremias, *Jesus' Promise to the Nations* (London: SCM, 1967), 11. The point about the time of Jesus being an unparalleled time of Jewish missionary activity is repeated more than once in the following pages; see 12, 19.

18. Jeremias, *Jesus' Promise*, 11, 19. On the resolution of this "riddle," see n. 99 below.

19. Riesner, "Jewish Mission?," 216; Sverre Aalen, *Die Begriffe "Licht" und "Finsternis" im Alten Testament, im Spätjudentum und im Rabbinismus*, Skrifter Utgitt av Det Norske Videnskaps-Akademi I Oslo. II, Hist.-Filos. Klasse (Oslo: I Kommisjon Hos Jacob Dybwad, 1951). Aalen insists on a distinction between proselytism and mission (206) and sees a "centripetal" rather than "centrifugal" force at work, attracting people toward Judaism (specifically understood in terms of notions of light, glory, and so on). His treatments of the topic of mission are on 202–32 and 282–306.

20. Scot McKnight, *A Light among the Gentiles: Jewish Missionary Activity in the Second Temple Period* (Minneapolis: Fortress, 1991); Goodman, *Mission and Conversion*; Will and Orrieux, *"Proselytisme Juif"*? Among other significant discussions, see Irina Levinskaya, *The Book of Acts in Its Diaspora Setting*, The Book of Acts in Its First Century Setting 5 (Grand Rapids: Eerdmans, 1996), 19–49, who also concludes "that sources from the first century do not support the view that there was large scale Jewish missionary activity" (49); Martin Goodman, "Jewish Proselytizing in the First Century," in *The Jews Among Pagans and Christians in the Roman Empire*, ed. Judith Lieu, John North, and Tessa Rajak (London: Routledge, 1992), 53–78; James Carleton Paget, "Hellenistic and Early Roman Period Jewish Missionary Efforts in the Diaspora," in *The Rise and Expansion of Christianity in the First Three Centuires of the Common Era*, ed. Clare K. Rothschild and Jens Schröter, WUNT 301 (Tübingen: Mohr Siebeck, 2013), 11–49. Note also the early challenge of A. T. Kraabel, "The Roman Diaspora: Six Questionable Assumptions," *JJS* 33 (1982): 445–64; and the weighty remarks of Fredriksen, "Judaism," 537–40.

time of Christian origins was not a proactively missionary religion.[21] As Michael Bird summarizes the picture, "There is no evidence for an organized campaign or a widely held ethos that endeavoured to recruit Gentiles to Judaism via the process of proselytizing."[22]

As many of the recent discussions make clear, questions of definition are crucial: needless to say, whether one finds Judaism to be a missionary religion or not depends on what is deemed to constitute such a religion. (In these particular discussions, the question about what it would mean to categorize Judaism as a "religion" is less often addressed.[23]) James Carleton Paget, for example, operates with the broad definition "that a missionary religion is one that makes it clear in a variety of ways that conversion to it is a desirable thing" but concedes to critics of his earlier article that this broad definition fails "to take sufficient account of an intention to convert"— though Carleton Paget insists that such intention is difficult to discern in the available evidence.[24] Perhaps better, then, is the tighter definition of Riesner: "A missionary religion intends to win converts, and this is accomplished actively by at least some of its members."[25] There is also the inevitable risk that both definitions and interpretations may be shaped by a Christian perspective, whether this emanates from a primary focus on the history of earliest Christianity or from the Christian context or commitment of the interpreter—or both these factors together, as in the early work of Harnack. But what these discussions of matters of definition helpfully highlight is the importance of distinguishing between the acceptance or welcome of those who seek to join and an active seeking of converts, even if the line between the two unavoidably remains blurry.

In what follows, I can offer no more than a brief and highly selective survey of the relevant evidence, which is discussed in much more detail in the extended treatments available elsewhere.[26] The key contours of this

21. For an overview of recent scholarship that reaches similar conclusions, see Michael F. Bird, *Crossing Over Sea and Land: Jewish Missionary Activity in the Second Temple Period* (Peabody, MA: Hendrickson, 2010). See also the cautious conclusions of Carleton Paget, "Jewish Missionary Efforts," which are especially notable given that he cautiously supports the notion of Judaism as a missionary religion, albeit defined in broad terms (see below); cf. Carleton Paget, "Jewish Proselytism."

22. Bird, *Crossing*, 149–50.

23. This is, however, one of the "questionable assumptions" that Kraabel, "Roman Diaspora," discusses, along with that of "missionary zeal."

24. Carleton Paget, "Jewish Missionary Efforts," 18.

25. Riesner, "Jewish Mission?," 223, italicized in the original.

26. See esp. McKnight, *Light*; Will and Orrieux, *"Proselytisme Juif"?*; Bird, *Crossing*. For

evidence will, however, provide an important basis for both the assessment of Judaism on its own terms and its comparison with early Christianity.

8.1.2 Evidence for Judaism's Popularity

One of the reasons Harnack took Judaism in the first century to be engaged in energetic missionary activity was that the Jewish population in this period seems to have been large and growing.[27] Such growth, it was assumed, would not have been possible solely through the reproduction, by birth, of new generations of *Ioudaioi* but must reflect the energy and success of Jewish missionary activity.[28] However, as various critics have pointed out, aspects of this reconstruction are fragile and flawed. For a start, the evidence for robust conclusions about ancient demography is limited: we have only imprecise estimates of the exact population sizes of cities and so on, let alone of the numbers of Jews and other groups within them; rural areas are even harder to assess. And the comments of writers such as Philo and Josephus on the size and spread of Jewish populations in many places may well be subject to a degree of exaggeration (see below). But most importantly, even if the numbers of people identified as Jewish was increasing and sympathizers and "converts" were joining, as seems likely, this need not reflect proactive missionary endeavour aimed at securing such conversions, as Harnack and others presume.[29]

There is, nonetheless, significant evidence both for the widespread existence of Jewish groups and communities throughout the Roman Empire

---

a thorough treatment of the sources in the context of a wider consideration of "patterns of universalism" in Judaism to 135 CE, see Terence L. Donaldson, *Judaism and the Gentiles: Jewish Patterns of Universalism (to 135 CE)* (Waco: Baylor University Press, 2007).

27. See Harnack, *Expansion*, 1:2–10.

28. Harnack, *Expansion*, 1:10–11; cf. also Louis H. Feldman, *Jew and Gentile in the Ancient World: Attitudes and Interactions from Alexander to Justinian* (Princeton: Princeton University Press, 1993), 293, 555n20.

29. See, e.g., the critical remarks of Goodman, *Mission and Conversion*, 84; Fredriksen, "Judaism," 538; Bird, *Crossing*, 52–54; Levinskaya, *Diaspora Setting*, 23–24, who affirms "that the size of the Jewish Diaspora was substantial and there was a certain growth in population" but points out that this does not confirm missionary activity; Carleton Paget, "Missionary Efforts," 21–22. Feldman, *Jew and Gentile*, 555n20, makes a valid point in questioning whether anything but conversions can explain a significant increase in the Jewish population. But, of course, such "conversions" need not be the result of proactive missionary activity.

and for the popularity and attractiveness of Jewish beliefs and practices.[30] Evidence for Judaism's popularity is found in both Jewish and non-Jewish sources, the latter being not infrequently hostile toward this phenomenon. Josephus, for example, remarks on the widespread adoption of Jewish laws by Greeks (*C. Ap.* 2.123) and comments that "the masses have long since shown a keen desire to adopt our religious observances [τῆς ἡμετέρας εὐσεβείας]" (*C. Ap.* 2.282 [Thackeray, LCL]). Indeed, Josephus claims that there is "not one city . . . nor a single nation [ἔθνος]" to which the Jewish custom of Sabbath rest has not spread (*C. Ap.* 2.282; cf. *B.J.* 2.398).[31] Likewise, Philo remarks that "almost every other people . . . have so far grown in holiness as to value and honour our laws" (*Mos.* 2.17 [Colson, LCL]; cf. 2.41–43). Elsewhere, Philo remarks on the size and spread of the Jewish people around the world (e.g., *Flacc.* 45–46; *Legat.* 281–82), as does Josephus (e.g., *B.J.* 7.43–45; *A.J.* 14.110). Such assertions may certainly be exaggerated but must have some basis in reality in order to have any plausibility and rhetorical force.[32] They also find confirmation in hostile or satirical comments from the non-Jewish side: Seneca, in a work known through quotations preserved in Augustine's *City of God*, complains that "the customs of this accursed race [*gens*] have gained such influence that they are now received throughout all the world."[33] Juvenal satirizes those who turn to Judaism due to the woeful influence of their parents (*Sat.* 14.96–106). More neutrally, Dio Cassius reports on the great increase in the number of Jews in Rome in the early to mid-first century CE (*Hist. Rom.* 57.18.5a; 60.6.6). Albeit negatively or critically, such texts seem to confirm both a widespread and growing number of people who identified as Jewish and a certain popular appeal of Jewish ways. Further evidence that indicates the existence of sympathizers and "converts" to Judaism will be discussed below.

---

30. For an extensive discussion, see esp. Feldman, *Jew and Gentile*, 177–287, who discusses the attractions of Judaism under the headings of its antiquity, its traditions and practice of virtue, and its ideal leader, Moses. See also Bernd Wander, *Gottesfürchtige und Sympathisanten: Studien zum heidnischen Umfeld von Diasporasynagogen*, WUNT 104 (Tübingen: Mohr Siebeck, 1998), 227.

31. See §5.3.1 above with n. 87 on this text and evidence for Sabbath observance.

32. Cf. Riesner, "Jewish Mission?," 228–29; Carleton Paget, "Missionary Efforts," 36–37.

33. Seneca, *De Superstitione*, quoted in Augustine, *Civ.* 6.11 (*GLAJJ*, §186); also in Bird, *Crossing*, 171; Donaldson, *Judaism*, 381–82 (with discussion).

8.1.3 *Sympathizers, Godfearers, and Patrons*

The evidence cited immediately above for the popularity and appeal of Judaism already makes it clear that many people not only found Judaism an attractive way of life—with its combination of religious, cultural, and ethical traditions—but also went some way toward adopting its beliefs and practices themselves. One way of expressing this move was to describe such people as "judaizing" (ἰουδαΐζειν, κτλ).[34] Some of the extant sources mention specific individuals—often (but not always) kings, foreign rulers, royal family members, lesser officials, or others in significant positions of some kind—who were more or less sympathetic toward Jewish customs and commitments.[35] Prominent examples include the queen mother Helena and her son King Izates (Josephus, *A.J.* 20.34–53, discussed below) and Nero's wife Poppea (Josephus, *A.J.* 20.195; cf. *Vita* 16).[36] The reason for a special interest in such prominent and influential figures is obvious. Even if some of these references indicate what Terence Donaldson calls "narrative wishful thinking," there are evidently instances in which a move to accept and adopt Jewish ways was made.[37] Other sources, as we have seen above, give more general indications of the appeal of Judaism among the population. As Donaldson has noted, there does not seem to be any clear definition concerning what level or extent of adoption of Jewish practices is necessary for someone to count as some kind of sympathizer or as someone who might be described as "judaizing": "the language was not used with any precision."[38] Shaye Cohen has helpfully set out a list of the ways in which sympathy and adherence to Judaism might be expressed, ranging from "admiring some aspect of Juda-

34. As in Esth 8:17 LXX; Josephus, *B.J.* 2.454, 463; Gal 2:14; Plutarch, *Cic.* 7.6. See also Donaldson, *Judaism*, 474, and his commentaries on the various primary texts. On the sense of the -ιζειν terminology, see Mason, "Jews, Judaeans, Judaizing, Judaism," 462–64; also Cohen, *Beginnings*, 175–97.

35. See Donaldson, *Judaism*, 470–72.

36. See also, e.g., Josephus, *A.J.* 13.69–71, 242–44; *C. Ap.* 2.45, 48. For an extensive list of examples, see Donaldson, *Judaism*, 472nn16, 18. For instances of support for and participation in Jewish custom and Temple by Roman imperial rulers, see, e.g., Philo, *Legat.* 157, 291, 295–98, 309–10, 319–20.

37. Donaldson, *Judaism*, 472, who cites as examples the various figures in 2 Maccabees; Ptolemy in the *Letter of Aristeas*; Alexander in Josephus, *A.J.* 11.331–36. By contrast, he notes the example of Helena and Izates as evidence that these narrative records are not always wishful thinking; on their tombs located near Jerusalem, see Pausanius, *Graec. descr.* 8.16.4–5 (*GLAJJ*, §358), with discussion there.

38. Donaldson, *Judaism*, 479; cf. also Carleton Paget, "Missionary Efforts," 27.

ism" to "converting to Judaism and 'becoming a Jew.'"[39] While there is a reasonably clear distinction between sympathizer and convert (a category we shall turn to below), there is no indication of "any concerted attempt to define a minimum level of sympathization such as would serve to create a distinct category or recognized class."[40] Nonetheless, as Donaldson summarizes the matter (noting that this is "widely recognized by scholars"), "there can be little doubt about the phenomenon itself: Gentile sympathizers existed throughout the area represented by these texts and in sufficient numbers that the phenomenon was widely recognized not only by Jews themselves but also by outsiders."[41]

One group of sympathizers who might seem to count as a "distinct category" or "recognized class" is the "Godfearers" (οἱ φοβούμενοι τὸν θεόν) or "worshippers of God" (σεβόμενοι τὸν θεόν) who appear in Acts (10:2, 22; 13:16, 26; 16:14; 18:7) and have been much discussed in New Testament scholarship.[42] While many have long regarded such "Godfearers" as a quasi-technical category of adherents to Judaism, others, notably A. T. Kraabel, have cast doubt on their existence, suggesting a peculiarly Lukan construction at work.[43] More recent scholarship, however, seems to have concluded, based on both literary and inscriptional evidence, that terms such as φοβουμένος τὸν θεόν, σεβομένος τὸν θεόν and θεοσεβής (the latter in the NT only at John 9:31) could indeed be applied to adherents and sympathizers who did not fully join as proselytes but who were evidently recognized among the Jewish communities (see, e.g., Josephus, A.J. 14.110).[44] Particularly significant has been an inscription from Aphrodisias that, though rather later than the period of earliest Christianity (probably third century CE), includes in a list of members and associates of the Jewish community some who are designated as θεοσεβεῖς (and some named as proselytes, on which see §8.1.4).[45]

---

39. Cohen, *Beginnings*, 140–62.

40. Donaldson, *Judaism*, 479; cf. also Wander, *Gottesfürchtige*, 229, 233.

41. Donaldson, *Judaism*, 475 with n. 44.

42. Among the most substantial recent treatments are Levinskaya, *Diaspora Setting*, and Wander, *Gottesfürchtige*. For a brief overview of the debate in relation to Luke-Acts, see Donaldson, *Judaism*, 415–19.

43. A. T. Kraabel, "The Disappearance of the 'God-fearers,'" *Numen* 28 (1981): 113–26; Kraabel, "Greeks, Jews and Lutherans in the Middle Half of Acts," *HTR* 79 (1986): 147–57.

44. See esp. Levinskaya, *Diaspora Setting*, 51–126; Wander, *Gottesfürchtige*.

45. For the text and commentary, see Reynolds and Tannenbaum, *Jews and God-Fearers*, 5–7. The Greek text and English translation are provided and discussed in Judge, *Jerusalem and Athens*, 121–29; the Greek with German translation is given in Wander, *Gottes-*

Neither the Aphrodisias inscription nor other pertinent evidence requires the view that "Godfearer" was a precise or clearly defined class of adherent. For a start, as Kirsopp Lake long ago pointed out, the language of "fearing" or "worshipping" God is often used of Jews, not least in the LXX (cf. Acts 13:43) and should not be assumed as a technical term for a special class of gentile adherents unless other evidence indicates that.[46] For this reason—and making a similar point—Louis Feldman argues that "sympathizer" rather than "Godfearer" is a better term for gentile adherents to Judaism.[47] Moreover, as Donaldson has pointed out, the Aphrodisias evidence does not indicate that the term θεοσεβής was used to denote a precisely defined group of people but rather "in a vague and non-technical sense" and could refer to gentiles with various kinds and degrees of involvement with the Jewish community.[48] Irina Levinskaya likewise remarks that the Aphrodisias inscription "shows how wide and how loose in reality the category of God-fearers was."[49] On face A of the inscription (lines 19–20), two people are each labeled "Godfearer" (θεοσεβής) and described, along with other proselytes and Jews, as people who "love study and praise constantly" (τῶν φιλομαθῶ[ν] τῶν κὲ παντευλογ[---ων], lines 4–5)—presumably referring to Torah study and worship of the Jewish God.[50] On face B, the people (also) described as "Godfearers" (θεοσεβῖς [*sic*], line 34) include some whose attachment to Judaism is likely to be somewhat more limited: nine of them are identified as civic officials, members of the town council (βουλεταί, lines 34–38). This, as Paula Fredriksen observes,

> is most intriguing, since it indicates that Gentiles whose status in the larger urban community necessitated their public idolatry (their office would re-

---

fürchtige, 235–39. For discussion, see also Levinskaya, *Diaspora Setting*, 70–80; Carleton Paget, "Missionary Efforts," 25–27.

46. Kirsopp Lake, "Note VIII: Proselytes and God-Fearers," in *Additional Notes to the Commentary*, vol. 5 of *The Beginnings of Christianity, Part 1: The Acts of the Apostles*, ed. Kirsopp Lake and Henry J. Cadbury (New York: Macmillan, 1933), 84–85.

47. Louis H. Feldman, "Jewish 'Sympathizers' in Classical Literature and Inscriptions," *TAPA* 81 (1950): 200–208; see also Feldman, *Jew and Gentile*, 342.

48. Donaldson, *Judaism*, 418; similarly, Carleton Paget, "Missionary Efforts," 26; Fredriksen, "Judaizing," 239.

49. Levinskaya, *Diaspora Setting*, 78.

50. See the lengthy discussion of this phrase in Reynolds and Tannenbaum, *Jews and God-Fearers*, 30–38, who suggest that it indicates that the members of the group devote themselves to study and prayer. Levinskaya, *Diaspora Setting*, 71, translates it as "the learned persons, also known as those who continually praise God."

quire their presence at sacrifices to the gods of the πόλις and the empire) could at the same time be active (if not, perhaps, fully integrated) participants in the synagogue community and worshippers, after their fashion, of the Jewish God.[51]

Some of those who were sympathizers or Godfearers may have embodied a form of support that was political and financial as much as—or even more than—"religious."[52] A famous inscription from Acmonia, in Phrygia, probably dating from the first century CE, records that a synagogue building "was erected [κατασκευασθέ(ν)τα] by Julia Severa."[53] The inscription goes on to list three others (two described as ἀρχισυνάγωγοι) who restored and further enhanced it "with their own funds." It seems clear that Julia Severa was the main benefactor who originally provided for the synagogue building. This prominent woman is also known from other evidence as a wealthy benefactor and civic leader; indeed, another inscription describes her as high priestess (ἀρχιέρεια)—probably of the imperial cult—and president of the games.[54] It is striking, then, as Donaldson has observed, "that the community was willing to accept benefaction from a Gentile who was so closely identified with pagan religion." Indeed, the community honored her in a very public way, "without either expecting that she demonstrate exclusive loyalty to the God of Israel or feeling that their own identity was somehow compromised or threatened in the process."[55] Donaldson also wisely remarks that

51. Fredriksen, "Judaism," 542. She goes on to note other evidence that supports this picture. See also Fredriksen, "Judaizing," 239; Donaldson, *Judaism*, 418; Carleton Paget, "Missionary Efforts," 26.

52. Carleton Paget, "Missionary Efforts," 27.

53. *MAMA* 6:264. For translation and commentary, see Paul R. Trebilco, *Jewish Communities in Asia Minor*, SNTSMS 69 (Cambridge: Cambridge University Press, 1991), 58–60; Donaldson, *Judaism*, 463–66; William M. Ramsay, *The Cities and Bishoprics of Phrygia*, 2 vols. (Oxford: Clarendon, 1897), 637–40 §530.

54. See Trebilco, *Jewish Communities*, 59; Donaldson, *Judaism*, 464; and the various inscriptions presented in Ramsay, *Cities and Bishoprics*, §§530, 549, 552–59; *MAMA* 6:263. It seems unlikely that she should be reckoned a "Jew," as Ramsay concludes (650); rather, as Trebilco argues, she is best seen as a sympathizer.

55. Donaldson, *Judaism*, 466 (both quotations). It is striking that Brigitte Kahl, *Galatians Re-Imagined: Reading with the Eyes of the Vanquished*, Paul in Critical Contexts (Minneapolis: Fortress, 2010), 241, implicitly criticizes this as an example of "tacit syncretism," "a model of acquiescence," "in glaring contrast to Paul's [laudably radical, anti-imperial] vision for his Galatian communities as he tries to challenge the smooth and prudent arrangement between the Jewish God and the imperial idols proposed by his 'opponents.'" This is one

we should not too quickly assume that Julia Severa's support for the Jewish community was only a matter of patronage and expressed no "religious" allegiance. On the contrary, it seems hard to imagine her making such a benefaction without some positive sense of sympathy toward the Jewish way of life, including its religious practices and beliefs.[56]

Nor should Julia Severa be seen as an exceptional case in this regard. Other examples of "pagan" benefactors are also known.[57] And as we noted above, "Godfearers" such as those named at Aphrodisias as members of the local council would also have been participants in the various "pagan" and imperial cults that were part of city life. It is important to emphasize, then, as Fredriksen has done, that despite the exclusive devotion to Israel's God required of Jews, Jewish communities were apparently often willing to accept such sympathizers, Godfearers, and patrons without requiring that they abandon their other forms of cultic and religious practice:

> all of these pagan sympathizers, to whatever degree they chose to participate in Jewish communal life, did so *as pagans*. They also continued in their native cults. No formal constraints from the Jewish side seem to have abridged what was an *ad hoc*, improvised and voluntary arrangement.[58]

It is important not to see only one side of the evidence, highlighting the inclusion and welcome that some Jewish communities apparently offered to sympathizers, supporters, and benefactors. There is also evidence for external hostility and internal separatism.[59] Nonetheless, not least in view of a common stress on Jewish exclusivism and separation, the evidence concerning the acceptance of various modes of affiliation with Jewish communities and their way of life is significant.[60] There is at least plentiful evidence for the existence of a wide range of sympathizers and adherents, some known and labeled as "Godfearers" (θεοσεβεῖς), who, for various reasons and to

---

indication of how work that is strenuously concerned to avoid any anti-Judaism (see Kahl, *Galatians*, 13–15) can still end up, it seems to me, replicating a sense of Christian superiority.

56. Donaldson, *Judaism*, 466.

57. See Lee I. Levine, *The Ancient Synagogue: The First Thousand Years* (New Haven: Yale University Press, 2000), 121, 479–81.

58. Fredriksen, "Judaizing," 239.

59. See McKnight, *Light*, 12–19 (on evidence for inclusion and integration), 19–25 (on evidence for separation and hostility).

60. On the evidence for Jews' own integration into various aspects of civic life, see Harland, *Associations*, 200–210.

varying extents, participated (but not exclusively) in the life of the Jewish communities and were accepted as such.

8.1.4 *Proselytes: Incomers and Joiners*

Just as there is no doubt about the existence of various kinds of sympathizers and adherents who supported and participated in Jewish communities to varying degrees, so too there is no doubt that there were proselytes—that is, those who took the step to fully join the Jewish people and adopt their way of life. The term προσήλυτος—predominantly found in Jewish discourse, though relatively rare outside the LXX and New Testament[61]—acquires its particular significance from the LXX, where it generally translates the Hebrew גר ("resident alien"). Like πάροικος, also used to render גר, in the LXX προσήλυτος seems to retain this sense of "resident alien," referring to those who come to live in or among the people of Israel.[62] Indeed, both the specific terminology and the general tendency of the Hebrew Bible's legislation to incorporate the resident alien fully into the life of the people provide a basis for the model of joining the Jewish people and their communities in the Hellenistic and Roman periods.[63] Nonetheless, προσήλυτος does not constitute the only established or standard label for those who chose to join in this way. Josephus, for example, nowhere uses the term,[64] though he does use etymologically related words, like the verb προσέρχομαι, to describe the process of what we call conversion; and Philo uses it only rarely, choosing instead words like ἔπηλυς (perhaps because they were in

---

61. See *TDNT* 6:727–44, esp. 731–32; Donaldson, *Judaism*, 486–87. LSJ, 1513, cite only biblical examples. The term appears around eighty-five times in the LXX and four times in the NT; each NT occurrence seems likely to refer to an incomer or "convert" to Judaism, most clearly in Matt 23:15 (see also Acts 2:11; 6:5; 13:43). However, a recently published inscription from the third century BCE (P.Duk. inv. 727r), without any specifically Jewish or "religious" context, uses προσήλυτος of an immigrant, resident alien, or "newcomer," indicating that the term (and its meaning) are not particular to Jewish texts; see David M. Moffitt and C. Jacob Butera, "P.Duk. inv. 727r: New Evidence for the Meaning and Provenance of the Word προσήλυτος," *JBL* 132 (2013): 159–78; Carleton Paget, "Missionary Efforts," 18–19.

62. See Matthew Thiessen, "Revisiting the προσήλυτος in 'the LXX,'" *JBL* 132 (2013): 333–50.

63. On the legislation regarding the "resident alien," see the overview in Donaldson, *Judaism*, 484–86.

64. See Rengstorf, *Complete Concordance*.

more general use and thus more widely comprehensible).[65] Indeed, both authors provide clear evidence of the existence of (and welcome for) "converts"—joiners or incomers—without using the term προσήλυτος, as also do a variety of texts and inscriptions where the word does appear.[66] As we shall see further below, the term "convert" is also open to question, implying a specifically "religious" kind of realignment; we might perhaps better speak of "incomers" or "joiners," though it is difficult to find concise alternative terms. Philo, for example, stresses in a number of places the welcome and full acceptance that is due to "incomers": Moses "commands all members of the nation [τοῦ ἔθνους] to love the incomers [τοὺς ἐπηλυτάς], not only as friends and kinsfolk [συγγενεῖς] but as themselves [ἑαυτούς] both in body and soul" (*Virt.* 103 [Colson, LCL]; cf. *Spec.* 1.51–53; *Legat.* 210–11).[67] Not all Jews, it seems, accepted that a gentile could "convert" or that circumcision would appropriately mark this joining of the people: Matthew Thiessen has drawn attention to evidence (especially in Jubilees) that suggests that for some Jews, only eighth-day circumcision was valid and "conversion" was impossible. However, as Thiessen himself acknowledges, this seems to be a comparatively rare position.[68]

In some instances, the motivation to "convert" may have had more to do with expediency or political loyalties than with what we might call religious factors. The Roman commander Metelius, for example, having surrendered with his garrison during the Jewish revolt against Rome, escapes being killed along with his soldiers by promising "to Judaize as far as circumcision" (μέχρι περιτομῆς ἰουδαΐσειν) (Josephus, *B.J.* 2.454).[69] A similar motivation may explain the process we find narrated in Esther 8:17 LXX, when, after the execution of Haman and a royal decree granting the Jews the right to kill any

---

65. Cf. *TDNT* 6:731–32; Donaldson, *Judaism*, 487.

66. For a brief overview of the inscriptional evidence, see Levinskaya, *Diaspora Setting*, 25–26, and the more extensive discussions in Ross S. Kraemer, "On the Meaning of the Term 'Jew' in Greco-Roman Inscriptions," *HTR* 82 (1989): 35–53; Kraemer, "Jewish Tuna and Christian Fish: Identifying Religious Affiliation in Epigraphic Sources," *HTR* 84 (1991): 141–62. Three of the persons listed in the Aphrodisias inscription are designated προσήλυτος (abbreviated differently in each case: A.13, 17, 22). On the evidence for proselytes more generally, see Donaldson, *Judaism*, 483–92.

67. On Philo's view of proselytes, see Will and Orrieux, *"Proselytisme Juif"?*, 81–99; Bird, *Crossing*, 106–7.

68. See, e.g., Thiessen, *Contesting Conversion*, 87, 107–108.

69. See the discussion in Donaldson, *Judaism*, 292–94. Cf. also Dio Cassius, *Hist. rom.* 66.5.4, on some of the Roman soliders who "went over" (μετέστησαν) to the Jewish side during the siege of Jerusalem (*GLAJJ*, §430).

who attack them (Esth 8:7–11), "many of the gentiles [πολλοὶ τῶν ἐθνῶν] were circumcised and judaized [περιετέμοντο καὶ ἰουδάϊζον]." Their action is, after all, described as being done "for fear of the Jews" (διὰ τὸν φόβον τῶν Ἰουδαίων).[70] That the book of Esther both presumes and positively accepts the possibility of such conversions seems clear, however, not least from the declaration that the feast of Purim will be celebrated by the people, their offspring, and "those who have joined themselves to them" (τοῖς προστεθειμένοις ἐπ᾽ αὐτῶν) (Esth 9:27).[71]

Another such mass joining is that of the Idumeans during the expansion of the Jewish kingdom under the Hasmonean ruler John Hyrcanus (see Josephus, *A.J.* 13.254–58; Strabo, *Geogr.* 16.2.34).[72] This joining entailed circumcision, observing Jewish law, and "making their manner of life conform in all other respects to that of the Jews" (*A.J.* 13.257–58 [Feldman, LCL]); the same requirements are noted in regard to the Itureans in a similar situation (see *A.J.* 13.318–19). Josephus's account may imply that this adoption by the Idumeans of the Jewish way of life was more or less forced, as some scholars have suggested, but Strabo's account does not, and others have argued that this was a willing acceptance of Judaism.[73] Whether this joining was voluntary or forced, it seems more to do with political alliance than what we might think of as religious conversion—though this once again serves to highlight the fact that such contemporary distinctions, not least concerning "religion," are often inadequate and inappropriate in the ancient context.[74] In any case, as Donaldson notes, "Josephus's language is strikingly categorical and unqualified": "from that time on they continued to be Jews" (ὥστε εἶναι τὸ λοιπὸν Ἰουδαίους) (*A.J.* 13.258).[75]

70. See Cohen, *Beginnings*, 181–82, though Cohen sees this fear-driven conversion as a pretence.

71. See Donaldson, *Judaism*, 32, though Donaldson perhaps downplays the motivation of fear in Esth 8:17 and sees a primarily positive attraction at work in such gentile proselytism (32–33).

72. Both texts are discussed by Donaldson, *Judaism*, 322–24, 374–76.

73. For this latter argument, see esp. Kasher, *Jews, Idumaeans, and Ancient Arabs*, 56–57; Kasher is followed by Richardson, *Herod*, 55. For an overview of the opinions, see Donaldson, *Judaism*, 322–23.

74. See the discussion in Smith, "Gentiles in Judaism."

75. This stands in some contrast to Josephus's reference to Herod, an Idumean, as ἡμιουδαῖος (*A.J.* 14.403). But that context is one in which Antigonus Mattathias, the Hasmonean ruler, is arguing before the Romans (besieging Judea with Herod, who has been designated king by the Romans) that Herod cannot rightly be king, as he is not ἐκ τοῦ γένους and is only a "half-Jew." As Benedikt Eckhardt argues in "Hasmoneans and Herodians," this

Other sources, both Jewish and non-Jewish, provide insight into the kinds of process through which someone might become a full convert, or proselyte. Among non-Jewish sources, probably the most famous example is found in the satires of Juvenal (*Sat.* 14.96–106 [Ramsey, LCL]).[76] Juvenal depicts how certain people, who seem to have learned or inherited certain Jewish ways and customs from their father—notably, keeping Sabbath and abstaining from pork—themselves "in time . . . take to circumcision" and "learn and practice and revere the Jewish law." What we have here, admittedly in a satirical form, is an indication that, through the generations, there might be a move from attachment to Judaism as a Godfearer or sympathizer—which is what the unnamed father appears to be—to full participation as a proselyte, signified here by circumcision. For Juvenal, this is a case where the father serves as a bad example and his sons go even further in this regrettable and deviant direction.

Another example, though a somewhat more complicated and difficult one, is found in Epictetus (*Diatr.* 2.9.19–22) and may also illustrate awareness of a distinction between some involvement with Judaism and full conversion to it. Here, in A. A. Long's words, "Epictetus chides his students *and himself* with merely acting the part of philosophers, drawing a fascinating comparison with vacillating or ambiguous Jews."[77] In drawing this illustrative comparison, Epictetus poses the question: "Why do you act the Jew, when you are a Greek?" (τὶ ὑποκρίνῃ Ἰουδαῖον ὢν Ἕλλην). He refers to the way in which people are called (πῶς ἕκαστος λέγεται) "Jew" (Ἰουδαῖος), "Syrian" (Σύρος), or "Egyptian" (Αἰγύπτος), then speaks of those who are seen to "play at both" (ἐπαμφοτερίζοντα). Such a person "is not a Jew, but is only acting the part" (οὐκ ἔστιν Ἰουδαῖος, ἀλλ᾽ ὑποκρίνεται). What is required is a proper commitment: "When he adopts the attitude of the man who has been baptized [βεβαμμένου] and has made his choice, then indeed he is and

---

is a very particular context in which Antigonus is contesting Herod's right to be king on the basis of an ancestral ideology that has not been the position of the Hasmonean dynasty (to which Herod is, in the Romans' eyes, related). It does not therefore tell us much about the position or status of Idumeans in general, nor about the possibility to affiliate with or "convert" to Judaism and then be regarded as a *Ioudaios*. What it does show, unsurprisingly, is that arguments about identity, genealogy, and ethnicity could be differently deployed depending on what was at stake.

76. For the text and commentary, see *GLAJJ*, §301; see also the discussion in Levinskaya, *Diaspora Setting*, 118–19; Donaldson, *Judaism*, 406–9.

77. A. A. Long, *Epictetus: A Stoic and Socratic Guide to Life* (Oxford: Clarendon, 2002), 110, italics original.

is called a Jew [τότε καὶ ἔστι τῷ ὄντι καὶ καλεῖται Ἰουδαῖος]."[78] Epictetus's reference to baptism or immersion here is puzzling and has been taken by some to suggest that the practice of immersion as part of an entrance ritual for proselytes is evidenced here and also that circumcision was (therefore) not always a requirement for male proselytes.[79] Another possibility is that he confused Jews and Christians (or saw them as part of the same grouping).[80] The broader evidence seems to confirm that circumcision remained at this time the standard requirement for male proselytes while immersion as part of the ritual process of conversion did not become standard until some time later.[81] But the significance of Epictetus's depiction here, assuming it does concern Jews (as its explicit terminology indicates), is that it demonstrates a familiarity with the possibility of what he regards as a "half-way" involvement with Judaism, as well as full conversion, which results in someone becoming truly a *Ioudaios* (ἔστι τῷ ὄντι . . . Ἰουδαῖος).[82]

An important and much-discussed example from a Jewish author, crucial also for the discussion of Jewish missionary activity, is Josephus's description of "how Helena, queen of Adiabene, and her son Izates became converts to Judaism" (Josephus, *A.J.* 20.17 [Feldman, LCL]; the story is recounted in 20.17–96).[83] As noted above, Josephus does not use the terminology for "proselytes" directly. The phrase translated above runs: εἰς τὰ Ἰουδαίων ἔθη τὸν βίον μετέβαλον; literally, "turned their life to the customs of the Jews" (cf. 20.35).

A Jewish merchant named Ananias "visited the king's wives and taught them to worship God [τὸν θεὸν σέβειν] after the manner of the Jewish tradition

78. Text and ET (slightly altered) from Oldfather, LCL; also see *GLAJJ*, §254. See the discussion in Donaldson, *Judaism*, 388–91.

79. See, e.g., McEleney, "Conversion," 328–33 (including Epictetus on 332). For counterarguments, see Nolland, "Uncircumcised Proselytes?," 179–82.

80. This is the view taken in Oldfather's translation in LCL (see xxvi and 272–73n1); the opposite case is made by Menahem Stern in *GLAJJ*, 1:543. Long, *Epictetus*, 110, notes the possibility but sees an allusion to Christians as "far from certain."

81. See the careful discussion in Chesnutt, *Death to Life*, 153–84. Chesnutt thereby shows that the "conversion" of Aseneth, which does not mention any ritual immersion, does not depart from the expected patterns of conversion in the period. See also p. 115 with n. 86 above.

82. Cf. Levinskaya, *Diaspora Setting*, 119.

83. For recent discussion, see Barclay, "Ἰουδαῖος," 50–52; Donaldson, *Judaism*, 334–38; Mason, "Jews, Judaeans, Judaizing, Judaism," 506–8; Mark D. Nanos, "The Question of Conceptualization: Qualifying Paul's Position on Circumcision in Dialogue with Josephus's Advisors to King Izates," in Nanos and Zetterholm, *Paul within Judaism*, 110–20.

[ὡς 'Ιουδαίοις πάτριον ἦν]" (*A.J.* 20.34). King Izates is "similarly won over." Meanwhile, his mother Helena had also "been instructed by another Jew and had been brought over to their laws" (20.35). Izates, learning of his mother's disposition toward Judaism, "was zealous [ἔσπευσε] to convert [μεταθέσθαι] to it himself"—his being "won over" does not yet constitute this full step, evidently—but considers that he would not be "genuinely a Jew [βεβαίως 'Ιουδαῖος] unless he was circumcised [εἰ μὴ περιτέμοιτο]" (20.38). Both his mother and Ananias, however, try to dissuade him from this step (20.39–42): "if his subjects should discover that he was devoted to rites that were strange and foreign to themselves, it would produce much disaffection and they would not tolerate the rule of a Jew over them" (20.39; cf. 47). Ananias insists that Izates "could worship God [τὸ θεῖον σέβειν] even without being circumcised [χωρὶς τῆς περιτομῆς]" (20.41). However, another Jew, Eleazar, who appears on the scene and is "extremely strict when it came to the ancestral laws," urges the king to proceed with circumcision, and so he does (20.44–46).

A number of things are striking about this account, besides its indications of the appeal and attractiveness of Judaism and indeed of the possibility of going over—"converting"—to it (a possibility nowhere queried in the narrative). One thing that is clear, as John Barclay has noted, is that

> for Izates to become a 'Ιουδαῖος is not a private or (in our terms) a merely "religious" decision: it identifies him fully with a "foreign" people, and therefore renders questionable his fitness to rule over the people of Adiabene. . . .
>
> This is about abandoning the customs, traditions, and practices of one people and adopting those of another, "foreign" nation. It makes little sense to describe this change as "religious" *as opposed to* "ethnic." . . . The change that Izates here undergoes concerns a package of social, cultural, and national traditions, which includes a special way of worshipping God (and of thinking about God), but only as part of a holistic shift in ethnic identity.[84]

Thus, as Mason has also stressed, "conversion" is an inadequate and problematic term to describe something that entailed what was regarded as a going over from one people's way of life (including its cultic and "religious" dimensions) to that of another—in effect leaving one people and joining another (see ch. 5 above).[85] As such, it is also an understandable focus for

---

84. Barclay, "'Ιουδαῖος," 51, italics original.

85. Mason, "Jews, Judaeans, Judaizing, Judaism," 505–10. See also Fredriksen, "Mandatory Retirement."

criticism, as is expressed in the risks to Izates highlighted by his mother and by Ananias. Philo's extended descriptions of the process through which "incomers" go is likewise rich in its depiction of a process of ethnic and religious reidentification: "Incomers" should be fully and warmly welcomed because they have abandoned "their kinsfolk by blood [γενεὰν μὲν τὴν ἀφ᾽ αἵματος], their country, their customs and the temples and images of their gods" and "taken the journey to a better home" (*Virt.* 102 [Colson, LCL]; cf. *Spec.* 1.52).

Another feature of interest is the role of circumcision in this process. For some, Josephus's account indicates that at least some Jews—represented here by Ananias—could reckon as fully a Jew a proselyte who had not been circumcised.[86] However, it seems rather that it is precisely the act of circumcision that would identify the king as having fully joined the Jewish people (cf. §5.3.1 above); hence Ananias's warning of reprisals if he should do so, and his insistence that in these (particular) circumstances, Izates can remain a "worshipper of God" (τὸ θεῖον σέβειν) (whether or not any specific sense of category is implied by this phrase) and will be pardoned by God for any failure to take the next step (*A.J.* 20.41–42). As Donaldson remarks, "The whole interchange rests on the assumption that if Izates were to be circumcised his subjects would consider him a Jew and would react accordingly, but if he did not take this step they would continue to view him as a Gentile."[87]

A final point of significance concerns the identity and aims of Ananias and Eleazar (and the unnamed Jew from whom Helena learned the ways of Judaism): Should they be seen as Jewish "missionaries," traveling with the aim of converting others to their way of life? There is little basis in Josephus's account for such a conclusion, as a number of recent scholars have rightly insisted,[88] though there may be some "element of initiative" in their activity.[89] Ananias is a "merchant" (ἔμπορος) (*A.J.* 20.34), and the text speaks of him (and the unnamed Jew who instructs Helena) as "teaching" (ἐδίδασκεν) these people Jewish ways. It is hard to be sure how far the initiative came from these Jews or from the members of the royal house of Adiabene, and all we can confidently glean from the narrative is that some Jews were at least willing and probably keen to instruct those who inquired about their way of life.[90] Eleazar's engagement begins with one who has already been

---

86. For references and discussion, see p. 158 n. 77.

87. Donaldson, *Judaism*, 336.

88. See, e.g., Bird, *Crossing*, 97–99; Goodman, *Mission and Conversion*, 84; McKnight, *Light*, 56.

89. Donaldson, *Judaism*, 337.

90. Cf. Wander, *Gottesfürchtige*, 224.

"won over" (20.35) to Judaism and has already wanted to be circumcised, only to be dissuaded; his role is to insist that full participation in this way of life is only possible (for a man) if he accepts the mark of circumcision. We might see Eleazar, then, as someone keen to encourage Godfearers and sympathizers to take the step toward fully belonging, though even this may go beyond what is reported here.[91]

Other texts, much briefer and more allusive in their depictions and written by non-Jews, have also been taken to suggest active mission on the part of Jews, specifically in Rome in the first two centuries BCE. One of these references, from Valerius Maximus, is known only from later epitomies and explains an expulsion of Jews from Rome on the basis that "they attempted to transmit their sacred rites to the Romans" (*Iudaeos . . . qui Romanis tradere sacra sua conati erant*).[92] Such a brief comment on action against Jews in Rome can scarcely form a basis for determining whether Jews were actively seeking to persuade others to join them or whether others were attracted to do so—or whether the sanction was based rather on the erection of altars to this new (to Rome) cult in public places.[93] Another such reference, from Horace's satires, has often been taken to indicate proselytizing activity on the part of Jews in Rome.[94] Having sought to make the case for his writing satire, Horace concludes by humorously "threatening" his readers that if they do not accept his arguments, a "mighty company of poets [*multa poetarum . . . manus*] will rally round to give me assistance . . . and, like the Jews, *cogemus in hanc concedere turbam*" (*Sat.* 1.4.141–43).[95] The interpretation of Horace's

91. Cf. McKnight, *Light*, 107.

92. For the text, translation, and commentary, see *GLAJJ*, §147.

93. On the complications of this text and its interpretation, see the comments of Goodman, *Mission and Conversion*, 82–83. McKnight, *Light*, 73, is perhaps overly confident in seeing in this text evidence that "speaks clearly of Jewish attempts to proselytize at some level"; even so, McKnight sees Rome as an exception in this regard (73–74).

94. Stern, in *GLAJJ*, 1:323, comments that the text "implies strong Jewish missionary activity in Rome." The same point is asserted by David Rokéah, "Ancient Jewish Proselytism in Theory and in Practice," *TZ* 52 (1996): 222. McKnight, *Light*, 73–74, accepts that such evidence points to Jewish missionary activity in Rome but sees this as an exception to the general picture. Others dispute that this is the implication, seeing only evidence of the attractions of Judaism and the antagonism caused by that attraction; e.g., Will and Orrieux, *"Proselytisme Juif"?*, 101–15; Bird, *Crossing*, 127–32.

95. ET from Niall Rudd, *Horace: Satires and Epistles; Persius: Satires* (London: Penguin, 1987), 60; Latin text from LCL. See also *GLAJJ*, §127; Donaldson, *Judaism*, 367–69. I am very grateful to John Barclay for helpful remarks on a draft of my comments on this passage.

language here, and particularly the last phrase I have left untranslated, is subject to considerable complexity and debate. It is generally translated as conveying the idea of compelling people to join the group, whether of Jews or poets: "We shall make you fall in with our happy band" (Rudd); "We shall compel you to make one of our throng" (Fairclough, LCL). But John Nolland makes a persuasive case that what Horace has in view in his comparison with what the Jews do is not "proselytizing" mission nor any kind of persuasion to "join" but rather the informal "political" activities through which the Jewish community in Rome sought to exert its influence and gain protection and permission for its way of life.[96] The sense, and the point of the comparison in its context, is that just as the Jewish community (according to Horace) pressures others to "accept," "allow," or "go along with" (*concedere*) its activity, so Horace seeks not that others "join" the band of poets but rather that they accept their activity, including his writing of satire. In this case, "it should not be taken as providing evidence for Jewish proselytizing activity."[97]

It is in this context that we should consider the single New Testament text that apparently refers to a zealous and outgoing Jewish proselytizing mission: Matt 23:15. It is indeed this text that has provided one of the major foundations for the view that first-century Judaism was an energetically missionary religion (see above).[98] Since this text is so singular in this regard and so clearly part of a viciously polemical passage, we should be very wary of taking it at face value and building a view of Judaism's proselytizing activity upon it.[99] However, for even sharp polemic to have force, it must reflect some connection with recognizable practices on the ground. One attempt to interpret it in the context of a view of Judaism as non-missionary is that of

96. John Nolland, "Proselytism or Politics in Horace Satires I, 4, 138–143?," *VC* 33 (1979): 347–55; Nolland is followed, e.g., by McKnight, *Light*, 64. Nolland (353) cites Cicero, *Flac.* 66–67, as an instance of this kind of collective Jewish political activity. See also Barclay, *Jews*, 295–96; Goodman, *Mission and Conversion*, 74.

97. Donaldson, *Judaism*, 369, following Nolland, "Proselytism or Politics." Cf. Barclay, *Jews*, 296: "The Jews are noticed as a social body able to pressurize others, with perhaps religious, but also social (and political?) consequences."

98. Indeed, on this text, Will and Orrieux, *"Proselytisme Juif"?*, 115, comment: "C'est là le seul texte . . . qui fasse une allusion dénuée d'ambiguïté à une activité missionnaire juive." Goodman, *Mission and Conversion*, 74, remarks that it often serves as *the* proof-text" for a Jewish mission to win converts. See also Bird, *Crossing*, 66–70; McKnight, *Light*, 106–8.

99. As Riesner, "Jewish Mission?," 234, remarks, the "riddle" noted by Jeremias (quoted above, p. 253 with n. 18)—"why this harsh saying about converts should be the only utterance of Jesus which we possess concerning the Jewish mission"—"is easily resolved" once the assumption of an "unparalleled" level of Jewish missionary activity is abandoned.

Martin Goodman, who argues that it refers instead to the practice of some Pharisaic Jews to "convert" other Jews to their particular form of Judaism.[100] The main difficulty with this view is that the term προσήλυτος is in the first-century context so clearly and uniformly associated with gentile converts to Judaism.[101] Matt 23:15 probably makes best sense, then, in comparison with a figure like Eleazar (described as "extremely strict when it came to the ancestral laws," *A.J.* 20.43): some Pharisaic Jews "were perceived as actively encouraging sympathizers to become full converts."[102] In other words, the most likely referent is those who had traveled beyond Judea and Galilee for other reasons (here Matthew's polemic recasts their reasons for travel) and, like Eleazar, encountered those already won over to Judaism but without having taken the step of full conversion and circumcision.

More generally, the relevant evidence—surveyed in detail in a number of recent works (see n. 20 above)—casts serious doubt on there having been any prominent ethos of Jewish missionizing. What does seem clear is that there were many outsiders who found Judaism appealing and attractive and that Jews were often keen to welcome and instruct such inquirers, to whatever degree they came to participate in Jewish customs and way of life.[103] As Levinskaya remarks, "No one working in the field of first-century Judaism would dream of denying the existence of Jewish proselytes at this time." However, she adds, "The sources from the first century do not support the view that there was large scale Jewish missionary activity."[104] Indeed, the etymology of the word προσήλυτος, as well as the wider range of terms used by Philo and Josephus, are consistent with such a scenario: the general picture is of people "coming in" (προσέρχομαι, κτλ.). As Riesner puts it, summarizing Aalen's work, Judaism exerted a form of "passive attraction" or centripetal force (so Aalen) which drew people in; but Jews did not—with a few

100. See Goodman, *Mission and Conversion,* 69–74; further supported by Levinskaya, *Diaspora Setting,* 36–46.

101. So, e.g., Carleton Paget, "Missionary Efforts," 41; Donaldson, *Judaism,* 414. Levinskaya's efforts (*Diaspora Setting,* 40–46) to strengthen Goodman's conclusion by pointing to later Christian examples (second century onward) that use the term to denote Christian converts or initiates more generally do not provide direct evidence for the particular case (Jew to Pharisee) argued by Goodman.

102. Donaldson, *Judaism,* 415. Cf. also McKnight, *Light,* 107.

103. Cf. Donaldson, *Judaism,* 492: "On the one hand, there is little evidence of an active mission designed to create interest where it did not already exist; on the other, many Jews were eager to instruct and encourage those who were attracted to Judaism and who took the initiative to seek them out" (see also 512).

104. Levinskaya, *Diaspora Setting,* 24, 49.

possible exceptions—"go out" to seek to win converts.[105] Josephus conveys precisely this impression when he writes, "To all who desire to come and live under the same laws with us, he [our legislator, Moses] gives a gracious welcome" (*C. Ap.* 2.210).[106]

A final issue regarding proselytes also deserves at least brief consideration: Were they now considered Jews ('Ιουδαῖοι)? Although most of the evidence, some already mentioned above, points toward a positive answer to this question, it is important to note some diversity on this point. As we have already noted in connection with the topic of marriage (§4.3), some Jewish texts—specifically those, such as Jubilees, that represent the kind of "holy seed" ideology rooted in Ezra-Nehemiah—seem to reject the idea that joining the people is possible, however impossible such exclusive purity is in practice.[107] At Qumran, for example, while some texts speak of the integration of the רג (proselyte? resident alien?) into the community—after priests, Levites, and the children of Israel (e.g. CD 14.3–6)—others suggest their exclusion (e.g., 4Q174 1.4), and it is debated whether the texts refer to proselytes in the sense of gentile converts to Judaism or, rather, to resident aliens in the land of Israel—and whether the community's view of (gentile) proselytes was purely theoretical, there being no such persons actually among them.[108] Philo, generally positive about the place of proselytes and the welcome to be shown to them, expresses a more cautious approach in the specific case of Egyptian proselytes on the basis of their history of maltreating the Israelites: Egyptians who wish to join the Jewish community should not be rejected, but only at the third generation do they fully share the rights of the "native born" (*Virt.* 106–8, drawing on Deut 23:7–8).[109] Elsewhere,

---

105. Riesner, "Jewish Mission?," 216; see his overall conclusions on 249–50. See also Donaldson, *Judaism*, 512.

106. As Barclay, *Against Apion*, 291n846, puts it, commenting on the theme of welcome here, "Judean communities rarely if ever engaged in active proselytization. . . . But 'friendly welcome' (active support) for those who wished to become proselytes may be presupposed."

107. For evidence concerning Jews who did not accept the possibility of valid gentile "conversions," see Thiessen, *Contesting Conversion*, in which the example of Jubilees is central. The ideology of racial purity is impossible to sustain, just as it is in other contexts, even on the texts' own terms: Ezra's exhortation to expel the "foreign wives" does not include the expulsion of the children of "mixed marriages," who presumably remained within the community (see, e.g., Ezra 10:11, 18–19; p. 125 above).

108. See Donaldson, *Judaism*, 195–215; see also the brief remarks of McKnight, *Light*, 38. Texts from García Martínez and Tigchelaar, *Dead Sea Scrolls: Study Edition*, 1:352–53, 572–73.

109. See McKnight, *Light*, 40. See also Philo, *Mos.* 1.147, where, narrating the Exodus

however, there is explicit evidence that proselytes were indeed regarded as Jews and designated as such. We have already seen some such indications in the writings of Josephus (*A.J.* 13.258; 20.38) and Epictetus (*Diatr.* 2.9.19–22). Dio Cassius also reports that the name *Ioudaioi* has been given not only to the people from the country of Judea but also to "the other people [τοὺς ἄλλους ἀνθρώπους], although of different ethnicities [καίπερ ἀλλοεθνεῖς ὄντες], who follow their laws [ὅσοι τὰ νόμιμα αὐτῶν . . . ζηλοῦσι]" (*Hist. Rom.* 37.16.5–17.1).[110] Indeed, Ross Kraemer cautiously suggests that some of the inscriptions that denote an individual as *Ioudaios/Ioudaia* may use the term specifically to indicate someone who has taken on this identity as a proselyte.[111]

The identification of incomers or proselytes as *Ioudaioi* does not mean that they cannot also be distinguished from (other) *Ioudaioi* in contexts in which it is relevant to differentiate those "born" from those "joining." Identity-language can be—and is—used in multiple ways, even at the same time:[112] Paul can variously, according to context, describe himself as a "Jew by birth" (Gal 2:15), as becoming occasionally "like a Jew" (1 Cor 9:20), and as someone who now counts such prior identifiers as "garbage" (Phil 3:7–8). His gentile converts can be *former* gentiles (1 Cor 12:2), or they can be currently so, when a distinction between Jewish and gentile believers is pertinent (Rom 11:13). Philo can distinguish members of the ἔθνος from those who are "incomers" (τοὺς ἐπηλύτας) precisely when urging the former to love and welcome the latter not only as "kinsfolk" (συγγενεῖς) but as their very selves (*Virt.* 103). But that proselytes entered fully into the Jewish way of life, were widely accepted as so doing, and were thus identified as Jewish seems to be evident in our sources.

8.1.5 Leaving the People: Defectors and Apostates

The counterpart to "converting" or coming into the Jewish way of life is, of course, abandoning it, an action that may be described as ἀποστασία (1 Macc

---

from Egypt, Philo distinguishes between the departing Israelites and those of mixed Hebrew and Egyptian parentage who had also come over to the Israelite people.

110. Text from LCL; my trans. This point is noted by Rokéah, "Ancient Jewish Proselytism," 207. See also *GLAJJ*, §406.

111. Kraemer, "Meaning of the Term 'Jew.'"

112. See Garroway, *Paul's Gentile-Jews*, 1–43, esp. 6–7, on multiple, hybrid, and negotiated identities and associated terminology.

2:15). This phenomenon, partly due to the relative paucity of evidence, has been rather less studied than sympathizing and proselytizing.[113] Moreover, defining apostasy and who should count as an apostate or defector is, as Stephen Wilson notes, a difficult issue, complicated by the fact that such judgments represent subjective and variable perspectives on the part of both the individuals involved and their wider communities—though this is also true of the wider phenomena of ethnic and religious identities.[114] As John Barclay stresses, identifying "apostates" is an act of labeling in which there is precisely disagreement and contention over what does or does not count as deviant.[115] Jews who went over to Greek ways are condemned as abandoning their ancestral traditions by the authors of 1 and 2 Maccabees, but they may not themselves have considered this level of assimilation an abandonment of their Jewish identity.[116] Moreover, once again, this is an area in which a distinction between "religion" and "ethnicity" cannot be clearly sustained, despite the fact that the language of "apostasy," like that of "conversion," implies (in modern discourse) the realm of religion rather than that of ethnic identity.

We have seen in an earlier chapter (§5.1.1) how following a certain (ancestral) "way of life" was constitutive of Jewish identity; as we have seen above, sympathizers and proselytes can similarly be described as turning to, or adopting, this way of life. This focus illustrates well why "religion" and "ethnicity" cannot in this case be separated. It is therefore no surprise that those who are seen to abandon their identity as Jews are described in comparable, albeit contrasting, terms. Antiochus's appeal for the unifying of "all the peoples" (πάντα τὰ ἔθνη) is said to require that they "abandon their particular customs [νόμιμα]"; Jews who did this are said to have sacrificed to idols and profaned the Sabbath (1 Macc 1:41–43; cf. Josephus, A.J. 12.240). Josephus can similarly describe the offspring of Alexander as those who

---

113. For a survey of the relevant evidence, both literary and epigraphic, see esp. Stephen G. Wilson, *Leaving the Fold: Apostates and Defectors in Antiquity* (Minneapolis: Fortress, 2004), 23–65.

114. Wilson, *Leaving*, 65.

115. See esp. John M. G. Barclay, "Deviance and Apostasy: Some Applications of Deviance Theory to First-Century Judaism and Christianity," in Esler, *Modelling*, 114–27; see also Barclay, "Who Was Considered an Apostate in the Jewish Diaspora?," in *Tolerance and Intolerance in Early Judaism and Christianity*, ed. Graham N. Stanton and Guy G. Stroumsa (Cambridge: Cambridge University Press, 1998), 80–98; and Barclay, "Paul among Diaspora Jews: Anomaly or Apostate?," *JSNT* 60 (1995): 89–120.

116. Cf. Wilson, *Leaving*, 25.

"abandoned from birth the observance of the ways of the Jewish land [τῶν Ἰουδαίοις ἐπιχωρίων] and went over [μετατάξαμενοι] to the Greek tradition [πρὸς τὰ Ἕλλησι πάτρια]" (*A.J.* 18.141 [Feldman LCL; slightly amended]). Prominent among these offspring of Alexander is his son, Tiberius Julius Alexander (nephew of Philo), whom Josephus describes as having failed "to continue [οὐκ ἐνέμεινεν] in his ancestral customs [τοῖς πατρίοις . . . ἔθεσιν]" (*A.J.* 20.100).[117]

In 3 Maccabees, a certain Dositheos, who acts to save the life of the Egyptian king Ptolemy Philopator, is described in similar terms: "one Dositheos, called the son of Drimylus, who was a Judean by race [τὸ γένος Ἰουδαῖος] but later [ὕστερον] changed his customs [μεταβαλὼν τὰ νόμιμα] and became estranged from his ancestral ways [τῶν πατρίων δογμάτων ἀπηλλοτριωμένος]" (3 Macc 1:3 [NETS; slightly amended]). As Louis Feldman notes, the name Dositheos likely confirms his Jewish origins, and extant papyri indicate his "apostate" status insofar as they record him "in the year 222 B.C.E. as the eponymous priest of Alexander and the deified Ptolemies, the highest priesthood in Hellenistic Egypt."[118]

The prominence of what we would term "religious" commitments in constituting "Jewish" identity is also illustrated, in relation to the theme of apostasy, by Philo's remarks on the danger posed by those who might encourage the people to join in the worship of other gods, attend their temples, and sacrifice to them (*Spec.* 3.315–17). In such cases, the ties of natural kinship count for little: such people become enemies worthy of death (3.316).[119]

> For we should have one tie of affinity [μία οἰκειότης], one accepted sign of goodwill [φιλίας ἓν σύμβολον], namely the willingness to serve God

117. For discussion of Tiberius Julius Alexander, see Barclay, "Deviance and Apostasy," 119–21; Wilson, *Leaving*, 29–33.

118. Feldman, *Jew and Gentile*, 82. See 79–83 for Feldman's general treatment of apostasy, which he seems overly to limit, concluding that "the net effect of the assimilation of the Greek language and culture by the Jews was not defection from Judaism but rather, on the contrary, the creation of a common bond of communication with Gentiles, through which at least some non-Jews were won over to Judaism" (83).

119. Whether Philo here not only indicates a contemporary problem with defectors but also supports violent vigilante action against them, as argued by Torrey Seland, *Establishment Violence in Philo and Luke: A Study of Non-Conformity to the Torah and Jewish Vigilante Reactions*, BibInt 15 (Leiden: Brill, 1995), is open to discussion. See the comments of Wilson, *Leaving*, 41–43, and Gregory E. Sterling, review of *Establishment Violence in Philo and Luke: A Study of Non-Conformity to the Torah and Jewish Vigilante Reactions*, by Torrey Seland, *JBL* 116 (1997): 368–70.

[ἡ πρὸς θεὸν ἀρέσκεια] and that our every word and deed promotes the cause of piety [εὐσεβείας]. But as for these kinships [συγγένειαι], as we call them, which have come down from our ancestors and are based on blood-relationship, or those derived from intermarriage or other similar causes, let them all be cast aside if they do not seek earnestly the same goal, namely, the honour of God [τὴν τοῦ θεοῦ τιμήν], which is the indissoluble bond of all the affection which makes us one [πάσης ἑνωτικῆς εὐνοίας]. (Philo, *Spec.* 3.316–17 [ET Colson, LCL])

Indeed, elsewhere Philo contrasts the virtuous devotion of "incomers" (ἐπηλύται) with the immorality of "those who rebel against the holy laws" (τοὺς τῶν ἱερῶν ἀποστάντας) (*Virt.* 182); the latter—whom Wilson describes as "Jews who drifted away from their community"—thus negate "the currency of their noble birth" (τὸ νόμισμα τῆς εὐγενείας) (*Praem.* 152).[120]

Philo's views are of course particular and cannot be taken as a generalizable Jewish perspective. Nonetheless, the "literary sources," only a small sample of which have been mentioned here, do, as Wilson remarks, "give us every reason to think that some Jews defected from their community, sometimes gradually and unobtrusively, sometimes suddenly in the face of a crisis, and sometimes violently."[121] Epigraphic evidence, notably (but not exclusively) the famous reference to "former Jews" (οἱ ποτὲ Ἰουδαῖοι) in a Hadrianic inscription from Smyrna, seems to support this picture.[122] Indeed, Gideon Bohak suggests that the ancient world was one "where the assimilation (or degeneration, depending on one's perspective) of immigrants into natives was virtually taken for granted."[123] Noting the decline and then disappearance of the ethnic marker *Ioudaios* in Egyptian papyri between 330 and 30 BCE, Bohak questions the assumption of Jewish "ethnic continuity" in Greco-Roman Egypt, arguing that the descendants of Jewish migrants to Egypt during the Hasmonean period "rarely were identified as 'Jews'—either because they migrated back to Judea or because they assimilated into their surrounding environment."[124] Whether those who assimilated, defected,

---

120. For discussion of these two texts, see Wilson, *Leaving*, 36–38 (quoted phrase from 36).

121. Wilson, *Leaving*, 52.

122. ISmyrna 697 = Smyrna 54 (see the Packard Humanities inscriptions database, https://epigraphy.packhum.org/text/254946?hs=1451–1472), on which see Wilson, *Leaving*, 53–56; see 52–65 for a broader overview of the epigraphic evidence.

123. Gideon Bohak, "Ethnic Continuity in the Jewish Diaspora in Antiquity," in *Jews in the Hellenistic and Roman Cities*, ed. John R. Bartlett (London: Routledge, 2002), 191.

124. Bohak, "Ethnic Continuity," 187; see appendix on 192.

or were seen as apostates continued to be regarded as *Ioudaioi* depends in part on perspective; apostasy is, as we have already noted, something that depends on who is making the judgment and on how an individual's view of themselves coheres with or differs from that expressed by others. Rabbinic halakha, for example, according to Lawrence Schiffman, may suggest that identity as a Jew is never lost.[125] But apart from the lateness (and obscurity) of this evidence, even if it is technically correct, it may have been sociologically irrelevant in the sense that, if Jewishness is visible only by association with the Jewish community (see §5.3.3), then just as those who joined came to be identified as *Ioudaioi*, so too those who left, who saw themselves as having left, and who assimilated fully to another way of life would, in practice (and in time), lose their identity as *Ioudaioi*.[126]

8.2 Early Christian Models of Mission

When it comes to the early Christian movement, its rapid spread and growth in numbers are generally attributed to an energetic missionary impulse. Stephen Neill, for example, affirms: "The Church of the first Christian generation was a genuinely missionary Church. . . . Every Christian was a witness. Where there were Christians, there would be a living, burning faith, and before long an expanding Christian community."[127] More recently, Howard Marshall comments: "It cannot be doubted that early Christianity was a missionary movement and that evangelism was practised. The church could not have spread and grown in the way that it did purely spontaneously without the Gospel being deliberately communicated to those who had not yet heard it or not yet responded positively to it."[128] Indeed, in contrast to the tendency of recent scholarship on Jewish missionizing to doubt the prevalence of such a proactive phenomenon, recent years have seen something of a growing interest in the missionary dimensions of earliest Christianity.[129]

---

125. Lawrence H. Schiffman, *Who Was a Jew? Rabbinic and Halakhic Perspectives on the Jewish-Christian Schism* (Hoboken, NJ: Ktav, 1985), 41–49.

126. Cf. the remarks of Wilson, *Leaving*, 131–33.

127. Stephen Neill, *A History of Christian Missions*, The Pelican History of the Church 6 (London: Hodder and Stoughton, 1964), 23–24.

128. Howard Marshall, "Who Were the Evangelists?," in Ådna and Kvalbein, *Mission*, 252.

129. E.g., Eckhard J. Schnabel, *Jesus and the Twelve*, vol. 1 of *Early Christian Mission* (Downers Grove: InterVarsity Press, 2004); Eckhard J. Schnabel, *Paul and the Early Church*,

Such historical studies are often explicitly motivated by a commitment to contemporary Christian mission.[130]

A range of New Testament texts points to a widespread conviction in the earliest Christian movement that the "good news" about Jesus was to be spread "to all nations" (Mark 13:10; Luke 24:47; Rev 14:6). The risen Jesus is presented as commissioning his disciples to this task (Matt 28:16–20; Acts 1:8). Yet there are also issues and questions to consider in assessing the nature and extent of this "missionary" activity.

First, paralleling the concern raised about drawing conclusions based on the extent of Jewish population growth in the period (see §8.1.1), we need to acknowledge the limited extent of our knowledge about the rate and extent of growth in Christian adherents across the first three centuries. Estimates are often given. For example, Eckhard Schnabel cites those of Bo Reicke: 40,000 Christians in 66 CE (ca. 0.07% of the total population of the empire), 320,000 in 100 CE, and 5 million in 300 CE (ca. 8.4% of the population). But, as Schnabel notes, "we have no statistical figures for the Christians in the Roman Empire," so these are only rough estimates and open to question.[131] We know from Paul's letters of Christian assemblies in specific places or provinces, including Rome, though the origins of Christianity's arrival there, clearly not one of Paul's achievements, remain unknown (cf. Rom 1:7–10; 15:20–24). And we have brief glimpses of, or later (possibly legendary) traditions about, other figures who were involved in the spread of the Christian message in its earliest years.[132] But even in the cases where we are best informed—concerning the assemblies to which Paul

---

vol. 2 of *Early Christian Mission* (Downers Grove: InterVarsity Press, 2004); Ådna and Kvalbein, *Mission*.

130. Note, e.g., the comments of Ådna and Kvalbein, *Mission*, 13: "This book is an expression of a hope that scholarly work with the Bible and with the origins of Christian mission may promote not only historical knowledge of the mission of the church, but also a personal commitment to the Great Commission from the Risen Lord"; see also Marshall, "Who Were the Evangelists?," 251; Schnabel, *Paul and the Early Church*, 1569–88; Edward L. Smither, *Mission in the Early Church: Themes and Reflections* (Cambridge: James Clarke, 2014).

131. Schnabel, *Jesus and the Twelve*, 4.

132. As well as the named associates in Paul's circles of activity, we know from Paul's letters something of the activities of Peter, James, and people associated with them (e.g. 1 Cor 9:5; Gal 2:7–12). Stories of the spread of Christianity by, e.g., Mark to Alexandria, Thomas to India, and Thaddeus to Edessa may be largely legendary. See Reidar Hvalvik, "In Word and Deed: The Expansion of the Church in the Pre-Constantinian Era," in Ådna and Kvalbein, *Mission*, 268–70.

wrote—we can offer only reasonable guesses as to the number of adherents. Jerome Murphy-O'Connor, for example, based on the names mentioned and estimates regarding size of households, suggests "between forty and fifty persons" for the church in Corinth.[133] And the possible rate of growth in the following century or so is largely a matter of speculative projection.[134] It is clear enough that the movement grew through "conversions"—sometimes, it seems, of individuals, sometimes of household groups[135]—though there is no standard term to denote such people.[136] There is little concrete evidence (and certainly no specific label) for "sympathizers" participating to some degree in the Christian communities, though there are enough hints to conclude that there may have been such people, as well as some who offered support or patronage.[137] Various kinds of "outsiders"—perhaps both sympathizers and nonbelievers—could be present at their meetings (1 Cor 14:23–24).[138] It is also evident from the early decades of the movement that

133. Jerome Murphy-O'Connor, *St. Paul's Corinth: Texts and Archaeology*, 3rd rev. and exp. ed. (Collegeville: Liturgical Press, 2002), 182.

134. See, e.g., the projections presented by Rodney Stark, *The Rise of Christianity: A Sociologist Reconsiders History* (Princeton: Princeton University Press, 1996).

135. Lukan references to the conversion of households may be somewhat schematized (see Acts 10:2; 11:14; 16:15, 31, 34; 18:8), but the Pauline letters give more incidental indications that households sometimes joined the Christian movement as a group (1 Cor 1:16; 16:15). The NT letters also indicate that individuals could convert in ways that left divisions in households between husbands and wives, or slaves and masters (1 Cor 7:12–16; 1 Pet 2:18–19; 3:1). It is striking that Philemon's slave, Onesimus, seems not to have converted at the same time as the head of the household but rather only on meeting Paul in prison (Phlm 2, 10). Richard S. Ascough, "The Thessalonian Christian Community as a Professional Voluntary Association," *JBL* 119 (2000): 311–28, has suggested that the Thessalonian congregation was formed through the group conversion of a voluntary association of (male) manual laborers, but this remains speculative.

136. Paul, for example, uses ἀπαρχή, "first-fruit," twice (Rom 16:5; 1 Cor 16:15); 1 Tim 3:6 uses νεόφυτος, "newly planted"; προσήλυτος is used of "converts" to Judaism (Matt 23:15; Acts 2:11; 6:5; 13:43) but not of converts to Christ.

137. One example of a sympathetic "sponsor" might be Jason (Acts 17:6–7). Nicodemus (John 3:1; 7:50; 19:39) has often been suggested to be some kind of supporter or crypto-disciple. Daniel R. Schwartz, "Non-Joining Sympathizers (Acts 5,13–14)," *Bib* 64 (1983): 550–55, finds evidence in Acts 5:13–14 for sympathizers who associated themselves to some degree with the Christian community.

138. The distinction drawn in 1 Cor 14 between ἰδιῶται and ἄπιστοι suggests that the former are not simply to be identified with the latter (*pace* Hans Conzelmann, *A Commentary on the First Epistle to the Corinthians*, Hermeneia [Philadelphia: Fortress, 1975], 243). Victor Paul Furnish, "Inside Looking Out: Some Pauline Views of the Unbelieving Public," in *Pauline Conversations in Context: Essays in Honor of Calvin J. Roetzel*, ed. J. C. Anderson,

members might, on occasion, be expelled (1 Cor 5:5) or leave the group, presenting the early church with one of its many dilemmas: whether to allow repentant apostates to rejoin.[139] Much of the historical detail concerning the spread of what became Christianity, however, remains lost to us.

Following on from this, and again paralleling a point often made in the discussion of Jewish missionary activity, the spread and growth of the Christian movement—whatever its rate and extent—does not in itself tell us the means by which converts were made. We may recall Riesner's definition, used in relation to the assessment of the Jewish evidence above: "A missionary religion intends to win converts, and this is accomplished actively by at least some of its members."[140] To what extent were converts to Christianity directly sought through proactive outreach and "evangelism," and to what extent were they attracted by the ethos and character of the movement (as seems often to have been the case with Judaism)? By whom was the task of articulating and promoting the Christian message mostly undertaken? I shall explore these issues in a few case studies—selective attempts to illustrate the nature of early Christian missionary activity.

8.2.1 *Matthew 28:18–20 and the Apostolic Commission*

The most iconic and important text expressing a missionary self-understanding within the early Christian movement is found at the conclusion of Matthew's Gospel, where the risen Jesus commissions the eleven disciples with the following words:

> All authority in heaven and on earth has been given to me. Go therefore and make disciples of all nations [μαθητεύσατε πάντα τὰ ἔθνη], baptizing

---

P. Sellew, and C. Setzer (Sheffield: Sheffield Academic Press, 2002), 122, suggests that the ἰδιῶται (cf. also 1 Cor 14:16) are those "on the margins of the community" (cf. BDAG, 468). Thiselton, *First Epistle*, 1114–15, 1127, suggests the meaning "uninitiated."

139. Hebrews gives a firmly negative answer to this question (Heb 6:4–6; 10:23–27), indicating at least that the risk of members leaving the group was already real. Discussion of such texts (including 1 Cor 5:5) has often been overly driven by theological convictions—Calvinist versus Arminian—about whether a "true" Christian can ever lose their salvation. On the history of interpretation of these passages in Hebrews, see B. J. Oropeza, "The Warning Passages in Hebrews: Revised Theologies and New Methods of Interpretation," *CurBR* 10 (2011): 81–100. Oropeza has also produced a three-volume study on apostasy in the NT communities: B. J. Oropeza, *Apostasy in the New Testament Communities*, 3 vols. (Eugene, OR: Cascade, 2011–2012).

140. Riesner, "Jewish Mission?," 223, italicized in the original.

them in the name of the Father and of the Son and of the Holy Spirit, and teaching them to obey everything that I have commanded you. And remember, I am with you always, to the end of the age. (Matt 28:18–20 NRSV)

Although comparable visions of the scope and task of Christian mission are expressed elsewhere (notably Luke 24:47; Acts 1:8; also Mark 16:15, perhaps derived from Matt 28),[141] Matt 28:18–20 is the most developed and emphatic apostolic commission, and, as such, an iconic text for the modern history of Christian missions.

The text may draw on earlier traditions, but in its present form, it seems most likely to be the composition of the evangelist, not least given its clear post-resurrection setting and proto-trinitarian baptismal formula—a development from the earlier wording which described baptism as done "in the name of the Lord Jesus" (cf. Acts 2:38; 10:48; Rom 6:3; Gal 3:27; see also §5.3.2).[142] The universal authority of the risen and exalted Jesus is, as Matthias Konradt comments, the basis for the universal commission.[143] One point of discussion is whether the phrase πάντα τὰ ἔθνη should be taken to include the Jewish people or whether Matthew's perspective is one that has already abandoned hope for the conversion of Israel—or does not see Israel as needing conversion— such that τὰ ἔθνη effectively refers to the gentiles. Given the universal perspective expressed in this passage, as well as the mission to Israel mandated in Matt 10:1–23, it would seem best to read the phrase inclusively: all are included within the scope of the apostles' task.[144] On this basis, some want to affirm the validity and necessity of contemporary

141. The closing twelve verses of Mark are widely seen as a later addition to the Gospel, derived at least in part from material in Matthew as well as the other Gospels and Acts. See, e.g., Morna D. Hooker, *The Gospel According to Saint Mark* (London: A. & C. Black, 1991), 388–94; Collins, *Mark*, 804–18.

142. See, e.g., Matthias Konradt, *Das Evangelium nach Matthäus*, NTD 1 (Göttingen: Vandenhoeck & Ruprecht, 2015), 459; Luz, *Matthew 21–28*, 616–17 ("this concluding section is largely Matthean"). For an attempt to discern early traditions in the passage, seen as "the *basic Jewish-Christian record of the apostolic mission to the world*," see Peter Stuhlmacher, "Matt 28:16–20 and the Course of Mission in the Apostolic and Postapostolic Age," in Ådna and Kvalbein, *Mission*, 17–43 (quotation from 30, italics original).

143. Konradt, *Matthäus*, 461: "Diese *universale* Vollmacht Jesu bildet die Voraussetzung für die universale Sendung" (italics original).

144. See Konradt, *Matthäus*, 462–63; Stuhlmacher, "Matt 28:16–20," 42; Luz, *Matthew 21–28*, 631, though Luz is cautious on this point, suggesting that "Matthew probably no longer has great hopes for it"—that is, "mission to Israel."

Christian mission to Jews[145]—a point of controversy and disagreement, not least given the lamentable history of Christian antisemitism.

One thing that is striking about the influence of Matt 28:18–20, as studies of its history of interpretation have shown, is that it does not serve as a prominent basis and motivation for ongoing Christian missionary activity until the modern period and the rise of Protestant missions in particular. As Reidar Hvalvik comments, texts like "Matt 28:18–20 are never quoted in the literature of the second and third centuries with the intention of encouraging missionary work."[146] Instead, when it is quoted in this period, it is as "a historical text," referring to the apparently completed work of the original apostles: "In the opinion of the early church, the Great Commission was given to the apostles, and they had fulfilled it."[147] As Ulrich Luz notes, it is only since the sixteenth century that this text—and the "Great Commission" of v. 19a in particular—has become "a decisive text for the mission of the church." More specifically, what Luz calls "the victory march" of this verse as the Great Commission begins only from the beginning of the nineteenth century, "especially in Protestantism."[148]

Two broader observations are significant, building on this finding. One is that appeals for evangelism and mission in the second and third centuries are hard to find.[149] Linked to this is the picture from the earliest times that mission was seen as the task of particular figures, predominantly the apostles—among whom Paul insists he belongs (1 Cor 9:1–2; 15:8–10)—and of others assigned a particular role, whether as teacher, bishop, or evangelist.[150] These observations stand in contrast, however, to the insistence of Neill, for example, that in the earliest church "every Christian was a witness," or Marshall's conclusion that "early congregations and individual believers did have an evangelistic function."[151] Since the Pauline evidence has been a crucial test case for such claims and provides our most extensive access to the

---

145. See, e.g., Stuhlmacher, "Matt 28:16–20," 42.

146. Hvalvik, "In Word and Deed," 277. See also Goodman, *Mission and Conversion*, 106–7.

147. Hvalvik, "In Word and Deed," 278. Hvalvik's conclusions are further reinforced in Oskar Skarsaune's study in the same volume: Oskar Skarsaune, "The Mission to the Jews—a Closed Chapter?," in Ådna and Kvalbein, *Mission*, 72–77. Cf. also Luz, *Matthew 21–28*, 626–28.

148. Luz, *Matthew 21–28*, 626.

149. See Hvalvik, "In Word and Deed," 275–80.

150. See Hvalvik, "In Word and Deed," 267–73.

151. Neill, *Christian Missions*, 24; Marshall, "Who Were the Evangelists?," 262.

earliest communities, we shall consider these issues through a brief look at the character of mission in the Pauline letters.

8.2.2 *Paul and the Earliest Communities*

Paul himself is explicit about his apostolic calling to take the "good news" to the nations (Rom 1:1–5; 15:15–24; 1 Cor 9:16–23; 15:9–10; Gal 1:15–16; Phil 1:12–18), and he clearly invested his time and energy in an itinerant ministry through which he pursued this vocation. A programmatic indication of his sense of his task is expressed in Rom 15:19, "that from Jerusalem and as far around as Illyricum I have fully proclaimed the good news of Christ [πεπληρωκέναι τὸ εὐαγγέλιον τοῦ Χριστοῦ]" (NRSV). Paul's conviction that he has "completed" (πεπληρωκέναι) his task across this geographical arc implies that he sees his work in terms of the strategic establishment of Christian communities in places where Christ has not previously been named (v. 20) rather than any kind of broader or more comprehensive outreach (cf. Rom 15:20–23). His plan, therefore, at the time of writing Romans, is to go on further, to Spain (Rom 15:24).[152]

Paul did not work alone but as part of a loosely connected team of collaborators and companions, some of whom are known to us by name (e.g., Aquila, Barnabas, Epaphroditus, Phoebe, Prisca, Silvanus, Timothy, Titus: see, e.g., Rom 16:1–3, 21; 1 Cor 4:17; 9:6; 2 Cor 1:1, 19; 2:13; 12:18; Phil 1:1; 2:25; 4:18; 1 Thess 1:1).[153] He also indicates that other apostles and their associates were involved in proclamation of the Christian message, at times with versions of that message in tension with Paul's own "gospel" (see, e.g., 1 Cor 9:5; 15:9–11; 2 Cor 11:1–15; Gal 2:1–9). There is no doubt, then, that Paul was one among a number of early Christian emissaries and traveling missionaries who saw it as their task to proclaim the message about Christ in the hope of winning converts.[154] Later references in the pseudo-Pauline

152. It seems unlikely that he ever made this journey, but for recent discussion of the possibility, see Armand Puig i Tàrrech et al., eds., *The Last Years of Paul: Essays from the Tarragona Conference, June 2013*, WUNT 352 (Tübingen: Mohr Siebeck, 2015).

153. See further Wolf-Henning Ollrog, *Paulus und seine Mitarbeiter: Untersuchungen zu Theorie und Praxis der paulinischen Mission*, WMANT 50 (Neukirchen-Vluyn: Neukirchener, 1979).

154. On the practical means by which Paul may have done this, working as an artisan, see Ronald F. Hock, *The Social Context of Paul's Ministry: Tentmaking and Apostleship* (Philadelphia: Fortress, 1980).

letters to certain figures as "evangelists" suggest a similar picture (Eph 4:11; 2 Tim 4:5; cf. Acts 21:8), even if such figures seem to fade from the picture after the second century.[155] In this sense, recalling Riesner's definition, the early Christian movement is clearly a "missionary religion"—notwithstanding issues concerning the definition and distinction of a "religion."

But given this, some features of the Pauline letters are striking. One is the complete absence of any direct exhortation to members of the early Christian communities to engage in evangelism or proselytism, to proclaim their message to those among whom they live in order to persuade others to join. This has led to some debate about whether Paul did or did not expect these "ordinary" Christians to engage in mission.[156] There are certain texts that might indicate that these community members did—and were positively expected to—engage in proclaiming their newfound faith.

In 1 Thess 1:8, in his opening thanksgiving for the Thessalonians' response to the message he proclaimed, Paul declares that "the word of the Lord sounded forth [ἐξήχηται] from you" and "your faith in God has gone forth [ἐξελήλυθεν] everywhere [ἐν παντὶ τόπῳ]" (ESV). It is clear enough that Paul sees the Thessalonians' faith in Christ as some kind of witness that has served to further promote the Christian message, the gospel ("the word of the Lord").[157] Whether this refers to missionary or evangelistic activity on their part depends in part on whether the two main parts of this (somewhat awkward) sentence are taken to be "connected but independent,"[158] with the first referring to missionary activity and the second to a wider reporting of their faith (so ESV), or as parallel and broadly equivalent declarations, with the second having a wider scope than the first (so NRSV).[159] If the latter, then the key point is that their *response* to Paul's message has become known,

---

155. See Hvalvik, "In Word and Deed," 266–73; see 268–69 specifically on "evangelists."

156. See e.g., John P. Dickson, *Mission-Commitment in Ancient Judaism and in the Pauline Communities*, WUNT 2.159 (Tübingen: Mohr Siebeck, 2003); Robert L. Plummer, *Paul's Understanding of the Church's Mission: Did the Apostle Paul Expect the Early Christian Communities to Evangelize?* (Carlisle: Paternoster, 2006); James P. Ware, *The Mission of the Church in Paul's Letter to the Philippians in the Context of Ancient Judaism*, NovTSup 120 (Leiden: Brill, 2005); Marshall, "Who Were the Evangelists?" All of these argue, though in diverse ways, that Paul does expect some kind of mission activity on the part of his converts. The contrary position was earlier argued by Paul Bowers, "Church and Mission in Paul," *JSNT* 44 (1991): 89–111.

157. For this gloss on "the word of the Lord," see Holtz, *Thessalonicher*, 51.

158. Marshall, "Who Were the Evangelists?," 259; cf. Earl J. Richard, *First and Second Thessalonians*, SP 11 (Collegeville: Liturgical Press, 1995), 70–73.

159. Cf. Holtz, *Thessalonicher*, 51–52.

sounding out as a witness to the gospel both within and beyond their own region.[160] This seems more plausible: even within the provinces of Macedonia and Achaia, and allowing for Pauline exaggeration, the spreading of a report or reputation from Thessaloniki seems more likely than their evangelistic activity as such. Moreover, what Paul reiterates in the following verses has nothing to do with witnessing or evangelizing but rather summarizes their response to his message (1:9–10).[161] And later in the letter, he urges them not to evangelistic activity, but, in a sense, to the opposite: "to live quietly [ἡσυχάζειν], and to mind your own affairs [πράσσειν τὰ ἴδια], and to work with your hands" (1 Thess 4:11, ESV).

A similar perspective concerning responsibility toward outsiders is suggested in 1 Cor 10:32–33, where, concluding his somewhat convoluted answer to a question about eating food that has been offered to idols, Paul urges the Corinthians to "give no offense [ἀπρόσκοποι . . . γίνεσθε] to Jews, or to Greeks, or to the church of God." Rather, they are, like Paul, to seek to please others in everything (πάντα πᾶσιν ἀρέσκω), seeking others' benefit, not their own (v. 33). Paul depicts this as an imitation of his own practice (1 Cor 11:1; cf. 9:19–23).

Another significant passage is Phil 2:14–16, in which Paul, after the famous Christ-hymn of 2:6–11, urges the Philippians to continue on the path to working out their salvation:

> Do all things without grumbling or questioning, that you may be blameless and innocent, children of God without blemish in the midst of a crooked and twisted generation, among whom you shine as lights [φωστῆρες] in the world, holding fast [ἐπέχοντες] to the word of life. (ESV)

Again, it is clear enough that the Philippians' life in Christ and their perseverance in their faith serves as some kind of witness in the world ("shining as lights"). But this seems primarily to be founded on the character of their conduct ("without grumbling or questioning"; showing humility, love, and internal harmony, 2:2–5) rather than their acting as missionaries or evangelists or proactively seeking converts.[162] They are urged to "hold on" (ἐπέχοντες) to the gospel, "the word of life" (cf. 1 Pet 1:23; 1 John 1:1) rather

---

160. See Bowers, "Church and Mission," 99.

161. Cf. Holtz, *Thessalonicher*, 52.

162. *Pace* Gordon D. Fee, *Paul's Letter to the Philippians*, NICNT (Grand Rapids: Eerdmans, 1995), 246–48.

than to proclaim or announce it.[163] Moreover, "light" may well serve as an image of witness in the sense of attraction rather than outreach as such, as Aalen discerned in the case of Jewish traditions—indicating, once again, that clear definitions of "missionary" activity are crucial to discerning the implications of particular texts.[164]

A final example is one of the rare places where Paul does actually mention explicitly the missionary impact that a Christian may have on an unbeliever: 1 Cor 7:12–16, where Paul advises Christians married to non-Christians not to seek or initiate a divorce. Paul explains this advice on the basis that the unbelieving partner is "made holy" (ἡγίασται) by (or in) the believing spouse and that the children of even such a "mixed" marriage are holy (ἅγια), an intriguing assertion we have already discussed (see §4.4). While he states that the Christian partner "is not bound" (δεδούλωται) if the unbeliever chooses to separate (7:15), he gives a final reason to maintain the marriage if possible: the Christian may "save" (σώσεις, active!) the non-Christian partner (7:16).[165] What Paul does not give here is any indication as to how this "saving" might take place, whether through the persuasive words of the Christian partner, their Christian pattern of conduct, or some combination of both.[166] The contagious holiness of the Christian spouse, in any case, does not (yet) seem enough to guarantee this outcome, though it is possible that Paul does see this as a basis for eventual salvation, if the unbeliever does not separate in the meantime. Whether this is conceivable or not, the passage indicates a "missionary motivation" for remaining in such a marriage, given both the desire and the potential for the unbelieving partner to be "saved."

It is indisputable, then, that we find in the letters of Paul evidence for what Riesner has defined as a "missionary religion" in the sense of an in-

---

163. Ware, *Mission of the Church*, 293–95, argues for the sense of "holding forth" (i.e., "offering") here; counterarguments are presented by Dickson, *Mission-Commitment*, 108–14.

164. Aalen, *Licht und Finsternis* (on which see §8.1.1 above). On the Jewish precedents and parallels for such an expression, see also Markus N. A. Bockmuehl, *The Epistle to the Philippians*, BNTC (London: A & C Black, 1998), 158.

165. Commentators have long discussed whether the questions in 1 Cor 7:16 imply a positive or a negative answer. It seems best, with Lightfoot, *Notes*, 227, to conclude that they are at least optimistic in outlook, expressing hope rather than doubt, "implying that there is a reasonable chance" of the unbeliever's salvation. See also Fee, *1 Corinthians*, 337–38; Schrage, *1 Kor 6,12–11,16*, 112. In favor of a more neutral or open interpretation, see Thiselton, *First Epistle*, 537–40.

166. Fee, *1 Corinthians*, 338: "Paul is referring to their 'evangelizing' or 'winning' them, whether by word or deed."

tention "to win converts . . . accomplished actively by at least some of its members."[167] Paul himself, and others with whom he collaborated (or, at times, competed), were clearly engaged in activity intended to announce the message about Jesus in the hope of winning converts. Yet on the other hand, the picture of the earliest Christian communities, at least as we glimpse them in Paul's letters, is much less clear about the nature of any missionary activity on the part of members of those communities. There are no clear exhortations to evangelize, and those passages that speak of what we might call the missionary witness of these communities seem to indicate that their faith and practice itself serve in this regard—more through "attraction" than through proselytization. That is to say, as we found in the case of Judaism, at least some of the missionary effect of the early Christian communities may have taken place through the attractiveness and appeal of their communal way of life, a picture that fits Phil 2:14–16 especially well. The extent of love and care offered to members of the community—not least those who were poor or sick—may also have been part of this appeal, among other things.[168] This model of "attraction" will also prove relevant as we explore another case study of the ethos and practice of early Christian mission: the first letter of Peter.

8.2.3 *Witness and Mission in 1 Peter*

The extent to which—and the ways in which—the author of 1 Peter urges his addressees to engage in some kind of missionary activity is also subject to some debate. One crucial text is 2:9, where the author, having drawn on a number of scriptural texts to depict the identity of the addressees as cho-

---

167. Riesner, "Jewish Mission?," 223, quoted more fully above. See also Michael Wolter's depiction of earliest Pauline Christianity as a "religion of conversion" or *Bekehrungsreligion*: Michael Wolter, "Die Entwicklung des paulinischen Christentums von einer Bekehrungsreligion zu einer Traditionsreligion," *EC* 3 (2010): 14–39; ET in Michael Wolter, "The Development of Pauline Christianity from a 'Religion of Conversion' to a 'Religion of Tradition,'" in *Paul and the Heritage of Israel: Paul's Claim upon Israel's Legacy in Luke and Acts in the Light of the Pauline Letters*, ed. David P. Moessner et al., LNTS 452 (London: T&T Clark, 2012), 49–69; see esp. 49–55.

168. On the charitable practices of the early Christian communities, see Longenecker, *Remember the Poor*. On care for the sick specifically, see Stark, *Rise of Christianity*, 73–94. The fact that an external critic could satirize this practice of care on the part of the Christians lends some weight to the suggestion that it was recognized as characteristic (Lucian, *Peregr.* 13, 16).

sen people of God (see §7.3), indicates that the purpose (ὅπως . . .) of their existence as such a people is "to declare the virtues [ἀρετάς] of the one who called you out of darkness into his marvelous light." As well as evoking the established Jewish imagery of light and darkness (see, e.g., Isa 9:2; 42:16), the author draws again on Isa 43:21 (τὰς ἀρετάς μου διηγεῖσθαι), having already drawn from this source the depiction of the people as a "chosen race" (γένος ἐκλεκτόν; cf. Isa 43:20). In place of Isaiah's verb διηγέομαι, the author of 1 Peter uses ἐξαγγέλλω, long noted by commentators to be a more vivid and striking word that conveys the sense of declaring or announcing things—often used when such things were previously unknown.[169]

One key question, then, is whether this act of declaring God's virtues (ἀρετάς) is primarily one directed toward God in worship—as argued by David Balch[170]—or one of explicit missionary witness to the world. In the LXX, clearly a source and influence for the author of 1 Peter, uses of ἐξαγγέλλω occur mostly in the Psalms, and in almost all of its occurrences (the exception is Prov 12:16) it refers either to the declaration of praises to God (Pss 9:15; 78:13; Sir 39:10; 44:15), the announcement of God's righteousness, deeds, and so on (Pss 70:15; 72:28; 106:22; 118:13; Sir 18:4), or the speaker's telling of their own experiences to God (Pss 55:9; 118:26). Most commentators see both worship and witness as pertinent in 1 Pet 2:9: declaring the praises of God is fundamentally an act of worship yet also an act of witness and proclamation in society (cf. 2:12; Pss 9:1, 11; 57:9–11; 96:1–3).[171] Yet it is important

---

169. See, e.g., Hort, *First Epistle of St. Peter*, 129 ("ἐξαγγέλλω is the more vivid word"); Edward Gordon Selwyn, *The First Epistle of St. Peter*, 2nd ed. (London: Macmillan, 1947), 167 ("a more striking word"). Cf. LSJ, 427 (διηγέομαι: "set out in detail, describe"), 580 (ἐξαγγέλλω: "tell out, proclaim, make known"). The two verbs appear in parallel in Sir 39:10; 44:15.

170. David L. Balch, *Let Wives Be Submissive: The Domestic Code in 1 Peter*, SBLMS 26 (Atlanta: Scholars Press, 1981), 133; also Torrey Seland, "The 'Common Priesthood' of Philo and 1 Peter: A Philonic Reading of 1 Peter 2:5, 9," *JSNT* 57 (1995): 87–119, esp. 116–18; repr. in Torrey Seland, *Strangers in the Light: Philonic Perspectives on Christian Identity in 1 Peter*, BibInt 76 (Leiden: Brill, 2005), 111–13, though he takes a somewhat different view in a more recent article, cited below. Michaels, *1 Peter*, 110, rejects any sharp distinction between worship and testimony but suggests that ἐξαγγέλλω "belongs in the category of worship, not missionary activity."

171. See Leonhard Goppelt, *I Peter*, 149–51; Reinhard Feldmeier, *The First Letter of Peter: A Commentary on the Greek Text*, trans. Peter H. Davids (Waco: Baylor University Press, 2008), 141; Joel B. Green, *1 Peter*, THNTC (Grand Rapids: Eerdmans, 2007), 62; Elliott, *1 Peter*, 439–40: "this proclamation of God's honor is fitting not only within but also *beyond* the boundaries of the Christian community." See also Stephen Ayodeji A. Fagbemi, *Who Are the Elect in 1 Peter? A Study in Biblical Exegesis and Its Application to the Anglican*

to emphasize that this proclamation takes place through the cultic practice of the Christian communities (cf. 2:5) rather than through any evangelism or verbal "outreach."[172] As we shall see elsewhere in the letter, it is visible practice rather than verbal proclamation—what is seen rather than what is said—that is the primary means of "witness" to outsiders.

This is confirmed in the immediately following verses, 2:11-12, which open the second major section of the letter body and shift the focus onto practical advice about life in a sometimes hostile world.[173] Here in v. 12, we find a theme that is emblematic for the rest of the letter—namely that of "doing good" (see 2:12-15, 20; 3:6, 11-17; 4:19). This pattern of conduct is presented as something that will cause their accusers to change their judgment on the basis of what they see (ἐκ τῶν καλῶν ἔργων ἐποπτεύοντες). And the result will be that "they glorify God on the day of visitation" (δοξάσωσι τὸν θεὸν ἐν ἡμέρᾳ ἐπισκοπῆς) (2:12). It is uncertain whether this recognition of good deeds and glorifying God signifies the "conversion" of their opponents or only that they will ultimately (and possibly to their regret) recognize and acknowledge the sovereignty of God (cf. Phil 2:11). Unlike the parallel in Matt 5:16, which is unspecific in this regard, here the time and occasion when unbelievers will glorify God is specified as "on the day of visitation" (ἐν ἡμέρᾳ ἐπισκοπῆς, a phrase drawn from Isa 10:3). Similar phrases, also with eschatological resonance, are found in LXX Jer 6:15; 10:15; Wis 3:7, 13; Sir 18:20, whether the time is depicted as one of vindication and blessing or

---

Church of Nigeria, StBibLit 104 (New York: Lang, 2007), 105-20; Torrey Seland, "Resident Aliens in Mission: Missional Practices in the Emerging Church of 1 Peter," *BBR* 19 (2009): 565-89, esp. 583-85, who (somewhat differently from his earlier work, cited above) opposes Balch and concludes that the term includes a sense of missionary proclamation.

172. *Pace*, e.g., Christoph Stenschke, "Mission and Conversion in the First Epistle of Peter," *Acta Patristica et Byzantina* 19 (2008): 221-63 (241: "This is a clear call for verbal proclamation of the gospel"); Seland, "Resident Aliens," esp. 583-89, who argues that 2:9 signifies "the missional, proclamatory act of the readers" (585) and that this implies "proclaiming the Word" (alongside their "good works") as part of what the author urged as their missionary strategy (589). Seland also takes the references to the readers' own conversion (1:12, 25, both using εὐαγγελίζω) as showing that "the author perceives the preaching of the Word to be pivotal in the lives of these Christians" (580). There seem to me too many Protestant presuppositions at work here in the assumption that "preaching of the Word" was central to the readers' conversion and must therefore be required of them in turn.

173. See Goppelt, *I Peter*, 155. On the section 2:9-12 as pivotal for the letter's sense of "holy engagement" with the world, see Douglas Holm, "Holy Engagement: 'Doing Good' as a Missional Response in 1 Peter," *Leaven* 20 (2012): 110-16; Holm, "Holy Engagement: Doing Good and Verbal Witness as Missional Activity in 1 Peter" (PhD diss., University of Bristol, 2014).

of judgment.[174] The Qumran texts also refer to a time of "visitation" (פקדה) as the eschatological ending of the present age (1QS 3.18; 4.6–8, 11–13, 18–19, 26).[175] The meaning of ἐπισκοπή in this context is that of scrutiny, of a time when deeds done will be exposed to God's evaluative gaze (cf. 2 Pet 3:10: τὰ ἐν αὐτῇ ἔργα εὑρεθήσεται). This seems most likely to refer to the final day of eschatological judgment,[176] though here, as elsewhere (3:12; 4:17–19), the letter leaves unspecified what the final fate of the "ungodly" will be, expressing neither optimistic nor pessimistic predictions.[177] Elsewhere, though, as we shall see, the possibility of conversion is certainly recognized.

As recent work by Douglas Holm and Travis Williams has shown, the emphasis on "doing good" in 1 Peter may be seen as central to the "missionary strategy" of the letter, or, more broadly put, its preferred mode of engagement with the wider world. Rather than seeing this call to do good, following Balch, as primarily an act of assimilation to the expectations of the wider society in the hope of lessening conflict and hostility, Holm and Williams, in their different ways, argue that "doing good" represents faithful adherence to what a way of life "in Christ" demands (3:16). In some respects this may cohere with conventional values and expectations (for example, in the submission of slaves to masters and wives to husbands, 2:18–3:6), but in others it may cause further hostility (for example, in resisting any demand to "worship" the emperor and in sanctifying Christ, 2:17; 3:15).[178]

---

174. See Michaels, *1 Peter*, 119; Elliott, *1 Peter*, 470–71 with n. 84.

175. See Michaels, *1 Peter*, 120.

176. *Pace* Selwyn, *First Epistle*, 171; Elliott, *1 Peter*, 471, who see this as a reference to an individual's time of testing that may lead to conversion—what Selwyn calls a "crisis of conversion" rather than "final Judgment."

177. It is significant where the author chooses to end the quotation of LXX Ps 33 in 3:12. The psalm continues immediately—as some later MSS of 1 Peter did, following the OT source—with the phrase τοῦ ἐξολεθρῦσαι ἐκ γῆς τὸ μνημόσυνον αὐτῶν ("to destroy the remembrance of them from earth," NETS). The omission seems likely to be deliberate, and as Michaels, *1 Peter*, 182, notes, reflects a certain "reluctance to fasten in detail on the fate of the ungodly."

178. Cf. Holm, "'Doing Good' as a Missional Response," 112: "The Christians at times suffer because of the backlash their good works provoke, suggesting that the Christian concept of good works did not always overlap with Hellenistic moral values." See also the arguments of Travis B. Williams, *Good Works in 1 Peter: Negotiating Social Conflict and Christian Identity in the Greco-Roman World* (Tübingen: Mohr Siebeck, 2014). For Balch's earlier arguments, see Balch, *Wives*; David L. Balch, "Hellenization/Acculturation in 1 Peter," in *Perspectives on First Peter*, ed. Charles H. Talbert (Macon, GA: Mercer University Press, 1986), 79–101. On the "polite resistance" implied in 2:17 and elsewhere in the letter, see Horrell, *Becoming Christian*, 211–38; Horrell, "Honour Everyone."

A particular example of this "missionary strategy" is found in 3:1–6, where, as part of the household code instruction (2:18–3:7), the author addresses wives, urging them to be submissive to their husbands.[179] While this instruction applies to all wives, the author shows a particular concern for wives married to unbelieving husbands (3:1). In such situations, their conduct serves a "missionary" purpose (cf. 1 Cor 7:15–16): "so that . . . they may be won over" (ἵνα . . . κερδηθήσονται) (3:1). This verb generally conveys the sense of "gaining" someone or something (as, e.g., in Matt 16:26; Phil 3:8), sometimes used with regard to the specific idea of winning someone over or restoring them to right relationship (Matt 18:15). Hence it may be used with the missionary sense of winning someone over to the Christian way—that is, securing their "conversion" (1 Cor 9:19–23).[180] Crucially, this "winning" of their husbands is to be done by the wives' conduct (διὰ τῆς τῶν γυναικῶν ἀναστροφῆς) and specifically "without a word" (ἄνευ λόγου).[181]

The exemplary and paradigmatic character of the behavior and lifestyle required of the wives becomes clear when we compare the instruction to wives in 3:1–6 with that addressed to the community as a whole in 3:13–17.[182] Verbal and thematic parallels are frequent, with references in both passages to the appropriate "way of life" (ἀναστροφή, 3:1–2, 16), to apposite fear but also the challenge "not to be afraid" (3:2, 6, 14, 16), to gentleness and hope (3:4–5, 15–16), to what is hidden in the heart (3:4, 15), and to "doing good" (3:6, 17).

As 2:12 also makes clear, it is fundamentally through a "good" and attractive way of life that Christians in general—and wives in particular—are meant to make their appeal to those who are currently nonbelievers: husbands who are "disobedient to the word" (3:1), or more generally the

179. For a more detailed study of this passage as an example of 1 Peter's missionary strategy, see Horrell, "Fear," on which I draw in the following paragraphs.

180. Schlosser, *Première épître de Pierre*, 182, describes it as "un terme technique du langage missionnaire."

181. Stenschke, "Mission and Conversion," 242, insists that "1 Peter 3.1 does *not* imply that these wives should be silent *in other circumstances*, nor does it mean that other women or men should abstain from verbal proclamation. . . . The silence of the Christian wives towards their non-Christian husbands is an *exception* to the rule." But where is this "rule" stated or even implied in 1 Peter?

182. See Horrell, "Fear," 419–20. Parallels between the two passages are briefly noted by Elliott, *1 Peter*, 619n230, and set out in more detail by Jeannine K. Brown, "Silent Wives, Verbal Believers: Ethical and Hermeneutical Considerations in 1 Peter 3:1–6 and Its Context," *WW* 24 (2004): 395–403. However, Brown's argument is that the conduct demanded of the wives is intended to be not paradigmatic but exceptional, on which see further below.

"gentiles" (ἔθνη) among whom they live (2:12; 4:3). The most significant difference in this regard between the pattern of instruction and exhortation in 3:1–6 and in 3:13–17 is that in 3:1 the wives are urged to make their appeal "without a word" whereas in 3:15 the addressees are told to be "ready to make a defence to anyone who asks you for an account concerning the hope that is in you." The question is which of these two patterns of conduct represents the author's "normal" expectation for the mode of Christian engagement.

It is important to notice, first, that the "defence" (ἀπολογία) is something to be given only in response to a request or inquiry (τῷ αἰτοῦντι ὑμᾶς). "Doing good" is the normal strategy for engagement with outsiders and critics; a verbal account (λόγος) should be ready (ἕτοιμοι ἀεί...) if it is called for. The specific contexts in which such an account might be demanded are a matter of debate. The dominant modern consensus is that the suffering and persecution evident in 1 Peter are "unofficial," a matter of public hostility and slander rather than "official" imperial persecution.[183] From this perspective, the situations in view in 3:15 are most likely everyday.[184] However, a number of words and phrases in 3:15—ἀπολογία, αἰτεῖν λόγον, κτλ.—may well imply a legal context (cf. Mart. Pol. 10.1–2) and that the character of the inquiry is hostile and accusatory.[185] Recent research has made the case that legal accusations and courtroom trials were at least part of the range of threats facing the Christians addressed by 1 Peter.[186] The internal depiction of the "account" as a description of the Christians' "hope" by no means indicates to the contrary (cf. Acts 26:1–23 [note the reference to "hope" in vv. 6–7]; Mart. Pol. 10.1–2; Acts of the Scillitan Martyrs 4; Martyrdom of Apollonius 4).[187] Whether the inquiry is judicial or not—and a range of situations is most likely included—it is notable that the outcome for those who inquire (or, more precisely, accuse) is not conversion or salvation but being put to shame (καταισχυνθῶσιν, 3:16). The good conduct of the Christians—their

---

183. For an extensive and more nuanced study of the history of research, see Travis B. Williams, "Suffering from a Critical Oversight: The Persecutions of 1 Peter within Modern Scholarship," *CBR* 10 (2012): 271–88; Williams, *Persecution in 1 Peter: Differentiating and Contextualizing Early Christian Suffering*, NovTSup 145 (Leiden: Brill, 2012), 4–15.

184. So, e.g., Elliott, *1 Peter*, 628.

185. See esp. Paul A. Holloway, *Coping with Prejudice: 1 Peter in Social-Psychological Perspective*, WUNT 244 (Tübingen: Mohr Siebeck, 2009), 199–205; see further Horrell, "Fear," 425–28.

186. See Horrell, "Χριστιανός," esp. 370–76; Horrell, *Becoming Christian*, 183–97; also Holloway, *Coping with Prejudice*, esp. 4–5, 65–73, 202–5, 220–27; Williams, *Persecution*.

187. *Pace* Elliott, *1 Peter*, 627.

ἀγαθὴν ἐν Χριστῷ ἀναστροφήν—will ultimately, the author hopes, lead not to their shaming (cf. 4:16) but rather to their vindication and the shaming of their opponents. This is hardly, then, primarily a strategy of "mission."

In 1 Peter, then, there is clearly hope that unbelievers and opponents will be won over, or at least driven (if only at the "end") to acknowledge the Christians' God. But the dominant mode of "missionary" engagement with the world is through Christian life and practice in both its cultic (2:5–9) and ethical dimensions (2:11–12). While verbal testimony can be given in certain situations if demanded, the main strategy urged upon wives and upon all is the quiet and gentle living of a good way of life—something that, as we have already seen (§5.1), eludes neat definition as specifically "religious" (or, indeed, "ethnic"). It seems here that the "attraction" model of mission again emerges as the dominant perspective.[188]

8.3 Conclusions

The main points of the preceding investigations may briefly be summarized. With regard to Judaism, there seems to be considerable evidence that it was widely found attractive and popular, though (sometimes for this very reason) it was also subject to criticism and satire. There were sympathizers or so-called Godfearers who affiliated themselves with the Jewish community and participated in its life to varying degrees and in various ways. There is also ample evidence for the existence of "proselytes" or "incomers" who took the steps to become full members of the Jewish people—something that, for males, entailed circumcision. Conversely, those who abandoned their Jewish customs and way of life could be seen as having committed apostasy or, in more sociological terms, as having defected or departed from the community and its people. The early Christian communities were clearly spreading through the addition of "converts," for whom, like Jewish proselytes, the process of joining involved a turn from their previous gods and cults to the God of Israel, seen as encountered in his son, Jesus Christ. This was an entry into a new community and group identity with a new way of life and its associated ethical demands. They were supposed to live no longer "like the gentiles." Expulsions and defections soon became part of the picture too.

---

188. See also Armand Puig i Tàrrech, "The Mission According to the New Testament: Choice or Need?," in *Einheit der Kirche im Neuen Testament*, ed. Anatoly Alexeev et al., WUNT 218 (Tübingen: Mohr Siebeck, 2008), 231–47.

Contrary to an earlier tradition of scholarship, it does not seem—so recent scholarship has largely agreed—that there is much evidence for proactive or zealous missionary activity on the part of Jews at the time. It seems that some at least were willing and even keen to instruct interested outsiders in their way of life and particular piety, but this does not itself constitute an active "going out" with the intention of gaining converts or persuading others to join this people's way of life. There may have been some instances where efforts were made to persuade sympathizers or adherents to become full proselytes—Eleazar would represent a particular example—but (aside from questionable interpretations of Matt 23:15) there is little indication that this was a widespread or prevalent pattern. The most prominent picture seems to be one of "passive attraction"—a centripetal rather than centrifugal force, drawing people in, as indeed the dominant terminology (προσέρχομαι, κτλ.) to describe such "incomers" implies.

There is some contrast here with the energetic missionary activity of the earliest Christian movement—the "going out" (πορεύομαι) to announce the message about Jesus in the hope of winning converts, as in the famous commission sending the disciples out (πορευθέντες) to all the nations in Matthew's Gospel.[189] But this call to go out and proclaim seems to have been the task of particular figures in the early Christian movement: the apostles and itinerant coworkers who engaged in the work of founding Christian assemblies across the Roman Empire. Paul, at least according to his own testimony and our extant literary records, did this with particular energy.

When it comes to the expectations and practices of the members of these early Christian assemblies, based on the (differing) depictions in Paul's letters and in 1 Peter, there is a striking lack of any call to proactive "mission" through proclaiming their message verbally to outsiders. The expectation was rather that community members would exercise a "missionary" function by exhibiting a pattern of life that was quiet and attractive such that the cultic and ethical life of the community itself served as a kind of "light," potentially attracting others to it. We must be candid about how little we know about the processes by which and the rate at which new members joined the Christian assemblies in the early generations. But in terms of this model of "attraction," there are notable similarities with the pattern in the Jewish evidence.

Indeed, while we might draw some contrast between the proactive missionary focus of the early Christian movement and the less proselytizing

189. On the contrasting terminology of "coming in" and "going out," see Riesner, "Jewish Mission?," 250.

approach of Jewish communities, it is clear enough that both Jewish and Christian communities—the latter seen as a particular kind of the former in the early years[190]—attracted others to join and that "incomers" or converts were generally welcomed and accepted. While the language we choose to denote the possibilities explored in this chapter might derive either from the modern discourse of religion ("mission," "conversion," "apostasy") or a more ethnic discourse ("customs," "way of life," "joining oneself to a people"), distinctions between "ethnicity" and "religion" cannot be clearly sustained, nor can Jewish and Christian perspectives be differentiated from one another in this way. There were, in both cases, possibilities for both joining and leaving. Given these various possibilities, the (significant) differences notwithstanding, there seems little basis for a categorical distinction between an "ethnic" Judaism, which people cannot join or leave, and a "Christian" identity that can welcome and include people of all ethnicities. Judaism too can be "multi-ethnic," with regard both to those already identified as *Ioudaioi* (as we saw in §6.1) and also those who might join. Despite a long-established tendency to depict the early Christian movement as a kind of "opening up" of Judaism to the gentiles, a broadening or universalizing of its appeal (cf. ch. 1), "Judaism itself," as Jon Levenson pithily remarks, "can also be Judaism for the gentiles."[191]

The tendency in the Christian-dominated fields of New Testament and early Christian studies is to depict the distinction in a way that locates the positive and hopeful possibilities on the side of the early Christian perspective, something we shall reflect on more in the following chapter. It is therefore worth considering—at least as a provocation to think differently—how these patterns and possibilities of inclusion (and exclusion) might be depicted otherwise. Judaism, we might stress, tended not to be characterized by the proselytizing zeal of the earliest Christians, but many Jewish communities were evidently more than willing to welcome and instruct those interested in the Jewish way of life. It hardly needs to be said that the Christian impetus to "go out" can be deeply problematic, especially when it is linked—as it has been in the modern history of Christianity—with imperialism and colonialism. It is no coincidence that, as noted above, the Great Commission

---

190. On the ways in which early Christian groups were, and would have been viewed as, a kind of Jewish phenomenon, particularly in their worship of the Jewish/Judean God and use of the Jewish scriptures, see Paul B. Duff, *Jesus Followers in the Roman Empire* (Grand Rapids: Eerdmans, 2017), 112–17.

191. Levenson, "Universal Horizon," 165.

of Matt 28:19 becomes an iconic text for Christian missions only from the sixteenth century onward, and especially in nineteenth- and twentieth-century Protestantism. Moreover, Jewish communities allowed people to affiliate and participate to varying degrees while remaining, in some cases, involved in other socio-religious networks—something that Paul, for example, seems less willing to accept. They could also join in fully and become Jewish. From a modern perspective, the Jewish option could appear more "tolerant" and "inclusive." Yet it is Christianity, and its iconic figures such as Paul, that tends to be credited with welcoming gentiles, modelling inclusion, diversity, and tolerance, or offering the possibility to join in the community that regarded itself as God's people. We might, for example, recall Harnack's comment that Judaism's failure to fully include gentiles as children of Abraham leaves scope for its successor to drive it from the field (§8.1.1), or Baur's depiction of Paul breaking through the boundaries of Jewish particularism to proclaim a universal religion, or the new perspective's contrast between Jewish ethnocentrism and Paul's inclusion of gentiles without "works of law," or the kinds of distinctions drawn more recently between Jewish ethnicity and the trans-ethnic inclusive identity offered in Christ, which allows all to retain their identities within an overarching identity in Christ (see ch. 1). If the historical and exegetical evidence points us in different directions, what might help us understand what is going on in these rosy depictions of the earliest Christian groups?

The task of the final chapter is to reflect on precisely this question, returning to the "structural dichotomy" outlined in chapter 1 and trying to understand how it might reflect its particular contexts of production. To what extent, and in what ways, might the various and changing contrasts drawn between Judaism and Christianity be shaped by the origins and context of New Testament scholarship in the white Western nations of Europe (and now the USA)?

PART III

Reflections on Location and Epistemology

Implicit Whiteness and Christian Superiority: The Epistemological Challenge

The previous chapter, drawing to a close a series of comparisons of early Jewish and Christian traditions, ended with a question arising from these comparisons concerning the extent to which the contrasts drawn between Judaism and Christianity in the field of New Testament scholarship—some of which were summarized in chapter 1—reflect the origins and context of that (Christian) tradition of scholarship in the white Western nations of Europe (and now the USA). This closing chapter, taking up that question, serves both to draw together the findings of the preceding studies and to offer some broader, and tentative, reflections on the "location" that they represent. It serves, therefore, both as a conclusion to the study as a whole and as a chapter in its own right, introducing a new and broader perspective of critical analysis.

The first part of this chapter, then, serves as a kind of conclusion to the preceding chapters, summarizing their main findings and offering some concluding arguments. The remainder of the chapter turns to broader issues of critical reflection on location and particularity within the discipline. This critical reflection is informed by insights from whiteness studies, which are briefly introduced and summarized below. This offers a perspective from which we may attempt to reflect on the religiously and racially particular location of the discipline of New Testament studies. As the title of this chapter indicates, I see this as raising fundamental issues of epistemology that should cause us to think hard about how to conceive and practice the discipline in which we work.

9.1 Retrospect, Summary, and Key Arguments Thus Far

I began this study with a selective overview of various phases of modern New Testament studies, from the nineteenth century to the present day, seeking to show how what I called a structural dichotomy—between an ethnically particular Judaism and a universal, inclusive, or trans-ethnic Christianity—features prominently from the early times of F. C. Baur right up to the most recent work. The specific terms and constructions change with changing historical and philosophical contexts and shifting scholarly paradigms, but the basic shape of the dichotomy seems to remain. Whether the distinction is cast in terms of particular versus universal, ethnocentric versus open, or ethnic versus trans-ethnic, there is a consistent pattern, and it is one in which Christianity—or faith in Christ, or Christ following—offers a positive and hopeful model, some way of either transcending the restrictions of its Jewish roots, incorporating both Jews and gentiles, or allowing diversity to remain in Christ—a point to which we shall return.

In order to establish a basis on which to critically probe the cogency and implications of this dichotomous categorization and to contextualize the present project in the landscape of scholarly research, the second chapter briefly surveyed the recent emphasis on early Jewish (or Judean) identity as "ethnic" within the broader context of scholarship on ethnicity and race in antiquity. It also examined some recent work, generated in particular by the stimulus of Denise Kimber Buell's *Why This New Race*, which has explored the ways in which early Christian texts construct identity in "ethnic" terms, deploying ethnic discourse and what Buell calls "ethnic reasoning" to do this. This focus on the discursive constructions of early Christian identity fits within a wider scholarly emphasis on the ways in which all ethnic and racial identities are constructed through discourse and social practice, something that has been a prominent emphasis in recent social-scientific discussion of ethnicity and race, as we saw in chapter 3. Following Rogers Brubaker's work supporting a "constructionist" view of ethnic and racial identities (see §3.1), we may see the focus of our inquiries not as seeking to ascertain whether this or that group is or is not "ethnic" (or, indeed, "religious") in character but rather as asking *how* "ethnic" or "religious" discourse and social practice are deployed in constructing a sense of group identity, or what Brubaker calls "groupness."

What we have come to call "religion" is often listed—along with culture, custom, or language—as a characteristic indicator of ethnicity, such that there is a significant intersection between these two facets of identity, though they are often treated as separate categories in modern scholarly discourse. Indeed, we need to take due account of the fact that both "ethnicity" and "religion" are modern categories of analysis that abstract certain features of human behavior and interaction into one or the other classification. In antiquity, and also in the present, the facets of social life that create and sustain senses of group identity are not so neatly or consistently distinguishable. As we saw in §3.3, the intersections between "religion" and "ethnicity" are intricate and strong, and attempts to distinguish them categorically are likely to be artificial. These theoretical perspectives therefore invite a reconsideration of the kinds of differences that might pertain between early Christian and Jewish identities—and the practices and discourses through which each was constructed.

One way to do this is to examine how various facets of what social scientists have identified as typical characteristics of ethnic groups appear in early Jewish and Christian texts. The central chapters in this book therefore examined in turn features such as appeals to ancestry and kinship, customs regarding marriage and children, the discursive and practical commitment to a particular way of life, the orientation toward a homeland, and the evidence for a sense of being a "people"—a "self-consciousness" about such identity. These chapters also included a theme not so commonly associated with ethnic groups but more often allocated to the category of religion: namely, that of mission and conversion. As I noted in chapter 8, however, this theme, like the other topics, crosses the categories of "religious" and "ethnic" (or national) identities because of such things as the role of religion in constituting or marking ethnic and national identities and the close connections between colonialism and mission. The purpose of these explorations, it should be stressed, is not to test a "category" question as to whether Jewish or early Christian identity is or is not "ethnic"—though I shall remark on this question further below—but rather to explore how various features, themes, and claims commonly associated with ethnic identity appear and to consider how far these characteristics are "religious" as well as "ethnic" in character.

The main results of these primarily historical and exegetical inquiries may briefly be summarized. First, in terms of ancestry, kinship, marriage, and family (ch. 4), the earliest Christian texts make considerable, if varied, use of discourses about ancestry and paternity to create narratives of identity for converts to Christ. These appeals to ancestry are in some ways different from the appeals found in Jewish texts, but they can nonetheless be seen together as diverse attempts to appeal to ancestors, especially Abraham, as a basis for group identity in the present. Jewish writers like Philo, as well as those we might categorize as early Christian, such as Paul, can depict ancestry as something that can be gained or lost, changed or abandoned, depending on conduct and orientation of life. A categorical contrast between "real" (Jewish, ethnic) ancestral claims on the one hand and "fictive" (Christian, non-ethnic) constructions seems difficult to maintain. (We might recall, for example, the strategic appeal recorded in 1 Maccabees to shared ancestry between Jews and Spartans [1 Macc 12:21; cf. Josephus, *A. J.* 12.225–27; see §4.1].) The same goes for kinship, also prominent in early Christian as well as Jewish discourse, for which shared ancestry provides one basis, despite the frequently encountered tendency to distinguish between "real" and "fictive" forms of kinship. All appeals to a large people-group as "brothers and sisters" are fictive, albeit in diverse and particular ways.

In terms of regulations concerning marriage and the identity of children, the New Testament, aside from instruction about divorce, contains very little. Paul, however, makes brief but significant moves that are influential on later Christian custom and practice, establishing a preference for inter-Christian endogamy and the notion of the passing on of Christian identity to children. Endogamy was the dominant principle of Jewish marriage rules, though it was understood and practiced in different ways. Since Jewish convictions about marriage, though again varied, often allowed marriage to a non-Jew if the gentile partner "converted," it again seems difficult to sustain a clear or consistent contrast between "real," "ethnic" Jewish endogamy and some kind of Christian principle based only on shared "religious" commitment.

In terms of key facets of what may be taken to constitute the distinctive "way of life" that sustains a sense of identity as Jewish or Christian, there are again significant points of similarity (ch. 5). In both traditions, adhering (or not adhering) to a particular way of life can be seen as determinative for continuing membership in the group. As the Christian movement developed into its second and third generations, there emerged significant emphasis on the socialization of children into this way of life, something that had long characterized Jewish exhortation and expectation. In both cases, there are distinctive practices that serve as particularly potent markers of belonging and identity—notably circumcision, food laws, and Sabbath observance in Judaism, and baptism, Lord's Supper, and Sunday meeting in early Christianity. It is not that such practices as such were necessarily unique to either group—circumcision, for example, was known to have been practiced by other peoples in the eastern regions of the Roman Empire (such as Egyptians and Idumeans)—so the practices themselves cannot stand *simpliciter*, devoid of interpretation, to denote either Jewish or Christian identity. Rather, it is the (identity-defining) significance placed upon certain actions, customs, and practices—their *salience*, to use a term prominent in Social Identity Theory[1]—that gives them this importance in terms of signaling belonging to the group. Although adherence to a particular way of life, with its cultural and religious dimensions, is often included among the constitutive characteristics of ethnic identity, "way of life" is also a category—rooted in the language of both Jewish and early Christian texts—that cuts across any distinction between ethnic or religious identity.[2]

When it comes to land, and the sense of territory or homeland that can be bound up, physically or symbolically, with a sense of being a people (ch. 6), scholarship has often drawn a clear distinction between the land-rootedness of Jewish identity and the deterritorialized perspective of early Christianity, an observation not unrelated to the Christian commitment to worldwide mission discussed in chapter 8. While some broad distinction along these lines should not entirely be dismissed, there is a much more nuanced and diverse picture to be discovered in both traditions, particularly when our interpretation is informed by recent theoretical work on space and place, which calls into question any sharp distinction between physical and symbolic space, emphasizing instead the intrinsic connections between "real" and "imagined" space (hence Soja's "real-and-imagined places"). For example, the Jewish scriptures include the idea that life on the earth is experienced as a "stranger," as one not at home—a theme taken up in some New Testament writings, notably Hebrews and 1 Peter. Later writers such as Philo can sustain and treasure an ongoing orientation toward Jerusalem as "motherland" while at the same time acknowledging that another land serves as homeland or πατρίς. This orientation toward Jerusalem, the heart of a symbolic configuration of the world, is expressed in a number of New Testament writings too—notably Paul, Hebrews, and Revelation. Gentile

---

1. See, for example, the often-quoted definition of social identity by one of the founders of modern Social Identity Theory, Henri Tajfel, *Human Groups and Social Categories* (Cambridge: Cambridge University Press, 1981), 255: "However rich and complex may be the individuals' view of themselves in relation to the surrounding world, social and physical, *some* aspects of that view are contributed by the membership of certain social groups or categories. Some of these memberships are more salient than others; and some may vary in salience in time and as a function of a variety of social situations."

2. See further David G. Horrell, "Religion, Ethnicity, and Way of Life: Exploring Categories of Identity," *CBQ* (forthcoming).

converts have their identity reconfigured in this topocentric way: Jerusalem comes to have a central significance, both as their "mother" (Gal 4:26) and as the focus of eschatological expectation. Rather than being detached from such "Jewish" geography, then, these early Christian constructions of space are clearly (and unsurprisingly) imbued with ongoing symbolic attachment and orientation to Judea and Jerusalem. It would be implausible to suggest that the early Christian traditions are oriented toward an ancestral land in the same ways or to the same extent as Jewish traditions, but it is equally implausible to invoke a categorical distinction between a territorial Judaism and a deterritorialized Christianity, dichotomizing the diversity within, as well as the commonalities between, both traditions.

One of the basic, almost tautologous, characteristics associated with ethnic or racial identities is a "self-consciousness" about being a "people" (ch. 7). Since "ethnicity" and "religion" are modern constructs, investigating this sense of "self-consciousness" is also an opportunity to focus on the ancient terminology and to ask how, where, and in what ways the language of "peoplehood" (particularly using ἔθνος, γένος, or λαός) is deployed to denote the group. A long-established—though variously expressed—sense of being a people is prominent in many Jewish texts. Unsurprisingly, since the New Testament texts emerge early in the process of Christianity's beginnings within Judaism, an explicit claim to Christian "peoplehood" is only glimpsed. In Paul's letters, it is only in his use of scriptural quotations that his (mostly gentile) addressees are identified as a "people" (λαός), specifically the "people of God." Scriptural language is also the source of the most forceful and emphatic application of "people" language to the addressees of an early Christian letter (1 Pet 2:9–10). This is a significant development. First Peter's use of γένος to identify the people inaugurates what became an influential facet of early Christian discourse: the identification of Christians as members of a particular γένος, often set alongside—and distinguished from—Greeks and Jews. In other words, we can see in early Christian discourse the gradual emergence of a self-conscious sense of "being a people," something that might be described as a process of "ethnicization," however we define the sense of "peopleness" that is exhibited.

Our final topic, mission and conversion, as I noted above, is not usually seen as characteristic of "ethnic" groups but rather as belonging to the realm of religion. However, it crosses and intersects the categories in various ways, not least in connection with a theme of the previous chapters: joining a "people" and following their way of life. The ways in which the possibilities for affiliating and joining are depicted are important to consider in our comparative juxtaposition of Jewish and early Christian perspectives. Despite ongoing debate, we can with reasonable confidence follow the majority of recent studies in concluding that Judaism at the time of Christian origins was not, on the whole, characterized by energetic efforts to proselytize. Nonetheless, it was clearly popular and seems to have been spreading at the time, a point noted by its ancient proponents and critics alike. It was possible to associate with Judaism in various ways: by adopting some of its customs and expressing some form of affiliation or association with the Jewish community (the kind of stance labeled "sympathization" or "godfearing") or by becoming a "proselyte" (or "incomer," "joiner")—that is, fully identifying oneself with the Jewish people, which for males entailed undergoing circumcision. Conversely, those who abandoned their Jewish way of life could be regarded as apostates or might simply assimilate fully into the people among whom they lived.

The early Christian movement is characterized by a more explicit sense of missionary commitment, though this seems to have been understood mainly in terms of a specific calling for particular early-generation figures— apostles or evangelists—rather than a general mandate for all. The absence from Paul's letters of any calls to members of the assemblies to engage in pro- active evangelism or outreach is one indication of this perspective. In Paul's letters, and also in 1 Peter, the "model of mission" seems to be more one of "passive attraction" than proactive proselytization, similar to the stance that seems to have characterized the appeal of Jewish communities. Again, join- ing and leaving are clearly possible, though there is little evidence for varying degrees of affiliation such as we see in Jewish texts and communities, with their affiliates, sympathizers, patrons, or Godfearers. One of the implications of this comparison, besides any reflections on whether we should character- ize these modes of "joining" in ethnic and/or religious terms, is that it raises questions about the kinds of contrast frequently drawn in scholarship—re- lated again to the dichotomy outlined in chapter 1—between an ethnocentric or exclusive Judaism and an open, inclusive, tolerant Christianity. We shall turn to further reflections on this important issue below.

For now, I want to clarify certain key points about the argument thus far. First, it is not my intention to dispute the notion that Judaism in this period may cogently be seen as an "ethnic" identity, both in the sense that Jews are recognized as an ancestral and established "people" (or ἔθνος) by ancient writers and that their way of life exhibits many of the characteristics com- monly seen by modern social scientists to typify ethnic groups.[3] Nor, indeed,

---

3. This is a point stressed by Mason and Esler, "Judaean and Christ-Follower Identi-

is it my intention to negate the significant gains made from highlighting the ways in which ancient "Jewish" identity may be understood in terms of being a "people," or ἔθνος, rather than being classified with the modern category of "religion."[4] However, I hope to have shown that this identity as "people" cannot adequately be understood simply by assigning it to a standard category—"ethnic group"—but only by examining the particular ways in which group identity is claimed, attained, defended, exhibited, sustained, or abandoned (cf. §3.1). We might recall Max Weber's remark, quoted already in chapter 3, that "the umbrella term 'ethnic'" is "entirely unusable" for any "truly rigorous investigation."[5] This would apply not only to the modern sociological category but also to ancient use of the term ἔθνος, since it was used of groups and peoples across a wide range of scales and types (see §7.1). Furthermore, there is the risk in using one primary category that we lose sight of the various other ways in which both Jewish and early Christian groups were identified—as associations, philosophical schools, ethnic or cultic groups, and so on.[6] Moreover, "religious" convictions and practices loom large in whatever Jewish identity is taken to be, making a distinction between "ethnicity" and "religion" in this case particularly hard to sustain.

Second, it is equally not my intention to claim that early Christian identity should be classified as "ethnic" or that the Christian groups should directly be identified as "ethnic groups." Again, such a clear and categorical "yes or no" classification is unlikely to be cogent or illuminating.[7] If,

---

ties," 496–504, responding in particular to David G. Horrell, "Ethnicisation, Marriage, and Early Christian Identity: Critical Reflections on 1 Corinthians 7, 1 Peter 3, and Modern New Testament Scholarship," *NTS* 62 (2016): 439–60.

4. See Mason and Esler, "Judaean and Christ-Follower Identities," 498, on "reacting against the continuing scholarly practice of comparing Judaism and Christianity as two religions." See also Mason, "Jews, Judaeans, Judaizing, Judaism," 457–512; and, on the problems with using the category in antiquity, Barton and Boyarin, *Imagine No Religion*. See the earlier discussion in §3.3.

5. Quoted in Brubaker, "Ethnicity without Groups," 186n29. For more detail, including the original quotation from Weber, see p. 74 with n. 30.

6. See further Horrell, "Judaean Ethnicity," 4–7; also §2.1 above.

7. Cf. my earlier comment in Horrell, "Ethnicisation," 458: "We should not, however, hastily and simplistically conclude that early Christian identity 'is' therefore 'ethnic,' or that the early Christian groups were 'ethnic groups'; such box-like categorisation is unlikely to be either cogent or illuminating. Indeed . . . it is much more likely that the categories are fuzzy and overlapping: ethnic, religious, cultural and social facets of group-identity intersect in complex ways. What is more relevant is the conclusion that in both discursive and practical ways, the texts . . . indicate how ethnic categories and features are deployed in the construc-

however, we ask whether the early Christians saw themselves, or were seen by others, as a "people"—when, where, how soon, in what ways, and so on—then the question might sound less incongruous, even if a complex and nuanced answer is still required. What I hope therefore to have shown in the previous chapters are some of the ways in which characteristics commonly associated with "ethnic" groups in general, and with Jewish groups in particular, are also prominent in the discourse and practice of early Christian identity-formation. Some of these suggest impulses in the direction of what we may call ethnicization—both in terms of discourse (e.g., in relation to self-description as a "people") and social practice (e.g., in relation to rules about marriage and the raising of children)—without that claim needing to imply the categorization of that peoplehood in terms of one or other of our modern categories. Insofar as early Christian texts deploy precisely the language of ἔθνος or γένος (or, indeed, πόλις-language) and associated characteristics, their constructions of group identity are at least competing within the realm identified by *ethnos* loyalties rather than in a sphere easily separated from them.[8]

Let us take one well-known example to illustrate the point, from Philo's description of what it is that "incomers" to the Jewish people have both left and joined: "their kinsfolk by blood [γενεὰν μὲν τὴν ἀφ' αἵματος], their country [πατρίδα], their customs [ἔθη] and the temples [ἱερά] and images of their gods [ἀφιδρύματα θεῶν]" (*Virt.* 102 [Colson, LCL]; cf. §8.1.4 above). Here it is clear that religious practices are inextricably integrated into a broader depiction of ethnic identity. As Philip Esler has noted, "All six of the diagnostic features [of an ethnic group] described by Hutchinson and Smith are found or implied here."[9] But if this is the case, then early Christian depictions—such as Paul's description of the transition made by gentile converts when they "turned to God from idols" (1 Thess 1:9) and adopted a way of life that was "not like the gentiles" (1 Thess 4:5), or 1 Peter's characterization of the turn away from a worthless "ancestral" way of life (1 Pet 1:18)—cannot easily be removed from the same kind of discursive and social context in which loyalty to or departure from an ethnicity-defining way

---

tion of Christian group-identity and that it is apposite to speak of this identity-construction as in some respects a form of ethnicisation, 'the making of a people.'"

8. For an extended presentation of the "classical paradigm" for "mapping peoples" in terms of *ethnos* and *polis*, see Mason, *History of Roman Judaea*, 97–146.

9. Esler, *God's Court*, 17. See also the application of these criteria to Josephus's *Contra Apionem* in Esler, "Josephus' *Against Apion*."

of life is in view.[10] Whatever one labels the early Christian groups, joining them—at least on the kind of basis that the New Testament letters depict— could hardly not be disruptive of ethnic identities, insofar as these are con- stituted, among other things, by loyalty to an ancestral way of life, including its religious and cultural practices.

Third, and building on these previous two points, what I am partic- ularly concerned with—as indicated both by the opening chapter of this book and by the comparisons of Jewish and Christian traditions in chapters 4–8—is a certain kind of juxtaposition of these two perspectives. That is to say, my concern is not to question per se the identification of ancient Judaism as an ethnic identity, in ancient or modern terms, nor to argue for the categorization of early Christian groups in the same way; both groups, as noted briefly above (and in §2.1), may be identified in various ways and are so identified in ancient sources, and there are reasons to question any univocal categorical distinction. Rather, my focus is on the ways in which Judaism and Christianity are juxtaposed so as to locate the capacity for of- fering an open, inclusive, or "superordinate" identity in the latter tradition. As I tried to show in chapter 1, the terminology used in such comparisons shifts considerably—from Baur's Hegelian particular versus universal to Es- ler's ethnic versus trans-ethnic, for example—but the common "structure" of these perspectives remains. And it is one in which the comparison is, to echo a phrase from my critics, "in the Christians' favour."[11]

What I hope to have shown in chapters 4–8, then, is that, however we categorize them, and notwithstanding their significant differences, both Jew- ish and Christian traditions exhibit the kinds of discourse and practice associ- ated in social-scientific taxonomies with ethnic groups. These features make both groups "particular," "exclusive," and, indeed, "ethnocentric"—"people- centered"—in terms of drawing identity-constituting boundaries between the group and outsiders and focusing on sustaining the common identity of

10. See further Horrell, "Religion, Ethnicity, and Way of Life."

11. In their response to my earlier article (Horrell, "Ethnicisation"), Mason and Esler, "Judaean and Christ-Follower Identities," 494, comment that "observers in antiquity knew Ju- daeans and Christ-followers to be two different kinds of group, but *this difference was not in the Christians' favour*" (my emphasis). This seems to me a crucial point, and one that has helped me to see that the critical issue with which I am concerned is not the categorization of Judaism and early Christianity as "ethnic" or "non-ethnic" as such but what significance is drawn from this distinction, particularly in the kinds of juxtapositions in which the positive achievement illuminated by the comparison seems clearly to be on the Christians' side. Whether either of my critics sees this as an appropriate lesson to learn from our exchange is another matter.

the in-group, for example through such practices as endogamy and socializing children into the group's way of life. What we would classify as "religious" practices also loom large in the self-definition of both identities. It is not only Christian groups that can be "multi-ethnic" (see pp. 189–91) or can welcome or encourage others to join (or lament their leaving). Indeed, while the early Christians—or at least specific figures among them—seem to have been driven, for better or worse, by a stronger proselytizing impulse, one might, as we remarked at the end of the previous chapter, see Jewish communities as offering more open, inclusive, tolerant models of affiliation and participation, given the evidence for various kinds of sympathizers, affiliates, patrons, and proselytes. Such a claim would, of course, also be open to plenty of questions, but it is worth making at least as a provocative contrast to the prevalent kind of comparison made in works that exhibit the sort of "structural dichotomy" outlined in chapter 1. If, then, both Jewish and early Christian traditions deploy aspects of ethnic discourse—often in the face of conflicts and challenges of various kinds—to construct their sense of group identity; if both traditions were open to outsiders joining (and to insiders leaving), and facilitated and managed this in various ways; if both can be seen as inclusive and open in their different ways, why is it that Judaism has so often been depicted as ethnocentric, particular, or limited by the boundaries of ethnicity or race while early Christianity has been seen as inclusive, open, trans-ethnic, or universal in its concerns?

Attempting to answer that question also returns us to the survey outlined in the opening chapter. There, we noted briefly how the kind of dichotomy between Jewish particularism and Christian universalism developed in the nineteenth century by F. C. Baur was framed in terms indebted to the philosophy of Hegel and, more generally, developed in the context of a wider narrative about European (racial and religious) superiority at a time of European colonial ambition. Our question then presses us to consider how, and in what ways, the construction of the contrast between Judaism and Christianity might bear the marks of its production in this particular historical and geographical context—one with specific religious and racial dimensions. And if I am right that the basic shape of this structural dichotomy, despite substantial changes and paradigm shifts, continues into recent work, then how, if at all, does this perspective—in both its elements of enduring consistency and its changes—continue to reflect its origins and ongoing production in this specific religious and racial context?

Such critical probing will inevitably and necessarily entail considering something other than the explicit intentions and arguments any of us presents. Indeed, the ideological and political tendencies, or the racial and religious identities, that shape our discipline's perspectives may run counter to our personal convictions, beliefs, or intentions. We may nonetheless be shaped by and implicated in such patterns of thought. As William Arnal comments in relation to the ways in which constructions of the historical Jesus reflect contemporary identity issues, "The question of *personal* agenda is irrelevant"; it is the "correspondence" between certain historical constructions and contemporary perspectives that is pertinent.[12] Our potential enmeshment in—the shaping of our thought by—the traditions, categories, and ideologies of our disciplinary, religious, racial, social, and geopolitical locations cannot be removed simply by declarations of intention or personal conviction, just as, say, declaring ourselves committed to nonsexism and gender equality does not mean that forms of unconscious and unintended ideological or practical bias—and, equally important, wider conventions and social practices—have thereby been eliminated.[13] And this applies even more so on the scale of disciplinary traditions and perspectives, into which each of us is inducted through our education and training. In order to inform a critical response to these issues and provide a framework to think with, I turn first to the field of "whiteness" studies.[14]

9.2 Insights and Questions from Whiteness Studies

Whiteness emerged as a particular focus of study within and beyond the field of critical race studies, in the USA in particular, in the early 1990s.[15]

---

12. William Arnal, "Jesus as Battleground in a Period of Cultural Complexity," in Moxnes, Blanton, and Crossley, *Jesus beyond Nationalism*, 104.

13. For just one example discussing these latter issues, see Helen Bond's blog post detailing the forms of sexism she has encountered in our discipline—most of which, I would think, emanate from colleagues (and I include myself here) who are unaware that this is what they are doing and whose explicit intentions and commitments run counter to such sexist practice: "Helen Bond on Sexism and NT Scholarship," *The Jesus Blog*, December 10, 2014, http://historicaljesusresearch.blogspot.com/2014/12/helen-bond-on-sexism-and-nt-scholarship.html. The broader issues of sexism and gender bias in, say, the Society for New Testament Studies (and other organizations), are complex, multifaceted, and in part historical and structural, such that they cannot simply be addressed at an individual level.

14. I thank my Exeter colleague Katharine Tyler for helpful comments on an initial draft of the following section and suggestions for further reading, though she of course bears no responsibility for what I present here. On major themes in "whiteness studies," see Katharine Tyler, *Whiteness, Class and the Legacies of Empire: On Home Ground* (Basingstoke: Palgrave Macmillan, 2012), 14–21.

15. Among the representative collections indicating the interest in the subject, see Ruth

Writing in 1999, for example, Thomas Nakayama and Judith Martin note "an emerging and interdisciplinary interest in whiteness and its reconfiguration in an era of increasing multiculturalism in everyday life," an interest "widespread across a number of academic fields."[16] Key works from the 1990s often identified as exemplifying and stimulating this emergence include David Roediger's *The Wages of Whiteness*, Ruth Frankenberg's *White Women, Race Matters*, and Richard Dyer's *White*—all works from writers identified as white, a point to which we shall return.[17] It is important, however, to trace the origins of a critical interest in whiteness, as Sara Ahmed insists, to the early work of Black feminists such as Audre Lorde and Toni Morrison—and, indeed, earlier to the work of W. E. B. DuBois—and their critique of "how whiteness works as a form of racial privilege."[18] Indeed, Roediger is acerbic in his critique of the tendency to depict the study of whiteness as "brand new and . . . a white thing": "Characterizing the study of whiteness as a project of white scholars . . . represents both a continued insistence on placing whites at the center of everything and a continuing refusal to take seriously the insights into whiteness that people of color offer."[19] Similarly, in the field of

---

Frankenberg, ed., *Displacing Whiteness: Essays in Social and Cultural Criticism* (Durham, NC: Duke University Press, 1997); Richard Delgado and Jean Stefancic, *Critical White Studies: Looking Behind the Mirror* (Philadelphia: Temple University Press, 1997); Thomas K. Nakayama and Judith N. Martin, eds., *Whiteness: The Communication of Social Identity* (Thousand Oaks, CA: Sage, 1999).

16. Thomas K. Nakayama and Judith N. Martin, "Introduction: Whiteness as the Communication of Social Identity," in Nakayama and Martin, *Whiteness*, vii. For the wide cross-disciplinary interest, see also, e.g., Tammie M. Kennedy et al., "Symposium: Whiteness Studies," *Rhetoric Review* 24 (2005): 359–402.

17. David Roediger, *The Wages of Whiteness: Race and the Making of the American Working Class* (London: Verso, 1991); Ruth Frankenberg, *White Women, Race Matters: The Social Construction of Whiteness* (Minneapolis: University of Minnesota Press, 1993); Richard Dyer, *White* (London: Routledge, 1997).

18. Ahmed, "Declarations of Whiteness," §2. See Audre Lorde, *Sister Outsider: Essays and Speeches*, The Crossing Press Feminist Series (Freedom, CA: Crossing Press, 1984); Toni Morrison, *Playing in the Dark: Whiteness and the Literary Imagination* (Cambridge, MA: Harvard University Press, 1992); W. E. B. DuBois, *Black Reconstruction in America* (London: Frank Cass; New York: Russell & Russell, 1966). Also to be noted as a landmark study is the 1993 essay by African American lawyer Cheryl I. Harris, "Whiteness as Property," *Harvard Law Review* 106 (1993): 1707–91.

19. David Roediger, *Colored White: Transcending the Racial Past* (Berkeley: University of California Press, 2002), 19, 20. Roediger's early study, *The Wages of Whiteness*, takes an important orientation from DuBois's insight into the "psychological wage" that being white paid (DuBois, *Black Reconstruction*, 700).

biblical studies, the pioneering work of African American, Asian, and other so-called minority perspectives needs to be credited with initiating a critical analysis of the racially-located traditions of European and North American exegesis, as we shall see in more detail below (§9.3.3).[20] Yet the specific interest in whiteness as a topic for critical analysis has only recently spread to the disciplines of theology[21] and biblical studies.[22]

A key reason for the emergence of this critical focus was the conviction that whiteness had remained largely "invisible" and thus unexamined in the field of race studies. It is important to make clear that this racialized construction of "whiteness" is not an objective or "essential" characteristic of those to whom it is assigned but rather a socially constructed, historically contingent, and ideologically loaded category; the division of people into white and non-white, formally or informally, bifurcates human diversity with an arbitrary line.[23] Yet whiteness has too often been an identity that, given

20. See, for example, Cain Hope Felder, ed., *Stony the Road We Trod: African American Biblical Interpretation* (Minneapolis: Fortress, 1991); R. S. Sugirtharajah, *Voices from the Margin: Interpreting the Bible in the Third World* (London: SPCK, 1991); Fernando F. Segovia and Mary Ann Tolbert, eds., *Reading from This Place*, 2 vols. (Minneapolis: Fortress, 1995).

21. Again, the work of African American theologians on the constructions of race, whiteness, and otherness is an important influence. See, for example, Carter, *Race*, who sees "the problem of whiteness . . . as the core theological problem of our times" (6) and "as the inner architecture of modern theology" (377); cf. Jennings, *Christian Imagination*. As indications of the recent interest in whiteness, see, e.g., George Yancy, ed., *Christology and Whiteness: What Would Jesus Do?* (London: Routledge, 2012); Deanna A. Thompson, "Calling a Thing What It Is: A Lutheran Approach to Whiteness," *Dialog* 53 (2014): 49–57; Garrigan, "Irish Theology"; David Clough, "Using Barth 'to Justify Doing Nothing': James Cone's Unanswered Critique of Barth Studies, 50 Years On" (paper presented at the Annual Karl Barth Conference: Karl Barth and the Future of Liberation Theology, Princeton, NJ, 2018).

22. Among these contributions are Jeffrey S. Siker, "Historicizing a Racialized Jesus: Case Studies in the 'Black Christ,' the 'Mestizo Christ,' and White Critique," *BibInt* 15 (2007): 26–53, esp. 47–53; Carey, "Introduction"; Denise Kimber Buell, "Anachronistic Whiteness and the Ethics of Interpretation," in Hockey and Horrell, *Ethnicity, Race, Religion*, 149–67; David G. Horrell, "Paul, Inclusion, and Whiteness: Particularising Interpretation," *JSNT* 40 (2017): 123–47. For a critical response to Siker's article, arguing that it does not sufficiently confront the problems of "white invisibility," see Wongi Park, "The Black Jesus, the Mestizo Jesus, and the Historical Jesus," *BibInt* 25 (2017): 190–205. There have also been some reflections specifically on and from the South African context: Gerrie Snyman, "African Hermeneutics' 'Outing' of Whiteness," *Neot* 42 (2008): 93–118; Jeremy Punt, "(Southern) African Postcolonial Biblical Interpretation: A White African Perspective" (paper presented at the SBL Annual Meeting, San Antonio, TX, November 2016).

23. See, for example, discussions of Irish identity and its changing relationship to white-

its dominant position in Western societies, could be taken as normative—a kind of unlabeled position that stands as universal, unmarked, unraced; a racialized identity not recognized as racial or racially particular by those deemed to inhabit it.[24] Thus Richard Dyer, in one of the landmark works of critical whiteness studies, speaks of "the invisibility of whiteness as a racial position,"[25] which he links with the tendency of the white perspective to function as the universal, ubiquitous, human perspective: "As long as race is something only applied to non-white peoples, as long as white people are not racially seen and named, they/we function as a human norm. Other people are raced, we are just people."[26] Ruth Frankenberg, another of the pioneers of contemporary whiteness studies, suggests that "the white Western self as a racial being has for the most part remained unexamined and unnamed."[27] Like Dyer, she highlights the "seeming normativity" and "structured invisibility" that result from the privileged and dominant position of white people.[28] More recent work continues to offer similar definitions: "Whiteness is defined as an identity that is neither problematized nor particularized within discourses on race because it assumes a status of normalcy."[29] In the field of biblical studies, Greg Carey suggests a similar definition of whiteness that indicates the importance of this self-critical interrogation: "'whiteness' functions as the attempt to define *other* groups as non-white without subjecting white identity itself to critical reflection."[30] It is important, though, to note

---

ness in Roediger, *Wages*, 133–63; Garrigan, "Irish Theology." On the artificial construction of "white" as a category in the USA and the costs of this categorization, see James Baldwin, "On Being 'White' . . . and Other Lies," in *Black on White: Black Writers on What It Means to Be White*, ed. David Roediger (New York: Schocken, 1998), 177–80.

24. See Tyler, *Whiteness*, 5: "White ethnicity often remains unmarked as an ethnic identity within everyday British society. . . . In identifying my research participants as 'White,' my aim is to make Whiteness a racially marked and visible category in the same way that non-White people are always already racially marked by the racial labels that are routinely used to describe them." This kind of point is regularly made in the literature on whiteness.

25. Dyer, *White*, 3.

26. Dyer, *White*, 1.

27. Frankenberg, *White Women*, 17.

28. Frankenberg, *White Women*, 6; see also 17–18.

29. Cleveland Hayes et al., "Toward a Lesser Shade of White: 12 Steps Towards More Authentic Race Awareness," in *Unhooking from Whiteness: The Key to Dismantling Racism in the United States*, ed. Cleveland Hayes and Nicholas D. Hartlep (Rotterdam: Sense Publishers, 2013), 2. See, similarly, George Yancy, "Introduction: Framing the Problem," in Yancy, *Christology and Whiteness*, 8: "Whiteness . . . functions, paradoxically, as that which signifies the 'superior' *race* while precisely obfuscating its status as *raced*."

30. Carey, "Introduction," 8.

Ahmed's observation that "whiteness is only invisible for those who inhabit it. For those who don't, it is hard not to see whiteness."[31] Indeed, we should also note that this "invisibility of whiteness" is itself a characteristic only of certain societies at certain points in time—perhaps most pertinently for the major works in whiteness studies, the multicultural Western societies of the latter decades of the twentieth and into the twenty-first century, where political commitment to racial equality coexists with the ongoing dominance and privileges enjoyed by those of us raced as white.[32]

According to Frankenberg, whiteness has three linked dimensions: "First, whiteness is a location of structural advantage, or race privilege. Second, it is a 'standpoint,' a place from which white people look at ourselves, at others, and at society. Third, 'whiteness' refers to a set of cultural practices that are usually unmarked and unnamed."[33] Similarly, Audrey Thompson notes the different ways in which "whiteness" may be understood as a category of analysis, depending in part on the political perspective of the interpreter: it may be associated primarily with skin color (a physiognomic feature), with European cultural heritage, or with a structural position of privilege.[34]

Whiteness studies calls for the critical interrogation of constructions of whiteness, probing especially the veiling of its particularity. "Naming 'whiteness,'" Frankenberg argues, "displaces it from the unmarked, unnamed status that is itself an effect of its dominance."[35] Dyer, likewise, sees the unmasking of the particularity of whiteness as a crucial task in unveiling and counteracting its power:

31. Ahmed, "Declarations of Whiteness," §1.

32. This is a point I owe to Mark Brett in a response he presented to a paper of mine touching on this topic. Brett notes, for example, the explicit declaration of the superiority of the white race by the first Australian Prime Minister, Edmund Barton, in 1901: "There is no racial equality. There is that basic inequality. These races are, in comparison with white races—I think no one wants convincing of this fact—unequal and inferior. The doctrine of the equality of man was never intended to apply to the equality of the Englishman and the Chinaman" ("Immigration Restriction Bill," Australian House of Representatives, September 26, 1901). Examples from other countries could be added, Apartheid South Africa being perhaps the most obvious example, as well as the recent rise of a kind of "alt-right" white supremacism in the USA.

33. Frankenberg, *White Women*, 1.

34. Audrey Thompson, "Reading Black Philosophers in Chronological Order," in *The Center Must Not Hold: White Women Philosophers on the Whiteness of Philosophy*, ed. George Yancy (Lanham, MD: Lexington, 2010), 31.

35. Frankenberg, *White Women*, 6.

There is no more powerful position than that of being "just" human. The claim to power is the claim to speak for the commonality of humanity. Raced people can't do that—they can only speak for their race. But non-raced people can, for they do not represent the interests of a race. The point of seeing the racing of whites is to dislodge them/us from the position of power, with all the inequities, oppression, privileges and sufferings in its train, dislodging them/us by undercutting the authority with which they/ we speak and act in and on the world.[36]

Rooting this construction of whiteness in the colonial expansion of Western Europe, Frankenberg suggests that "one effect of colonial discourse is the production of an unmarked, apparently autonomous white/Western self, in contrast with the marked, Other racial and cultural categories with which the racially and culturally dominant category is coconstructed."[37] As Dyer puts it:

It has become common for those marginalised by culture to acknowledge the situation from which they speak, but those who occupy positions of cultural hegemony blithely carry on as if what they say is neutral and unsit-uated—human but not raced. As I shall argue later, there is something es-pecially white in this non-located and disembodied position of knowledge, and thus it seems especially important to try to break the hold of whiteness by locating and embodying it in a particular experience of being white.[38]

The goal of Frankenberg's early study, then, as of critical whiteness stud-ies more generally, is to probe the ways in which whiteness, precisely as a racialized identity, is constructed and maintained. As Frankenberg empha-sizes, this does not imply that race and racial difference are somehow "real" in any essentialist (let alone physiological or biological) way, but rather that "race, like gender, is 'real' in the sense that it has real, though changing, effects in the world and real, tangible, and complex impact on individuals' sense of self, experiences, and life chances."[39] In this way, it is hoped that

36. Dyer, *White*, 2.

37. Frankenberg, *White Women*, 17. On the centrality of the colonial project in the mak-ing of modern Europe and its ideological (racial) foundations, see also Walter D. Mignolo, "Epistemic Disobedience, Independent Thought and De-Colonial Freedom," *Theory, Culture & Society* 26 (2009): 16; Jennings, *Christian Imagination*; Robert Young, *White Mythologies*.

38. Dyer, *White*, 4.

39. Frankenberg, *White Women*, 11.

what is too often presented as an unsituated, non-specific, universal human perspective might be unmasked and made specific, identified, contextualized. Dyer expresses the challenge as follows: "White people need to learn to see themselves as white, to see their particularity. In other words, whiteness needs to be made strange."[40]

Whiteness studies thus calls for the critical interrogation of the constructions and effects of whiteness, probing especially the veiling of its particularity. This forms part of the wider critical project of following through the implications of the realization that knowledge is produced by located subjects, a fundamental issue of epistemology. One of the important claims that has emerged from both feminist and critical race studies, pertinent across many academic fields, is that knowledge is not to be seen as an innocent, neutral, or "disembodied" product. In Walter Mignolo's words, "the knower is always implicated, geo- and body-politically, in the known"; and what is known is always known by "a racially marked body in a geo-historical marked space."[41] Barbara Applebaum, for example, comments on the assumption in modern Western philosophy that "knowledge is exclusively a function of the mind" such that the discipline of philosophy "prides itself on a disembodied epistemology." She goes on to encapsulate the warnings of "both feminists and critical race scholars" that "what is considered essentially and universally human is a mystified version of what is masculine, white, able-bodied, heterosexual and Western."[42] It is one thing, of course, to assert this particularity of knowledge and another to demonstrate how it might be visible in specific disciplinary areas—which is part of the task I shall attempt in the following section. It is also challenging to navigate the terrain between the assumption that knowledge is simply knowledge—abstract, disembodied, universal—and the insistence that it is embodied and particular. Siding with the latter conviction should not be allowed to imply the assumption that all members of a certain group, whether identified on the basis of gender, race, or religion, see things the same way such that any one person might "represent" the perspective of their identity-grouping.[43]

40. Dyer, *White*, 10.

41. Mignolo, "Epistemic Disobedience," 4 and 2 respectively.

42. Barbara Applebaum, "White Ignorance and Denials of Complicity: On the Possibility of Doing Philosophy in Good Faith," in Yancy, *The Center Must Not Hold*, 13.

43. Peggy McIntosh lists as one of the privileges of whiteness "never [being] asked to speak for all the people of my racial group"; see Peggy McIntosh, "White Privilege: Unpacking the Invisible Knapsack," National Seed Project, https://www.nationalseedproject.org/images/documents/Knapsack_plus_Notes-Peggy_McIntosh.pdf; orig. in *Peace and*

Nor should it be taken to mean that people of different genders, ethnicities, races, and religions cannot develop informed, critical, and valuable perspectives on traditions and groups not their own.[44] Nor should it be used as a basis for evading rigorous and reasoned argument intended to evaluate and discern more and less convincing perspectives, whether historical, political, or ethical—though what passes for "rigorous and reasoned" should also be subject to critical suspicion in terms of differentials of power and assumption about what constitutes knowledge.[45] But it can, and should, lead us to (self)-critical investigation of scholarly traditions and the extent to which they might be seen as products of particular locations.[46]

It is also important to stress that the project of whiteness studies, for all its critical intent, aims fundamentally to explore and particularize the perspective of whiteness. It insists that one facet—and a crucial one at that—of the identity that shapes the way we see and understand the world is that of race or ethnicity, socially constructed though these categories are, and that whiteness is one racialized identity that needs to be interrogated explicitly and critically, just as much as—and perhaps, given its historical dominance and claims to universality, more than—other such identities. As is clear, for example from Frankenberg's early study based on interviews with a range of white women, the aim is to explore the various ways in which whiteness as identity is constructed, including among those with clear and explicit commitments to racial equality and anti-racist action. Indeed, both Frankenberg and Dyer identify themselves within the focus of their critical investigations of whiteness; their projects are, in part at least, a probing of their own identity and its implications as those who are constructed—by others as well as by themselves—as white. In other words, to recall Carey's phrase, it is a matter of "subjecting white identity itself to critical reflection."[47]

Freedom Magazine, July/August 1989, 10–12. Developing a critical perspective on whiteness should not mean that the expectation of "speaking on behalf of one's race" is extended to those raced as white.

44. See further the reflections on white scholars researching and teaching black history in Thompson, "Reading Black Philosophers."

45. On the particular forms that reason and rationality take in the (white) Western philosophical tradition, see, e.g., Cynthia Kaufman, "Is Philosophy Anything If It Isn't White?," in Yancy, *The Center Must Not Hold*, 245–63.

46. See further Young, *White Mythologies*, on the connections between epistemology, the writing of history, and European colonialism, or "the link between structures of knowledge and the forms of oppression of the last two hundred years: a phenomenon that has become known as Eurocentrism" (2).

47. Carey, "Introduction," 8.

There are, as Ahmed points out, risks to be identified in the project of critical whiteness studies: that whiteness itself may be "essentialized" or reified as an object of study; that whiteness will thus be sustained "at the centre of intellectual inquiry"; that the discourse may even become a focus for the positive appreciation of whiteness—for people "learning to love their own whiteness." Moreover, Ahmed highlights the risk that the critical interrogation of whiteness may become valorized in itself, as if the identification of the constructions of whiteness of itself achieves anti-racist goals when changes in practice and relationship still remain as challenges.[48] Yet this critical interrogation is, if not sufficient, clearly necessary in order to bring to light how a certain racialized identity, often overlooked, unmarked, or presented as universal, is itself the product of a particular bodily location in the world. Particularizing whiteness and subjecting it to critical scrutiny is one way to dethrone this perspective from a position of assumed universality and disembodied rationality and to place it alongside—not "above"—other embodied and particular perspectives.

9.3 Particularizing (White, Western, Christian) New Testament Studies

Returning to the field of New Testament studies after an overview of whiteness studies may seem a sharp disjunction, but I hope to show that insights from reflection on "whiteness" may inform our critical reflection in two main ways, focused in turn on the "religious" and the "ethnoracial" aspects of the discipline's location, even though these aspects cannot be neatly separated. Indeed, as I shall suggest further below, there are particular reasons to connect these issues in the field of New Testament studies, given the links between "Christianness" and "whiteness" and the ways that this "white Christian" identity is constructed in relation to Jewish and to "non-white" peoples. In the first section, the insights of studies of whiteness, linked with recent discussions of "Christian privilege," are used to provoke a parallel consideration of "Christianness" and its influence on interpretation: How might some of the themes identified as problematic aspects of the white gaze on the world—presumed normativity, implicit superiority, and universalizing of particularity—enable us to think about the way that (white) Christian identity and commitment shape New Testament interpretation? Might there

48. Ahmed, "Declarations of Whiteness," esp. §§3–12, with quotations from §§4 and 5 respectively.

be some value, adapting Dyer's goal for the critical evaluation of whiteness, in "making Christianness strange"? In the second section, we turn more directly to the subject of whiteness, considering how far the perspectives in the dominant traditions of New Testament studies are not only Christianly particular but also racially particular, the product of an essentially white, Eurocentric or Western view of the world—not because individuals intend, self-identify with, or promote this perspective but rather because, in both the past and the present, it forms the context that shapes the discipline's modes of thinking.

9.3.1 *Making Christianness Strange?*

There are of course clear and significant differences between "whiteness" and "Christianness": the former denotes a racialized identity while the latter refers to a religious commitment that may be held by people of all races, ethnicities, and nationalities. Even if the overlaps between religious and ethnic or racial identities are more profound and complex than often acknowledged (see §3.3), there can be no blanket collation of these two labels. Nonetheless, in contexts where both combine to define the dominant majority, there are strong connections between them.[49] Some recent studies from the US context have suggested both parallels and certain intersections between "white privilege" and "Christian privilege."[50] As Amy-Jill Levine suggests, in such contexts, we can "extrapolate from studies of racial privilege and fragility to interrogate the structural systems of Christian privilege and Christian

49. For example, a 2017 Pew Research Center survey (Stokes, "What It Takes") revealed that in the USA, 57 percent of white evangelical Protestant respondents felt that it was "very important" to be Christian in order to truly share the national identity of "American" (for Americans overall, the figure was 32 percent).

50. See, e.g., on the specifically Christian privilege that operates in the US education system, Kevin J. Burke and Avner Segall, *Christian Privilege in U.S. Education: Legacies and Current Issues*, Studies in Curriculum Theory (London: Routledge, 2017); and on the parallels and connections between "white privilege" and "Christian privilege," Jason A. Mahn, *Becoming a Christian in Christendom: Radical Discipleship and the Way of the Cross in America's "Christian" Culture* (Minneapolis: Fortress, 2016), 29–52 (this is a chapter on "unpacking Christian privilege," consciously alluding to the work of Peggy McIntosh on white privilege; see n. 43 above). Also on these connections, specifically related to the problem of anti-Judaism in Christian preaching, see Amy-Jill Levine, "Christian Privilege, Christian Fragility, and the Gospel of John," in *The Gospel of John and Jewish-Christian Relations*, ed. Adele Reinhartz (Lanham, MD: Lexington, 2018), 87–110.

fragility," since "these phenomena are analogous to, and often reinforced by, white privilege and white fragility."[51] Likewise, Jason Mahn, in "unpacking Christian privilege," does so through an "excursion in the problem of white privilege because of how well it aligns with the experience of being identified as a Christian in the United States today."[52] We may thus explore how the Christian location of the interpreter—whether that location is a matter of personal commitment, institutional affiliation, or disciplinary tradition—shapes interpretation and depictions of the "structural dichotomy" in particular, more profoundly than may be intended or acknowledged, and in ways that might be illuminated by the parallels with the critical investigation of whiteness. By highlighting the extent and nature of this Christian influence, I want not only to identify and particularize it but also to render it strange, just as Dyer refers to the goal of whiteness studies as "making whiteness strange."[53]

The focus of the kinds of studies surveyed in chapter 1, notwithstanding their significant differences, is on the (potential) achievement of early Christianity—or the Jesus movement, Christ-groups, or whatever neologisms are used. And almost inevitably, given the context of Christian origins, this achievement, potential, or value is articulated in relationship to Judaism. This may be expressed in the Hegelian language of F. C. Baur, with Judaism's servile particularity overcome (*aufgehoben*) by Christianity's universality and freedom; or in the new perspective's contrast between Jewish ethnocentrism and Christian openness; or in more recent discussions of the way in which a "trans-ethnic" identity "in Christ" can unite and affirm both Jews and gentiles, transcending but preserving their diversity. Much recent scholarship, as we have seen, tends to stress how this inclusion takes place without erasing or even devaluing the existing identities of those who join: Jews remain Jews and gentiles gentiles while finding a common group identity in Christ. Being in Christ transcends religious and ethnic distinctions and thus provides hope for a (contemporary) world divided along such

---

51. Levine, "Christian Privilege," 88 and 87 respectively. By "fragility" in this context, Levine refers, quoting Robin DiAngelo, to the "defensive moves" that may be triggered by stress related to racial or religious identity, leading to "anger, fear, and guilt" (88). See further Robin DiAngelo, *What Does It Mean to Be White? Developing White Racial Literacy*, rev. ed., Counterpoints: Studies in the Postmodern Theory of Education 497 (New York: Lang, 2016), 245–53; DiAngelo, *White Fragility: Why It's So Hard for White People to Talk about Racism* (Boston, MA: Beacon, 2018).

52. Mahn, *Becoming a Christian*, 37.

53. Dyer, *White*, 4.

lines. What remains broadly consistent across these diverse perspectives is the focus on the potential of the Christian message to provide some kind of basis for this positive outcome, the depiction of which changes over time, as we shall explore in more detail below. Conversely, the potential of the Jewish traditions to offer their own modes of inclusion, participation, and multi-ethnic group identity tends not to be the focus. Indeed, the emphasis on Jewish particularity—or, in more recent terminology, on its ethnic character—may serve to show how as an ethnic group it comes into conflict with other ethnic groups such that peaceable co-existence may be enabled by the kind of "superordinate," "trans-ethnic" identity provided in Christ.[54] What may instead be highlighted are less appealing characteristics supposedly typical of Jewish communities: ethnic pride, ethnocentrism, exclusivism, and so on. Commentary on Gal 3:28 often exemplifies such contrasts. For example, Leon Morris writes that

> in the first century the Jews despised the Gentiles (even proselytes were not fully accepted) [this assertion lacks any evidence], the Greeks looked down on uncultured people outside their race, the Romans felt themselves superior to those they had conquered, and so on. . . . Jews divided the whole human race into Jews and Gentiles and they saw only themselves as making up the people of God. . . . The Jews were very proud of the fact that they were the descendants of the great patriarch [Abraham] and physically his heirs.[55]

These proud and divisive viewpoints are starkly contrasted with Paul's insistence

> that the great divide between Jew and Gentile that meant so much to the Jews in general is meaningless. . . . When people are saved by Jesus Christ they are brought into a marvellous unity. . . . Even the major divisions in the human race cannot do away with this unity.[56]

54. Cf. Esler, *Conflict and Identity*, discussed above in §1.3.

55. Leon Morris, *Galatians: Paul's Charter of Christian Freedom* (Leicester: Inter-Varsity Press, 1996), 121, 124.

56. Morris, *Galatians*, 121, 123. Very similar comments are made by William Hendriksen, *New Testament Commentary: Exposition of Galatians* (Grand Rapids: Baker, 1968), 149–50; and by Herman N. Ridderbos, *The Epistle of Paul to the Churches of Galatia*, NICNT (Grand Rapids: Eerdmans, 1953), 149–50. For further discussion of the interpretive history of Gal 3:28 in this regard, see Horrell, "Paul, Inclusion, and Whiteness."

Scholars sometimes note that the other obvious contender for a comparable offer of trans-ethnic inclusion at the time of Christian origins was the Roman Empire itself, but the oppression and violence associated with this form of "inclusion" are negatively juxtaposed—and thus easily rejected by comparison—with the positive vision of peaceable affirmation of diversity seen in the earliest Christian vision.[57] By ignoring the violence and oppression with which Christianity soon enough began to enact its program of universal inclusion, once it had the means at its disposal, this inequitable comparison is again able (on its own terms) to depict the Christian option as superior. It is not hard to see that it is the Christianness of these scholarly perspectives that shapes both the focus and the conclusions and leads to the depiction of the Christian identity as literally superior—in the sense that other identities can "nest" beneath it or be transcended by it more positively than in competing alternatives.

Several critical observations may be made. The first, part of the task of making Christianness "strange," is to question the assumption underlying appeals to the attractiveness of this Christian vision. Whatever its positive promise—whether expressed in Baurian terms of freedom and spirit or in the more modern terms of the valuing of ethnic, racial, or religious diversity—the focus of the vision on Christ may make it attractive for Christians, but for others it may sound more like a threat of religious, cultural, or political imperialism, as Daniel Boyarin has stressed.[58] The demand for exclusive commitment to Christ does not necessarily allow diversity or existing identities to continue any more than does a commitment to Jewish Torah or other comparable commitments.[59] As we have seen (ch. 8), there is substantial evidence to indicate not only the appeal of Jewish customs and practices to outsiders but also a widespread openness to various levels of participation—whether as sympathizer, Godfearer, or full proselyte. Why should adopting this identity equate to "eliminating diversity"—self-evidently a bad thing—whereas joining Christ, becoming a Christian, is to join a group that

---

57. See, e.g., Kuecker, *Spirit and the "Other,"* 226; Ehrensperger, *Paul at the Crossroads,* 158, 172–73. See above pp. 40–42 with nn. 70, 81–82.

58. Boyarin, *Radical Jew.*

59. Contrast, for example, Peter Oakes's comment on Gal 3:28: Paul's aim "is to preserve social diversity rather than to eliminate it" and "to be inclusive," whereas "it is Paul's opponents who are seeking to eliminate diversity. They want gentiles to adopt circumcision, to Judaize, to become Jews, losing their distinction in identity. Paul wants unity between gentiles as gentiles and Jews as Jews, all together in Christ"; Peter Oakes, *Galatians,* Paideia Commentaries on the New Testament (Grand Rapids: Baker Academic, 2015), 128–29.

embodies hope for human unity and positive tolerance of diversity? Paul is insistent, for example, that people must become Christian—or, if one rejects that specific label as anachronistic, that they make being an "in-Christ" (cf. 2 Cor 12:2) the defining center of their identity. Moreover, the claims for the potential of this Christian vision—whether as universal, inclusive, open, or trans-ethnic—depend on its being placed above other forms of religious, ethnic, or social identification such that they can "nest" beneath its umbrella. The religio-ethnic particularity of early Christian identity—its exclusionary boundaries and specific people-like sense of belonging, its "ethnicizing" or "ethnocentric" tendencies—is often left aside or downplayed, despite the extent to which, as we have seen in chapters 4–8, this "Christian" identity is formed precisely by drawing on various facets of what is typically seen as "ethnic" discourse and practice.[60] On the contrary, the attractiveness of this specifically "Christian" vision is often universalized—implicitly or explicitly—by depicting it as offering hopeful potential to the modern world.

Just as whiteness studies has criticized the tendency of white authors to write as if they did so from a general, universal, unraced location, so too we might critically question the extent to which scholarship on Christian origins presents itself as offering a historically grounded, rationally argued, "human" view of the earliest Christian groups—and of the positive potential of their ideas for the contemporary world—while that perspective is in fact particular, and particularly Christian. There may be a parallel between the tendency of white people, subjected to critical analysis in whiteness studies, to speak as if from a universal "human" perspective without acknowledging their (racialized) particularity and the tendency of Christian scholars insufficiently to acknowledge the influence of their Christian particularity on their depictions of the attractions and contemporary relevance of the early Christian achievement. This may be especially so when whiteness and Christianness coincide, given the tendency highlighted in whiteness studies for this perspective to presume a certain universality and non-particularity. The particularity of this Christian viewpoint may be insufficiently acknowledged in two crucial respects. First, the depiction of the early Christian groups as open, inclusive, trans-ethnic, or universal often downplays their exclusiveness and particularity. Second, the particularity of the implicitly Christian

---

60. It is interesting to note a move toward emphasizing the "ethno-social particularity" of Paul's vision of Christian community in the recent work of N. T. Wright, following the work of Love Sechrest in this regard. See Wright, *Paul and the Faithfulness of God*, 1443–49; Sechrest, *A Former Jew*; and the discussion in Horrell, "Grace, Race."

perspective itself, from which the analysis of the early Christian movement is conducted in ostensibly historical terms, is inadequately acknowledged.

The reason why perspectives that implicitly reflect Christian commitment and a sense of Christianity's superiority are dominant in the discipline is not hard to discern: many scholars who work on the New Testament are motivated to do so by their own Christian commitment, and/or they teach in institutions with a Christian foundation—sometimes institutions where Christian clergy are trained—and they research and write (in part at least) for a wider Christian readership. More broadly, the discipline is shaped by its origins and location in this Christian context. Let me stress that these connections between academic discipline and religious commitment are not in my view any cause for lament or criticism. But there are implications that require serious and ongoing critical reflection. Because of the focus, purpose, and audience of much New Testament scholarship, the tasks of historical reconstruction and "theologizing" through exegesis of a text are often closely intertwined.[61] This means that it is not always clear how far an author is seeking to describe the historical setting and comparisons in the light of relevant evidence or to rearticulate and reiterate what the text itself is claiming. This carries particular risks in our field, especially in terms of the comparisons drawn with Judaism.[62] Whatever Paul intends to claim in Gal 3:28, for example—which *might*, potentially, include the idea expressed by Morris, that this community represents a "marvellous unity" far superior to the alternatives on offer—Morris's comments on the text (quoted above) not only affirm such a view but undergird it with ostensibly historical information about the pride with which Jews distinguished themselves from the despised gentiles and so on. The risks of reinscribing such depictions still need to be stressed, as the events discussed at the opening of this book make clear.[63] The strongly Christian character of New Testament studies means

61. E.g., in the prologue to his study of Paul's theology, James D. G. Dunn, *The Theology of Paul the Apostle* (Edinburgh: T&T Clark, 1998), 24, describes his aims as "first of all, so far as possible, to get inside the skin of Paul, to see through his eyes, to think his thoughts from inside . . . [and] at the same time . . . to theologize *with* Paul" (italics original).

62. For just one exposé of the ways in which Christian assumptions shape exegetical and historical argument, see Amy-Jill Levine, "Discharging Responsibility: Matthean Jesus, Biblical Law, and Hemorrhaging Woman," in *Treasures New and Old: Contributions to Matthean Studies*, ed. David R. Bauer and Mark Allan Powell, SBL Symposium Series 1 (Atlanta: Scholars Press, 1996), 379–97.

63. On the continuing prevalence of such anti-Jewish characterizations in Christian preaching, see, e.g., Levine, "Christian Privilege," 89–91; and more generally in Christian

that self-critical probing—attempts to remind ourselves how "strangely" Christian are the perspectives and arguments often developed—is vital, as are opportunities and efforts to learn from those who do not approach the texts from the same perspective.

9.3.2 Whiteness and Constructions of the Early Christian Vision

There may, then, be a certain parallel—and indeed, particular connections—between the "white" identity that whiteness studies seeks to particularize and the Christian identity that so shapes the interpretation of early Christianity and also needs, I have suggested, to be particularized. But there is a further question to be probed, one that invites us to consider whether the correlation between whiteness and Christianness and their mutual implicatedness in the interpretation of the New Testament might be even closer. To what extent is the implicit superiority granted to what is taken to be the early Christian vision purely an issue of "religion," a perspective deriving from the fact that most of the New Testament's modern interpreters are located, either personally or institutionally, within the Christian tradition? In other words, is there also a racial dimension to the particular constructions of the early Christian vision as depicted in New Testament scholarship?

Modern historical-critical New Testament scholarship developed in Western Europe precisely during the period when European colonialism was at its height and in which mission and empire coincided in an awkward (and sometimes uneasy) alliance. As we saw in the opening chapter, through the example of Hegel and Baur in particular, Orientalist views of the Western European races in comparison with their African and Asian (and Jewish) counterparts are infused into the early work of the discipline. Thus, woven into the discipline's early fabric is an ideology of religious and racial superiority that reflects its specifically European origins: it is in Christianity that humanity finds its highest freedom and calling and in the peoples of Western Europe that this is first and most clearly realized. We need also to remember the profound irony that the lofty humanistic ideals of the European Enlightenment—the context for the emergence of New Testament studies as a modern discipline—were being articulated precisely in an era when Europeans were brutally subduing, exploiting, enslaving, and killing vast numbers of

---

scholarship and theology, see Amy-Jill Levine, *The Misunderstood Jew: The Church and the Scandal of the Jewish Jesus* (New York: HarperOne, 2006).

other peoples around the world, a disjunction only made possible, it seems, through racial ideologies that cast these (mostly) dark-skinned others as less than fully human.[64] The irony is expressed in a typically direct manner by Frantz Fanon in one of the seminal texts of the decolonial struggle:

> The violence with which the supremacy of white values is affirmed and the aggressiveness which has permeated the victory of these values over the ways of life and thought of the colonized mean that, in revenge, the colonized person laughs in mockery when Western values are mentioned in front of him.[65]

This is, however, another point at which the connections between "whiteness" and "Christianness" become significant: the racial ideologies that legitimated colonial projects also undergirded European antisemitism. Robert Young remarks that "fascism was simply colonialism brought home to Europe."[66] As noted in the introduction, other scholars have made the broader case that the modern Western ideologies of race find their origin in Christianity's construal of its relationship to Judaism.

Another of the main observations—and key claims—made in chapter 1 is that the "structural dichotomy" between Judaism and Christianity that we find formulated so clearly by critics such as Baur continues to be replicated in varying forms through the later history of New Testament studies up to the present day, despite the shifts to new paradigms, perspectives, and methods. If this basic "shape" continues, in at least some prominent repre-

---

64. See, e.g., Young, *White Mythologies*, 119, 121: "European thought since the Renaissance would be as unthinkable without the impact of colonialism as the history of the world since the Renaissance would be inconceivable without the effects of Europeanization. . . . Humanism itself, often validated amongst the highest values of European civilization, was deeply complicit with the violent negativity of colonialism, and played a crucial part in its ideology." See also Mignolo, "Epistemic Disobedience," 16.

65. Frantz Fanon, *The Wretched of the Earth*, trans. Constance Farrington (London: Penguin, 1967), 33. I have altered the original translation of *des colonisés* and *le colonisé* as "native" in both places to "colonized." For the French original (from 1961), see Frantz Fanon, *Les damnés de la terre* (Paris: Éditions La Découverte, 1987), 31. Young, *White Mythologies*, 119–20, describes Fanon's text as "both a revolutionary manifesto of decolonization and the founding analysis of the effects of colonialism upon colonized peoples and their cultures." For another seminal analysis of the relationships between colonizer and colonized, see Albert Memmi, *The Colonizer and the Colonized* (New York: Orion Press; London: Souvenir Press, 1965).

66. Young, *White Mythologies*, 125.

sentations, then we may wonder whether the discipline has yet sufficiently faced the challenge of escaping from the formative influences of this early context—though we shall return to this point, and the voices that have been raised, in the following section. In this regard, there are some features that are unique to the discipline of New Testament studies: its focus on the origins of Christianity and on (part of) the canonical scriptures of that religion, which bear continued status and authority for Christians, not least for many of the scholars and institutions who conduct this research. But there are also features in common with many other academic disciplines, which also trace their modern origins to post-Enlightenment Europe and the period of its colonial expansion. In many such disciplines there has been critical questioning of the extent to which European racial ideologies of superiority may be bound into the orientation and construction of the discipline and associated calls for the radical reshaping of methods and focus. Whether this be anthropology and geography with their tendency to exoticize the (non-Western) other,[67] or classics with its linking of the roots of European civilization to the (Western) Greek and Roman traditions,[68] or philosophy with its construction of a white, Western tradition of thought that dominates teaching and research[69]—in each case the legacy of the discipline's context of origin has been recognized as something that needs sustained and reflective critique.

67. E.g., on the efforts of anthropology to reconfigure itself away from a traditional orientation toward Western observation of non-Western or "primitive" societies, see Talal Asad, "Introduction," in *Anthropology and the Colonial Encounter*, ed. Talal Asad (London: Ithaca, 1973), 9–19; Edward W. Said, "Representing the Colonized: Anthropology's Interlocutors," *Critical Inquiry* 15 (1989): 205–25. As James Clifford, "Introduction: Partial Truths," in *Writing Culture: The Poetics and Politics of Ethnography*, ed. James Clifford and George Marcus (Berkeley: University of California Press, 1986), 23, comments, "Ethnography in the service of anthropology once looked out at clearly defined others, defined as primitive, or tribal, or non-Western, or pre-literate, or nonhistorical. . . . Now ethnography encounters others in relation to itself, while seeing itself as other." For one example of this shift in perspective, as well as the ongoing challenges, see Mwenda Ntarangwi, *Reversed Gaze: An African Ethnography of American Anthropology* (Champaign: University of Illinois Press, 2010).

68. Consider, e.g., the debates in classics around the arguments of Martin Bernal, *The Fabrication of Ancient Greece 1785–1985*, vol. 1 of *Black Athena: The Afroasiatic Roots of Classical Civilisation* (London: Free Association Books, 1987); Martin Bernal, *The Archaeological and Documentary Evidence*, vol. 2 of *Black Athena: The Afroasiatic Roots of Classical Civilisation* (London: Free Association Books, 1991).

69. See, e.g., the critical reflection on the whiteness of philosophy in Yancy, *The Center Must Not Hold*; Robert Bernasconi, "Waking Up White and in Memphis," in *White on White/ Black on Black*, ed. George Yancy (Lanham, MD: Rowman & Littlefield, 2005), 17–25.

Part of this critical task is to demonstrate not only the early ideological influences on the formation of such disciplines but also the ways in which those disciplines continue to be shaped by their sociopolitical, religious, and racialized contexts. In the discipline of New Testament studies, one way in which this contextualized production of our perspectives can become evident is through attending to the *shifts* in language that occur through the various reproductions of the structural dichotomy. Baur's depiction of the contrast between Judaism and Christianity as one between servitude and freedom, flesh and spirit, childhood and maturity (see §1.1) would cause a post-Sanders "new perspective" scholar to cringe. Likewise, a scholar writing in a post-Holocaust, (notionally) decolonized, ecumenical era of inter-religious dialogue would be unlikely to interpret Paul's vision in Gal 3:28 as "an inspiring picture of the world under one universal religion," as Ernest DeWitt Burton did in his 1921 commentary.[70] Yet as we have seen, the post-Holocaust, post-1967, post-Sanders representations of early Christianity in relation to Judaism, while they generally avoid caricaturing the latter with the labels associated with legalism, continue to reproduce the structural dichotomy with new language of ethnocentrism versus openness and inclusion in Christ (see §1.2): for example, Jewish exclusivism, represented by the "profound barrier" of the law is seen to be brought to an end by the offer of inclusion for all who have faith in Christ;[71] Paul's vision of human community, defined "over against ethnic Israel," is seen as "a vision of humankind and human unity that still challenges us today."[72]

Along with this shift in language, we may also observe a tendency, as we saw in chapter 1, to emphasize the idea that "Christian" identity—or "being in Christ"—allows previous identities to be preserved and valued rather than erasing, abolishing, or nullifying them. The diverse identities of Jew and gentile are affirmed but enabled to peaceably coexist under the inclusive, trans-ethnic umbrella of being in Christ. These changes in language and focus correlate with a shift in the kind of relationship that the Christian West has with the rest of the world and in the ideological convictions of the West. In an era of the United Nations, decolonization, inter-religious—not least Jewish-Christian—dialogue, and so on, it is no longer plausible or

---

70. Ernest DeWitt Burton, *A Critical and Exegetical Commentary on the Epistle to the Galatians*, ICC (Edinburgh: T&T Clark, 1921), 206.

71. James D. G. Dunn, *The Epistle to the Galatians*, BNTC (London: A. & C. Black, 1993), 206.

72. Ben Witherington III, *Grace in Galatia: A Commentary on Paul's Letter to the Galatians* (Edinburgh: T&T Clark, 1998), 271, 281.

attractive to speak of Christianity as the "absolute" and universal religion, which marks humanity's progress from "servitude to freedom" (see §1.1). It is significant that in an era when overt imperial ambition has tended to be replaced by language about the valuing of difference, tolerance of diversity, and so on, these more acceptable notions are precisely the kinds of things that are now seen in the early Christian vision, Paul's version of it in particular. In other words, this language itself reflects its own sociopolitical context, in which certain ways of talking of difference are more acceptable and attractive than others.[73] The modern Western model of political liberalism—the aim to create a just framework for the co-existence and tolerance of differences (not least religious differences)—has (now) been "found" in early Christianity and expressed through exegesis of the New Testament texts. Drawing attention to these parallels of ideology and language may help to indicate that such readings of the New Testament are much more enmeshed in their contemporary context than their authors generally assume, despite their ostensibly historical focus.[74] Moreover, by finding in early Christianity precisely the model of tolerant inclusion of difference that is so valorized in Western liberalism, interpreters not only reflect but also add legitimation to that contemporary model, providing it with biblical precedents and foundations. There is a non-coincidental structural similarity—a "correspondence," to recall Arnal's comment[75]—between the scholarly construal of the early Christian vision and the kind of vision that undergirds the project of Western (post-)Christian political liberalism: to create societies in which there is tolerant space for a diversity of cultural and religious identities peacefully to coexist. The intentions and commitments may be laudable, but insofar as it is the Christian worldview that offers the "umbrella" under which identities may safely nest—rather than, say, imagining a framework for co-existence in which Christians nest beneath some other encompassing framework—it may

73. On the ways in which the new perspective reflects and fits within the cultural context of multiculturalism, see John M. G. Barclay, "'Neither Jew nor Greek': Multiculturalism and the New Perspective on Paul," in Brett, *Ethnicity and the Bible*, 197–214.

74. This also suggests that finding *analogies* between the biblical text and the contemporary situation may be a prominent (but implicit) strategy in this kind of biblical interpretation, just as it is a more explicit strategy in (for example) African American biblical interpretation; see Love L. Sechrest, "Double Vision for Revolutionary Religion: Race Relations, Moral Analogies, and African-American Biblical Interpretation," in Hockey and Horrell, *Ethnicity, Race, Religion*, 202–18. Making the analogies—and the search for them—explicit is preferable insofar as it makes the connections clear and thus invites critical analysis of both sides of the comparison.

75. Arnal, "Jesus as Battleground," 104.

seem, in Willie James Jennings's words, that "Western Christian intellectuals still imagine the world from the commanding heights."[76]

In order to be clear that this is not a critique from which I exempt my own work, let me illustrate how such analysis might raise questions about my earlier work on Pauline ethics, *Solidarity and Difference*.[77] This project, one might observe, is thoroughly "Western" in its orientation, setting as a methodological framework for reading Paul the liberal-communitarian debate in ethical theory exemplified by the contrasting work of Jürgen Habermas and Stanley Hauerwas—potentially problematic in ways that I did not fully appreciate at the time.[78] The primary conundrum is that central to the Western liberal project: how to nurture forms of communal solidarity while at the same time preserving and tolerating difference and diversity. And it is Paul, and his attempts to foster both solidarity and difference in Christ, who serves as the primary focus for reflections on how contemporary plural societies might negotiate and sustain their peaceable existence. I am not uncritical of Paul in this study, and I try to make clear that Paul's focus on Christ as the basis for communal solidarity is not superior to, but simply different from, a Jewish focus on Torah as central to corporate life.[79] I also make clear that any use of the Pauline approach to social solidarity and toleration of difference will need to go beyond and even against Paul's own intentions. Nonetheless it is the Pauline moral vision that stands at the center of reflection on contemporary social challenges. It is a work, then, which displays the marks of its production in a specific historical, religious, and geopolitical context.

As another specific example of this kind of correspondence, rooted in contemporary political discourse, we might consider the ways in which recent British Prime Ministers—David Cameron especially—have spoken about Britain's identity as "a Christian country," with values that derive from the Bible, providing a "home to many different faith communities" and have promoted the "British values" that include "individual liberty and

---

76. Jennings, *Christian Imagination*, 8.

77. Horrell, *Solidarity*.

78. On the "implicit racism" and sense of "the superiority of Western ways" that may be woven into Habermas's work, see, e.g., Kaufman, "Is Philosophy Anything If It Isn't White?," 254–57 (quoted phrases from 255, 257). For critique of Hauerwas's failure to address issues of race and whiteness, see, e.g., James Logan, "Liberalism, Race, and Stanley Hauerwas," *Cross Currents* 55 (2006): 522–33; Derek Woodard-Lehman, "Body Politics and the Politics of Bodies: Racism and Hauerwasian Theopolitics," *JRE* 36 (2008): 295–320; Kristopher Norris, "Witnessing Whiteness in the Ethics of Hauerwas," *JRE* 47 (2019): 95–124.

79. See, e.g., Horrell, *Solidarity*, 214n87, 215, 223–24 with n. 100.

mutual respect and tolerance of other faiths and beliefs."[80] Indeed, under the "Prevent" legislation introduced in 2011, designed to prevent people being drawn into extremism and terrorism, "vocal or active opposition" to these "fundamental British values" is proscribed by law.[81] Teachers, among others, have a statutory duty to "promote British values" and to monitor and report those who may be displaying opposition to them, however problematic that duty might be.[82] What is significant to note here are the parallels between the kind of politically liberal vision Cameron sets out and the depiction of the structure of the early Christian communities prominent in recent scholarship: a Christian framework provides the umbrella beneath which other identities can be tolerated and included—in a way that rather masks the extent to which this Christian framework is itself both particular and "intolerant," within its own prescribed parameters.[83] I should be clear that in making this point I do not intend to imply any rejection of the values of tolerance and diversity but primarily to identify their specific context of production and the kinds of "correspondence" that exist between contemporary ideology and historical reconstruction. It is also clear, moreover, that the articulation and impact of what are depicted as "British values" deserve critical analysis, partly because of the brute force that has sometimes accompanied attempts to impose similar values in other parts of the world

80. For the connections between the Bible and British values, see David Cameron, "Prime Minister's King James Bible Speech" (speech delivered at 10 Downing Street, December 16, 2011, https://www.gov.uk/government/news/prime-ministers-king-james-bible-speech). See also David Cameron, "Easter Reception at Downing Street Speech" (speech delivered at 10 Downing Street, April 9, 2014, https://www.gov.uk/government/speeches/easter-reception-at-downing-street-2014); David Cameron, "British Values," June 16, 2014, https://www.gov.uk/government/news/british-values-article-by-david-cameron. For discussion, see James G. Crossley, *Harnessing Chaos: The Bible in English Political Discourse since 1968*, rev. ed. (London: Bloomsbury, 2016), 283–97.

81. See the "Prevent strategy" policy paper on GOV.UK at https://www.gov.uk/government/publications/prevent-strategy-2011.

82. On the policy guidance for schools, see "The Prevent Duty: Departmental Advice for Schools and Childcare Providers," UK Department of Education, https://assets.publishing.service.gov.uk/government/uploads/system/uploads/attachment_data/file/439598/prevent-duty-departmental-advice-v6.pdf. For critical discussion, see the articles in a special themed issue of *Journal of Education for Teaching* 42.3 (2016), which are introduced and contextualized by the guest editor, Vini Lander, "Introduction to Fundamental British Values," *Journal of Education for Teaching* 42 (2016): 274–79. I am grateful to Ruth Flanagan for an orientation to the Prevent legislation and its implications for schoolteachers.

83. On the limits of this liberal notion of tolerance and its parallels in Paul, see Horrell, *Solidarity*, 212–24.

(giving a certain enduring relevance to Fanon's acerbic critique, quoted above) but also because of the ways in which Christianness and Britishness are woven together in the particular articulation of the foundations of these values.

Indeed, in the context of such remarks and policy enactments, it is notable that the 2015 report on religion and belief in British public life, *Living with Difference*, highlighted the complex overlaps between "race" and "religion" and drew attention to the fact that some "religious groups and communities" can suffer forms of prejudice and exclusion that "prevent them from seeing themselves as belonging fully to the national story."[84] The report therefore recommends that "there needs to be a better understanding of how race, ethnicity and religion overlap" and consideration of whether outstanding anomalies need to be addressed by changes in the law.[85] As Vini Lander remarks in the context of the debate about promoting "British values" in schools:

> Teachers and students rely on nostalgic imperialist constructions of Britishness . . . re-inscribing . . . the whiteness associated with this national identity. . . . The discourse of civic nationalism which purports to accommodate plurality . . . serves to exclude the very members of its society that are constructed as the terrorist "other" within and whose religious identity is racialized and conceived as the binary opposite against which the discourse of civic nationalism is constructed.[86]

Such critical assessments help to show how appeals to values of tolerance, inclusion, and so on are also enmeshed and implicated in ethnic, racial, and religious constructions of identity, belonging, and implicit superiority. Construals of the early Christian vision that exhibit a similar structure and set of values to those promoted in Western liberalism are, then, enmeshed in, and products of, a contemporary context—specifically that of the white Christian West. Just as whiteness studies have drawn attention to the ways in which whiteness operates in an unmarked, unacknowledged way, masking its

84. Commission on Religion and Belief in British Public Life, *Living with Difference: Community, Diversity and the Common Good* (Cambridge: Woolf Institute, 2015), 74 (available at https://corablivingwithdifference.files.wordpress.com/2015/12/living-with -difference-online.pdf). On the (perceived) correlations between religious and national identity, see Stokes, "What It Takes," and §3.3 above.

85. Commission on Religion and Belief in British Public Life, *Living with Difference*, 78.

86. Lander, "Introduction," 276.

own particularity as a universal, so too in these articulations of the tolerant inclusiveness of the early Christian vision we may suspect the particularity of Western Christian universalism to be lurking. Such scholarly depictions are written, on the whole, as if speaking from a non-particularized "historical" perspective but represent a production of knowledge from within a quite particular location—and one that has racial as well as religious aspects to it.

In the specific context of New Testament studies, it is Judaism that constitutes the particular "particular" in the context of which the early Christian achievement is found, such that this specific nexus of engagement forms the site at which this Western Christian identity—with its religious and racializing core—is developed. Judaism constitutes the "other" to which early Christian inclusivism is contrasted. One risk of such perspectives, as Buell remarks in reflections on this issue, is that "definitions of Christianity's racially inclusive ideal will perpetuate a racially loaded form of anti-Judaism if the implied point of contrast to Christianity's inclusiveness is Jewishness."[87] This does not mean, of course, that contemporary antisemitism is the sole focus for concern about religious and racial prejudice today but rather that this is the historical site for the articulation of a Christian vision that can express both religious and racial superiority in ways that carry broader implications in terms of the constructions of particularities and differences.

One way to pursue this further is, in Levine's words, "to recognize the intersectionality of racism and anti-Semitism,"[88] a theme we highlighted at the opening of this book.[89] Long ago, for example, Fanon remarked that "an anti-Semite is inevitably anti-Negro."[90] More recently, in response to incidents such as the killing and wounding of protestors against the "Unite the Right" rally in Charlottesville, Virginia, in 2017 by a domestic terrorist holding neo-Nazi and white supremacist views—a rally at which the chants included "the Jews will not replace us"—Levine stresses the need to reject bigotry in the form of both anti-Black racism and antisemitism.[91] Elucidat-

87. Buell, *Why This New Race*, 12.

88. Levine, "Christian Privilege," 106.

89. On the need to integrate the study of antisemitism more fully into analyses of race and racism, see Les Back and John Solomos, "Introduction: Theorising Race and Racism," in Back and Solomos, *Race and Racism*, 10–11.

90. Frantz Fanon, "The Fact of Blackness," in Back and Solomos, *Race and Racism*, 264; orig. published in 1952.

91. Levine, "Christian Privilege," 107. For an overview of the event, and specifically of the fatal attack, see "Deadly Car Attack, Violent Clashes in Charlottesville: What We Know Now," *USA Today*, August 13, 2017, https://eu.usatoday.com/story/news/nation

ing the nature of these intersections is not straightforward: racism and antisemitism are not simply identical, nor are white privilege and Christian privilege the same, nor can racial and religious prejudices be elided—even while all these cannot neatly be parceled out and separately categorized.[92] The relationship of Jewish identity to whiteness, for example—different in different contexts, of course—is subject to considerable discussion. In a historical study of nineteenth- and twentieth-century America, for example, Eric Goldstein richly documents "how Jews have *negotiated* their place in a complex racial world where Jewishness, whiteness, and blackness have all made significant claims upon them."[93] Steve Garner, looking specifically at the USA and the UK, sees Jews as an "inbetween group" occupying "a space of peripherality . . . marginal to the dominant culture," though this plays out differently at different times and in different places.[94] While they may be identified as white, there can also be times and contexts in which they are treated as other, or, conversely, where the identification as ethnically white seems to threaten their ability to preserve and record a sense of distinctiveness as a people.[95] Linking the (often implicit) operations of Christian privilege and white privilege in contexts where these define the dominant identity in numerical, historical, or structural terms is one way to understand how racism and antisemitism may align and to subject both to critical examination.

/2017/08/13/charlottesville-protests-what-we-know-now/562911001/. On the connections between anti-Black racism and antisemitism at the Charlottesville rally, see Emma Green, "Why the Charlottesville Marchers Were Obsessed with Jews," *The Atlantic*, August 15, 2017, https://www.theatlantic.com/politics/archive/2017/08/nazis-racism-charlottesville/536928/.

92. As Levine "Christian Privilege," 106, notes, e.g., preaching in Black churches might express anti-Jewish attitudes; but she argues for a recognition of "the intertwined nature of racism and anti-Semitism" such that "potential allies" are not "lost in the struggle against racism."

93. Eric L. Goldstein, *The Price of Whiteness: Jews, Race, and American Identity* (Princeton: Princeton University Press, 2006), 5, italics original. On the complex and disputed negotiations between the categories of race and religion in pre–World War I USA, see 86–115.

94. Steve Garner, *Whiteness: An Introduction* (New York: Routledge, 2007), 99; see 99–118. On the shifting depictions of Jews' blackness and moves toward whiteness and the enduring "taint" of Jewishness, see also Sander L. Gilman, "Are Jews White? Or, The History of the Nose Job," in Back and Solomos, *Race and Racism*, 229–37.

95. See, e.g., Goldstein, *Price of Whiteness*, 226–27, for discussion of the US census of 2000, which did not include Jewish as an option for racial or ethnic identification: "The absence of a Jewish category on the census, however, did not stop many Jews from 'writing in' Jewish as an alternative to the options listed" (227).

9.3.3 *Critique from the "Margins"—and the Center?*

Having tried to link "Christianness" and "whiteness" as facets that shape the dominant traditions and perspectives of New Testament studies, and thus linked concerns about antisemitism with broader racial ideologies, it should be clear, as already hinted above, that contributions and perspectives from those who do not inhabit that dominant and privileged position warrant particular attention. Such scholars have already raised critical questions, in various ways, about the Eurocentric character of established approaches in New Testament studies in terms of both its religious and its racial character. Given the focus of the two immediately preceding sections, it should already be apparent that Jewish and so-called "minority" perspectives constitute two main sources of such critique.

As noted in chapter 1, Jewish scholars raised objections to the depictions of Judaism in New Testament scholarship long before E. P. Sanders's epoch-making work.[96] It is not merely coincidental that it was the work of an American Protestant scholar that had the most impact on the field. The sensitivities of Christian scholars, chastened by the horrors of the Holocaust, have no doubt shifted such that there is much greater concern to avoid anti-Jewish readings of New Testament texts and to grapple with the legacies of anti-Jewish interpretation and supercessionist theology.[97] Recent efforts to read New Testament writers, not least Paul, firmly "within Judaism"—with Jewish scholars prominent among those pressing for such a shift in perspective—are another indication of the reconfigurations of the discipline.[98]

---

96. See p. 29 with n. 27.

97. A voluminous literature could be cited on this point. Indicative of the concern and reflection among the predominantly Christian guild of NT scholars are Craig A. Evans and Donald A. Hagner, eds., *Anti-Semitism and Early Christianity: Issues of Polemic and Faith* (Minneapolis: Fortress, 1993); Reimund Bieringer, Didier Pollefeyt, and Frederique Vandecasteele-Venneuville, eds., *Anti-Judaism and the Fourth Gospel* (Louisville: Westminster John Knox, 2001); Reimund Bieringer and Didier Pollefeyt, eds., *Paul and Judaism: Crosscurrents in Pauline Exegesis and the Study of Jewish-Christian Relations*, LNTS 463 (London: Bloomsbury T&T Clark, 2012). See also the recent remarks of Philip F. Esler, "Intergroup Conflict," 38–59; and Esler, "Giving the Kingdom," 196. Among attempts to read NT texts from a Christian theological perspective while avoiding supercessionism are Douglas Harink, *Paul among the Postliberals: Pauline Theology beyond Christendom and Modernity* (Grand Rapids: Brazos, 2003); Givens, *We the People*.

98. See esp. Nanos and Zetterholm, *Paul within Judaism*. For an overview of the emergence of this grouping, see Matthew V. Novenson, "Whither the Paul within Judaism Schule?," *JMJS* 5 (2018): 79–88.

However, as Jewish scholars have continued to point out, explicit or implicit commitments to Christianity often lead, whether intentionally or unconsciously, to various kinds of depictions in which the positive appeal of the Christian vision is set against the backdrop of a negative Jewish comparison, even when the particular form of Christian vision promoted is intended to be emancipatory or to avoid anti-Jewish implications.[99] Whether it be the liberation of women from patriarchal Jewish customs and oppressive laws, the inclusion of all people within the one new humanity God is calling together in Christ, or other themes and foci in New Testament research, Jewish (and non-Jewish) scholars have pointed out how such perspectives can easily convey historically questionable contrasts or problematic contemporary implications.[100] It would seem fair to conclude, though, that the field of New Testament studies, through the critical reflection provoked in the field by Jewish, Christian, and non-religious scholars, has shifted significantly in response to an awareness of the risks of anti-Jewish readings, with their legacy and impact in preaching as well as wider social attitudes and prejudices. Few would suggest, however, that the difficulties and challenges lie only in the past; on the contrary, as recent events have highlighted, the need to address antisemitism remains.[101]

Criticism of the Eurocentric character of established approaches in New Testament studies (and biblical studies more generally) has also long been expressed in the fields of African American hermeneutics, Asian hermeneutics, and other forms of what has come to be known as minority criticism(s).

---

99. For just two examples, see Levine, "Discharging Responsibility"; Nanos, "Inter-Christian Approaches."

100. For example, on the problems with early feminist readings of the NT in this regard, see Katharina von Kellenbach, *Anti-Judaism in Feminist Religious Writings*, AAR Cultural Criticism Series (Atlanta: Scholars Press, 1994), 57–74; on the problems for Jewish identity of the vision of Gal 3:28, see Boyarin, *Radical Jew*. Recent examples that illustrate the problems can readily be found. For example, in an essay intended to help preachers, clergy, and teachers with the "difficult text" of 1 Tim 2:11–15, Amy J. Erickson, "Difficult Texts: 1 Timothy 2:11–15," *Theology* 122 (2019): 200–203, sees the text as confronting a local form of false teaching derived from the Artemis cult, exacerbated "by the deficiency in theological education due to Jewish custom (which Paul's injunction in 1 Timothy 2:11 decisively combats)" (202). A note at this point cites a rabbinic text about the dangers of teaching women Torah as a contrast to "the gospel's revolutionary perspective on the theological education of women" (203n9).

101. For a recent volume grappling with the ongoing issues related to the interpretation and legacy of John's Gospel, see Reinhartz, *Gospel of John*; also Levine, *Misunderstood Jew*, 167–90.

(How this area of biblical criticism relates to the issues raised about the depictions of Judaism, and the contributions of Jewish scholars, is a point to which I will return, briefly, in the following section.) Indeed, as Emerson Powery and Rodney Sadler have recently shown, nineteenth-century narratives written by African American slaves (or the formerly enslaved) already represent "an early history of African American biblical hermeneutics":[102] these early interpreters exhibit many of the key moves fundamental to more recent scholarly approaches to biblical hermeneutics.

Among the other significant landmarks, we might mention the early work of James Cone, whose radical theology of Black power and liberation includes the claiming of Jesus as Black—a claim that relates not primarily to the color of the historical Jesus's skin but rather to Christ's contemporary significance.[103] Again, this claim is anticipated in the much earlier declaration of Henry McNeal Turner, in 1895, that "God is a Negro."[104] For Cone, Jesus is Black "because and only because Christ *really* enters into our world where the poor, the despised, and the black are, disclosing that he is with them, enduring their humiliation and pain and transforming oppressed slaves into liberated servants."[105] The claim that "Jesus is Black" is provocative, as Cone notes, partly because of its jarring collision with the dominant construction—albeit often an implicit and unexamined one—of Jesus as white.[106] As

102. Emerson B. Powery and Rodney S. Sadler Jr., *The Genesis of Liberation: Biblical Interpretation in the Antebellum Narratives of the Enslaved* (Louisville: Westminster John Knox, 2016), 161.

103. See James H. Cone, *God of the Oppressed*, rev. ed. (Maryknoll, NY: Orbis, 1997), 122–26 (the section entitled "Jesus Is Black"). Cone writes: "I begin by asserting once more that *Jesus was a Jew*. It is on the basis of the soteriological meaning of the particularity of his Jewishness that theology must affirm the Christological significance of Jesus's present blackness. He *is* black because he *was* a Jew" (123). "The 'blackness of Christ,' therefore, is not simply a statement about skin color, but rather, the transcendent affirmation that God has not ever . . . left the oppressed alone in struggle" (126). On Cone's depiction of Jesus, see also Siker, "Racialized Jesus," 30–35, and the broader discussion in Carter, *Race*, 157–93. There is, however, at least potentially, the risk in this move that Jesus's Jewishness becomes part of his *past* and not present identity, raising other difficulties.

104. See Andre E. Johnson, "God Is a Negro: The (Rhetorical) Black Theology of Bishop Henry McNeal Turner," *Black Theology* 13 (2015): 29–40.

105. Cone, *God of the Oppressed*, 125–26.

106. See Cone, *God of the Oppressed*, 123: "The same white theologians who laughingly dismiss Albert Cleage's 'Black Messiah' say almost nothing about the European (white) images of Christ plastered all over American homes and churches. I perhaps would respect the integrity of their objections to the Black Christ on scholarly grounds, if they applied the same vigorous logic to Christ's whiteness."

Cone remarks, "Much of the present negative reaction of white theologians to the Black Christ is due almost exclusively to their *whiteness*, a cultural fact that determines their theological inquiry, thereby making it almost impossible for them to relate positively to anything black."[107]

In another significant expression of such concerns in the context of the development of African American biblical interpretation, William Myers reflects on the "Eurocentric approach" that dominates the field of biblical studies and the difficulties this poses "for the African American biblical student," particularly when they are being trained and examined in this method.[108] "The challenge to Eurocentrism as evident in the historical-critical method occurs," he remarks, "because opponents and some proponents recognize that few of its results have moved us any closer to an appreciation of other people's . . . ways of interpreting the text."[109]

As Myers's comment suggests, part of the challenge lies in recognizing and critically probing the extent to which the established methods of ("Eurocentric") biblical criticism are the product of a particular historical and contemporary context. Indeed, it is precisely this need to focus on the "social location" of the interpreter, whatever the context and tradition in which they stand, that provides the rationale for the project that culminated in the publication of the two-volume *Reading from This Place*.[110] These volumes also include (self-)critical reflection by white scholars on what Daniel Patte calls "the contextual character of male, European-American critical exegeses."[111]

---

107. Cone, *God of the Oppressed*, 123.

108. William H. Myers, "The Hermeneutical Dilemma of the African American Biblical Student," in Felder, *Stony the Road*, 41. See also the more recent comments of Musa W. Dube, "Introduction: The Scramble for Africa as the Biblical Scramble for Africa: Postcolonial Perspectives," in *Postcolonial Perspectives in African Biblical Interpretations*, ed. Musa W. Dube, Andrew M. Mbuvi, and Dora R. Mbuwayesango (Atlanta: Society of Biblical Literature, 2012), 17–18: "Mainstream academic biblical studies and theology is steeped in Eurocentric perspectives. . . . Those of us who come from former colonies drink our fill, as we inevitably become colonized by the terms of the discipline."

109. Myers, "Hermeneutical Dilemma," 47.

110. Segovia and Tolbert, *Reading from This Place*.

111. Daniel Patte, "Acknowledging the Contextual Character of Male, European-American Critical Exegeses: An Androcritical Perspective," in Segovia and Tolbert, *Reading from This Place*, 1:35–55. See also Daniel Patte, *Ethics of Biblical Interpretation: A Reevaluation* (Louisville: Westminster John Knox, 1995). The unacknowledged "contextual" character of mainstream Western exegesis has also been recently highlighted in specific ways through a contrast with community readings from Namibia: see Helen C. John, *Biblical Interpretation and African Traditional Religion: Cross-Cultural and Community Readings in Owamboland, Namibia*, BibInt 176 (Leiden: Brill, 2019).

In the light of the issues raised by whiteness studies, it is interesting to consider how these critiques and alternatives have fared. We may recall Dyer's observation that "it has become common for those marginalized by culture to acknowledge the situation from which they speak, but those who occupy positions of cultural hegemony blithely carry on as if what they say is neutral and unsituated—human but not raced." For Dyer, this legitimates and motivates the programme of whiteness studies: the attempt to show how "this non-located and disembodied position of knowledge"[112] is peculiarly and distinctively white and thus to particularize (and problematize) its claims.

Dyer's remarks may provoke us to think about the history of recent biblical studies—in which, as we have briefly noted, there have long been critiques of the dominant white tradition of historical-critical exegesis, with its European origins and American continuation—along with an insistence on the locatedness of all interpreters. Alternative perspectives exist in the academy, and are labeled in ways that, in Dyer's words, "acknowledge the situation from which they speak": African American, Latin American, Asian hermeneutics and so on. Together they may identify as "minority criticism."[113] Yet this labeling not only acknowledges their particularity but also contributes to their remaining "at the margins."[114] What remains at the center—despite the explicit intentions of the "minority" critique[115]—is (simply) "biblical studies": the unspecified, unmarked, but largely white, Western, Christian project of a particular kind of historical exegesis.[116] Here the

---

112. Dyer, *White*, 4.

113. See, e.g., Randall C. Bailey, Tat-siong Benny Liew, and Fernando F. Segovia, eds., *They Were All Together in One Place? Toward Minority Biblical Criticism*, SemeiaSt 57 (Atlanta: Society of Biblical Literature, 2009).

114. I echo here the title of R. S. Sugirtharajah, ed., *Still at the Margins: Biblical Scholarship Fifteen Years after the Voices from the Margin* (London: Bloomsbury T&T Clark, 2008), which takes stock of the field fifteen years after the landmark publication of Sugirtharajah, *Voices from the Margin*.

115. See, e.g., Randall C. Bailey, Tat-siong Benny Liew, and Fernando F. Segovia, "Toward Minority Biblical Criticism: Framework, Contours, Dynamics," in Bailey, Liew, and Segovia, *All Together in One Place?*, 27: "Minority criticism sees itself as ultimately relativizing, and hence mortally undoing, dominant criticism as well, insofar as it presses the question of location and agenda as applicable to and inescapable in all situations, not only at the periphery but also at the center."

116. See R. S. Sugirtharajah, "Muddling Along at the Margins," in Sugirtharajah, *Still at the Margins*, 8–21, who, asking how much has changed since the publication of *Voices from the Margin* in 1991, remarks: "Not much, as far as the attitude of the mainstream is

parallel with whiteness studies is illuminating: it is precisely the dominant mode of seeing and knowing that remains unidentified, and thereby implicitly universal(izable)—"untainted" by its contextual origins in the same way as other critical perspectives.

As we noted above, whiteness studies can trace its origins to those Black authors like Audre Lorde and Toni Morrison who saw the hegemonic power of whiteness; yet some of the key contributions in critical whiteness studies are those of white authors, like Dyer and Frankenberg, seeking—from within, as it were—"to break the hold of whiteness by locating and embodying it in a particular experience of being white."[117] Acknowledging the important and seminal contributions of those non-white writers and scholars who have criticized the Eurocentric orientation and assumptions of biblical studies, the critical challenge, as Carey suggests, is for "white interpreters also [to] invest themselves in the conversation."[118]

The particular ways in which I have sought to identify the religious and racial locatedness of dominant streams within contemporary New Testament studies are of course open to question. Others may conclude that what I have called the structural dichotomy between (particular, ethnic) Judaism and (universal, inclusive) Christianity is not a particularly crucial site for revealing the contemporary "location" of such scholarship. But the broader claim would remain: that New Testament studies, as a Western European production precisely concurrent with the period of European imperialism (and its associated racist ideologies) is shaped by and implicated in that wider socio-historical context and specifically in its ideologies of religion and race. Given no major rupture in the fundamental orientation of the discipline—as chapter 1 has sought to show—despite new perspectives and challenges, often

---

concerned. The practice of treating American and European interpretation as 'the' interpretation and labeling the enterprise of others—'Asian,' 'African' and so on, or in gender or ethnic terms—persists. Those who work on the margins are unable to shake off the exotic tag attached to them" (8). Likewise, Mary Ann Tolbert, "Writing History, Writing Culture, Writing Ourselves: Issues in Contemporary Biblical Interpretation," in Lozada and Carey, *Soundings*, 27, comments that "the writers who omit any indication of their assumptions, ideologies, and agendas are largely white males of dominant Western cultures, while those acknowledging their concerns are overwhelmingly minority and two-thirds world writers."

117. Dyer, *White*, 4.

118. Carey, "Introduction," 6. Wongi Park, *The Politics of Race and Ethnicity in Matthew's Passion Narrative* (London: Palgrave Macmillan, 2019), e.g., refers to both "minority" and "dominant" biblical scholarship that draws on "insights from ethnoracial theory, whiteness studies, and minority criticism" (3 with nn. 10–11).

policed at the margins, it is likely still tied to those Western religio-racial ideologies in ways that are profoundly formative, if difficult to discern.

The point may be expressed in the form of a question: Can we plausibly imagine that our reconstructions of the earliest Christian communities and our exegesis of New Testament and early Christian texts are not shaped, inflected, by our contemporary social, political, religious, and racial location? And though it may be uncomfortable to acknowledge it, is not our racialized identity one significant part of that complex intersection of facets of identity to which we should—indeed must—pay attention? It is easier to see how the past of New Testament studies was implicated in religious and racializing ideologies than to identify such things in the present. But the challenge remains—not least for those of us who inhabit the still dominant malestream of the discipline—to develop critical analyses of how this particularity becomes visible in our exegesis. Assuming that our interpretation is uncontextualized—unmarked, unlocated, un*raced*—is hardly a cogent option.

9.4 Moving Forward?

As the previous section has made clear, others, and particularly those from minoritized locations, have long raised critical questions about the implicit Eurocentrism—with its racial, colonial, and religious dimensions—bound up in the dominant methods and perspectives of New Testament studies. Interest in critical reflection on whiteness, particularly on the part of those for whom this involves self-critique, is recent but clearly part of this trajectory of examination. My own attempt to reflect on the locatedness—and the whiteness—of particular constructions of the early Christian achievement in the field of New Testament studies has emerged from a primarily historical and exegetical study, informed by contemporary social science, which has examined the various ways in which Jewish and Christian traditions construct group identity by drawing on characteristics of discourse and social practice commonly associated with ethnic groups. It is, as it were, an analysis from "within" the tradition I am also seeking to subject to critique. As such, it may seem far too wedded to "the master's tools"—to echo Audre Lorde's famous declaration—to play any part in the critical dismantling of "the master's house."[119]

119. Lorde, *Sister Outsider*, 110–13, 123. For further discussion, see Wei Hsien Wan,

But that raises the question of how we might continue to move forward, to learn from our different perspectives and approaches, from the diverse productions of knowledge emanating from different traditions and locations. Once the locatedness and specificity of interpretations has been acknowledged, Daniel Patte's proposal is "to affirm the legitimacy of a plurality of interpretations" and to depict the task of critical biblical studies as "the bringing to critical understanding of ordinary readings, including those other than our own."[120] We might then seek to articulate and appreciate a range of "readings"—and to identify the white, Euro-American tradition of reading as one specific and contextually shaped kind of reading. One problem, though, as Stephen Moore and Yvonne Sherwood observe, is that the multiplicity of perspectives produced by what they concisely label "reading as" "can easily be accommodated to the democratic ethos of the discipline . . . and accorded a place in it—but precisely on its margins, where they can be both visible from the mainstream of the discipline and extraneous to it, and need have no deep or lasting effect on how mainstream practitioners of biblical scholarship go about their daily business."[121] There is equally the risk of assuming that readings reflect their context of production to the extent that any individual's reading is taken to represent the perspective of their identity-group—such that a "Jewish" reading or an "Asian American" reading or, indeed, a "white British" reading might be predictably correlated with the identity of their author. Such presumptions should be resisted.[122] We should, then, not only juxtapose different readings but also continue to seek ways to evaluate them rigorously and critically, whoever their authors might be. The contextual production of such scholarship, including in the so-called mainstream, should not only be identified but also subjected to ongoing critical analysis, not least by those who practice it—though this

---

"Re-examining the Master's Tools: Considerations on Biblical Studies' Race Problem," in Hockey and Horrell, *Ethnicity, Race, Religion*, 219–29.

120. Patte, *Ethics of Biblical Interpretation*, 27, 113.

121. Stephen D. Moore and Yvonne Sherwood, *The Invention of the Biblical Scholar: A Critical Manifesto* (Minneapolis: Fortress, 2011), 117–18.

122. This would simply replicate one of the problems highlighted by Peggy McIntosh in her list of "white privileges": that of being expected to speak on behalf of one's racial group (see n. 43 above). A similar problem is evident in the expectation that a Jewish interpreter might convey "what the Jews think." For one report of such an expectation, see Paula Fredriksen's comment on an earlier experience of Amy-Jill Levine's in the "Concluding Roundtable," in Caputo and Alcoff, *St. Paul among the Philosophers*, 182; see also Amy-Jill Levine, "A Jewess, More and/or Less," in *Judaism since Gender*, ed. Miriam Peskowitz and Laura Levitt (London: Routledge, 1996), 149.

critical task will also surely require a diverse range of voices and insights, both religiously and racially.

That last point indicates the profound importance of thinking about the ways in which we accept, welcome, and attend to difference.[123] If it is the case that knowledge is, as Mignolo stresses, the product of particular bodies (with their different racial, sexual, religious, and social identities) located in different geopolitical spaces, disciplinary traditions, and systems of education, then any attempt to gain greater knowledge and deeper understanding necessarily requires both the participation of and a profound attentiveness to the epistemological insights of as wide as possible a range of people—though without assuming any easy identification of person and perspective. It is especially incumbent on those of us who inhabit the traditionally dominant positions to listen attentively and patiently to the perspectives of those who have been marginalized and harmed by that dominant tradition[124]—"to listen *desperately*," as Barbara Applebaum puts it.[125] That does not mean that we simply affirm a range of perspectives: proposals, interpretations, and reconstructions should still be subjected to rigorous critical examination, with comparison and communication across the boundaries of difference. Yet we cannot recognize the particularity and partiality of our own insights unless we hear those of others. At the annual SBL meeting, for example, an "unmarked" session such as "Pauline Epistles" is usually very well attended, while far smaller numbers of people attend, say, "African American Hermeneutics"—most of whom would identify as African American.[126] Why do more people not want "to listen desperately"?

In terms of moving forward, one thing that seems to me worth observing is that the integration of Jewish perspectives into the discipline seems

123. On the crucial importance of recognizing difference and attending to it rather than merely tolerating it, see Lorde, *Sister Outsider*, 113, 115–16, 122, et passim; Wan, "Reexamining the Master's Tools," 227–28.

124. At the end of his study of the appeals to the Bible in the American slavery debates, Wayne A. Meeks, "The 'Haustafeln' and American Slavery: A Hermeneutical Challenge," in *Theology and Ethics in Paul and His Interpreters: Essays in Honor of Victor Paul Furnish*, ed. Eugene H. Lovering Jr. and Jerry L. Sumney (Nashville: Abingdon, 1996), 252–53, concludes by suggesting certain moral principles for the interpretation of the Bible: "the habit of listening to the weaker partner in every relationship of power" and "to make sure that among the voices interpreting the tradition are those of the ones who have experienced harm from that tradition."

125. Applebaum, "White Ignorance," 15, summarizing a point made by Audrey Thompson.

126. See also the remarks of Buell, "Anachronistic Whiteness," 153–56.

to proceed differently—and rather separately—from what has come to be known as "minority" criticism.[127] There are various reasons for this, not least the long-standing tradition of close study of Jewish texts as part of the historical-critical method, but it seems to me that there might be more scope for alliance between Jewish and other "minority" perspectives in the field of New Testament studies. In contexts where both coincide to define the dominant majority, the impact of Christian privilege and of white privilege should, as Levine has suggested, be seen together rather than separate, just as concerns about antisemitism and anti-Black racism should be connected.[128] Is there more scope for such communication and collaboration here, despite profound disagreements about Israel and Palestine?[129]

But for those of us identified, in whatever ways, with the white, Christian traditions at the center of the discipline, the aspiration to attend to the insights of a range of voices and perspectives cannot properly be attempted without attending to differentials of power at both micro- and macro-structural levels and the ways in which these affect and distort any communication of and across differences. Unless we recognize and address the ways in which our discipline and its conventions, research foci, career structures, language-traditions, publishing opportunities, and so on shape our interactions, then it will be naïve and unrealistic to speak of (truly) hearing a range of different perspectives as a crucial (and not merely optional) means to move closer to plausible, robust, and significant knowledge.[130]

In the end, I do not think it sufficient merely to articulate our diverse and contextually produced readings and to hold them alongside one another as equally authentic and valid interpretations of the texts. They need to be brought into robust and meaningful critical dialogue, to have their plausibility and implications tested, though this can only be validly done to the

127. It is notable that Jewish voices are not often explicitly represented in collections of "minority" perspectives, which tend to focus on other ethnic and/or geographically labeled identities. See, e.g., Segovia and Tolbert, *Reading from This Place*; Bailey, Liew, and Segovia, *All Together in One Place?* For a critique of the kinds of anti-Jewish perspectives that can emerge in some such "located" and "liberatory" readings, see Levine, *Misunderstood Jew*, 167–90, esp. 179–81.

128. Levine, "Christian Privilege."

129. See, e.g., the robust and valuable exchange of perspectives in Michael J. Sandford, ed., *The Bible, Zionism, and Palestine: The Bible's Role in Conflict and Liberation in Israel-Palestine*, Bible in Effect 1 (Dunedin, New Zealand: Relegere Academic Press, 2016).

130. See also the comments of Ma. Marilou S. Ibita, "Exploring the (In)Visibility of the Christ-Believers' 'Trans-ethnicity': A Lowland Filipina Catholic's Perspective," in Hockey and Horrell, *Ethnicity, Race, Religion*, 190–97; Buell, "Anachronistic Whiteness," 163–64.

extent that distortions of power and inequality are removed. That means, I think, more willingness on the part of those of us who do inhabit the dominant (white, Western, Christian) malestream of biblical studies to fully recognize—and to enact in the ways we do our scholarship[131]—that our production of knowledge about Christian origins and about the contemporary appropriations of the New Testament texts requires the insights of scholars representing a wide range of other religious, cultural, geographical, and ethnic or racial perspectives. What we see will continue to be the product of a white, Western, Christian location unless the epistemological insights of those who do not share that location are truly given due weight, not only as "particular," labeled approaches to interpretation but also as contributions to knowledge that precisely in their particularity can help to reshape the equally perspectival and particular contributions of Western exegesis.

131. This would include what Sara Parks, "Historical-Critical Ministry? The Biblical Studies Classroom as Restorative Secular Space," *New Blackfriars* 100 (2019): 235–40, has called "the politics of citation."

Bibliography

Aalen, Sverre. *Die Begriffe "Licht" und "Finsternis" im Alten Testament, im Spät-judentum und im Rabbinismus.* Skrifter Utgitt av Det Norske Videnskaps-Akademi I Oslo. II, Hist.-Filos. Klasse. Oslo: I Kommisjon Hos Jacob Dy-bwad, 1951.

Aasgaard, Reidar. *"My Beloved Brothers and Sisters!" Christian Siblingship in Paul.* JSNTSup 265. London: T&T Clark, 2004.

——. "'Role Ethics' in Paul: The Significance of the Sibling Role for Paul's Ethical Thinking." *NTS* 48 (2002): 513–30.

Achtemeier, Paul J. *1 Peter.* Hermeneia. Philadelphia: Fortress, 1996.

Adams, Edward. *The Stars Will Fall from Heaven: Cosmic Catastrophe in the New Testament and Its World.* LNTS 347. London: T&T Clark, 2007.

Adams, Edward, and David G. Horrell, eds. *Christianity at Corinth: The Quest for the Pauline Church.* Louisville: Westminster John Knox, 2004.

Ådna, Jostein, and Hans Kvalbein. "Introduction." Pages 1–13 in *The Mission of the Early Church to Jews and Gentiles.* Edited by Jostein Ådna and Hans Kvalbein. WUNT 127. Tübingen: Mohr Siebeck, 2000.

Ådna, Jostein, and Hans Kvalbein, eds. *The Mission of the Early Church to Jews and Gentiles.* WUNT 127. Tübingen: Mohr Siebeck, 2000.

Ahmed, Sara. "Declarations of Whiteness: The Non-Performativity of Anti-Racism." *Borderlands* 3.2 (2004).

Alexander, Loveday. "Mapping Early Christianity: Acts and the Shape of Early Church History." *Int* 57 (2003): 163–73.

Alexander, Philip S. "Jerusalem as the *Omphalos* of the World: On the History of a Geographical Concept." Pages 104–19 in *Jerusalem: Its Sanctity and Centrality to Judaism, Christianity, and Islam.* Edited by Lee I. Levine. New York: Continuum, 1999.

——. Review of *Jesus and Judaism,* by E. P. Sanders. *JJS* 37 (1986): 103–6.

Alikin, Valeriy A. *The Earliest History of the Christian Gathering: Origin, Development and Content of the Christian Gathering in the First to Third Centuries.* VCSup 102. Leiden: Brill, 2010.

Amaru, Betsy Halpern. "Land Theology in Josephus' 'Jewish Antiquities.'" *JQR* 71 (1981): 201–29.

American Anthropological Association. "AAA Statement on Race." May 17, 1998. https://www.americananthro.org/ConnectWithAAA/Content.aspx?ItemNumber=2583.

Anson, Edward M. "Greek Ethnicity and the Greek Language." *Glotta* 85 (2009): 5–30.

Applebaum, Barbara. "White Ignorance and Denials of Complicity: On the Possibility of Doing Philosophy in Good Faith." Pages 1–25 in *The Center Must Not Hold: White Women Philosophers on the Whiteness of Philosophy*. Edited by George Yancy. Lanham, MD: Lexington, 2010.

Arnal, William. "Jesus as Battleground in a Period of Cultural Complexity." Pages 99–117 in *Jesus beyond Nationalism: Constructing the Historical Jesus in a Period of Cultural Complexity*. Edited by Halvor Moxnes, Ward Blanton, and James G. Crossley. BibleWorld. London: Equinox, 2009.

Asad, Talal. *Formations of the Secular: Christianity, Islam, Modernity*. Cultural Memory in the Present. Stanford: Stanford University Press, 2003.

———. "Introduction." Pages 9–19 in *Anthropology and the Colonial Encounter*. Edited by Talal Asad. London: Ithaca, 1973.

Ascough, Richard S. "The Thessalonian Christian Community as a Professional Voluntary Association." *JBL* 119 (2000): 311–28.

Ascough, Richard S., Philip A. Harland, and John S. Kloppenborg. *Associations in the Greco-Roman World: A Sourcebook*. Berlin: De Gruyter, 2012.

Attridge, Harold W. *The Epistle to the Hebrews*. Hermeneia. Philadelphia: Fortress, 1989.

Augoustinos, Martha, and Stephanie De Garis. "'Too Black or Not Black Enough': Social Identity Complexity in the Political Rhetoric of Barack Obama." *European Journal of Social Psychology* 42 (2012): 564–77.

Avruch, Kevin. "Culture and Ethnic Conflict in the New World Disorder." Pages 72–82 in *Race and Ethnicity: Comparative and Theoretical Approaches*. Edited by John Stone and Rutledge Dennis. Blackwell Readers in Sociology. Malden, MA: Blackwell, 2003.

Bacchiocchi, Samuele. *From Sabbath to Sunday: A Historical Investigation of the Rise of Sunday Observance in Early Christianity*. Rome: Pontifical Gregorian University Press, 1977.

Backhaus, Knut. "Das Land der Verheißung: Die Heimat der Glaubenden im Hebräerbrief." *NTS* 47 (2001): 171–88.

Badiou, Alain. *Saint Paul: The Foundation of Universalism*. Translated by Ray Brassier. Cultural Memory in the Present. Stanford: Stanford University Press, 2003.

Bailey, Randall C., Tat-siong Benny Liew, and Fernando F. Segovia. "Toward Minority Biblical Criticism: Framework, Contours, Dynamics." Pages 3–43 in *They Were All Together in One Place? Toward Minority Biblical Criticism*. Edited by Randall C. Bailey, Tat-siong Benny Liew, and Fernando F. Segovia. SemeiaSt 57. Atlanta: Society of Biblical Literature, 2009.

Bailey, Randall C., Tat-siong Benny Liew, and Fernando F. Segovia, eds. *They Were All Together in One Place? Toward Minority Biblical Criticism*. SemeiaSt 57. Atlanta: Society of Biblical Literature, 2009.

Baker, Cynthia M. "'From Every Nation under Heaven': Jewish Ethnicities in the Greco-Roman World." Pages 70–99 in *Prejudice and Christian Beginnings: Investigating Race, Gender, and Ethnicity in Early Christian Studies*. Edited by Laura Nasrallah and Elisabeth Schüssler Fiorenza. Minneapolis: Fortress, 2009.

Balch, David L. "Hellenization/Acculturation in 1 Peter." Pages 79–101 in *Perspectives on First Peter*. Edited by Charles H. Talbert. Macon, GA: Mercer University Press, 1986.

———. *Let Wives Be Submissive: The Domestic Code in 1 Peter*. SBLMS 26. Atlanta: Scholars Press, 1981.

Baldwin, James. "On Being 'White' . . . and Other Lies." Pages 177–80 in *Black on White: Black Writers on What it Means to Be White*. Edited by David Roediger. New York: Schocken, 1998.

Balibar, Étienne. "The Nation Form: History and Ideology." Pages 86–106 in *Race, Nation, Class: Ambiguous Identities*. Edited by Immanuel Wallerstein and Étienne Balibar. London: Verso, 1991.

Balla, Peter. *The Child-Parent Relationship in the New Testament and Its Environment*. WUNT 155. Tübingen: Mohr Siebeck, 2003.

Banks, Robert. *Paul's Idea of Community: The Early House Churches in Their Historical Setting*. Rev. ed. Peabody, MA: Hendrickson, 1994.

Barclay, John M. G. *Against Apion*. Vol. 10 of *Flavius Josephus: Translation and Commentary*. Leiden: Brill, 2007.

———. "Deviance and Apostasy: Some Applications of Deviance Theory to First-Century Judaism and Christianity." Pages 114–27 in *Modelling Early Christianity*. Edited by Philip F. Esler. London: Routledge, 1995.

———. "'Do We Undermine the Law?' A Study of Romans 14.1–15.6." Pages

287–308 in *Paul and the Mosaic law*. Edited by James D. G. Dunn. WUNT 89. Tübingen: Mohr Siebeck, 1996.

———. "The Family as the Bearer of Religion in Judaism and Early Christianity." Pages 66–80 in *Constructing Early Christian Families: Family as Social Reality and Metaphor*. Edited by Halvor Moxnes. London: Routledge, 1997.

———. "Ἰουδαῖος: Ethnicity and Translation." Pages 46–58 in *Ethnicity, Race, Religion: Identities and Ideologies in Early Jewish and Christian Texts and in Modern Biblical Interpretation*. Edited by Katherine M. Hockey and David G. Horrell. London: Bloomsbury T&T Clark, 2018.

———. *Jews in the Mediterranean Diaspora from Alexander to Trajan (323 BCE–117 CE)*. Edinburgh: T&T Clark, 1996.

———. "'Neither Jew nor Greek': Multiculturalism and the New Perspective on Paul." Pages 197–214 in *Ethnicity and the Bible*. Edited by Mark G. Brett. BibInt. Leiden: Brill, 1996.

———. *Paul and the Gift*. Grand Rapids: Eerdmans, 2015.

———. "Paul among Diaspora Jews: Anomaly or Apostate?" *JSNT* 60 (1995): 89–120.

———. "Paul, Philemon and the Dilemma of Christian Slave-Ownership." *NTS* 37 (1991): 161–86.

———. *Pauline Churches and Diaspora Jews*. WUNT 275. Tübingen: Mohr Siebeck, 2011.

———. "Universalism and Particularism: Twin Components of Both Judaism and Early Christianity." Pages 207–24 in *A Vision for the Church: Studies in Early Christian Ecclesiology in Honour of J. P. M. Sweet*. Edited by Markus Bockmuehl and Michael B. Thompson. Edinburgh: T&T Clark, 1997.

———. "Who Was Considered an Apostate in the Jewish Diaspora?" Pages 80–98 in *Tolerance and Intolerance in Early Judaism and Christianity*. Edited by Graham N. Stanton and Guy G. Stroumsa. Cambridge: Cambridge University Press, 1998.

Barreto, Eric D. *Ethnic Negotiations: The Function of Race and Ethnicity in Acts 16*. WUNT 2.294. Tübingen: Mohr Siebeck, 2010.

Barrett, C. K. *A Critical and Exegetical Commentary on the Acts of the Apostles*. Vol. 2. ICC. London: T&T Clark, 1998.

———. *The First Epistle to the Corinthians*. 2nd ed. BNTC. London: A & C Black, 1971.

———. *The Gospel According to St. John*. London: SPCK, 1955.

Bartchy, S. Scott. "Undermining Ancient Patriarchy: The Apostle Paul's Vision of a Society of Siblings." *BTB* 29 (1999): 68–78.

Barth, Fredrik. "Introduction." Pages 9–38 in *Ethnic Groups and Boundaries: The*

Social Organization of Culture Difference. Edited by Fredrik Barth. Boston: Little, Brown, 1969.

Barth, Fredrik, ed. *Ethnic Groups and Boundaries: The Social Organization of Culture Difference.* Boston: Little, Brown, 1969.

Barton, Carlin, and Daniel Boyarin. *Imagine No Religion: How Modern Abstractions Hide Ancient Realities.* New York: Fordham University Press, 2016.

Barton, Stephen C. "The Communal Dimension of Earliest Christianity: A Critical Survey of the Field." *JTS* 43 (1992): 399–427.

———. *Discipleship and Family Ties in Mark and Matthew.* SNTSMS 80. Cambridge: Cambridge University Press, 1994.

———. "The Relativisation of Family Ties in the Jewish and Graeco-Roman Traditions." Pages 81–100 in *Constructing Early Christian Families: Family as Social Reality and Metaphor.* Edited by Halvor Moxnes. London: Routledge, 1997.

Bassler, Jouette M. *Navigating Paul: An Introduction to Key Theological Concepts.* Louisville: Westminster John Knox, 2007.

Bauckham, Richard J. "James, 1 and 2 Peter, Jude." Pages 303–17 in *It Is Written: Scripture Citing Scripture.* Edited by D. A. Carson and Hugh G. M. Williamson. Cambridge: Cambridge University Press, 1988.

———. *James: Wisdom of James, Disciple of Jesus the Sage.* New Testament Readings. London: Routledge, 1999.

———. "The Lord's Day." Pages 221–50 in *From Sabbath to Lord's Day: A Biblical, Historical and Theological Investigation.* Edited by D. A. Carson. Grand Rapids: Zondervan, 1982.

———. "Sabbath and Sunday in the Post-Apostolic Church." Pages 251–98 in *From Sabbath to Lord's Day: A Biblical, Historical and Theological Investigation.* Edited by D. A. Carson. Grand Rapids: Zondervan, 1982.

———. *The Theology of the Book of Revelation.* New Testament Theology. Cambridge: Cambridge University Press, 1993.

Bauman-Martin, Betsy J. "Speaking Jewish: Postcolonial Aliens and Strangers in First Peter." Pages 144–77 in *Reading 1 Peter with New Eyes: Methodological Reassessments of the Letter of First Peter.* Edited by Robert L. Webb and Betsy Bauman-Martin. LNTS 364. London: T&T Clark, 2007.

Baur, Ferdinand Christian. *Ausgewählte Werke in Einzelausgaben.* Edited by Klaus Scholder. 2nd ed. 5 vols. Stuttgart-Bad Cannstatt: Friedrich Frommann, 1963–75.

———. *The Church History of the First Three Centuries.* Translated by Allan Menzies. 3rd ed. 2 vols. London: Williams & Norgate, 1878–1879.

————. *Paul the Apostle of Jesus Christ: His Life and Works, His Epistles and Teachings.* 2nd ed. 2 vols. London: Williams & Norgate, 1873–1875.

Bauspiess, Martin, Christof Landmesser, and David Lincicum, eds. *Ferdinand Christian Baur und die Geschichte des Urchristentums.* WUNT 333. Tübingen: Mohr Siebeck, 2014.

Beard, Mary, John North, and Simon Price. *A History.* Vol. 1 of *Religions of Rome.* Cambridge: Cambridge University Press, 1998.

Beare, Francis W. *The First Epistle of Peter.* 3rd ed. Oxford: Blackwell, 1970.

Behr, John. *Asceticism and Anthropology in Irenaeus and Clement.* OECS. Oxford: Oxford University Press, 1999.

Benko, Andrew. *Race in John's Gospel: Toward an Ethnos-Conscious Approach.* Lanham: Lexington, 2019.

Benko, Stephen. *Pagan Rome and the Early Christians.* Bloomington: Indiana University Press, 1985.

Berger, Klaus. *Das Buch der Jubiläen.* JSHRZ 2/3. Gütersloh: Gerd Mohn, 1981.

Bernabé Ubieta, Carmen. "'Neither *xenoi* nor *paroikoi, sympolitai* and *oikeioi tou theou*' (Eph 2:19): Pauline Christian Communities: Defining a New Territoriality." Pages 260–80 in *Social Scientific Models for Interpreting the Bible: Essays by the Context Group in Honor of Bruce J. Malina.* Edited by John J. Pilch. Leiden: Brill, 2001.

Bernal, Martin. *The Fabrication of Ancient Greece 1785–1985.* Vol. 1 of *Black Athena: The Afroasiatic Roots of Classical Civilisation.* London: Free Association Books, 1987.

————. *The Archaeological and Documentary Evidence.* Vol. 2 of *Black Athena: The Afroasiatic Roots of Classical Civilisation.* London: Free Association Books, 1991.

Bernasconi, Robert. "Waking Up White and in Memphis." Pages 17–25 in *White on White/Black on Black.* Edited by George Yancy. Lanham, MD: Rowman & Littlefield, 2005.

Berquist, Jon L., and Claudia V. Camp, eds. *Theory, Geography, and Narrative.* Vol. 1 of *Constructions of Space.* LHBOTS 481. London: T&T Clark, 2007.

————, eds. *The Biblical City and Other Imagined Spaces.* Vol. 2 of *Constructions of Space.* LHBOTS 490. London: T&T Clark, 2008.

Betz, Hans Dieter. *Galatians: A Commentary on Paul's Letter to the Churches in Galatia.* Hermeneia. Philadelphia: Fortress, 1979.

Bieringer, Reimund, and Didier Pollefeyt, eds. *Paul and Judaism: Crosscurrents in Pauline Exegesis and the Study of Jewish-Christian Relations.* LNTS 463. London: Bloomsbury T&T Clark, 2012.

Bieringer, Reimund, Didier Pollefeyt, and Frederique Vandecasteele-Venneuville, eds. *Anti-Judaism and the Fourth Gospel*. Louisville: Westminster John Knox, 2001.

Bigg, Charles. *A Critical and Exegetical Commentary on the Epistles of St. Peter and St. Jude*. ICC. Edinburgh: T&T Clark, 1901.

Bird, Michael F. *Crossing Over Sea and Land: Jewish Missionary Activity in the Second Temple Period*. Peabody, MA: Hendrickson, 2010.

Bobichon, Philippe, ed. *Justin Martyr, Dialogue avec Tryphon: Édition critique, traduction, commentaire*. 2 vols. Paradosis 47/1–2. Fribourg, Switzerland: Academic Press Fribourg, 2003.

Bockmuehl, Markus N. A. *The Epistle to the Philippians*. BNTC. London: A & C Black, 1998.

Bohak, Gideon. "Ethnic Continuity in the Jewish Diaspora in Antiquity." Pages 175–92 in *Jews in the Hellenistic and Roman Cities*. Edited by John R. Bartlett. London: Routledge, 2002.

Boin, Douglas. "Hellenistic 'Judaism' and the Social Origins of the 'Pagan-Christian' Debate." *JECS* 22 (2014): 167–96.

Borgen, Peder, Kåre Fuglseth, and Roald Skarsten. *The Philo Index: A Complete Greek Word Index to the Writings of Philo of Alexandria*. Grand Rapids: Eerdmans, 2000.

Bormann, Lukas. "'Auch unter politischen Gesichtspunkten sehr sorgfältig ausgewählt': Die ersten deutschen Mitglieder der Studiorum Novi Testamenti Societas (SNTS) 1937–1946." *NTS* 58 (2012): 416–52.

———. "Griechen und Juden—Skythen und Barbaren: Ethnizität, kulturelle Dominanz und Marginalität im Neuen Testament." Pages 116–33 in *Alternative Voices: A Plurality Approach for Religious Studies. Essays in Honor of Ulrich Berner*. Edited by Afe Adogame, Magnus Echtler, and Oliver Freiberger. Critical Studies in Religion/Religionswissenschaft 4. Göttingen: Vandenhoeck & Ruprecht, 2013.

Botermann, Helga. *Das Judenedikt des Kaisers Claudius: Römischer Staat und Christiani im 1 Jahrhundert*. Hermes Einzelschriften 71. Stuttgart: Franz Steiner, 1996.

Bowers, Paul. "Church and Mission in Paul." *JSNT* 44 (1991): 89–111.

Boyarin, Daniel. *Judaism: The Genealogy of a Modern Notion*. Key Words in Jewish Studies 9. New Brunswick, NJ: Rutgers University Press, 2019.

———. *A Radical Jew: Paul and the Politics of Identity*. Berkeley: University of California Press, 1994.

———. "Rethinking Jewish Christianity: An Argument for Dismantling a Dubious Category (to Which Is Appended a Correction of My *Border Lines*)." *JQR* 99 (2009): 7–36.

Brett, Mark G. "Interpreting Ethnicity: Method, Hermeneutics, Ethics." Pages 3–22 in *Ethnicity and the Bible*. Edited by Mark G. Brett. BibInt. Leiden: Brill, 1996.

Brooke, George J. "Miqdash Adam, Eden, and the Qumran Community." Pages 285–301 in *Gemeinde ohne Tempel/Community without Temple: Zur Substituierung und Transformation des Jerusalemer Tempels und seines Kults im Alten Testament, antiken Judentum und frühen Christentum*. Edited by Beate Ego, Armin Lange, and Peter Pilhofer. WUNT 118. Tübingen: Mohr Siebeck, 1999.

Brown, Jeannine K. "Silent Wives, Verbal Believers: Ethical and Hermeneutical Considerations in 1 Peter 3:1–6 and Its Context." *WW* 24 (2004): 395–403.

Brown, Peter. *The Body and Society: Men, Women and Sexual Renunciation in Early Christianity*. Columbia Classics in Religion. 20th anniv. ed. New York: Columbia University Press, 2008.

Brox, Norbert. "Das 'irdische Jerusalem' in der altchristlichen Theologie." *Kairos* 28 (1986): 152–73.

Brubaker, Rogers. "Ethnicity without Groups." *European Journal of Sociology* 43 (2002): 163–89.

———. *Ethnicity without Groups*. Cambridge, MA: Harvard University Press, 2004.

———. *Grounds for Difference*. Cambridge, MA: Harvard University Press, 2015.

———. *Trans: Gender and Race in an Age of Unsettled Identities*. Princeton: Princeton University Press, 2016.

Brueggemann, Walter. *The Land: Place as Gift, Promise, and Challenge in Biblical Faith*. 2nd ed. OBT. Minneapolis: Fortress, 2002.

Buell, Denise Kimber. "Anachronistic Whiteness and the Ethics of Interpretation." Pages 149–67 in *Ethnicity, Race, Religion: Identities and Ideologies in Early Jewish and Christian Texts and in Modern Biblical Interpretation*. Edited by Katherine M. Hockey and David G. Horrell. London: Bloomsbury T&T Clark, 2018.

———. "Challenges and Strategies for Speaking about Ethnicity in the New Testament and New Testament Studies." *SEÅ* 79 (2014): 33–51.

———. "Early Christian Universalism and Modern Forms of Racism." Pages 109–31 in *The Origins of Racism in the West*. Edited by Eliav-Feldon, Benjamin Isaac, and Joseph Ziegler. Cambridge: Cambridge University Press, 2009.

———. "Ethnicity and Religion in Mediterranean Antiquity and Beyond." *RelSRev* 26 (2000): 243–49.

———. "God's Own People: Specters of Race, Ethnicity, and Gender in Early

Christian Studies." Pages 159–90 in *Prejudice and Christian Beginnings: Investigating Race, Gender, and Ethnicity in Early Christian Studies*. Edited by Laura Nasrallah and Elisabeth Schüssler Fiorenza. Minneapolis: Fortress, 2009.

———. "Race and Universalism in Early Christianity." *JECS* 10 (2002): 429–68.

———. "Rethinking the Relevance of Race for Early Christian Self-Definition." *HTR* 94 (2001): 449–76.

———. *Why This New Race: Ethnic Reasoning in Early Christianity*. New York: Columbia University Press, 2005.

Buell, Denise Kimber, and Caroline Johnson Hodge. "The Politics of Interpretation: The Rhetoric of Race and Ethnicity in Paul." *JBL* 123 (2004): 235–51.

Burchard, Christoph. *Der Jakobusbrief*. HNT 15/1. Tübingen: Mohr Siebeck, 2000.

———. "Joseph and Aseneth." Pages 177–247 in *Old Testament Pseudepigrapha*, vol. 2. Edited by James H. Charlesworth. New York: Doubleday, 1985.

———. *Joseph und Aseneth*. Pseudepigrapha Veteris Testamenti Graece 5. Leiden: Brill, 2003.

Burke, Kevin J., and Avner Segall. *Christian Privilege in U.S. Education: Legacies and Current Issues*. Studies in Curriculum Theory. London: Routledge, 2017.

Burton, Ernest DeWitt. *A Critical and Exegetical Commentary on the Epistle to the Galatians*. ICC. Edinburgh: T&T Clark, 1921.

Butticaz, Simon. "The Church in Acts: Universality of Salvation, Ethnicity, and Philanthropy." *Annali di Storia dell'Esegesi* 36 (2019): 433–52.

———. "Paul and Ethnicity between Discourse and Social Practices." *EC* 8 (2017): 309–35.

Byrne, Brendan. "Jerusalems Above and Below: A Critique of J. L. Martyn's Interpretation of the Hagar-Sarah Allegory in Gal 4.21–5.1." *NTS* 60 (2014): 215–31.

Byron, Gay L. *Symbolic Blackness and Ethnic Difference in Early Christian Literature*. London: Routledge, 2002.

Calvin, John. *The First Epistle of Paul the Apostle to the Corinthians*. Calvin's Commentaries. Edinburgh: Oliver & Boyd, 1960.

Cambe, Michel. *Kergyma Petri: Textus et Commentarius*. Corpus Christianorum: Series Apocryphorum 15. Turnhout: Brepols, 2003.

Campbell, William S. *Paul and the Creation of Christian Identity*. LNTS 322. London: T&T Clark, 2006.

Caputo, John D., and Linda Martin Alcoff, eds. *St. Paul among the Philosophers*. Indiana Studies in the Philosophy of Religion. Bloomington: Indiana University Press, 2009.

Carey, Greg. "Introduction and a Proposal: Culture, Power, and Identity in White New Testament Studies." Pages 1–13 in *Soundings in Cultural Criticism: Perspectives and Methods in Culture, Power, and Identity in the New Testament*. Edited by Francisco Lozada Jr. and Greg Carey. Minneapolis: Fortress, 2013.

Carleton Paget, James. "Hellenistic and Early Roman Period Jewish Missionary Efforts in the Diaspora." Pages 11–49 in *The Rise and Expansion of Christianity in the First Three Centuries of the Common Era*. Edited by Clare K. Rothschild and Jens Schröter. WUNT 301. Tübingen: Mohr Siebeck, 2013.

———. "Jewish Proselytism at the Time of Christian Origins: Chimera or Reality?" *JSNT* 62 (1996): 65–103.

———. "The Reception of Baur in Britain." Pages 335–86 in *Ferdinand Christian Baur und die Geschichte des Urchristentums*. Edited by Martin Bauspiess, Christof Landmesser, and David Lincicum. WUNT 333. Tübingen: Mohr Siebeck, 2014.

———. "Some Observations on Josephus and Christianity." *JTS* 52 (2001): 539–624.

Carson, D. A. *The Gospel According to John*. Grand Rapids: Eerdmans, 1991.

Carson, D. A., ed. *From Sabbath to Lord's Day: A Biblical, Historical and Theological Investigation*. Grand Rapids: Zondervan, 1982.

Carter, J. Kameron. *Race: A Theological Account*. Oxford: Oxford University Press, 2008.

Casey, Robert Pierce. *The Excerpta ex Theodoto of Clement of Alexandria*. SD 1. London: Christophers, 1934.

Catchpole, David. "The Synoptic Divorce Material as a Traditio-Historical Problem." *BJRL* 57 (1974–75): 92–127.

Chapman, Cynthia R. "'Oh That You Were Like a Brother to Me, One Who Had Nursed at My Mother's Breasts.' Breast Milk as a Kinship-Forging Substance." *JHebS* 12 (2012): 1–41.

Chesnutt, Randall D. *From Death to Life: Conversion in Joseph and Aseneth*. JSPSup 16. Sheffield: Sheffield Academic Press, 1995.

———. "The Social Setting and Purpose of Joseph and Aseneth." *JSP* 2 (1988): 21–48.

Cheung, Alex T. *Idol Food in Corinth: Jewish Background and Pauline Legacy*. JSNTSup 176. Sheffield: Sheffield Academic Press, 1999.

Church, Philip. "'God Has by No Means Rejected His People' (Rom 11:1): A Response to the Accusation of 'Replacement Theology.'" Pages 147–57 in *The Gospel and the Land of Promise: Christian Approaches to the Land of the Bible*. Edited by Philip Church, Peter Walker, Tim Bulkeley, and Tim Meadowcroft. Eugene, OR: Pickwick, 2011.

———. "'Here We Have No Lasting City' (Heb 13:14): The Promised Land in the Letter to the Hebrews." Pages 45–57 in *The Gospel and the Land of Promise: Christian Approaches to the Land of the Bible*. Edited by Philip Church, Peter Walker, Tim Bulkeley, and Tim Meadowcroft. Eugene, OR: Pickwick, 2011.

Church, Philip, Peter Walker, Tim Bulkeley, and Tim Meadowcroft, eds. *The Gospel and the Land of Promise: Christian Approaches to the Land of the Bible*. Eugene, OR: Pickwick, 2011.

Clarke, Fern K. T. "God's Concern for the Poor in the New Testament: A Discussion of the Role of the Poor in the Foundation of Christian Belief (Early to Mid First Century CE)." PhD diss., University of Exeter, 2000.

———. "'Remembering the Poor': Does Galatians 2.10a Allude to the Collection?" *ScrB* 31 (2001): 20–28.

Clifford, James. "Introduction: Partial Truths." Pages 1–26 in *Writing Culture: The Poetics and Politics of Ethnography*. Edited by James Clifford and George Marcus. Berkeley: University of California Press, 1986.

Clough, David. "Using Barth 'to Justify Doing Nothing': James Cone's Unanswered Critique of Barth Studies, 50 Years On." Paper presented at the Annual Karl Barth Conference: Karl Barth and the Future of Liberation Theology. Princeton, NJ, 2018.

Cohen, Shaye J. D. *The Beginnings of Jewishness: Boundaries, Varieties, Uncertainties*. Berkeley: University of California Press, 1999.

———. "From Permission to Prohibition: Paul and the Early Church on Mixed Marriage." Pages 259–91 in *Paul's Jewish Matrix*. Edited by Thomas G. Casey and Justin Taylor, 259–91. Bible in Dialogue 2. Rome: Gregorian and Biblical Press, 2011.

Commission on Religion and Belief in British Public Life. *Living with Difference: Community, Diversity and the Common Good*. Cambridge: Woolf Institute, 2015. https://corablivingwithdifference.files.wordpress.com/2015/12/living-with-difference-online.pdf.

Concannon, Cavan W. *"When You Were Gentiles": Specters of Ethnicity in Roman Corinth and Paul's Corinthian Correspondence*. Synkrisis: Comparative Approaches to Early Christianity in Greco-Roman Culture. New Haven: Yale University Press, 2014.

Cone, James H. *God of the Oppressed*. Rev. ed. Maryknoll, NY: Orbis, 1997.

Conzelmann, Hans. *A Commentary on the First Epistle to the Corinthians*. Hermeneia. Philadelphia: Fortress, 1975.

————. *The Theology of St Luke.* Translated by Geoffrey Buswell. London: Faber and Faber, 1960.

Cook, John Granger. *Roman Attitudes toward the Christians: From Claudius to Hadrian.* WUNT 261. Tübingen: Mohr Siebeck, 2010.

Cornell, Stephen, and Douglas Hartmann. *Ethnicity and Race: Making Identities in a Changing World.* Sociology for a New Century. Thousand Oaks, CA: Pine Forge, 2007.

Countryman, L. William. *Dirt, Greed, and Sex: Sexual Ethics in the New Testament and Their Implications for Today.* Rev. ed. Minneapolis: Fortress, 2007.

Cromhout, Markus. *Walking in Their Sandals: A Guide to First-Century Israelite Ethnic Identity.* Eugene, OR: Cascade, 2010.

Crossley, James G. *The Date of Mark's Gospel: Insight from the Law in Earliest Christianity.* JSNTSup 266. London: T&T Clark, 2004.

————. *Harnessing Chaos: The Bible in English Political Discourse since 1968.* Rev. ed. London: Bloomsbury, 2016.

————. *Jesus in an Age of Terror: Scholarly Projects for a New American Century.* London: Equinox, 2008.

————. "Jesus the Jew since 1967." Pages 119–37 in *Jesus beyond Nationalism: Constructing the Historical Jesus in a Period of Cultural Complexity.* Edited by Halvor Moxnes, Ward Blanton, and James G. Crossley. BibleWorld. London: Equinox, 2009.

Dahl, Nils Alstrup. *Studies in Paul.* Minneapolis: Augsburg, 1977.

Dalton, William J. *Christ's Proclamation to the Spirits: A Study of 1 Peter 3:18–4:6.* AnBib 23. 2nd ed. Rome: Pontifical Biblical Institute, 1989.

Daube, David. *Ancient Jewish Law: Three Inaugural Lectures.* Leiden: Brill, 1981.

Davies, W. D. *The Gospel and the Land: Early Christianity and Jewish Territorial Doctrine.* Berkeley: University of California Press, 1974.

————. *The Territorial Dimension of Judaism.* Berkeley: University of California Press, 1982.

Davies, W. D., and Dale C. Allison. *A Critical and Exegetical Commentary on the Gospel According to Saint Matthew.* ICC. 3 vols. Edinburgh: T&T Clark, 1988–1997.

De Ste. Croix, Geoffrey E. M. "Why Were the Early Christians Persecuted?" *Past and Present* 26 (1963): 6–38.

Deines, Roland, Volker Leppin, and Karl-Wilhelm Niebuhr, eds. *Walter Grundmann: Ein Neutestamentler im Dritten Reich.* Arbeiten zur Kirchen- und Theologiegeschichte 21. Leipzig: Evangelischer Verlagsanstalt, 2007.

Delgado, Richard, and Jean Stefancic. *Critical White Studies: Looking Behind the Mirror.* Philadelphia: Temple University Press, 1997.

Delling, Gerhard. *Studien zum Neuen Testament und zum hellenistischen Judentum: Gesammelte Aufsätze 1950–1968*. Göttingen: Vandenhoeck & Ruprecht, 1970.

DeMaris, Richard E. *The New Testament in Its Ritual World*. London: Routledge, 2008.

Descourtieux, Patrick, ed. *Clément d'Alexandrie, Les Stromates: Stromate VI*. SC 446. Paris: Cerf, 1999.

DiAngelo, Robin. *What Does It Mean to Be White? Developing White Racial Literacy*. Rev. ed. Counterpoints: Studies in the Postmodern Theory of Education 497. New York: Lang, 2016.

———. *White Fragility: Why It's So Hard for White People to Talk about Racism*. Boston, MA: Beacon, 2018.

Dickson, John P. *Mission-Commitment in Ancient Judaism and in the Pauline Communities*. WUNT 2.159. Tübingen: Mohr Siebeck, 2003.

Donaldson, Terence L. *Judaism and the Gentiles: Jewish Patterns of Universalism (to 135 CE)*. Waco: Baylor University Press, 2007.

Doran, Robert. "2 Maccabees." Pages 734–50 in *The Oxford Bible Commentary*. Edited by John Barton and John Muddiman. Oxford: Oxford University Press, 2001.

———. *2 Maccabees: A Critical Commentary*. Hermeneia. Minneapolis: Fortress, 2012.

Dube, Musa W. "Introduction. The Scramble for Africa as the Biblical Scramble for Africa: Postcolonial Perspectives." Pages 1–26 in *Postcolonial Perspectives in African Biblical Interpretations*. Edited by Musa W. Dube, Andrew M. Mbuvi, and Dora R. Mbuwayesango. Atlanta: Society of Biblical Literature, 2012.

DuBois, W. E. B. *Black Reconstruction in America*. London: Frank Cass; New York: Russell & Russell, 1966.

Duff, Paul B. *Jesus Followers in the Roman Empire*. Grand Rapids: Eerdmans, 2017.

Duling, Dennis C. "The Matthean Brotherhood and Marginal Scribal Leadership." Pages 159–82 in *Modelling Early Christianity*. Edited by Philip F. Esler. London: Routledge, 1995.

Dunn, James D. G. "Boundary Markers in Early Christianity." Pages 49–68 in *Gruppenreligionen im römischen Reich: Sozialformen, Grenzziehungen und Leistungen*. Edited by Jörg Rüpke. STAC 43. Tübingen: Mohr Siebeck, 2007.

———. *The Epistle to the Galatians*. BNTC. London: A & C Black, 1993.

———. *Jesus, Paul and the Law*. London: SPCK, 1990.

———. "The New Perspective on Paul." *BJRL* 65 (1983): 95–122.

———. "Paul: Apostate or Apostle of Israel?" *ZNW* 89 (1998): 256–71.

———. *Romans 9–16*. WBC 38B. Waco: Word, 1988.

———. *The New Perspective on Paul*. Rev. ed. Grand Rapids: Eerdmans, 2008.

———. *The New Perspective on Paul: Selected Essays*. WUNT 185. Tübingen: Mohr Siebeck, 2005.

———. *The Theology of Paul the Apostle*. Edinburgh: T&T Clark, 1998.

———. "Was Judaism Particularist or Universalist?" Pages 57–73 in *Judaism in Late Antiquity Part Three: Where We Stand: Issues and Debates in Ancient Judaism*. Edited by Jacob Neusner and Alan J. Avery-Peck. Vol. 2. Leiden: Brill, 1999.

———. "Who Did Paul Think He Was? A Study of Jewish-Christian Identity." *NTS* 45 (1999): 174–93.

Dunning, Benjamin H. *Aliens and Sojourners: Self as Other in Early Christianity*. Divinations: Rereading Late Ancient Religion. Philadelphia: University of Pennsylvania Press, 2009.

———. "Strangers and Aliens No Longer: Negotiating Identity and Difference in Ephesians 2." *HTR* 99 (2006): 1–16.

Dyer, Richard. *White*. London: Routledge, 1997.

Eastman, Susan. "'Cast Out the Slave Woman and Her Son': The Dynamics of Exclusion and Inclusion in Galatians 4.30." *JSNT* 28 (2006): 309–36.

Eckhardt, Benedikt. "'An Idumean, That Is, a Half-Jew': Hasmoneans and Herodians between Ancestry and Merit." Pages 91–115 in *Jewish Identity and Politics between the Maccabees and Bar Kokhba: Groups, Normativity, and Rituals*. Edited by Benedikt Eckhardt. JSJSup 155. Leiden: Brill, 2012.

Ehrensperger, Kathy. *Paul at the Crossroads of Cultures: Theologizing in the Space-Between*. LNTS 456. London: Bloomsbury T&T Clark, 2013.

———. "Paul, His People and Racial Terminology." *Journal of Early Christian History* 3 (2013): 17–32.

———. "Paulus, sein Volk und die Rasseterminologie: Kritische Anfragen an den 'Race'-Diskurs in neuerer englischsprachiger Paulus-Forschung." *Kirche und Israel* 27 (2012): 119–33.

———. "What's in a Name? Ideologies of *Volk*, *Rasse*, and *Reich* in German New Testament Interpretation Past and Present." Pages 92–112 in *Ethnicity, Race, Religion: Identities and Ideologies in Early Jewish and Christian Texts and in Modern Biblical Interpretation*. Edited by Katherine M. Hockey and David G. Horrell. London: Bloomsbury T&T Clark, 2018.

Eisen, Ute E., Christine Gerber, and Angela Standhartinger. "Doing Gender— Doing Religion. Zur Frage nach der Intersektionalität in den Bibelwissenschaften: Eine Einleitung." Pages 1–33 in *Doing Gender—Doing Religion:*

Fallstudien zur Intersektionalität im frühen Judentum, Christentum und Islam. Edited by Ute E. Eisen, Christine Gerber, and Angela Standhartinger. WUNT 302. Tübingen: Mohr Siebeck, 2013.

Eisenbaum, Pamela. "Jewish Perspectives: A Jewish Apostle to the Gentiles." Pages 135–53 in *Studying Paul's Letters: Contemporary Perspectives and Methods.* Edited by Joseph A. Marchal. Minneapolis: Fortress, 2012.

———. *Paul Was Not a Christian: The Original Message of a Misunderstood Apostle.* New York: HarperCollins, 2009.

Elliott, John H. *The Elect and the Holy: An Exegetical Examination of 1 Peter 2:4–10 and the Phrase* basileion hierateuma. NovTSup 12. Leiden: Brill, 1966.

———. *1 Peter: A New Translation with Introduction and Commentary.* AB 37B. New York: Doubleday, 2000.

———. *A Home for the Homeless: A Social-Scientific Criticism of 1 Peter, Its Situation and Strategy.* 2nd ed. Minneapolis: Fortress, 1990.

———. "Jesus the Israelite Was Neither a 'Jew' nor a 'Christian': On Correcting Misleading Nomenclature." *Journal for the Study of the Historical Jesus* 5 (2007): 119–54.

Erickson, Amy J. "Difficult Texts: 1 Timothy 2:11–15." *Theology* 122 (2019): 200–203.

Eriksen, Thomas H. "Ethnicity, Race, Class and Nation." Pages 28–31 in *Ethnicity.* Edited by John Hutchinson and Anthony D. Smith. Oxford Readers. Oxford: Oxford University Press, 1996.

Esler, Philip F. *Community and Gospel in Luke-Acts: The Social and Political Motivations of Lucan Theology.* SNTSMS 57. Cambridge: Cambridge University Press, 1987.

———. *Conflict and Identity in Romans: The Social Setting of Paul's Letter.* Minneapolis: Fortress, 2003.

———. "From *Ioudaioi* to Children of God: The Development of a Non-Ethnic Group Identity in the Gospel of John." Pages 106–37 in *In Other Words: Essays on Social Science Methods and the New Testament in Honor of Jerome H. Neyrey.* Edited by Anselm C. Hagedorn, Zeba A. Crook, and Eric Stewart. Social World of Biblical Antiquity, Second Series 1. Sheffield: Sheffield Phoenix, 2007.

———. *Galatians.* New Testament Readings. London: Routledge, 1998.

———. "Giving the Kingdom to an *Ethnos* That Will Bear Its Fruit: Ethnic and Christ-Movement Identities in Matthew." Pages 177–96 in *In the Fullness of Time: Essays on Christology, Creation, and Eschatology in Honor of Richard Bauckham.* Edited by Daniel M. Gurtner, Grant Macaskill, and Jonathan T. Pennington. Grand Rapids: Eerdmans, 2016.

———. *God's Court and Courtiers in the Book of the Watchers: Re-interpreting Heaven in 1 Enoch 1–36*. Eugene, OR: Cascade, 2017.

———. "Group Boundaries and Intergroup Conflict in Galatians: A New Reading of Galatians 5:13–6:10." Pages 215–40 in *Ethnicity and the Bible*. Edited by Mark G. Brett. BibInt. Leiden: Brill, 1996.

———. "Intergroup Conflict and Matthew 23: Towards Responsible Historical Interpretation of a Challenging Text." *BTB* 45 (2015): 38–59.

———. "Jesus and the Reduction of Intergroup Conflict: The Parable of the Good Samaritan in the Light of Social Identity Theory." *BibInt* 8 (2000): 325–57.

———. "Judean Ethnic Identity and the Matthean Jesus." Pages 193–210 in *Jesus—Gestalt und Gestaltungen: Rezeptionen des Galiläers in Wissenschaft, Kirche und Gesellschaft. Festschrift für Gerd Theißen zum 70. Geburtstag*. Edited by Petra von Gemünden, David G. Horrell, and Max Küchler. NTOA 100. Göttingen: Vandenhoeck & Ruprecht, 2013.

———. "Judean Ethnic Identity in Josephus' *Against Apion*." Pages 73–91 in *A Wandering Galilean: Essays in Honour of Seán Freyne*. Edited by Zuleika Rodgers, Margaret Daly-Denton, and Anne Fitzpatrick McKinley. Leiden: Brill, 2009.

Evans, Craig A., and Donald A. Hagner, eds. *Anti-Semitism and Early Christianity: Issues of Polemic and Faith*. Minneapolis: Fortress, 1993.

Fagbemi, Stephen Ayodeji A. *Who Are the Elect in 1 Peter? A Study in Biblical Exegesis and Its Application to the Anglican Church of Nigeria*. StBibLit 104. New York: Lang, 2007.

Fanon, Frantz. "The Fact of Blackness." Pages 257–65 in *Theories of Race and Racism: A Reader*. Edited by Les Back and John Solomos. Routledge Student Readers. London: Routledge, 2000.

———. *Les damnés de la terre*. Paris: Éditions La Découverte, 1987 [1961].

———. *The Wretched of the Earth*. Translated by Constance Farrington. London: Penguin, 1967.

Fee, Gordon D. *The First Epistle to the Corinthians*. Rev. ed. NICNT. Grand Rapids: Eerdmans, 2014.

———. *Paul's Letter to the Philippians*. NICNT. Grand Rapids: Eerdmans, 1995.

Felder, Cain Hope, ed. *Stony the Road We Trod: African American Biblical Interpretation*. Minneapolis: Fortress, 1991.

Feldman, Louis H. *Jew and Gentile in the Ancient World: Attitudes and Interactions from Alexander to Justinian*. Princeton: Princeton University Press, 1993.

———. "Jewish 'Sympathizers' in Classical Literature and Inscriptions." *TAPA* 81 (1950): 200–208.

Feldmeier, Reinhard. *Die Christen als Fremde: Die Metapher der Fremde in der antiken Welt, im Urchristentum und im 1. Petrusbrief.* WUNT 64. Tübingen: Mohr Siebeck, 1992.

———. *The First Letter of Peter: A Commentary on the Greek Text.* Translated by Peter H. Davids. Waco: Baylor University Press, 2008.

Fenton, Joseph Clifford. "New Testament Designations of the Catholic Church and of its Members." *CBQ* 9 (1947): 127–46.

Ferguson, Everett. *Baptism in the Early Church: History, Theology, and Liturgy in the First Five Centuries.* Grand Rapids: Eerdmans, 2009.

Filtvedt, Ole Jakob. *The Identity of God's People and the Paradox of Hebrews.* WUNT 2.400. Tübingen: Mohr Siebeck, 2015.

Foerster, Werner. *Patristic Evidence.* Vol. 1 of *Gnosis: A Selection of Gnostic Texts.* Translated by R. McL. Wilson. Oxford: Clarendon, 1972.

Frankel, David. *The Land of Canaan and the Destiny of Israel: Theologies of Territory in the Hebrew Bible.* Siphrut: Literature and Theology of the Hebrew Scriptures 4. Winona Lake, IN: Eisenbrauns, 2011.

Frankenberg, Ruth. *White Women, Race Matters: The Social Construction of Whiteness.* Minneapolis: University of Minnesota Press, 1993.

Frankenberg, Ruth, ed. *Displacing Whiteness: Essays in Social and Cultural Criticism.* Durham, NC: Duke University Press, 1997.

Fredriksen, Paula. "Judaism, the Circumcision of Gentiles, and Apocalyptic Hope: Another Look at Galatians 1 and 2." *JTS* 42 (1991): 532–64.

———. "Judaizing the Nations: The Ritual Demands of Paul's Gospel." *NTS* 56 (2010): 232–52.

———. "Mandatory Retirement: Ideas in the Study of Christian Origins Whose Time Has Come to Go." *SR* 35 (2006): 231–46.

———. *Paul: The Pagans' Apostle.* New Haven: Yale University Press, 2017.

———. Review *Paul and the Faithfulness of God*, by N. T. Wright. *CBQ* 77 (2015): 387–91.

———. "What 'Parting of the Ways'? Jews, Gentiles, and the Ancient Mediterranean City." Pages 35–63 in *The Ways That Never Parted: Jews and Christians in Late Antiquity and the Early Middle Ages.* Edited by Adam H. Becker and Annette Yoshiko Reed. TSAJ 95. Tübingen: Mohr Siebeck, 2003.

Furnish, Victor Paul. "Inside Looking Out: Some Pauline Views of the Unbelieving Public." Pages 104–24 in *Pauline Conversations in Context: Essays in Honor of Calvin J. Roetzel.* Edited by J. C. Anderson, P. Sellew, and C. Setzer. Sheffield: Sheffield Academic Press, 2002.

————. *II Corinthians*. AB 32A. New York: Doubleday, 1984.

Furstenberg, Yair. "Defilement Penetrating the Body: A New Understanding of Contamination in Mark 7.15." *NTS* 54 (2008): 176–200.

Gabriel, Sharmani P. "The Meaning of Race in Malaysia: Colonial, Post-Colonial and Possible New Conjunctures." *Ethnicities* 15 (2015): 782–809.

Gager, John G. *Reinventing Paul*. Oxford: Oxford University Press, 2000.

García Martínez, Florentino, and Eibert J. C. Tigchelaar. *The Dead Sea Scrolls Study Edition*. 2 vols. Leiden: Brill; Grand Rapids: Eerdmans, 2000.

Garner, Steve. *Whiteness: An Introduction*. New York: Routledge, 2007.

Garrigan, Siobhán. "Irish Theology as White Theology: A Case of Mistaken Identity?" *Modern Theology* 30 (2014): 193–218.

Garrow, Alan. *The Gospel of Matthew's Dependence on the Didache*. JSNTSup 254. London: T&T Clark, 2004.

Garroway, Joshua D. *Paul's Gentile-Jews: Neither Jew nor Gentile, but Both*. New York: Palgrave Macmillan, 2012.

Gaston, Lloyd. *Paul and the Torah*. Vancouver: University of British Columbia Press, 1987.

Geiger, Joseph. "The Jew and the Other: Doubtful and Multiple Identities in the Roman Empire." Pages 135–46 in *Jewish Identities in Antiquity: Studies in Memory of Menahem Stern*. Edited by Lee I. Levine and Daniel R. Schwartz. TSAJ 130. Tübingen: Mohr Siebeck, 2009.

George, Mark K., ed. *Further Developments in Examining Ancient Israel's Social Space*. Vol. 4 of *Constructions of Space*. LHBOTS 569. London: Bloomsbury T&T Clark, 2013.

Georgi, Dieter. *The Opponents of Paul in Second Corinthians: A Study of Religious Propaganda in Late Antiquity*. Edinburgh: T&T Clark, 1987.

Gerdmar, Anders. "Baur and the Creation of the Judaism-Hellenism Dichotomy." Pages 107–28 in *Ferdinand Christian Baur und die Geschichte des Urchristentums*. Edited by Martin Bauspiess, Christof Landmesser, and David Lincicum. WUNT 333. Tübingen: Mohr Siebeck, 2014.

Gil-White, Francisco J. "Are Ethnic Groups Biological 'Species' to the Human Brain? Essentialism in Our Cognition of Some Social Categories." *Current Anthropology* 42 (2001): 515–53.

————. "How Thick Is Blood? The Plot Thickens . . . : If Ethnic Actors Are Primordialists, What Remains of the Circumstantialist/Primordialist Controversy?" *Ethnic and Racial Studies* 22 (1999): 789–820.

Gillihan, Yonder Moynihan. "Jewish Laws on Illicit Marriage, the Defilement of Offspring, and the Holiness of the Temple: A New Halakic Interpretation of 1 Corinthians 7:14." *JBL* 121 (2002): 711–44.

Gilman, Sander L. "Are Jews White? Or, The History of the Nose Job." Pages 229–37 in *Theories of Race and Racism: A Reader*. Edited by Les Back and John Solomos. Routledge Student Readers. London: Routledge, 2000.

Girsch, Katherine Anne. "Begotten Anew: Divine Regeneration and Identity Construction in 1 Peter." PhD diss., Durham University, 2015. http://etheses.dur.ac.uk/11349/.

Givens, Tommy. *We the People: Israel and the Catholicity of Jesus*. Minneapolis: Fortress, 2014.

Goldstein, Eric L. *The Price of Whiteness: Jews, Race, and American Identity*. Princeton: Princeton University Press, 2006.

Goodman, Alan H., Yolanda T. Moses, and Joseph L. Jones. *Race: Are We So Different?* Chichester: Wiley-Blackwell, 2012.

Goodman, Martin. "Jewish Proselytizing in the First Century." Pages 53–78 in *The Jews Among Pagans and Christians in the Roman Empire*. Edited by Judith Lieu, John North, and Tessa Rajak. London: Routledge, 1992.

———. *Mission and Conversion: Proselytizing in the Religious History of the Roman Empire*. Oxford: Clarendon, 1994.

Goppelt, Leonhard. *A Commentary on I Peter*. Grand Rapids: Eerdmans, 1993.

Grässer, Erich. *An die Hebräer (Hebr 1–6)*. EKKNT 17.1. Zürich: Benziger; Neukirchen-Vluyn: Neukirchener, 1990.

Green, Joel B. *1 Peter*. THNTC. Grand Rapids: Eerdmans, 2007.

Gruen, Erich S. *Diaspora: Jews amidst Greeks and Romans*. Cambridge, MA: Harvard University Press, 2002.

———. "Kinship Relations and Jewish Identity." Pages 101–16 in *Jewish Identities in Antiquity: Studies in Memory of Menahem Stern*. Edited by Lee I. Levine and Daniel R. Schwartz. TSAJ 130. Tübingen: Mohr Siebeck, 2009.

———. *Rethinking the Other in Antiquity*. Martin Classical Lectures. Princeton: Princeton University Press, 2011.

———. Review of *Why This New Race: Ethnic Reasoning in Early Christianity*, by Denise Kimber Buell. *CBQ* 72 (2010): 365–67.

Guttenberger, Gudrun. "Ethnizität im Markusevangelium." Pages 125–52 in *Jesus—Gestalt und Gestaltungen: Rezeptionen des Galiläers in Wissenschaft, Kirche und Gesellschaft: Festschrift für Gerd Theißen zum 70. Geburtstag*. Edited by Petra von Gemünden, David G. Horrell, and Max Küchler. NTOA 100. Göttingen: Vandenhoeck & Ruprecht, 2013.

Habel, Norman C. *The Land Is Mine: Six Biblical Land Ideologies*. OBT. Minneapolis: Fortress, 1995.

Hadas-Lebel, Mireille. "Les mariages mixtes dans la famille d'Hérode et la Halakha prétalmudique sur la patrilinéarité." *Revue des Etudes Juives* 152 (1993): 397–404.

Hadot, Pierre. *Philosophy as a Way of Life: Spiritual Exercises from Socrates to Foucault.* Oxford: Blackwell, 1995.

Hägg, Henny Fiskå. *Clement of Alexandria and the Beginnings of Christian Apophaticism.* OECS. Oxford: Oxford University Press, 2006.

Hagner, Donald A. *Matthew 14–28.* WBC 33B. Grand Rapids: Zondervan, 1995.

Hall, Jonathan M. *Ethnic Identity in Greek Antiquity.* Cambridge: Cambridge University Press, 1997.

———. *Hellenicity: Between Ethnicity and Culture.* Chicago: University of Chicago Press, 2002.

Hannaford, Ivan. *Race: The History of an Idea in the West.* Washington, DC: Woodrow Wilson Center; Baltimore: Johns Hopkins University Press, 1996.

Hansen, Bruce. *"All of You Are One": The Social Vision of Galatians 3.28, 1 Corinthians 12.13 and Colossians 3.11.* LNTS 409. London: T&T Clark, 2010.

Harink, Douglas. *Paul among the Postliberals: Pauline Theology beyond Christendom and Modernity.* Grand Rapids: Brazos, 2003.

Harland, Philip A. *Associations, Synagogues, and Congregations.* Minneapolis: Fortress, 2003.

———. *Dynamics of Identity in the World of the Early Christians: Associations, Judeans, and Cultural Minorities.* London: T&T Clark, 2009.

Harnack, Adolf von. *The Expansion of Christianity in the First Three Centuries.* Translated by James Moffatt. Vol. 1. London: Williams and Norgate, 1904.

———. *Die Mission und Ausbreitung des Christentums in den ersten drei Jahrhunderten.* Leipzig: Hinrichs, 1902.

———. *Die Mission und Ausbreitung des Christentums in den ersten drei Jahrhunderten.* 4th ed. 2 vols. Leipzig: Hinrichs, 1924.

Harrill, J. Albert. "Ethnic Fluidity in Ephesians." *NTS* 60 (2014): 379–402.

———. *Paul the Apostle: His Life and Legacy in Their Roman Context.* Cambridge: Cambridge University Press, 2012.

Harrington, Wilfrid J. *Revelation.* SP 16. Collegeville: Liturgical Press, 1993.

Harris, Cheryl I. "Whiteness as Property." *Harvard Law Review* 106 (1993): 1707–91.

Harris, Horton. *The Tübingen School.* Oxford: Clarendon, 1975.

Harris, J. Rendel, and J. Armitage Robinson. *The Apology of Aristides on Behalf of the Christians.* TS 1.1. Cambridge: Cambridge University Press, 1891.

Hartin, Patrick J. *James.* SP 14. Collegeville: Liturgical Press, 2009.

Hartman, Lars. *"Into the Name of the Lord Jesus": Baptism in the Early Church.* Edinburgh: T&T Clark, 1997.

Harvey, David. *The Condition of Postmodernity: An Inquiry into the Origins of Cultural Change*. Oxford: Blackwell, 1989.

———. *Spaces of Hope*. Edinburgh: Edinburgh University Press, 2000.

Hastings, Adrian. "The Clash of Nationalism and Universalism within Twentieth-Century Missionary Christianity." Pages 15–33 in *Missions, Nationalism, and the End of Empire*. Edited by Brian Stanley. Studies in the History of Christian Missions. Grand Rapids: Eerdmans, 2003.

Hatch, Edwin, and Henry A. Redpath. *A Concordance to the Septuagint and the Other Greek Versions of the Old Testament (Including the Apocryphal Books)*. 2 vols. Graz-Austria: Akademische Druck, 1954.

Hayes, Christine E. *Gentile Impurities and Jewish Identities: Intermarriage and Conversion from the Bible to the Talmud*. Oxford: Oxford University Press, 2002.

Hayes, Cleveland, Brenda G. Juárez, Matthew T. Witt, and Nicholas D. Hartlep. "Toward a Lesser Shade of White: 12 Steps Towards More Authentic Race Awareness." Pages 1–16 in *Unhooking from Whiteness: The Key to Dismantling Racism in the United States*. Edited by Cleveland Hayes and Nicholas D. Hartlep. Rotterdam: Sense Publishers, 2013.

Hegel, Georg Wilhelm Friedrich. *Lectures on the Philosophy of World History: Introduction: Reason in History*. Translated by H. S. Nisbet. Cambridge: Cambridge University Press, 1975.

Heid, Stefan. *Chiliasmus und Antichrist-Mythos: Eine frühchristliche Kontroverse um das Heilige Land*. Hereditas: Studien zur Alten Kirchengeschichte 6. Bonn: Borengässer, 1993.

Hellerman, Joseph H. *The Ancient Church as Family*. Minneapolis: Fortress, 2001.

———. *Jesus and the People of God: Reconfiguring Ethnic Identity*. New Testament Monographs 21. Sheffield: Sheffield Phoenix, 2007.

Hendriksen, William. *New Testament Commentary: Exposition of Galatians*. Grand Rapids: Baker, 1968.

Heng, Geraldine. *The Invention of Race in the European Middle Ages*. Cambridge: Cambridge University Press, 2018.

Hengel, Martin. *The "Hellenization" of Judaea in the First Century after Christ*. Translated by John Bowden. London: SCM Press; Philadelphia: Trinity Press International, 1989.

———. *Judaism and Hellenism: Studies in Their Encounter in Palestine During the Early Hellenistic Period*. Translated by John Bowden. 2 vols. London: SCM Press, 1974.

Heschel, Susannah. *Abraham Geiger and the Jewish Jesus*. Chicago: University of Chicago Press, 1998.

———. *The Aryan Jesus: Christian Theologians and the Bible in Nazi Germany.* Princeton: Princeton University Press, 2008.

———. "Historiography of Antisemitism versus Anti-Judaism: A Response to Robert Morgan." *JSNT* 33 (2011): 257–79.

Hicks-Keeton, Jill. *Arguing with Aseneth: Gentile Access to Israel's Living God in Jewish Antiquity.* Oxford: Oxford University Press, 2018.

Hock, Ronald F. *The Social Context of Paul's Ministry: Tentmaking and Apostleship.* Philadelphia: Fortress, 1980.

Hoek, Annewies van den. "The 'Catechetical' School of Early Christian Alexandria and Its Philonic Heritage." *HTR* 90 (1997): 59–87.

Holloway, Paul A. *Coping with Prejudice: 1 Peter in Social-Psychological Perspective.* WUNT 244. Tübingen: Mohr Siebeck, 2009.

Holm, Douglas. "Holy Engagement: 'Doing Good' as a Missional Response in 1 Peter." *Leaven* 20 (2012): 110–16.

———. "Holy Engagement: Doing Good and Verbal Witness as Missional Activity in 1 Peter." PhD diss., University of Bristol, 2014.

Holtz, Gudrun. *Damit Gott sei alles in allem: Studien zum paulinischen und frühjüdischen Universalismus.* BZNW 149. Berlin: De Gruyter, 2007.

Holtz, Traugott. *Der erste Brief an die Thessalonicher.* EKKNT 13. Zürich: Benziger; Neukirchen-Vluyn: Neukirchener, 1986.

Honigman, Sylvie. "*Politeumata* and Ethnicity in Ptolemaic and Roman Egypt." *Ancient Society* 33 (2003): 61–102.

Hooker, Morna D. "1 Thessalonians 1.9–10: A Nutshell—But What Kind of Nut?" Pages 435–48 in *Frühes Christentum.* Vol. 3 of *Geschichte—Tradition—Reflexion: Festschrift für Martin Hengel zum 70. Geburtstag.* Edited by Hermann Lichtenberger. Tübingen: Mohr Siebeck, 1996.

———. *The Gospel According to Saint Mark.* London: A & C Black, 1991.

Horrell, David G. "Aliens and Strangers? The Socioeconomic Location of the Addressees of 1 Peter." Pages 176–202 in *Engaging Economics: New Testament Scenarios and Early Christian Reception.* Edited by Bruce W. Longenecker and Kelly Liebengood. Grand Rapids: Eerdmans, 2009.

———. *Becoming Christian: Essays on 1 Peter and the Making of Christian Identity.* LNTS 394. London: Bloomsbury T&T Clark, 2013.

———. "Between Conformity and Resistance: Beyond the Balch-Elliott Debate Towards a Postcolonial Reading of 1 Peter." Pages 111–43 in *Reading 1 Peter with New Eyes: Methodological Reassessments of the Letter of First Peter.* Edited by Robert L. Webb and Betsy Bauman-Martin. LNTS 364. London: T&T Clark, 2007.

———. "'Das im Unglauben verharrende Judenvolk': 1 Pet 2:4–10 and Its History of Interpretation in Germany (1855–1978), and the Important Contribution of Leonhard Goppelt." Pages 327–51 in *Bedrängnis und Identität: Studien zu Situation, Kommunikation und Theologie des 1. Petrusbriefes*. Edited by David S. Du Toit. BZNW 200. Berlin: De Gruyter, 2013.

———. *The Epistles of Peter and Jude*. Epworth Commentaries. London: Epworth, 1998.

———. "Ethnicisation, Marriage, and Early Christian Identity: Critical Reflections on 1 Corinthians 7, 1 Peter 3, and Modern New Testament Scholarship." *NTS* 62 (2016): 439–60.

———. "Fear, Hope, and Doing Good: Wives as a Paradigm of Mission in 1 Peter." *EstBib* 73 (2015): 409–29.

———. *1 Peter*. New Testament Guides. London: T&T Clark, 2008.

———. "From ἀδελφοί to οἶκος θεοῦ: Social Transformation in Pauline Christianity." *JBL* 120 (2001): 293–311.

———. "Grace, Race, and the People of God." Pages 191–210 in *One God, One People, One Future: Essays in Honour of N. T. Wright*. Edited by John Anthony Dunne and Eric Lewellen. Minneapolis: Fortress, 2018.

———. "'Honour Everyone . . .' (1 Pet. 2.17): The Social Strategy of 1 Peter and Its Significance for the Development of Christianity." Pages 192–210 in *To Set at Liberty: Essays on Early Christianity and Its Social World in Honor of John H. Elliott*. Edited by Stephen K. Black. Sheffield: Phoenix, 2014.

———. "Idol-Food, Idolatry and Ethics in Paul." Pages 120–40 in *Idolatry: False Worship in the Bible, Early Judaism and Christianity*. Edited by S. C. Barton. London: T&T Clark, 2007.

———. "Judaean Ethnicity and Christ-Following Voluntarism? A Reply to Steve Mason and Philip Esler." *NTS* 65 (2019): 1–20.

———. "The Label Χριστιανός: 1 Pet 4:16 and the Formation of Christian Identity." *JBL* 126 (2007): 361–81.

———. *The Making of Christian Morality: Reading Paul in Ancient and Modern Contexts*. Grand Rapids: Eerdmans, 2019.

———. "Paul, Inclusion, and Whiteness: Particularising Interpretation." *JSNT* 40 (2017): 123–47.

———. "Physical and Symbolic Geography: Constructions of Space and Early Christian Identities." *Annali di Storia dell'Esegesi* 36 (2019): 375–92.

———. "'Race,' 'Nation,' 'People': Ethnic Identity-Construction in 1 Peter 2.9." *NTS* 58 (2012): 123–43.

———. "Religion, Ethnicity, and Way of Life: Exploring Categories of Identity." *CBQ* (forthcoming).

———. "Re-Placing 1 Peter: From Place of Origin to Constructions of Space."

Pages 271–86 in *The Urban World and the First Christians*. Edited by Steve Walton, Paul R. Trebilco, and David Gill. Grand Rapids: Eerdmans, 2017.

———. *The Social Ethos of the Corinthian Correspondence: Interests and Ideology from 1 Corinthians to 1 Clement*. SNTW. Edinburgh: T&T Clark, 1996.

———. "Social Sciences Studying Formative Christian Phenomena: A Creative Movement." Pages 3–28 in *Handbook of Early Christianity: Social Science Approaches*. Edited by Anthony J. Blasi, Jean Duhaime, and Paul-André Turcotte. Walnut Creek, CA: Alta Mira, 2002.

———. *Solidarity and Difference: A Contemporary Reading of Paul's Ethics*. 2nd ed. Cornerstones. London: Bloomsbury T&T Clark, 2016.

Horsley, G. H. R., ed. *A Review of the Greek Inscriptions and Papyri Published in 1977*. Vol. 2 of *New Documents Illustrating Early Christianity*. North Ryde: Macquarie University, 1982.

Hort, F. J. A. *The First Epistle of St. Peter I.1–II.17: The Greek Text with Introductory Lecture, Commentary, and Additional Notes*. 1898. Repr. Eugene, OR: Wipf & Stock, 2005.

Howard-Brook, Wes, and Anthony Gwyther. *Unveiling Empire: Reading Revelation Then and Now*. Maryknoll, NY: Orbis, 1999.

Hurtado, Larry W. *Destroyer of the Gods: Early Christian Distinctiveness in the Roman World*. Waco: Baylor University Press, 2016.

Hutchinson, John, and Anthony D. Smith. "Introduction." Pages 3–14 in *Ethnicity*. Edited by John Hutchinson and Anthony D. Smith. Oxford Readers. Oxford: Oxford University Press, 1996.

Hutchinson, John, and Anthony D. Smith, eds. *Ethnicity*. Oxford Readers. Oxford: Oxford University Press, 1996.

Hvalvik, Reidar. "In Word and Deed: The Expansion of the Church in the Pre-Constantinian Era." Pages 265–87 in *The Mission of the Early Church to Jews and Gentiles*. Edited by Jostein Ådna and Hans Kvalbein. WUNT 127. Tübingen: Mohr Siebeck, 2000.

Ibita, Ma. Marilou S. "Exploring the (In)Visibility of the Christ-Believers' 'Trans-ethnicity': A Lowland Filipina Catholic's Perspective." Pages 183–201 in *Ethnicity, Race, Religion: Identities and Ideologies in Early Jewish and Christian Texts and in Modern Biblical Interpretation*. Edited by Katherine M. Hockey and David G. Horrell. London: Bloomsbury T&T Clark, 2018.

Isaac, Benjamin. *The Invention of Racism in Classical Antiquity*. Princeton: Princeton University Press, 2004.

Jackson, Peter, and Jan Penrose. "Introduction: Placing 'Race' and 'Nation.'" Pages 1–23 in *Constructions of Race, Place and Nation*. Edited by Peter Jackson and Jan Penrose. London: UCL Press, 1993; Minneapolis: University of Minnesota Press, 1994.

Jacobs, Andrew S. "The Remains of the Jew: Imperial Christian Identity in the Late Ancient Holy Land." *Journal of Medieval and Early Modern Studies* 33 (2003): 23–45.

———. *Remains of the Jews: The Holy Land and Christian Empire in Late Antiquity.* Divinations: Rereading Late Ancient Religion. Stanford: Stanford University Press, 2004.

Jefford, Clayton N. *The Epistle to Diognetus (with the Fragment of Quadratus): Introduction, Text, and Commentary.* Oxford Apostolic Fathers. Oxford University Press, 2013.

Jenkins, Claude. "Origen on I Corinthians." *JTS* 9–10 (1908): (I) 9:231–47, (II) 9:353–72, (III) 9:500–514, (IV) 10:29–51.

Jenkins, Richard. "Rethinking Ethnicity: Identity, Categorization, and Power." Pages 59–71 in *Race and Ethnicity: Comparative and Theoretical Approaches.* Edited by John Stone and Rutledge Dennis. Blackwell Readers in Sociology. Oxford: Blackwell, 2003.

Jennings, Willie James. *The Christian Imagination: Theology and the Origins of Race.* New Haven: Yale University Press, 2010.

Jeremias, Joachim. *Jesus' Promise to the Nations.* London: SCM, 1967.

Jewett, Robert. *Romans.* Hermeneia. Minneapolis: Fortress, 2007.

John, Helen C. *Biblical Interpretation and African Traditional Religion: Cross-Cultural and Community Readings in Owamboland, Namibia.* BibInt 176. Leiden: Brill, 2019.

Johnson, Aaron P. *Ethnicity and Argument in Eusebius' "Praeparatio Evangelica."* OECS. Oxford: Oxford University Press, 2006.

Johnson, Andre E. "God Is a Negro: The (Rhetorical) Black Theology of Bishop Henry McNeal Turner." *Black Theology* 13 (2015): 29–40.

Johnson Hodge, Caroline. *If Sons, Then Heirs: A Study of Kinship and Ethnicity in the Letters of Paul.* Oxford: Oxford University Press, 2007.

———. "'Mixed Marriage' in Early Christianity: Trajectories from Corinth." Pages 227–44 in *Corinth in Contrast: Studies in Inequality.* Edited by Steven J. Friesen, Sarah A. James, and Daniel N. Schowalter. NovTSup 155. Leiden: Brill, 2014.

Jones, Christopher. "Ancestry and Identity in the Roman Empire." Pages 111–24 in *Local Knowledge and Microidentities in the Imperial Greek World.* Edited by Tim Whitmarsh. Cambridge: Cambridge University Press, 2010.

Jones, Siân. "Identities in Practice: Towards an Archaeological Perspective on Jewish Identities in Antiquity." Pages 29–49 in *Jewish Local Patriotism and*

Self-Identification in the Graeco-Roman Period. Edited by Siân Jones and Sarah Pearce. JSPSup 31. Sheffield: Sheffield Academic Press, 1998.

Jones, Steve. *The Language of the Genes: Biology, History and the Evolutionary Future.* Rev. ed. London: Flamingo HarperCollins, 2000.

Judge, Edwin A. *Jerusalem and Athens: Cultural Transformation in Late Antiquity.* Edited by Alanna Nobbs. WUNT 265. Tübingen: Mohr Siebeck, 2010.

Kahl, Brigitte. *Galatians Re-imagined: Reading with the Eyes of the Vanquished.* Paul in Critical Contexts. Minneapolis: Fortress, 2010.

Käsemann, Ernst. *The Wandering People of God: An Investigation of the Letter to the Hebrews.* Minneapolis: Fortress, 1984.

Kasher, Aryeh. *Jews, Idumaeans, and Ancient Arabs: Relations of the Jews in Eretz-Israel with the Nations of the Frontier and the Desert during the Hellenistic and Roman Era (332 BCE–70 CE).* TSAJ 18. Tübingen: Mohr Siebeck, 1988.

Kaufman, Cynthia. "Is Philosophy Anything If It Isn't White?" Pages 245–63 in *The Center Must Not Hold: White Women Philosophers on the Whiteness of Philosophy.* Edited by George Yancy. Lanham, MD: Lexington, 2010.

Keener, Craig S. "Interethnic Marriages in the New Testament (Matt 1:3–6; Acts 7:29; 16:1–3; cf. 1 Cor 7:14)." *CTR* 6, no. 2 (2009): 25–43.

Kelhoffer, James A. "Response to Denise Kimber Buell: A Plea for Clarity in Regard to Examining Ethnicity in, Based on, or in Scholarship on the New Testament." *SEÅ* 79 (2014): 53–59.

Kellenbach, Katharina von. *Anti-Judaism in Feminist Religious Writings.* AAR Cultural Criticism Series. Atlanta: Scholars Press, 1994.

Kelley, Shawn. *Racializing Jesus: Race, Ideology and the Formation of Modern Biblical Scholarship.* London: Routledge, 2002.

Kennedy, Liam. *Race and Urban Space in Contemporary American Culture.* Tendencies: Identities, Texts, Cultures. Edinburgh: Edinburgh University Press, 2000.

Kennedy, Tammie M., Joyce Irene Middleton, Krista Ratcliffe, Kathleen Ethel Welch, Catherine Prendergast, Ira Shor, Thomas R. West, Ellen Cushman, Michelle Kendrick, and Lisa Albrecht. "Symposium: Whiteness Studies." *Rhetoric Review* 24 (2005): 359–402.

Kidd, Colin. *The Forging of Races: Race and Scripture in the Protestant Atlantic World, 1600–2000.* Cambridge: Cambridge University Press, 2006.

Klauck, Hans-Josef. *4. Makkabäerbuch.* Edited by Hermann Lichtenberger. JSHRZ 3/6. Gütersloh: Gütersloher Verlagshaus, 1989.

Konradt, Matthias. *Das Evangelium nach Matthäus.* NTD 1. Göttingen: Vandenhoeck & Ruprecht, 2015.

———. *Israel, Church, and the Gentiles in the Gospel of Matthew.* Baylor-Mohr

Siebeck Studies in Early Christianity. Tübingen: Mohr Siebeck; Waco: Baylor University Press, 2014.

Konstan, David. "*To Hellēnikon ethnos:* Ethnicity and the Construction of Ancient Greek Identity." Pages 29–50 in *Ancient Perceptions of Greek Ethnicity.* Edited by Irad Malkin. Center for Hellenic Studies Colloquia 5. Cambridge, MA: Harvard University Press, 2001.

Kraabel, A. T. "The Disappearance of the 'God-Fearers.'" *Numen* 28 (1981): 113–26.

———. "Greeks, Jews and Lutherans in the Middle Half of Acts." *HTR* 79 (1986): 147–57.

———. "The Roman Diaspora: Six Questionable Assumptions." *JJS* 33 (1982): 445–64.

Kraemer, Ross S. "Jewish Tuna and Christian Fish: Identifying Religious Affiliation in Epigraphic Sources." *HTR* 84 (1991): 141–62.

———. "On the Meaning of the Term 'Jew' in Greco-Roman Inscriptions." *HTR* 82 (1989): 35–53.

Kraft, Henricus. *Clavis Patrum Apostolicorum.* Munich: Kösel, 1963.

Kuecker, Aaron J. *The Spirit and the "Other": Social Identity, Ethnicity and Intergroup Reconciliation in Luke-Acts.* LNTS 444. London: T&T Clark, 2011.

Lake, Kirsopp. "Note VIII: Proselytes and God-Fearers." Pages 74–96 in *Additional Notes to the Commentary.* Vol. 5 of *The Beginnings of Christianity, Part 1: The Acts of the Apostles.* Edited by Kirsopp Lake and Henry J. Cadbury. New York: Macmillan, 1933.

Lampe, Peter. "Das korinthische Herrenmahl im Schnittpunkt hellenistisch-römischer Mahlpraxis und paulinischer Theologia Crucis (1 Kor 11, 17–34)." *ZNW* 82 (1991): 183–213.

Lander, Vini. "Introduction to Fundamental British Values." *Journal of Education for Teaching* 42 (2016): 274–79.

Langton, Daniel R. *The Apostle Paul in the Jewish Imagination.* Cambridge: Cambridge University Press, 2010.

———. "Modern Jewish Identity and the Apostle Paul: Pauline Studies as an Intra-Jewish Ideological Battleground." *JSNT* 28 (2005): 217–58.

———. "The Myth of the 'Traditional View of Paul' and the Role of the Apostle in Modern Jewish-Christian Polemics." *JSNT* 28 (2005): 69–104.

Lans, Birgit van der. "Belonging to Abraham's Kin: Genealogical Appeals to Abraham as a Possible Background for Paul's Abrahamic Argument." Pages 307–18 in *Abraham, the Nations, and the Hagarites: Jewish, Christian, and Islamic Perspectives on Kinship with Abraham.* Edited by Martin Goodman,

Guert Henrik van Kooten, and Jacques T. A. G. M. van Ruiten. TBN 13. Leiden: Brill, 2010.

Lattke, Michael. "Die Wahrheit der Christen in der Apologie des Aristides: Vorstudie zu einem Kommentar." Pages 215–35 in *Ein neues Geschlecht? Entwicklung des frühchristlichen Selbstbewusstseins*. Edited by Markus Lang. NTOA/SUNT 105. Göttingen: Vandenhoeck & Ruprecht, 2014.

Law, Timothy Michael, and Charles Halton, eds. *Jew and Judean: A Forum on Politics and Historiography in the Translation of Ancient Texts*. Los Angeles: Marginalia Review of Books, 2014.

Lefebvre, Henri. *The Production of Space*. Translated by Donald Nicholson-Smith. Oxford: Blackwell, 1991.

Lehmkuhl, Augustus. "Divorce I: In Moral Theology." Pages 54–64 in *The Catholic Encyclopedia*. Edited by Charles G. Herbermann, Edward A. Pace, Condé B. Pallen, Thomas J. Shahan, and John J. Wynne. New York: Robert Appleton, 1909.

Levenson, Jon D. "The Universal Horizon of Biblical Particularism." Pages 143–69 in *Ethnicity and the Bible*. Edited by Mark G. Brett. BibInt. Leiden: Brill, 1996.

Levine, Amy-Jill. "Christian Privilege, Christian Fragility, and the Gospel of John." Pages 87–110 in *The Gospel of John and Jewish-Christian Relations*. Edited by Adele Reinhartz. Lanham, MD: Lexington, 2018.

———. "Discharging Responsibility: Matthean Jesus, Biblical Law, and Hemorrhaging Woman." Pages 379–97 in *Treasures New and Old: Contributions to Matthean Studies*. Edited by David R. Bauer and Mark Allan Powell. SBL Symposium Series 1. Atlanta: Scholars Press, 1996.

———. "*The Gospel and the Land* Revisited: Exegesis, Hermeneutics, and Politics." In *Peace and Faith: Christian Churches and the Israeli-Palestinian Conflict*. Edited by Cary Nelson and Michael C. Gizzi. Forthcoming.

———. "A Jewess, More and/or Less." Pages 149–57 in *Judaism since Gender*. Edited by Miriam Peskowitz and Laura Levitt. London: Routledge, 1996.

———. *The Misunderstood Jew: The Church and the Scandal of the Jewish Jesus*. New York: HarperOne, 2006.

Levine, Lee I. *The Ancient Synagogue: The First Thousand Years*. New Haven: Yale University Press, 2000.

———. "Jewish Identities in Antiquity: An Introductory Essay." Pages 12–40 in *Jewish Identities in Antiquity: Studies in Memory of Menahem Stern*. Edited by Lee I. Levine and Daniel R. Schwartz. TSAJ 130. Tübingen: Mohr Siebeck, 2009.

Levinskaya, Irina. *The Book of Acts in Its Diaspora Setting*. The Book of Acts in Its First Century Setting 5. Grand Rapids: Eerdmans, 1996.

Lietzmann, Hans. *Mass and Lord's Supper*. Leiden: Brill, 1979.

Lieu, Judith M. *Christian Identity in the Jewish and Graeco-Roman World*. Oxford: Oxford University Press, 2004

———. "Circumcision, Women and Salvation." *NTS* 40 (1994): 358–70.

———. "Identity Games in Early Christian Texts: The *Letter to Diognetus*." Pages 59–72 in *Ethnicity, Race, Religion: Identities and Ideologies in Early Jewish and Christian Texts and in Modern Biblical Interpretation*. Edited by Katherine M. Hockey and David G. Horrell. London: Bloomsbury T&T Clark, 2018.

———. *Neither Jew nor Greek? Constructing Early Christianity*. SNTW. Edinburgh: T&T Clark, 2002.

———. "The Race of the God-Fearers." *JTS* 46 (1995): 483–501.

Lightfoot, J. B. *Notes on Epistles of St. Paul from Unpublished Commentaries*. London: Macmillan, 1904.

———. *St. Paul's Epistle to the Galatians: A Revised Text with Introduction, Notes, and Dissertations*. London: Macmillan, 1869.

Lindars, Barnabas. *The Theology of the Letter to the Hebrews*. Cambridge: Cambridge University Press, 1991.

Lindemann, Andreas. ". . . ἐκτρέφετε αὐτὰ ἐν παιδείᾳ καὶ νουθεσίᾳ κυρίου (Eph 6.4): Kinder in der Welt des frühen Christentums." *NTS* 56 (2010): 169–90.

Llewelyn, S. R. "The Use of Sunday for Meetings of Believers in the New Testament." *NovT* 43 (2001): 205–23.

Logan, James. "Liberalism, Race, and Stanley Hauerwas." *Cross Currents* 55 (2006): 522–33.

Lona, Horacio E. "An Diognet." Pages 208–25 in *Die Apostolischen Väter: Eine Einleitung*. Edited by Wilhelm Pratscher. Göttingen: Vandenhoeck & Ruprecht, 2009.

Long, A. A. *Epictetus: A Stoic and Socratic Guide to Life*. Oxford: Clarendon, 2002.

Long, Burke O. "Bible Maps and America's Nationalist Narratives." Pages 109–25 in *Constructions of Space*. Vol. 1: *Theory, Geography, and Narrative*. Edited by Jon L. Berquist and Claudia V. Camp. LHBOTS 481. London: T&T Clark, 2007.

Longenecker, Bruce W. *Remember the Poor: Paul, Poverty, and the Greco-Roman World*. Grand Rapids: Eerdmans, 2010.

Lopez, Davina C. *Apostle to the Conquered: Reimagining Paul's Mission*. Paul in Critical Contexts. Minneapolis: Fortress, 2008.

Lorde, Audre. *Sister Outsider: Essays and Speeches*. The Crossing Press Feminist Series. Freedom, CA: Crossing, 1984.

Luz, Ulrich. *Matthew 21–28: A Commentary*. Hermeneia. Minneapolis: Fortress, 2005.

Maaren, John van. "Does Mark's Jesus Abrogate Torah? Jesus' Purity Logion and Its Illustration in Mark 7:15–23." *JMJS* 4 (2017): 21–41.

MacDonald, Margaret Y. *Early Christian Women and Pagan Opinion: The Power of the Hysterical Woman*. Cambridge: Cambridge University Press, 1996.

———. *The Pauline Churches: A Socio-Historical Study of Institutionalization in the Pauline and Deutero-Pauline Writings*. SNTSMS 60. Cambridge: Cambridge University Press, 1988.

———. *The Power of Children: The Construction of Christian Families in the Greco-Roman World*. Waco: Baylor University Press, 2014.

———. "Women Holy in Body and Spirit: The Social Setting of 1 Corinthians 7." *NTS* 36 (1990): 161–81.

MacDonald, Margaret Y., and Leif E. Vaage. "Unclean but Holy Children: Paul's Everyday Quandary in 1 Corinthians 7:14c." *CBQ* 73 (2011): 526–46.

Mahn, Jason A. *Becoming a Christian in Christendom: Radical Discipleship and the Way of the Cross in America's "Christian" Culture*. Minneapolis: Fortress, 2016.

Maier, Christl M. "Der Diskurs um interkulturelle Ehen in Jehud als antikes Beispiel von Intersektionalität." Pages 129–53 in *Doing Gender—Doing Religion: Fallstudien zur Intersektionalität im frühen Judentum, Christentum und Islam*. Edited by Ute E. Eisen, Christine Gerber, and Angela Standhartinger. WUNT 302. Tübingen: Mohr Siebeck, 2013.

Malherbe, Abraham J. *The Letters to the Thessalonians*. AB 32B. New York: Doubleday, 2000.

Marcar, Katherine. *Begotten Anew: Metaphor, Divine Regeneration and Ethnic Identity Construction in 1 Peter*. SNTSMS. Cambridge: Cambridge University Press, forthcoming.

Marchand, Suzanne L. *German Orientalism in the Age of Empire: Religion, Race, and Scholarship*. Cambridge: Cambridge University Press; Washington, DC: German Historical Institute, 2009.

Marcus, Joel. *Mark 1–8: A New Translation with Introduction and Commentary*. AB 27. New York: Doubleday, 1999.

Marohl, Matthew J. *Faithfulness and the Purpose of Hebrews: A Social Identity Approach*. Princeton Theological Monograph Series. Eugene, OR: Pickwick, 2008.

Marshall, Howard. "Who Were the Evangelists?" Pages 251–63 in *The Mission of the Early Church to Jews and Gentiles*. Edited by Jostein Ådna and Hans Kvalbein. WUNT 127. Tübingen: Mohr Siebeck, 2000.

Martin, Dale B. "Paul and the Judaism/Hellenism Dichotomy: Toward a Social History of the Question." Pages 29–61 in *Paul Beyond the Judaism/Hellenism Divide*. Edited by Troels Engberg-Pedersen. Louisville: Westminster John Knox, 2001.

Martin, Troy W. *Metaphor and Composition in 1 Peter*. SBLDS 131. Atlanta: Scholars Press, 1992.

———. "The TestAbr and the Background of 1 Pet 3,6." *ZNW* 90 (1999): 139–46.

Martyn, J. Louis. *Galatians: A New Translation with Introduction and Commentary*. AB 33A. New York: Doubleday, 1997.

———. *Theological Issues in the Letters of Paul*. SNTW. Edinburgh: T&T Clark, 1997.

Mason, Steve. "Das antike Judentum als Hintergrund des frühen Christentums." *ZNT* 19 (2016): 11–22.

———. "Jews, Judaeans, Judaizing, Judaism: Problems of Categorization in Ancient History." *JSJ* 38 (2007): 457–512.

———. *Orientation to the History of Roman Judaea*. Eugene, OR: Cascade, 2016.

Mason, Steve, and Philip F. Esler. "Judaean and Christ-Follower Identities: Grounds for a Distinction." *NTS* 63 (2017): 493–515.

Masuzawa, Tomoko. *The Invention of World Religions: Or, How European Universalism Was Preserved in the Language of Pluralism*. Chicago: University of Chicago Press, 2005.

Matlock, R. Barry. "Almost Cultural Studies? Reflections on the 'New Perspective' on Paul." Pages 433–59 in *Biblical Studies/Cultural Studies: The Third Sheffield Colloquium*. Edited by J. Cheryl Exum and Stephen D. Moore. Sheffield: Sheffield Academic Press, 1998.

———. "Sins of the Flesh and Suspicious Minds: Dunn's New Theology of Paul." *JSNT* 72 (1998): 67–90.

Maughan, Stephen S. *Mighty England Do Good: Culture, Faith, Empire, and World in the Foreign Missions of the Church of England, 1850–1915*. Grand Rapids: Eerdmans, 2014.

May, Alistair S. *"The Body for the Lord": Sex and Identity in 1 Corinthians 5–7*. JSNTSup 278. London: T&T Clark, 2004.

McCoskey, Denise Eileen. *Race: Antiquity and Its Legacy*. Ancients and Moderns. London: I. B. Tauris, 2012.

McEleney, Neil J. "Conversion, Circumcision and the Law." *NTS* 20 (1974): 319–41.

McGowan, Andrew B. *Ascetic Eucharists: Food and Drink in Early Christian Ritual Meals*. OECS. Oxford: Clarendon, 1999.

McInerney, Jeremy. "Ethnos and Ethnicity in Early Greece." Pages 51–73 in *Ancient Perceptions of Greek Identity*. Edited by Irad Malkin. Centre for Hellenic Studies Colloquia 5. Cambridge, MA: Harvard University Press, 2001.

McIntosh, Peggy. "White Privilege: Unpacking the Invisible Knapsack." National Seed Project. https://www.nationalseedproject.org/images/documents/Knapsack_plus_Notes-Peggy_McIntosh.pdf.

McKnight, Scot. *A Light among the Gentiles: Jewish Missionary Activity in the Second Temple Period*. Minneapolis: Fortress, 1991.

Meadowcroft, Tim. "The Gospel and the Land of Promise: A Response." Pages 158–65 in *The Gospel and the Land of Promise: Christian Approaches to the Land of the Bible*. Edited by Philip Church, Peter Walker, Tim Bulkeley, and Tim Meadowcroft. Eugene, OR: Pickwick, 2011.

Meeks, Wayne A. "The 'Haustafeln' and American Slavery: A Hermeneutical Challenge." Pages 232–53 in *Theology and Ethics in Paul and His Interpreters: Essays in Honor of Victor Paul Furnish*. Edited by Eugene H. Lovering Jr. and Jerry L. Sumney. Nashville: Abingdon 1996.

———. *The First Urban Christians: The Social World of the Apostle Paul*. New Haven: Yale University Press, 1983.

Meer, Nasar. "Racialization and Religion: Race, Culture and Difference in the Study of Antisemitism and Islamophobia." *Ethnic and Racial Studies* 36 (2013): 385–98.

———. "Semantics, Scales and Solidarities in the Study of Antisemitism and Islamophobia." *Ethnic and Racial Studies* 36 (2013): 500–515.

Meggitt, Justin J. *Paul, Poverty and Survival*. SNTW. Edinburgh: T&T Clark, 1998.

Memmi, Albert. *The Colonizer and the Colonized*. New York: Orion Press; London: Souvenir Press, 1965.

Mendels, Doron. *The Rise and Fall of Jewish Nationalism*. 2nd ed. Grand Rapids: Eerdmans, 1997.

Meneses, Eloise Hiebert. "Science and the Myth of Biological Race." Pages 33–46 in *This Side of Heaven: Race, Ethnicity, and Christian Faith*. Edited by Robert J. Priest and Alvaro L. Nieves. Oxford: Oxford University Press, 2007.

Michaels, J. Ramsey. *1 Peter*. WBC 49. Waco: Word, 1988.

Mignolo, Walter D. "Epistemic Disobedience, Independent Thought and De-Colonial Freedom." *Theory, Culture & Society* 26 (2009): 1–23.

Milbank, John. *Theology and Social Theory: Beyond Secular Reason.* Oxford: Blackwell, 1990.

Miller, David M. "Ethnicity Comes of Age: An Overview of Twentieth-Century Terms for *Ioudaios.*" *CurBR* 10 (2012): 293–311.

Mitchell, Claire. "Behind the Ethnic Marker: Religion and Social Identification in Northern Ireland." *Sociology of Religion* 66 (2005): 3–21.

———. "The Religious Content of Ethnic Identities." *Sociology* 40 (2006): 1135–52.

Mitton, C. Leslie. "The Relationship between 1 Peter and Ephesians." *JTS* 1 (1950): 67–73.

Moffitt, David M., and C. Jacob Butera. "P.Duk. inv. 727r: New Evidence for the Meaning and Provenance of the Word προσήλυτος." *JBL* 132 (2013): 159–78.

Moore, George Foot. "Christian Writers on Judaism." *HTR* 14 (1921): 197–254.

Moore, Nicholas J. "'In' or 'Near'? Heavenly Access and Christian Identity in Hebrews." Pages 185–98 in *Muted Voices of the New Testament: Readings in the Catholic Epistles and Hebrews.* Edited by Katherine M. Hockey, Madison N. Pierce, and Francis Watson. LNTS 565. London: Bloomsbury T&T Clark, 2017.

Moore, Stephen D. *Untold Tales from the Book of Revelation: Sex and Gender, Empire and Ecology.* RBS 79. Atlanta: Society of Biblical Literature, 2014.

Moore, Stephen D., and Yvonne Sherwood. *The Invention of the Biblical Scholar: A Critical Manifesto.* Minneapolis: Fortress, 2011.

Moore, Stewart. *Jewish Ethnic Identity and Relations in Hellenistic Egypt: With Walls of Iron?* JSJSup 171. Leiden: Brill, 2015.

Morgan, Jonathan David. "Land, Rest and Sacrifice: Ecological Reflections on the Book of Leviticus." PhD diss., University of Exeter, 2010.

———. "Transgressing, Puking, Covenanting: The Character of Land in Leviticus." *Theology* 112 (2009): 172–80.

Morgan, Teresa. *Roman Faith and Christian Faith:* Pistis *and* Fides *in the Early Roman Empire and Early Churches.* Oxford: Oxford University Press, 2015.

———. "Society, Identity, and Ethnicity in the Hellenic World." Pages 23–45 in *Ethnicity, Race, Religion: Identities and Ideologies in Early Jewish and Christian Texts and in Modern Biblical Interpretation.* Edited by Katherine M. Hockey and David G. Horrell. London: Bloomsbury T&T Clark, 2018.

Morris, Leon. *Galatians: Paul's Charter of Christian Freedom.* Leicester: Inter-Varsity Press, 1996.

Morrison, Toni. *Playing in the Dark: Whiteness and the Literary Imagination.* Cambridge, MA: Harvard University Press, 1992.

Moxnes, Halvor. "From Ernest Renan to Anders Behring Breivik: Continuities in Racial Stereotypes of Muslims and Jews." Pages 113–29 in *Ethnicity, Race, Religion: Identities and Ideologies in Early Jewish and Christian Texts and in Modern Biblical Interpretation*. Edited by Katherine M. Hockey and David G. Horrell. London: T&T Clark, 2018.

———. *Jesus and the Rise of Nationalism: A New Quest for the Nineteenth-Century Historical Jesus*. London: I. B. Tauris, 2012.

Munck, Johannes. *Paul and the Salvation of Mankind*. London: SCM, 1959.

Muraoka, T. *A Greek-English Lexicon of the Septuagint*. Leuven: Peeters, 2009.

Murphy-O'Connor, Jerome. *Keys to First Corinthians: Revisiting the Major Issues*. Oxford: Oxford University Press, 2009.

———. *Keys to Second Corinthians: Revisitng the Major Issues*. Oxford: Oxford University Press, 2010.

———. *St. Paul's Corinth: Texts and Archaeology*. 3rd rev. and exp. ed. Collegeville: Liturgical Press, 2002.

———. "Works without Faith in I Cor., VII, 14." *RB* 84 (1977): 349–61.

Myers, William H. "The Hermeneutical Dilemma of the African American Biblical Student." Pages 40–56 in *Stony the Road We Trod: African American Biblical Interpretation*. Edited by Cain Hope Felder. Minneapolis: Fortress, 1991.

Nakayama, Thomas K., and Judith N. Martin. "Introduction: Whiteness as the Communication of Social Identity." Pages xii–xiv in *Whiteness: The Communication of Social Identity*. Edited by Thomas K. Nakayama and Judith N. Martin. Thousand Oaks, CA: Sage, 1999.

Nakayama, Thomas K., and Judith N. Martin, eds. *Whiteness: The Communication of Social Identity*. Thousand Oaks, CA: Sage, 1999.

Nanos, Mark D. "How Inter-Christian Approaches to Paul's Rhetoric Can Perpetuate Negative Valuations of Jewishness—Although Proposing to Avoid that Outcome." *BibInt* 13 (2005): 255–69.

———. "The Question of Conceptualization: Qualifying Paul's Position on Circumcision in Dialogue with Josephus's Advisors to King Izates." Pages 105–52 in *Paul within Judaism: Restoring the First-Century Context to the Apostle*. Edited by Mark D. Nanos and Magnus Zetterholm. Minneapolis: Fortress, 2015.

Nanos, Mark D., and Magnus Zetterholm, eds. *Paul within Judaism: Restoring the First-Century Context to the Apostle*. Minneapolis: Fortress, 2015.

Neill, Stephen. *A History of Christian Missions*. The Pelican History of the Church 6. London: Hodder and Stoughton, 1964.

Neusner, Jacob. "Mr. Sanders' Pharisees and Mine: A Response to E. P. Sanders, *Jewish Law from Jesus to the Mishnah*." *SJT* 44 (1991): 73–95.

Neutel, Karin B. "'Neither Jew nor Greek': Abraham as a Universal Ancestor."

Pages 291–306 in *Abraham, the Nations, and the Hagarites: Jewish, Christian, and Islamic Perspectives on Kinship with Abraham*. Edited by Martin Goodman, Guert Henrik van Kooten, and Jacques T. A. G. M. van Ruiten. TBN 13. Leiden: Brill, 2010.

Niederwimmer, Kurt. *The Didache*. Hermeneia. Minneapolis: Fortress, 1998.

Niemand, Christoph. Review of *Jesus and the People of God*, by Joseph H. Hellerman. *TLZ* 134 (2009): 1059–63.

Nolland, John. "The Gospel Prohibition of Divorce: Tradition History and Meaning." *JSNT* 58 (1995): 19–35.

———. "Proselytism or Politics in Horace Satires I, 4, 138–143?" *VC* 33 (1979): 347–55.

———. "Uncircumcised Proselytes?" *JSJ* 12 (1981): 173–94.

Nongbri, Brent. *Before Religion: A History of a Modern Concept*. New Haven: Yale University Press, 2013.

Norris, Kristopher. "Witnessing Whiteness in the Ethics of Hauerwas." *JRE* 47 (2019): 95–124.

Novenson, Matthew V. "Whither the Paul within Judaism Schule?" *JMJS* 5 (2018): 79–88.

Ntarangwi, Mwenda. *Reversed Gaze: An African Ethnography of American Anthropology*. Champaign: University of Illinois Press, 2010.

Oakes, Peter. *Galatians*. Paideia Commentaries on the New Testament. Grand Rapids: Baker Academic, 2015.

Öhler, Markus. "Essen, Ethnos, Identität—der antiochenische Zwischenfall (Gal 2,11–14)." Pages 158–99 in *Der eine Gott und das gemeinschaftliche Mahl: Inklusion und Exklusion biblischer Vorstellungen von Mahl und Gemeinschaft im Kontext antiker Festkultur*. Edited by Wolfgang Weiß. Biblisch-Theologische Studien 113. Neukirchen-Vluyn: Neukirchener, 2011.

———. "Ethnos und Identität: Landsmannschaftliche Vereinigungen, Synagogen und christliche Vereinigungen." Pages 221–48 in *Kult und Macht: Religion und Herrschaft im syropalästinensischen Raum: Studien zu ihrer Wechselbeziehung in hellenistisch-römischer Zeit*. Edited by Anne Lykke and Fredrich T. Schipper. WUNT 2.319. Tübingen: Mohr Siebeck, 2011.

Ok, Janette H. "Who You Are No Longer: Constructing Ethnic Identity in 1 Peter." PhD diss., Princeton Theological Seminary, 2018.

Økland, Jorunn, J. Cornelis de Vos, and Karen J. Wenell, eds. *Constructions of Space*. Vol. 3: *Biblical Spatiality and the Sacred*. LHBOTS 540. London: Bloomsbury T&T Clark, 2016.

Ollrog, Wolf-Henning. *Paulus und seine Mitarbeiter: Untersuchungen zu Theo-*

rie und Praxis der paulinischen Mission. WMANT 50. Neukirchen-Vluyn: Neukirchener, 1979.

O'Neill, John Cochrane. "1 Corinthians 7,14 and Infant Baptism." Pages 357–61 in *L'Apôtre Paul: Personnalité, Style et Conception du Ministère*. Edited by A. Vanhoye. BETL 73. Leuven: Peeters, 1986.

Oropeza, B. J. *Apostasy in the New Testament Communities*. 3 vols. Eugene, OR: Cascade, 2011–12.

———. "The Warning Passages in Hebrews: Revised Theologies and New Methods of Interpretation." *CBR* 10 (2011): 81–100.

Otto, Jennifer. *Philo of Alexandria and the Construction of Jewishness in Early Christian Writings*. OECS. Oxford: Oxford University Press, 2018.

Park, Wongi. "The Black Jesus, the Mestizo Jesus, and the Historical Jesus." *BibInt* 25 (2017): 190–205.

———. *The Politics of Race and Ethnicity in Matthew's Passion Narrative*. London: Palgrave Macmillan, 2019.

Parks, Sara. "Historical-Critical Ministry? The Biblical Studies Classroom as Restorative Secular Space." *New Blackfriars* 100 (2019): 229–44.

Patte, Daniel. "Acknowledging the Contextual Character of Male, European-American Critical Exegeses: An Androcritical Perspective." Pages 35–55 in *Social Location and Biblical Interpretation in the United States*. Vol. 1 of *Reading from This Place*. Edited by Fernando F. Segovia and Mary Ann Tolbert. Minneapolis: Fortress, 1995.

———. *Ethics of Biblical Interpretation: A Reevaluation*. Louisville: Westminster John Knox, 1995.

Paulsen, Henning. "Das Kerygma Petri und die urchristliche Apologetik." *ZKG* 88 (1977): 1–37.

———. *Zur Literatur und Geschichte des frühen Christentums*. WUNT 99. Tübingen: Mohr Siebeck, 1997.

Pearce, Sarah. "Belonging and Not Belonging: Local Perspectives in Philo of Alexandria." Pages 69–105 in *Jewish Local Patriotism and Self-Identification in the Graeco-Roman Period*. Edited by Siân Jones and Sarah Pearce. JSPSup 31. Sheffield: Sheffield Academic Press, 1998.

———. "Jerusalem as 'Mother-City' in the Writings of Philo of Alexandria." Pages 19–36 in *Negotiating Diaspora: Jewish Strategies in the Roman Empire*. Edited by John M. G. Barclay. LSTS 45. London: T&T Clark, 2004.

———. "Notes on Philo's Use of the Terms ἔθνος and λαός." *The Studia Philonica Annual: Studies in Hellenistic Judaism* 28 (2016): 205–26.

Peppard, Michael. "Personal Names and Ethnic Hybridity in Late Ancient Galilee: The Data from Beth She'arim." Pages 99–113 in *Religion, Ethnicity, and*

Identity in Ancient Galilee: A Region in Transition. Edited by Jürgen Zangenberg, Harold W. Attridge, and Dale B. Martin. WUNT 210. Tübingen: Mohr Siebeck, 2007.

Perrone, Lorenzo. "'The Mystery of Judaea' (Jerome, *Ep.* 46): The Holy City of Jerusalem between History and Symbol in Early Christian Thought." Pages 221–39 in *Jerusalem: Its Sanctity and Centrality to Judaism, Christianity, and Islam.* Edited by Lee I. Levine. New York: Continuum, 1999.

Petersen, Norman R. *Rediscovering Paul: Philemon and the Sociology of Paul's Narrative World.* Philadelphia: Fortress, 1985.

Philonenko, Marc. *Joseph et Aséneth: Introduction, texte critique, traduction et notes.* Studia Post-Biblica. Leiden: Brill, 1968.

Pierce, Chad T. *Spirits and the Proclamation of Christ: 1 Peter 3:18–22 in Light of Sin and Punishment Traditions in Early Jewish and Christian Literature.* WUNT 2.305. Tübingen: Mohr Siebeck, 2011.

Plummer, Robert L. *Paul's Understanding of the Church's Mission: Did the Apostle Paul Expect the Early Christian Communities to Evangelize?* Carlisle: Paternoster, 2006.

Porter, Stanley E. *Idioms of the Greek New Testament.* 2nd ed. Sheffield: Sheffield Academic Press, 1994.

Pouderon, Bernard, Marie-Joseph Pierre, Bernard Outtier, and Marina Guiorgadzé. *Aristide, Apologie: Introduction, Textes Critiques, Traductions et Commentaire.* SC 470. Paris: Cerf, 2003.

Powery, Emerson B., and Rodney S. Sadler Jr. *The Genesis of Liberation: Biblical Interpretation in the Antebellum Narratives of the Enslaved.* Louisville: Westminster John Knox, 2016.

Prinsloo, Gert T. M., and Christl M. Maier, eds. *Constructions of Space.* Vol. 5: *Place, Space and Identity in the Ancient Mediterranean World.* LHBOTS 576. London: Bloomsbury T&T Clark, 2013.

Puig i Tàrrech, Armand. "The Mission According to the New Testament: Choice or Need?" Pages 231–47 in *Einheit der Kirche im Neuen Testament.* Edited by Anatoly Alexeev, Christos Karakolis, Ulrich Luz, and Karl-Wilhelm Niebuhr. WUNT 218. Tübingen: Mohr Siebeck, 2008.

Puig i Tàrrech, Armand, John M. G. Barclay, Jörg Frey, and Orrey McFarland, eds. *The Last Years of Paul: Essays from the Tarragona Conference, June 2013.* WUNT 352. Tübingen: Mohr Siebeck, 2015.

Punt, Jeremy. "(Southern) African Postcolonial Biblical Interpretation: A White African Perspective." Paper presented at the SBL Annual Meeting. San Antonio, TX, November 2016.

Quasten, J. *The Ante-Nicene Literature After Irenaeus.* Vol. 2 of *Patrology.* Utrecht: Spectrum, 1958.

Rajak, Tessa. *The Jewish Dialogue with Greece and Rome: Studies in Cultural and Social Interaction.* Leiden: Brill, 2002.

Ramsay, William M. *The Cities and Bishoprics of Phrygia.* 2 vols. Oxford: Clarendon, 1897.

Reasoner, Mark. *The Strong and the Weak: Romans 14.1–15.13 in Context.* SNTSMS 103. Cambridge: Cambridge University Press, 1999.

Rebillard, Éric. *Christians and Their Many Identities in Late Antiquity, North Africa 200–450 CE.* Ithaca: Cornell University Press, 2013.

Reed, Annette Yoshiko, and Shaul Magid, eds. "Daniel Boyarin's *Judaism*: A Forum." *Marginalia: Los Angeles Review of Books.* July 5, 2019. https://marginalia.lareviewofbooks.org/daniel-boyarins-judaism-forum/.

Reicke, Bo. *The Disobedient Spirits and Christian Baptism: A Study of 1 Pet. III.19 and Its Context.* ASNU 13. Copenhagen: Ejnar Munksgaard, 1946.

Reinhartz, Adele. "Parents and Children: A Philonic Perspective." Pages 61–88 in *The Jewish Family in Antiquity.* Edited by Shaye J. D. Cohen. Brown Judaic Studies 289. Atlanta: Scholars Press, 1993.

Reinhartz, Adele, ed. *The Gospel of John and Jewish-Christian Relations.* Lanham, MD: Lexington, 2018.

Reinhartz, Adele, and Kim Shier. "Josephus on Children and Childhood." *SR* 41 (2012): 364–75.

Renan, Ernest. *The Life of Jesus.* London: Trübner, 1864.

Rengstorf, Karl Heinrich. *A Complete Concordance to Flavius Josephus.* 5 vols. Leiden: Brill, 1973–1983.

Reynolds, Joyce, and Robert Tannenbaum. *Jews and God-Fearers at Aphrodisias: Greek Inscriptions with Commentary.* Cambridge Philological Society Supplementary Series 12. Cambridge: Cambridge Philological Society, 1987.

Richard, Earl J. *First and Second Thessalonians.* SP 11. Collegeville: Liturgical Press, 1995.

Richardson, Peter. *Herod: King of the Jews and Friend of the Romans.* Edinburgh: T&T Clark, 1999.

———. *Israel in the Apostolic Church.* SNTSMS 10. Cambridge: Cambridge University Press, 1969.

Ridderbos, Herman N. *The Epistle of Paul to the Churches of Galatia.* NICNT. Grand Rapids: Eerdmans, 1953.

Riesner, Rainer. "A Pre-Christian Jewish Mission?" Pages 211–50 in *The Mission of the Early Church to Jews and Gentiles.* Edited by Jostein Ådna and Hans Kvalbein. WUNT 127. Tübingen: Mohr Siebeck, 2000.

Roediger, David. *Colored White: Transcending the Racial Past*. Berkeley: University of California Press, 2002.

———. *The Wages of Whiteness: Race and the Making of the American Working Class*. London: Verso, 1991.

Roetzel, Calvin J. "No 'Race of Israel' in Paul." Pages 230–44 in *Putting Body and Soul Together: Essays in Honor of Robin Scroggs*. Edited by Virginia Wiles, Alexandra Brown, and Graydon F. Snyder. Valley Forge: Trinity Press International, 1997.

Rokéah, David. "Ancient Jewish Proselytism in Theory and in Practice." *TZ* 52 (1996): 206–23.

Rudd, Niall. *Horace: Satires and Epistles; Persius: Satires*. Penguin Classics. London: Penguin, 1987.

Ruether, Rosemary Radford. *Faith and Fratricide: The Theological Roots of Anti-Semitism*. New York: Seabury; London: Search Press, 1975.

Runesson, Anders. "Particularistic Judaism and Universalistic Christianity? Some Critical Remarks on Terminology and Theology." *ST* 54 (2000): 55–75.

———. "The Question of Terminology: The Architecture of Contemporary Discussions on Paul." Pages 53–77 in *Paul within Judaism: Restoring the First-Century Context to the Apostle*. Edited by Mark D. Nanos and Magnus Zetterholm. Minneapolis: Fortress, 2015.

Safrai, S. "Education and the Study of the Torah." Pages 945–70 in *The Jewish People in the First Century*. Edited by S. Safrai and M. Stern. Vol. 2. CRINT 2. Assen: Van Gorcum, 1976.

———. "Home and Family." Pages 728–92 in *The Jewish People in the First Century*. Edited by S. Safrai and M. Stern. Vol. 2. CRINT 2. Assen: Van Gorcum, 1976.

Sagnard, François. *Clément d'Alexandrie, Extraits de Théodote: texte grec, introduction, traduction et notes*. SC 23. Paris: Cerf, 1970.

Said, Edward W. "Representing the Colonized: Anthropology's Interlocutors." *Critical Inquiry* 15 (1989): 205–25.

Saïd, Suzanne. "The Discourse of Identity in Greek Rhetoric from Isocrates to Aristedes." Pages 275–99 in *Ancient Perceptions of Greek Identity*. Edited by Irad Malkin. Centre for Hellenic Studies Colloquia 5. Cambridge, MA: Harvard University Press, 2001.

Saldarini, Anthony J. *Matthew's Christian-Jewish Community*. Chicago: Chicago University Press, 1994.

Sanders, E. P. *Jesus and Judaism*. London: SCM, 1985.

————. *Paul and Palestinian Judaism: A Comparison of Patterns of Religion*. London: SCM, 1977.

————. "Paul's Jewishness." Pages 51–73 in *Paul's Jewish Matrix*. Edited by Thomas G. Casey and Justin Taylor. Bible in Dialogue 2. Rome: Gregorian and Biblical Press, 2011.

Sanders, E. P., and Margaret Davies. *Studying the Synoptic Gospels*. London: SCM, 1989.

Sandford, Michael J., ed. *The Bible, Zionism, and Palestine: The Bible's Role in Conflict and Liberation in Israel-Palestine*. Bible in Effect 1. Dunedin, New Zealand: Relegere Academic Press, 2016.

Sandmel, Samuel. "Philo's Place in Judaism: A Study of Conceptions of Abraham in Jewish Literature: Part II." *HUCA* 26 (1955): 151–332.

Sänger, Dieter. "Ἰουδαϊσμός—ἰουδαΐζειν—ἰουδαϊκῶς: Sprachliche und semantische Überlegungen im Blick auf Gal 1,13f. und 2,14." *ZNW* 108 (2017): 150–85.

Sargent, Benjamin. *Written to Serve: The Use of Scripture in 1 Peter*. LNTS 547. London: Bloomsbury T&T Clark, 2015.

Schäfer, K. *Gemeinde als "Bruderschaft": Ein Beitrag zum Kirchenverständnis des Paulus*. Europäische Hochschulschriften 333. Frankfurt: Peter Lang, 1989.

Schaller, Berndt. "Philon von Alexandria und das 'Heilige Land.'" Pages 172–87 in *Das Land Israel in biblischer Zeit*. Edited by Georg Strecker. Göttinger Theologische Arbeiten 25. Göttingen: Vandenhoeck & Ruprecht, 1983.

Schermerhorn, Richard A. *Comparative Ethnic Relations: A Framework for Theory and Research*. Chicago: University of Chicago Press, 1978.

Schiffman, Lawrence H. "Community Without Temple: The Qumran Community's Withdrawal from the Jerusalem Temple." Pages 267–84 in *Gemeinde ohne Tempel/Community without Temple: Zur Substituierung und Transformation des Jerusalemer Tempels und seines Kults im Alten Testament, antiken Judentum und frühen Christentum*. Edited by Beate Ego, Armin Lange, and Peter Pilhofer. WUNT 118. Tübingen: Mohr Siebeck, 1999.

————. *Who Was a Jew? Rabbinic and Halakhic Perspectives on the Jewish-Christian Schism*. Hoboken, NJ: Ktav, 1985.

Schlosser, Jacques. *La première épître de Pierre*. Commentaire biblique: Nouveau Testament 21. Paris: Cerf, 2011.

Schmeller, Thomas. *2 Kor 1,1–7,4*. Vol. 1 of *Der zweite Brief an die Korinther*. EKKNT 8.1. Neukirchen-Vluyn: Neukirchener; Ostfildern: Patmos, 2010.

Schnabel, Eckhard J. *Jesus and the Twelve*. Vol. 1 of *Early Christian Mission*. Downers Grove, IL: InterVarsity Press, 2004.

———. *Paul and the Early Church.* Vol. 2 of *Early Christian Mission.* Downers Grove, IL: InterVarsity Press, 2004.

Schneemelcher, Wilhelm. "The Kerygma Petrou." Pages 94–102 in *New Testament Apocrypha.* Edited by E. Hennecke and Wilhelm Schneemelcher. Vol. 2. London: Lutterworth, 1965.

Schneider, Johannes. *Die Briefe des Jakobus, Petrus, Judas und Johannes: Die Katholischen Briefe.* NTD 10. Göttingen: Vandenhoeck & Ruprecht, 1961.

Schoedel, William R. *Ignatius of Antioch: A Commentary on the Letters of Ignatius of Antioch.* Hermeneia. Philadelphia: Fortress, 1985.

———. "Theological Norms and Social Perspectives in Ignatius of Antioch." Pages 30–56 in *The Shaping of Christianity in the Second and Third Centuries.* Vol. 1 of *Jewish and Christian Self-Definition.* Edited by E. P. Sanders. Philadelphia: Fortress, 1980.

Schrage, Wolfgang. "Der erste Petrusbrief." Pages 60–121 in *Die "Katholischen" Briefe: Die Briefe des Jakobus, Petrus, Johannes und Judas.* By Horst Balz and Wolfgang Schrage. NTD 10. Göttingen: Vandenhoeck & Ruprecht, 1993.

———. *1 Kor 6,12–11,16.* Vol. 2 of *Der erste Brief an die Korinther.* EKKNT 7.2. Neukirchen-Vluyn: Neukirchener, 1995.

Schröder, Bernd. *Die "väterlichen Gesetze": Flavius Josephus als Vermittler von Halachah an Griechen und Römer.* TSAJ 53. Tübingen: Mohr Siebeck, 1996.

Schüssler Fiorenza, Elisabeth. *In Memory of Her: A Feminist Theological Reconstruction of Christian Origins.* London: SCM, 1983.

Schutter, William L. *Hermeneutic and Composition in 1 Peter.* WUNT 2.30. Tübingen: Mohr Siebeck, 1989.

Schwartz, Daniel R. "Non-Joining Sympathizers (Acts 5,13–14)." *Bib* 64 (1983): 550–55.

———. *Studies in the Jewish Background of Christianity.* WUNT 60. Tübingen: Mohr Siebeck, 1992.

Schwarz, Eberhard. *Identität durch Abgrenzung: Abgrenzungsprozesse in Israel im 2. vorchristlichen Jahrhundert und ihre traditionsgeschichtlichen Voraussetzungen: Zugleich ein Beitrag zur Erforschung des Jubiläenbuches.* Europäische Hochschulschriften 162. Frankfurt: Peter Lang, 1982.

Scott, James M. *Geography in Early Judaism and Christianity: The Book of Jubilees.* SNTSMS 113. Cambridge: Cambridge University Press, 2002.

———. *Paul and the Nations: The Old Testament and Jewish Background of Paul's Mission to the Nations with Special Reference to the Destination of Galatians.* WUNT 84. Tübingen: Mohr Siebeck, 1995.

Sechrest, Love L. "Double Vision for Revolutionary Religion: Race Relations, Moral Analogies, and African-American Biblical Interpretation." Pages

202–18 in *Ethnicity, Race, Religion: Identities and Ideologies in Early Jewish and Christian Texts and in Modern Biblical Interpretation*. Edited by Katherine M. Hockey and David G. Horrell. London: Bloomsbury T&T Clark, 2018.

———. *A Former Jew: Paul and the Dialectics of Race*. LNTS 410. London: T&T Clark, 2009.

Segovia, Fernando F., and Mary Ann Tolbert, eds. *Reading from This Place*. 2 vols. Minneapolis: Fortress, 1995.

Seland, Torrey. "The 'Common Priesthood' of Philo and 1 Peter: A Philonic Reading of 1 Peter 2:5, 9." *JSNT* 57 (1995): 87–119.

———. *Establishment Violence in Philo and Luke: A Study of Non-Conformity to the Torah and Jewish Vigilante Reactions*. BibInt 15. Leiden: Brill, 1995.

———. "Resident Aliens in Mission: Missional Practices in the Emerging Church of 1 Peter." *BBR* 19 (2009): 565–89.

———. *Strangers in the Light: Philonic Perspectives on Christian Identity in 1 Peter*. BibInt 76. Leiden: Brill, 2005.

Selwyn, Edward Gordon. *The First Epistle of St. Peter*. 2nd ed. London: Macmillan, 1947.

Shimada, Kazuhito. "Is I Peter Dependent on Ephesians? A Critique of C. L. Mitton." *AJBI* 17 (1991): 77–106.

———. *Studies on First Peter*. Tokyo: Kyo Bun Kwan, 1998.

Shipley, Graham. *Pseudo-Skylax's* Periplous*: The Circumnavigation of the Inhabited World: Text, Translation and Commentary*. Exeter: Bristol Phoenix, 2011.

Siker, Jeffrey S. "Historicizing a Racialized Jesus: Case Studies in the 'Black Christ,' the 'Mestizo Christ,' and White Critique." *BibInt* 15 (2007): 26–53.

Sim, David C. *The Gospel of Matthew and Christian Judaism*. SNTW. Edinburgh: T&T Clark, 1998.

Skarsaune, Oskar. "The Mission to the Jews—a Closed Chapter?" Pages 69–83 in *The Mission of the Early Church to Jews and Gentiles*. Edited by Jostein Ådna and Hans Kvalbein. WUNT 127. Tübingen: Mohr Siebeck, 2000.

Sleeman, Matthew. "Critical Spacial Theory 2.0." Pages 49–66 in *Constructions of Space*. Vol. 5: *Place, Space and Identity in the Ancient Mediterranean World*. Edited by Gert T. M. Prinsloo and Christl M. Maier. LHBOTS 576. London: Bloomsbury T&T Clark, 2013.

———. *Geography and the Ascension Narrative in Acts*. SNTSMS 146. Cambridge: Cambridge University Press, 2009.

Smith, Anthony D. *The Antiquity of Nations*. Cambridge: Polity, 2004.

———. *Chosen Peoples*. Oxford: Oxford University Press, 2003.

———. *The Ethnic Origins of Nations*. Oxford: Blackwell, 1986.

————. *National Identity*. London: Penguin; Reno: University of Nevada Press, 1991.

————. *Nationalism: Theory, Ideology, History*. Key Concepts. Cambridge: Polity, 2010.

Smith, Dennis E. *From Symposium to Eucharist: The Banquet in the Early Christian World*. Minneapolis: Fortress, 2003.

Smith, Jonathan Z. "Religion, Religions, Religious." Pages 269–84 in *Critical Terms for Religious Studies*. Edited by Mark C. Taylor. Chicago: University of Chicago Press, 1998.

Smith, Morton. "The Gentiles in Judaism 125 BCE–CE 66." Pages 192–249 in *The Early Roman Period*. Vol. 3 of *The Cambridge History of Judaism*. Edited by William Horbury, W. D. Davies, and John Sturdy. Cambridge: Cambridge University Press, 1999.

Smith, R. R. R. "Simulacra Gentium: The Ethne from the Sebasteion at Aphrodisias." *JRS* 78 (1988): 50–77.

Smith, Wilfred Cantwell. *The Meaning and End of Religion*. Minneapolis: Fortress, 1991.

Smither, Edward L. *Mission in the Early Church: Themes and Reflections*. Cambridge: James Clarke, 2014.

Snowden, Frank M., Jr., *Before Color Prejudice: The Ancient View of Blacks*. Cambridge, MA: Harvard University Press, 1983.

Snyman, Gerrie. "African Hermeneutics' 'Outing' of Whiteness." *Neot* 42 (2008): 93–118.

Soja, Edward W. *Thirdspace: Journeys to Los Angeles and Other Real-and-Imagined Places*. Oxford: Blackwell, 1996.

Sollors, Werner. "Foreword: Theories of American Ethnicity." Pages x–xliv in *Theories of Ethnicity: A Classical Reader*. Edited by Werner Sollors. New York: New York University Press, 1996.

Solomos, John, and Les Back. "Introduction: Theorising Race and Racism." Pages 1–28 in *Theories of Race and Racism: A Reader*. Edited by Les Back and John Solomos. Routledge Student Readers. London: Routledge, 2000.

Solomos, John, and Les Back, eds. *Theories of Race and Racism: A Reader*. Routledge Student Readers. London: Routledge, 2000.

Sordi, Marta. *The Christians and the Roman Empire*. London: Routledge, 1994.

Southwood, Katherine E. *Ethnicity and the Mixed Marriage Crisis in Ezra 9–10: An Anthropological Approach*. Oxford: Oxford University Press, 2012.

Stanley, Christopher. *Arguing with Scripture: The Rhetoric of Quotations in the Letters of Paul*. London: Continuum, 2004.

Stanton, Graham N. *A Gospel for a New People: Studies in Matthew.* Edinburgh: T&T Clark, 1992.

Stark, Rodney. *The Rise of Christianity: A Sociologist Reconsiders History.* Princeton: Princeton University Press, 1996.

Stavrakopoulou, Francesca. *Land of Our Fathers: The Roles of Ancestor Veneration in Biblical Land Claims.* LHBOTS 473. London: T&T Clark, 2010.

Stegemann, Wolfgang. *Jesus und seine Zeit.* Biblische Enzyklopädie 10. Stuttgart: Kohlhammer, 2010.

———. "Religion als Teil von ethnischer Identität: Zur aktuellen Debatte um die Kategorisierung des antiken Judentums." *Kirche und Israel* 25 (2010): 47–59.

Stendahl, Krister. "The Apostle Paul and the Introspective Conscience of the West." *HTR* 56 (1963): 199–215.

———. *Paul among Jews and Gentiles.* London: SCM, 1977.

Stenschke, Christoph. "Mission and Conversion in the First Epistle of Peter." *Acta Patristica et Byzantina* 19 (2008): 221–63.

Sterling, Gregory E. Review of *Establishment Violence in Philo and Luke: A Study of Non-Conformity to the Torah and Jewish Vigilante Reactions*, by Torrey Seland. *JBL* 116 (1997): 368–70.

Stewart, Eric C. "New Testament Space/Spatiality." *BTB* 42 (2012): 139–50.

Still, Todd D., and David G. Horrell, eds. *After the First Urban Christians: The Social-Scientific Study of Pauline Christianity Twenty-Five Years Later.* London: T&T Clark, 2009.

Stokes, Bruce. "What It Takes to Truly Be 'One of Us.'" Washington, DC: Pew Research Center, 2017. http://www.pewglobal.org/2017/02/01/what-it-takes-to-truly-be-one-of-us/.

Stone, John. "Max Weber on Race, Ethnicity, and Nationalism." Pages 28–42 in *Race and Ethnicity: Comparative and Theoretical Approaches.* Edited by John Stone and Rutledge Dennis. Blackwell Readers in Sociology. Oxford: Blackwell, 2003.

Stone, John, and Rutledge Dennis, eds. *Race and Ethnicity: Comparative and Theoretical Approaches.* Blackwell Readers in Sociology. Oxford: Blackwell, 2003.

Storm, Ingrid. "'Christianity Is Not Just about Religion': Religious and National Identities in a Northern English Town." *Secularism and Nonreligion* 2 (2013): 21–38.

Stowers, Stanley K. *A Rereading of Romans: Justice, Jews and Gentiles.* New Haven: Yale University Press, 1994.

———. Review of *Why This New Race: Ethnic Reasoning in Early Christianity*, by Denise Kimber Buell. *JAAR* 75 (2007): 727–30.

Strecker, Georg. "Das Land Israel in frühchristlicher Zeit." Pages 188–200 in *Das Land Israel in biblischer Zeit*. Edited by Georg Strecker. Göttinger Theologische Arbeiten 25. Göttingen: Vandenhoeck & Ruprecht, 1983.

Strom, Mark. "From Promised Land to Reconciled Cosmos: Paul's Translation of 'Worldview,' 'Worldstory,' and 'Worldperson.'" Pages 14–27 in *The Gospel and the Land of Promise: Christian Approaches to the Land of the Bible*. Edited by Philip Church, Peter Walker, Tim Bulkeley, and Tim Meadowcroft. Eugene, OR: Pickwick, 2011.

Stuhlmacher, Peter. "Matt 28:16–20 and the Course of Mission in the Apostolic and Postapostolic Age." Pages 17–43 in *The Mission of the Early Church to Jews and Gentiles*. Edited by Jostein Ådna and Hans Kvalbein. WUNT 127. Tübingen: Mohr Siebeck, 2000.

Sugirtharajah, R. S. "Muddling Along at the Margins." Pages 8–21 in *Still at the Margins: Biblical Scholarship Fifteen Years after the Voices from the Margin*. Edited by R. S. Sugirtharajah. London: Bloomsbury T&T Clark, 2008.

———, ed. *Still at the Margins: Biblical Scholarship Fifteen Years after the Voices from the Margin*. London: Bloomsbury T&T Clark, 2008.

———. *Voices from the Margin: Interpreting the Bible in the Third World*. London: SPCK, 1991.

Tajfel, Henri. *Human Groups and Social Categories*. Cambridge: Cambridge University Press, 1981.

Taussig, Hal. *In the Beginning Was the Meal: Social Experimentation and Early Christian Identity*. Minneapolis: Fortress, 2009.

Theissen, Gerd. *Neutestamentliche Wissenschaft vor und nach 1945: Karl Georg Kuhn und Günther Bornkamm*. Schriften der Philosophisch-historischen Klasse der Heidelberger Akademie der Wissenschaften 47. Heidelberg: Universitätsverlag, 2009.

———. *Social Reality and the Early Christians: Theology, Ethics, and the World of the New Testament*. Edinburgh: T&T Clark, 1993.

Theissen, Gerd, and Dagmar Winter. *The Quest for the Plausible Jesus: The Question of Criteria*. Louisville: Westminster John Knox, 2002.

Thiessen, Matthew. *Contesting Conversion: Genealogy, Circumcision, and Identity in Ancient Judaism and Christianity*. Oxford: Oxford University Press, 2011.

———. *Paul and the Gentile Problem*. Oxford: Oxford University Press, 2016.

———. "Revisiting the προσήλυτος in 'the LXX.'" *JBL* 132 (2013): 333–50.

Thiselton, Anthony C. *The First Epistle to the Corinthians*. NIGTC. Grand Rapids: Eerdmans, 2000.

Thomas, James M. "The Racial Formation of Medieval Jews: A Challenge to the Field." *Ethnic and Racial Studies* 33 (2010): 1737–55.

Thompson, Audrey. "Reading Black Philosophers in Chronological Order." Pages 27–50 in *The Center Must Not Hold: White Women Philosophers on the Whiteness of Philosophy*. Edited by George Yancy. Lanham, MD: Lexington, 2010.

Thompson, Deanna A. "Calling a Thing What It Is: A Lutheran Approach to Whiteness." *Dialog* 53 (2014): 49–57.

Thorsteinsson, Runar M. *Roman Christianity and Roman Stoicism: A Comparative Study of Ancient Morality*. Oxford: Oxford University Press, 2010.

Thrall, Margaret E. *A Critical and Exegetical Commentary on the Second Epistle to the Corinthians*. Vol. 1. ICC. Edinburgh: T&T Clark, 1994.

Tite, Philip L. "Nurslings, Milk and Moral Development in the Greco-Roman Context: A Reappraisal of the Paraenetic Utilization of Metaphor in 1 Peter 2.1–3." *JSNT* 31 (2009): 371–400.

Tolbert, Mary Ann. "Writing History, Writing Culture, Writing Ourselves: Issues in Contemporary Biblical Interpretation." Pages 17–30 in *Soundings in Cultural Criticism: Perspectives and Methods in Culture, Power, and Identity in the New Testament*. Edited by Francisco Lozada Jr. and Greg Carey. Minneapolis: Fortress, 2013.

Torres, Rodolfo D., Louis F. Mirón, and Jonathan Xavier Inda, eds. *Race, Identity, and Citizenship: A Reader*. Oxford: Blackwell, 1999.

Trebilco, Paul R. *Jewish Communities in Asia Minor*. SNTSMS 69. Cambridge: Cambridge University Press, 1991.

———. *Self-Designations and Group Identity in the New Testament*. Cambridge: Cambridge University Press, 2012.

Tucker, J. Brian. *Remain in Your Calling: Paul and the Continuation of Social Identities in 1 Corinthians*. Eugene, OR: Pickwick, 2011.

Tucker, J. Brian, and Coleman A. Baker, eds. *T&T Clark Handbook to Social Identity in the New Testament*. London: Bloomsbury T&T Clark, 2014.

Tyler, Katharine. *Whiteness, Class and the Legacies of Empire: On Home Ground*. Basingstoke: Palgrave Macmillan, 2012.

UNESCO [United Nations Educational, Scientific and Cultural Organization], "The Race Question." Paris: UNESCO, 1950. http://unesdoc.unesco.org/images/0012/001282/128291eo.pdf.

Vaage, Leif E. "The Translation of 1 Cor 7:14C and the Labile Social Body of the Pauline Church." *RB* 116 (2009): 557–71.

Vahrenhorst, Martin. "Land und Landverheißung im Neuen Testament." Pages 123–47 in *Heiliges Land*. Edited by Marie-Theres Wacker and Ralf Koerrenz. Jahrbuch für Biblische Theologie 23. Neukirchen-Vluyn: Neukirchener, 2009.

Vair, Richard James. "The Old Testament Promise of the Land as Reinterpreted in First and Second Century Christian Literature." PhD diss., Graduate Theological Union, 1979.

Vogel, Manfred. "Modelle jüdischer Identitätsbildung in hellenistisch-römischer Zeit." Pages 43–68 in *Religionsgemeinschaft und Identität: Prozesse jüdischer und christlicher Identitätsbildung im Rahmen der antike*. Edited by Markus Öhler. Biblisch-Theologische Studien 142. Neukirchen-Vluyn: Neukirchener, 2013.

Vollenrieder, Samuel. "Are Christians a New 'People'? Detecting Ethnicity and Cultural Friction in Paul's Letters and Early Christianity." *EC* 8 (2017): 293–308.

Vos, Craig S. de. "Popular Graeco-Roman Responses to Christianity." Pages 869–89 in *The Early Christian World*. Edited by Philip F. Esler. London: Routledge, 2000.

Vos, J. Cornelis de. "Die Bedeutung des Landes Israel in den jüdischen Schriften der hellenistisch-römischen Zeit." Pages 75–99 in *Heiliges Land*. Edited by Marie-Theres Wacker and Ralf Koerrenz. Jahrbuch für Biblische Theologie 23. Neukirchen-Vluyn: Neukirchener, 2009.

Wacker, Marie-Theres, and Ralf Koerrenz, eds. *Heiliges Land*. Jahrbuch für Biblische Theologie 23. Neukirchen-Vluyn: Neukirchener, 2009.

Wallace, Daniel B. *Greek Grammar beyond the Basics: An Exegetical Syntax of the New Testament*. Grand Rapids: Zondervan, 1996.

Walzer, Richard. *Galen on Jews and Christians*. Oxford Classical and Philosophical Monographs. Oxford: Oxford University Press, 1949.

Wan, Sze-kar. "'To the Jew First and Also to the Greek': Reading Romans as Ethnic Construction." Pages 129–55 in *Prejudice and Christian Beginnings: Investigating Race, Gender, and Ethnicity in Early Christian Studies*. Edited by Laura Nasrallah and Elisabeth Schüssler Fiorenza. Minneapolis: Fortress, 2009.

Wan, Wei Hsien. *The Contest for Time and Space in the Roman Imperial Cults and 1 Peter: Reconfiguring the Universe*. LNTS 611. London: Bloomsbury T&T Clark, 2019.

———. "Reconfiguring the Universe: The Contest for Time and Space in the Roman Imperial Cults and 1 Peter." PhD diss., University of Exeter, 2016.

———. "Re-examining the Master's Tools: Considerations on Biblical Studies' Race Problem." Pages 219–29 in *Ethnicity, Race, Religion: Identities and Ideologies in Early Jewish and Christian Texts and in Modern Biblical Interpretation*. Edited by Katherine M. Hockey and David G. Horrell. London: Bloomsbury T&T Clark, 2018.

————. "Repairing Social Vertigo: Spatial Production and Belonging in 1 Peter." Pages 287–303 in *The Urban World and the First Christians*. Edited by Steve Walton, Paul R. Trebilco, and David Gill. Grand Rapids: Eerdmans, 2017.

————. "Whose Time? Which Rationality? Reflections on Empire, 1 Peter, and the 'Common Era.'" *Postscripts: The Journal of Sacred Texts and Contemporary Worlds* 7 (2011): 279–94.

Wander, Bernd. *Gottesfürchtige und Sympathisanten: Studien zum heidnischen Umfeld von Diasporasynagogen*. WUNT 104. Tübingen: Mohr Siebeck, 1998.

Ward, Roy B. "Musonius and Paul on Marriage." *NTS* 36 (1990): 281–89.

Ware, James P. *The Mission of the Church in Paul's Letter to the Philippians in the Context of Ancient Judaism*. NovTSup 120. Leiden: Brill, 2005.

Watson, Francis. *Paul and the Hermeneutics of Faith*. London: T&T Clark, 2004.

————. *Paul, Judaism and the Gentiles: Beyond the New Perspective*. Revised and expanded ed. Grand Rapids: Eerdmans, 2007.

Weber, Max. *Economy and Society: An Outline of Interpretive Sociology*. New York: Bedminster Press, 1968.

————. "Race Relations." Translated by Eric Matthews. Pages 359–69 in *Max Weber: Selections in Translation*. Edited by W. G. Runciman. Cambridge: Cambridge University Press, 1978.

————. *Wirtschaft und Gesellschaft*. Vol. 3 of *Grundriss der Sozialökonomik*. 2nd ed. Tübingen: Mohr Siebeck, 1925.

Weima, Jeffrey A. D. *1–2 Thessalonians*. BECNT. Grand Rapids: Baker Academic, 2014.

Weiss, Daniel H. "Born into Covenantal Salvation? Baptism and Birth in Early Christianity and Classical Rabbinic Judaism." *JSQ* 24 (2017): 318–38.

Wenell, Karen. *Jesus and Land: Sacred and Social Space in Second Temple Judaism*. LNTS 334. London: T&T Clark, 2007.

Werman, Cana. "Jubilees 30: Building a Paradigm for the Ban on Intermarriage." *HTR* 90 (1997): 1–22.

Westerholm, Stephen. *Perspectives Old and New on Paul: The "Lutheran" Paul and His Critics*. Grand Rapids: Eerdmans, 2004.

Whitelam, Keith W. *The Invention of Ancient Israel: The Silencing of Palestinian History*. London: Routledge, 1996.

Whitmarsh, Tim. *Greek Literature and the Roman Empire: The Politics of Imitation*. Oxford: Oxford University Press, 2001.

Whittaker, Molly. *Jews and Christians: Graeco-Roman Views*. Cambridge Commentaries on Writings of the Jewish and Christian World, 200 BC to AD 200, 6. Cambridge: Cambridge University Press, 1984.

Wilken, Robert L. *The Land Called Holy: Palestine in Christian History and Thought*. New Haven: Yale University Press, 1992.

Will, Edouard, and Claude Orrieux. *"Proselytisme Juif"? Histoire d'une erreur*. Paris: Les Belles Lettres, 1992.

Williams, Travis B. *Good Works in 1 Peter: Negotiating Social Conflict and Christian Identity in the Greco-Roman World*. Tübingen: Mohr Siebeck, 2014.

———. *Persecution in 1 Peter: Differentiating and Contextualizing Early Christian Suffering*. NovTSup 145. Leiden: Brill, 2012.

———. "Suffering from a Critical Oversight: The Persecutions of 1 Peter within Modern Scholarship." *CBR* 10 (2012): 271–88.

Wilson, Stephen G. *Leaving the Fold: Apostates and Defectors in Antiquity*. Minneapolis: Fortress, 2004.

Windisch, Hans. *Die Katholischen Briefe*. HNT 15. 2nd ed. Tübingen: Mohr Siebeck, 1930.

Wire, Antoinette C. *The Corinthian Women Prophets: A Reconstruction through Paul's Rhetoric*. Minneapolis: Fortress, 1990.

Witherington, Ben. *Grace in Galatia: A Commentary on Paul's Letter to the Galatians*. Edinburgh: T&T Clark, 1998.

Wohlenberg, G. *Der erste und zweite Petrusbrief und der Judasbrief*. Kommentar zum Neuen Testament 15. Leipzig: Deichert'sche Verlagsbuchhandlung, 1915.

Wolter, Michael. "The Development of Pauline Christianity from a 'Religion of Conversion' to a 'Religion of Tradition.'" Pages 49–69 in *Paul and the Heritage of Israel: Paul's Claim upon Israel's Legacy in Luke and Acts in the Light of the Pauline Letters*. Edited by David P. Moessner, Daniel Marguerat, Mikael C. Parsons, and Michael Wolter. LNTS 452. London: T&T Clark, 2012.

———. "Die Entwicklung des paulinischen Christentums von einer Bekehrungsreligion zu einer Traditionsreligion." *EC* 3 (2010): 14–39.

———. "Ein neues 'Geschlecht'? Das frühe Christentum auf der Suche nach seiner Identität." Pages 282–98 in *Ein neues Geschlecht? Entwicklung des frühchristlichen Selbstbewusstseins*. Edited by Markus Lang. NTOA/SUNT 105. Göttingen: Vandenhoeck & Ruprecht, 2014.

———. "Ethnizität und Identität bei Paulus." *EC* 8 (2017): 336–53.

Woodard-Lehman, Derek. "Body Politics and the Politics of Bodies: Racism and Hauerwasian Theopolitics." *JRE* 36 (2008): 295–320.

Wright, David F. "A Race Apart? Jews, Gentiles, Christians." *BSac* 160 (2003): 131–41.

Wright, N. T. *The Climax of the Covenant: Christ and the Law in Pauline Theology*. Edinburgh: T&T Clark, 1991.

———. *The New Testament and the People of God*. Christian Origins and the Question of God 1. London: SPCK, 1992.

———. *Paul and His Recent Interpreters: Some Contemporary Debates*. London: SPCK, 2015.

———. *Paul and the Faithfulness of God*. Christian Origins and the Question of God. 2 vols. London: SPCK; Minneapolis: Fortress, 2013.

———. "The Paul of History and the Apostle of Faith." *TynBul* 29 (1978): 61–88.

———. *Pauline Perspectives: Essays on Paul, 1978–2013*. Minneapolis: Fortress, 2014.

Yancy, George. "Introduction: Framing the Problem." Pages 1–18 in *Christology and Whiteness: What Would Jesus Do?* Edited by George Yancy. London: Routledge, 2012.

Yancy, George, ed. *The Center Must Not Hold: White Women Philosophers on the Whiteness of Philosophy*. Lanham, MD: Lexington, 2010.

———, ed. *Christology and Whiteness: What Would Jesus Do?* London: Routledge, 2012.

Yarbro Collins, Adela. *Mark: A Commentary*. Hermeneia. Minneapolis: Fortress, 2007.

Yarbrough, O. Larry. *Not Like the Gentiles: Marriage Rules in the Letters of Paul*. SBLDS 80. Atlanta: Scholars Press, 1985.

———. "Parents and Children in the Jewish Family of Antiquity." Pages 39–59 in *The Jewish Family in Antiquity*. Edited by Shaye J. D. Cohen. Brown Judaic Studies 289. Atlanta: Scholars Press, 1993.

Young, Norman H. "'The Use of Sunday for Meetings of Believers in the New Testament': A Response." *NovT* 65 (2003): 111–22.

Young, Robert. *White Mythologies: Writing History and the West*. London: Routledge, 1990.

Zetterholm, Magnus. *Approaches to Paul: A Student's Guide to Recent Scholarship*. Minneapolis: Fortress, 2009.

Cover Illustrations Credits

The cover art includes the following images:

Black Madonna of Częstochowa, ca. 1382, Jasna Góra Monastery, Częstochowa, Poland.

Sandro Botticelli, *Christ Crowned with Thorns*, ca. 1500, tempera on panel, Accademia Carrara, Bergamo, Italy.

Jean Bourdichon, *Christ Blessing*, ca. 1480, oil on panel, Museum of Fine Arts of Tours, France.

Christ and the Twelve Apostles (detail), ca. 1100, painting on wood, National Art Museum of Catalonia, Barcelona, Spain.

Christ Entering Jerusalem, Russian icon painting, sixteenth century, National Museum of Fine Arts, Stockholm, Sweden.

The Christ from the Vision of Ezekiel, ca. 1130, fresco, Frauenchiemsee convent, Chiemsee, Germany.

Christ in the Tomb, late fifteenth century, tempera on wood, Museum of Icons, Recklinghausen, Germany.

Christ Pantocrator Surrounded by the Tetramorph, 1200–1210, altar frontal, tempera on panel, Museo del Prado, Madrid, Spain.

Christ with Beard, late fourth to early fifth century, mural painting, catacomb of Commodilla, Rome, Italy.

Gustave Doré, *Jesus*, late 1800s.

Double diptych icon pendant from Ethiopia, early eighteenth century, tempera on wood, Metropolitan Museum of Art, New York, NY.

Albin Egger-Lienz, *Christ's Resurrection*, 1924, oil on canvas.

Giampetrino, *Christ with the Symbol of the Trinity*, early sixteenth century, oil on canvas, Hermitage Museum, St. Petersburg, Russia.

Jesus Wearing a Crown of Thorns, graffiti, photo by Jon Tyson on Unsplash, 2018.

The Madonna as Advocate, ca. 1150, tempera on canvas mounted on panel, National Gallery of Ancient Art, Rome, Italy.

Vladimir Makovsky, *Jesus Christ*, 1894, oil on canvas, Tomsk Regional Art Museum, Russia.

The Miracle of Turning Water into Wine at the Wedding in Cana, tenth century, from *Codex Egberti*, ms. 24, fol. 20v, City Library, Trier, Germany.

Antônio Parreiras, *Jesus Christ on the Edge of Golgotha*, 1907, oil on canvas, art gallery Barão de Santo Ângelo, Porto Alegre, Brazil.

The Passion of Christ, most recently attributed to Giovanni da Oriolo, fifteenth century, oil on panel, Faenza Art Gallery, Italy.

Antonio Sicurezza, *The Nazarene*, 1977, oil on canvas, private collection.

Luca Signorelli, *Christ and the Doubting Thomas*, fresco, 1477–1482, Basilica della Santa Casa, Loreto, Italy.

Enrique Simonet, study of Jesus for his 1892 painting *Flevit super illam* (*He Wept over It*), 1890–1891, oil on canvas.

Henry O. Tanner, *Nicodemus*, 1899, oil on canvas, Pennsylvania Academy of the Fine Arts, Philadelphia, PA.

Uber painter, *Jesus of Africa,* 2015.

Index of Modern Authors

Aalen, Sverre, 253, 271, 286
Aasgaard, Reidar, 106n41, 107n45, 108, 111
Achtemeier, Paul J., 103n27, 103n29, 234n91, 235n96
Adams, Edward, 23n5, 212n135
Ådna, Jostein, 277n129, 278n130
Ahmed, Sara, 83, 311, 314, 318
Alcoff, Linda Martin, 44n90, 342n122
Alexander, Loveday, 196n77
Alexander, Philip S., 31, 32n34, 185n31
Alikin, Valeriy A., 166n107, 168n114, 168n116, 171n122, 173n128
Allison, Dale C., 98n12, 231n76
Amaru, Betsy Halpern, 191
Anson, Edward M., 54
Applebaum, Barbara, 316, 343
Arnal, William, 310, 329
Asad, Talal, 83n71, 88n94, 327n67
Ascough, Richard S., 222n25, 279n135
Attridge, Harold W., 54n38, 183n23, 206n120, 209n127, 209n128
Augoustinos, Martha, 69n9
Avruch, Kevin, 69, 70n11

Bacchiocchi, Samuele, 170n119, 171n125, 172n126
Back, Les, 3n9, 333n89, 333n90, 334n94
Backhaus, Knut, 207, 209n129, 210n131
Badiou, Alain, 43–44
Bailey, Randall C., 339n113, 339n115, 344n127
Baker, Coleman A., 37n57

Baker, Cynthia M., 13n35, 189–90, 192n63, 194
Balch, David L., 288, 290
Baldwin, James, 312n23
Balibar, Étienne, 218
Balla, Peter, 151n52, 152n60
Banks, Robert, 107
Barclay, John M. G., 13n33, 21n1, 32n35, 50, 101n19, 108n49, 109n55, 115n85, 115n86, 116n89, 132n157, 139n12, 139n13, 141n25, 142n26, 151, 153, 158n78, 159n81, 160n85, 161n87, 178, 191n58, 191n61, 266n83, 267, 270n96, 270n97, 272n106, 274, 275n117, 329n73
Barreto, Eric D., 60
Barrett, C. K., 118n98, 131n154, 168n113, 170n120, 170n121, 229n69
Bartchy, S. Scott, 110n62
Barth, Fredrik, 52, 69, 71, 155
Barton, Carlin, 87, 88n97, 306n4
Barton, Stephen C., 37n54, 123n117, 132n157, 152n59
Bassler, Jouette M., 35
Bauckham, Richard J., 171n123, 171n125, 211n134, 212, 230n75, 232n86
Bauman-Martin, Betsy J., 234
Baur, Ferdinand Christian, 22–29, 35–36, 45–46, 296, 308–9, 320, 325, 326, 328
Bauspiess, Martin, 23n4
Beard, Mary, 55n41, 87n91
Beare, Francis W., 103n27
Behr, John, 244n134

Benko, Andrew, 99n13
Benko, Stephen, 156n73
Berger, Klaus, 120n104
Bernabé Ubieta, Carmen, 204n111
Bernal, Martin, 327n68
Bernasconi, Robert, 327n69
Berquist, Jon L., 180n12
Betz, Hans Dieter, 199
Bieringer, Reimund, 335n97
Bigg, Charles, 235n98
Bird, Michael F., 254, 255n29, 256n33,
    263n67, 268n88, 269n94, 270n98
Bobichon, Philippe, 213n142, 236n100
Bockmuehl, Markus N. A., 286n164
Bohak, Gideon, 276
Boin, Douglas, 48n4, 51n20, 139, 149n44,
    246n141
Borgen, Peder, 225n52, 226n61, 227n66
Bormann, Lukas, 28–29, 48n3, 63–64,
    236n101,
Botermann, Helga, 236n102
Bowers, Paul, 284n156, 285n160
Boyarin, Daniel, 48n4, 87, 88n97, 138n8,
    183n22, 306n4, 322, 336n100
Brett, Mark G., 70n14, 314n32
Brooke, George J., 192n66
Brown, Jeannine K., 291n182
Brown, Peter, 120n106, 123n116, 123n118
Brox, Norbert, 196, 213n141, 213n142
Brubaker, Rogers, 9, 72–75, 76n40, 77, 149,
    217, 228, 235, 300, 306n5
Brueggemann, Walter, 183n21, 201n98, 216
Buell, Denise Kimber, 5–6, 7n26, 8, 16n41,
    21n1, 41n73, 51n19, 56–61, 66, 70n13,
    82n65, 83–84, 86n83, 87n87, 87n88,
    90n100, 95, 111, 219n11, 236n99, 241n120,
    242–43, 248, 300, 312n22, 333, 343n126,
    344n130
Burchard, Christoph, 114n80, 115n83,
    115n84, 115n86, 144n33, 230n75
Burke, Kevin J., 319n50
Burton, Ernest DeWitt, 328
Butticaz, Simon, 64–65, 196n76
Byrne, Brendan, 199n90, 199n91, 200

Calvin, John, 127n134, 252n13
Cambe, Michel, 237n104, 237n105, 238n106
Camp, Claudia V., 180n12, 185n31
Campbell, William S., 42–43, 44n91,
    44n93
Caputo, John D., 44n90, 342n122
Carey, Greg, 11, 312n22, 313, 317, 340
Carleton Paget, James, 35n50, 240n117,
    252n13, 253n20, 254, 255n29, 256n32,
    257n38, 258n45, 259n48, 260n51,
    260n52, 262n61, 271n101
Carson, D. A., 170n119, 170n121
Carter, J. Kameron, 4–5, 6n24, 217–18,
    312n21, 337n103
Casey, Robert Pierce, 244n137
Catchpole, David, 116n91
Chapman, Cynthia R., 104, 115n82, 124
Chesnutt, Randall D., 115n83, 115n86,
    266n81
Cheung, Alex T., 166n106
Church, Philip, 207, 216n145, 216n146,
    216n147
Clarke, Fern K. T., 197n83
Clifford, James, 327n67
Clough, David, 312n21
Cohen, Shaye J. D., 50–51, 52, 112–13,
    115n82, 117n92, 119n100, 119n102, 121n110,
    121n111, 121n112, 122, 124, 125n125,
    125n127, 125n128, 138n9, 173–74, 176,
    190n57, 257–58, 264n70
Concannon, Cavan W., 21n1, 60
Cone, James H., 337–38
Conzelmann, Hans, 195, 279n138
Cook, John Granger, 112n68
Cornell, Stephen, 69n7, 69n8, 69n9, 69n10,
    70, 71n19, 72, 78–79, 82, 90–91
Countryman, L. William, 124n121
Cromhout, Markus, 50n15
Crossley, James G., 36, 166n104, 331n80

Dahl, Nils Alstrup, 21n1
Dalton, William J., 163n96
Daube, David, 114n81, 124n122, 125n127,
    125n128
Davies, Margaret, 116n90

Davies, W. D., 98n12, 179n5, 183n24, 184n28, 185n31, 185n32, 186, 187, 192n64, 192n65, 192n66, 195n73, 196–97, 198n84, 201, 231n76

De Garis, Stephanie, 69n9

Deines, Roland, 28n24

Delgado, Richard, 310n15

Delling, Gerhard, 126n129

DeMaris, Richard E., 162–63

Dennis, Rutledge, 83n70

Descourtieux, Patrick, 237n105, 238n107

De Ste. Croix, Geoffrey E. M., 156n73, 172n127

Dickson, John P., 284n156, 286n163

Donaldson, Terence L., 254n26, 256n33, 257–60, 261n56, 262n61, 262n63, 263n65, 263n66, 263n69, 264, 265n76, 266n78, 266n83, 268, 269n95, 270n97, 271n101, 271n102, 271n103, 272n105, 272n108

Doran, Robert, 138n6

Dube, Musa W., 338n108

DuBois, W. E. B., 311

Duff, Paul B., 295n190

Duling, Dennis C., 111n63

Dunn, James D. G., 32–34, 35, 35n50 37, 46, 156n72, 157n75, 198n85, 324n61, 328n71

Dunning, Benjamin H., 147n39, 148n40, 203n104, 211n133

Dyer, Richard, 311, 313, 314–16, 317, 319, 320, 339, 340

Eastman, Susan, 199n90, 200

Eckhardt, Benedikt, 157n76, 264n75

Ehrensperger, Kathy, 42, 61n73, 62, 63n79, 80n60, 82n66, 238n109, 242, 322n57

Eisen, Ute E., 86n82

Eisenbaum, Pamela, 15n39, 43, 45n95

Elliott, John H., 14n38, 49n11, 103n27, 103n29, 108, 109n58, 163n96, 202–5, 232, 233n87, 235, 288n171, 290n174, 290n176, 291n182, 292n184, 292n187

Erickson, Amy J., 336n100

Eriksen, Thomas H., 75n33

Esler, Philip F., 14n38, 37–39, 44–46, 49,

50n12, 51n19, 53–54, 55n39, 72n20, 80n60, 82n66, 87–88, 143n29, 178n2, 190, 222n30, 274n115, 305n3, 306n4, 307, 308, 321n54, 335n97

Evans, Craig A., 335n97

Fagbemi, Stephen Ayodeji A., 288n171

Fanon, Frantz, 326, 332, 333

Fee, Gordon D., 117n93, 118n96, 119n100, 131n153, 285n162, 286n165, 286n166

Felder, Cain Hope, 312n20

Feldman, Louis H., 255n28, 255n29, 256n30, 259, 275

Feldmeier, Reinhard, 186, 205n112, 288n171

Fenton, Joseph Clifford, 239n111

Ferguson, Everett, 162n91, 162n92, 162n93, 164n97

Filtvedt, Ole Jakob, 229n70, 230n72

Foerster, Werner, 244n137

Frankel, David, 183n21

Frankenberg, Ruth, 310n15, 311n17, 313, 314, 315, 317, 340

Fredriksen, Paula, 35n49, 87, 158n77, 161n88, 198n84, 253n20, 255n29, 259–60, 261, 267n85

Fuglseth, Kåre, 225n52, 226n61, 227n66

Furnish, Victor Paul, 119n103, 279n138

Gabriel, Sharmani P., 77n47

Gager, John G., 36n52, 59

García Martínez, Florentino, 114n77, 272n108

Garner, Steve, 334,

Garrigan, Siobhán, 85n77, 312n21, 312n23

Garrow, Alan, 164n98

Garroway, Joshua D., 174n133, 273n112

Gaston, Lloyd, 36n52, 59

Geiger, Joseph, 173n129, 174n132

George, Mark K., 180n12

Georgi, Dieter, 252

Gerber, Christine, 86n82

Gerdmar, Anders, 25n13

Gillihan, Yonder Moynihan, 128, 130n148

Gilman, Sander L., 334n94

Girsch, Katherine Anne, 60–61, 99n13, 100, 104–5, 192n65, 205n115, 205n116
Givens, Tommy, 217–18, 232n80, 251n8, 335n97
Goldstein, Eric L., 334
Goodman, Alan H., 77n47
Goodman, Martin, 115–16, 245n139, 253, 255n29, 268n88, 269n93, 270n96, 270n98, 271, 282n146
Goppelt, Leonhard, 103n27, 288n171, 289n173
Grässer, Erich, 206n120
Green, Joel B., 288n171
Gruen, Erich S., 57n49, 80n62, 97n7, 161n89, 189n50, 191n62, 192n63
Grundmann, Walter, 28–29
Guttenberger, Gudrun, 63
Gwyther, Anthony, 212n137

Habel, Norman C., 183
Hadas-Lebel, Mireille, 125n127
Hägg, Henny Fiskå, 244n134
Hagner, Donald A., 231n77, 335n97
Hall, Jonathan M., 38, 52–54, 57, 70, 76n43, 90, 95, 111, 189, 220, 223, 243n128
Halton, Charles, 13n33
Hannaford, Ivan, 67n1, 68n2, 68n5, 77, 80n61
Hansen, Bruce, 59, 223n32
Harink, Douglas, 335n97
Harland, Philip A., 111n63, 161n89, 222n25, 261n60
Harnack, Adolf von, 238, 240n116, 241–42, 251–52, 254–55, 296
Harrill, J. Albert, 59n62, 158n77
Harrington, Wilfrid J., 212n136
Harris, Cheryl I., 311n18
Harris, Horton, 22, 23n6, 24n8, 26n16
Harris, J. Rendel, 239n111
Hartin, Patrick J., 230n75
Hartlep, Nicholas D., 313n29
Hartman, Lars, 162n94, 164n97
Hartmann, Douglas, 69n7, 69n8, 69n9, 69n10, 70, 71n19, 72, 78–79, 82, 90–91
Harvey, David, 180, 181

Hastings, Adrian, 250–51
Hatch, Edwin, 137n4, 140n21, 187n41, 224n43, 224n46, 226n56, 227n62
Hayes, Christine E., 113–14, 116, 117n92, 119n102, 120n106, 121n108, 125, 130n147
Hayes, Cleveland, 313n29
Hegel, Georg Wilhelm Friedrich, 23–24
Heid, Stefan, 213
Hellerman, Joseph H., 40–41, 50n15, 110
Hendriksen, William, 321n56
Heng, Geraldine, 80n61
Hengel, Martin, 139
Heschel, Susannah, 28, 29n27
Hock, Ronald F., 283n154
Hoek, Annewies van den, 245
Holloway, Paul A., 292n185, 292n186
Holm, Douglas, 289n173, 290
Holtz, Gudrun, 21n1, 35n46, 35n50
Holtz, Traugott, 143, 144n33, 284n157, 284n159, 285n161
Honigman, Sylvie, 189n52
Hooker, Morna D., 143n30, 281n141
Horsley, G. H. R., 111n63
Hort, F. J. A., 109, 225n50, 226n55, 230n74, 288n169
Howard-Brook, Wes, 212n137
Hurtado, Larry W., 41, 87n92
Hutchinson, John, 68n4, 69n7, 71–72, 83n70, 136n2, 178n1, 307
Hvalvik, Reidar, 278n132, 282, 284n155

Ibita, Ma. Marilou S., 344n130
Inda, Jonathan Xavier, 83n70
Isaac, Benjamin, 6n24, 75–76, 78, 80

Jackson, Peter, 69n9
Jacobs, Andrew S., 214
Jefford, Clayton N., 239n114
Jenkins, Claude, 121n112
Jenkins, Richard, 79
Jennings, Willie James, 5, 312n21, 315n37, 330
Jeremias, Joachim, 252–53, 270n99
Jewett, Robert, 198n85
John, Helen C., 338n111

Johnson, Aaron P., 58n52, 245n139
Johnson, Andre E., 337n104
Johnson Hodge, Caroline, 14n37, 21n1, 36, 42, 43, 59, 60, 100n16, 101–2, 117n92, 117n94, 119n99, 121n111
Jones, Christopher, 95n4
Jones, Joseph L., 77n47
Jones, Siân, 73n26
Jones, Steve, 76, 77
Judge, Edwin A., 86, 87n85, 258n45

Kahl, Brigitte, 260n55
Kant, Immanuel, 5
Käsemann, Ernst, 210
Kasher, Aryeh, 158n78, 264n73
Kaufman, Cynthia, 317n45, 330n78
Keener, Craig S., 127n134
Kelhoffer, James A., 58n55
Kellenbach, Katharina von, 336n100
Kelley, Shawn, 24–25, 27
Kennedy, Liam, 181n13
Kennedy, Tammie M., 311n16
Kidd, Colin, 68n2, 76, 86n84
Kittel, Gerhard, 28–29
Klauck, Hans-Josef, 109n55
Kloppenborg, John S., 222n25
Koerrenz, Ralf, 183n21
Konradt, Matthias, 220n16, 231, 232n80, 232n81, 232n82, 232n84, 281
Konstan, David, 54n33
Kraabel, A. T., 253n20, 254n23, 258
Kraemer, Ross S., 263n66, 273
Kraft, Henricus, 142n27
Kuecker, Aaron J., 39–40, 44–45, 322n57
Kuhn, Karl Georg, 29
Kvalbein, Hans, 277n129, 278n130

Lake, Kirsopp, 169n118, 259
Lampe, Peter, 167n111
Lander, Vini, 331n82, 332
Landmesser, Christof, 23n4
Langton, Daniel R., 29n27
Lans, Birgit van der, 96n6, 97
Lattke, Michael, 239n111
Law, Timothy Michael, 13n33

Lefebvre, Henri, 180–82
Lehmkuhl, Augustus, 118n97
Leppin, Volker, 28n24
Levenson, Jon D., 21n1, 295
Levine, Amy-Jill, 12, 179n5, 319–20, 324n62, 324n63, 333–34, 336n99, 336n101, 342n122, 344
Levine, Lee I., 51n21, 173n129, 261n57
Levinskaya, Irina, 253n20, 255n29, 258n42, 258n44, 259, 263n66, 265n76, 266n82, 271
Lietzmann, Hans, 168n113
Lieu, Judith M., 57n50, 58n52, 66, 148n40, 165, 227, 235n96, 236n99, 237n105, 239n111, 239n114, 241n122, 246n140
Liew, Tat-siong Benny, 339n113, 339n115, 344n127
Lightfoot, J. B., 117n93, 118, 131, 199, 286n165
Lincicum, David, 23n4
Lindars, Barnabas, 206n120
Lindemann, Andreas, 126n129, 130n150, 153n61, 153n63, 162n93
Llewelyn, S. R., 170n119, 171n122
Lona, Horatio E., 239n114
Long, A. A., 265, 266n80
Long, Burke O., 185n31
Longenecker, Bruce W., 197n83, 287n168
Lopez, Davina C., 221n20
Lorde, Audre, 311, 340, 341, 343n123
Luz, Ulrich, 231n76, 232n81, 232n83, 232n84, 281n142, 281n144, 282

MacDonald, Margaret Y., 117n94, 128–29, 152n58, 152n60, 153
Mahn, Jason A., 319n50, 320
Maier, Christl M., 113n71, 180n12
Malherbe, Abraham J., 120n105, 143n32, 144n33
Marchand, Suzanne L., 26n18
Marohl, Matthew J., 208n126
Marshall, Howard, 277, 278n130, 282, 284n156, 284n158
Martin, Dale B., 25n13, 54n38
Martin, Judith N., 311

Martin, Troy W., 102n26, 110n59
Martyn, J. Louis, 200n92, 200n96
Mason, Steve, 12n31, 13n33, 47–48, 49, 51n17, 51n19, 51n20, 62, 138–39, 140n17, 140n21, 145n36, 146n37, 148–49, 178n2, 220n19, 221, 222, 223n31, 239n115, 257n34, 266n83, 267, 305n3, 306n4, 307n8, 308n11
Matlock, R. Barry, 32n34, 35
Maughan, Stephen S., 250n4
May, Alistair S., 166n105
McCoskey, Denise Eileen, 54
McEleney, Neil J., 158n77, 266n79
McGowan, Andrew B., 167, 168n113
McInerney, Jeremy, 220, 222
McIntosh, Peggy, 316n43, 319n50, 342n122
McKnight, Scot, 253, 254n26, 261n59, 268n88, 269n91, 269n93, 269n94, 270n96, 270n98, 271n102, 272n108, 272n109
Meadowcroft, Tim, 216n146
Meeks, Wayne A., 37, 107n43, 164n99, 343n124
Meer, Nasar, 3, 5, 86
Meggitt, Justin J., 168n116
Memmi, Albert, 326n65
Mendels, Doron, 187n45, 192n64, 219n10
Meneses, Eloise Hiebert, 76n43
Michaels, J. Ramsey, 103n27, 103n29, 205, 234n91, 235n96, 288n170, 290n174, 290n175
Mignolo, Walter D., 315n37, 316, 326n64, 343
Milbank, John, 83n71
Miller, David M., 68n3, 68n4
Mirón, Louis F., 83n70
Mitchell, Claire, 85
Mitton, C. Leslie, 202n99
Moore, George Foot, 29n27
Moore, Nicholas J., 208n126
Moore, Stephen D., 212n138, 342
Moore, Stewart, 50n15, 51–52
Morgan, Jonathan, 184n27
Morgan, Teresa, 52n24, 54, 208n125, 219n12, 220
Morris, Leon, 321, 324
Morrison, Toni, 311, 340

Moses, Yolanda T., 77n47
Moxnes, Halvor, 26n17, 36n53, 47n7
Munck, Johannes, 198n84
Muraoka, T., 139n15, 140n19
Murphy-O'Connor, Jerome, 119n101, 126–27, 129n140, 279
Myers, William H., 338

Nakayama, Thomas K., 311
Nanos, Mark D., 15n39, 59n58, 200, 266n83, 335n98, 336n99
Neill, Stephen, 277, 282
Neusner, Jacob, 32n34
Neutel, Karin B., 102n24
Niebuhr, Karl-Wilhelm, 28n24
Niederwimmer, Kurt, 154n66, 164n98, 168n115, 169n118, 171n124
Niemand, Christoph, 41n73
Nolland, John, 116n91, 158n77, 266n79, 270
Nongbri, Brent, 84
North, John, 55n41, 87n91
Novenson, Matthew V., 335n98
Ntarangwi, Mwenda, 327n67

Oakes, Peter, 100n16, 322n59
Öhler, Markus, 62–63, 147n39
Ok, Janette H., 61
Økland, Jorunn, 180n12
Ollrog, Wolf-Henning, 283n153
O'Neill, John Cochrane, 127
Oropeza, B. J., 280n139
Orrieux, Claude, 252n13, 253, 254n26, 263n67, 269n94, 270n98

Park, Wongi, 312n22, 340n118
Parks, Sara, 345n131
Patte, Daniel, 338, 342
Paulsen, Henning, 237n105, 238n108, 238n110, 241n121
Pearce, Sarah, 188–89, 193n68, 225n52, 226n56, 226n61
Penrose, Jan, 69n9
Peppard, Michael, 54
Perrone, Lorenzo, 213
Petersen, Norman R., 108n49
Philonenko, Marc, 115n83, 115n84

Pierce, Chad T., 163n96
Plummer, Robert L., 284n156
Pollefeyt, Didier, 335n97
Porter, Stanley E., 130n145
Powery, Emerson B., 337
Price, Simon, 55n41, 87n91
Prinsloo, Gert T. M., 180n12
Puig i Tàrrech, Armand, 283n152, 293n188
Punt, Jeremy, 312n22

Quasten, J., 240n116

Rajak, Tessa, 227n66
Ramsay, William M., 110n61, 260n53,
    260n54
Reasoner, Mark, 159n80
Rebillard, Éric, 149, 162n90, 173n128, 174,
    176
Redpath, Henry A., 137n4, 140n21, 187n40,
    224n43, 224n46, 226n56, 227n62
Reicke, Bo, 163n96, 278
Reinhartz, Adele, 112n69, 150n48, 151n55,
    151n57, 336n101
Renan, Ernest, 26
Rengstorf, Karl Heinrich, 140n18, 225n53,
    226n61, 227n66, 262n64
Reynolds, Joyce, 185n33, 258n45, 259n50
Richard, Earl J., 284n158
Richardson, Peter, 158n78, 234n89, 235n96,
    264n73
Ridderbos, Herman N., 321n56
Riesner, Rainer, 251n9, 252n13, 253, 254,
    256n32, 270n99, 271, 272n105, 280, 284,
    286–87, 294n189
Robinson, J. Armitage, 239n111
Roediger, David, 311, 312n23
Roetzel, Calvin J., 34n44, 80n60
Rokéah, David, 269n94, 273n110
Rudd, Niall, 269n95, 270
Ruether, Rosemary Radford, 5
Runesson, Anders, 14n38, 21n1

Sadler, Rodney S., Jr., 337
Safrai, S., 113n73, 124n19, 149n47, 150
Sagnard, François, 244n137
Said, Edward W., 327n67

Saïd, Suzanne, 53, 54n33, 136n1
Saldarini, Anthony J., 220n16, 231n78,
    231n79, 232n80
Sanders, E. P., 28–36, 116n90, 119n99,
    120n107, 335
Sandford, Michael J., 344n129
Sandmel, Samuel, 193
Sänger, Dieter, 51n17
Sargent, Benjamin, 232n86
Schäfer, K., 107n48
Schaller, Berndt, 186n39, 187n45, 188n48,
    192n63, 193
Schermerhorn, Richard A., 71, 72, 78, 89,
    189, 217
Schiffman, Lawrence H., 192n65, 192n66,
    277
Schlosser, Jacques, 103n27, 291n180
Schmeller, Thomas, 119n103
Schnabel, Eckhard J., 277n129, 278
Schneemelcher, Wilhelm, 237n105,
    238n107
Schneider, Johannes, 234n90
Schoedel, William R., 120, 138n7, 148n41,
    148n43, 149n45, 168n115, 168n116,
    169n117
Schrage, Wolfgang, 117n92, 117n93, 118n98,
    119n100, 235n96, 286n165
Schröder, Bernd, 140n21, 141n24, 142n28
Schüssler Fiorenza, Elisabeth, 37
Schutter, William L., 232n86
Schwartz, Daniel R., 13n35, 50n16, 192n65,
    279n137
Schwarz, Eberhard, 234n93
Scott, James M., 185n31, 190n55, 196n76,
    196n77, 197n82, 198n88, 224n43, 225
Sechrest, Love L., 34n44, 51, 59, 60, 72n20,
    102, 179, 222, 223, 238n109, 323n60,
    329n74
Segall, Avner, 319n50
Segovia, Fernando F., 312n20, 338n110,
    339n113, 339n115, 344n127
Seland, Torrey, 275n119, 288n170, 288n171,
    289n172
Selwyn, Edward Gordon, 288n169,
    290n176
Sherwood, Yvonne, 342
Shier, Kim, 112n69, 150n48

Shimada, Kazuhito, 202n99
Shipley, Graham, 221
Siker, Jeffrey S., 312n22, 337n103
Sim, David C., 231n79
Skarsaune, Oskar, 282n147
Skarsten, Roald, 225n52, 226n61, 227n66
Sleeman, Matthew, 180n11, 181n13, 181n14, 181n15, 195n75, 196n77, 198, 206
Smith, Anthony D., 49, 50, 69n7, 71–72, 74, 75n33, 82, 83n70, 85, 89, 136, 178, 179, 180n8, 189, 211, 215, 218, 219n9, 219n10, 247, 249–50, 307
Smith, Dennis E., 166, 167, 168n113
Smith, Jonathan Z., 84n73, 88
Smith, Morton, 13n34, 264n74
Smith, R. R. R., 178n2, 221n20, 222n28
Smith, Wilfred Cantwell, 84, 87n87, 88
Smither, Edward L., 278n130
Snyman, Gerrie, 312n22
Soja, Edward W., 180, 181–82, 194, 201, 206, 303
Sollors, Werner, 68n4
Solomos, John, 3n9, 333n89
Sordi, Marta, 172n127
Southwood, Katherine E., 113n72
Standhartinger, Angela, 86n82
Stanley, Christopher, 101n18
Stanton, Graham N., 231, 232n80
Stark, Rodney, 279n134, 287n168
Stavrakopoulou, Francesca, 97n10, 183n21, 187n42
Stefancic, Jean, 310n15
Stegemann, Wolfgang, 12n32, 48, 49n6, 51n17, 62,
Stendahl, Krister, 30n30
Stenschke, Christoph, 289n172, 291n181
Sterling, Gregory E., 275n119
Stewart, Eric C., 180n11
Still, Todd D., 37n56
Stokes, Bruce, 84n75, 319n49, 332n84
Stone, John, 69n9, 70–71, 83n70
Storm, Ingrid, 84n75
Stowers, Stanley K., 21n1, 57n49, 59
Strecker, Georg, 179n5
Strom, Mark, 197

Stuhlmacher, Peter, 281n142, 281n144, 282n145
Sugirtharajah, R. S., 312n20, 339n114, 339n116

Tajfel, Henri, 303n1
Tannenbaum, Robert, 185n33, 258n45, 259n50
Taussig, Hal, 167n111
Theissen, Gerd, 29n26, 37n54, 122n115, 152n59
Thiessen, Matthew, 100n16, 101n18, 158n77, 200n96, 262n62, 263, 272n107
Thiselton, Anthony C., 118n96, 119n100, 127, 279n138, 286n165
Thomas, James M., 5
Thompson, Audrey, 314, 317n44, 343n125
Thompson, Deanna A., 312n21
Thorsteinsson, Runar M., 108n52
Thrall, Margaret E., 119
Tigchelaar, Eibert J. C., 114n77, 272n108
Tite, Philip L., 105n37
Tolbert, Mary Ann, 312n20, 338n110, 339n116, 344n127
Torres, Rodolfo D., 83n70
Trebilco, Paul R., 107n44, 131n151, 131n152, 228n67, 260n53, 260n54
Tucker, J. Brian, 37n57, 42n80
Tyler, Katharine, 310n14, 313n24

Vaage, Leif E., 128–29
Vahrenhorst, Martin, 185n34, 187n45, 188n48, 201, 206n120
Vair, Richard James, 183, 201n97, 204n108, 213n142
Vandecasteele-Venneuville, Frederique, 335n97
Vogel, Manfred, 51n17
Vollenrieder, Samuel, 64–65
Vos, Craig S. de, 172n127
Vos, J. Cornelis de, 180n12, 187n45, 188n48, 191n61, 193n70

Wacker, Marie-Theres, 183n21
Wallace, Daniel B., 130

Walzer, Richard, 55n40
Wan, Sze-kar, 198
Wan, Wei Hsien, 17–18, 203, 204, 205–6, 341n119, 343n123
Wander, Bernd, 256n30, 258n40, 258n42, 258n44, 258n45, 268n90
Ward, Roy B., 123n118
Ware, James P., 284n156, 286n163
Watson, Francis, 101n18, 158n77
Weber, Max, 9, 68, 70–71, 74, 78, 95, 101, 106, 306
Weiss, Daniel H., 124n120, 130n148, 131–32
Wenell, Karen J., 180n12, 195n73
Werman, Cana, 113n74, 114n76
Westerholm, Stephen, 31n32 142n23
Whitelam, Keith W., 183n21
Whitmarsh, Tim, 155
Whittaker, Molly, 159n79, 159n82, 160n86
Wilken, Robert L., 183n23, 184, 185n34, 186n37, 187, 188n48, 193, 206, 207n121, 210n132, 213n142, 214n143, 215
Will, Edouard, 252n13, 253, 254n26, 263n67, 269n94, 270n98
Williams, Travis B., 290, 292n183, 292n186

Wilson, Stephen G., 274, 275n117, 275n119, 276, 277n126
Windisch, Hans, 234n90
Winter, Dagmar, 122n115
Wire, Antoinette C., 117n94
Witherington, Ben, III, 328n72
Wohlenberg, G., 235n94
Wolter, Michael, 64, 65, 236n102, 237n103, 238n108, 238n109, 239, 241n119, 242n125, 287n167
Wright, David F., 236n99
Wright, N. T., 22, 32n36, 34, 35n49, 35n50, 119n99, 161n88, 323n60

Yancy, George, 312n21, 313n29, 327n69
Yarbro Collins, Adela, 166n104, 281n141
Yarbrough, O. Larry, 119n100, 120n105, 123n118, 130, 149n47, 150, 151n57
Young, Norman H., 170n119, 170n120
Young, Robert, 27n23, 315n37, 317n46, 326

Zetterholm, Magnus, 14n38, 15n39, 31n32, 59n58, 266n83, 335n98

Index of Subjects

African American biblical interpretation, 329n74, 336–38, 343

American Anthropological Association, 75

anastrophe (ἀναστροφή), as way of life, 140, 145–47

ancestry, 95, 301–2; in early Jewish sources, 96–98, 140–41; in 1 Peter, 102–5; in Galatians, 100–102; in NT, 98–100, 133

antisemitism, 1–3, 28–29; links with racism, 3–5, 326, 333–34, 344

baptism, 162–65, 265–66; of infants, 131, 153, 162

boundaries, of groups, 71, 119n99, 128, 131, 139, 155–56, 246, 308, 323

British values, 330–32

children: in early Judaism, 123–26; holiness and identity of in 1 Cor 7:14, 126–33, 134; socialization of, 149–55

Christian: attitudes toward Muslims and Jews, 4; links with national identity, 84–86; perspectives in NT studies, 323–35; use of term, 13–16

circumcision, 157–59, 164–65, 173–75, 263–64, 265–66, 267, 268, 269, 302–3

colonialism, 10, 27, 75, 215, 295, 315, 325, 327

Common Era, as label, 16–18

conversion, 41–42, 114–15, 124, 143–44, 249, 255, 295; in early Christianity, 279–80, 287, 289–90; to Judaism, 258, 262–73; as problematic term, 267–68

endogamy. *See* marriage

epistemology, 7, 10, 299, 316–17, 343, 344, 345

ethnic groups, definitions and characteristics of, 71–74, 89, 217, 222, 301

ethnicity: as alternative term to "race," 68; constructivist and primordial definitions of, 69–74, 78–79, 89–90; in German-language NT scholarship, 61–64; links with religion, 3, 5, 74, 83–89, 144, 146, 176, 267, 274, 295, 300–301, 332

ethnicization, 9, 65, 91, 134–35, 146, 155, 218, 235, 247, 304, 307; definition of, 79

ethnic reasoning, 56–57, 243

ethnocentrism, 6, 9, 33, 35, 296, 305, 308, 309, 320, 321, 323, 328

ethnos (ἔθνος): in ancient Greek, 220–23; in early Christian literature, 245n139; in Jewish literature, 224, 226–27; in NT, 228n68, 230, 233–35

eucharist, 166–69

Eurocentrism, 17, 336, 338, 340, 341

food: in early Christian practice, 165–69; and Jewish identity, 159–61

genealogy. *See* ancestry

genos (γένος): in ancient Greek, 223;

in early Christian (post-NT) literature, 236–45; in Jewish literature, 224,
226–27; in NT, 228n68, 230, 233–35;
translation of, 242
Godfearers, 257–62
Greek, as ethnic or cultural identity, 52–54,
136
groupism, critique of, 72–73, 217

inclusivism, 6, 43, 295–96, 305, 308, 309,
320–23, 328, 333
Islamophobia, 2–3

Jerusalem, 184–85, 187, 190–92, 194–201,
204, 210–15, 303–4; as mother-city
(μητρόπολις), 188–89, 191n60, 201, 303
Jew/Judean: choice of term, 12–13; as
ethnic identity, 47–52, 305–6, 308; as
multi-ethnic identity, 50–51, 189–91,
194, 273, 295; as religious identity,
50–51, 275–76
Jewish scholarship, 29, 335–36, 343–44

kinship: as ἀδελφότης in 1 Peter and
beyond, 108–10; in early Christian
discourse, 106–11; in Jewish sources,
106; "real" and fictive, 70–71, 90, 95,
106, 111, 133, 301

laos (λαός): in ancient Greek, 223–24; in
Jewish literature, 224, 226–27; in NT,
226, 228–30, 233
liberalism, Western, 10, 329, 330–33

marriage: among Jews, 112–16, 134; rules
and debates in NT and early Christianity, 116–23, 134
minority criticism, 336, 339, 344
mission, 249–51, 304; in early Judaism,
251–55, 268–72, 293–96, 305; in NT and
early Christianity, 277–96, 305

new perspective on Paul, 2, 32–36, 320

paideia (παιδεία), as cultural formation,
136, 150–55
people-terms, 219–20, 242, 245–48, 304,
307. See also *ethnos*; *genos*; *laos*; tribe
proselytes, Jewish: as *Ioudaioi*, 272–73. *See
also* conversion

race: as a term, 67–68; definitions of,
75–80; DNA and genes, 76–78; use of
term for antiquity, 34n44, 56, 58, 80–83
racialization, 5, 27, 82, 189, 341; definition
of, 79
Rasse (race), 62, 68n3, 238n109, 242
religion: in antiquity, 48, 86–89; linked
with ethnicity and race, 3, 5, 74, 83–89,
144, 146, 176, 247, 267, 274–76, 295,
300–301, 332; and national identity,
84–86, 217–18, 249–51

Sabbath, as marker of Jewish identity,
160–61, 171–72
spatial theory, 180–82, 206, 211, 215, 303
Sunday, as Christian practice, 169–72
supersessionism, 5, 218, 234–35
sympathizers, of Judaism. *See* Godfearers

third race, 231, 236–42
tribe (φυλή), 223, 224n46, 230n73

UNESCO (United Nations Educational,
Scientific and Cultural Organization),
68, 83

whiteness, 2–5, 10, 310–20, 323, 325, 332,
334, 338, 339–41, 345; definition of,
312–14

Index of Ancient Sources

Note: Since this book represents the perspective of an author trained in the Protestant Christian tradition, it seems best to acknowledge that particularity by using the categories of that tradition to organize biblical references, recognizing that these represent a perspective not shared by other Christian traditions or by Jews, whose scriptural canons are different, and differently organized. The comments above on BC/BCE and AD/CE (pp. 16–18) are relevant to this decision.

OLD TESTAMENT

Genesis

1:11–12	226
1:21	226
1:24–25	226
2:2	209
2:24	120
4:17–5:32	96
10	185n31, 198n88, 225
10:1–32	96
10:5	224n46
10:18	224n46
11:6	227
11:10–29	96
12:1	183
12:2	183, 225
12:3	100, 224n46, 225n49
12:5	186n36
13:15	101n18
15:5	183
15:6	100
15:7	183
15:8–20	185
15:18–21	187
16:1–4	199
16:2	102
17:4–7	183
17:5	96
17:8	101n18, 183, 186n36
17:9–14	157
18:12	102n26
18:18	100n17, 225
21:1–18	199
21:7	104
22:18	225
23:4	185, 186, 202, 209
24:3	112
25:19–26	96
26:4	225
28:14	225n49
32:28	96
37:1	186n36
37:2–3	96
41:45–50	115
49:1–28	96
50:24	96n5

Exodus

1:9	224, 227n63
2:7–9	104
2:11	106
2:16–21	116
3:8	187
3:16	96
3:17	187
4:18	106
5:14	227n63
18	137
18:20	137
19:5	233n88
19:5–6	113, 233, 234
19:6	225
20:2–6	137

20:8–11	160	11:19	150	**Ezra**	121		
20:12	149	12:9–10	207	9:2	113		
23:22	225n50	13:5	137	10:3	125		
24:4	224n46	14:2	233n88	10:10–11	116		
28:21	224n46	14:21	233n88	10:10–19	133		
31:13–17	160	15:3–7	106	10:11	125, 272n107		
34:11–16	112	21:18–21	149	10:18–19	125, 227n107		
34:24	224	23:2–3	112	10:44	125n126		
		23:7–8	272				
Leviticus		32:8–9	224, 228	**Nehemiah**	272		
10:6	106	32:18	100, 105	9:7–8	183		
18:24	224			9:8	187		
19:3	149, 160	**Joshua**	184	9:14	160		
20:17–18	226			10:31	160		
21:13–14	226	**Ruth**		13:15–22	160		
21:14	112	1:8–12	104	13:23–27	116		
21:17	226	1:15–16	114				
23:3	160	1:16	114	**Esther**			
24:10	124	4:13–17	104	2:27	264		
24:10–16	125	4:16	115	3:13	227n63		
25:18	184			6:13	227n63		
25:23	185	**1 Samuel**		8:7–11	264		
25:46	106	13:19	186	8:17	257n34, 263		
26:3–13	184			9:19	188n47		
26:12	228	**2 Samuel**		9:27	264		
26:27–33	184	7:12	101n18				
		20:19	188n47	**Psalms**	288		
Numbers				9:1	288		
1:4–49	224	**1 Kings**		9:11	288		
11:12	100	7:13–14	124	9:15	288		
		11:1–4	116	14:7	198n85		
Deuteronomy				33 LXX	290n177		
1:8	96, 184	**2 Kings**		34:8	105n39		
5	137	11:4	121	39:10	154n66		
5:7–10	137	13:23	96n5	39:12	185		
5:12–15	160			53:6	198n85		
5:16	149	**1 Chronicles**		55:9	288		
5:33	137	1–8	96	57:9–11	288		
6:7	150	2:17	124	70:15	288		
6:10	96	2:34–36	124	72:28	288		
7:1	187	29:15	185, 209	78:13	288		
7:1–4	112			78:54	184n30		
7:6	225, 233n88, 234	**2 Chronicles**		95:7–8	208		
7:6–7	224, 228	2:12–14	124	95:7–11	207		
9:5	96	20:7	183	95:11	208		
9:6	191n59			96:1–3	288		

106:22	288
118:13	288
118:26	288
119	137
127:3–5	149

Proverbs

1:8	150
2:20	137
4:1	150
4:1–4	150
4:13	150
8:10	150
10:17	150
12:16	288
13:24	150
19:18	150
22:6	150
22:15	150, 155n68

Isaiah

1:26	188
2:1–4	184n29
2:3	198n85
8:21	140n21
9:2	288
10:3	289
22:4	227n63
25:8	212
27:13	184n29
30:19	233n88
41:8	97
42:5	227n63
42:6	224n45
42:16	288
43:20	227n63, 235n94,
	244n135, 244n136, 288
43:20–21	233
43:21	288
49:6	224n45
51:1–2	96, 105
52:1–9	184n29
56:1–6	160
57:13	184n30
58:13	160

59:20	198
59:20–21	198n85
60:11–22	184n29
60:21	185n34
61:7	185n34
65:4	159
65:17	212
65:19	212
66:7–9	100
66:10–20	184n29
66:17	159
66:22	212

Jeremiah

6:15	289
6:16	137
7:23	137
9:25–26	158n78
10:15	289
17:19–27	160
22:10	187n41
26:16 LXX	187n41
29:4–14	184, 191
31:23	184n30
31:31–32	237
31:33	228
38:1	227n63
38:35	227n63
38:37	227n63
41:16	187n41
51:45	229

Ezekiel

5:5	185
20:40	184n30
23:15	187n41
37:27	212, 228
38:12	185
40–48	212
47:13–48:29	212
48:30–35	212
48:35	212

Hosea

1–2	233
1:6	233

1:9	233
2:3 LXX	233
2:25 LXX	233
12:1 LXX	233n88

Joel

2:1	184n30

Amos

9:14–15	184

Micah

4:1–3	184

Zechariah

2:12	184

Deutero-
canonical Books

Tobit	113
4:3–19	150
4:12	121
4:12–13	113
4:13	106
4:14	140n19
14:6	144n33

Judith	227
5:10	227n65
6:2	227n65
6:5	227n65
6:19	227n65
8:20	227n65
8:32	227n65
9:14	227n65
11:10	227n65
12:3	227n65
13:20	227n65
15:9	227n65
16:17	224, 227n65
16:24	227n65

Additions to Esther

8:21	227n63

Wisdom of Solomon

3:7	289
3:13	289
6:17	150
10:15	224
12:3–7	186
17:2	225n50
19:11	226

Sirach   140n21, 150

1:27	150
3:1–18	149
6:18	150
7:23	150
18:4	288
18:20	289
22:3–6	150
25:7	149
30:1–13	150
39:10	288
44:15	288
44:19–21	96

1 Maccabees

1:11–15	138
1:13–15	138n5
1:14–15	165
1:15	157
1:41–43	274
1:43–45	160
1:60–61	157
1:62–63	159
2:15	273–74
2:20–21	138
2:34–38	160
2:40–41	106
2:41	160
2:46	157
2:51–61	97
5:2	226
12:1–7	97
12:10	109
12:17	109
12:21	97, 226, 302
15:33	187

2 Maccabees   138n6, 145, 146, 148–49

1:1	106
1:2	96n5
1:7	184
2:21	138, 139
2:23	138
4:9–12	138n5
4:10	139
4:10–15	139
4:12	157n76
4:13	138, 139, 140
5:8	140
5:22	226, 227n65
5:25–26	160
6:1	141
6:7–9	138n5
6:10	157
6:12	155n68, 227n65
6:18	159
6:23	140
6:24	140
7:1	159
7:2	141
7:8	141
7:16	227n65
7:21	141
7:24	141
7:27	141
7:28	227
7:33	155n68
7:37	141
7:38	227n65
8:1	138, 139
8:9	224, 227n65
8:21	187
8:23	187
8:24–28	160
11:25	141
12:31	227n65
12:37	141
12:38	160
13:10	187
13:14	187
14:8–9	227n65
14:18	187

14:38	138, 139
15:1–5	160
15:29	141

1 Esdras

1:4	225n47
1:32	225n47, 227n63
1:34	225n47
1:49	225n47
2:5	225n47
5:9	225n47
8:10	225n47
8:13	225n47
8:64	225n47
8:66	225n47
9:36	125n126

3 Maccabees   140n21

1:3	141, 275
3:2	227n65
6:4	227n65
6:9	227n65
6:13	227n65
6:32	141
7:10	227n65

4 Maccabees   139, 141

1:11	187
4:20	187
4:23	141
4:25	157
5:1–6:30	138n5
5:2	159
5:6	159
5:33	141
6:15	159
6:17	97
6:17–20	97
6:22	97
7:19	96n5
8:7	141
9:1	141
9:23	109
9:24	141
9:29	141
10:3	109

10:15	109
13:17	96n5
13:19	109
13:27	109
14:20	97
15:28	97
16:16	140n21
16:25	96n5
17:6	97
17:21	187
18:1	97
18:4	187
18:5	141
18:9–19	150

OLD TESTAMENT PSEUDEPIGRAPHA

Jubilees

8–9	185n31
8:12	185
8:19	185
16:17–18	113
30:7–15	114
30:15	120n104
40:10	113n73

Odes of Solomon

8:14	105
19:1–4	105

Psalms of Solomon

7:9	155n68
9:9	97
18:3	97

Testament of Abraham

	102n26

Testament of Job

1:5	244n135

DEAD SEA SCROLLS

CD

6.20	106

7.2	106
14.3–6	272

1QS

3.18	290
4.6–8	290
4.11–13	290
4.18–19	290
4.26	290
6.10	106
6.22	106
8.4–11	192

4Q174

1.4	272

4QMMT

B75–82	114

ANCIENT JEWISH WRITERS

Josephus

Antiquitates judaicae

1.158	97
1.214	97
1.221	97
1.239	97
1.241	97
2.301	226n51
3.86–87	191n59
4.115–16	192
4.260–65	150
7.289	191n60
8.191–92	112
10.269	191n60
11.140	112
11.151–52	112
11.160	191n60
11.331–36	257n37
11.340	191n60
12.187	112
12.225–27	97, 302
12.240	274
12.259	160
12.274–78	160n84
12.280	141
12.303	141
13.12	160n84
13.45	111
13.69–71	257n36
13.242–44	257n36
13.254–58	264
13.257–58	264
13.258	141, 264, 273
13.318–19	264
13.397	141
14.64	160n84
14.110	256, 258
14.194	141
14.213–14	141
14.290	225n53
14.403	264n75
16.163–64	160
16.225	115
17.345	140n18
18.6	225n53
18.63–64	172
18.64	240
18.65–84	55n41
18.139–41	125n127
18.141	141, 275
18.173	140n18
18.349	112
18.354	160n84
18.359	140n18
19.28	140n18
19.90	140n18
20.17	266
20.17–96	266
20.34	267, 268
20.34–53	257
20.35	266, 267
20.38	267, 273
20.38–46	158n77
20.39	267
20.39–42	267
20.41	267
20.41–42	268
20.43	271
20.44–46	267

20.47	267	2.137	157, 159	1.51–53	263
20.100	275	2.141	159	1.52	268
20.139	115	2.141–42	158	1.317	142
20.142	190	2.144	141	2.228–31	151
20.195	257	2.160	191n59	2.232–33	150
		2.171	151	2.247–48	150
Bellum judaicum		2.171–89	151n54	3.29	112
1.122	226n61	2.182–83	141	3.110–16	147
1.232	225n53	2.202	147	3.315–17	275
1.550	226n61	2.204	151	3.316	275
1.581	225n53	2.210	141–42	3.316–17	275–76
2.122	106	2.216–17	150	*De virtutibus*	
2.282	225n53	2.220	225n53	102	144, 268, 307
2.398	256	2.237	141	103	145, 263, 273
2.400	191n60	2.277	187	106–8	272
2.421	191n60	2.282	159, 160–61, 192,	182	276
2.454	257n34, 263		256	195	98, 142
2.463	257n34	2.282–83	141	206–7	98
3.29	191n60	2.288	227	211–16	98
4.239	191n60				
4.267–68	191n60	*Vita*		*De vita contemplativa*	
7.43–45	256	16	257	18	188
7.375	191n60	414–15	112		
		426–27	112	*De vita Mosis*	
Contra Apionem				1.147	126, 272n109
1.1	97	**Philo**		2.17	256
1.1–2	227			2.21–22	161
1.1–46	97	*De Abrahamo*		2.41–43	256
1.30–36	98, 112	31–39	98n11	2.193	125
1.59	227	60–68	193		
1.60	151, 191n61	67	98n11	*Hypothetica*	
1.103	191n61	251	98n11	6.1	186
1.106	227			6.5	186
1.130	227	*De confusione linguarum*		6.6	186
1.160	227	78	188		
1.169–71	158	78–82	186	*In Flaccum*	
1.174	191n61	79	185n33	45	192
1.176	191n58			45–46	256
1.179–80	191n58	*De migratione Abrahami*		46	188
1.210	187, 272	62	226n61	53–54	189
1.212	187	89–93	158n77		
		91	160	*Legatio ad Gaium*	
2.8	227	92	157	3–4	227
2.30	178			74–113	156
2.38–42	191	*De praemiis et poenis*		115	142, 151, 156
2.45	257n36	152	276	117	142, 225n52
2.48	257n36	*De specialibus legibus*		119	225n52
2.123	256	1.2	158	134	142

137	225n52	2:15	143n29	14:22–25	168
153	142	3:9	99	16:7	195
155	142	5:5	185n34	16:15	281
157	257n36	5:13	185n34	16:16	163
161	225n52	5:16	289		
170	142	5:17–20	166n104	**Luke**	195–96
200	142	5:22–24	107	1:1	143n29
200–202	193	5:31–32	116	1:9	142
201	227	7:3–5	26	2:32	224n44
202	191n61, 193	8:11	96n5	3:8	99
205	191n61	8:17	143n29	3:23	99
208	142	10:1–23	281	3:23–38	99
210	142, 151	12:27–28	130n145	6:41–42	26
210–11	263	15:17–18	166n104	7:5	225n54
265	227	16:18	231	9:51	195
278	188n48	16:26	291	9:51–19:28	195
279	225n52	18:15	291	12:30	225n48
281	188	18:15–22	107	13:22	195
281–82	256	18:17	231	14:26	132
281–84	192	19:3–9	116	16:18	116
291	257n36	19:5–6	120	17:11	195
295–98	257n36	19:28	230n73	18:31	195
309–10	257n36	21:33–46	231	19:28	195
319–20	257n36	21:43	231–32, 234	20:9–19	231
361–62	159	23:15	253, 262n61,	22:15–20	168n112
			270–71, 279n136, 294	22:30	230n73
Quaestiones et solutiones		26:26–29	168n112	22:32	107
in Exodum		27:25	30	22:39	142
2.2	158n77	28:7	195–96	23:2	225n54
2.13	193	28:16–20	278	24:6	195–96
		28:18–20	280–82	24:25–27	143n29
Quaestiones et solutiones		28:19	163, 164, 225n48,	24:30	168
in Genesin			231–32, 296	24:35	168
3.47	158			24:47	278, 281
				24:47–49	196
Quod Deus sit immutabilis		**Mark**		24:52	196
72	140n18	1:9–10	164		
		3:31–35	132	**John**	
NEW TESTAMENT		7:1–23	166	1:9–13	39
		7:19	159, 166	1:12–13	99
Matthew	164n98	9:1	152	3:1	279
1:1	98	10:2–12	116	3:3–8	99
1:1–16	98	10:7–8	120	6:53–56	173
1:3–6	127n134	11:17	225n48	7:35	203
1:17	98	12:1–12	231	7:50	279
1:18–25	98	13:10	278	8	99
1:22	143n29	13:30	152		

8:37	99	10:48	281	24:14	15, 143, 146
8:39–44	82, 99	11:14	279n135	24:17	225n54
8:44	6	11:21	143	25:16	142
8:48	99	11:26	15	26:1–23	292
9:31	258	13:16	258	26:3	142
11:48	226	13:26	228n68, 258	26:4	225n54
11:50–52	226	13:43	259, 262, 279n136	26:17	226n60
18:35	226	13:44–46	229	26:23	224n44, 225n48,
19:39	279	13:47	196		226n60
19:40	142	14:2	107	26:28	15
20:19	170	14:5	224n44, 225n48	27:33–36	168n114
20:26	170	14:15	143	27:35	168
21:23	107	14:19	229	28:14	196
		15:1	107, 142	28:16	196
Acts	195–96	15:1–2	158	28:17	142
1:4	196	15:4	229	28:19	225n54
1:8	196, 278, 281	15:19	143		
1:15	107	15:19–20	159	**Romans**	27, 38, 44
2:5	190	15:28–29	159	1:1–5	283
2:5–14	13	16:1–5	60	1:5	228n68
2:9–11	190	16:14	258	1:7	131, 228
2:11	262, 279n136	16:15	162n93, 279n135	1:7–10	278
2:14	196	16:21	142	1:13	107
2:14–36	143n29	16:31	279n135	2:14	228n68
2:38	163, 281	16:34	279n135	3:6	130n146
2:42	168	16:35–40	60	3:29	228n68
2:42–47	196	17:5–9	229	4:3	100
2:46	168	17:6–7	279n137	4:13	201
3:13	96n5	17:28–29	99	4:17–18	228n68
4:27	224n44, 226n60	18:2	190	6	163
4:32–37	196	18:5–6	229	6:1–11	163
5:13–14	279n137	18:7	258	6:3	281
6:5	262, 279n136	18:8	162n93, 279n135	6:3–4	164
6:14	142	18:10	229	9	233n87
7:6	202	18:24	190	9:4	201
7:19	68, 228n68	19:1–6	162n92	9:25–26	228
7:29	127n134, 202	19:21	196	9:33	233n87
7:49	208n124	20:7	168, 170	11:1	230n73
8:36	163	20:11	168	11:1–2	226n60
9:2	15, 143, 146	21:8	284	11:6	130n145, 130n146
9:30	107	21:21	142	11:11–13	228n68
9:35	143	21:39	190	11:13	273
10–15	39	22:4	15, 143, 146	11:17–24	143
10:2	258, 279n135	23:11	196	11:22	130n146
10:22	225n54, 258	24:2	225n54	11:23	102
10:44–48	162n92	24:10	225n54	11:25	107

11:26	198	7:12–16	117, 132, 279n135,	14:23–24	279	
14:1–7	159		286	15:8–10	282	
14:1–15:13	38	7:14	117, 122, 126, 132,	15:9–10	283	
14:5–6	160		134, 153	15:9–11	283	
14:10–21	107	7:15	118	15:29	130n146	
14:14	165	7:15–16	291	15:51–52	123, 152	
15:4	229	7:16	117, 286n165	16:2	170	
15:10	224n44, 226n60,	7:29–31	123	16:15	107, 279n135,	
	228n68	7:39	120, 121, 122, 134		279n136	
15:11	226n60	8:1–11:1	166	16:20	173n128	
15:15–24	283	8:11–13	107			
15:19	197, 283	9:1–2	282	**2 Corinthians**		
15:20–23	283	9:5	278n132, 283	1:1	131, 283	
15:20–24	278	9:6	283	1:19	283	
15:23–24	198	9:16–23	283	2:13	283	
15:24	283	9:19–23	60, 285, 291	3:4–18	200	
15:25–27	197	9:20	273	3:17–18	60	
15:27	198	10:1	143, 229	6:14	121	
15:30	107	10:1–11	163	6:14–7:1	119, 229	
16:1–3	283	10:1–13	60	6:16	228	
16:5	279n136	10:1–22	65	11:1–15	283	
16:16	173n128	10:4	230	11:18	130n146	
16:21	283	10:11	152	11:26	224n44, 228n68	
		10:14	167	12:2	15, 323	
1 Corinthians		10:14–21	167	12:18	283	
1:2	15, 131, 228	10:18	235	13:3	130n146	
1:10	107	10:25	165	13:12	173n128	
1:12	23	10:25–32	159			
1:13–17	163	10:32	64, 236	**Galatians**		
1:16	162n93, 279n135	10:32–33	285	1:11	107	
1:18–25	64	11:1	285	1:13	145	
1:22–24	236n102	11:11	119n99	1:13–14	145	
1:23	228n68	11:20	167, 170	1:14	142, 228n68	
3:16	229	11:23–26	168n112	1:15–16	283	
4:17	283	11:25	200	1:16–24	197	
5:5	280	11:27–30	168	2:1–9	283	
5:10	129n144	12–14	167n111	2:7–12	278n132	
5:11	145	12:2	229, 273	2:10	197n83	
6:1–2	131	12:10	228n68	2:11–21	65	
6:5–8	107	12:13	163	2:14	257n34	
6:15–17	121	12:28	228n68	2:14–15	224n44, 228n68	
6:16	119	14	279n138	2:15	273	
7	118	14:10	228n68	2:16	100n15	
7:2–5	123	14:12	130n146	2:16–21	15	
7:10–11	117, 129	14:16	130n146, 279n138	2:16–3:5	100	
7:12–13	118	14:21	228	3	100–102	

3:6–29	143n29	2:11	289	**2 Timothy**		
3:7	100	2:14–16	285–86, 287	1:5	132	
3:8	100, 228n68	2:25	283	4:5	284	
3:17–20	101n19	3:3–9	15			
3:26–29	165	3:5	228n68, 230n73	**Titus**		
3:27	164, 281	3:7–8	273	1:14	230	
3:27–28	163	3:8	291	2:1–10	152n59	
3:27–29	102	3:20	147	2:14	234	
3:28	43, 62, 165,	4:1–2	119	3:5	100	
	236n102, 249, 321,	4:18	283			
	322n59, 324, 328,			**Philemon**		
	336n100	**Colossians**		2	279	
3:29	143	1:10	146	7	108	
4:21–31	199, 210	2:12	163	10	279	
4:22–24	199	2:16	160	16	108	
4:26	199, 204, 304	3:9–10	145, 164	20	108	
4:26–31	103	3:11	63			
4:28	199	3:18	119n99	**Hebrews**	206–11, 229, 303	
4:31	199	3:18–4:1	147, 152	3–4	210	
5:1–4	158, 199	3:20	152	3:1	107	
5:2	165			3:7–11	208	
5:6	236n102	**1 Thessalonians**		3:7–4:11	207	
6:15	236n102	1:1	283	3:11	208n124	
		1:8	284	3:12–15	208	
Ephesians		1:9	307	3:17–18	208	
2:19	147, 202, 204	1:9–10	167	3:18	208	
2:21	119n99	1:9b	143	3:19	208	
4:1	146	3:8	119n99	4:1	208	
4:5	163	4:1–11	146	4:2–5	208	
4:11	284	4:3–8	120	4:3	208n124	
4:22	145	4:5	307	4:4	209	
4:22–24	145, 164	4:11	285	4:5	208n124	
5:8	119n99	4:13–18	123	4:7	208	
5:21–6:9	152	4:13–5:11	152	4:8	208	
5:22–6:9	147	5:12	119n99	4:9	209, 230n74	
6:1	119n99	5:14	107	4:10	208n124, 209	
6:1–3	152	5:26	173n128	4:11	208, 209	
6:2	149			5:3	229	
6:4	126n129, 153	**2 Thessalonians**	107	6:4–6	280n139	
				6:4–8	208	
Philippians		**1 Timothy**		7:5	229	
1:1	131, 283	2:1–2	156	7:11	229	
1:12	107	2:11–15	336n100	7:14	230n73	
1:12–18	283	3:1–15	152n59	7:18–19	235	
1:27	146, 147	3:6	279n136	8:6–13	235	
2:2–5	285	4:12	145	8:8–10	237	

8:10	229	1:6–9	210	3:6	102–3, 289, 291
9:7	229	1:9	204	3:8	108
9:11–15	235	1:11	230	3:11–17	289
9:19	229	1:15	145n35, 146, 228	3:12	290
9:25	229	1:17	147n39, 202, 204	3:13–17	203, 291, 292
9:26	129	1:18	145, 146, 307	3:14	291
10:23–27	280n139	1:22	108	3:15	290, 291, 292
10:25	142	1:23	61, 104, 243n132,	3:15–16	291
10:30	229		285	3:16	102, 146, 290, 291
11	209	2:1–2	243n132	3:17	291
11:8	209	2:1–3	61, 104	3:20	163
11:8–16	207	2:4–5	232	3:21	163
11:9	183, 207, 209	2:4–7	205	4:2–3	145
11:10	209	2:4–8	205	4:2–4	146
11:13	202	2:4–10	232–34	4:3	292
11:13–14	211	2:5	61, 204, 205, 234, 289	4:8	108
11:13–16	209	2:5–9	293	4:16	15, 293
11:14	209	2:6–8	233	4:17	204
11:15–16	209	2:7	205	4:17–19	290
11:16	210	2:9	60, 68, 225, 228,	4:19	289
11:25	230n74		230n74, 235, 243–44,	5:9	108, 109n55, 206
12:1	210		287–89	5:12	108
12:11	155n68	2:9–10	105, 230, 233,	5:13	203
12:22	210		235n96, 243, 245,	5:14	108, 173n128
13:7	145		247, 304		
13:12	230n74	2:11	147n39, 202	**2 Peter**	
13:14	210	2:11–12	289, 293	2:1	226n60
13:22	107	2:11–4:11	232	2:7	145n35
		2:12	146, 289, 291, 292	3:10	290
James		2:12–15	289	3:11	145
1:1	203, 230	2:17	108, 109n55, 157,		
1:2	107		290	**1 John**	
2:15	107	2:18	205	1:1	285
3:13	145	2:18–19	279n135	2:9–11	107
4:11	107	2:18–3:6	290	2:29	99
		2:18–3:7	147, 291	3:9	99
1 Peter	61, 102–4, 202–6,	2:20	289	3:10–17	107
	287–93	3:1	291, 292	4:7	99
1:1	147n39, 202, 203, 228	3:1–2	146, 291	5:4	99
1:3	104, 243n132	3:1–6	291, 292	5:18	99
1:3–5	61, 104	3:1–7	132		
1:3–12	104	3:2	291	**3 John**	
1:3–2:10	61, 232	3:4	291	10	107
1:4	204	3:4–5	291		
1:5	204	3:5–6	102	**Jude**	
				12	168

Revelation	211–14
1:9	230n73
1:10	170
2:20	159, 166
2:26	225n48
3:7–13	211
3:12	211
5:5	212, 230n73
5:9	230n73
7:4–8	230n73
7:9	230n73
14:6	230n73, 278
18:4	229, 230n74
21:1	212
21:1–22:5	211
21:3	229
21:3–4	212
21:16	212
21:17	212
21:22	212

MISHNAH

'Abot
5.21	150n51

Yebamot
6.6	123–24

APOSTOLIC FATHERS

Barnabas
5.7	239n113
11.1	163
13.1–6	230n71
15.8	172
15.9	172
16.5–8	235
19.5	154

1 Clement
1.3	153
2.8	147
3.4	147
6.1	147

21.1	147
21.6	153
21.7–8	153–54
21.8	154, 155
44.6	147
51.2	147
54.4	147
59.4	230n71

2 Clement
2.3	230n71
6.9	163

Didache
1–4	146
4.9	154
6.3	166
7.1–4	164
7.2–3	164
7.4	164
9.1–5	169
10.1–6	169
10.7	169
11–13	169
14.1	168, 171

Diognetus
1.1	146, 173, 239
2	167
2.1–4.6	148
4.1	157n75
5.1	147, 173
5.6	147
5.17	147

Hermas

Mandates
8.10	109

Similitudes
9.17.5	236

Visions
2.3	155n68
3.3	163
3.7	163

Ignatius

To the Ephesians
13.1	169, 169n77
20.2	168

To the Magnesians
8.1	171
9.1	171
10.1	148
10.3	148

To the Philadelphians
4.1	169
6.1	148

To Polycarp
5.2	120
6.2	163

To the Romans
3.3	148n42

To the Smyrnaeans
7.1	169
8.1–2	168n116, 169
8.2	163

Martyrdom of Polycarp
3.2	236
9.2	156
10.1–2	292
14.1	236
17.1	236

Polycarp

#### To the Philippians	109n58
4.2	154
5.1–2	146, 147

NEW TESTAMENT APOCRYPHA

Acts of John
106	171

Acts of Peter
30	171
34	118n94

Gospel of Peter

35	171
50	171

**Preaching of Peter
(Kerygma Petrou)** 241, 242

5	236–38

OTHER EARLY CHRISTIAN LITERATURE

Acts of the Scillitan Martyrs

4	292

Aristides

Apologia

2.2	238–39
15.1	239

Augustine

De civitate Dei

6.11	256n33

Clement of Alexandria

Adumbrationes in epistulas canonicas 243–44

Excerpta ex Theodoto

4–5	244n137
4.1	244

Paedagogus

1.6.32.4	243

Protrepticus

4.59.3	243
12.120.2	243n127

Stromateis

3.10.70.1–2	242
5.14.98.4	243
6.5.41.6–7	237
6.5.42.2	242

6.6.50.4	244n135
6.13.106.4	242
6.17.159.9	243
7.7.35.2	244
7.10.58.6	244
7.12.73.5	244

Cyprian (and Pseudo-Cyprian) 241

Ad Quirinum testimonia adversus Judaeos

1.12	244n135
3.62	121

De Pascha computus (Pseudo-Cyprian)

17	240

Epistulae

63.8	244n135

Eusebius

Historia ecclesiastica

1.4.2	245n139
1.11.7–9	240n117
4.7.11	172n127
4.14.9	109
5.1.14	172n127
5.1.26	172n127
6.45.1	110
9.5.2	172n127
9.9a.1–6	245n139

Praeparatio evangelica

7.1–20	186n38
8.6.1–9	186n38

John Chrysostom

Homiliae in epistulam i ad Corinthios

19.4	118n95

Justin Martyr

Apologia i

26	172n127

Apologia ii

2	118n94
12	172n127

Dialogus cum Tryphone

80.1–5	213
80.5	213
81.4	213
113.3–5	213
116.3	234, 236
119.3	236

Martyrdom of Apollonius

4	292

Origen

Commentarii in Romanos

5.9.11	162n93

Contra Celsum

5.61	241n122

Exhortatio ad martyrium

22.13	140n16

Fragmenta ex commentariis in epistulam i ad Corinthios

35.70–71	121
36	122
36.20	122

Tertullian

Ad nationes

1.7.34	240
1.8.1	240
1.20.4	240–41

Ad uxorem

2.2	117n92, 121
2.2–5	121n109
2.2.2	117–18
2.3	121

Adversus Marcionem

3.5.3	244n135
5.7	121n109

Apologeticus

2.5	172n127
6.11–7.5	172n127
18.4	132n156

De baptismo

2	164
6	164
11–14	164
18	162n93, 163

De corona militis

13	121n109

De monogamia

7	121n109
11	121n109

Scorpiace

10.10	240

GREEK AND ROMAN LITERATURE

Aelius Aristides

Orationes

45.1	223n33

Appian

Bella civilia

2.2.13	222n25
3.35.140	222n25
26.107	222n25

Aristotle

Politica

7.2.5 (1324b)	222n25

Aulus Gellius

Noctes atticae

12.1.1–24	105n37

Cicero

Pro Flacco

66–67	270n96

Dio Cassius

Historia Romana

36.41.1	222n25
37.16.5–17.1	273
57.18.5a	256
60.6.6	256
66.5.4	263n69
67.14.2	156

Dio Chrysostom

Ad Nicomedienses

15	109

Diodorus Siculus

Bibliotheca historica

1.28.3	158n78
1.55.5	158n78

Epictetus

Diatribai

2.9.19–22	265–66, 273

Herodotus

Historiae

1.56–57	223n37
1.57	220n15
1.101	223n36
2.104.2	158n78
5.77	220n15
7.161	220n15
8.73	220n15
8.144	53, 179

Homer

Ilias

2.87	220n14
2.91	220n14
2.365	223n40
2.459	220n14
2.469	220n14
2.852	223n33
3.32	220n14

12.23	223n33
13.108	223n40
13.354	223n34

Odyssea

3.305	223n40
15.267	223n34

Horace

Satirae

1.4.141–43	269–70

Isocrates

Panegyricus

50	53, 136

Juvenal

Satirae

14.96–106	157n75, 256, 265

Lucian

De morte Peregrini

13	287n168
16	287n168

Macrobius

Saturnalia

5.15	105n37

Petronius

Fragmenta

37	157n75

Satyricon

102	158

Pliny the Younger

Epistulae

10.96.7	172

Plutarch

Cicero

7.6	257n34

De superstitione
8   160

Moralia
5E   105n37
363D   179n7

Quaestionum convivialum
4.4.4   160

Romulus
26.3   224n42

Seneca

De superstitione (apud Augustine)   256

Epistulae morales
108.17–22   159n80

Sophocles

Oedipus tyrannus
1383   223n34

Strabo

Geographica
2.5.32   221–22
2.5.33   178n2
16.2.34   264

16.4.9   158n78
17.2.5   158n78

Suetonius

Divus Augustus
76.2   160

Domitianus
12.2   158–59, 165

Nero
16.2   172, 240

Tiberius
36   55

Tacitus

Annales
2.85   55n41
15.44   112, 172

Historiae
5.4.2   160n83
5.5   112, 156, 161

Vettius Valens

Anthologia
1.1.45   109
1.1.89   109

INSCRIPTIONS AND PAPYRI

Duke Papyrus Archive
727   262n61

Greek Papyri in the British Museum
42   111n64

Inscriptiones Graecae
2.1283   222n25

Inscriptions of Aphrodisias
8.210   109n56

Inscriptions of Smyrna
697   276n122

Monumenta Asiae Minoris Antiqua
4.37[1]   109n56
6.263   260n54
6.264   260n53

Oxyrhynchus Papyri
120   111n64
528   111n64
744   111n64